HANDBOOK OF
EUROPEAN HISTORY
1400–1600

HANDBOOK OF EUROPEAN HISTORY 1400–1600

Late Middle Ages, Renaissance, and Reformation

VOLUME II
VISIONS, PROGRAMS, AND OUTCOMES

Edited by

Thomas A. Brady, Jr. ❖ Heiko A. Oberman
James D. Tracy

WILLIAM B. EERDMANS PUBLISHING COMPANY
GRAND RAPIDS, MICHIGAN

First published in the Netherlands 1995 by
E. J. Brill, Leiden

This edition published in the United States of America 1996
through special arrangement with Brill by
Wm. B. Eerdmans Publishing Co.
255 Jefferson Ave. S.E., Grand Rapids, Michigan 49503
All rights reserved

Printed in the United States of America

02 01 00 99 98 97 96   7 6 5 4 3 2 1

Library of Congress Cataloging-in-Publication Data

Handbook of European history, 1400-1600: late Middle Ages,
Renaissance, and Reformation / edited by Thomas A. Brady, Jr.,
Heiko A. Oberman, James D. Tracy.
p.   cm.
Originally published: Leiden; New York: E. J. Brill, 1994-   .
Includes index.
Contents: v. 1. Structures [i.e.] Structures and assertions.
ISBN 0-8028-4194-5. — ISBN 0-8028-4195-3
1. Europe — History — 15th century. 2. Europe — History — 1492-1648.
I. Brady, Thomas A. II. Oberman, Heiko Augustinus. III. Tracy, James D.
D203.H36   1996
940.2 — dc20   95-50652
                                                CIP

CONTENTS

VOLUME 1: STRUCTURES AND ASSERTIONS

CONTENTS

VOLUME 2: VISIONS, PROGRAMS, OUTCOMES

EDITORS' PREFACE

A project of this *Handbook*'s magnitude—forty-one authors from nine countries and seven language areas—bears a history of successes and failures. These ran together. The successes began with the concept, which arose within the firm of E. J. Brill, and were capped by the recruitment of top specialists for nearly every subject. Yet, some subjects had to be abandoned. Of these the greatest loss is perhaps the chapter on the Reformation and gender relations, but other important lacunae include the history of Ashkenazic Jewry and many aspects of high culture and the history of ideas.

The balance sheet aside, the three editors and the editorial assistant have produced two volumes which realize fairly well the original intention: to provide an up-to-date, reliable, and interestingly written guide to the histories of the European peoples during the heart of the late Middle Ages, Renaissance, and Reformation. Special care has been taken with the aids. These include the bibliographies, the maps, and two appendices reproduced from vol. 1: the lists of rulers and John H. Munro's excellent and original appendix on money. They support in an important way the editors' desire to produce a work which does not cap or summarize a field so much as open it to further study by bringing current expertise both to the future experts and to the educated general readers in all countries where English is widely read.

A project of this magnitude also incurs many debts. The translators, who are named at the end of their respective chapters, are collectively due the editors' thanks. Our thanks also go to Professor Gerald D. Feldman, director of the University of California Center for German and European Studies, who helped with the editorial costs. Jan Steyaert, professor of art history at the University of Minnesota, helped select illustrations for the dust jackets. Drs. Elisabeth Venekamp of the publishing firm of E. J. Brill watched over the project for more than five years.

Finally, the editors express their thanks to Katherine G. Brady. As editorial assistant to the project, she managed the correspondence, conversion of electronic files, and recruitment of translators; she did the lion's share of the preparation of manuscripts and the reading of proofs.

May 1, 1995
Berkeley, Tucson, Minneapolis

Thomas A. Brady, Jr.
Heiko A. Oberman
James D. Tracy

LIST OF ABBREVIATIONS

AÉSC	=	*Annales. Économies, Sociétés, Civilisations*
AGKN	=	*Archief voor de Geschiedenis van de Katholieke Kerk in Nederland*
AHR	=	*American Historical Review*
AKG	=	*Archiv für Kulturgeschichte*
AM	=	*Annales du Midi*
ARG	=	*Archiv für Reformationsgeschichte*
BFPLL	=	Bibliothèque de la Faculté de Philosophie et Lettres de l'Université de Liège
BHR	=	*Bibliothèque d'Humanisme et Renaissance*
BSHPF	=	*Bulletin de la Société de l'Histoire du Protestantisme Français*
CEH	=	*Central European History*
CH	=	*Church History*
CHR	=	*Catholic Historical Review*
CRR	=	Classics of the Radical Reformation
DB	=	Doopsgezinde Bijdragen
DIP	=	*Dizionario degli istituti di perfezione* (Rome, 1974-)
GG	=	*Geschichte und Gesellschaft*
HistJ	=	*The Historical Journal*
HJ	=	*Historisches Jahrbuch*
HWJ	=	*History Workshop Journal*
HZ	=	*Historische Zeitschrift*
IMU	=	*Italia medioevale e umanistica*
JBS	=	*Journal of British Studies*
JEccH	=	*Journal of Ecclesiastical History*
JGPÖ	=	*Jahrbuch der Gesellschaft für die Geschichte des Protestantismus in Österreich*
JIH	=	*Journal of Interdisciplinary History*
JMH	=	*Journal of Modern History*
JMRS	=	*Journal of Medieval and Renaissance Studies*
JSH	=	*Journal of Social History*
KLK	=	Katholisches Leben und Kämpfen im Zeitalter der Glaubensspaltung
MQR	=	*Mennonite Quarterly Review*
NCE	=	*New Catholic Encyclopedia*
PaP	=	*Past and Present*
QFRG	=	Quellen und Forschungen zur Reformationsgeschichte
RenQ	=	*Renaissance Quarterly*
RGPGS	=	Rijks Geschiedkundige Publicatiën, Grote Serie
RGPKS	=	Rijks Geschiedkundige Publicatiën, Kleine Serie
RHEF	=	*Revue d'Histoire de l'Eglise de France*
RHFFL	=	Renaissance Humanism: Foundations, Forms, and Legacy, ed. Albert Rabil, Jr., 3 vols. (Philadelphia, 1988)
RQ	=	*Römische Quartalschrift für christliche Altertumskunde und Kirchengeschichte*
RSCHS	=	*Records of the Scottish Church History Society*
RSCI	=	*Rivista di Storia della Chiesa in Italia*
RSI	=	*Rivista Storica Italiana*

SCJ	=	*Sixteenth Century Journal*
SCES	=	Sixteenth Century Essays & Studies
SFN	=	Spätmittelalter und Frühe Neuzeit. Tübinger Forschungen zur Geschichtswissenschaft
SH	=	*Social History*
SIA	=	*Storia d'Italia. Annali*
SKRG	=	Schriften zur Kirchen- und Rechtsgeschichte
SAMH	=	Studies in Anabaptist and Mennonite History
SMRT	=	Studies in Medieval and Reformation Thought
SHCT	=	Studies in the History of Christian Thought
SVRG	=	Schriften des Vereins für Reformationsgeschichte
TAPS	=	Transactons of the American Philosophical Society
THR	=	Travaux d'Humanisme et Renaissance
TRE	=	*Theologische Realenzyklopädie*
TRS	=	*Transactions of the Royal Historical Society*
VIEG	=	Veröffentlichungen des Instituts für Europäische Geschichte Mainz
VKLBW	=	Veröffentlichen der Kommission für geschichtliche Landeskunde in Baden-Württemberg
WA	=	Martin Luther, *Kritische Gesamtausgabe* (Weimar, 1883-1983)
WdF	=	Wege der Forschung
ZBLG	=	*Zeitschrift für bayerische Landesgeschichte*
ZfG	=	*Zeitschrift für Geschichtswissenschaft*
ZHF	=	*Zeitschrift für Historische Forschung*
ZKiG	=	*Zeitschrift für Kirchengeschichte*
ZSRG, KA	=	*Zeitschrift der Savigny-Stiftung für Rechtsgeschichte, Kanonistische Abteilung*

LIST OF MAPS

LIST OF TABLES

INTRODUCTION:
THE UNSETTLING SETTLEMENTS

The halfway-point of this *Handbook* is exactly the place to pause in our exploration of two centuries of European history in order to reflect on the development of this field, its advances achieved and pitfalls encountered on paths long trodden. Our successors in the next century will more readily grasp the blind spots concealed in our value judgements, the capriciousness in our selectiveness, and the timebound nature of our intuitive apperceptions. Yet from our present perspective, it seems safe to say that this *Handbook* is presented at a favorable junction in time. The very material extension of the scope of historical knowledge—through intensive archival research, the availability of more and better annotated critical editions, and the expansion of geographical coverage—has muted the bold claims to a single, comprehensive, and indeed inclusive Grand Narrative.

In striking humility, the emerging field of twentieth-century history, the emancipated child of political journalism, shows its origins in a search for 'trends'; historians of modern Europe boast greater hindsight by looking for the still fluid but already more definite category of 'dynamics'. In our field the search is on for 'processes', which are far more enticing than mere trends or dynamics. This search suggests a reality which the historian encounters rather than invents. Whenever one of these processes—in themselves not realities but models for organizing the painfully limited knowledge we have about some aspect of the past—is singled out as the conduit of the 'true dynamics' of history, we approach the cradle where a new Grand Narrative is given birth.

One essential function of this *Handbook* is to provide such abundant information and broad perspectives that the reader will suspect the word 'process' in the singular and, at most, consider it as a working hypothesis, bold and challenging. Early modern historians agree on two questions: was there such a thing as modernization, and if so, how does one unravel its multiple threads? This high standard for measuring historiographical advance will admit 'settlements' only as stages on an open-ended trajectory. These settlements—be they national, confessional, regional or political—can only be designated as such to high-light their unsettled, transitory nature.

※ ※ ※

Renaissance and Reformation history owe much of their appeal to their perceived role in the modernization of Europe. Today, however, scholars in these two fields have become noticeably reticent. The emancipation thesis, the tale of the liberation from the 'Dark Ages' to the 'modernity' of the Italian Renaissance, first met major resistance from within the ranks of intellectual historians who assailed this high wall of separation between the Middle Ages and the Renaissance. His unparalleled grasp of primary sources allowed Paul Oskar Kristeller to muster ample evidence for continuity, while carefully chronicling a new beginning in the humanist reform of education. Particularly after Peter Burke questioned the relation between high culture and the several strata in society, the modernity thesis of Jacob Burckhardt rapidly lost support in the world of English-speaking Renaissance scholarship, with only occasional reprises in Germany.[1]

While this debate subsided, the view of Hans Baron, articulated forty years ago in a German publication, refocused attention on the arena of political history: 'In confrontation with imperial and papal claims to universal rule, a new awareness emerged stressing the political function and historical role of the autonomous state'.[2] Though this thesis of secular emancipation grew out of Baron's study of Calvin,[3] Reformation historians have paid strikingly little—and increasingly less—attention to this line of pursuit. Either subsumed—and therefore disguised—under the umbrella of 'anticlericalism' or rendered suspect by means of the anachronistic term 'whiggish',[4] today political emancipation does not play a central role in determining an innovative dimension of Luther and his movement. Both the catholic qualification of Luther's reformation as the 'reformation of the princes', the dead end of the 'Fürstenreformation',[5] and the protestant insistence on the theological nature of the early Reformation—in a 'Lutherische Engführung'[6]—mark the boundaries of the present debate in which political history must struggle to regain its place side by side with religious and social history. The first signs of such a recovery can be found in a perspective which accounts both for discontinuity and continuity with a fresh sense of the porous demarcation line separating the later Middle Ages from the Reformation.[7]

※ ※ ※

Advances, shifts, and present preoccupations can be best measured in the distant mirror of past achievements. Just over a century ago Friedrich von Bezold (1848-1928) denied the very idea of a sixteenth-century 'settlement' in an encompassing Handbook, innovative both in vision and scope. Bezold's *Geschichte der deutschen Reformation*[8] formed an essential part of Wilhelm Oncken's impressive project to present 'world history' in a cohesive series of monographs. Throughout we are reminded of the high standards set by what is often disdainfully called the age of 'historicism'. Reared with the ideals of his revolutionary birth year (1848),[9] Bezold approached the Reformation epoch by shifting away from Ranke's emphasis on politics and princes as well as from Treitschke's pursuit of a uniquely German national 'spirit': Bezold offers a study of the German people from about 1400 until 1555. Completed in the year in which Leopold von Ranke (1795-1886) died, this promising reorientation was swept aside by the prevailing winds of nationalism, as the legacy of Heinrich von Treitschke (1834-1895) gave momentum to an increasingly radical confidence, a conviction that a superior destiny awaited the German nation. It deserves to be recalled here.

In his Introduction Bezold does not yet reveal his new vision, but rather he seems to combine the prevailing German version of British imperialism with the usual central casting of Luther as prophet of Christian Freedom: the greatest threat to the hegemony of the medieval church, more formidable than the military prowess of the Emperor and the secular spirit of Renaissance humanism, was the 'awakening of the German conscience'.[10] Even the final passage of the volume can still be read in this vein: 'Without Luther we would not have had a Kant or a Goethe; without the protestant and anti-imperial origins of the Prussian state we would not have our new German Reich. Not without grief, and yet moved by profound gratitude we may look back today upon the most revolutionary upheaval in our national history'.[11]

Yet, Bezold's acknowledgment of this sense of grief—his word 'Trauer' oscillates between 'sorrow' and 'mourning'—is in keeping with the major underlying thesis: the Reformation, *the* epoch of revolution—as a matter of fact, of a series of revolutions—failed to reshape the social and political landscape of Germany. Contesting the convictions of his conservative colleagues, Bezold's presentation of the Peasant's War—the 'Revolution' of the peasants—dwarfed the hallowed revolt of the knights. The uprising of the cities and the resistance of the princes are likewise placed in the framework of political and social history. Luther, though treated at length, is not canonized as a national liberator; he is even censured for being 'excessive' at crucial times; but above all, he lacks a vital grasp of the interconnection between religious and social ferment.[12] Bezold points to Luther's stance 'between God and the Devil' to explain why Luther recoils before revolts in every form as machinations of Satan rather than aspirations of human agents.[13] Yet in the long-term view, the true drama of the failed revolution of 1525 was not so much a matter of religion but of social control: from here a line can be drawn to the emergence of the German police state.[14] The Peasant War spawned strict supervision and state control which modern research tends to associate with 'confessionalization', a development today relegated to the later-half of the century.

One more point will highlight the wider perimeters of this achievement. Friedrich von Bezold wrote at a time when German universities were still on the forefront of medieval and Renaissance studies, before the forced exodus of Jewish scholars and the resulting *translatio imperii* in the thirties. For him it is therefore a matter of course to include the fifteenth century as part of the Reformation era. Accordingly, his story starts around 1400 and highlights what we call today structural 'long-term developments' in church and society, enlarging the scope of that cultural history which in 1860 Jacob Buckhardt had identified with the Italian Renaissance. Moreover, Bezold's geographical range is remarkable. Even for the period 1525-1555, the traditional German focus suggested by the title broadens to encompass Europe from Italy to Scandinavia, from Spain to Austria, and from the Low Countries to the Ottoman Empire.

Looking at modern scholarship from this vantage point, one is most struck by the study's grand dimensions. Today no single scholar could write—or would dare to write—a work of such scope. Our two-volume *Handbook* brings forty-one leading scholars together, not out of some democratic sentiment of 'equal representation', but because each contributor is acutely aware of a fundamental limitation: each has only mastered individual strands of a complex lived reality in the fifteenth and sixteenth centuries. In itself this is not the dramatic drawback oft cited by those lamenting 'specialization'—provided that the results of microscopic research are integrated into the totality of the known past. This *Handbook* is at once a necessary and challenging resource for information and re-orientation, illuminating avenues of investigation

which otherwise would remain blind alleys. Specialization only becomes counterproductive when a historian canonizes a selection of
themes as the sole carrier of the Grand Narrative, claimed as the
'Mother of all Stories' either by virtue of a theory of causation or by a
prophetic vision of transcendent reality.

A second observation goes beyond matters of material grasp and
geographical scope. The treatment of the period 1400-1600 has been
the privileged battleground of conflicting ideological presuppositions
and competing confessions. At times wrapped in nostalgic dreams
about a harmonious union of church and state, about liberal education
or a global Reformation, these controlling conceptions, never receding
far, often simmered just beneath the surface and thus eluded complete
elimination. The very choice of the chronological perimeters 1400-
1600 raises a significant barrier to the confessional canonization of one
isolated phase, privileging either the Late Middle Ages, the Renaissance, or the Reformation.

This vision of the entire field, which takes in both the center and the
periphery, could not but affect the status of intellectual history. This
scholarly tradition was already in fierce competition with a new interest in impersonal, material factors as the decisive forces shaping the
course of history. While classical Marxism continued to esteem the
progressive course of ideas as illuminating social reality, the emphasis
on the determining role of economic and social conditions marginalized Renaissance humanism as the preserve of the cultural elite; and the
Reformation movement appeared at best as an accelerator in the mechanical transformation of the middle class from citizen to subject.

Whereas Bezold had already pointed to the importance of 'conditions', he had avoided their association with the loaded pre-Enlighten-
ment concept of 'destiny', so subtly but forcefully present in the work
of Ranke.[15] Whatever the typical blinders of our day may be, this
Handbook is published at an auspicious time, in so far as the concepts
'destiny' and 'determination' have become suspect. Yet long after a supernatural vision of the goal of history and its concomitant teleology
had been abandoned, derivative forms are still operational wherever a
political or economic concatenation of causes is posited. In our period
this can take the form of a late medieval economic depression marking
the end of feudalism, or the birth of the nation state as the necessary
access route to modernity. Echoes of the former language of determin-
ism can still be heard in the use of supposedly innocent and seemingly
descriptive expressions as 'of course', and 'process'. But precisely the

explanatory force of Max Weber's rationalization thesis or of Norbert Elias' discovery of the interrelation between state control and self-discipline[16] has pointed to multiple processes: each alone cannot lay claim to present the sole explanatory historical force. A multifaceted perspective gained a substantial following in the post-World War II era under the influence of Marc Bloch and Lucien Febvre, who in 1929 founded the *Annales d'histoire économique et sociale*. Not intended as a new school—a premise which later interpreters are not always willing to honor[17]—the structuralist shift of emphasis from 'events' to factors of 'long duration' never evolved into a stringent orthodoxy. It did serve, however, to demythologize the confessional divide between the later Middle Ages and early modern times—today associated with the mythological year 1500 only by incunabula-collectors.

✖ ✖ ✖

This *Handbook* is heir to more than a new sense of periodization.[18] Novel insights pertaining to the beginning and to the end of our period directly affect the agenda of issues to be dealt with in the period between the long fourteenth and the seventeenth centuries.

While the division of these two volumes into 'Structures' and 'Settlements' evokes the older distinction between 'long-term developments' and 'events', the third focal point of the *Annales*, 'mentalité', functions here in a new way. Increasingly reinterpreted as 'subjective reality'— how people perceive themselves and their world—this concept has its own dynamics and cannot easily be confused with statistically measurable social and economic conditions. Aaron Gurevich has advanced a concise formulation of this role of mentality: 'The objective processes of history in themselves are only potential causes for the behavior of people; they become its effective causes only after they have been transformed into facts of social consciousness.'[19] This assessment of the creative response of social groups not only allows for the revalidation of the study of the 'elite' speakers for such groups, but more generally bridges the treacherous, pervasive gap between social and intellectual history—provided the latter can be coaxed from its splendid tower of isolation to become once more a major player on the fields below.

Such bridging is already well advanced in the treatment of the end of our epoch. The settlements here treated are collectively interpreted as the initiation of a new era, the era of 'confessionalization'.[20] The language of 'process' with its 'necessary' outcomes is still applied to the emergence of the modern state. On closer inspection, however, a multitude of processes are identified in order to describe the historical dynamics in the rise of modernity, a development observed in far more than state formation. It is best described as a paradigm change, the interconfessional emergence of a new, early-modern mentality, expressed simultaneously in the domains of religious, social, and political culture. This designation of the outcome of the era of reformations as the Age of Confessionalization 'emphasizes the dynamic and revolutionary character of the period as well as the political and social implications of its religious and ecclesiastical change'.[21]

※ ※ ※

Looking back over the path travelled in about one hundred years, it is clear that the once dominant German perspective has been thoroughly Europeanized. Furthermore, the former preoccupation with the early modern state has been reoriented to the emergence of early modern society. As in the past, the quest for order is seen as pervasive in our period, while the stability and the legitimacy of the old order—Church and Empire—was put to the test. Whether this era actually marks the arrival of a disciplined, ordered Europe, depends both on the evaluation of the settlements achieved and on the geographical areas studied: the Dutch Republic will yield discoveries which differ greatly from conclusions reached in either France or England, in Spain or Scandinavia. The suggested processes must be grasped as explanatory devices which function better in extrapolating ordered sequences than in accounting for the manifold contingent anomalies. However, they do allow for the kind of intercontinental comparative history which sees in the world beyond Europe more than the discoveries of colonizing sailors, bent on the export of civilization and the exploitation of the uncivilized.

A balanced view of history will be concerned with the large-scale dynamics without losing sight of subjective reality, the taste and touch of a time, the experience of daily life. In these two volumes the contributors have gathered materials and gleaned insights which provide the basic ingredients necessary for that kind of history which seeks 'to see every idea, value, and practice in tension between at least two voices, whether Catholic and Protestant, southern and northern, local and national, rich and poor, powerful and powerless, lettered and unlettered, clerical and lay, or female and male'.[22]

NOTES

1. See August Buck, "Säkularisierende Grundtendenzen der italienischen Renaissance," in *Studien zum 15. Jahrhundert. Festschrift für Erich Meuthen*, Band 2, ed. Johannes Helmrath and Heribert Müller with Helmut Wolff (Munich, 1994), 609-22.
2. "Die politische Entwicklung der italienischen Renaissance," in *HZ* 174 (1952): 31-54, here at 35.
3. *Calvins Staatsauffassung und das konfessionelle Zeitalter*, Historische Zeitschrift, Beihefte 1-3, (Berlin, 1924).
4. For a precise description of genuine "whiggish" thought, perceptions and politics, see Patrick Collinson, "The Elizabethan Exclusion Crisis and the Elizabethan Polity," *Proceedings of the British Academy* 84 (1994): 51-92.
5. Erwin Iserloh, "Die Protestantische Reformation," in *Handbuch der Kirchengeschichte*, vol. 4, Reformation, Katholische Reform und Gegenreformation, ed. E. Iserloh, J. Glazik, and H. Jedin, (Freiburg, 1967), 145.
6. See Bernd Moeller, "Was wurde in der Frühzeit der Reformation in den deutschen Städten gepredigt?" *ARG* 75 (1984): 176-93, here at 193. Terminologically modified as "evangelische Engführung" in *Reformationstheorien* (as in note 7), 21 note 22.
7. See Manfred Schulze, *Fürsten und Reformation*, Spätmittelalter und Reformation, Neue Reihe, vol. 2 (Tübingen, 1991); Berndt Hamm, "Einheit und Vielfalt der Reformation—oder: was die Reformation zur Reformation machte," in Berndt Hamm, Bernd Moeller, and Dorothea Wendebourg, *Reformationstheorien. Ein kirchenhistorischer Disput über Einheit und Vielfalt der Reformation*, (Göttingen, 1995), 57-127.
8. Berlin: G. Grote'sche Verlagsbuchhandlung, 1886. The very publication date of Bezold's Reformation history is something of a mystery. Whereas 1886 appears on the title page of some copies, in all modern bibliographies the date of publication is given as 1890. See *Neue Deutsche Biographie*, vol. 2 (1955): 210-11. (The reprint by AMS Press, New York, 1971, reproduces the 1890 edition.) The explanation is that the volume was produced in installments—the total typesetting ran from 2 January 1886 until 13 June 1890. The first 168 pages were published in 1886 covering medieval social history until the "armer Konrad" (1514) and the politics preceding the election of Charles V (1519).
9. Thus Fritz Kern, "Friedrich von Bezold: 29 April 1928. Gedächtnisworte am Sarg, *AKG* 18 (1928): 241-45, here at 243. See the more extensive article by Gisbert Beyerhaus, who could draw on private correspondence, in "Friedrich von Bezold," *HZ* 141 (1930): 315-26, here at 316.
10. "Gefährlicher als die Romfahrten der mächtigsten Kaiser, zerstörender als das schleichende Gift des humanistischen Heidentums wurde für die All-

macht der Hierarchie das Erwachen des deutschen Gewissens." Bezold, *Geschichte der deutsche Reformation*, 17.

11. "Ohne Luther hätten wir keinen Kant und Goethe, ohne die protestanti-sche und antikaiserliche Herkunft des preußischen Staats nicht unser neu-es Deutsches Reich. Nicht ohne Trauer, aber doch mit dankbarer Erhe-bung dürfen wir heute auf die gewaltigste Umwälzung unserer nationalen Geschichte zurückschauen." Ibid., 872.

12. Ibid., 445-48.

13. "Wir müssen uns gegenwärtig halten, daß Luther ganz in dem Gedanken eines höchst persönlichen Kampfs mit dem Teufel lebte, daß er jedes sei-nem Evangelium entgegenstehende Hinderniß auf satanischen Ursprung zurückführte." Ibid., 447.

14. "Der Gedanke, daß die Obrigkeit im Kleinsten wie im Größten ganz nach Gutdünken schalten könne, ist durch den Bauernkrieg wesentlich geför-dert worden; in diesem Sinn mag die furchtbare Katastrophe für eine von den Vorbedingungen jenes modernen Staatswesens gelten, wie es sich da-mals in den deutschen Territorien entwickelte." Ibid., 511.

15. The most revealing statement is not to be found, as one might expect, in Ranke's history of the Reformation but 'hidden' in his *Französiche Ge-schichte vornehmlich im sechzehnten und siebzehnten Jahrhundert*: "... so erschien, als die Zeit gekommen war,—denn alles auf Erden hat durch ein göttliches Geschick seine Zeit und Stunde—aus den inneren Trieben des europäischen Lebens erwachsend, der Protestantismus" Vol. 1 (Leipzig, 1876 [1852]): 109.

16. For the profile and impact of Elias (1897-1990) see *Human History and Social Process*, ed. Johan Goudsblom, et al. (Exeter, 1989). For the con-vergence of interests between Weber (1864-1920) and Elias, see Edward Portis, "Max Weber's theory of personality," *Sociological Inquiry* 48 (1978): 113-20. See Colin Gordon, *Max Weber: Rationality and Moder-nity*, ed. S. Whimster and Scott Lash (London, 1987).

17. Thus Lutz Raphael, *Die Erben von Bloch und Febvre. 'Annales'— Geschichtschreibung und 'nouvelle histoire' in Frankreich 1945 bis 1980* (Stuttgart, 1994).

18. For its wide acceptance, see the literature quoted in the Introduction to Volume 1 of this *Handbook*, xxiv note 19.

19. *Historical Anthropology of the Middle Ages*, ed. Jana Howlett (Chicago, 1992), 48.

20. For its most concise formulation, see Heinz Schilling, "Luther, Loyola, Calvin und die europäische Neuzeit," *ARG*, 85 (1994): 5-31, here at 8-9, 28-29.

21. Heinz Schilling, *Religion, Political Culture and the Emergence of Early Modern Society. Essays in German and Dutch History*, SMRT, vol. 50, (Leiden, 1992), 301.

22. Thomas A. Brady, Jr., "'The Reformation in Germany and Europe'— Reflections," in *Die Reformation in Deutschland und Europa: Interpreta-tionen und Debatten*, eds. H.R. Guggisberg and G.G. Krodel, Sonderband ARG (Gütersloh, 1993), 683-91, here at 685.

Part 1.
Visions of Reform

IDEAS OF *REFORMATIO* AND *RENOVATIO* FROM THE MIDDLE AGES TO THE REFORMATION

Gerald Strauss
(Amherst, Massachusetts)

"... to bring the affairs of the Holy Church and the
Holy Roman Empire into good and right order"

Throughout the later Middle Ages the call for reform and renewal was near-universal in Europe, and in the sixteenth century the responses made to its persistent sounding became a test for judging what was, and what was not, being done in the enactment of the Reformation. No other words carried the conceptual richness and emotive power of the pair *reformatio-renovatio*, which—as organizing image, object and expression of hope, and rallying slogan resonated in nearly every segment of society. Scrutinized by scholars for well over a century now, the two words, along with their satellite terms *instauratio*, *restauratio*, *reparatio*, continue to be of great interest to students of late medieval and early modern culture because the investigation of them leads one directly and deeply into the language and thought of the era that gave them currency.

Awareness of being present at a historical moment of fateful change must have been pervasive in the sixteenth century, for talk about it was abundant, almost obsessive. From learned commentary and programmatic assertions made in high places to popular preaching and soothsaying, the voices of observers promised, intimated, urged and cajoled, cautioned about, exulted in or at times deplored far-reaching mutations in all areas of life: "a new and thoroughgoing reformation,"[1] "a total alteration and reformation in the Christian Church,"[2] "an amelioration of the faith and a renovation of the clergy,"[3] "a reformation and renewal of Christian life,"[4] "a reformation of the spiritual and temporal estates,"[5] "a reforming of our life and actions by [Christ's] word,"[6] "a reformation and improvement of public morals in this land,"[7] and so on. Addressing the Fifth Lateran Council convened by Pope Julius II at its opening session in May 1512, the noted scholar, orator, and Augustinian vicar-general Aegidius of Viterbo implored those present to recognize that even as "celestial and human things,

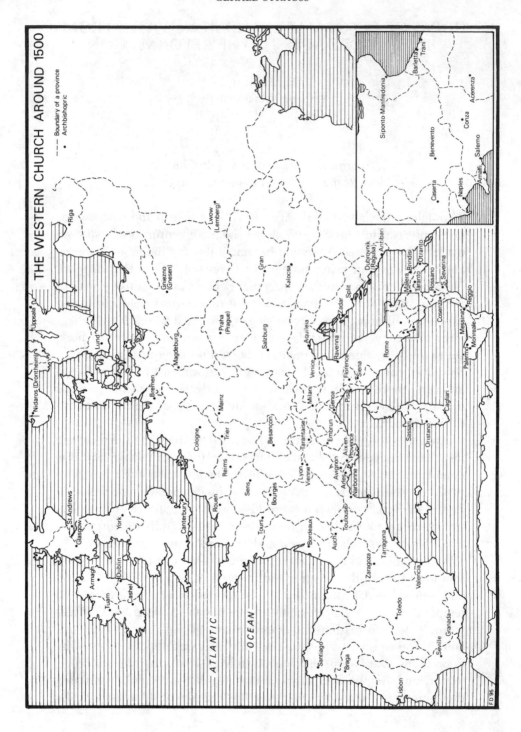

which are subject to motion, crave renewal," so the Church must be "restored to its ancient splendor and purity."[8] From the cosmos to the human body renewal was deemed necessary and was desired, demanded, and expected. Assurances by medical practitioners that their panaceas could bring about "a *Restauratio, Renovatio*, purgation and renewal of the whole body"[9] suggested compelling analogies to corporations such as Church and community whose ills had long been resisting less systemic prescriptions for a cure. When Martin Luther was eulogized upon his death as the "God-sent Reformer of the Church"[10] who had broken down the gates of the Babylonian prison by inaugurating *diese endliche Reformation*—this reformation-in-the-nick-of-time, this long-awaited, long-overdue, often-predicted but ever-delayed reformation at the last possible moment "before Judgment Day"[11]—the words must have suggested to those who heard and read them that, Luther having now "led us back to the pure source of Scripture,"[12] the longed-for renewal of faith and religion had actually been accomplished. By no means everyone agreed that this was so (Martin Luther himself refused to be cast in the part of "reformer"). But the mental and verbal charge of hopes and anticipations carried by "reform" and "renewal" was so high that it could not have failed to release itself upon so spectacular a public figure and the well publicized struggles of his embattled career.

How this came to be so by the middle of the sixteenth century—how "reform" and "renewal" became the "key terms" and "catchwords" of the age[13]—is a long story that, as noted, has been closely studied but does not stale in the retelling. What needs to be conveyed by an account that reaches from Greek antiquity to early modern times in Europe is not only the provenance, the long life, and the rich signification of *reformatio-renovatio* as ideas. To the historian, at least, what matters above all is the place of these ideas in the collective experience of Europeans, and their relevance to some major events and prominent groups and persons whose self-perception and view of the world, and of their roles in it, were substantially shaped by their understanding of reform and renewal as imperatives, norms, and warrants. In the late Middle Ages, ideas and notions of reform and renewal surged in historical importance, causing great agitation and commotion. It has been said that there was scarcely a major figure in Europe at the time who did not concern himself with them.[14] But ordinary people were also caught up in the excitement. An explanation of reform-renewal in their historical setting must suggest something of the great swell of enthusiasm that gathered around this notional cluster in the mid- and late fourteen hundreds, and the powerful momentum that carried this wave into the sixteenth century. The present essay will concentrate on the late Middle Ages before returning to the Reformation which, as the title acquired by the evangelical movement even in its own time makes clear,[15] was seen, at least by its early partisans, as the long-delayed fulfillment of the cherished promise of reform.

1. CHRISTIAN IDEAS OF REFORM AND THEIR SOURCES

The pregnancy of "reform" and "renewal" as descriptive and evocative terms, and their enduring hold on Christian Europe, results in the first place from their compelling use in the New Testament and, in the second, from the echoes of pagan antiquity resounding in the thought world of that document, particularly in its Pauline portion.[16] The crucial place is Romans 12:2: "et nolite conformari huic saeculo, sed reformamini in novitate sensus vestri;" "Do not be conformed to this world, but be transformed by the renewal of your mind," the Greek *metamorphousthe*, Latin *reformamini*, suggesting a "creative transformation" or "making over" or "anew" of an existing state or condition.[17] The prefix "re" introduces the evocative register of the word, recalling, and recalling to, an earlier, better state of being or of affairs. In this sense *reformare* had been used by Roman writers to point to the need for, and possibility of, moral restoration,[18] while *reformatio/metamorphosis* as structural mutation, suggesting an alteration of form, goes back to Ovid and Apuleius. Given the inevitability of corruption and deformation in nature and time, "reforming" a thing mandated a change in the direction of a return, a restitution or reparation. Thus the early uses of the term connoted reversion rather than forward motion, no sort of progress being suggested—though the notion of an advance toward a desirable and attainable goal was to be introduced at a later moment in the Middle Ages, with explosive consequences, as we shall see.

That the healing reversion to a prior norm should be seen as a *renovatio* was implicit in the very image of such a return. But this interpretation drew further strength from ancient notions of cosmological and vitalistic renewal that never lost their original vigor and appeal under the Christian dispensation. The possibility of reform-by-return was therefore greatly enhanced by lingering, if vaguely expressed, beliefs in eternal recurrence, cyclical cosmic rejuvenation, and—more immediate to experience—seasonal vegetative revivals. The allure and longevity of such beliefs is expressed in language used throughout the Middle Ages to describe the recovery of vital energy by things and institutions: *revisco* (to be revived), *reviresco* (greening), *recalesco* (grow warm again), *refloresco* (bloom again), as well as regenerate, recuperate, resuscitate, and so forth.[19] Without the presence of such terms in the public discourse, the notion of a "renaissance" would not have been possible. *Renascor* (to spring up again, to be returned to life) was understood as a natural process guaranteed by the divine arrangement of things. Thus reform-transform-renew constituted a conceptual cluster, each term evoking and implying the others,[20] as in the verse from Romans (*sed reformamini in novitate sensus vestri*) and in many related New Testament passages such as Eph. 4:23 "And be renewed in the spirit of your minds," Titus 3:5 "he saved us... by the washing of regeneration and renewal in the Holy Spirit," 2 Cor. 4:16 "Though our outer nature is wasting away, our inner nature is being renewed every day," Col. 3:10 "the new nature, which is being renewed in knowledge after the image of his creator," God's image (Gen. 1:26) being the norm the reversion to which constitutes the renewing rectification held out as the only remedy for the deformations all natural things are heir to.

Pagan antiquity also furnished the material for a program of political restoration which, grafted onto Christian ideas of historical change, generated much of the reform momentum evident in Church and state throughout the Middle Ages. Given the enormous weight of ancient Rome in the European past, and its even more formidable presence in the historical imagination, it is not surprising that the possibility of a rebirth of the glory that had once been Rome was widely believed in, aspired to, and at times striven for.[21] Thus the coronation of Charlemagne by Pope Leo III, in Rome in the year 800, was represented as a "restoration of the Roman Empire [*renovatio imperii Romanorum*]," and this political restoration, in turn, encouraged endeavors to "repair [*reparare*]" arts and learning and to "recall [*revocare*]" other aspects of what, in retrospect, seemed to have been a political and cultural Golden Age. By the time the Saxon emperors Otto I and Otto III sought once again to "renew" the realm of the Caesars, in the 960s and 990s, repectively, "the Roman past, formerly only occasionally alluded to, had become an indispensable argument in the theory of legitimation with which the western empire advanced and defended its claims."[22]

In the eleventh century the "revival of Rome" became the objective also of a more aggressive papacy, which saw in Rome's place as "head of the world [*caput mundi*]" its own warrant for ecumenical primacy, particularly in its rivalry with secular states for this preeminence. For help in this competition both sides turned to the surviving body of Roman law. Justinian's *Corpus Juris Civilis* having been reintroduced into European jurisprudence in the eleventh century, the *renovatio* of the *Corpus Juris* was thought to be an effective instrument for reviving a political system whose constitutional and administrative mainstay it had been. Existing laws were "reformed" by bringing them into accord with Roman principles and procedures—another way in which the idea of *reformatio* (from then on the accepted term for an improving redaction of an older code)[23] merged with that of *renovatio*.

While certain analytical distinctions can therefore be drawn between the two terms (*reformatio* occurs when an improvement is made in something that, though deformed, has not ceased to exist, while *renovatio* suggests the revival of an entity or condition that had become defunct)[24] in ordinary usage, throughout the medieval period, reform and renewal presupposed and complemented each other as notions signifying necessary and desirable change—change that would not merely remedy defects, but also reverse a decline by infusing affected matter with fresh vitality. In this sense, the overriding object of "reform" was always the Christian faith and the institutions that enshrined and transmitted it. Corruption in the Church was universally seen as the root cause of all other problems besetting Christendom. Overcoming corruption meant a return to first principles and original practices, and such a return became the great imperative of all medieval reform.

A clear expression of it is the monastic reform movement. Cluny, in the tenth century, was for a time the model for the disciplined regular life validated normatively by a return to the rule of St. Benedict. In the twelfth century, it was above all the Cistercians who stood for a thoroughgoing attempt to undertake a restoration of the authentic spirit of pristine Christianity: renunciation, labor, imitation of Christ in all things. To "reform" individuals and institutions, i.e., "make them better [*reformare in melius*]," it was necessary to "restore [*restaurare*]" them to these original virtues. Although most orders relaxed the reforming impulse sooner or later, monasticism itself never lost the impetus to achieve this restoration, nor did the Church as a whole lack proponents of renewal, some merely urging meliorating steps to put its house in order, others exhorting to a drastic course of regeneration by returning it, somehow, to its original apostolic form.[25]   Contention about the goals and processes of Church reform is one of the grand themes of medieval ecclesiastical history. In no other undertaking was the contrast between ideal and reality so stark, or the tension as great between what was observed and what could be imagined. The perennial incentive to reform was a natural product of this contrast and this tension.

2. THE FRANCISCANS AND THE JOACHITE LEGACY

The Franciscan Spirituals

It was the Franciscan Order more than any other ecclesiastical corporation that came to embody the perennial drive to reform and renew. Having grown with astonishing speed from a band of intimate companions to the charismatic Francis of Assisi, who took the Christian command to humility literally, the *fratres minores* (from *minuere*, to make smaller, lessen: they considered themselves ministers to the poor and lowly) developed to its full revolutionary potential Christ's call to absolute poverty as a precondition for renewal. When soon after Francis's death in 1226 the Order split over the strict application of this command—specifically over the binding force of Francis's testament in which the founder had enjoined his followers never to deviate from the rule of unconditional poverty—a party of rigorists began to pursue an independent course. These "Spirituals," who included most of the early associates of Francis, vehemently opposed "relaxers" in the Order, men who were prepared to modify the New Testament command to "take nothing for your journey" (Luke 9:3). Spirituals stood for the strictest interpretation and application of Francis's rule and testament, and they were prepared to live accordingly. Eventually given separate standing in the Order by Pope Celestine V, an unworldly recluse who was chosen to the throne of St. Peter's (from which he resigned after five months) in 1294, the Spirituals were so unyielding in their advocacy of Christian ideals as laid down to them by their founder, and so militant in their attacks on a Church they saw operating at a huge distance from these ideals, that they soon incurred charges of heresy. While the more moderate wing of Franciscans, the Conventuals, adapted to the institutional demands of an established monastic Order, the Spirituals adhered to their principles, which they offered as the only means of effecting Christian reform in the world.

In this effort they were both impelled and supported by their becoming the apostles of the doctrine of the Eternal Gospel of Joachim a
Fiore, the Calabrian prophet who had left upon his death in 1202 a
body of revelatory writings that were to furnish succeeding ages with
one of western tradition's most powerful ideologies of renewal. Starting from the common conviction that, as events given in the Old Testament prefigure what comes to pass in the New, it must be possible to
foretell the course of the future from the past, but relying ultimately on
illuminations that came to him while working on the interpretation of
the Revelation of St. John, Joachim taught that history was moving
through three grand phases, or *status*, which corresponded to the three
Persons of the Trinity. The first of these phases, under the sovereignty
of the Father and the Old Testament, lasted to the birth of Christ. The
second, that of the New Testament and under the aegis of the Son, encompassed the history of the Church from its beginnings to the thirteenth century, the age on the threshold of which Joachim was writing.
Counting (with Matthew) forty-two generations from Abraham to
Christ, and reckoning a generation to be thirty years in length, Joachim
computed each *status* to be 1260 years in duration, which meant that
the second *status* would end, and the third and final one begin, in
about the middle of the thirteenth century. This third *status*, Joachim
predicted, would inaugurate an altogether new condition for humankind. Under the dispensation of the Holy Ghost and in accordance
with the revelation of an Everlasting Gospel (mentioned in Rev. 14:6),
old institutions and authorities would give way to a spiritual state
based on fullness of knowledge, true Christian love, and universal concord. The new age would not arrive without travail. The Church
would become more corrupt than ever, Antichrist and other enemies
would rise. But through the turmoil the certain way to the third state
would be led by two new religious orders whose work was to prepare
for the supplanting of the corrupt *ordo clericorum* of the second state
by an *ordo monachorum* in the third. They were to be representatives
of, and guides to, the Apostolic life whose simplicity, mutuality, and
joy in contemplation would become the models for all.[26]

The Joachite Legacy

Joachim's writings have puzzled interpreters down to our own time.
To a considerable extent it is the lack of precision—characteristic of
prophets—on many points in his works that accounts for his growing
influence in the centuries that followed. But two things, at least, are

clear about his doctrine of the Eternal Gospel (the title under which Joachim's writings were gathered after his death, explicitly suggesting that they themselves constituted the promised *evangelium aeternum*). First, it offered an unprecedented vision of a better future situated in real time, close at hand, and drastically different from everything that had preceded it in human affairs. In proposing this vision, it raised older expectations of renewal to a much higher pitch. Strictly speaking there is no *renovatio* in Joachim, no return to origins (although he does use the traditional term *reformatio* to characterize the coming transition). In Joachim's view, history moves forward to a higher state: it will be an *innovatio*. While he is certain that the world will end, he writes as the seer of things that will happen until the end comes.[27] It was this orientation that enabled Joachimism to generate the kind of intellectual and emotional enthusiasm peculiar to progressive readings of history, of which Joachim's doctrine is the exemplar.

Secondly, the vagueness inherent in Joachim's predictive scheme allowed for the appearance on the medieval scene of a proliferation of claimants to the role of inaugurator of the new age, a consequence that lent Joachimism an unusually direct historical relevance. Franciscans, in particular, took to its promulgation as a gospel of hope. From the 1240s (when the Spiritual John of Parma, an adherent of Joachim, was minister-general of the Order), they began to cast themselves as the *viri spirituales* of the third *status*, a distinction for which they believed themselves to be qualified by their devotion to the ideal of absolute poverty. They became prophets of the *evangelium aeternum*, which some of them identified with the rule of St. Francis. This, they taught, would supplant the laws and instruments of a worldly Church. They predicted the election of a *papa angelicus*, an "Angelic Pope (who, some claimed, would be a second Celestine, the pontiff who had first recognized the Spirituals) to take over from the Roman pope.[28] No instruments of governance would be needed in the coming *ecclesia spiritualis* whose guiding lights were to be ascetic and contemplative monks. Even the sacraments, according to Joachim, would disappear. Given this response, the Joachimite scheme of three world ages was bound to be distrusted, and at times condemned, by the Church as adherents began to claim that the third *status* had already begun, and as Spiritual Franciscans, the self-proclaimed bearers of Joachim's message, moved ever closer to what the Church had to regard as subversion.[29] On the other hand, it is not surprising that Joachimism should have continued to be highly influential (Dante, in his Divine Comedy

[Paradiso XII] placed Joachim in Paradise). First taken up by monastic zealots, Joachim's doctrines eventually entered society at large, where "they worked underground in the following centuries, from time to time springing to new life in a group or an individual. Their vital quality arose from the fact that they worked in the imagination, moving to hope and to action."[30]

Concretely, what was this hope? In general terms, it was the sense—palpable in the European consciousness from at least the fourteenth century onward—that the many defects burdening the institutions of religious and temporal life could and would be removed, and that the clean sweep to be made of deformed conditions would create the basis for a different and better state of being. As interpreted by his followers, some of whom took large liberties in reading and explaining him, even producing spurious treatises ascribed to him,[31] Joachim a Fiore's scheme offered those who longed for such a change the assurance that a great *reformatio* was destined to take place, that it would come in the near, perhaps the very near, future, and that it would be brought about by suprahuman intervention, ordinary mortals having long ago lost their ability to mend things by their own powers. In outline, at least, Joachimism sketched the scenario for this transition; it also cast the leading actors in the impending drama of reform and renewal: Peace Emperor, *papa sanctus*, *pastor bonus*; Antichrist, Simoniac Pope, *malleus ecclesiae*. As a prophetic model it was flexible enough to allow its interpreters to combine Joachim's progressivism with the backward-reaching propensity of traditionalists for whom the desirable future was inscribed in a Christian or humanistic Golden Age of the ancient past. Adjusted and readjusted to suit particular interests and circumstances, Joachimism served far into the sixteenth century as an ideological armature for prophets of renewal and advocates of corrective agendas.

More specifically, hopes for renewal and restoration embraced all institutions and processes of public life: Church, clergy, empire and states, law, the conditions of spiritual and material existence, relations of rulers to the governed, work and its rewards, apportionment of resources, the common welfare. Concerning the Church, the prescription for reform was given in its history, spelled out in its foundation charters: reform had to be a return to its state of origin in the apostolic age.[32] How could such a restoration be effected in time to avert ruination at the hands of heaven-sent chastizers or secular destroyers? Generations of churchmen and theologians attempted to give answers, always assuming that—as the fourteenth-century ecclesiastic William Durant argued—improvement in the world would never come without prior reform in the Church.[33] Nor could Church reform be partial. It must be total: "Reform in head and members." Durant's call for periodic General Councils to correct abuses top to bottom and prevent their recurrence continued to be taken up in his and the following two centuries, both within and outside the Church.

The Conciliar Movement

The Conciliar movement formed in response to this call proved especially productive of designs for the restructuring of the Church and the larger society in which it was the most influential presence. From inside the Church, Pierre d'Ailly's *De reformatione ecclesiae*, written when this prominent church politician was a member of a commission set up by the Council of Constance (1415-1418), suggested a scheme of total reform. So did his more famous colleague Nicholas of Cusa, whose *De concordantia catholica*—"the agenda for the Council of Basel for which all Europe waited impatiently"—and *Reformatio generalis*, a draft bull Cusa submitted to Pius II in 1459, suggested a way of leading the Church back to its original form (*ad formam primam reducere*).[34] These treatises are representative of a multitude of similar proposals that sprang up in the decades following the papal schism of 1378.[35] Their circulation helped give currency to the idea of reform as the removal of abuses. Meanwhile temporal rulers and their political agents pursued the objective of Church reform with somewhat different goals in mind. Sensing that all striving for an internal structural change was bound to come to grief over the Church's inability to resolve the inherent contradiction between trying to become spiritual and remaining institutionally viable, they utilized the universal demand for reform as a handy legitimizing warrant for extending their own authority over the Church in their respective realms. In the process of doing so, they produced "a distinct shift in the power relations between Church and territorial state" as more and more of the social functions traditionally reserved to the former came into the hands, or at least fell under the supervision, of the latter.[36]

3. INTIMATIONS OF REFORM AROUND 1500

But these words and deeds from high places do not convey the full measure of anticipation on the eve of the sixteenth century. Expectations of reform and renewal flowed like a great waterway into the age of the Reformation, nourished by tributaries each of which carried its own freight of wishes, hopes, and anxieties. Few in society failed to be swept along by this swelling stream, from which issued the great outpouring that bore Martin Luther and the evangelical movement on its crest, and which continued past the events of the early Reformation into the period of state churches and orthodoxy late in the sixteenth century.

Signs and Portents of Change
What gave these expectations of impending change their compelling force was the sense of urgency generated in the populace by the most abundant of tributary sources: the proliferation of warnings, promises, admonitions, and predictions that gushed from printing presses and pulpits, touching people's lives at every level of the social order. Astrology was the weightiest authority for such foretellings and forwarnings, most of them announcing an imminent crisis in the affairs of Church and states. Corruption and disintegration are everywhere. The end is clearly in sight; all portents point to it. Wherever one looks, one sees "a pitiful disintegration of Christendom, destruction of good customs and laws, misery of all estates, raging of plagues, inconstancy in all things, dreadful events befalling everyone."[37] And worse is to come. "Injustice and treachery will grow monstrously. The innocent will suffer persecutions." "So much screaming and moaning will be heard among Christians that one will say to the other, were it not better we had perished in our mother's womb?"[38]

Such was the opinion of prescient observers on how things were and were to be; but it was only half their message. The other part, offered with equal confidence, announced a *reformatio* or *renovatio* of worldly conditions, in the course of which a fundamental turnabout would occur only just in time to avert total destruction. "Thus things may still get better, though now all is wretched."[39] Few prognosticators thought that human strength sufficed to wield "the weapons of a reformation, transformation, edification, and amelioration of things."[40] Most promised help from a higher power. A "prophet" will "renew laws" and establish "new ceremonies." A "saintly pope" will be chosen and he will command the gospel to be preached. A "holy man" will lead followers to a more Christian life. A "reformer [*reformirer*]" will cleanse away all "filth and impurity [*unsauberkeit*]."[41] From the late fifteenth throughout the sixteenth and into the seventeenth centuries such predictions were written, printed, reprinted, read, and—presumably—talked about.[42] Some drew what, in retrospect, came to seem like an indisputable connection with events in Wittenberg. In his biography of Luther, written soon after the reformer's death, Johann Mathesius quoted the assertion of Johann Hilten, a fifteenth-century Franciscan interpreter of Daniel and Revelation, that "in the year 1516 he will come who will reform you and will cause my prophecies against you to come true."[43] These predictions were alarming enough to Church authorities to cause them to issue a decree in 1516 prohibiting clerics from foretelling future evils and calamities without prior approval by their superiors.[44] There is no doubt that, taken together, such proclamations of a coming *reformatio* contributed substantially to the widespread readiness of people in all ranks of society to believe that the time was near when "there will occur a veritable renewal and transformation."[45]

Shapes of the Coming Reform
If the forecasts of astrologers, while offered with confidence, are usually lacking in concreteness, other voices gave highly specific prescriptions for the renewal to come. In the realm of politics, the wish to reexperience ancient Rome restored to its full vigor had led, in the mid-fourteenth century, to the—briefly successful—attempt by Cola di Rienzo to stage a revival of the Republic. Fusing Joachimite and Spiritual Franciscan religious convictions about the coming age of the Holy Ghost[46] with a fierce longing for the revenance of Roman political might and brilliance, Rienzo—who was convinced of the imminence of Joachim's third *status*—filled his many pronouncements during and after his seven-months' term of office as tribune with mystical references to the "resurgence" of the Church, the "reform" of justice, the "regeneration" of the city of Rome, the "renewal" of all Italy under Roman leadership, and a "universal reformation," part of God's plan, which he hoped to launch with the help of pope and emperor.[47] A century and a half later another great politico-religious resurgence was predicted, in Florence, by the Dominican friar Savonarola, who announced from his pulpit, in 1494, that his city "will be the reformation of all Italy, and from here the renewal will begin and spread every-

where."[48] Savonarola's reading of Revelation and the prophets in the light of recent events had told him that "this is the time of the renewal of the Church and of your city [il tempo di rinovarsi la Chiesa e la città tua]."[49] "I predicted," Savonarola wrote a year later, "that by this reformation the city would become more glorious, more powerful, and richer than it had been up to now."[50] But it could not be done with the citizens' own powers. Too weak and corrupt to restore themselves, men can receive regeneration only through divine intervention, brought into their lives by agents of God. Both Rienzo's visions in the fourteenth, and Savonarola's at the end of the fifteenth century, evoked responses far beyond their immediate local effects. Their fusion of religious and political motives and goals, the projection of their respective cities as a New Jerusalem rising from a renewal of self and of the community, and the passionate energy with which their message was promoted, imparted to their ideals a powerful, if short-lived, ideological thrust.

In Germany renewal expectations were fed by an equally potent, but much more enduring, combination of political and religious images. Since the middle of the thirteenth century, Joachimite annunciations of a soon-to-come Age of the Spirit had, in the Holy Roman Empire, merged with promises—derived from other sources—of the advent of a peace-bringing ruler, an Emperor of the Last Days whose reign would establish the hoped-for Good Time. Launched originally by propagandists for the Hohenstaufen dynasty as an ideological weapon against papal and Italian efforts (also drawn from Joachim) to portray Frederick II and his successors as vicious destroyers of the Church,[51] the image of the Emperor of the New Age gained independent life in subsequent centuries. It was shaped and sustained by other prophetic traditions—Sibylline oracles and the revelations of St. Bridget, and Hildegard of Bingen[52]—in which a conquering hero was envisioned who would convert, or annihilate, all adversaries, purify the Church, re-establish justice, and bring about a blessed reordering of all things. Increasingly, and notably in the fifteenth century, descriptions of the ensuing reign of peace and prosperity, and of the preceding struggle to establish it, took on the character of a critique of existing social conditions. As such, the many prophecies of a coming Friedenskaiser, a peace emperor, seem to have reflected the aspirations of ordinary folk whose needs for significant social change had little chance of success in the real world of Church and national politics.[53]

The Emperor and Reform of the Empire

But the figure of a new, or Third, Friedrich (with suggestive plays on *Fried*—peace and *rich/reich*—rich in or realm of) as a *deus ex machina* to usher in the long-awaited *renovatio mundi* evidently stirred hearts and minds in all social ranks, and the sometimes extravagant, occasionally bizarre, and frequently violent language in which the shape of coming events was indicated should not lead one to suspect German emperor prophecies of being a species of rabble rousing. They were a common article of belief in an age without firm distinctions between the political and religious mentalities of the poor and the culture of the well-to-do. By far the most widely known of the fifteenth century's many reform writings, the so-called *Reformation of the Emperor Sigismund*, written in 1439, in German, by an unknown author in Basel, and purporting to contain the emperor's thoughts on the reform of religion and society, exerted its influence for a long time on the highest political and intellectual circles in the empire.[54] It opens with a ringing declaration: "Obedience is dead. Justice is grievously abused. Nothing stands in its proper order."[55] It proposes sweeping alterations to be made in ecclesiastical and worldly affairs so as to curb greed, ambition, the arrogance of power, and the exploitation of the weak. These reforms, though they are announced in sometimes inflammatory language,[56] are conservative in that they proceeded from the claimed remembrance of a sound and right order of things in the past, the return to which is mandated by the disarray into which things have fallen. The *Reformatio Sigismundi* has much to say about practical steps to be taken in that direction. In the end, however, the success of the great transformation will depend on the intervention of a higher power, in this case a priest-ruler, whose appearance will signal the imposition of "the holy blessed new order." This truth, it is stated, was communicated to Sigismund by a voice he heard "toward dawn on Ascension Day." It told him that "He who will come after you is a priest through whom God will accomplish many things ... His name shall be Friedrich, and he shall bring peace to the empire ... Though stern at first, his rule will grow mild; he may appear strange now, but will become familiar ... All men await his coming. The time is near when it shall be fulfilled."[57]

The prospects for a superhuman peace bringer seem to have been considered excellent in the fifteenth century, though he was slow in making his appearance. "When will the emperor come? God's mercy has come, but peace comes slowly ... You will find a man of honor and strength, who will counsel us in the law and will know what is right."[58] Around 1500, a wordy treatise offering a blueprint for a drastically changed society to be inaugurated by a brotherhood of religious—though not monkish—reformers, announced the arrival, soon after 1500, of a "Peace King from the Black Forest" who will make justice prevail, reform the Church, and establish order in the empire:

> Our future King is sent to us by God.... He will bear upon his breast a yellow cross as a sign of his mission to abolish evil and reestablish the good ... The Cumaean Sibyl says: "He will reform and discipline both estates!" Saint Bridget of Sweden writes "Be of good cheer. A pious man will enter into the garden of the Virgin," by which she means the Black Forest and Alsace. And Jesus, a Son of God, said: "Greater works than these shall he do." ... His name signifies Man of God, Lover of Right, Bringer of Peace. For this reason he is called Friedrich, rich in peace.[59]

Such hopes enjoyed vigor and a long life in the volatile religious and political climate of the empire, In 1521 Martin Luther speculated that the old prophecies of a New Friedrich were in his day being fulfilled in the person of his territorial lord, Duke Frederick of Saxony. The Elector had figuratively liberated the Holy Sepulcher, Luther contended, as the oracles predicted he would, by releasing Holy Scripture from the tomb in which the papists had buried it. And as he had been the imperial electors' original choice in the recent election, he might well have become emperor, which "is enough to fulfill the prophecy."[60] More extravagant claims that mantic predictions were being realized in an exalted figure of the day were concentrated on the Emperor Charles V, whose name linked him with a rival prophetic tradition that anticipated the imperial redeemer in the person of a returned Charlemagne. Readiness to see in Charles the fulfillment of these ancient forecasts transcended the boundaries of social station. Popular ballads circulating at the time of the imperial election of 1519 acclaimed him as the answer to "a multitude of prophecies" and saw in him a ruler who would "totally reform the world."[61] Astrologers ascertained "from all the old prophecies that the invincible Roman Emperor Charles V is He who shall carry out the Reform and conquer the Empire from east to west."[62] If this has the ring of populism in its naive linkage of soothsaying and history, humanists and theologians displayed no smaller confidence in the proposition that, with the ascent of the Burgundian-Austrian-Spanish Habsburg, a heaven-sent hero had arrived who would undertake, at long last, the promised *renovatio* of the world.[63]

Trying to come to terms with such effusions, which are plentiful in the sources, late-twentieth-century scholars will do well to restrain their interpretive impulses. Unable to think our way deeply into the minds and psyches of people from a distant time, we cannot tell whether, and how, they managed in their private understanding of things to distinguish the real (as it will seem to us now) from the fanci-ful in their experience. Without clues to their habits of sorting out facts from fantasies, we have no choice but to exercise hermeneutic caution. Nor can we be confident in attaching a label to the common hope for the appearance on the scene of a divinely appointed bringer of renewal. Was it chiliasm? The idea of a millennium based on Rev. 20:1-5 and other Jewish sources depicting a future deliverer sent to annihilate enemies and reign over the whole world[64] was rejected by the Church but survived in the popular imagination, whence it materialized repeatedly throughout the Middle Ages in the form of popular movements. Protestants, too, opposed the belief in a thousand years-long "worldly realm" of the pious from which all the godless would be eliminated.[65] Millenarian hopes proved inextinguishable, however, and in the figure of a peace-bringing ruler of the final days they received their most dramatic articulation.

A longing for justice, fair play, and spiritual comfort was perhaps the most heartfelt impulse driving these hopes.[66] Or it may have been the wish for a restoration of order and unity, for it was said to be the mission of the *Friedenskaiser* above all other things to put a permanent end to the fragmentation and internal strife that had been the unhappy lot of humankind throughout its history. How this grand pacification was imagined to work in practice we cannot say. Descriptions of it[67] tended to be vague and conventional, mixing elements of Christian eschatology,[68] Golden Age primitivism,[69] Roman law and government, apostolic egalitarianism, and Paradisical perfection. In general, change was believed to come in the form of a reversal: the mighty will fall, the hungry will eat, all that should not be will be abolished. Precedents existed for truly radical reconstructions of the world, as in the articles written for Tabor in 1420, where "nothing is mine and nothing thine, but all is common. Christ himself shall rule."[70] More often, Utopian goals remained shadowy. But three points about the great transformation seem of special importance. First, the acceptance of even the possibility of such an event coming to pass is likely to have greatly expanded people's horizon of expectation at the beginning of the sixteenth century: wishful thinking, ceaselessly stimulated, leading to

visions of wish fulfillment.[71] Second, this expectation, in turn, must
have bred a mental and emotional state of readiness, a tense condition
in which people were prepared to recognize in a figure such as Martin
Luther—far from imperial though he was in his bearing—the leader so
ardently promised in so many prophecies. Third, the sense of impending crisis generated by apocalyptic announcements of a great transformation preceded by a comprehensive purification (sometimes spoken
of as the analogue of an alchemical process)[72] must have infused the
mental and psychological atmosphere with great urgency. Without
this work of preparation, and in the absence of this climate of urgency,
it is difficult to imagine that the events beginning in Wittenberg in
1517 could have followed the course that shaped them into The Reformation.

4. Ideas of Reform in the Protestant and
Catholic Reformations

Ideas of Reform in the German Reformation
Luther, as already noted, decisively rejected for himself the role of reformer. What he meant by this disclaimer is made clear in a comment
he wrote on the Ninety-Five Theses in 1518: It's not within the powers of one man—be he pope, cardinal, or anyone else—to reform the
Church, desperately needed though reform is, he wrote. If such a reform is to be effective, it must be part of a reconditioning of the whole
world, a task no one but God Himself can undertake. "But the time of
this reformation is known to Him alone who has created the ages."[73]
In other words, the renewal anticipated by so many of Luther's contemporaries, and later credited to him by his supporters, was not his to
achieve, or even to inaugurate. It could only be God's work.

On the other hand, Luther did, at times, allude—and not without
evident pleasure—to his personal success as an initiator of reforms. "I
must praise myself for once … I think I have made … a reformation to
make the papists' ears ring."[74] "Thanks be to God, I have done more
reforming with my Gospel than [the papists] have been able to do in
five councils."[75] In these passages, and in several others scattered
through his polemical *Address to the Christian Nobility* of 1520,[76]
Luther gave "reform" a much more limited and pragmatic signification, referring to inroads made on the Church, and to partial modifications attempted in the religious and ecclesiastical state of affairs. True

reform, an authentic improvement (*besserung*) in God's realm, must be God's endeavor, not his.[77] Some contemporaries were even more pessimistic than Luther concerning the likelihood of success in human tinkering with things. "The pious emperor Sigismund ... wanted to make matters right with a reformation," wrote Sebastian Franck in his *Chronicle and History Book*. "Reformation, indeed! Who is there to make one? Those who should do it, the ones who sit in the high seats of courts and councils, are themselves guilty. So no one may attempt a reformation until everything shall be reformed on Judgment Day."[78] In general, however, Luther's implicit distinction between fundamental renewal on the one hand, and small-scale corrections (with occasional large consequences) on the other, reflected common sixteenth-century assumptions and usage. In ordinary language, the word meant remedial or improving action, as in "A Reformation, necessary to Christendom, concerning priests and their serving maids,"[79] "What we must do to reform the clergy,"[80] "A much-needed reformation through restoring an old Christian custom."[81]

It was recognized that even such piecemeal "reformations" might do violence to existing structures. Printings of the "Twelve Articles of the Swabian Peasantry" of 1525 took pains to deny that it was the peasants' aim "to reform, eradicate, perhaps even put to death spiritual and secular authorities."[82] Warnings were sounded concerning the dangers attending an excessive zeal in launching reforms; among critics who made this point (anti-Philippists, for example) *reformirer* turned into a pejorative tag.[83] But despite such cavils and qualifications, it was the corrective sense of the term that prevailed. Before long, it became the hallmark of the Wittenberg movement itself. Organized Lutherans referred to themselves early on as "evangelically reformed" and to their church as *ecclesia reformata*. Later, from the time of the Formula of Concord of 1577, "reformed" tended to be applied more often to those Protestants who had not accepted that agreement, while signatories of the Formula were known as "Lutherans" or "evangelicals."[84] Ultimately, of course, "Reformation" came to be the identifying sign, at least among Protestants, for the entire process begun in 1517 by Martin Luther, as in Veit Ludwig von Seckendorff's *Comprehensive History of Lutheranism and of the Salutary Reformation Happily Completed by Martin Luther*[85] or in the definition given in Johann Heinrich Zedler's *Lexicon of All the Sciences and Arts*: "Reformation we call simply the actions of D. Martin Luther of blessed memory in which, impelled and supported by God, he cleansed the Christian religion of

the errors and abuses that had dominated it."[86] Gradually, thus, in the
discourse on the great religious change of the sixteenth century, the interpretation of this turning point as a transforming renewal or fundamental reversal in the human situation receded in favor of its representation as a much more circumscribed, modest, and practical undertaking.

Ideas of Reform in the Catholic Revival

Sixteenth-century Catholic usage moved in the same direction, elaborating—though in more concrete and urgent terms—the proposals for
reform that had long been mooted in the Church. Aegidius of Viterbo,
when he spoke to the Fifth Lateran Council in 1512, still described the
enterprise of reform as one in a succession of renewals the Church
must undergo from time to time if it is to remain vital: a *renovatio* ne-
cessitating profound mutations in the institution's ethos and in the
character of its officers.[87] But the dangers inherent in such a totalizing
demand were all too obvious. In the aftermath of the Joachimite
agitations of the preceding centuries, the Church was naturally suspicious of renewal schemes threatening to supplant, or at least curtail, its
authority and that of its tradition. When it became obvious that Protestants had seized the initiative and might well, in a very concrete way,
fulfill the Joachimite prediction of the founding of a new Church, prelates and theologians began to approach reform with plans for more re-
alistic steps that had a chance of yielding a quicker return. Johann Eck
proposed top-down improving measures from papal declarations of
policy to better parish preaching.[88] Training the priesthood became a
paramount concern.[89] The principle *docendus est populus* directed reform toward its most essential task of holding on to the loyalty of the
faithful through effective instruction and preaching.[90] Marian congregations, founded by the Jesuits, extended reform to particular groups
among the laity, whose allegiance the organization needed to secure
and retain.[91] Conceding success to the efforts of Lutheran theologians
to bring religion to the people, churchmen attempted to produce religious and edificatory books to match Protestant writings in popular
appeal—without lasting success, however, as the example of Berthold
Pirstinger's *German Theology*—an earnest attempt at comprehensive
religious instruction with a common touch—showed.[92]

Ideas of Reform and the Temporal Rulers

Among secular authorities, whose voice in organized religion became ever more assertive as the Reformation settled into its established phase, this "reformation" altogether lost the character of a renewal. For obvious reasons, promises of a *renovatio* with its always implied, and often very explicit, program for overturning existing structures, did not appeal to those whose positions depended on the survival of these institutions. Practicing reform as an ameliorating process, on the other hand, presented few perils. Here authorities could build on established procedures. The sense of *reformatio* as remedial action had long been familiar in legal circles; during the fifteenth century it had also gained currency as a rhetorical marker in the contention of governments that they, in the persons of Christian rulers and magistrates, and not the Church as personified by wordly prelates, were best able to make significant improvements in religion. The German territorial princes' claim to possess the *jus reformandi* is the end result of this contention.[93] In practice, their exercise of this right meant a shift of administrative and, to a sometimes significant extent, doctrinal authority to the agencies of the state, ultimately yielding *Kirchenhoheit*—real sovereignty over the Church. To secular rulers and their spokesmen, "reformation" meant the completion of this transfer.

A clue to contemporary conceptualizations of this important change is contained in the frequent association in the sources of *reformation* with *Ordnung*—order. The intentions of those in a position to act on the Right to Reform, and perhaps also the desires of all who had been swept along by the centuries-long excitement about the promise of such a reform, were for the establishment of *eine gute Ordnung und Reformation.*[94] Throughout the Middle Ages, "Order" had stood for the harmony of parts and the smooth and purposeful operation of the whole. This is the *rechte ordenung*—the "right order"—the collapse of which is lamented by the *Reformatio Sigismundi*. To "put things in order" meant not merely to make them work, but also to bring them into accord with, or to restore them to, right—that is, God-ordained—reason. Reform was the procedure that effected such a restoration. There could be no order without prior reform; conversely, only actions aiming at the institution and preservation of order could properly be called reform. In 1411, upon his election as German king, the future Emperor Sigismund (ostensible author of the *Reformatio Sigismundi*) pledged that he would

turn seriously and with God's help to the task of bringing the affairs
of the Holy Church and the Holy Roman Empire into good and
right order, to repair justice and the common weal which have been
too long suppressed, ... and to check the ruination of the Holy
Church and extend help and succor to the Holy Roman Empire.[95]
A sixteenth-century printing of the *Reformatio Sigismundi*, which aug-
ments that most famous of all late medieval reform writings with laws
and decrees issued by subsequent rulers, bears the title "*Reformation*
or *Ordnung* of All Estates, Spiritual and Secular." It declares it to be
the aim of a reformation "to bring everything into better order and
condition" and to assure "a stable order" in all things.[96] Promulga-
tions of new laws and regulations were often designated *Reformation
und Ordnung*[97] as the two terms blended into one in the usage of early
modern chancelleries.

Contemporaneously with this coupling, and in step with narrowing
and pragmatizing adjustments in the meaning of "reform," there occurred a modification in the ordinary sense of "order." This change
came as a result of the word's usurpation by governments which
sought in their official declarations to gain sanction for their directives
by claiming that it was the purpose and rationale of orders to promote
and guarantee Order.[98] Order was a framework built of laws and
regulations. Within it pious and useful lives could be lived. The linkage of *Ordnung*, in this sense, and *Reformation*, with the full reso-
nance supplied by that word's long history, created an ideological
thrust which affected the relations of religion and politics at least into
the seventeenth century. To the support of aggressive governments it
brought the momentum, built up over centuries, of popular hopes for
meaningful reform. Reciprocally, by insisting that order requires discipline and dutiful submission to salutary rules, it served to control the
extravagant expectations of religious and secular change aroused by
the more free-wheeling proponents of reform. The established reformation resulting from this merger was far from the great *renovatio* predicted by prophets and preachers. As a *reformatio*, too, its scope had
shrunk and its center shifted. But it was this reformation, articulated
in a host of church constitutions, ecclesiastical and political legislation,
school ordinances, and catechisms, which came to define the interac-
tions of state and church throughout the early modern period.

NOTES

1. "... eyn nawe ernstliche reformacion ..." Hieronymus Emser, *Wider das unchristenliche buch Martini Luthers* ... (Würzburg, 1521), B iv^v.
2. "... ein gantze veranderung und reformation der christlichen kirchen ..." Johann Carion, *Prognosticatio und Erklerung der grossen Wesserung* ... (Leipzig, 1522), A iv^r.
3. Johann Virdung, *Practica Teutsch* ... (Oppenheim, 1522), C iii^v.
4. Melchior Ambach, *Vom Ende der Welt und zukunfft des Endtchrists* ... (Frankfurt am Main, 1550), B^v.
5. *Ein Reformation des geistlichen und weltlichen Stands* (Strasbourg, 1520).
6. "... unser leben und thun nach seinem Wort reformiern ..." Melchior Ambach, *Vom Ende der Welt...* (Frankfurt am Main, 1550), A iv^v.
7. "Darumb würt disem land einer reformation und besserung gemeyner sitten von nöten sein." "Proinde opus esse natione huic publica morum emendatione reor ... ." Ulrich von Hutten, *Inspicientes. Die Anschawenden* (1520) in *Ulrichs von Hutten Schriften*, ed. Eduard Böcking, vol. 4 (Leipzig, 1860):301.
8. "celestes vero atque humanae agitationi obnoxiae, instaurationem desiderant." "... in antiquum splendorem munditiamque restitui." Giovanni Domenico Mansi, ed., *Sacrorum Conciliorum ... Collectio* (reprint Graz, 1961), vol. 32, cols. 669, 676. An English translation is in John C. Olin, ed., *The Catholic Reformation: Savonarola to Ignatius Loyola* (New York, 1969), 44-53. Aegidius's entire speech is replete with references to renewal.
9. "... ein *Restauratio, Renovatio*, Reinigung und Ernewerung dess gantzen Leibs." Georg am Wald, *Kurtzer Bericht, wie ... und warumb das Panacea am Waldina ... anzuwenden seye* (Frankfurt am Main, 1595), C ii^v.
10. "... diesen hohen Lerer und Propheten und von Gott gesandten Reformatorn der Kirchen... ." Johann Bugenhagen, *Eine christliche Predigt uber der Leich und begrebnis ... D. Martini Luthers* (Frankfurt am Main, 1546), A iii^r.
11. Johann Mathesius, *Historien von des Ehrwirdigen... Doctoris Martini Anfang, lehr, leben und sterben...* (Nuremberg, 1566), A ii^v.
12. Ibid.
13. Lortz and Iserloh (1969), 14; Molitor (1921), 1.
14. O'Malley (1967), 531-32.
15. See Mathesius, *Historien*: "diese ... Reformation."
16. Important sources for the following paragraphs are: Wolgast (1984), 313-60; Ladner (1952), (1959), (1964) and (1982); Brunner (1967); Burdach (1910) and (1926); Schramm (1984).
17. Brunner (1967), 161.

18. E.g., Seneca: "reformatio morum," *Letters to Lucilius*, Letter 58:26.
19. Giles Constable, in Benson and Constable (1982), 37-67.
20. Richard Reitzenstein, *Die Hellenistischen Mysterienreligionen nach ihren Grundlagen und Wirkungen*, 3rd ed. (Leipzig, 1927 [reprint, Darmstadt, 1977]), 262, shows that in the language of Hellenistic mystery religions, and in authors who wrote about them such as Apuleius, the terms *reformatio, regeneratio, metamorphosis, renasci*, etc., are identical in meaning and are used interchangeably.
21. On this entire issue see Schramm (1984).
22. Schramm (1984), 101. See Burdach, "Rienzo und die geistige Wandlung seiner Zeit," in Burdach and Piur (1913-28), vol. 1 (1913), 186-87. For a somewhat different view of the function of *renovatio* in the history of the western medieval empire, see Brackmann (1932), 346-74. Brackmann argues that particular, practical interests, not ideal images, determined the policies of Charlemagne, Otto III, Frederick I, etc. He does not doubt, however, that the *renovatio* idea had lasting influence, at least in rhetoric and propaganda.
23. See the article "Reformation (Rechtsquelle)" in Adalbert Erler and Ekkehard Kaufmann, eds., *Handwörterbuch zur deutschen Rechtsgeschichte*, vol. 4 (Berlin, 1990): cols. 468-72.
24. Wolgast (1984), 318.
25. Bonet-Maury (1904).
26. Grundmann (1927), esp. 56-118, on the course of history toward the third *status*. Generally on Joachimism see Reeves (1969).
27. Grundmann (1927), 57; McGinn (1985), 16, 190-91.
28. Grundmann (1929), 77-159.
29. Burr (1989), 172-89.
30. Reeves (1969), 135.
31. Grundmann (1927), 158-80; Reeves (1969), chap. VII; Lee, Reeves, and Silano (1989), 3-88; Reeves (1976).
32. See Leff (1971); for a discussion of the problematics of reform-by-return-to-tradition, see Backmund (1980).
33. Fasolt (1991), 129.
34. Molitor (1921), 77; Iserloh (1965).
35. Heimpel (1974).
36. To observe this process in detail, see the excellent article by Stievermann (1985).
37. Joseph Grünpeck, *Speculum naturalis, coelestis et propheticae visionis* (Nuremberg, 1508); I use *Spiegel der natürlichen himlischen und prophetischen sehungen...* (Leipzig, 1522), B iii^r.
38. From Johann Lichtenberger's *Pronosticatio* (1488), printed in a collection *Propheceien und Weissagungen: Künftige Sachen, Geschicht und Zufäll* (Frankfurt am Main, 1548), 33 verso; Joseph Grünpeck, *Spiegel...*, B iv^r.
39. *Auslegung der verborgenen Weissagung Doctor Johannis Carionis...* (n.p., 1546), C iv recto.
40. Grünpeck, *Speculum naturalis...*, C iiii^v. Grünpeck, who remained Catholic, seems to have changed his mind later. In 1532 he feared that things had become so bad "das man nicht kann noch mag ein rechtschaffene weiss einer guten ordnung und Reformation erfinden." *Pronostication ... vom 32. bis auff das 40. Jar* (Nuremberg, 1532), A i^v.

41. Lichtenberger in *Propheceien und Weissagungen*, 68^v-69^r; 74^v-75^r; *Das Buch M. Joseph Grünpecks von der Reformation der Christenheyt...* (written c. 1500) in *Propheceien und Weissagungen*, 84^v.

42. They are surveyed and discussed by Barnes (1988).

43. Johann Mathesius, *Historien...* (as in note 11), IV^v: "im 1516. wird der kommen der euch reformiren und meine weissagung wider euch war machen wird." Hilten was kept locked up in a monastery from 1477 to his death in about 1500.

44. Minnich (1992).

45. "... so gar wirdt ein erneüerung werden und verenderung..." From a collection of prophecies taken from Lichtenberger, Carion, Grünpeck, etc., *Propheceien und Weissagungen* (Frankfurt am Main, 1548), 18^v. For a dramatic depiction of the acceleration of prophesying in the fourteenth and fifteenth centuries, see J. von Döllinger, *Der Weissagungsglaube und das Prophetenthum in der christlichen Zeit (Historisches Taschenbuch, 5. Folge I [Leipzig, 1871])*, 259-92.

46. See Rienzo's letter to Charles IV (who thought him a dangerous fantasist), in Burdach and Piur (1913-28), vol. 2, part 3, 193-94.

47. Burdach (1910), 600-646 (reprinted in Burdach [1926]); Burdach, *Rienzo und die geistige Wandlung seiner Zeit*, in Burdach and Piur (1913-28), vol. 1:397-98. See Robert L. Benson, in Benson and Constable (1982).

48. Girolamo Savonarola, *Prediche sopra Aggeo*, ed. Luigi Firpo (Rome, 1965), 166. See Weinstein (1970), 143.

49. *Prediche sopra Aggeo*, 234; see also ibid., 236, 238. Weinstein (1970), 234.

50. Savonarola, *Compendio di Rivelazioni* (1495), translated by Bernard McGinn, *Apocalyptic Spirituality* (New York, 1979), 207.

51. For the context, see Töpfer (1964); Reeves (1969), 306-18.

52. McGinn (1979), 19-21; 49-50; Reeves (1969), 299-302.

53. For a catalogue of these prophecies, see Struve (1977); also Töpfer (1964), 154-210; Reeves (1969), 332-46. Older but highly informative treatments of emperor prophecies and legends are Hermann Grauert, "Zur deutschen Kaisersage," *Historisches Jahrbuch* 13 (1892): 100-43, and Franz Kampers, *Die deutsche Kaiseridee in Prophetie und Sage*, 2d ed. (Munich, 1896).

54. Struve (1978).

55. Heinrich Koller, ed., *Reformation Kaiser Siegmunds*, Monumenta Germaniae Historica. Staatsschriften des späteren Mittelalters, vol. 6 (Stuttgart, 1964), 50.

56. Struve (1978) emphasizes the variations in contents and terminology of the several redactions of the *Reformation Siegmunds*, each with its special target audience.

57. Koller, ed., *Reformation Kaiser Siegmunds*, 332, 342, 344.

58. From a placard posted in Regensburg on the occasion of a diet held there in 1471. Quoted in Boockmann (1979), 541.

59. From *Das Buch der Hundert Kapitel und der Vierzig Statuten des sogenanten Oberrheinischen Revolutionärs*, ed. Gerhard Zschäbitz and Annelore Franke (Berlin, 1967), 369-70, 375. Discussion of authorship, context, and meaning in Lauterbach (1985). Unlike other interpreters of this text (which survives in only one manuscript), Lauterbach sees the "Upper Rhenish revolutionary" as a pragmatic thinker, firmly rooted in reality.

60. Martin Luther, "Vom Missbrauch der Messe," in *WA*, vol. 8 (Weimar 1889): 561-62; the Latin version is in ibid., 475-76.
61. Von im [Charles V] gar menge profecei
gesaget hat und noch darbei,
wie wunder gross beschehen wirt
bei seiner zeit, so er regiert.
Er wirt die welt ganz referrmirn
und sie in besser ordnung firn.
"An den grossmechtigsten fürsten Karolum ... ein supplication ... " (1520) in Rochus von Liliencron, ed., *Die historischen Volkslieder der Deutschen*, vol. 3 (Leipzig, 1867): 345. This is one of many such ballads composed for this and similar occasions. See also ibid., vol. 3:230; vol. 4:5, 359.
62. *Kaiserliche Praktika und prognostication aus allen alten weissagungen... das eben der unüberwindtlichst Rö. K. Carolus V der sey, so Reformiren und allein das Regimen von Orient biss in Occident erobern soll* (Munich, 1519). On this subject generally, see Kurze (1966).
63. Examples in Reeves (1969), 364-72; id., "Cardinal Egidio of Viterbo: a Prophetic Interpretation of History," in Reeves (1992), 104; id., "A Note on Prophecy and the Sack of Rome (1527)," in Reeves (1992), 271-78.
64. Nigg (1967); McGinn (1979), 1-36.
65. Article 17 of the Augsburg Confession condemned "Jewish opinions that before the resurrection of the dead the godly shall take possession of the kingdom of the world... ." See Luther's warnings in his preface to Revelation, in *WA Deutsche Bibel*, vol. 7 (Weimar, 1931): 406-08, 416.
66. See the devastating critique of Norman Cohn's *Pursuit of the Millennium* by Herbert Grundmann (in *HZ* 196 [1963]: 661-65), who rejects Cohn's contention that social-economic motives were always paramount in driving expectations of an *Endkaiser*.
67. In greatest detail in *Buch der Hundert Kapitel und der Vierzig Statuten* (see note 59), 422-529.
68. As elaborated, for example, by Guillaume Postel. See Bouwsma (1957), 275-92.
69. Reeves (1969), 429-51.
70. Kaminsky (1967), 335-36.
71. I take the terms "horizon of expectation (*Erwartungshorizont*)" and "wishful thinking (*Wunschbilder*)" from Alfred Doren, "Wunschräume und Wunschzeiten," *Vorträge der Bibliothek Warburg 1924-1925* (Berlin, 1927), 158-205.
72. *Propheceien und Weissagungen ... Doctor Paracelsi, Lichtenberger, Grünpeck, Carionis...* (Frankfurt am Main, 1548), 8ʳ.
73. *Resolutiones disputationum de indulgentiarum virtute*, Conclusio 89. *WA*, vol. 1:627.
74. In his preface to Stephan Klingebeil's *Von Priester Ehe* (1528), in *WA*, vol. 26:530: "Ich mus mich ein mal rhümen, ... Ich meine ja, ich hab ein Concilium angericht und eine reformation gemacht das den Papisten die ohren klingen." Bernhard Lohse, *Lutherdeutung heute* (Göttingen, 1968), 62, takes the meaning of this reference as "obviously ironic."
75. "Ein Brief D. Mart. Luth. von seinem Buch der Winckelmessen (1534)," in *WA*, vol. 38:271.
76. *WA*, vol. 6:422, 425, 438. See also Luther's *Commentary on Galatians* of 1519, in *WA*, vol. 2:609.

77. "Der 101 Psalm, durch D. Mar. Luth. Ausgelegt (1534)," in *WA*, vol. 53:660. See Maurer (1957); "Das Reformatorische bei Martin Luther," a panel discussion by Hubert Jedin, Walther von Loewenich, et al., in August Franzen, *Um Reform und Reformation* (Münster, 1968), 33-52.

78. *Chronica, Zeytbuch und geschychtbibel von anbegyn biss in diss gegenwertig MDxxxi jar* (Strasbourg, 1531), D xxx^v.

79. Hans Kolb, *Ein Reformation notturfftig in der Christenheit mit den Pfaffen und iren Mägden* (Strasbourg, 1523).

80. Martin Bucer, *Ein schöner dialogus und gesprech ... betreffend alle ubel des Standes der geystlichen* (Erfurt, 1521), B iv^v.

81. Andreas Carlstadt, *Von abtuhung der Bylder ...* (Wittenberg, 1522), A i^v.

82. "... geistliche und weltliche oberkeyten zu reformiren, ausszureutten, ja vielleicht gar erschlagen." *Die gründtlich und rechten hawpt Artickel aller Pawrschafft ...* (n.p., 1525), A^v.

83. Johannes Wigand, *Vom Straff Ampt der Sünden...* (Magdeburg, 1560), D 5^r: "ihr klugen, hochverstendigen reformirer und meister des kirchenampts"; F 5^v: "die aller künsten reformirer des Predigampts." Among the "Turks" who suppress God's Word in Cyriacus Spangenberg's *Ein schön geistlich Lied. Erhalt uns Herr bey deinem Wort* are:
Die grossen Herrn, die also plagn
Dein treue Knecht und sie verjagn.
Dein heiligen Geist auch Reformiern.
Den grossen Hauffen zu hofiern.
Philipp Wackernagel, ed., *Das deutsche Kirchenlied*, vol. 4 (Leipzig, 1874): 175, no. 249.

84. Heinrich Heppe, *Ursprung und Geschichte der Bezeichnungen 'reformierte' und 'lutherische' Kirche* (Gotha, 1859).

85. *Ausführliche Historie des Lutherthums und der heilsamen Reformation welche der theure Martin Luther ... glücklich ausgeführet* (Leipzig, 1714).

86. *Grosses vollständiges Universal-Lexicon ...* vol. 30 (Leipzig and Halle, 1741): col. 1676.

87. See note 8 above. Also F. X. Martin, "The Problem of Giles of Viterbo," *Augustiniana* 10 (1960): 60; Minnich (1969).

88. Smolinsky (1988a).

89. Föllinger (1988); Anton Schindling, "Die katholische Bildungsreform zwischen Humanismus und Barock," in *Vorderösterreich in der frühen Neuzeit*, ed. Hans Maier and Volker Press (Sigmaringen, 1989), 137-76.

90. Smolinsky (1988b).

91. E. Villaret, *Les congrégations mariales* I (Paris, 1947); M. V. Sattler, *Geschichte der Marianischen Congregationen in Bayern* (Munich, 1864).

92. Berthold Pirstinger, *Tewtsche Theologey* (Munich, 1528). Pirstinger's 100 chapters touch all aspects of the Catholic faith and present them in simple language and vivid examples, free of theological jargon. The book is, however, dry and schoolmasterish in tone, no match for the vigorous language of so much Lutheran popular religious writing. Above all, its tone is sad, as though Pirstinger knew that the game was lost to the Church.

93. It is explained in its historical context by Justus Hashagen, "Die vorreformatorische Bedeutung des spätmittelalterlichen landesherrlichen Kirchenregiments," *ZKiG* 41 (1922): 63-93.

94. Paul Egricens, *Trewhertzige Ermanung der Zeichen so für dem Jüngsten Tage hergehen* (Eisleben, 1560), B vii^r.

95. *Deutsche Reichstagsakten unter Kaiser Sigmund*, vol. 1, 2d ed. (Göttingen, 1956), 56.
96. "... alles in bessere ordnung und wesen zu bringen;" "... in ein bestendige Ordnung zu bringen.:" *Reformation oder Ordnung aller Ständen, Geistlicher und Weltlicher...* (Basel, 1577), title page and A i^r.
97. E.g., *Reformation und Landtgerichts Ordnung unserer ... Hertzogen zu Mecklenburgk...* (Rostock, 1558), A ii^v: "... diese unser Reformation und Ordnung." In ordinary usage, *reformation* was often a synonym for law, as in Hans Sachs's *Lobspruch der statt Nürnberg*:
Auch seind die amptleut one zal
Zu allen dingen überal
Ir gsetz und reformation
ist fürgeschriben yedermon.
Hans Sachs, ed. Adelbert von Keller, vol. 4 (Stuttgart, 1870; reprint, Hildesheim, 1964): 194.
98. For a development of this argument see Gerald Strauss, "The Idea of Order in the Reformation," in id., *Enacting the Reformation in Germany: Essays on Institution and Reception* (Aldershot, 1993), xiv, 1-16.

BIBLIOGRAPHY

Backmund, Norbert. "Spätmittelalterliche Reformbestrebungen im Prämonstratenserorden." *Analecta Praemonstratensia* 56 (1980), 198-204.

Barnes, Robin Bruce. *Prophecy and Gnosis. Apocalypticism in the Wake of the Lutheran Reformation.* Stanford, 1988.

Benson, Robert L. "Political *Renovatio*: Two Models from Roman Antiquity." In Benson and Constable (1982), 339-86.

Benson, Robert L., and Giles Constable, eds. *Renaissance and Renewal in the Twelfth Century.* Cambridge, Mass., 1982.

Bonet-Maury, Gaston. *Les précurseurs de la reforme et de la liberté de la conscience dans les pays latins du XIIe au XVe siècle.* Paris, 1904. Reprint. Geneva, 1969.

Boockmann, Hartmut. "Zu den Wirkungen der 'Reform Kaiser Siegmunds.'" *Deutsches Archiv fur Erforschung des Mittelalters* 35 (1979).

Bouwsma, William J. *Concordia Mundi. The Career and Thought of Guillaume Postel (1510-1581).* Cambridge, Ma., 1957.

Brackmann, Albert. "Der 'Römische Erneuerungsgedanke' und seine Bedeutung für die Reichspolitik der deutschen Kaiserzeit." *Sitzungsberichte der preussischen Akademie der Wissenschaften*, phil-hist. Klasse, vol. 16 (1932).

Brunner, Peter. "Reform-Reformation. Einst-Heute." *Kerygma und Dogma* 13 (1967): 159-83.

Burdach, Konrad. *Reform, Renaissance, Humanismus.* 2d ed. Berlin, 1926 [1918].

Burdach, Konrad. "Sinn und Ursprung der Worte Renaissance und Reformation." In *Sitzungsberichte der königl. preussischen Akademie der Wissenschaften*, vol. 32:594-646. Berlin, 1910.

Burdach, Konrad, and Paul Piur, eds. *Briefwechsel des Cola di Rienzo.* 2 vols. Berlin, 1913-28.

Burr, David. *Olivi and Franciscan Poverty: the Origins of the Usus Pauper Controversy.* Philadelphia, 1989.

Constable, Giles. "Renewal and Reform in Religious Life: Concepts and Realities." In Benson and Constable (1982), 37-67.

Fasolt, Constantin. *Council and Hierarchy. The Political Thought of William Durant the Younger.* Cambridge, 1991.

Föllinger, Georg. "Zur Priesterausbildung in den Bistümern Köln, Paderborn und Konstanz nach dem Tridentinum." *Ecclesia militans. Studien zur Konzilien- und Reformationsgeschichte, Remigius Bäumer gewidmet*, vol. 1:367-97. Paderborn, 1988.

Grundmann, Herbert. "Die Papstprophecien des Mittelalters." *Archiv für Kulturgeschichte* 19 (1929): 77-159.

Grundmann, Herbert. *Studien über Joachim von Floris.* Leipzig, 1927.

Heimpel, Hermann. "Studien zur Kirchen- und Reichsreform des 15. Jahrhunderts, part 2." *Sitzungsberichte der Heidelberger Akademie der Wissenschaften, philos.-hist. Klasse*, vol. 1. Heidelberg, 1974.

Iserloh, Erwin. *Reform der Kirche bei Nikolaus von Kues.* Wiesbaden, 1965.

Kaminsky, Howard. *A History of the Hussite Revolution.* Berkeley and Los Angeles, 1967.

Kurze, Dietrich. "Nationale Regungen in der spätmittelalterlichen Prophetie." *HZ* 202 (1966): 1-23.

Ladner, Gerhart B. "Erneuerung." *Reallexikon für Antike und Christentum*, vol. 6 (1964), cols. 240-75.

Ladner, Gerhart B. *The Idea of Reform. Its Impact on Christian Thought and Action in the Age of the Fathers.* Cambridge, Ma., 1959.

Ladner, Gerhart B. "Die mittelalterliche Reform-Idee und ihr Verhältnis zur Idee der Renaissance." *Mitteilungen des Instituts für österreichische Geschichtsforschung* 60 (1952): 31-59.

Ladner, Gerhart B. "Terms and Ideas of Renewal." In Benson and Constable (1982), 1-33.

Lauterbach, Klaus H. *Geschichtsverständnis, Zeitdidaxe und Reformgedanke an der Wende zum sechzehnten Jahrhundert. Das oberrheinische "Buchli der hundert Capiteln" im Kontext des spätmittelalterlichen Reformbiblizismus.* Freiburg im Breisgau, 1985.

Lee, Harold, Marjorie Reeves, and Giulio Silano. *Western Mediterranean Philosophy: the School of Joachim of Fiore and the Fourteenth-Century Breviloquium.* Toronto, 1989.

Leff, Gordon. "The Making of the Myth of a True Church in the Later Middle Ages." *JMRS* 1 (1971): 1-15.

Lortz, Joseph, and Erwin Iserloh. *Kleine Reformationsgeschichte.* Freiburg im Breisgau, 1969.

McGinn, Bernard. *The Calabrian Abbot: Joachim of Fiore in the History of Western Thought.* New York, 1985.

McGinn, Bernard. *Visions of the End: Apocalyptic Traditions in the Middle Ages.* New York, 1979.

Maurer, Wilhelm. "Was verstand Luther unter der Reformation der Kirche?" *Luther. Mitteilungen der Luther Gesellschaft* 28 (1957): 49-62.

Minnich, Nelson H. "Concepts of Reform Proposed at the Fifth Lateran Council." *Archivum Historiae Pontificiae* 7 (1969): 163-251.

Minnich, Nelson H. "Prophecy and the Fifth Lateran Council (1512-1517)." In *Prophetic Rome in the High Renaissance Period*, ed. Marjorie Reeves, 63-87. Oxford, 1992.

Molitor, Erich. *Die Reichsreformbstrebungen des 15. Jahrhunderts.* Breslau, 1921.

Nigg, Walter. *Das ewige Reich.* Munich, 1967.

O'Malley, John W., S.J. "Historical Thought and the Reform Crisis of the Early Sixteenth Century." *Theological Studies* 28 (1967).

Reeves, Marjorie. *The Influence of Prophecy in the Later Middle Ages: a Study in Joachimism.* Oxford, 1969.

Reeves, Marjorie. *Joachim of Fiore and the Prophetic Future.* Bungay, Suffolk, 1976.

Reeves, Marjorie, ed. Prophetic Rome in the High Renaissance Period. Oxford, 1992.

Schramm, Percy Ernst. *Kaiser Rom und Renovatio. Studien zur Geschichte des römischen Erneuerungsgedankens...* 4th ed. Darmstadt, 1984.

Smolinsky, Heribert. "'Docendus est populus.' Der Zusammenhang zwischen Bildung und Kirchenreform in Reformordnungen des 16. Jahrhunderts." *Ecclesia militans. Studien zur Konzilien- und Reformationsgeschichte, Remigius Bäumer gewidmet,* vol. 1:539-59. Paderborn, 1988b.

Smolinsky, Heribert. "Die Reform der Kirche in der Sicht des Johannes Eck." In *Johannes Eck (1486-1543) im Streit der Jahrhunderte,* ed. Erwin Iserloh, 155-73. Münster, 1988a.

Stievermann, Dieter. "Die württembergischen Klosterreformen des 15. Jahrhunderts." *Zeitschrift für württembergische Landesgeschichte* 44 (1985): 65-103.

Struve, Tilman. "Reform oder Revolution? Das Ringen um eine Neuordnung in Reich und Kirche im Lichte der 'Reformatio Sigismundi' und ihrer Überlieferung." *Zeitschrift für die Geschichte des Oberrheins* 126 (1978): 73-129.

Struve, Tilman. "Utopie und gesellschaftliche Wirklichkeit. Zur Bedeutung des Friedenkaisers im späten Mittelalter." *HZ* 225 (1977): 65-95.

Töpfer, Bernhard. *Das kommende Reich des Friedens.* Berlin, 1964.

Weinstein, Donald. *Savonarola and Florence.* Princeton, 1970.

Wolgast, Eike. "Reform, Reformation." In *Geschichtliche Grundbegriffe*, vol. 5:313-60. Stuttgart, 1984.

VISIONS OF ORDER IN THE CANONISTS AND CIVILIANS

Constantin Fasolt
(University of Chicago)

1. Definition of the Subject

Like the other chapters in this book, this one focuses attention on Europe in space and the period from about 1400 to 1600 in time. Unlike them, it is limited to visions of order held by canonists and civilians. What precisely does or does not qualify as a vision of order may be difficult to say in specific cases, but this much is certain: visions of order are mental phenomena. They consist of thoughts about the proper way of arranging things. Who precisely does or does not qualify as a canonist or civilian is also difficult to say sometimes, but here again something is certain: canonists and civilians were living human beings. More specifically, they were people who had mastered a certain body of legal knowledge and relied upon that knowledge to lead a certain kind of life. Jurists, for short.

The following chapter is devoted to a certain type of ideas held by a certain kind of people. That raises an obvious question: what is the reason for putting people and ideas together in this way? It is assuredly not that all canonists and civilians had the same vision of order. The plural in the title of the chapter is quite intentional: canonists and civilians had many different visions of order, and sometimes they proved to be difficult, if not impossible, to reconcile. The more closely you look, the more finely differentiated varieties become discernible until the subject threatens to disintegrate in a burst of caleidoscopic multiplicity.

Conversely, few if any of these visions were the exclusive property of canonists and civilians. They were shared by theologians, humanists, and many other people. Seeing that canonists and civilians disagreed with each other over the most basic issues, how could it have been otherwise? Perhaps more important, the ideas of canonists and civilians were shared in a limited but significant sense by everybody who had to obey canon and civil law—and during our period the number of people who did happens to have grown at an unprecedented rate.

In short, canonists and civilians did not all have the same ideas about order, and the ideas they did have were not theirs alone. Hence there is nothing in the record to which one could point with confidence and say, look, there are the visions of order in the canonists and civilians. To the contrary, the more precisely you try to identify the meaning of the words in the title of this chapter, the more likely you are going to narrow your focus to a point where there is nothing left to see, or broaden it to a scope where it includes everything. That is embarrassing.

A better reason for putting ideas and people together in this way consists of what we nowadays believe has to be done in order to understand the past. Once upon a time (or so it is believed) historians divided the people of the past into a small group that had ideas and a large group that merely lived. Historians interested in ideas paid no attention to the people that merely lived, and not enough to the people who had ideas. What mattered were the ideas alone. Historians interested in people meanwhile paid no attention to ideas and only very little to the tiny minority of people who called themselves civilians and canonists. What mattered was how the majority of people lived, especially how they worked, ate, and reproduced.

Those times are changing—slowly, perhaps, and not to the same degree in France, Italy, Germany, England, the United States, and other places, but changing nonetheless. Social historians have proved to the satisfaction of most observers that people whose income stems from rents, for example, will for that reason sometimes think and act quite differently from people whose income stems from wages. Hence intellectual historians have tried to learn more about the social setting in which ideas took shape. But it is a fact as well that sometimes people think and act in certain ways for no other apparent reason than what they believe to be true and right—or fun. Hence social historians have begun to look more closely at what people thought. Those efforts have paid off handsomely. We now know more about the reasons why people thought what they did than we ever have before, and there is a burgeoning literature on what might be called the intellectual history of ordinary people, a huge, fascinating, and previously almost totally uncolonized territory. Historians seem to be tentatively moving to a consensus that what people thought and how they lived is one subject, not two.

That helps to understand the growth of interest in the history of law. Law and history used to be kept at arm's length. They were studied and practiced in different institutions by different people with different methodologies and different goals. Law seemed technical, forbidding, and ahistorical to historians. History seemed shiftless and devoid of legal substance to jurists. "Today," however, as Franz Wieacker said some time ago, "the walls between the various national schools of law, between romanists, germanists, and canonists, indeed, even those between social, cultural, and legal historians have been more thoroughly taken apart than at any time since the beginnings of modern historical research in the nineteenth century."[1] And with good reason. There are not many other places where ideas have such immediate and obvious effects on life as they do in law, nor are there many more imposing bodies of evidence from which to learn about life in the past.[2]

In a small way the title of this chapter thus reflects a trend in contemporary historical thought. Unfortunately it reflects as well that a trend does not amount to a solution. We have already reached a point where excitement over the insights to be learned from neighboring disciplines is giving way to the recognition that our neighbors are struggling with the same problems, except that they call the problems by different names. It is good that we are abandoning the sterile kind of dualism that divides the world into ideas and things and then wonders which is more basic than the other. But in so doing we have also lost two mutually exclusive and, perhaps for that reason, successful definitions of what history was about. Now what? How exactly are we to understand the relationship between ideas and life? Is it enough to compile a list of things certain people usually considered to have been canonists and civilians happen to have said about principles of order in early modern times? Is this chapter about anything besides a trend in contemporary historical thought? Does it perhaps have no subject whatsoever?

Readers who have taken the title as a promise that they will be reading about something rather than nothing will not, I hope, be disappointed. But they should also consider themselves to have been warned that the subject is elusive. Questions like the ones just raised are difficult to answer without reconsidering the categorical division of the world into thinking things and material things of which the most familiar spokesman is René Descartes (1596-1650). There are reasons to believe that such a reconsideration may be underway. But if so, it is far from complete. Notwithstanding the enthusiasm with which alternatives are being advanced in any number of contemporary intellectual experiments, our notions of what is and what is not a subject worthy of investigation—of what does and does not constitute a decent explanation—continue to rely on the Cartesian metaphysical inheritance, and it makes little difference whether they do so with or without acknowledgment.[3]

Under those circumstances it is best to proceed with caution, jump to no conclusions, and keep basic questions clearly in view. In the present context these questions are: what, if anything, united canonists and civilians? What divided them? And do their ideas about order follow any patterns?

2. CANONISTS AND CIVILIANS: THE COMMON GROUND

One thing obviously did unite canonists and civilians: all of them had gone to university and studied law. That may not seem like much but it is something. It meant, first of all, that they had to have an opportunity to go to university. Most of their contemporaries did not: no woman did, and the vast majority of men did not because they happened to work on a rural estate in one or another form of servitude and knew not how to read or write and were not free to leave. Few jurists came from the village. Most came from the city. And all were men.

In the second place these men had to have a motive to study law. Most of those who had the opportunity did not have the motive. Members of the nobility, for example, had little reason to go to university to study anything at all. As time passed there was a growing number of exceptions. But in principle the study of law was most attractive to men who would have liked to have been noble, not for those who were—especially since a doctorate in law did in fact entitle you to consider yourself as having joined the ranks of the nobility. Something similar can be said about men in the highest levels of urban society. Their wealth was of a different sort from that of the nobility, but its presence, or the prospect of enjoying it, and the responsibilities associated with either made an academic career unattractive to bankers, long-distance merchants, great entrepreneurs, and their sons. On the whole the study of law was not for men who had a fortune but for those who wanted one.

The typical jurist, in other words, was one of a small group of literate ambitious men who lived in cities and owed their standing in society to their mastery of a very special kind of knowledge. Having relied on his talents to rise to the top, he was likely to prefer merit to birth as a basic criterion of social order. To that extent he favored liberty and equality over hierarchy. Having relied on knowledge to rise to the top, he was likely to oppose custom on the grounds of reason, and unlikely to have much sympathy for, or understanding of, the uneducated, whether they had a title of nobility or not. To that extent he may be considered a reformer and a progressive. And since he lacked any power of his own, he had little choice but to ally himself with those among the powerful who were most likely to draw on his knowledge in return for a salary, which is to say kings, princes, and urban governments attempting to establish control over, and extract taxes from, their subjects—whether they had a title of nobility or not. To that extent he may be considered an instinctive supporter of the state.

It should go without saying that these few words capture only very little and nothing without exception. But there may not be much more that can be said about late medieval and early modern jurists in general. If there is, we do not know it. The evidence is fragmentary and complex. Even simple questions like how many students studied law at a given university, precisely what they studied, and what they went on to do thereafter, are impossible to answer until technical problems of great difficulty have been solved, and often remain impossible to answer even then. The state of our knowledge is best described as a great darkness interrupted by bursts of brightness in a few widely separated spots where the evidence is plentiful and someone has spent years studying it.[4] Under those circumstances the little that has just been said is already too much.

There was, however, one other thing to unite canonists and civilians: their allegiance to a definite and relatively small number of books collected in two sets that have since the sixteenth century been called *Corpus Iuris Civilis* and *Corpus Iuris Canonici*, the body of civil and canon law, respectively.[5] The jurists believed that these books contained "reason in writing," as they sometimes put it. More specifically, they believed that these books were sanctioned by God's universal representatives, pope and emperor, and contained universally valid answers to questions of right and wrong.

This had two main consequences, both of which are fundamental for an understanding of their notions of order. First, no jurist worth his salt was willing to give, or allow others to give, answers to questions of right and wrong that could not be found in, derived from, or reconciled with, the texts of the civil and canon law. All jurists were pledged to a definite method. The method did not always work. It depended on the skill of individual jurists and often resulted in contradictory answers. But it was an enormously powerful tool to sanction certain views of right and wrong and reject others.

Second, the jurists were bound to the doctrines and concepts contained in the body of canon and civil law. Many of these were in dispute and they are far too numerous even to adumbrate in outline. But three may be singled out for mention because they are basic and conveniently gathered at the very beginning of the *Corpus Iuris Civilis* and the *Corpus Iuris Canonici*. First, law was divided into two basic types: natural law and human law. The former was universal and directly founded on reason. The latter was limited to specific communities and founded on reason only in a qualified sense. Second, according to natural law human beings were free and equal. And third, law was distinguished from custom: law was written and formally promulgated, custom was not. The precise meaning of any one of these terms was never settled (and always different from its meaning in modern times). But one thing was settled: if anyone was going to determine the meaning correctly, it would be properly trained jurists.

This tended to put the jurists at odds with two other types of men: those who preferred to answer questions of right and wrong by referring to other books and those who preferred to refer to no books at all—or at least not to books written in Latin. Theologians did the former, followers of custom the latter. Theologians worried that jurists would exceed the limits of their authority and forget that the most important questions of right and wrong were answered by the Bible, also a collection of books and in some ways overlapping with Roman and canon law, but containing writings of a different sort that were thought to have been directly revealed by God himself. Their worries were only increased by the opening words of the *Digest* according to which jurists

> are deservedly called priests, because we cultivate justice and profess
> knowledge of the good and the equitable, separating what is
> equitable from what is iniquitable, discriminating between the licit
> and the illicit, desiring to produce good conduct not merely through
> fear of punishment but also through the promise of rewards,
> teaching, if I am not mistaken, true, not feigned, philosophy.[6]

Followers of custom, meanwhile, were dismayed to learn that experts in Roman and canon law, far from practicing the good and the equitable, were quick to brush aside conventions they did not know, reject cases that had not been brought according to the proper procedure, and ignore wrongs for which they found no admissible evidence.

Theologians and followers of custom shared a suspicion that the jurists' allegiance to civil and canon law was dishonest because it sometimes appeared to fly in the face of the will of God or the obvious facts of the case. On occasion, as during the reformation, that suspicion could fuel powerful alliances and undermine the jurists' self-confidence. But in the long run it always proved to be weaker than the ties by which those who had received a professional education were joined to each other and divided from those who had not.

3. CANONISTS AND CIVILIANS: THE CONTRASTS AND DIVERGENCES

Canon law and civil law were two separate bodies of texts. One was rooted in the church, the other in the Roman Empire. Each had its own characteristic doctrines, and sometimes they conflicted with each other. Canon lawyers, for example, regularly identified natural law with divine law. Roman lawyers were less willing to do so. The most obvious division among canonists and civilians thus was the division of canonists from civilians. It was turned into law in 1219 when Pope Honorius III (r. 1216-27) prohibited priests and members of religious orders from studying civil law. To a certain extent it also coincided with a geographic boundary. In Italy and southern France, where knowledge of Roman law was most extensive, jurists were often laymen. In the rest of Europe, where canon law played a more important role, they were almost invariably clerics. It was only in the period considered in this essay that university-trained jurists who did not belong to the clergy began to outnumber those who did even in northern Europe.

Important though it is, however, the division of canonists from civilians must not be exaggerated, as happens all too easily when modern observers forget how deeply the church was rooted in the Roman Empire. For the most part and in the long run relations between canon and civil law were far more peaceful than the decision of Honorius III might suggest. Canon law not only borrowed texts and principles directly from Roman law but also drew on Roman law in indirect ways. In the absence of Roman law canon law would have been incomplete and, in parts, unintelligible. Hence many clerics did study civil law, especially those in lower orders whom the prohibition of Honorius III did not affect because they did not (yet) exercise the care of souls or belong to a religious order.[7] "The church lives by Roman law" was a familiar and entirely appropriate maxim. Roman law, meanwhile, was not enough for any lawyer worth his salt in an age when marriages and testaments—perhaps the two most important instruments for the massive transfer of property known to the world—fell under the jurisdiction of the church. Hence it became increasingly common for jurists to study both kinds of law, call themselves "doctor of both laws [*doctor utriusque iuris*]," and look down upon colleagues who knew only one kind of law. Fundamentally, the relationship between canonists and civilians was one of complementarism, not contradiction. No one else managed to pay more balanced respect to texts coming from classical antiquity and what is sometimes called the Judeo-Christian tradition.

Different levels of training and different careers made for more important lines of demarcation. In the first place many of the people who knew something about Roman and canon law did not really qualify as canonists or civilians strictly speaking. This includes scribes and notaries who had studied the art of writing letters (*ars dictaminis*) or the art of authenticating documents by entering them in a public register (*ars notariatus*). Scribes and notaries had to know at least parts of the law and they far outnumbered fully trained jurists. More than anyone else they helped to spread knowledge of Roman and canon law in everyday use. But they ranked far below doctors of law. There were also distinguished individuals like Lorenzo Valla (1407-57), the son of a doctor of both laws who is justly regarded as one of the most important figures in early modern legal thought, but who never received a formal legal education. And we ought not to forget people who did study law for a while, but dropped out in disgust, like Ulrich von Hutten (1488-1523).

In the second place some doctors and licentiates of law cannot be considered civilians or canonists except in a purely formal sense because they devoted their careers to rather different pursuits, like Leon Battista Alberti (1404-72), Johann Reuchlin (1454/5-1522), Andreas Karlstadt (1480-1541), and John Calvin (1509-64), all of whom are serviceable examples of professionally trained lawyers not generally known for their legal expertise.

In the third place canonists and civilians in the full sense of the word went on to use their knowledge in very different ways. A few of the most popular ways are worth specifying. One was to become a professor of law. Another was to work in the courts of the church. But above all university-trained jurists were ever more often employed in government, first in the church, then in the state. Their particular combination of expertise and pliancy made them exceptionally desirable members of the councils of state on which early modern monarchs relied in their struggle to bring the nobility to heel. There they left their most important imprint, and there they had a chance to rise to positions of great power themselves. In the church they often rose to the very top.[8]

Conspicuously absent from this list of typical careers for canonists and civilians are the courts of lay society and what you might call private practice. From the beginning of our period both were well represented in Italy. But outside of Italy the courts of the laity were usually staffed, and the laity given legal advice, by followers of custom. University-trained professionals replaced them only during our period, slowly at first, very rapidly towards the end, but in any event only after they had proved their worth as councillors, chancellors, and diplomats to the rulers of Europe.

Finally, and most important for the purposes of this essay, canonists and civilians were divided over the meaning of the laws they studied. They debated more issues and disagreed more deeply in more ways than one can even begin to suggest without a detailed examination of the evidence. Four issues may nonetheless be singled out for special attention because they were fundamental and especially clearly related to conceptions of order.

The first was where to locate supreme authority in the church. Conciliarists like Francisco Zabarella (c. 1339-1417) argued that supreme authority rested with general councils, that such councils derived their authority directly from Christ, and that even legitimate popes could be compelled to obey them in matters concerning the unity, the faith, and the reform of the church in general.[9] Papalists like Pedro de Luna (c. 1328-1423), better known as Pope Benedict XIII (r. 1394-1417), argued that supreme authority in the church rested with the pope, that he was exempt from the judgment of any human being, including human beings assembled in a general council, and that no council could be regarded as legitimate unless it had been approved by the pope.[10] The issue had been debated since the twelfth century, but it was not fully joined until the outbreak of the great schism in 1378. For about three generations the champions of general councils engaged the champions of the papacy in an intellectual and political struggle involving all of Europe. When the dust settled in about 1450 the papacy had recovered its balance. Thereafter it made very sure that no council would ever again contest its control over the church. Nonetheless conciliarists continued to maintain their cause throughout the early modern period and, in the view of some, had the last word in the Glorious Revolution of 1688 and in the writings of John Locke (1632-1704).[11]

The second issue dividing canonists and civilians concerned the question how to resolve differences over the meaning of canon and especially Roman law. Many jurists believed that the best way to proceed was to build on the interpretations that had been worked out by the so-called glossators and commentators since the eleventh century. Typically they stayed close to the texts of individual laws and dealt with them in the order in which they appeared in the *Corpus Iuris Civilis*. They are often called Bartolists, after Bartolus of Sassoferrato (1313/14-57), one of the most influential jurists of the later middle ages, and their method "scholastic" or "the Italian manner" (*mos italicus*) because it had been perfected in Italian schools of law and continued to flourish there, but by no means only there, until well into the early modern period.[12] The others believed that it was necessary to make a fresh start because the older interpretations were written in atrocious Latin, founded on corrupt versions of the texts, and marred not only by logical inconsistencies but also ignorance of history. Typically they spent much effort on philology and grammar in order to reconstruct the original text of the ancient laws and expose what they considered to be the errors of the Bartolists. They also liked to interpret the law by devising broad conceptual schemes that seemed more rational than a text-bound approach. They are usually called legal humanists and their method "the French manner" (*mos gallicus*) because their most famous practitioners taught at French universities like Orléans, Toulouse, and above all Bourges.[13] Legal humanists captured a great deal of attention because of the novelty of their discoveries, the elegance of their style, and the trenchancy of their analysis. Bartolists, however, were by no means ready to concede and continued to predominate in less conspicuous but no less important places, both because of the sheer weight of tradition and their unparalleled ability to settle specific legal difficulties in specific settings, including the setting where it often mattered the most, namely, in court.

The third issue was, of course, the Reformation. The main question with which the Reformation confronted canonists and civilians was this: could the doctrine of salvation by faith alone be reconciled with canon and Roman law, or could it not? Many jurists thought that it could not. They recoiled in horror from ideas that threatened not only to deprive them of their professional existence but also to throw the entire world into turmoil. They went on to defend the law by editing new and improved versions of the basic texts and glosses, collecting the best existing legal scholarship, and rethinking their positions from the bottom up. Two of their efforts are worth mentioning: the first authoritative edition of the *Corpus Iuris Canonici* and the so-called *Tractatus Universi Iuris*, down to the present day the most comprehensive single collection of the best that romano-canonical jurisprudence had to offer.[14] Others, meanwhile, were convinced that Roman and canon law could very well be reconciled with salvation by faith alone if only they were correctly distinguished from divine and natural law properly speaking and recognized as products of human action and historical circumstance. They, too, had their brilliant successes, among which we may mention the investigations into the history of law by French Huguenots, an edition of the *Corpus Iuris Civilis* with a new set of glosses by Dionysius Gothofredus (1549-1622), the proliferation of ecclesiastical legislation in Protestant territories, and the veritable explosion of public law in the Holy Roman Empire just after the end of our period.[15]

The fourth and final issue was the question whether or not supreme authority in the state was to be given to the people or to their sovereign ruler. This was in many ways a replay of the debate between conciliarists and papalists. It resulted from a schism between two confessions and pitted temporal constitutionalists against temporal absolutists, just as a schism between different papal obediences had pitted ecclesiastical constitutionalists against ecclesiastical absolutists. It involved similar arguments and it often drew on the same sources. It had also been in the air since the high middle ages, but it was not fully joined until the very end of our period, and it was most effectively joined in France. On the one hand it was argued that rulers were servants of the common good and subject to the laws. Hence the people had a right to resist and depose rulers who violated the law—and if not the people as such, then at least the magistrates who represented the people in general assemblies. Among the most important authors taking this point of view was François Hotman (1524-90), who had studied Roman law in Orléans.[16] On the other hand it was argued that public order was impossible to preserve unless rulers had the right to put an end to public controversies without possibility of resistance or appeal. Such rulers were not above divine and natural law, but they were above, or absolute from, human law. Among the most important defenders of that position was Jean Bodin (1529/30-96), who had studied Roman law in Toulouse.[17]

This sketch of the main issues dividing canonists and civilians is both rough and incomplete, but it is enough to make a point and raise a question. The point is that wherever and whenever fundamental issues of order were debated in early modern times, canonists and civilians can be found on both sides of the debate. Moreover, the stand a jurist took on any one of these issues did not determine his stand on any of the others. Supporters of papal supremacy sometimes maintained and sometimes denied that people had a right to resist their sovereign rulers. So did the followers of Luther and practitioners of the *mos gallicus*. Supporters of absolute monarchy sometimes supported Luther and sometimes the pope. So did theorists of resistance and practitioners of the *mos italicus*. No stereo-type stands up to scrutiny, especially not the one according to which experts in Roman law were born supporters of absolute monarchy, experts in canon law born allies of the papacy, and both sworn enemies of Luther.[18] The question is whether canonists and civilians took their positions according to chance or some discernible pattern.

4. LEGALITY AND LEGITIMACY

In order to deal with this question it may be useful to make a distinction. Law consists of rules that tell you how to behave. These rules are not necessarily good and they can be broken. Hence people using laws have two entirely different ways of doing wrong (or right): they can do wrong (right) by breaking a rule that is good (bad), but they can also do wrong (right) by following a rule that is bad (good).

This is a source of endless confusion. In order to keep matters straight, theorists of law distinguish between legality and legitimacy.[19] Legality has to do with conduct. Conduct is legal if it agrees with the rules and illegal if it does not. Legitimacy has to do with the rules. The rules are legitimate if they deserve to be followed, and illegitimate if they deserve to be changed or broken. Conduct is lawful in the full sense of the word only if it comprises both elements: it must follow the law and the law must be legitimate.[20]

The question is, of course: who decides what is legitimate and how? It is a simple question. But the answer is necessarily uncertain. It could be certain if, and only if, it could be given according to some rules. But rules are precisely what the question is about. Since the legitimacy of every rule can reasonably be questioned the answer cannot be founded on any rule without begging the question. This is not obvious so long as any rules remain that have not yet been questioned. But once they are, the distinction between legality and legitimacy breaks down and questions about conduct turn out to be impossible to keep apart from questions about rules. In the end there remains no surer way to answer questions of right and wrong than to do the best one can and wait and see whether or not others will agree.[21]

Some people believe that the trouble with legitimacy is unique to modern western societies governed by complex bodies of written law under conditions of capitalist production.[22] That seems unlikely. Questions about conduct can be distinguished from questions about rules of conduct wherever and whenever people rely on rules that can be broken, regardless of whether these rules are customary, legal, moral, ethical, religious, written, unwritten, natural, or unnatural. Distinctions like those between the letter and the spirit of the law, natural and human law, custom and abuse, *nomos* and *physis*, and perhaps even the distinction between right and wrong itself suggest that the trouble with legitimacy is as old as the inclination, or ability, of people to break rules. To that extent small societies of hunters and gatherers following customs transmitted by word of mouth or imitation are exactly like large industrial societies governed by written codes of law.

At the same time writing down the rules does have important consequences. Above all it makes them easier to identify. That has definite advantages. If you want to know whether an alleged but unwritten rule does in fact exist, you have no option but to ask as many people as you can whether or not they have heard of the rule in question and hope they are willing and able to answer. If they are not, you have little choice but to wash your hands of the question or perhaps impose a rule of your own devising. In either case it will be difficult to tell whether the dispute is about rules or about conduct and force is likely to be used not only when undisputed rules call for some wrong to be avenged or punished (or prevented), but also when the rules are in dispute and it is not at all clear whether any wrong has even been committed. That can make for real injustice.

Not so with written law. If you want to know whether an alleged law does in fact exist, you need ask no one. You merely need to look it up. Most of the time that is enough. If it is not, because the law in question is doubtful, obscure, or poorly suited to the circumstances of the case, you may have to do some careful thinking until you arrive at a satisfactory answer, but you will have no good reason to use force until the question about the law has been settled. When law is written down questions of legality are easier to distinguish from questions of legitimacy. That increases the chances that force will be used to make conduct conform to the rules, but not to settle questions about the rules. Written law thus makes the use of force more predictable and helps to avoid the kind of injustice that occurs when someone is punished for breaking a rule unawares or in good faith.

These are the advantages people have in mind when they call the jurists' method rational. But written law has disadvantages, too. One is that written laws can exist without being known because the books in which they are written can exist without being read. For most of recorded history most people could not read books, and even nowadays most of the people who can read books do not read books of law. Hence it is not only possible but likely that most of the people living in a society governed by written laws do not know those laws—especially if the laws happen to be written in a foreign language, as was the case with Roman and canon law in the middle ages. That is a source of considerable doubt about the legitimacy of the law.

The other disadvantage is that written law is harder in some ways to change than custom. This is not only because old laws stay on the books forever unless someone takes the trouble to remove them. It is also because written laws are more easily turned into a foundation for coherent logical systems. And it is above all because people who understand coherent logical systems tend to identify with them. The more coherent the system, the more difficult it will become for them to change the law without threatening the system, and the more they are invested in the system, the more likely the law will lag behind social realities. That is a second source of considerable doubt about the legitimacy of the law.

These doubts can reinforce each other. There is nothing like a thoroughly developed legal system to pinpoint the need for change. But what if the law itself needs to be changed? Who can change a thoroughly developed legal system peacefully? Not the people, because they do not know what it is, and not the jurists, because their existence depends on it. Under such circumstances violence may seem, not an attractive, but the only option. If written law is preferable to custom in that it prevents the unpredictable use of force most of the time, it can also make the unpredictable use of force inevitable some of the time and thus lead into a crisis of legitimacy more intractable than anything imaginable under custom.

5. History of the Subject

Precisely such a crisis occurred in late medieval and early modern Europe. It began roughly when the defeat of Emperor Frederick II (r. 1220-50) proved that the emperor was powerless to rule the world. That raised the question: which law is good? In the past the jurists had answered: the law is good if God approves of it, and God approves of the laws written in the *Corpus Iuris Civilis* and the *Corpus Iuris Canonici*. Now that answer was no longer quite acceptable. When about fifty years later Pope Boniface VIII (r. 1294-1303) was, for all intents and purposes, assassinated by the lieutenants of the king of France and the papacy forced to take up residence in Avignon, it became even less acceptable. The crisis ended when a new answer found general agreement. That answer was: the law is good if it is approved by a sovereign ruler—and it is to be hoped, but impossible to know, if God approves of it as well. The history of visions of order among canonists and civilians from 1400 to 1600 consists largely of the answers that were given in between.

One of the earliest answers was also one of the most brilliant, even in the very long run of European legal history. It was given in Italy, which is no accident, because Italy was the place where the professional study of law had been invented and where the authority of pope and emperor had been most strikingly undermined. Its author was Bartolus of Sassoferrato. Bartolus pointed out that the refusal of the Italian cities to obey the emperor did not violate the authority of Roman law in and of itself because the authority of Roman law was universal whereas the authority of the Italian cities was not. The laws made by cities were as valid as the laws of the emperor, except that they were valid only for the city concerned whereas the laws of the emperor were valid for the world as a whole, but only for the world as a whole and not necessarily for any particular place. The laws of the cities and Roman law thus ranged on different planes of legal reality. The well-known formula for this solution was that the emperor was *dominus mundi* ("lord of the world") and *Princeps* with a capital P—and Bartolus insisted that anyone who denied the emperor's right to rule the world as a whole was in danger of heresy—while cities became "princes unto themselves [*sibi princeps*, with a small p]." The same solution helped to account for kings and princes who denied the emperor the right to interfere in the affairs of their realms, like those of France or England.[23]

Bartolus thus rescued the legitimacy of Roman law by distinguishing universally valid law from locally valid law. But the distinction had a cost, and the cost was the possibility of tyranny. So long as Roman law was thought to apply to each and every place in the world, tyrants were easy to identify: they violated the law. But if local governments were allowed to make their own laws, tyrants were harder to recognize. What if a tyrant seized control of a local government and started making bad law? How could you tell the difference between the laws of a tyrant and the laws of a legitimate government? There was a very real possibility that following the law might actually be wrong—and it is worth reading the opening pages of Bartolus' tract on tyranny for an expression of the stomach-turning horror which that possibility provoked.[24]

Bartolus responded with a legal theory of tyranny that was squarely founded on the distinction between legality and legitimacy. Tyranny came in two forms: tyranny by title and tyranny by conduct. Tyrants by title were both illegitimate and illegal because they acquired and exercised their power in evident violation of the law. That was the easy case. Tyrants by conduct were illegitimate in fact, but appeared to conform to the standards of legality. That was the hard case. But Bartolus was convinced that even tyranny by conduct could be proved and controlled by legal means that included a prominent role for pope and emperor in their capacity as chief guardians of universal law. There is no space to analyze his reasoning, fascinating though it is, in any more detail. The point to keep in mind is this: Bartolus identified tyranny as the main danger to the legitimacy of law and, as his very choice of the term tyranny suggests, tried to solve it by relying on existing law. That established the terms of the debate.

Those terms were confirmed by the conciliar movement. When the papacy tried to escape from French tutelage and returned to Rome, the result was the great schism (1378-1417) between two and eventually three popes. Everyone knew there could be only one legitimate pope, but no one knew which one it was. If anything ever raised the spectre of tyranny in medieval times, that did. The conciliarists banished the spectre by elaborating a theory of conciliar government that was squarely founded on existing canon law. They argued that on matters concerning the universal church the pope was obliged to obey a general council. If he did not, he could be legally deposed in spite of the papacy's basic exemption from human judgment. With the active support of the emperor they put their views into practice in a series of councils that met during the first half of the fifteenth century. The conciliar movement may thus be interpreted as an attempt to do for the church and canon law what Bartolus had done for the Italian cities and Roman law: restore legitimacy by relying on existing law.

The views of Bartolus and the conciliarists amount to something of a European prototype for dealing with tyranny by legal means. They remained influential far into the early modern period and have in some ways never been overtaken. But they had a serious weakness: they presupposed the very law that was in doubt. The weakness was quickly exposed by Jean Petit's (d. 1411) advocacy of tyrannicide and John Hus' (c. 1370-1415) attack on the hierarchical church, to choose two examples from the conciliar movement. The fathers at the council of Constance (1414-18) condemned the former and executed the latter. That was consistent with their understanding of the law. But the consistency was lost on people who wondered why the fathers were allowed to attack the papacy whereas John Hus was not. When the council of Basel (1431-49) turned on an undisputed pope, even supporters of the conciliar cause began to think that general councils displaced, but did not solve, the problem of tyranny.

At this point the terms laid down by Bartolus and the conciliarists were exhausted. Yet there was no plausible alternative. The period following the demise of the conciliar movement is therefore best characterized as an ambiguous mixture of veiled tyranny, official legality, and an intensive search of the records for better terms. Tyranny was everywhere suspected, but nowhere talked about—except as regards the Turks, whose conquest of Constantinople in 1453 confirmed the fear of tyranny while helpfully distracting attention from tyranny at home. Reform was everywhere demanded, and yet expressions of popular piety reached unprecedented heights while papal, imperial, and princely courts presided over spectacular achievements in patronage. Meanwhile the jurists began to look more carefully at ancient sources of the law and to experiment with new interpretations. But far from establishing common ground they undermined the law still further by fueling new debates and demonstrating that some of the most famous parts of law, including the Donation of Constantine and the Pseudo-Isidorian decretals, were outright forgeries.

The ambiguities were not resolved until Niccolò Machiavelli (1469-1527) and Martin Luther (1483-1546) proposed alternatives to law. Machiavelli and Luther could hardly have been more different from each other. One was an Italian diplomat and humanist, the other a German monk and theologian. One sought legitimacy from the mastery of politics and time, the other from faith in the eternal word of Christ. But they were united on one point: both rejected law as a source of legitimacy. Both thought that law and tyranny went happily together. Both insisted that the gap between legitimacy and legality—faith and works in Luther's terms, how we ought to live and how we do live in Machiavelli's—was utterly unbridgeable. And both defined virtue in ways that flew in the face of law as it was understood by jurists. Machiavelli and Luther made it possible to call someone prince whom Bartolus called tyrant, and Antichrist whom the established church called pope.

In point of principle the solutions offered by Luther and Machiavelli were equally plausible—and equally capable of throwing societies founded on law into upheaval. That may explain why some contemporaries lumped them together and why they continue to be controversial nowadays. Their view that virtue is incommensurate with rules was heresy then and still is heresy today—one measure of the extent to which the jurists have managed to hold their own. But in point of practice there was an important difference: Luther spoke to everyone; that made him dangerous. Machiavelli spoke to princes and humanists; that made him safe, which may explain why he did not acquire the reputation of having justified every conceivable form of immorality until after Luther's views had inspired popular uprisings that put the fear of God into established governments. Fear of God and people forced princes to realize that they could not do without law, converted them to anti-machiavellianism, and helped to save the jurists from danger of extinction.

The solution the jurists adopted in the end was as ingenious as it was simple. Since Bartolus they had been wondering how to restore legitimacy to the law without begging the question. But begging the question had turned out to be inevitable except at the cost of uncontrolled violence. That left but one choice: question-begging must be turned into a point of principle. The principle was stated by Jean Bodin, one of the greatest civilians of the later sixteenth century. Bodin agreed with Luther and Machiavelli that the gap between legality and legitimacy could not be bridged by any of the means so far considered. But he refused to trust in faith or politics. Like Bartolus he placed his trust in law. But unlike Bartolus he thought that rulers had to have absolute control over the law. The word for that control was sovereignty. Sovereign was he who made the law, and law was what the sovereign said it was. Sovereignty was "the absolute and perpetual power of a commonwealth," and its validity as unconditional as that of a tautology.[25]

Sovereignty changed the terms of the debate for good and made law legitimate again. What was left was to elaborate the consequences. The boundaries between natural, divine, and human law needed to be redrawn. The content of each kind of law needed to be identified. Natural and divine law could no longer be considered enforcable unless a sovereign decided otherwise. The history of human laws needed to be investigated. Sovereigns had to decide which parts of Roman and canon law they would accept and why. New laws needed to be developed in order to regulate relations between sovereigns—a task most expeditiously completed by Hugo Grotius (1583-1645), a doctor of both laws with a degree from Orléans and, next to Bodin, perhaps the most important thinker to put an end to the debate about the legitimacy of the law. In short, the period to follow saw a profusion of legislation and writings on all kinds of law and legal questions. Many of these, like those on canon law and those from Spain, are poorly understood. But none of them went back on principles that were effectively summed up by Jean-Jacques Rousseau (1712-78):

> What is good and in conformity with order is such by the very nature of things and independently of human agreements. All justice comes from God, who alone is its source; and if only we knew how to receive it from that exalted fountain, we should need neither government nor laws. There is undoubtedly a universal justice which springs from reason alone, but if that justice is to be acknowledged as such it must be reciprocal. Humanly speaking, the laws of natural justice, lacking any natural sanction, are unavailing among men.[26]

Sovereignty had advantages. It defined an institution whose legitimacy remained intact even where the law was in dispute. It thus settled the violence that had erupted all over Europe. But it did so by transforming the distinction between tyrants and legitimate rulers from a matter of law into a matter of conscience. At a time of political, religious, and military turmoil that was a plausible concession. But after four hundred years of experience with sovereignty, in a century that has

strained conscience beyond the breaking point, it may be worth giving
Luther and Machiavelli a second hearing.

❊ ❊ ❊

Three separate processes can be distinguished in this account. The first
is the gradual replacement of custom by written law. The second is the
shift in control over written law from pope and emperor to sovereign
nation states. And the third is the elaboration of different national traditions of law and attitudes to law.

The first of these three processes began long before the period here
under consideration, in the eleventh century, and culminated long after
in the great codifications of the nineteenth and twentieth centuries. It
spread from Italy, where the connection to ancient Roman law was
strongest, to the rest of Europe and, more recently, the world. It was
led by clerics in medieval, and laymen in modern, times. It went
through different phases at different speeds. But it has not been reversed for close to a thousand years.

The second process coincides more closely with the period under
consideration. It is in fact one of the reasons to regard the period as a
unit. It was fueled by doubts about the legitimacy of Roman and
canon law and the two universal institutions claiming responsibility for
that law. Because it undermined those institutions it could be, and
was, mistaken as a reversal in favor of the good old law so heartily desired by ordinary people. But because it shifted the responsibility for
law from universal institutions to the sovereign rulers of territorial
states, it actually increased the authority of written law still further.

The third process may explain why the conciliarists met in southwestern Germany, why an Italian wrote the Prince, why the Reformation began in Saxony, and why a lawyer from Angers invented sovereignty. But it is not nearly as well understood as the other two. There
are some trenchant analyses of nations and nationalism from the perspective of the social sciences.[27] They suggest that nation states are
made by literate elites. Since jurists figure prominently among those
elites, the different experiences of jurists in countries completely, half,
or barely familiar with written law may well explain some of the differences between Italy, France, and Germany—not to mention England,
the only European country with a class of professional jurists trained
outside the universities. But most historians either presuppose that nations have existed since the origins of time or else dismiss them as un-

worthy of attention. Most national histories thus reproduce more than explain the differences between the nations.[28]

From hindsight these processes are relatively easy to distinguish. In historical reality, however, they are inseparably connected. That accounts for the complexity of the subject, confusing both contemporaries and historians. Luther, to take a case that illustrates the source of the confusion clearly, went out of his way to prove that he was utterly uninterested in conduct. What interested him was faith.[29] To use the terms of this essay: he was interested in what made the law legitimate, not in legality. But since there was no general agreement on what made law legitimate—not even agreement on the distinction between legitimacy and legality itself—it was impossible to say whether his views undermined or strengthened existing law or conduct. For the same reason it was impossible to say whether the views of Bartolus, the conciliarists, Machiavelli, and Bodin undermined or strengthened existing law or conduct—and it is possible to say from hindsight only on the assumption that today's ideas about the law will not be overturned tomorrow. That helps to understand why German peasants thought they could rely on Luther to support their rebellion against the princes. But it also helps to understand why Luther condemned the peasants with as much conviction as he declared to be concerned with nothing but the faith.

The history of visions of order among the canonists and civilians from 1400 to 1600 is thus best described as part of a protracted struggle to win agreement on the benefits of written law. Precisely how that agreement could be won depended entirely on circumstance. Hence jurists could be found on both sides of every debate. At the same time a single thread of historical and intellectual continuity leads from the early days of the discovery and study of the *Digest* in Bologna to today's disputes about the law. That thread consists of the reasonably constant loss of control on the part of local communities and individuals to centrally organized bureaucracies increasingly staffed by jurists administering written law. The battles pitting papalists against conciliarists, Bartolists against legal humanists, catholics against protestants, and champions of popular sovereignty against absolute monarchy thus are somewhat misleading. They obscure the success the literate have consistently enjoyed over the illiterate. Whether or not that is about to end, and the progress of written law about to be reversed by "decodification" in favor of local, customary, and oral arrangements, it seems reasonable to consider, but too early to decide.[30]

NOTES

1. Wieacker (1967), 19 note 18.
2. For current thinking about the relationship between law, history, and social history times see Grossi (1986); Schnur (1986); and Bossy (1983). For the anthropological perspective see Roberts (1979); and Antony Allott and Gordon R. Woodman, eds., *People's Law and State Law: the Bellagio Papers* (Dordrecht, 1985). For a quick introduction to the literature on early modern law see Rowan (1986). For an indication of the volume of the literature read Scupin, Scheuner, and Wyduckel (1973), vol. 1:xi-xxxix, esp. xvii.
3. The extent of our devotion to that inheritance is best appreciated by reading critics as direct as Alfred North Whitehead, *Science and the Modern World* (New York, 1925); and Paul Feyerabend, *Against Method*, rev. ed. (London, 1988).
4. Among the brightest spots are the studies of Suzanne and Sven Stelling-Michaud (1955) on Swiss students of law at the University of Bologna and their subsequent careers; Coing (1964); Richard Kagan's *Students and Society in Early Modern Spain* (Baltimore, 1974); Kagan (1981), and the quantitative analyses of Ranieri (1985). They supply numbers that, although never as hard as they look, at least suggest orders of magnitude. For example: in the sixteenth century the University of Padua had 20 salaried, that is, full, professors of law; most German universities had no more than 4, 5, or 6 professors of law, half teaching Roman, half, canon law; in 1394 there were 256 bachelors and 368 scholars of law registered at the University of Orléans; in the second half of the fifteenth century an average of about 1,000 students are estimated to have been studying law in Germany at any given time. Coing (1984), 61, 66-67. The supreme court of the Holy Roman Empire tried about 9,900 cases during the first fifty-five years of its existence from 1495 to 1550, and almost twice as many, 19,300, during the next fifty years from 1550 to 1600. Ranieri (1985), vol. 1:135-37. One may add Carlo Cipolla's estimate that there were 5 physicians, 20 lawyers, and 250 notaries per 10,000 inhabitants in the city of Milan in 1288, and 5 physicians, 7 lawyers, and 26 notaries per 10,000 inhabitants in the city of Verona in 1545. Carlo M. Cipolla, *Before the Industrial Revolution: European Society and Economy, 1000-1700*, 2d ed. (New York, 1980), 83.
5. The *Corpus Iuris Civilis* was issued by Emperor Justinian in the sixth century and consisted of four books: the *Institutes*, the *Digest*, the *Code*, and the *Novels*. The *Corpus Iuris Canonici* consisted of four books that were issued over a period of time from 1140 to 1317: the *Decretum* of Gratian (about 1140), the *Liber Extra* of Pope Gregory IX (1234), the *Liber Sextus* of Pope Boniface VIII (1298), and the *Clementinae* of Pope Clem-

ent V (1317). The medieval version of the *Corpus Iuris Civilis* also contained certain constitutions of medieval emperors, and the *Corpus Iuris Canonici* a number of so-called extravagants that were not reliably identified until the early modern period. For basic information with further bibliography, see Roger E. Reynolds, "Law, Canon: To Gratian," in *Dictionary of the Middle Ages*, ed. Joseph R. Strayer (New York, 1982-89), vol. 7:395-413; Stanley Chodorow, "Law, Canon: After Gratian," in ibid., vol. 7:413-17; and Charles Donahue Jr., "Law, Civil-Corpus Iuris, Revival and Spread," in ibid., vol. 7:418-25.

6. *Digest* 1.1.1.

7. Genzmer (1966) vol. 2:1207-36.

8. Among the thirty-three popes who ruled from 1400 to 1600 fifteen had studied law, eleven were doctors of law, and four had at one time been professors of law. This includes the four popes who are sometimes referred to as anti-popes and is based on information taken from entries under individual popes' names in the *New Catholic Encyclopedia*, 18 vols. (New York, 1967-89).

9. Brian Tierney, *Foundations of the Conciliar Theory: the Contribution of the Medieval Canonists from Gratian to the Great Schism* (Cambridge, 1955), 220-37; Thomas E. Morrissey, "The Decree 'Haec Sancta' and Cardinal Zabarella," *Annuarium historiae conciliorum* 10 (1978):145-76.

10. Alexander Lamont Glasfurd, *The Antipope. Peter de Luna, 1342-1423: a Study in Obstinacy* (London, 1965).

11. Figgis (1916); Francis Oakley, "On the Road from Constance to 1688: the Political Thought of John Major and George Buchanan," *JBS* 2 (1962):1-31.

12. Mario Astuti, *Mos italicus e mos gallicus nei dialogi "De iuris interpretibus" di Alberico Gentili* (Bologna, 1937).

13. Maffei (1956); Kisch (1960).

14. *Decretum Gratiani emendatum et notationibus illustratum, una cum glossis* (Rome, 1582); *Decretales D. Gregorii Papae IX suae integritati una cum glossis restitutae* (Rome, 1584); and *Tractatus universi iuris, duce, & auspice Gregorio XIII. Pontifice Maximo in unum congesti*, 18 vols. in 25 (Venice, 1584-86). Both of these efforts came to fruition under the leadership of Pope Gregory XIII (1572-85), a doctor of both laws who had taught at the University of Bologna from 1531 to 1539 and counted future cardinals like Reginald Pole (1500-58) and Alessandro Farnese (1520-89) among his students. *New Catholic Encyclopedia*, vol. 6:779-81.

15. Kelley (1970); Stolleis (1988).

16. Donald Kelley, *François Hotman: a Revolutionary's Ideal* (Princeton, 1973).

17. Julian Franklin, *Jean Bodin and the Rise of Absolutist Theory* (Cambridge, 1973).

18. One of the last bastions of stereotype has just been conquered by Gelderen (1992), 273, concluding for the importance of Roman law to the Calvinist leaders of the Dutch revolt against Philip II.

19. The point of the distinction is not affected by the different terms that can be used to make it. Plausible alternatives to legitimacy include authority, validity, equity, morality, and justice.

20. Hence law is often defined as consisting of two elements, whether it is Thomas Aquinas defining law as "a certain dictate of reason for the Common Good [ergo legitimate], made by him who has the care of the community and promulgated [ergo legal]," or Philip Selznick defining the elementary legal act as an "appeal from an asserted rule, however coercively enforced [ergo legal], to a justifying rule [ergo legitimate]". See St. Thomas Aquinas, *The Treatise on Law*, ed. and transl. R. J. Henle, S. J. (Notre Dame and London, 1993), 145; Philip Selznick, "The Sociology of Law," in *International Encyclopedia of the Social Sciences*, ed. David L. Sills (New York, 1968-79), vol. 9:52.

21. Attempts are sometimes made to remove the uncertainty by distinguishing between two kinds of rules: rules that tell you how to behave and rules that tell you how to distinguish legitimate rules from illegitimate rules. For a modern example, see Herbert Lionel Adolphus Hart, *The Concept of Law* (Oxford, 1961). But that distinction breaks down as well because, although there may be two kinds of rules, there is only one kind of people and they have to apply both kinds of rules.

22. See William Connolly, ed. *Legitimacy and the State* (New York, 1984).

23. Interpreters of Bartolus are sharply divided on this crucial issue. See, e.g., Marcel David, "Le Contenu de l'hégémonie impériale dans la doctrine de Bartole," in *Bartolo da Sassoferrato: Studi e documenti per il VI centenario* (Milan, 1962), vol. 2:199-216 (to whom I owe the point about *Princeps* with a capital P); Keen (1965), 105-26; Skinner (1978), vol. 1:9-10. My own interpretation is based on a close reading of Bartolus' commentary on *Digest* 6.1.1 in Bartolus of Sassoferrato, *Opera*, 12 vols. (Venice, 1570-71), vol. 1:172 recto col. b, s.v. *per hanc actionem*, nrs. 1-2, and on *Digest* 49.15.24 in Bartolus, *Opera*, vol. 6:228 recto col. a, s.v. *hostes* nrs. 3-7, along with the cross-references given there.

24. Bartolus of Sassoferrato, "On the Tyrant," trans. Julius Kirshner in *The Renaissance*, ed. Eric Cochrane and Julius Kirshner (Chicago, 1986), 7-30, here at 9-10, and "Tractatus de tyranno," in Diego Quaglioni, ed., *Politica e diritto nel Trecento italiano* (Florence, 1983), 171-213, here at 175.

25. "For although one can receive law from someone else, it is as impossible by nature to give one's self a law as it is to command one's self to do something that depends on one's own will. As the law says, *Nulla obligatio consistere potest, quae a voluntate promittentis statum capit*—which is a rational necessity and clearly demonstrates that a king cannot be subject to the laws." Jean Bodin, *On Sovereignty: Four Chapters from Six Books of the Commonwealth*, book 1, chapter 8, ed. and trans. Julian H. Franklin (Cambridge, 1992), 12-13. Hence Bodin rejected the Aristotelian distinction between good and bad governments, considered tyrants to be sovereigns, described sovereignty as an unconditional gift, distinguished categorically between contracts (which are binding on the sovereign) and laws (which are not), and drew the stunning conclusion that "it is a kind of legal absurdity to say that it is in the power of the prince to act dishonestly, since his power should always be measured by the standard of justice." Ibid., pp. 1-2, 6-8, 13-15, 39.

26. Rousseau, *The Social Contract*, book 2, chapter 6, trans. Maurice Cranston (Harmondsworth, 1968), 80-81.

27. See especially Ernest Gellner, *Nations and Nationalism* (Ithaca, 1983) and Benedict Anderson, *Imagined Communities: Reflections on the Origin and Spread of Nationalism*, 2d ed. (London and New York, 1991).
28. For an outstanding exception see J.G.A. Pocock, *The Ancient Constitution and the Feudal Law*, rev. ed. (Cambridge, 1987).
29. See, for example, his statement in the letter he sent to Pope Leo X in 1520: "There is no dispute about conduct between me and anyone else, only about the word of truth." Martin Luther, "Epistola Lutheriana ad Leonem decimum summum pontificem," in WA (Weimar, 1883-), vol. 7:43. The word translated as "conduct" is *mores*, a term uniting conduct with rules of conduct in a way that Luther's distinction was designed to explode.
30. See Bellomo (1991).

BIBLIOGRAPHY

The purpose of the bibliography is to give readers unfamiliar with the field a means of orientation. It is divided into three sections. The section entitled "reference" lists bibliographies, handbooks, surveys, dictionaries, basic texts of canon and civil law, and the like. The section entitled "perspectives" is meant for readers seeking frames of reference. The section entitled "studies" lists works that have made a major contribution to our understanding of the field, or represent a particular approach to it particularly clearly, or both. In order to include as many different authors as possible I have with rare exceptions mentioned no more than one title per author per section. Since lack of space made it impossible to include a balanced selection of works written by the individual canonists and civilians themselves—not to mention philosophers or theologians with ideas about law—I have mentioned no such works at all. I have similarly excluded reference works limited to specific national traditions. For guidance to such works readers will have to rely on the tools listed in the reference section.

Reference
Allen, John William. *A History of Political Thought in the Sixteenth Century.* London, 1928.
Berger, Adolf. *Encyclopedic Dictionary of Roman Law.* TAPS, new series, vol. 43, pt. 2. Philadelphia, 1953.
Burns, James Henderson, ed. *Cambridge History of Medieval Political Thought, c. 350 - c. 1450.* Cambridge, 1988.
Burns, James Henderson, and Mark Goldie, eds. *Cambridge History of Political Thought, 1450-1700.* Cambridge, 1991.
Carlyle, Robert Warrand, and Alexander James Carlyle. *A History of Mediaeval Political Theory in the West.* 6 vols. Edinburgh and London, 1903-36.
Coing, Helmut. *Europäisches Privatrecht.* 2 vols. Munich, 1985-89.
Coing, Helmut, ed. *Handbuch der Quellen und Literatur der neueren europäischen Privatrechtsgeschichte.* 3 vols. Veröffentlichungen des Max-Planck-Instituts für europäische Rechtsgeschichte. Munich, 1973- .
Dawson, John Philip. *The Oracles of the Law.* Thomas M. Cooley lectures. Ann Arbor, 1968.
Erler, Adalbert, and Ekkehard Kaufmann, eds. *Handwörterbuch zur deutschen Rechtsgeschichte.* Berlin, 1964-.
Feine, Hans Erich. *Kirchliche Rechtsgeschichte.* Vol. 1, *Die katholische Kirche.* 5th ed. Cologne, 1972.
Friedberg, Emil Albert, ed. *Corpus Iuris Canonici.* 2 vols. Leipzig, 1879-81.
Justinian. *Corpus Iuris Civilis.* Ed. Theodor Mommsen, Paul Krüger, Rudolf Schoell, and Wilhelm Kroll. 3 vols. Berlin, 1872-95.
Justinian. *The Digest of Justinian.* Ed. Theodor Mommsen and Paul Krüger. 4 vols. Trans. Alan Watson, et al. Philadelphia, 1985.
Justinian. *Justinian's Institutes.* Trans. Peter Birks and Grant McLeod. Ithaca, 1987.
Koschaker, Paul. *Europa und das Römische Recht.* Munich, 1953.
Le Bras, Gabriel, ed. *Histoire du droit et des institutions de l'Eglise en Occident.* Paris, 1955-.
Mesnard, Pierre. *L'Essor de la philosophie politique au XVIe siècle.* Paris, 1936.
Naz, Raoul, ed. *Dictionnaire de droit canonique.* 7 vols. Paris, 1935-65.
Robinson, O. F., T. D. Fergus, and William M. Gordon. *An Introduction to European Legal History.* Abingdon, Oxon., 1985.

Rowan, Steven W. *Law and Jurisprudence in the Sixteenth Century: an Introductory Bibliography.* Sixteenth Century Bibliography, no. 26. St. Louis, 1986.
Scupin, Hans Ulrich, Ulrich Scheuner, and Dieter Wyduckel, eds. *Althusius-Bibliographie. Bibliographie zur politischen Ideengeschichte und Staatslehre, zum Staatsrecht und zur Verfassungsgeschichte des 16. bis 18. Jahrhunderts.* 2 vols. Berlin, 1973.
Skinner, Quentin. *The Foundations of Modern Political Thought.* 2 vols. Cambridge, 1978.
Société d'histoire des droits de l'antiquité. Ius Romanum Medii Aevi. Milan, 1961-.
Wieacker, Franz. *Privatrechtsgeschichte der Neuzeit, unter besonderer Berücksichtigung der deutschen Entwicklung.* 2d ed. Jurisprudenz in Einzeldarstellungen, vol. 7. Göttingen, 1967.

Perspectives
Coing, Helmut. "Das Recht als Element der europäischen Kultur." *HZ* 238 (1984): 1-15.
Donahue, Charles, Jr. *Why the History of Canon law is Not Written.* Selden Society lectures, 1984. London, 1986.
Genzmer, Erich. *Mittelalterliches Rechtsdenken.* Schriftenreihe zur europäischen Integration. Sonderdrucke, vol. 2. Hamburg, 1961.
Keen, Maurice H. "The Political Thought of the Fourteenth-Century Civilians." In *Trends in Medieval Political Thought*, ed. Beryl Smalley, 105-26. Oxford, 1965.
Kelley, Donald R. "Civil Science in the Renaissance: Jurisprudence Italian Style." *HistJ* 22 (1979): 777-94.
Kunkel, Wolfgang. "The Reception of Roman Law in Germany: an Interpretation." In *Pre-Reformation Germany*, ed. Gerald Strauss, 263-81. New York, 1972.
Le Goff, Jacques. "Histoire médiévale et histoire du droit: Un dialogue difficile." In *Storia sociale e dimensione giuridica*, ed. Paolo Grossi, 23-63. Per la storia del pensiero giuridico moderno, vol. 22. Milan, 1986.
Oakley, Francis. "Legitimation by Consent: The Medieval Roots." *Viator* 14 (1983): 303-35.
Roberts, Simon. "The Study of Dispute: Anthropological Perspectives." In Bossy (1983), 1-24.
Selznick, Philip, Leon Mayhew, Philippe Nonet, Jerome E. Carlin, and Paul Bohannan. "Law." In *International Encyclopedia of the Social Sciences*, ed. David L. Sills, vol. 9:49-78. New York, 1968-79.
Skinner, Quentin. "The State." In *Political Innovation and Conceptual Change*, ed. Terence Ball, James Farr, and Russell Hanson, 90-131. Ideas in context. Cambridge and New York, 1989.
Stein, Peter. *Roman Law and English Jurisprudence Yesterday and Today: an Inaugural Lecture.* London, 1969.
Tierney, Brian. "Hierarchy, Consent, and the 'Western Tradition.'" *Political Theory* 15 (1987): 646-52.
Ullmann, Walter. *The Relevance of Medieval Ecclesiastical History: an Inaugural Lecture.* Cambridge, 1966.
Weber, Max. "The Types of Authority and Imperative Co-ordination." In Max Weber, *The Theory of Social and Economic Organization*, trans. A. M. Henderson and Talcott Parsons, 324-423. New York, 1947.
Wieacker, Franz. "Zum heutigen Stand der Rezeptionsforschung." In *Festschrift für Joseph Klein zum 70. Geburtstag*, ed. Erich Fries, 181-201. Göttingen, 1967.

Studies
Alberigo, Giuseppe. *Chiesa conciliare: identità e significato del conciliarismo.* Testi e ricerche di scienze religiose, vol. 19. Brescia, 1981.
Bellomo, Manlio. *L'Europa del diritto comune.* 5th ed. Rome, 1991.

Berman, Harold J. *Law and Revolution: the Formation of the Western Legal Tradition.* Cambridge, Mass., 1983.

Black, Antony. *Monarchy and Community: Political Ideas in the Later Conciliar Controversy, 1430-1450.* Cambridge, 1970.

Bossy, John, ed. *Disputes and Settlements: Law and Human Relations in the West.* Past and Present Publications. Cambridge, 1983.

Brunner, Otto. *Land and Lordship: Structures of Governance in Medieval Austria.* Trans. Howard Kaminsky and James Van Horn Melton. Philadelphia, 1992.

Calasso, Francesco. *I glossatori e la teoria della sovranità.* 3d ed. Milan, 1957.

Coing, Helmut. *Römisches Recht in Deutschland.* Ius Romanum Medii Aevi, part V, vol. 6. Milan, 1964.

Cortese, Ennio. *La norma giuridica: Spunti teorici nel diritto comune classico.* 2 vols. Ius nostrum. Studi e testi, pubblicati dall'Istituto di storia del diritto italiano dell'Università di Roma, vol. 6. Milan, 1962-64.

Figgis, John Neville. *Studies of Political Thought from Gerson to Grotius, 1414-1625.* 2d ed. Cambridge, 1916.

Franklin, Julian H. *Jean Bodin and the Sixteenth-Century Revolution in the Methodology of Law and History.* New York, 1963.

Gelderen, Martin van. *The Political Thought of the Dutch Revolt, 1555-1590. Ideas in context.* Cambridge, 1992.

Genzmer, Erich. "Kleriker als Berufsjuristen im späten Mittelalter." In *Etudes d'histoire du droit canonique, dédiées à Gabriel Le Bras,* vol. 2:1207-36. *Revue de droit canonique,* vol. 16. Paris, 1966.

Gierke, Otto Friedrich von. *Community in Historical Perspective: A Translation of Selections from Das deutsche Genossenschaftsrecht (The German Law of Fellowship).* Ed. Antony Black. Trans. Mary Fischer. Cambridge, 1990.

Gilmore, Myron P. *Argument from Roman Law in Political Thought, 1200-1600.* Harvard Historical Monographs, vol. 15. Cambridge, Mass., 1941.

Grossi, Paolo, ed. *Storia sociale e dimensione giuridica: Strumenti d'indagine e ipotesi di lavoro. Atti dell'incontro di studio, Firenze, 26-27 aprile, 1985.* Per la storia del pensiero giuridico moderno, vol. 22. Milan, 1986.

Heckel, Johannes. *Lex charitatis: eine juristische Untersuchung über das Recht in der Theologie Martin Luthers.* 2d ed. by Martin Heckel. Cologne and Vienna, 1973.

Helmholz, Richard H. *Roman Canon Law in Reformation England.* Cambridge Studies in English Legal History. Cambridge, 1990.

Kagan, Richard. *Lawsuits and Litigants in Castile, 1500-1700.* Chapel Hill, 1981.

Kantorowicz, Ernst. *The King's Two Bodies: a Study in Mediaeval Political Theology.* Princeton, 1957.

Kantorowicz, Hermann Ulrich. *Rechtshistorische Schriften.* Eds. Helmut Coing and Gerhard Immel. Freiburger rechts- und staatswissenschaftliche Abhandlungen, vol. 30. Karlsruhe, 1970.

Kelley, Donald R. *Foundations of Modern Historical Scholarship: Language, Law, and History in the French Renaissance.* New York, 1970.

Kelley, Donald R. *The Human Measure: Social Thought in the Western Legal Tradition.* Cambridge, Mass., 1990.

Kisch, Guido. *Erasmus und die Jurisprudenz seiner Zeit: Studien zum humanistischen Rechtsdenken.* Basler Studien zur Rechtswissenschaft, vol. 56. Basel, 1960.

Kuehn, Thomas. *Law, Family & Women: Toward a Legal Anthropology of Renaissance Italy.* Chicago, 1991.

Kuttner, Stephan. *The History of Ideas and Doctrines of Canon Law in the Middle Ages.* London, 1980.

Lagarde, Georges de. *La naissance de l'ésprit laïque au déclin du Moyen Age.* 3d ed. 5 vols. Louvain, 1956-70.

Langbein, John. *Prosecuting Crime in the Renaissance: England, Germany, France.* Studies in Legal History. Cambridge, Mass., 1974.

Maclean, Ian. *Interpretation and Meaning in the Renaissance: The Case of Law.* Ideas in context. Cambridge, 1992.

Maffei, Domenico. *Gli inizi dell' umanesimo giuridico.* Milan, 1956.
Maitland, Frederic William. *English Law and the Renaissance.* Rede lectures, 1901. Cambridge, 1901.
Martines, Lauro. *Lawyers and Statecraft in Renaissance Florence.* Princeton, 1968.
Meinecke, Friedrich. *Machiavellism: the Doctrine of Raison d'Etat and its Place in Modern History.* Trans. Douglas Scott. New Haven, 1957.
Oakley, Francis. *Natural Law, Conciliarism, and Consent in the Late Middle Ages.* London, 1984.
Pennington, Kenneth. *The Prince and the Law, 1200-1600: Sovereignty and Rights in the Western Legal Tradition.* Berkeley and Los Angeles, 1993.
Pocock, John Grenville Agard. *The Machiavellian Moment: Florentine Political Thought and the Atlantic Republican Tradition.* Princeton, 1975.
Post, Gaines. *Studies in Medieval Legal Thought: Public Law and the State, 1100-1322.* Princeton, 1964.
Prodi, Paolo. *Il sacramento del potere: Il giuramento politico nella storia costituzionale dell'Occidente.* Collezione di testi e di studi. Storiografia. Bologna, 1992.
Quaglioni, Diego. *Civilis sapientia: Dottrine giuridiche e dottrine politiche fra medioevo ed età moderna.* Saggi per la storia del pensiero giuridico moderno, vol. 21. Rimini, 1989.
Ranieri, Filippo. *Recht und Gesellschaft im Zeitalter der Rezeption: eine rechts- und sozialgeschichtliche Analyse der Tätigkeit des Reichskammergerichts im 16. Jahrhundert.* 2 vols. Quellen und Forschungen zur höchsten Gerichtsbarkeit im alten Reich, vol. 17. Cologne, 1985.
Roberts, Simon. *Order and Dispute: an Introduction to Legal Anthropology.* New York, 1979.
Salmon, John Hearsey McMillan. *Renaissance and Revolt: Essays in the Intellectual and Social History of Early Modern France.* Cambridge Studies in Early Modern History. Cambridge, 1987.
Schnur, Roman, ed. *Die Rolle der Juristen bei der Entstehung des modernen Staates.* Berlin, 1986.
Stelling-Michaud, Suzanne, and Sven Stelling-Michaud. *L'université de Bologne et la pénétration du droit romain et canonique en Suisse au XIIIe et XIVe siècles.* THR, vol. 17. Geneva, 1955.
Stolleis, Michael. *Geschichte des öffentlichen Rechts in Deutschland.* Vol. 1, *Reichspublizistik und Policeywissenschaft, 1600-1800.* Munich, 1988.
Strauss, Gerald. *Law, Resistance, and the State: the Opposition to Roman Law in Reformation Germany.* Princeton, 1986.
Tierney, Brian. *Religion, Law, and the Growth of Constitutional Thought, 1150-1650.* The Wiles Lectures given at the Queen's University of Belfast. Cambridge, 1982.
Troje, Hans Erich. *Graeca leguntur. Die Aneignung des byzantinischen Rechts und die Entstehung eines humanistischen Corpus iuris civilis in der Jurisprudenz des 16. Jahrhunderts.* Forschungen zur neueren Privatrechtsgeschichte, vol. 18. Cologne, 1971.
Tuck, Richard. *Natural Rights Theories: Their Origin and Development.* Cambridge and New York, 1979.
Ullmann, Walter. *Principles of Government and Politics in the Middle Ages.* 2d ed. London, 1966.
Villey, Michel. *La formation de la pensée juridique moderne: Cours d'histoire de la philosophie du droit.* 4th ed. Paris, 1975.
Vinogradoff, Paul. *Roman Law in Medieval Europe.* 2d ed. by F. de Zulueta. Oxford, 1929.
Watson, Alan. *The Evolution of Law.* Baltimore, 1985.
Willoweit, Dietmar. *Rechtsgrundlagen der Territorialgewalt: Landesobrigkeit, Herrschaftsrechte und Territorium in der Rechtswissenschaft der Neuzeit.* Forschungen zur deutschen Rechtsgeschichte, vol. 11. Cologne and Vienna, 1975.

VOICES OF REFORM FROM HUS TO ERASMUS

Erika Rummel
(Wilfried Laurier University)

After the Leipzig Disputation of 1519, in which Luther defended articles condemned by the Council of Constance, he was both branded and
hailed as a second Hus.[1] A continuity of thought between Luther and
another suspected heretic, Desiderius Erasmus, was expressed by the
popular saying, "Erasmus laid the egg, and Luther hatched it."[2]
Nowadays, the readiness of protagonists in the Reformation debate to
embrace a "forerunner" theory is recognized by modern scholars for
what it was: a polemical strategy rather than a historical thesis. In his
programmatically titled *Forerunners of the Reformation*, Heiko Oberman notes, on the one hand, the concept's utility as a guard against
rigid periodization and, on the other, its encouragement of a simplistic
notion of linear intellectual development from the "forerunners" to
Luther and other leaders of the Reformation in the sixteenth century.[3]
Alister McGrath also sounds a note of caution. Although he emphasizes the continuity of theological thought and the Reformation's intellectual debt to earlier centuries, he prefers to search out trends that
foreshadow later developments rather than to identify individual carri-
ers of pre-reformation thought.[4] Alternatively—and this is the approach adopted here—we may examine prominent voices of reform
without losing sight of the fact that the Reformation of the sixteenth
century blended the voices of "forerunners" in a manner that ultimately precludes an analysis into separate intellectual genealogies.

It follows that the names of Hus and Erasmus in this chapter's title
merely mark the peripheries of our investigation. Standing between
these two men were many writers, preachers, and church administrators who contributed to the process that culminated in the Reformation. Some, such as the humanists Lorenzo Valla, Elio Nebrija, and
Jacques Lefèvre, applied philological skills to Biblical studies with the
aim of providing a better and clearer source text. Others, such as
Wessel Gansfort and John Colet, spread the message of reform to lecture halls, recalling students to the Bible and the inner piety recommended by St. Paul. Preachers added emotional force to the call for re-

form, whether they adopted the apocalyptic language of Girolamo
Savonarola or the earthy humour of Johann Geiler von Kaysersberg. A
number of churchmen used their positions of authority in the church
hierarchy to protect advocates of reform and became themselves active
reformers, notably Guillaume Briçonnet, Francisco Ximénes de
Cisneros, and Giles of Viterbo. At the end of this stream, Erasmus expressed the whole range of concerns that came to the forefront during
the century bracketed by the death of Hus and the rise of Luther: outrage over ecclesiastical abuses; a new focus on patristic and scriptural
studies; spiritual renewal and greater personal piety; and a more
broadly conceived church of all believers rather than a rigidly hierarchical one.

1. Jan Hus' Reforming Vision

The story of Jan Hus (1370-1415) unfolds against the background of
the crisis of the papacy during the Great Schism (1378-1417). The
Council of Constance, called to restore unity, also confronted the tasks
of defending orthodoxy and initiating a reformation of the church in
head and members. Hus' views on the church, rooted in the fourteenth-century Bohemian reform movement, were further shaped by
John Wyclif, whose books had found avid readers at Hus' University of
Prague. In 1402 he entered the priesthood and was appointed preacher
at Bethlehem Chapel in Prague, where he inveighed against the clergy's
venality and moral corruption and called for spiritual renewal and voluntary poverty. Preaching in a vernacular, he attracted a strong following but was soon caught up in a web of politics. When he spoke
out against the indiscriminate condemnation of Wyclif, whose books
had been confiscated and burned by the archbishop's command, he
was ordered to cease preaching and, upon defying the order, excommunicated. His condemnation of the sale of indulgences, which had
royal approval, and the resulting tumult brought him into direct conflict with King Wenceslaus. The situation was expected to be resolved
at the Council of Constance, where Hus was to present himself for examination.

The main target of Hus' preaching had been clerical corruption,
which occupied him more than matters of doctrine. Yet it was his orthodoxy that became the focus of the investigation at Constance,
where Hus was associated with the condemned practice of utraquism,

the administering of communion to the faithful under both species, which he had approved rather than initiated. Even more dangerous in the eyes of the Council was Hus' affinity to Wyclif's teaching on a number of points: the rejection of the church's hierarchy, the promotion of a democratic ecclesiology, and the insistence that all disputes be settled by reference to the Bible. Hus had given expression to these controversial ideas in his treatise *On the Church* (*De ecclesia*) of 1413. He plainly deprecated church traditions that were not founded on Scripture:

> Every Christian is expected to believe explicitly and implicitly all the truth which the Holy Spirit has put in Scripture, and in this way a man is not bound to believe the sayings of the saints which are apart from Scripture, nor should he believe papal bulls, except in so far as they speak out of Scripture, or in so far as what they say is founded in Scripture simply.[5]

Summoned before the Council, Hus dissociated himself from some of the heretical articles attributed to him but refused to accept without reserve the Council's condemnation of Wyclif. After he rejected a moderate formula of abjuration proposed to him, he was sentenced as an obdurate heretic and, an Imperial safe-conduct not withstanding, relaxed to the temporal ruler for execution.

Hus' death at the stake did not prevent the movement named for him from becoming a social, religious, and political force. The Hussites anticipated the Protestant Reformation in adopting a vernacular liturgy, allowing the clergy to marry, dispensing with auricular confession, and forbidding the veneration of saints. In its extreme form the movement found expression in the "Articles of Tabor" (1420), which decreed the destruction of churches as places of idolatry and proclaimed the community of goods. Although the Council of Basel in 1436 reached a compromise with the more moderate representatives of the movement, the "Bohemian heresy" continued to occupy the minds of sixteenth-century theologians, who at every opportunity raised the Hussite spectre in their polemics against the reformers. Luther's pronouncement, "We are all Hussites," gave epigrammatic force to the notion that the reformers were resurrecting views that had been condemned as unorthodox by the Church.

2. THE BEGINNINGS OF BIBLICAL HUMANISM

Following the road leading from Hus to Erasmus, we first direct our attention to the Biblical humanists, whose scholarship prepared the way for the exegetical approach adopted by the Protestant reformers. It was they who translated the humanist call to turn to the sources of classical antiquity into an appeal to investigate the sources of Christian faith and to turn to the Christian "classics", that is, Scripture and the Fathers. Thus the reformers' interest in the Biblical languages and in a philological approach to scriptural exegesis may, to some extent, be seen as a derivative of secular humanism. In the context of Reformation polemics, at any rate, Catholic protagonists routinely blamed the schism on the preparatory work of the "theologizing humanists [*humanistae theologizantes*]."[6] Valla, Lefèvre, and Erasmus form the usual roundup of suspects, but other "meddling" humanists, such as Gianozzo Manetti, Aurelio Brandolini, and closer to the Reformation era, Elio Nebrija and Johann Reuchlin, did not escape the wrath of conservative critics or, in many cases, Inquisitorial attention.

Lorenzo Valla
Lorenzo Valla (c. 1407-57), who taught at the universities of Pavia and Rome and enjoyed the patronage of the king of Naples, was appointed toward the end of his life secretary to Pope Calixtus, a position he had long coveted. As a student of classical antiquity, Valla was largely an autodidact. The self-reliance fostered by this approach to learning, combined with a natural penchant for polemics, made him one of the sharpest critics of tradition in his time. He challenged the teachings of Aristotle, which had long formed the core of the university curriculum; he challenged the hierarchy that assigned greater merit to the regular clergy than to secular priests or to lay Christians; he challenged the authenticity of the "Donation of Constantine," the document which formed the legal basis of papal territorial rights and claims to predominance over secular rulers; and he cast doubt on the correctness of the Vulgate, the church's *textus receptus* of the Bible. His scholarly probings earned him a charge of heresy in 1444, but he escaped serious consequences through the intervention of King Alfonso V of Naples, whose secretary and counsellor he then was.

There are three principal areas in which Valla's thought shows affinities with the Protestant reformers' ideals. He advocated turning, first, from philosophical speculation to faith, second, from external observances to inner piety, and third, from scholastic to patristic commentaries and to the Scriptures themselves. He also commented on doctrinal issues that became subject to intensive debate during the Reformation.

In *On the Mystery of the Eucharist* (*De mysterio Eucharistiae*) Valla wrote on a matter that informed the sacramentarian debate in the sixteenth century. It is notable, however, that he refrained from speculating on the process of transubstantiation or determining the question whether the celebration of the Eucharist repeats Christ's sacrifice or constitutes a commemorative act. In his opinion such questions lay within the realm of faith rather than reason. "If we can give no probable explanation why the bread is converted into God," he declared, "we should not regard ourselves lacking in religion or theology. For we know that faith proper means believing in God as we do in a friend whose truthfulness we have tested and ascertained. Hence it is written 'Blessed are those who did not see, yet believed.'"[7]

In *On Free Will* (*De libero arbitrio*, begun in 1435) Valla goes so far as to deny the possibility of reconciling faith with reason. He promotes a Pauline emphasis on faith and love, which he contrasts with the intellectual approach taken by scholastic theologians. "I would prefer," he writes, "that those who are called theologians would not depend so much on philosophy or devote so much energy to it, making it almost an equal and sister (I do not say patron) of theology, for it seems to me that they have a poor opinion of our religion if they think it needs the protection of philosophy." As for Valla's position on free will, it is significant that Erasmus lists him, together with Hus and Wyclif, among those sharing Luther's views on the subject.[8]

In *On Religious Vows* (*De professione Religiosorum*) Valla attacks the special claims to piety made by members of religious orders. Discounting the merit of vows and emphasizing spiritual devotion over ritual action, he writes: "It is not the external man but the inner one who pleases God."[9] Interpreted in a broader sense, his tract *On the Donation of Constantine* (*De Constantini Donatione*, 1440), in which he questions the historical foundation of papal claims, may be considered yet another attack on the preoccupation of the institutional church with external things and the secular world.

One of the most significant features of Valla's reform thought was his appeal to return to the sources of Christian teaching. His *In Praise of St. Thomas* (*Encomium Sancti Thomae*) shows a preference for patristic over scholastic theology. It was not only the method of exegesis that attracted Valla to the Fathers, but also their command of language. In his opinion, "anyone devoid of eloquence [was] quite unworthy of speaking on theological matters."[10]

The result of Valla's Biblical studies, gathered in the *A Collation of the New Testament* (*Collatio Novi Testamenti*), was a pioneering work of textual and literary criticism.[11] Valla did not provide a new text, but he noted variants, briefly stated his preference for one over the other, and pointed out inaccuracies, ambiguities, and solecisms in the Vulgate translation. The innovative character of his work prompted sharp criticism.[12] In an apologetic preface to the *Collatio* Valla explained the nature of his enterprise. Scripture, he said, is the precious material from which Christian doctrine is fashioned. "The individual words of divine scripture are like individual gems and precious stones, out of which the heavenly Jerusalem is constructed . . . I myself do not build a new edifice, but attempt to support the roof of this city and temple as far as I am able to do so, for if this is not done it will necessarily rain into the temple so that holy matters cannot remain in it safely."[13] Answering accusations that he "had shown disdain for Scripture by asserting that there was much in it that was not right", Valla reminded his critics that Scripture and the Vulgate were not one and the same thing. Many regarded the Vulgate as Jerome's translation, commissioned and authorized by Pope Damasus. Valla replied defiantly:

> If Jerome came back to life, he would correct what has been vitiated
> and corrupted in some places . . . . To say it briefly: If I emend the
> text, I do not emend Scripture but a translation of it. In doing so, I
> am not scornful, but rather pious, and I merely offer a better version
> than the previous translator, so that my version should be called
> authentic rather than his. And if Holy Writ is, properly speaking,
> what the saints themselves wrote in Hebrew or Greek, the Latin text
> is nothing of this sort.[14]

There are a number of annotations in the *Collatio* that reflect on doctrinal questions taken up by the reformers of the sixteenth century.[15] Accordingly, Valla's name was frequently invoked by polemicists in the Reformation debate. He was praised by Luther and Calvin, and put on the Index by the Catholic Church, verdicts that reflect the public perception of his doctrinal positions at the time. In the assessment of modern historians, however, Valla did not provide the necessary premises leading to Luther's conclusions.[16]

Elio Nebrija

If Valla exemplifies Biblical humanism in Italy, in Spain that honour goes to Elio Antonio de Nebrija (c. 1444-1522). After obtaining a bachelor of arts from the University of Salamanca, Nebrija continued his studies at the University of Bologna. He went to Italy, he said, "not to obtain a benefice or learn the formulae of civil and canon law, or do business, but . . . to restore the long-lost authors of Latin, who have now been exiled from Spain for many centuries." During the 1460s while in Italy he absorbed the ideals of humanism and promoted them vigorously on his return to Salamanca, where he was appointed to the chair of grammar in 1505. The uncompromising manner in which Nebrija championed the New Learning, and his undisguised disdain for those who failed to espouse it, caused resentment among his colleagues and eventually led to his departure from the university in 1513.[17] Nebrija's interests had led him to apply his philological skills to the Bible, and it was a natural progression that Cardinal Ximénes de Cisneros invited him to join the team of scholars he had assembled at Alcalá to produce a new edition of the Bible.

Nebrija had begun his Biblical studies at Bologna. The papers containing the results of his researches were, however, confiscated by the Inquisitor General, Diego de Deza, on suspicion of heresy. When Ximénes succeeded Deza, Nebrija recovered his manuscripts and published them under the title *The Third Fifty Observations* (*Tertia Quinquagena*) in 1516.[18] His *Extracts from the Epistles of Paul, Peter, James, and John* (*Segmenta ex epistolis Pauli, Petri, Iacobi et Ioannis*) appeared that same year. There he explained that the Latin translators had vitiated Paul's language and that the text had been mutilated by inattentive scribes. He had therefore exceeded his original commission from Juan de Fonseca, Bishop of Burgos, to normalize spelling and punctuation, and had added scholia and paraphrases of some obscure passages.[19]

The fact that Nebrija, a philologist and a layman, was engaged in Biblical studies, offended some conservative minds. In an apologia, written while his work was being investigated by Deza, Nebrija answered the objections of his critics. They claimed "that a person trained only in grammar had no right to touch Holy Writ." It was ironic, Nebrija noted, that he could have chosen to write about trifles and enjoyed popularity, but because he had devoted himself to that most important study of Scripture, he suffered persecution, was labelled "a bold and sacrilegious falsifier, and came close to being charged with impiety, shackled, and forced to defend [himself] in court." His research aimed at clearing up ambiguities and correcting mistakes in the Septuagint and the Vulgate by consulting the texts in the original language, a practice recommended by both Augustine and Jerome.[20]

Nebrija was convinced of the importance of philology for an understanding of Scripture:

> We lack a knowledge of the language on which our religion and Christian commonwealth is based . . . . The result of this ignorance is that those who are engaged in the study of Sacred Scripture cannot understand the books of [the Fathers] . . . and content themselves with reading other [inferior medieval authors] who write in a style they can understand.

Elsewhere he wrote: "Since the Christian religion derives from the three languages which were written on the inscription on the cross and thus have been consecrated by the triumph of our divine Saviour, we must acquire a knowledge of Hebrew, Greek, and Latin."[21] Thus we find in Nebrija the twin emphasis on Scripture in the original languages and on patristic exegesis, a platform also adopted by sixteenth-century reformers.

The multi-lingual Bible known as the *Complutensian Polyglot*,[22] on which Nebrija collaborated, was an ambitious undertaking. It supplied, in parallel columns, the text of the complete Bible in Greek and Latin. To this were added the Hebrew text for the Old Testament and the Syriac text for the Pentateuch, as well as an apparatus of vocabularies and a Hebrew grammar. The printing began in 1514 but publication was delayed until a papal privilege could be obtained in 1521. Although the edition drew on a remarkable pool of scholarly talent, it ultimately reflected the conservative attitude of its mastermind, Ximénes. Presenting the texts side by side, rather than emending the Latin version on the basis of the original language from which it was drawn, relieved the editors of making critical choices. Furthermore, no scholia were provided other than a revised version of a commentary on textual divergences in the Old Testament by the medieval exegete Nicholas of Lyra. The edition thus represents a compromise between the perceived need to uphold the authority of the traditional text and a desire to accommodate scholarly principles of textual criticism. It is significant in this context that Nebrija could not reconcile his methods with the approach taken by Ximénes and departed from the project. He had come to Alcalá, he wrote to the cardinal, "to take part in the correction of the Latin which is commonly corrupted in all the Latin Bibles, by comparing it with the Hebrew, Chaldaic, and Greek . . . but then Your Reverence told me to do what the rest are doing, that is, not to make any changes in what is commonly found in the old books."[23] Nor would the cardinal give in to Nebrija's protests against including Remigius' lexicon of names, a medieval work that did not meet humanist standards. Thus the *Complutensian Polyglot*, while an impressive scholarly enterprise and a tribute to Spanish scholarship, was not an instrument of reform in the sense in which the contemporary editions of Lefèvre and Erasmus undoubtedly were.

Jacques Lefèvre

Jacques Lefèvre d'Etaples (c. 1460-1536) studied and later taught at the Collège du Cardinal Lemoine in Paris. He undertook several journeys to Italy, where he met, among other distinguished humanists, Ermolao Barbaro, who encouraged his work of purifying the Aristotelian corpus from its medieval corruptions and accretions. His subsequent editions, paraphrases, and commentaries on Aristotelian works earned him the respect of fellow scholars throughout Europe. He became the central figure of a circle of French humanists which included Josse Clichtove, Charles de Bovelles, and Gérard Roussel. In 1507 he retired from teaching to take up residence with his patron Guillaume Briçonnet, the reform-minded abbot of Saint-Germain-des-Prés. He followed Briçonnet to Meaux, when the latter became bishop in 1515, and took an active part in his reform programme.

Lefèvre's thought was shaped by the mystical writings of Ramón Lull and Pseudo-Dionysius. He devoted himself to scriptural studies, believing that studying the Bible and patristic writings was a first step toward true piety. "Proceed from [Aristotelian writings] to a reverent reading of the Scripture, guided by . . . the Fathers," was his advice.[24] His spiritual goal was a piety at once eloquent and evangelical. The first-fruit of his Biblical studies was the *Quincuplex Psalterium* (Paris, 1509), which contained in parallel columns the so-called Roman, Gallic, and Hebrew versions of the Psalter[25] as well as the Old Latin version and the Vulgate text with some corrections. The texts were accompanied by an exposition, concordances, and annotations. He redefined the meaning of "literal sense:" "Let us call 'literal sense' that which is in accord with the spiritual and which the Holy Spirit shows us . . . . I have carefully sought to elicit this sense, as far as is in the gift of the Holy Spirit."[26]

He next turned his attention to the Pauline Epistles. In 1512 he published in parallel columns the Vulgate text of the Epistles and his own revision based on the original Greek, followed by a commentary. The edition constitutes an important step in the reformation of exegetical methods, moving away from a speculative to a philological and homiletic approach. Anticipating criticism, Lefèvre defended his work:

> They will accuse or rather condemn me for being bold and daring
> . . ., but they will pardon me when they realize that I have made no
> daring move against the translation of St. Jerome, but against the
> Vulgate, which existed long before Jerome, that blessed and glorious
> light of the church. He himself joins me in criticizing this edition.

He carps at it, proves it wrong, and calls it the old Vulgate edition.[27] The criticism anticipated by Lefèvre soon surfaced and was taken up by the faculty of theology at the University of Paris, which investigated his works on the initiative of its syndic Noël Béda. The conflict between Lefèvre and the faculty deepened with his involvement in the reform movement at Meaux, where he had been made Briçonnet's vicar-general *in spiritualibus*. The reservations of the theologians were reinforced when Lefèvre published in quick succession French translations of the Gospels and Epistles and homiletic "exhortations." Conservative theologians saw Lefèvre as one of the "pestilential heretics who, having made themselves a covering shed out of the bark of the Scriptures, brought in all sorts of abominable ravings."[28] In 1525, accordingly, the Faculty censured passages from Lefèvre's work as containing "many impious, scandalous, schismatic, and heretical things."[29] The hostile climate forced Lefèvre to seek refuge in Strasbourg. After his return he retired to Nérac, the estate of the King's sister, Marguerite of Navarre, who afforded him protection until his death.

Lefèvre was labelled by his critics "the teacher of Luther."[30] His influence on the reformer is undeniable. Luther owned a copy of Lefèvre's *Quincuplex Psalterium* and based his lectures on them.[31] For Lefèvre's influence on the Strasbourg reformers we have Guillaume Farel's testimony: "When God . . . made himself known to me through the gentle guidance of a saintly brother [Lefèvre] . . . things took on a new appearance. Scripture began to be full of meaning, the Prophets plain, the Apostles clear, the voice of the Shepherd, Master, and Teacher Christ recognized."[32]

In the context of Reformation thought Lefèvre's views on justification by faith and on the nature of sacraments are significant. He emphasized the spiritual and participatory element in sacramental action. Celebrations of the Eucharist, he said, were "not repeated offerings, but rather a remembrance and recollection of the same victim who has been offered once only." It was not the action of the priest, but the congregation's faith that made them recipients of sacramental grace: "The sacrament does not effect anything without faith." Similarly he said of confession: "Unless you first confess to God . . . I judge confession of this kind to men, whether as it was formerly or as it is now of little worth."[33]   Although his position on the relative merits of faith and works was not unequivocal, it is significant that he used the expressions *sola gratia, sola fide*, which were to become catchphrases of reformed theology.[34]   One of the censures by the faculty of theology at Paris in the condemnation of his writings read: "This proposition which indicates that faith alone is required and suffices for the remission of sins and for justification . . . is Lutheran heresy."[35]   The final verdict stated that the censured passages "detract from good works and contend that satisfaction for sins is not necessary for salvation, that human laws and ecclesiastical sanctions are of no consequence, . . . reject the cult of the saints and their holy days together with Catholic expositions of Holy Scripture, . . . recalling the heresies of the Manicheans, Waldensians, Wycliffites, and Lutherans".[36]

Lefèvre's work as textual critic and exegete demonstrates his commitment to scriptural studies and eventually led him to embrace the scriptural principle.   "To know nothing beyond the Gospel is to know everything," he wrote in the introduction to his commentaries on the four gospels (1522). He added: "Christ . . . does not proffer the Gospel to be understood but to be believed".[37]   Erasmus, who prepared his edition of the New Testament at the same time as Lefèvre was working on the Epistles, remained for some time unaware of the parallel efforts of the French humanist.[38]   A discussion of Erasmus' contribution to Biblical scholarship will be deferred to the end of the chapter. We now turn from the Biblical humanists to four advocates of moral reform and spiritual renewal: Wessel Gansfort and John Colet, who disseminated their ideas from the lectern, and Girolamo Savonarola and Geiler von Kaysersberg, who spread the reform message from the pulpit.

3. Teaching and Preaching Reform

Voices for a spiritual and moral reform of the church in the fifteenth century owed much to the *Devotio Moderna*, the movement that sought a deepening of inner piety and personal morality through meditation. Originating in the circle of Gerard de Groote (1340-84), it soon spread from the Low Countries to Germany, France, and Italy. Among the men associated with the *Devotio Moderna*, the reformers of the sixteenth century paid special tribute to Wessel Gansfort.

Wessel Gansfort

In a prefatory letter to the *Farrago rerum theologicarum*, which contained works by Gansfort, Luther reflected on the remarkable parallels between their views: "If I had read his works earlier, my enemies might think that Luther had absorbed everything from Wessel, his spirit is so in accord with mine."[39] Elsewhere he praised "the purity of theological thought" found in the writings of Gansfort and expressed the hope that the dissemination of his works would bring it about that "shortly there will be no Thomist or Albertist or Scotist in our world. Rather all will be simple children of God and true Christians."[40] In his own time Gansfort (c. 1420-89) inspired both admiration and disdain. His disciples called him the "light of the world [*lux mundi*]"; his detractors, referring to his controversial views, called him the "professor of contradiction [*magister contradictionis*]."[41] He studied scholastic theology at Cologne, Paris, and Louvain, taught, and wrote extensively on theological subjects.[42] At Paris he was a spirited participant in the disputations between Nominalists and Realists, but ultimately he expressed dissatisfaction with scholastic theology. Of his years at Paris he said: "The study of the sacred sciences, when it is merely superficial and not animated by a higher spirit, is not in itself particularly acceptable to God."[43] He was critical of the scholastic doctors also for their academic shortcomings. With a proud disdain familiar from the writings of later reformers, he notes: "Thomas hardly knew Latin, and it was the only language he did know; whereas I am master of the three principal tongues."[44]

Gansfort's focus on Scripture and his emphasis on language studies that would allow the theologian to inspect the text in the original anticipate the demands of humanists and reformers in the sixteenth century. While Gansfort recognized the traditions of the church as normative and did not propound the principle of *sola scriptura*, other views proffered in his writings approached positions later identified as Protestant. Parallels are found, for example, in his views on justification by faith and on the sacraments of penance and the Eucharist. Divine grace was not the consequence of a mechanical act, Gansfort said. Rather the sacramental act provided a suitable setting for receiving divine grace. Indeed, the receptive mind and the faith of the believer were of principal importance: "He who believes feeds upon the body of Christ, even though it be nowhere externally offered to him."[45] Similarly, the sacrament of penance did not depend on the external process of confession, absolution, and acts of penance. The priest did not have judicial power, and indulgences were useless. Divine grace was given freely to the repentant soul. Gansfort also embraced the concept of a priesthood of all believers. Priestly authority was given to anyone "who wished to be God's minister. But every son of God ministers to him as to the first-born."[46] Although the striking parallels between Gansfort's views and those of later reformers led one modern biographer to entitle a chapter "Wessel as a Protestant,"[47] it should be noted that his works were not widely disseminated before 1522, when a selection appeared almost simultaneously in two centres of the Reformation: Wittenberg and Basel.[48] Thus Gansfort's writings mainly served to corroborate the views of the reformers. Indeed, Luther testifies that he was confirmed in his beliefs by reading Gansfort's works: "Now I have not the slightest doubt that I have been teaching the truth, since he, living at so different a time, under another sky, in another land, and under such diverse circumstances, is so consistently in accord with me in all things."[49] In his lifetime, Gansfort may have influenced more minds through his teaching and homiletic activity than through his writings. He taught and acted as spiritual adviser to the boys at the school of the Brethren of the Common Life in Zwolle. He was in close contact with the Canons Regular of St. Agnietenberg near Zwolle, with the Cistercians at the monastery of Aduard near Groningen, and often read and discussed Scripture with the Poor Clares of Groningen, where he lodged in his old age.

John Colet

In England, John Colet (c. 1466-1519) presents a case similar to Wessel Gansfort's in that the personal impact he had on the minds of his contemporaries was proportionately greater than the dissemination of his written work.[50] In fact, a generation after his death, Thomas Harding was under the impression that Colet had "left no workes".[51]

This lack of readily available written documentation of Colet's thought may have led the first chroniclers of the Reformation to portray him as a more radical spirit than he was. Both Erasmus and More paid eloquent tribute to his character and learning. Their praise raised Colet's reputation as a spiritual leader to mythical proportions. Tyndale and Latimer made him out a reformer in danger of being martyred for his beliefs, an image that was preserved in John Foxe's *Book of Martyrs*. The view of Colet as a forerunner of the Reformation, perpetuated by later biographers, is enshrined in Frederic Seebohm's *The Oxford Reformers* of 1867. However, contemporary studies of Colet's work, much of which remained unpublished until the nineteenth century, put some qualifications on the traditional portrait of Colet the reformer. They do not find in his works the catchphrases of the Reformation, although they do find the characteristic turning away from scholastic commentaries to Scripture as the source of Christian philosophy, outspoken criticism of the wordliness of the clergy, and a call to inner piety.

Colet studied at the universities of Cambridge and Oxford, where he obtained a doctorate in theology. He interrupted his studies from 1493-96 to travel in Italy, but returned curiously untouched by the humanism which flourished there. He admired the neo-platonism of Ficino but made no effort to learn Greek—the accomplishment *de rigueur* for aspiring humanists—and showed no interest in classical pagan authors. All his efforts were focused on gaining an understanding of the Word of God. The lectures he gave at Oxford on Matthew and the Pauline epistles clearly show that, unlike his contemporaries Lefèvre and Erasmus, he saw no propedeutic value in humanist studies. "If anyone should say—as is often said—that to read heathen authors is of assistance for the right understanding of Holy Writ, let them reflect whether the very fact of such reliance being placed upon them does not make them a chief obstacle to such understanding," he wrote in his *Lectures on Corinthians*. Colet modified his position somewhat in later years, however, as the statutes of the boys' school show which he founded at St. Paul's in 1512. Although the emphasis there was to be on catechization, he also wanted students to be instructed in Latin and Greek literature and, on going over Erasmus' edition of the New Testament, he admitted: "I am sorry that I never learnt Greek, without some skill in which we can get nowhere."[52]

Although Colet focused his lectures on the revealed text as the foundation of the Christian religion, he was no advocate of *sola scriptura*.

Rather he believed in an esoteric tradition, precepts received by the apostles directly from Christ, to which the institutional church was heir. "Hence we must believe that the sacrifices, rites, and customs in the church, and the church itself, have grown from the laws laid down by the apostles".[53] In taking this position Colet places himself firmly in the Catholic tradition, but in his views on justification he approaches more closely to the reformers. "The just man," he wrote, "is the man who believes and trusts in God, while the man who trusts in created things of any sort is impious and unjust."[54] In his rejection of the superstitious veneration of saints and the anxious observance of auricular confession he likewise adopted a stand taken by the reformers.[55]

In 1510 Colet was asked to address the Convocation, that is, a synod of the higher clergy of Canterbury.[56] The sermon he gave is a significant call to reform. "Put the reformation of the church on your agenda," Colet urged the assembly. "And this reformation or restoration of the church must begin with you, our elders." From there, he said, it would spread to the clergy, and finally to the laity. He deplored the worldliness of the clergy, their mercenary interests, their moral corruption, their lack of vocation. It was not enough for a priest to receive academic training that enabled him to "propose insignificant questions and sophistical answers, but much more important are a good and holy life, moral integrity, a measure of scriptural knowledge, an understanding of the sacraments, and before all else, fear of God and love of Heaven." There was widespread criticism of the church in his time, Colet noted. "We see the opposition of the laity. But they are not as inimical to us as we are to ourselves. Nor is their opposition as harmful as the evil life we are leading, which puts us in opposition to God and Christ." Clearly aware of clerical corruption and the dangers it posed to the spiritual wellbeing of the Christian community, Colet nevertheless remained a devout Catholic. It is not surprising, then, that Erasmus, confronted with the spectre of schism in 1521, held up Colet as a man who could promote reform without promoting discord.[57]

Girolamo Savonarola

The spoken rather than the written word also served two preachers, famous in their time, though very different in their style of address: Girolamo Savonarola and Geiler von Kaysersberg. Sermons to the faithful were their principal means of calling for the conversion and reform of church and society. Although Savonarola's impact can be understood as a political phenomenon—a charismatic individual taking

charge in a crisis—as much as the manifestation of a spiritual current—
a millenarian vision of redemption and the conversion of Florence into
the New Jerusalem—it is in the latter capacity that his thought lived on
and can be said to have contributed to a general movement toward reform.

Girolamo Savonarola (1452-98) came from a prominent family in
Ferrara and entered the Dominican order against the wishes of his parents. After studying theology at Bologna and Ferrara, he taught at the
Studium of his order in Florence and was appointed prior of the Convent of San Marco in 1491. His prophetic sermons, castigating the
abuses of the church and threatening divine retribution, had attracted
attention for some time, when he gained political ascendancy in Florence after the invasion of Italy by Charles VIII and the overthrow of
Piero de' Medici. As Savonarola intensified his campaign of moral reform, his political opponents marshalled their forces. Pope Alexander
VI, whose support they enlisted, excommunicated Savonarola in an attempt to silence his outspoken criticism of the church. As the number
of Savonarola's opponents grew, his position became vulnerable. He
was imprisoned, tried, and executed as a heretic under turbulent circumstances.

In 1496 he had written *A Compendium of Revelations* (*Compendium Revelationum*), a summary and defense of his beliefs. He saw
himself as a divine instrument, whose preaching was directly inspired
by God and therefore prophetic. "I continually set forth three things,"
he wrote: "first, that the renovation of the Church would come about
in these times; second, that all of Italy would be mightily scourged before God brought about this renovation; third, that these two things
would come about soon."[58] Only repentance and conversion could
stay the judgement of God. Savonarola's most famous sermon, "On
the Renovation of the Church," preached at Florence in January 1495,
was published immediately and enjoyed wide dissemination.[59] Here,
too, Savonarola insisted on his divine inspiration. "Florence," he said,
"you heard with your ears, not me, but God." In the sermon he laid
the blame of Italy's troubles on a corrupt clergy. "O tonsured ones,
tonsured ones, through you this tempest has arisen." The Roman
church, he said, was "full of simony and evils," the congregation
lacked faith, and theology was vitiated by philosophy. "We must
struggle against lukewarm piety and against the division of wisdom . . .
[into] philosophy and knowledge of Sacred Scripture."

While Savonarola's role as a "forerunner" of the Reformation is disputed, it should be noted that Luther wrote a commendatory preface to an edition of his prison meditations (Wittenberg, 1523).[60] We may speculate, therefore, that Luther absorbed Savonarola's message. The paucity of references to this source in Luther's works is seen by at least one historian as political and characteristic of his efforts "to obscure the traces of his own beginnings" as a reformer.[61]

Johann Geiler von Kaysersberg

Rather different in style from Savonarola but equally effective was Johann Geiler von Kaysersberg (1445-1510), one of the most famous preachers north of the Alps. The son of a city scribe, Geiler studied at the universities of Freiburg and Basel, where he obtained a doctorate in theology in 1475. A few years later, he abandoned his academic career to take up an endowed preachership at Strasbourg and embarked on the moral and spiritual formation of his congregation. Although Geiler was considered by his contemporaries an innovative and provocative preacher, he cannot be called a radical. He held progressive views in some areas later developed by the reformers, but on the whole maintained conservative doctrinal positions, occasionally manifesting a decidedly "medieval" cast of mind. His feelings concerning the scholastics were mixed. He praised the scholastic method of exegesis, but ridiculed the wranglings of Thomists and Scotists who, he said, reminded him of "a cat dragging a piece of cloth to and fro."[62] Nor did he approve of preachers displaying their learning and introducing scholastic reasoning into their sermons, failing to address the spiritual needs of their audience. Geiler himself focused the attention of his hearers on the Word of God, but at the same time upheld the teaching authority of the church. The idea of a priesthood of all believers would have shocked him. He did not approve of vernacular translations of the Bible or of the unguided reading of Scripture by lay persons: "It is not good to print the Bible in German, for it does not suffice to read it as one reads any other book. One does not profit from it, if one does not have the requisite knowledge." Interpreting the Bible was a skill for which one needed training and an apprenticeship as in any other skilled trade, he said. It was the business of the theologians to teach, of the congregation to believe: "You have the creed, the Our Father, and the Ten Commandments. That's all you need to go to heaven."[63] He was, however, an vocal advocate of moral reform, a relentless critic of ecclesiastic abuses and of the hypocrisy of the laity, whose piety was confined to an outward observance of rites. They prayed mechanically, while their thoughts were elsewhere: "OUR FATHER, you say, and then to your wife or servant: When are you going to serve up the soup? WHO ART IN HEAVEN—Heintz, boy, saddle my horse so it will be ready. HALLOWED BE THY NAME . . . "[64] He urged his listeners to become Christians in spirit. Using the earthy images that were the hallmark of his sermons, he likened perfect Christians to sausages: "Sausages are made of minced meat, and perfect Christians have crucified their flesh by suppressing vice and evil desire; they have minced their meat with the knives of abstinence in fasting and chastity."[65]

In 1482 Geiler was asked to give the opening address at the Strasbourg synod and took the opportunity to call for reform.[66] He contrasted the worldly and corrupt practices of the clergy with the lives of Jesus and the apostles and appealed to the clergy to become the true guardians of Christian philosophy. In a vivid comparison, he likened them to "guard dogs" and "walls that protect a city." He demanded that candidates for church office be able and willing to take on the task of protecting the flock entrusted to them and deplored the acquisition of such offices through simony. "It is no longer the Holy Spirit who confers these offices, but the devil. If someone wants to become pope, he need only bribe the cardinals." Even the pope himself was not immune to bribes, he said. "He looks at the coins with the images of princes in armour and says: 'Who can resist the attack of such warriors?'" The Word of God must remain the basis of Christian thought and the simple precepts of the Bible must not be overshadowed by human laws. "In truth, divine law is so encumbered with human statutes, that it is almost impossible to uncover it. Neither pope nor emperor have the right to pass decrees contrary to divine law, and if they do so, one is not only allowed to disobey but obliged by one's conscience not to observe them."

Geiler was keenly aware that the church of his time was corrupt and saddened to see that his own call for reform yielded no tangible results. In the end he despaired of institutional reform: "You say: is it not possible to have a general reform? I say it isn't. There is no hope that the condition of Christendom will improve . . . therefore let each individual stick to his neck of the woods and see that he keep God's commandment and do what is right so that he may obtain salvation".[67]

Although Geiler published few of his sermons, they appeared in several collections after his death and became enormously popular with preachers looking for inspiration and with lay readers who appreciated an uplifting message expressed in down-to-earth language. It is significant that Matthias Flacius listed Geiler in his *Catalogus testium veritatis*. An anecdote related by another sixteenth century chronicler confirms Geiler's status as "forerunner" in the eyes of his generation. Questioned by Pope Adrian VI about the spread of the "Lutheran heresy" in Strasbourg, the city council replied that they were not qualified to pass judgment on what constituted heresy, but what was being preached now was not much different from "what [they] had heard more than twenty years ago, that is, a very long time before the Lutheran question arose. At that time, Dr. Geiler preached in the cathedral, and he . . . enjoyed the support of Bishop Albrecht".[68]

4. PATRONS OF REFORM

We have seen that several of the writers mentioned in our account had the active support of reform-minded churchmen in positions of authority. Among ecclesiastical leaders who recorded their misgivings about the corrupt state of the church and promoted spiritual reform from within were Ximénes de Cisneros in Spain, Guillaume Briçonnet in France, and Giles of Viterbo in Italy.

Francisco Ximénes de Cisneros
Ximénes de Cisneros (1436-1517) studied canon law at the University of Salamanca, entered the Franciscan order, and in 1492 became confessor and trusted adviser to Queen Isabella. Twice, during periods of political crisis, he served as regent of Castile. Appointed archbishop of Toledo and primate of Spain in 1495, cardinal and inquisitor-general in 1507, he had the authority not only to call for reforms but also to implement them. And he did so with determination and in the face of considerable opposition from those who stood to benefit from the *status quo*.

His earnest concern for church reform is borne out by the visitations he undertook, first among the Franciscan convents and subsequently among the houses of other orders, and the corresponding programme of spiritual renewal that he instituted for the benefit of the secular clergy in Spain. His goal was that the orders return to the original intentions of their founders and the clergy as a whole embrace the apostolic example as the normative pattern of their conduct.

Ximénes' care for the spiritual well-being of the church was paral-

leled and complemented by a concern for the status of theological studies. In this area his reform plans began with the foundation in 1499 of
a new university at Alcalá, which was to provide lectures in theology,
canon law, and the liberal arts.[69] Courses were inaugurated in 1508
under well qualified masters, most of whom had studied and taught at
the prestigious University of Paris, on whose statutes the constitution
of the new university was modelled.[70] Unlike Paris, however, Alcalá
embraced the humanist creed. Its statutes declared that grammar and
rhetoric were fundamental sciences and that training in the Biblical
languages was essential because they were the vehicles of the Word of
God, and "Scripture must be the principal end of theologians".[71] The
new university not only repatriated Spanish scholars from Paris, but
also benefited from squabbles at Salamanca, the premier university in
Spain. Both Alfonso Zamora, a prominent Hebraist, and Elio Nebrija,
the most highly regarded philologist in Spain at the time, came to
Alcalá after a falling out with the more conservative authorities of
Salamanca. We have already mentioned Ximénes' role in the publication of the *Complutensian Polyglot* and his patronage of humanist
learning. The impact of his policies on the church of Spain was such
that it has been claimed, with some exaggeration, that Ximénes' reforms prevented the Reformation from taking root in the Iberian peninsula. More balanced is John Elliott's view: "Cisneros helped give
the Spanish Church a new strength and vigour at the very moment
when the Church was everywhere under heavy attack. At a time when
the desire for radical ecclesiastical reform was sweeping through Christendom, the rulers of Spain personally sponsored reform at home."[72]

Guillaume Briçonnet

Guillaume Briçonnet (1472-1534) was one of the most powerful champions of reform within the French church. The son of a cardinal who
had turned to an ecclesiastical career after the death of his wife,
Briçonnet was in a privileged position, but unlike others he did not
abuse his connections. After his appointment to the abbacy of Saint-
Germain-des-Prés, he supported the reform efforts under way there.
His repeatedly stated aim was "to maintain the regular observance in
the said abbey according to the statutes there and according to their
Rule."[73] When Briconnet's increased honours and duties no longer allowed him to supervise the abbey personally, he appointed Etienne de
Bussy, a vicar sympathetic to his goals, "that the tender shoot of life
and religious rule which we planted there some time ago by the grace

of God may rise up with the help of a spiritual shower, grow and become strong".[74]

As bishop of Meaux, Briçonnet continued to pursue his reform goals, as his speech before the synod of 1519 demonstrates.[75] In it he castigated the worldliness of the clergy and their neglect of pastoral duties: "Some have fallen so low that they lavish on hunting dogs the care they should give to souls . . . . They correct them if they make a mistake in the course of a chase, but when it comes to giving direction to souls—grievous to say!—they show no interest." He lamented the times, in which "laymen are better men than priests," in which "faith has vanished, religion is in exile, good is confounded with evil . . . and all the [candidates] admitted [to clerical office] are boorish and ignorant and trained, not to lead the Christian soldiers, but to mislead them." Briçonnet concluded his speech with an appeal for the cooperation of those present: "Help me, comrades-in-arms, help me, give me your support . . . . Do not pasture yourselves, but, on the contrary, pasture the flock entrusted to you!"

It was under Briçonnet's spiritual leadership that Meaux developed into a haven for scholars sympathetic to the Reformation, but he adopted a more cautious and conservative policy after his conduct came under investigation and he was fined for allowing "heresy" to spread in his diocese. Briçonnet's seemingly changed attitude toward the Reformation has been denounced as cowardice, insincerity, and pandering to political expediencies. Henry Heller describes Briçonnet in somewhat more moderate terms as an "ecclesiastic whose aspirations toward reform were mixed in an ultimately unstable combination, with a strong sense of political realism".[76]

Giles of Viterbo

Giles of Viterbo (Egidio da Viterbo, 1469-1532) was a member of the Augustinian Hermits, whose Vicar General he became in 1506. On good terms with both Julius II and Leo X, he undertook a number of embassies to the imperial court on behalf of the papal court. He was in touch with prominent humanists, and his classicizing sermons reflect their literary tastes.

Peace and concord within the church and the harmonization of Christian and non-Christian thought were constant themes in Giles' writings. Both are rooted in his belief in a divine plan of salvation embracing all mankind: "For God guides all in recognizing the road to salvation, the elementary form of truth, and the way to happiness."[77]

Giles' beliefs are further characterized by Christocentricity, a focus he
shares with many reformers: "I place my hope, not on Pythagoras, not
on Plato, not on Socrates, nor any of the other philosophers . . . nor on
any of the saints, nor on Abraham, nor on Moses, but on Christ incar-
nated." He took pride in his activity as a preacher: "Like the apostle
[Paul], I profess to know nothing but Christ and him crucified. I have
preached Christ now for many years in all cities of Italy, with very little
learning, perhaps, but with great zeal for the salvation of the people
and for Christian liberty." Giles was a traditionalist in accepting the
laws of the church, but he joined in the call for a greater focus on the
law of the gospel: "Only by taking up the gospels, listening to them,
reading them, and preserving them in one's life, can a person be filled
with certain hope and say: I trust in God." His praise for the role of
language studies in scriptural exegesis appears progressive, but his emphasis was on the mystical quality of the original languages, rather
than on human philological skills which might lead to a better understanding. Similarly, Giles' thought on the nature of sacraments has a
certain affinity to reformed theology, but is ultimately conservative.
With reference to the Eucharist, for example, he stated that, unless the
congregation attended with fervent devotion, the celebration was a
meaningless ceremony and incapable of sanctifying the participants.
At the same time, however, he maintained the Catholic emphasis on
the mediating role of the priest, "not because God was unable to save
humanity, but because he wanted human beings to be of help to each
other." In view of the priest's essential role in salvation, it was lamen-
table that the clergy included so many unsuitable individuals: "a lazy,
inexperienced throng without order and self-discipline, gamblers,
youngsters, buyers and sellers, often also soldiers and fighters, not to
say, pimps and usurers." As General of his order Giles conducted visitations and implemented a programme of reform, punishing transgres-
sions of the order's rules and appointing superiors capable of enforcing
them.[78]

Among Giles' sermons, the address to the Fifth Lateran Council
(1512) is the most important document of his reform thought.[79] Striking an apocalyptic tone reminiscent of Savonarola's sermons, Giles asserted that his listeners "would see great agitation and destruction in
the Church and would one day behold its correction." They were wit-
nessing God's warning. Vice had reached its zenith: "When has our
life been more effeminate? When has ambition been more unre-
strained, greed more burning? When has the license to sin been more

shameless? When has temerity in speaking, in arguing, in writing against piety been more common or more unafraid? When has there been among the people not only a greater neglect but a greater contempt for the sacred, for the sacraments, for the keys [the symbol of papal authority], and for the holy commandments?"

Giles saw the council as a means of curing these ills. His trust in its mission was so great that he did not hesitate to use strong terms: "Without Councils, faith cannot stand firm." Councils were the "seedbed and revival of virtues." Their examination of the state of the church corrected the wicked and provided incentives for the good, "with the result that people take courage, decide on the better course of action, undertake to give up vice and pursue virtue, and strive after nothing that is not honourable and lofty." Giles' reform plan, then, called for the purification of the church in its head and members, a rejuvenation of authentic practices and a rekindling of religious fervour and inner piety which had grown cold.

5. DESIDERIUS ERASMUS

Among the "forerunners" of the Reformation, Erasmus had no doubt the largest audience. The success of his works was due to a combination of factors. He offered both relevance and historical depth. He had his finger on the pulse of society, but he also represented the aspirations of a century. And he had a writer's sensitivity that allowed him to speak in terms that rang true. His pacifist tracts voiced the yearning of a wartorn Europe for peace; his educational philosophy embraced the ideals of the New Learning; his style reflected Renaissance esthetics; and his doctrinal, exegetical, and devotional writings offered a scholarly comment on the subjects that dominated the Reformation debate.

Desiderius Erasmus (c. 1469-1536) was the illegitimate son of a priest. Orphaned early in life, he was obliged by his guardians to enter the Order of Augustinian Canons Regular. He studied for some years at the University of Paris, but departed without a degree, feeling a strong distaste for the brand of scholastic theology taught there. He briefly lectured at Cambridge and was instrumental in the organization of a trilingual college at Louvain but never became part of the academic establishment. The financial support of patrons, pensions from his church benefices, and an (irregularly paid) salary as imperial coun-

cillor, allowed him to live the life of an independent scholar. He would
have preferred to stay aloof from the Lutheran controversy, but he was
too much a part of the intellectual world of his time to be allowed to
withdraw from the stage. His apparent support for the theological
platform of the reformers made him the subject of an investigation by
the Inquisition in Spain as well as an official condemnation by the faculty of theology at Paris, and assured that his works were placed on the
Index of Prohibited Books. Conversely, his refusal to break with the
Old Church and his public conflict with Luther over the question of
free will in 1524 deprived him of support in the reformers' camp as
well. Erasmus found himself under attack from both Catholics and
Protestants during the last decade of his life.

A vocal critic of the church, Erasmus castigated the lack of vocation
in the clergy, their patent ignorance, immorality, and greed, the pervasive secularism of the leaders of the church, who accumulated benefices
through simony and kept a lavish court rivalling that of princes. His
criticism was effective because his writing was vivid and eminently
quotable. Satirical pieces like the famous *Praise of Folly* and the best-
selling *Colloquies* are peopled with quibbling theologians, monks
fleecing dying men, fraudulent clerics posing as alchemists and necro-
mancers, pilgrims duped into paying for relics of questionable authenticity, petitioners making insincere promises to saints, abbots despising
learning and discipline, and other caricatures of piety. Tendering his
criticism in a serious vein, Erasmus wrote:

> I could see that the common body of Christians was corrupt not
> only in its affections but in its ideas. I pondered on the fact that
> those who profess themselves pastors and doctors for the most part
> misuse these titles, which belong to Christ, for their own advantage.
> . . . Is there any religious man who does not see with sorrow that this
> generation is far the most corrupt there has ever been?[80]

Erasmus did not stop short at criticizing the church but put forward his
own proposals for reform. They centered on the "philosophy of
Christ" as expounded in the gospels and placed a Pauline emphasis on
inner piety as opposed to the observance of ceremonies. In his blueprint of spiritual renewal, the *Enchiridion*, he called on his fellow
Christians to rise from concerns for the visible world to a love of invis-
ible things:

> I do not disapprove in any way of the external ceremonies of
> Christians and the devotions of the simple-minded, especially when
> they have been approved by the authority of the church, for they are

often signs of supports of piety . . . But to worship Christ through visible things for the sake of visible things and to think of this as the summit of religious perfection . . . would be to desert the law of the gospel, which is spiritual, and to sink into a kind of Judaism [i.e. the legalism that characterizes the Old Testament].[81]

As a Biblical scholar, Erasmus refined and expanded on the philological approach pioneered by Valla, repeating in their common defense some of the arguments first advanced by the Italian scholar: the philological method was a valid approach to an understanding of the Bible. It was neither a challenge to Jerome, whose revision had been corrupted by scribes, nor to the principle of divine inspiration, which did not extend to the translator. Reaching beyond the immediate aim of establishing a correct Biblical text, Erasmus further suggested curricular reforms that would make training in philological skills mandatory for theologians. "Our first care must be to learn the three languages, Latin, Greek, and Hebrew," he wrote, "for it is plain that the mystery of all Scripture is revealed in them . . . I would say it matters a great deal whether you take something from the sources or from some puddles."[82] He recommended that theology students concentrate on the Scriptural text and rely on patristic rather than scholastic commentaries for an exposition of its meaning.

Erasmus did not embrace the scriptural principle, but he queried practices of the church that had no clear basis in the New Testament: celibacy, auricular confession, feastdays, and laws regulating choice of foods. He was careful, however, to cast his remarks in the form of suggestions and subject them to the teaching authority of the church. Erasmus' reluctance to pronounce on doctrinal matters was interpreted by some of his contemporaries as hypocrisy or lack of commitment, although it was clearly rooted in his definition of orthodoxy. Articles of faith, he said, were based on "unequivocal Scriptural passages, publicly accepted creeds, or universal synods".[83] He therefore rejected the accusation that he was equivocating:

> They are looking for a certain and definitive pronouncement on
> every single point . . . I would ask those who demand this from me
> to join me in embracing unquestioningly what the Church—
> indisputedly inspired by the Holy Spirit—has handed down to us;
> and in doubtful matters . . . join me in awaiting the verdict of the
> Church, suspending their own judgment.[84]

It is clear from these statements that the pun circulated by Catholic controversialists, "Either Erasmus lutherizes or Luther erasmianizes,"

and other popular dicta linking Erasmus with the reformer were not
based on fact. The two men's doctrinal positions were significantly
different. Erasmus' role in the dissemination of ideas is therefore less
that of a forerunner of the Reformation than that of a synthesizer of
many of the currents of thought that fed into the Reformation. He advocated the ideal of inner piety fostered by the *Devotio Moderna*; he
voiced the widespread disgust with the flagrant abuses of the Church
and the nostalgia for a simpler and purer faith based on the Gospel; he
popularized new trends in learning which shifted attention from scholasticism to the *studia humanitatis* and, in the realm of theology, from
medieval commentaries to Scripture and patristic exegesis. It is his eloquent advocacy of these ideas that makes Erasmus the outstanding representative of an age in which the call for reform came to fruition.

NOTES

1. Peter Fabisch and Erwin Iserloh, eds., *Dokumente zur Causa Lutheri (1517-1521)* (Münster, 1988), vol. 1:343; vol. 2:437, 521.
2. Rummel (1989), vol. 2:91.
3. Oberman (1966), 39: "The category of Forerunners does not function to establish the *nature of the cause* but to describe the *structure of the change.*"
4. McGrath (1987), 31.
5. *The Church*, trans. David Schaff (New York, 1915; reprint, Westport, Conn., 1974), 71, 168.
6. The term was used by Noël Béda, who attacked the work of Jacques Lefèvre and Desiderius Erasmus. See Rummel (1989), vol. 2:35.
7. Quoted by Trinkaus (1970), vol. 2:838 note 73.
8. Ernst Cassirer, et al. eds., *The Renaissance Philosophy of Man* (Chicago, 1975), 155; Erasmus *Hyperaspistes* in *Opera omnia Des. Erasmi Roterodami*, ed. Jean Leclerc, 10 vols. (Leiden, 1703-6), vol. 10: col. 1315A-C.
9. *The Profession of the Religious and The Falsely Believed and Forged Donation of Constantine*, trans. Olga Pugliese (Toronto, 1985), 46.
10. *Opera Omnia* (Basel, 1540; reprint, Turin, 1962), 120^v.
11. Published in 1505 at Erasmus' initiative.
12. See Salvatore Camporeale, "Lorenzo Valla tra Medioevo e Rinascimento: Encomion s. Thomae, 1457," *Memorie Domenicane* 7 (1976): 3-190.
13. *Collatio Novi Testamenti*, ed. Alessandro Perosa (Florence, 1970), 6-7.
14. *Antidotum Primum*, ed. Ari Wesseling (Amsterdam, 1978), para. 135-36.
15. See the examples in Trinkaus (1970), vol. 2:575-76.
16. See Salvatore Camporeale in "Lorenzo Valla ed il 'De falso credita donatione': Retorica, libertà ed ecclesiologia nel '400," *Memorie Domenicane* 19 (1981): 284.
17. In his *Introductiones latinae* Nebrija described his relationship with the other masters at Salamanca as a battle against barbarians. Cf. Olmedo (1942), 39.
18. The title probably indicates that this represents a third redaction, incorporating earlier material.
19. For the text of the introduction, see Olmedo (1942), 155-56.
20. *Apologia earum rerum quae illi obiiciuntur* (n.p., n.d.). The first quotation comes from a manuscript letter in the copy of the book at the British Library. The other quotations are on sigs. a1 recto and b1 recto, respectively.
21. *Introduciones latinae* (Salamanca, 1486), a.i^v; *Tertia Repetitio* (Salamanca, 1506), cited by Olmedo (1942), 35-36.
22. So named after "Complutense," the Latin name of Alcalá, its place of publication.

23. For the Latin text of the letter see *Revista de Archivos, Bibliotecas y Museos* 8 (1903): 493-96. The passage translated here appears on 495.

24. Quoted by Rice (1972), xvi.

25. I.e., the three revisions of the Old Latin text made by Jerome.

26. Quoted by Rice (1972), 195-96.

27. Ibid., 299.

28. Quoted by Farge (1985), 181.

29. Ibid., 184.

30. Noël Béda, *Annotationes* (Paris, 1526), fols. iv, cxx, cxxxiii.

31. See Bedouelle (1976), 181.

32. Aimé Herminjard, ed., *Correspondance des réformateurs dans les pays de langue française* (Geneva and Paris, 1866-97), vol. 2:42ff.

33. In his annotations on Heb. 7:26-28, John 6:15, 5:16, quoted by Hughes (1984), 87, 89, 93.

34. In his annotations on Rom. 3:19-20 and 3:28, quoted by Hughes (1984), 97. For his conjunction of faith with works see *Epistola ad Rhomanos...* (Paris, 1512), fols. 75, 76$^{r\cdot v}$; and Rice (1972), xxii.

35. Michael Screech, ed., *Jacques Lefèvre d'Etaples et ses disciples: Epistres et Evangiles pour les cinquante et deux sepmaines de l'an* (Geneva, 1964), 41.

36. Ibid., 51.

37. Rice (1972), 435-36.

38. See *Opera omnia Des. Erasmi Roterdami*, ed. Jean Leclerc, 10 vols. (Leiden, 1703-6), vol. 9:19 B-C.

39. Preface to *Farrago* (Wittenberg, 1522), trans. in Miller (1917), vol. 1:232.

40. Quoted by Benrath (1968), 9.

41. As reported by Albert Hardenberg and Rudolph Agricola. Miller (1917), vol. 2:324-25.

42. What survives of his works can be found in the *Opera* (Groningen, 1614; reprint, Nieuwkoop, 1966).

43. Miller (1917), vol. 1:77.

44. Quoted by Gerhard Geldenhouwer in *Germaniae inferioris historia*, for which see Miller (1917), vol. 2:345.

45. Miller (1917), vol. 1:145.

46. Ibid., 139-41.

47. Miller's chapter 8 is so entitled. He does, however, comment on the "anomaly" of the term. Miller (1917), vol. 1:128.

48. Cf. Miller (1917), vol. 1:232.

49. Ibid.

50. "The influence he had exerted in his lifetime by the spoken word soon became generalized and anonymous," Colet's modern editors, Bernard O'Kelly and Catherine Jarrot, observe in *John Colet's Commentary on First Corinthians* (Binghamton, 1985), 10.

51. *A reioindre to M. Jewels Replie* (Antwerp, 1566), fol. 44 verso.

52. In a letter to Erasmus, in *Collected Works of Erasmus. The Correspondence of Erasmus*, ed. R. A. B. Mynors, et al. (Toronto, 1974-), no. 423:14-15.

53. *Two Treatises on the Hierarchies of Dionysius*, ed. John Lupton (London, 1869), 197.

54. From a letter to John Kidderminster, quoted by Gleason (1989), 173.

55. See Erasmus on Colet in *Correspondence of Erasmus*, no. 1211:513-35.

56. Gleason (1989), 279-81.
57. *Correspondence of Erasmus*, no. 1211:687-88.
58. Weinstein (1970), 69.
59. Olin (1969), 5-6, 10, 13.
60. *WA*, vol. 12:248.
61. Josef Nolte says that Luther is intent "die Spuren seiner Anfänge...[zu] verwischen" (Nolte [1978], 88).
62. Quoted by Charles Schmidt, *Histoire littéraire de l'Alsace à la fin du XVe et au commencement du XVIe siècle*, 2 vols. (Paris, 1879; reprint, Hildesheim, 1966), vol. 1:431 note 174.
63. Ibid., vol. 1:422 note 141, 423.
64. Ibid., vol. 1:454 note 259.
65. Ibid., vol. 1:408 note 102.
66. The quotations in this paragraph come from ibid., vol. 1:441-42.
67. Ibid., vol. 1:460 note 286.
68. Douglass (1966), 9 note 1.
69. See D. Vincente de la Fuente, *Historia de las universidades, colegios y demàs establicimientos de enseñanza en España* (Madrid, 1885), vol. 2:appendix 13.
70. See Basil Hall, *Humanists and Protestants: 1500-1900* (Edinburgh, 1990), 8-10.
71. Quoted by Bernardino Llorca, *Historia de la Iglesia Católica* (Madrid, 1967), vol. 3:632.
72. John Elliott, *Imperial Spain 1469-1716* (New York, 1963), 103. See the discussion in Marcel Bataillon, *Erasmo y España* (Mexico, 1950; 4th repr. 1991), 1-3; Jocelyn Hillgarth, *The Spanish Kingdoms, 1250-1516* (Oxford, 1978), vol. 2:406-9.
73. Quoted by Veissière (1974), 70 note 42.
74. Ibid., 77.
75. H. Tardif and M. Veissière, "Un discours synodal de G. Briçonnet (1519)," *Revue d'Histoire Ecclesiastique* 71 (1976):96, 99-100, 102, 105, 108.
76. See Heller (1973), 250.
77. The quotions in this and the next paragraph come from O'Malley (1968), 22 note 3, 33 note 1, 69 notes 2 and 9, 119 note 1, 133 note 3.
78. O'Malley (1968), 150.
79. Olin (1990), 48, 50, 52.
80. *Correspondence of Erasmus*, no. 858:167-77.
81. *Collected Works of Erasmus*, vol. 66:73-74.
82. *Ausgewählte Werke*, eds. Hajo and Annemarie Holborn (Munich, 1933), 151-52.
83. *Opera Omnia Des.Erasmi*, ed. Jean Leclerc, vol. 9:1091C.
84. *Annali di Storia del Diritto*, vol. 9,1:256-58.

BIBLIOGRAPHY

Andrés Martín, Melquiades. "Corrientes culturales en tiempo de los Reyes Católicos y recepción de Erasmo." In *El Erasmismo en España*, ed. Manuel Revuelta Sañudo and Ciriaco Morón Arroyo, 73-96. Santander, 1986.

Antonetti, Pierre. *Savonarole. Le prophète désarmé*. Paris, 1991.

Augustijn, Cornelis. *Erasmus: His Life, Works and Influence*. Toronto, 1991.

Becker, Reinhard, ed. *German Humanism and the Reformation*. New York, 1982.

Bedouelle, Guy. *Lefèvre d'Etaples et l'intelligence des écritures*. Geneva, 1976.

Benrath, Gustav, ed. *Reformtheologen des 15. Jahrhunderts: Johann Pupper von Goch, Johann Ruchrath von Wesel, Wessel Gansfort*. Gütersloh, 1968.

Camporeale, Salvatore. *Lorenzo Valla. Umanesimo e teologia*. Florence, 1972.

Centi, Tito. *Girolamo Savonarola. Il frate che sconvolse Firenze*. Rome, 1988.

Chaunu, Pierre. *Le temps des réformes, histoire religieuse et système de civilization: la crise de la chrétienté, 1250-1550*. Paris, 1976.

Chrisman, Miriam Usher. *Strasbourg and the Reform: a Study in the Process of Change*. New Haven, 1967.

Cordero, Franco. *Savonarola*. 4 vols. Bari, 1986-88.

D'Amico, John. "Humanism and Pre-Reformation Theology." In *Renaissance Humanism: Foundations, Forms, and Legacy*, ed. Albert Rabil, 349-79. Philadelphia, 1988.

Douglass, E. Jane Dempsey. *Justification in Late Medieval Preaching: A study of John Geiler of Keisersberg*. SMRT, vol. 1. Leiden, 1966.

Elm, Kaspar, ed. *Reformbemühungen und Observanzbestrebungen im spätmittelalterlichen Ordenswesen*. Berlin, 1989.

Farge, James. *Orthodoxy and Reform in Early Reformation France: The Faculty of Theology of Paris, 1500-1543*. SMRT, vol. 32. Leiden, 1985.

Fois, Mario. *Il pensiero cristiano di Lorenzo Valla nel quadro storico-culturale del suo ambiente*. Rome, 1969.

García de la Concha, Victor, ed. *Nebrija y la introducción del renacimiento en España*. Salamanca, 1983.

García Oro, José. *El Cardenal Cisneros. Vida y empresas*. Madrid, 1992.

Gleason, John. *John Colet*. Berkeley and Los Angeles, 1989.

Hay, Denys. *The Church in Italy in the Fifteenth Century*. Cambridge, 1977.

Heller, Henry. "The Briçonnet Case Reconsidered." *JMRS* 2 (1973): 223-50.

Hendrix, Scott "In Quest of the *Vera Ecclesia*: The Crises of Late Medieval Ecclesiology." *Viator* 7 (1976): 347-78.

Hudson, Anne. *The Premature Reformation. Wycliffite Texts and Lollard history*. Oxford, 1988.

Hughes, Philip. *Lefèvre d'Etaples: Pioneer of Ecclesiastical Renewal in France*. Grand Rapids, 1984.

Huizinga, Johan. *The Waning of the Middle Ages: a Study of the Forms of Life, Thought, and Art in France and the Netherlands in the 14th and 15th Centuries*. London, 1924.

Kaminsky, Howard. *A History of the Hussite Revolution*. Berkeley and Los Angeles, 1967.

Kittelson, James, and Pamela Transue, eds. *Rebirth, Reform, and Resilience: Universities in Transition, 1300-1700*. Columbus, Ohio, 1984.

Lortz, Josef. *How the Reformation Came*. Trans. Otto Knab. New York, 1964.

Lovy, René-Jacques. *Les origines de la Réforme française: Meaux 1518-1546.* Paris, 1959.

McConica, James K. *Erasmus.* Oxford, 1991.

McGrath, Alister. *The Intellectual Origins of the European Reformation.* Oxford, 1987.

Miller, Edward. *Wessel Gansfort: His Life and Writings.* 2 vols. New York, 1917.

Nauert, Charles. "The Clash of Humanists and Scholastics: An Approach to Pre-Reformation Controversies." *SCJ* 4 (1973): 1-18.

Oakley, Francis W. "Religious and Ecclesiastical Life on the Eve of the Reformation." In *Reformation Europe: a Guide to Research*, ed. Steven Ozment, 5-32. St. Louis, 1982.

Oberman, Heiko Augustinus, ed. *The Dawn of the Reformation: Essays in Late Medieval and Early Reformation Thought.* Grand Rapids, 1986. Reprint. Edinburgh, 1992.

Oberman, Heiko Augustinus. *Forerunners of the Reformation: the Shape of Late Medieval Thought.* New York, 1966.

Oberman, Heiko Augustinus. "Gansfort, Reuchlin and the 'Obscure Men': First Fissures in the Foundations of Faith." In *Studien zum 15. Jahrhundert. Festschrift für Erich Meuthen*, ed. Johannes Helmrath and Heribert Müller, 717-35. Munich, 1994.

Oberman, Heiko Augustinus, and Charles Trinkaus, eds. *The Pursuit of Holiness in Late Medieval and Renaissance Religion.* SMRT, vol. 10. Leiden, 1974.

Olin, John. *Catholic Reform: From Cardinal Ximenes to the Council of Trent, 1495-1563.* New York, 1990.

Olin, John. *The Catholic Reformation: Savonarola to Ignatius Loyola.* New York, 1969.

Olmedo, Felix. *Nebrija (1441-1522): debelador de la barbarie, comentador eclesiástico, pedagogo, poeta.* Madrid, 1942.

O'Malley, John. *Giles of Viterbo on Church and Reform: a Study in Renaissance Thought.* SMRT, vol. 5. Leiden, 1968.

Pettegree, Andrew, ed. *The Early Reformation in Europe.* Cambridge, 1992.

Phillips, Margaret Mann. *Erasme et les débuts de la Réforme française (1517-1536).* Paris, 1934. Reprint. Geneva, 1978.

Post, R. R. *The Modern Devotion: Confrontation with Reformation and Humanism.* SMRT, vol. 3. Leiden, 1968.

Rapp, Francis. *Réformes et Réformation à Strasbourg: église et société dans le diocèse de Strasbourg (1450-1525).* Paris, 1974.

Renaudet, Auguste. *Préréforme et humanisme à Paris pendant les premières guerres d'Italie, 1494-1517.* Paris, 1953.

Rice, Eugene. *The Prefatory Epistles of Jacques Lefèvre and Related Texts.* New York, 1972.

Rico, Francisco. *Nebrija frente a los bárbaros.* Salamanca, 1978.

Rummel, Erika. *Erasmus and His Catholic Critics.* 2 vols. Nieuwkoop, 1989.

Spinka, Matthew. *John Hus: a Biography.* Princeton, 1968.

Spitz, Lewis. *The Religious Renaissance of the German Humanists.* Cambridge, 1963.

Steinmetz, David, ed. *The Bible in the Sixteenth Century.* Durham, 1990.

Stöhr, Martin. *Die erste Reformation.* Frankfurt am Main, 1987.

Strauss, Gerald, ed. *Manifestations of Discontent in Germany on the Eve of the Reformation.* Bloomington, 1971.

Tracy, James. *Erasmus: the Growth of a Mind.* Geneva, 1972.

Trinkaus, Charles. *In Our Image and Likeness: Humanity and Divinity in Italian Humanist Thought.* 2 vols. Chicago, 1970.

Veissière, Michel. "Guillaume Briçonnet, abbé renovateur de Saint-Germain de-Prés (1507-1534)." *RHEF* 55 (1974): 65-84.

Weinstein, Donald. *Savonarola and Florence: Prophecy and Patriotism in the Renaissance.* Princeton, 1970.

Werner, Ernst. *Jan Hus. Welt und Umwelt eines Prager Frühreformators.* Weimar, 1991.

THE HUMANIST MOVEMENT

Ronald G. Witt
(Duke University)

Although Italian renaissance humanists themselves referred to their studies as *studia humanitatis* already in the fourteenth century, the term "humanista" arose as part of university jargon late in the fifteenth century and that of "humanismus" only in 1818.[1] Because of their rich polyvalence, both "humanist" and "humanism" have invited a wide variety of interpretations of the intellectual movement they were designed to designate. Since Jacob Burckhardt's *Civilisation of the Italian Renaissance in Italy* (1860) a strong current of scholarship has approached humanism as essentially the study of the writings of the ancient Greeks and Romans directed to articulating a new emphasis on worldly, human concerns in contemporary life. The result has been to lump together an extensive range of intellectual activities from literature and historical writing to philosophy and theology. The ambiguity of "humanism," moreover, has even led some scholars to consider the mere appearance of a secular orientation in a renaissance writer as sufficient to mark him as a humanist.

In a series of lectures given between 1944 and 1945 and then elaborated in subsequent publications, Paul O. Kristeller offered a more precise definition of humanism and humanist which has gained wide currency in the field. Although initially focused on the Italian development, Kristeller's definition has been extended to northern humanism as well. Considering the humanists along professional lines as primarily grammarians and rhetoricians, Kristeller relates humanism to five basic areas of learning: grammar, poetry, oratory, historical writing and ethics.[2] In their professional capacity, the humanists worked as either teachers of grammar and rhetoric or as notaries and judges in official positions in communal or princely governments. Kristeller's position has been challenged on a number of grounds: (1) the two leading humanists of the fourteenth century, Petrarch and Boccaccio, were neither professional teachers nor public officials; (2) it cannot account for the many patrician humanists of the fifteenth century: and (3) certain humanists, especially Salutati and Valla, drew theological and philosophical consequences from their grammatical and rhetorical investigations. Nonetheless, despite these objections, Kristeller's conception of the five basic areas of humanist endeavor and of the professional status of the core group of humanists has proved extremely valuable in clarifying contemporary approaches to humanism.

Humanism began in the second half of the thirteenth century when a passionate interest in close study of ancient literature combined with a stylistic principle which made imitation of ancient Latin authors *the* aesthetic goal.   Until the emergence of Ciceronianism in the late fifteenth century, humanist stylistic imitation or "classicizing" consisted not so much in imitating the style of a particular pagan author, but rather in using ancient models as analogies from which to learn ancient syntax, vocabulary, and turns of phrases. Without a good grasp of ancient writings the endeavor to classicize would have been impossible, while creative imitation of ancient style in their own work enhanced the ability of scholars to lay hold of the emotional and intellectual dimensions of the ancient world. At the same time over the long run the attempt of humanists to capture the spirit of antiquity in their own writings produced "a reorganization of consciousness," which contributed to a restructuring of their own mentality.[3] Involved was a gradual historicizing of culture and ideas, the development of historical perspective on past, present and future. Over the decades as the ancient world became increasingly defined, antiquity emerged as "a cultural alternative" to the present one and transformed a scholarly movement into a powerful engine for the reform of contemporary culture and society.[4]

1. Humanism in Italy to 1400

Commonly called "protohumanists" simply because predecessors of Petrarch, the first two generations of Italian humanists were with a few possible exceptions all from the Veneto mainland. Lovato dei Lovati (1240-1309), a Paduan judge and notary, is generally considered to have been the first to have combined an intense interest in studying the ancient Latin poets with the composition of poetry in classicizing Latin. One of a number of Latin poets in the middle decades of the thirteenth century endeavoring to imitate ancient poetry, Lovato stands out not only for his poetic achievements but also for his wide knowledge of pagan poets, some ignored for centuries, and for the quality of his philological studies. These latter were especially centered on Seneca's tragedies, which he himself had recovered. Lovato's literary studies, moreover, were closely tied to contemporary concerns. Many of his poems—among his least classicizing, perhaps for want of an ancient model—dealt with the frequent crises facing his city state of Padua. As a prose stylist, however, Lovato remained loyal to the medieval *ars dictaminis*, a highly codified method of letter writing, beginning around 1100 which subsequently came to impose its rules generally on prose composition.

For his most brilliant disciple, Albertino Mussato (1261-1329), also a notary and leader of the second generation of Paduan humanism, literary studies were even more intimately related to current political affairs. Like his master, an admirer of Senecan tragedy, Mussato composed in 1315 a Senecan drama, *Ecerinis*, to warn his fellow Paduans of the dangers of tyranny at a moment when they contemplated offering the lordship of the city to Mastino della Scala of Verona. In this same period he began the composition of a series of histories dealing with contemporary events, *Historia augusta*, the account of the fateful expedition of Emperor Henry VII to Italy between 1310 and 1313. The first conscious attempt consistently to imitate ancient prose among the humanists, the work, stylistically imitating Livy, betrays by its awkward periodic construction the relative difficulty of classicizing prose by comparison with poetry. Attacked by a local Dominican among others for his devotion to pagan poetry, Mussato in a series of poetic letters defended the ancients as divinely inspired and tried to establish the similarity between pagan beliefs and the Christian religion. In what might have been the last months of his life, however, he repented by damning the ancients for their ignorance of God and reserving poetry only for celebrating Christian truth.

Neighboring Vicenza and Verona produced a number of scholars contemporary with Mussato who, though not of the same stature, helped to diffuse the new approach to the ancients through philological and literary writings. Outside the Veneto humanism appeared in only two centers, Arezzo and Bologna, in the early decades of the fourteenth century. Of Paduan descent possibly with continuing ties to that city, Giovanni del Vigilio (c. 1327) occupied the first chair of poetry in an Italian university. He is best known for having provoked Dante, at the very end of the latter's life, to revive Vergilian bucolic poetry. Dante was exiled in 1302 from Florence, which remained untouched by humanistic influence until mid-century, and his late classicizing poetry

doubtless reflects his many years of residence in the Veneto. Another
Tuscan city in Mussato's generation, however, was to engender a major humanist, Geri d'Arezzo (c. 1270-1339), a lawyer by training who
dared challenge the supremacy of medieval *ars dictaminis* by
classicizing the style of private letters and restoring their personal character in line with ancient precedents.

The contribution of Petrarch (1304-74), often called the Father of
Italian Humanism, should be seen against this background. Born in
Arezzo of Florentine parents, he reached maturity in and around Avignon. Giuseppe Billanovich has established at least an indirect connection between Petrarch and the Paduan humanists through members of
the papal court and, as a student of law in Bologna between 1320 and
1326, he very probably came to know Giovanni del Virgilio. With his
father, ser Petracco, a learned notary, he edited the *Aeneid* in 1325 and
then in 1329, apparently on his own, the historical works of Livy, an
edition of lasting significance for the future of that author.

Like the Paduans convinced of the relevance of ancient literature
and history for his own world, he explicitly articulated the Ciceronian
link between eloquence and moral philosophy and established moral
reform as the guiding principle of humanism. For Petrarch logical arguments spoke only to the reason, whereas eloquence had the capacity
to move the will, the affective, active part of the soul. He defined the
humanists as moral therapists.[5] While like the Paduans he was a vigorous defender of Italy as the home of ancient Roman culture, in contrast
to them Petrarch, raised in exile, remained free of local prejudice. Except for a brief unhappy flirtation with politics in the form of Cola da
Rienzo's revolution in Rome (1347), Petrarch's reform ideas did not
extend to government *per se*: the moral character of rulers was far
more important to him than the constitutional character of the government.

Although he denounced the worldly orientation of the Avignon
popes, his residence in the capital of Christendom probably contributed to the Christian context in which he tried to develop his moral
teachings. Sincerely troubled by the tension between pagan letters and
Christian doctrine, he reached an uneasy resolution to the problem by
affirming himself preeminently a Christian and insisting on the value of
the pagan heritage in constructing a Christian character. This commitment constituted a reversal of the secular tendencies of two generations
of humanism and answered the charges of its opponents including
those of Mussato himself in his last few years.

Besides his formulation of the humanist program, one of Petrarch's greatest contribution to the movement was to deepen interest in ancient history. For two generations the leaders of humanism had sought contemporary relevance for their studies of antiquity and, where history was concerned, current events had largely been the focus of writing. Petrarch's genius was to legitimate the antiquarian currents of his time represented by the scholars at Avignon like his Colonna patrons, Landolfo (c. 1250-1331) and Giovanni (d. 1348), within the compass of humanism's general practical goal of moral reform. In this he succeeded so well that, while humanists concentrated during the next decades on ancient history, humanistic treatment of contemporary events was subject to a hiatus of seventy years.

His intimacy with the lives of ancient Latin writers humanized them and encouraged Petrarch to approach them as equals. Although he admired many among them, especially Cicero, he refused to recognize them as unquestioned authorities in anything. Indeed, so strong was his sense of self that, barring religious authority, he assumed responsibility for decisions of truth and falsehood. This reliance on self affected his stylistic preferences as well: each man should create his own style as a mirror of his personality. Consequently, although mindful of ancient models, Petrarch's Latin, at least his prose style, was by choice less classicizing than that of Mussato. As such, he enjoyed greater flexibility in dealing with Christian ideas which a more classical language might have expressed awkwardly.

Handsome, a gifted vernacular poet as well as brilliant scholar with a gift for dramatizing his work, Petrarch was a successful publicist for humanism. Had he not, however, given its progress a more religious orientation making it less threatening to traditional values, it could not have made the advances it did in the second half of the century not only in Italy but also in court circles like Paris and Prague. When after 1400 Italian humanism generally resumed its secular course, it ceased to nourish those outposts abroad and an interval of decades separates the first and abortive appearance of humanist influence in Germany and France and the establishment of the movement in those countries.

Only his close friend, the Florentine Giovanni Boccaccio (1313-75), who felt himself far inferior, could in any way rival Petrarch's scholarly and literary achievements. Having as a younger man won wide recognition for his vernacular writings culminating in the *Decamerone* in 1350, in maturity Boccaccio gained in stature as a Latin scholar. His major humanist endeavor, *De geneologia deorum*, an enormous study

of the ancient myths as allegories, displayed an extensive knowledge of
classical poetry. Deeply religious in his later years, Boccaccio never felt
completely comfortable as had Petrarch with the suitability of a Christian studying pagan letters.

That the city of Florence assumed direction of the humanistic enterprise after Petrarch's death was not the work of Boccaccio, who died a
year later, but of Coluccio Salutati (1331-1406), a notary and later
Chancellor of Florence between 1375 and 1406. During this thirty-
one year period, by means of an enormous correspondence, the prestigious chancellor made Florence the nerve center for the movement. On
his death distinguished Florentine disciples, principally Leonardo
Bruni and Poggio Bracciolini, inherited his leadership.

A devoted disciple of Petrarch, Salutati, a layman and the leading
public servant of a republican government, reflected in his thought the
tensions present in the master's particular amalgam of pagan and
Christian elements. His well-recognized Florentine patriotism conflicted with the detached character of a political treatise like the *De
tyranno* (1400) and his praise of the contemplative life, *De seculo et
religione* (1381/2). While it is possible to some degree to resolve these
contradictions by an appeal to circumstances and chronology, nonetheless, at one level they stemmed from a tension between the medieval
spirituality enshrined in Petrarch's humanistic program and the demands of an active communal life.

Close to that of Petrarch, Salutati's Latin was somewhat more ecumenical. Not only was it for him a language of Christian piety as for
Petrarch but, incorporating in a limited way scholastic terminology, it
served for discussions of theological and philosophical ideas. While
Salutati utilized this generally reformed Latin for his personal letters
and treatises, as chancellor he showed himself a master of *ars
dictaminis*. If the content of his greatest public letters reflected to a degree his humanist background, the style remained essentially traditional. His surviving orations as well followed medieval prescriptions
laid down either by the secular manuals of *ars arengandi* or by those
for sermons in manuals of *ars praedicandi*.

2. FIFTEENTH-CENTURY ITALIAN HUMANISM

The advent of classicizing oration around 1400 indicates that by this
date humanist education had been sufficiently diffused within the

larger community to make possible oral delivery of reformed prose. At the same time the prestige surrounding humanism which made such oratory fashionable increasingly attracted new adherents among the upper classes. Ambitious fathers came to realize the political advantages of a humanist education. A reputation for such learning not only earned respect in the councils of state but also the ability to deliver an oration in the new style proved a distinct advantage for ambassadors. Indeed, by the mid-fifteenth century the extended, expensive humanist education became characteristic of upper class status in many Italian cities.

With the stylistic reform of the oration Cicero emerged as the fundamental model for humanist style. Although Cicero had been a major ancient author for Petrarch and Salutati, Seneca had been more important for the fourteenth century on all counts. Initially attractive because of his tragedies, his brand of pietistic moralism appealed to Petrarch and his followers. The acceptance of Cicero as the stylistic model for the generation of humanists after Salutati coincided with a renewed secular emphasis in humanist writings.

The first example of humanist oration in Florence, *Laudatio urbis Florentinae* written by Leonardo Bruni (1370-1444), was at the same time the first clear statement of what Hans Baron calls "civic humanism."[6] According to Baron, Petrarcan humanists tended to be politically passive and to consider monarchy as the best form of goverment. The near fall of Florence to Giangaleazzo Visconti in 1402, however, awoke Florentine humanists to the value of their republican heritage. Bruni's *Laudatio* with its historical and psychological arguments for republicanism constituted the first fruit of the new political consciousness.

Although scholars have generally accepted Baron's conception of two phases of humanism, critics have assailed the belief that Bruni was the first European to defend republicanism as superior to monarchy.[7] They point to a strong republican tradition both among scholastic thinkers and vernacular writers. Some consider Bruni's republican position grossly hypocritical when applied to the Florentine regime, which around 1400 rested in the hands of a limited number of families. Like most of the early Florentine humanists, such as Salutati and Poggio, he came from the provinces and he must have hoped the patriotic work would gain him recognition. However, to the extent that Bruni's *Laudatio* represented a clearly formulated republican position, it reflects a departure from Petrarcan humanism. Doubtless he drew heavily for his political sentiments on the Ciceronian orations, which his generation of humanists prized. Whether or not Bruni was sincere, within a decade Florentine leaders appear to have been debating public policy among themselves in terms of the republicanism found in that speech.

Florentine civic humanism found a ready response in the "despotic humanism" of the Visconti chancery. Through public letters, poetry and tracts young scholars like Antonio Loschi (1369-1441) and Uberto Decembrio (c. 1350-1427) applied their humanistic learning to defend their employer from charges of tyranny. In his drama *Achilles*, set in the Trojan War, Loschi, for instance, praised the order brought by lordship as opposed to the license encouraged by freedom.

Although infused with the decidedly anti-monarchical spirit of Cicero, Bruni derived the formal organization of the *Laudatio* from a Greek model, just as he was to do more than two decades later when he based a funeral oration for a Florentine general on the speech of Pericles in Thucydides. If the most gifted, Bruni was only one of a number of young Florentines of his generation who had availed themselves of Greek lessons given by Chrysoloras (c. 1350-1415) in the Florentine *studio* from 1397 to 1400. A brilliant teacher, Chrysoloras on his departure in 1400 left behind him a handful of students sufficiently trained so that they could make headway in the language on their own. Plutarch and Plato were the preferred authors for the first translators, but over the next century much of the pagan Greek heritage as well as many of the writings of the Greek Church Fathers and Byzantine Greeks found their way into Latin translation. Greek learning was never to be as diffused as Latin—it generally remained the second ancient language of the schools—but through intensive efforts at translation over the next hundred and fifty years not only religious and literary texts became available, but the vast array of scientific and mathematical material amassed by the Greek world.

The issues involved in the process of translation emerged as a major concern to fifteenth-century humanists. The traditional method of word-for-word translation, long rejected in practice in Tuscan translations of Latin texts, rested on the assumptions made by speculative grammar, that is, words were originally assigned to things and were designed to reflect cosmic reality in themselves and their syntactical relationships. By contrast humanists looked at language from a rhetorical perspective. Historically conditioned, language should be utilized so as to make the ideas it articulates active in the world. For this reason they insisted on rendering the sense of the original Greek text in an eloquent Latin capable of moving an audience.

On the basis of the conception of the historicity of language, the Roman humanist Lorenzo Valla (1405/7-57) in his *Elegantiae linguae latinae* drew the conclusion that Latin was a "dead" or artificial language. In modern times Latin, he argued, no longer underwent development. Contemporaries learned their Latin not as the ancient Romans did at their mothers' knees but rather from grammar books and from diligent study of the ancient authors. Thus, because language no longer drew life from popular usage as it had in ancient times, Latin usage should conform to the syntactical and lexical practices of the period when Latin attained its greatest height of expression. In its six books *Elegantiae* offered a full account of the language found in the authors of the first century B.C. and first and second centuries A.D. The theological consequences he drew from his historical conception of Latin are discussed below.

Valla would, however, never have approved of Ciceronianism, an important stylistic movement among humanists in early sixteenth century Italy and especially at the papal *curia*. Although since 1400 Cicero had been the primary model for Latin prose in a general way, the Ciceronians after 1500 demanded strict adherence to Cicero's use of language, barring any compromise with eclectic tendencies. Faithful imitation of the best style produced by Latin antiquity, they argued, was not only the path to eloquent speech, but would permit appreciation of the purest traditions of ancient culture and abet reform of both modern style and thought. Perhaps this aggressive Ciceronianism had been provoked by two stylistic tendencies in the second half of the fifteenth century which rejected Cicero's primacy. Humanists such as Giorgio Valla and Angelo Poliziano (1454-94) advocated a return to the eclectic position of Petrarch while others like Paolo Cortese embraced the obscure, baroque style of Apuleius.

In what was to be the best known critique of Ciceronianism, *Ciceronianus* (1528), Erasmus (1469-1536) argued that, given the historical changes intervening between Cicero and the present, such slavish imitation of a pagan author produced ridiculous results especially in the expression of Christian ideas and attitudes. He suggested in fact that Ciceronianism might be a sign of covert pagan sympathies in its proponents. The Sack of Rome in 1527 scattered the papal Curia, home of the core group of Ciceronians, but with the *Ciceronianus* the issue became a major issue of debate among humanists throughout Europe.

If humanists showed themselves divided between a Ciceronian or more electic approach to Latin style, general agreement prevailed on the need to revamp the traditional educational system. From the earliest humanist treatise on education, *De ingenuis moribus* of Pier Paolo Vergerio in 1402, writers offered their advice on curricular and pedagogic reform. Two schools in the second quarter of the century, the *Giocosa* of Vittorino da Feltre (c. 1379-1446) in Mantua and the school of Guarino da Verona (1370-1460) in Ferrara, provided working models of what could be achieved. De-emphasizing corporal punishment and stressing the importance of physical exercise to proper learning, these two schools in line with the treatises insisted on intensive training in Greek and Latin literature and history as well as in Latin composition.

Although humanists made much of their efforts to create highly educated moral leaders, in practice their teaching appeared oriented toward producing scholars like themselves. Exacting attention to detail, insistence on memorizing and repetition at all levels of linguistic proficiency characterized the methodology of these humanist schools.[8] If instructional techniques differed little from medieval ones, nonetheless, in the course of the fifteenth century the teaching material with which the students worked became increasingly marked by linguistic reform.

Until recent decades Eduard Fueter's classic *Geschichte der neueren Historiographie* (1911), which presented humanist historiography as essentially moralizing and bombastic, strongly influenced the modern scholarly assessment of the humanist contribution to historical writing. Currently that contribution receives a more positive evaluation. Three humanists stand out in the fifteenth century as significantly developing the historical concerns of their fourteenth-century predecessors, Leonardo Bruni, Lorenzo Valla and Flavio Biondo. While Bruni's *Historia florentini populi* (1415-44) retained Petrarch's moralistic orientation, Bruni broadened it to include political ideals, those of civic humanism. Rejecting fables and much of the traditional, Bruni presented the history of Florence from its inception under Rome down to his own day, judiciously utilizing the ancient and medieval sources at his disposal, but blending all with a consistently classicizing style. Coherently organized and concerned with causal explanations, Bruni's work became a model for succeeding generations. Particularly important for him were the psychological ingredients in historical events; these he manifested by dialogues and orations.

In contrast Valla's reputation as a historian derives not from his historical writing proper but from his masterful use of textual criticism in interpreting historical, legal and literary sources. Inordinately eager for fame, Valla was, nevertheless, also driven in his historical labors by his devotion to the ideal of Roman culture which through law and language still exercised a certain sovereignty over western civilization. Nowhere in his works does the breadth of his historical vision merge more brilliantly with his skill as a textual critic than in his *De falso credita et ementita Constantini donatione* (1440). In his assault on the authenticity of the purportedly fourth-century *Donatio*, Valla utilized a variety of arguments ranging from the psychological character of Constantine to the anachronistic nature of the language employed and of the customs and objects alluded to by the document. Having established it as a forgery, Valla then moves to indict the Roman papacy which, following the conversion of the empire, increasingly took on itself imperial powers, thereby destroying through its laws and institutions the Christian liberty of believers.[9] In his later *De professione religiosorum* (c. 1441) he likewise ties to the fourth century the origins of the monastic ideal, which falsely raised the religious professionals above laymen and, departing from the intent of the Sermon on the Mount, devalued "civic" Christianity.

Perhaps the greatest historian of the century, however, was Flavio Biondo (1392-1463). In his *Roma instaurata* (1444-46) Biondo identified the ruins of the city and their history with the help of architectural details along with epigraphic, numismatic and literary materials. A decade later he attempted in his *Roma triumphans* (1457-59) to provide an overview of the political, military, and religious institutions. Biondo's desire to strengthen Western resolve against the Turkish menace constituted a strong motivation for both works. In between these two histories, joining topographical with historical and antiquarian material, Biondo authored *Italia illustrata* (1448-53), a topographical ordering of historical materials covering the whole of the Italian peninsula. Finally his *Historiarum ab inclinatione romanorum imperii decades* (1438-53 and 1462-63) provided a view of Roman history and of the European territories it had encompassed from 410 down to his own day. Of major importance for later historians, Biondo identified the fall of Rome as associated with the invasions of the barbarians and severe internal divisions and conceptualized the centuries after the fall as the rise of Christian Europe.

Because of their generally critical approach to the sources, the variety of materials they utilized for evidence beyond historical and literary writings, i.e. archaeology, epigraphy, numismatics, legal codes, psychology, and topography, and their powers of definition, clear expression and sense of organization drawn from rhetoric, these three men stood at the beginning of modern historiography. Although the greatest Italian historians of the sixteenth century, Machiavelli (1469-1527) and Guicciardini (1483-1540), wrote in the vernacular, they both had been prepared for their work by humanistic education.

Inherent in the humanists' devotion to the ancient texts was the belief that, were the ancient writings to be brought back to their original state, they could not help but exert an influence on their readers. From the earliest days of the movement, therefore, textual criticism played a role in the humanist enterprise, but with limited results.[10] Until the second half of the fifteenth century Italy lacked stable libraries with large collections of manuscripts containing multiple copies of the same text for collation and until the invention of printing scholars were without editions of ancient authors to serve as the standard basis for further correction and specific line and page references.

After mid-century as conditions for exegesis and textual criticism decidedly improved with the growth of important library collections, these activities became the central focus of much of the humanists' interest. The line-by line commentary, wherein the author had ample space to expatiate learnedly on issues raised by the text, became fashionable as a literary work. Within a few decades, however, the attraction of concentrating on the more difficult passages of a text without considering the rest led fame-seeking scholars to move to a new format. With titles like *Observationes* or *Annotationes* the authors directed these works not to students but rather to fellow scholars. The first technical treatise of philology since antiquity, the commentaries devoted to detailed research on specific details of a text laid the basis of the modern profession of classical philology.

In his *Miscellanea* (1489), the leading philologist of the fifteenth century, Antonio Poliziano took this tendency one step further. In a conscious effort to imitate the *Noctes Atticae* of Aulius Gellius, Poliziano abandoned the commentary tradition tied to specific texts and organized his work according to different categories with a separate chapter assigned to each. To this new format he joined a rare scrupulosity in his use of texts, usually identifying the specific manuscripts he consulted or, in cases where the material came to him second-hand, the intermediary. While his predecessors had at times reconstructed manuscript traditions, Poliziano surpassed them in his systematic approach. Where manuscripts agreed on a reading, he sought to determine whether one was derived from another. He aimed to simplify by identifying independent versions of the same text.

Poliziano's superiority at literary exegesis matched that of his textual criticism. His generation generally recognized the value of Greek literature for exegetical work on Latin texts, but the superiority of his particular use of the comparative method derived from his sense of the variety of ways in which a Roman author could imitate a Greek model, for example intellectually rather than verbally. Poliziano's mastery of Greek literature and of the critical tradition surrounding it not only aided his understanding of Latin texts but permitted him partially to reconstruct lost Greek works. Regrettably no disciple of stature remained after his death to continue his philological labors. Only late in the next century did a scattering of scholars begin building on the foundations he had laid.

In a more general sense Poliziano's career marked a break in the development of Italian humanism. Whereas from the first generation of humanists the *studia humanitatis* had been oriented toward practical goals of reform, according to Poliziano philological research, if not self-justifying, should furnish models for one's own literary efforts. To interpret antiquity in terms of present concerns necessarily distorted the historical past. In this he articulated what was to become an increasingly important position in sixteenth-century Italy as the scholarly disciplines, turning inward, shut out the broader vision of their role in serving the cause of reforming contemporary society.

As Paul O. Kristeller has pointed out, the one major philosophical theme important to Italian humanism involved the dignity of man.[11] A large number of Italian humanists spoke to the issue even if not specifically in philosophical terms. The ancient pagan and patristic traditions surrounding the topic offered a wide range of positions on which writers could draw according to their own experience. While Petrarch and Salutati often expressed very negative views of the potentialities of earthly life, on the whole both believed that through their work as scholars and teachers, always aided by divine grace, they could work toward the moral improvement of themselves and others. Salutati's disciple, Poggio Bracciolini, however, saw only misery in the human condition and essentially placed his hope for happiness in life after death. In this he was followed by other humanists, such as Bartolomeo Fazio (1400-57) and Giovanni Garzoni (1419-1506).[12]

By contrast still other fifteenth century humanists, inheriting the

strong voluntaristic emphasis of Petrarch and Salutati, offered essentially optimistic interpretations of man's earthy state. Although freely
admitting the imperfection of human existence, writers such as
Lorenzo Valla, Giannozzo Manetti (1396-1459), Benedetto Morandi
(d. 1478) and Aurelio Brandolini (1440-97/98) exalted the creative
power of man by which he remolded both himself and his world.
Drawing on Cicero and Hermetic texts as well as those of the Church
Fathers, these humanists transformed what in their sources were relatively static traits of human nature, stature, beauty, reason and the like,
into a dynamic vision of man as the creator of civilization.

Already in the previous century, like Cicero but also parallel to contemporary nominalist thinkers north of the Alps, Petrarch had called
into question reason's power to create architectonic metaphysical systems. While his position rested primarily on the preeminent importance of morality, Petrarch paralleled the nominalists by maintaining
the superiority of the will to the intellect. Salutati endorsed both these
positions of Petrarch, but he did so utilizing a number of arguments
drawing heavily on scholastic writers of the previous hundred years.
Therefore, if only a few Italian humanists of the next century explicitly
identified the will as the superior human faculty, nonetheless,
voluntarism had roots in the movement.

So pervasive indeed was this voluntaristic tendency in the Italian
Renaissance that it exercised a significant influence on the reception of
Platonic thought beyond humanistic circles in the second half of the fifteenth century. At least the two major philosophers of Florentine
Platonism, Marsilio Ficino (1433-99) and Giovanni Pico della Miran-
dola (1462/3-94), substituted a volitional experience, the eternal enjoy-
ment of God as the final state of the blessed rather than the eternal contemplation of God, which one would have expected in the Platonic
heaven so oriented toward the visual. Moreover, in his conception of
human nature, Pico went beyond any humanist in assigning no essence
to man save the capacity through will to outdo the angels in heaven or
sink to the lowest depths.

Apart from occasional criticism of the sophistry of the dialecticans,
the humanists did not on the whole oppose scholasticism. Most felt
perfectly free to draw on scholastic thinkers for and against the dignity
of man and in their analysis of the relationship between will and intellect. Perhaps scholastics found Lorenzo Valla to be their bitterest opponent in this century. Not only did he assail the imaginary entities
they created by ontologizing abstract philosophic terms, but he re-

buked them for relying so extensively on pagan philosophers in their philosophical and theological constructions.

His critique of scholasticism in fact was of a piece with his general one of the contemporary Church. Just as the Church since Constantine wrongly considered itself heir to the imperial tradition, so scholasticism, by its embrace of ancient rationalism with its constellation of values, distorted the mysteries of the Christian faith. Placing the history of the Church in historical perspective, Valla called for a return to the original ideals of Christianity when theologians followed St. Paul by basing themselves solely on Scripture, and the civic life of laymen, fulfilling their baptismal vows, was considered of equal spiritual value to the clerical life.

More specifically, he identified the principle of analogy as the foundation of scholastic theology, the basis on which scholastic theologians justified their application of Greek metaphysical categories to understand revealed scriptural truth. While admitting the absolute difference between finite and divine being, they insisted on the presence of enough analogical similitude to afford an approximate understanding of the divine nature. Valla, however, absolutely denied ontological proportionality between finite being, the province of philosophy, and infinite being, that of theology. Deprived of access to the divine through analogy, Christians could only approach divine truth through linguistic, semantic and historical analyses of biblical language. The theologian must become the philologist. Valla, therefore, redirected the tools of textual criticism and exegesis developed for ancient pagan literature to interpretation of the bible. In two works, *Collatio Testamenti* (1442) and *Adnotationes in Novum Testamentum* (1453-57), he collated the Latin Vulgate with the Greek New Testament, submitted the latter to a philological analysis, compared the adequacy of the Vulgate translation, and focused on interpreting a selection of difficult passages. Behind his work lay the assumption that (1) only the Hebrew and Greek versions of the bible could claim authority and (2) only the scholar properly trained in textual criticism could determine the meaning of the word of God. Therefore, in as much as the ancient texts contained significant knowledge for all branches of learning from the arts to mathematics and natural sciences and because the philologist alone could determine their meaning, philology could well claim to have become the queen of the sciences.

In addition to establishing biblical humanism, Valla also attempted to legitimize the pursuit of pleasure as a natural drive behind human

action and to prove that Christianity permitted the maximum realization of that desire. Given the natural condition of man in the ancient
world, Epicureanism with its emphasis on seeking pleasure proved
more fitting to human needs than the self-abnegation of Stoicism or the
middle-of-the-road way of Peripateticism. By contrast, Christianity
with its promise of eternal life in paradise fulfills this central human desire even more satisfactorily. In view of such future bliss, the Christian
should be willing to forego certain worldly pleasures for its attainment.
Such ultimate pleasure, which is really love of God, could only be
reached with the inspiration of divine grace. Inciting in the believer a
new orientation, grace transforms his values and pattern of action so
that he might finally find the fruition of love in the eternal possession
of God.

Both Erasmus and Lefèvre d'Etaples would draw on Valla's biblical
humanism, and in Erasmus' case the contrast between biblical and medieval Christianity would be sharpened further. Valla's positive stance
on pleasure reappeared in the work of his disciple Platina, who might
have acted as intermediary between Valla and Aurelio Brandolini in
this regard. The Christian Epicureanism of More and Erasmus almost
certainly drew some of its inspiration from Valla's writings. To Luther
Valla's *Declamatio* revealed the trickery which lay at the basis of the
contemporary church and the means by which "Christian liberty" had
been lost.[13]

3. The Outcome of Italian Humanism

The history of Italian humanism after 1500 becomes muddled by the
very extent of its success in transforming the educational organization
of the Italian schools. Products of humanistic education, vernacular
writers often reflected in their work the influence of Latin training. For
example, while highly original and drawing extensively on their personal experience, Machiavelli and Guicciardini were heavily indebted
to their education both for the formal structuring of their work and
their historical perspective. Again, the humanists handed over to theologians, philosophers, mathematicians and natural scientists the relevant textual treasures of the ancient world in reasonably intelligible
forms. As they became informed with a humanistic education, scholars in these other fields increasingly became able themselves to deal
with the philological problems involved in interpreting the texts. Ac-

cordingly, it becomes difficult for modern scholars to identify in many cases who should be included among the humanists.

At the same time, even where individuals were clearly continuing research in areas traditionally dominated by the humanists, the whole enterprise changed character. Poliziano already heralded the advent of the re-orientation of Italian humanism's priorities in the sixteenth century. What in effect occurred was that the reform zeal which served as the glue holding the various scholarly enterprises of the movement together became unstuck. While humanistic researches in history, legal history, literary criticism, and classical philology continued to deepen, the connection between the fields grew increasingly tenuous and independent of an overarching goal.

To an extent specialization reflected the maturity of the humanist movement in this century, but more practical considerations were involved as well. Both the despotic character of political power throughout the peninsula and the gradual restriction of freedom of thought by a church fighting for its existence discouraged a discourse of broad political, religious and moral reform. Dependent as they largely were on the patronage of the establishment, humanists found safety in the narrow compartments of scholarship where their work threatened no one but their scholarly competitors.

4. Humanism in England and France

Petrarchan humanism had certain resonances in fourteenth-century northern Europe, primarily in the imperial court at Prague and in Paris. But the interest in these places apparently could not yet be self-sustaining, and the changed character of Italian humanism after 1400 both in style and orientation exercised for a time little appeal north of the Alps. The renewal of religious concerns first with Valla and then with Florentine Platonism again made humanism attractive to northern Europeans and inspired native humanist movements there. Scholars who have insisted that northern humanism began largely in independence from Italy have failed to make a strong case. Nevertheless, as could be expect, northern pioneers of humanism adapted the Italian inheritance according to their own intellectual traditions and needs.

An intense exchange of students between northern and southern European institutions of learning had existed since the eleventh century, but whereas the students going to Italy before the mid-fifteenth century had principally sought legal instruction at Bologna or another of the Italian *studia*, from this time on a growing number came to pursue the new grammatical and literary studies. Not only did they become the transmitters of the new scholarship, but after 1475 the printing presses of northern Europe provided northern readers with a flood of works by the great Italian scholars and in some cases the scholars themselves moved north to occupy prestigious positions at Paris and Oxford and in courtly circles of great northern rulers.

By the early decades of the sixteenth century the relationship between northern and Italian humanists, previously one of dependency, changed dramatically. The increasing demand for political stability and control of cultural life by Italian rulers within their relatively centralized domains had a chilling effect on humanist creativity and encouraged conformity. By contrast, the extensive realms of northern monarchies favored a greater degree of cultural pluralism which, when humanism moved north, led to a rejuvenation of the movement.

England

Both in late fifteenth-century England and France Italian philological techniques and especially the emphasis on Greek found great favor in university circles, but not because of any strong interest in the pagan literary inheritance. Although some ancient Greek literary works both in the original and in translation circulated in the period, Greek was largely prized by scholastic theologians and philosophers for its use in understanding ancient Greek philosophical texts as well as the writings of the Greek Church Fathers.

Visiting Italian professors at Oxford and Cambridge initiated a new approach to rhetoric in 1465 and 1478 respectively. One of the earliest effort at humanist reform of education by an Englishman occurred at Oxford, when John Anwykyll (d. 1487) introduced a new Latin grammar text at Magdalen about 1480.[14]   William Grocin (1446-1519) may have learned at Oxford what Greek he knew before leaving for Italy in 1488, but the first solid evidence of Greek instruction coincides with the arrival of the Italian Cornelio Vitelli at Oxford in 1490.[15]

Although he wrote little, Grocin devoted his knowledge of Greek largely to study of the Church Fathers. Similarly, John Colet (1466?-1519) brought back from his contact with Ficino and Pico in Florence a strong interest in Plato and Plotinus and a pre-occupation with the Pauline epistles. Convinced of the need to substitute the writings of the

Church Fathers for those of scholastic writers of theology, Colet not only directed Erasmus' attention to the importance of biblical and patristic scholarship, but also embodied his ideal of Christian learning in the curriculum of St. Paul's School, which he founded in 1510.

The establishment of the Latin secretaryship by Henry VII clearly signaled the royal government's awareness of the prestige of reformed Latin style. The career of Thomas Bekynton early demonstrated that classicizing eloquence could carry its possessor far in royal service and the creation of the new post by Henry VII served to institutionalize that recognition. During his reign, however, humanistic activity at court was primarily in the hands of foreigners, mostly Italians. Only under Henry VIII did humanistically trained Englishmen come to predominate in this milieu.

Basically utilitarian in their approach to humanism, the first two generations of humanists, Anwykyll, Bekynton, Grocin and Colet as well as Thomas Linacre (1460-1524) and William Lily (1468?-1522) were all clerics. Consequently, Thomas More (1478-1535) stands out as something of a pioneer as regards the participation of laymen in the humanist movement. A student of Linacre in Greek at Oxford, More constructed for himself an active life as a lawyer yet one congenial to intellectual, scholarly pursuits. Devoted to Greek literature, especially Lucianic satire, More added a literary dimension to English humanism hitherto lacking. The best known product of the English renaissance, his *Utopia* sparkles with wit and the free rein of an imagination inspired by the excitement surrounding the discovery of a new world. Driven by largely traditional values, More combined a virulent critique of his own society with the description of a fantasy whose implications for practical reform are not at all clear.

A friend to the new philological studies in theology, More staunchly defended Erasmus' edition of the Greek New Testament and in 1518 willingly accepted the royal charge to defend the study of Greek for theology against a strong conservative group of theologians at Oxford who feared that study of Greek would lead to a paganizing of Christianity.[16] His later, violent, often scatalogical invectives against the Protestant menace are difficult to reconcile with the reasonableness of his earlier writings.

The presence of John Fisher at Cambridge perhaps averted a similar conservative reaction of theologians against humanism there. The brief residence of Erasmus at Cambridge from 1511-14 certainly helped to protect as it certainly encouraged the new studies. In the second decade of the century the founding at Cambridge of St. John's College, based on a trilingual program in Latin, Greek and Hebrew, together with Richard Fox's establishment of Corpus Christi College at Oxford, specifically designed to foster humanist learning, solidly anchored humanism within the universities and drove scholasticism into retreat.

By the generation after that of More the student body in the new schools and colleges became increasingly lay in composition while the tie between royal government and the schools intensified. Confronted with the task of constructing a new religious settlement, the government naturally sought the talents of well-trained clerics, but opportunities for humanistically educated laymen in royal service expanded more dramatically. Consistent from the first generation, English humanists tended to see humanistic training primarily as utilitarian, as a means to ends other than scholarship or literary achievement.

France

As in England the earliest serious interest of French scholars in Italian humanism came from its potential service to theological studies. Belonging as they did primarily to university faculties, French humanists worked to adapt humanistic approaches to learning to the traditional curriculum of the schools. The origin of such interest within the University of Paris can be traced to the 1450s when Gregorio Tifernate (d. 1466) of Città di Castello received an appointment to teach Greek at the Sorbonne (1458). Within a few years Guillaume Fichet (b. 1433), returning from a long sojourn in Italy, began teaching rhetoric, which he viewed as integrally connected with the study of theology. Scholastically trained like his colleague Fichet, Robert Gaguin (1433-1501) learned some Greek from Tifernate and produced the first humanist history of France. Nonetheless, the ultimate goal of learning was to reform what he saw as the decayed state of university education and the corruption of ecclesiastical institutions.

A new concern for philological questions marks the work of the next generation, who passed beyond the composition of manuals of rhetoric and grammar. The scholars of this generation led by Erasmus and Lefèvre d'Etaples (1450-1536) focused their attention on obtaining accurate texts of both classical and Christian authors. Still within the framework of the university curriculum, Lefèvre endeavored to renew the study of Aristotle by commentaries and translations based directly on the Greek text. Committed to the belief in a natural ethic compatible with Christianity, he focused his philological efforts particularly on the ancient philosopher's political and ethical writings.

Like Colet, Lefèvre returned from an extended period of study in Italy inspired by his contact with Ficino in Florence. However, whereas Ficino redirected both men to the study of scripture, he further awakened Lefèvre to the importance of the ancient and medieval mystic tradition. Lefèvre devoted much of the remainder of his life to editing and commenting on parts of scripture, especially the Psalms and the Pauline Epistles, editing patristic works and finding and publishing mystic treatises. Although his Greek was uneven, his historical sense defective, and his judgement at times quixotic, Lefèvre played a role only second to that of Erasmus in demonstrating the need for a theology securely grounded on philological research.

Lefèvre's younger contemporary, Guillaume Budé (1468-1540) was similarly knowledgeable in Greek and Hebrew, but significantly more gifted as a scholar. A lawyer by profession, Budé composed two important treatises, *Annotationes in Pandectas* (1508) and *De asse* (1515) which went far beyond the specific subject of Roman law and Roman coinage to explore Roman institutions and the ancient way of life in general. Whereas Lefèvre committed himself to the reconciliation of pagan and Christian thought, Budé like Valla affirmed the superiority of Christian culture over paganism and eyed the attractions of ancient literature with suspicion.

Solidly within the French humanistic tradition, Budé conceived of humanistic studies not as ends in themselves, but rather as the best preparation for understanding scripture. Both Guillaume Farel (1489-1565), disciple of Lefèvre at Paris, and John Calvin (1509-64), professionally a lawyer but deeply imbued with humanistic learning, agreed with him. In Geneva, his place of exile, Calvin established a humanist curriculum for the schools which became a model in both Protestant and Catholic Europe.

5. HUMANISM IN SPAIN

During the last three decades of the fifteenth century Italian humanists found a warm reception both at the Castillian court and at Salamanca, the leading university of the kingdom. Pomponio Mantovano began lecturing on the ancient Latin poets at Salamanca in 1473 and Pietro Martire joined him there in 1488. The latter also held the post of secretary for Latin letters for some time under Ferdinand and Isabella. This position had earlier been occupied by the prolific Alfonso de Palencia (1423-92), the Castilian who had studied for some years in Italy and acquired a classicizing style which he demonstrated in his *Decades*, a commentary on contemporary history.

The nascent humanism of Palencia was far surpassed in the work of Antonio de Nebrija (l441/4-1522), who after a ten-year sojourn in Italy returned to Spain where he taught grammar at Salamanca from 1473-86 and again from 1505-13. He devoted the last ten years of his life (1513-22) to teaching grammar at the new university of Alcalá, founded in 1508 by Cardinal Ximenes (1436-1517), primate of Spain. Concerned in his early years with a wide range of humanist subjects from archeology to grammar, by the mid-1490s Nebrija narrowed his interests to focus primarily on biblical scholarship. When in 1505/6 his research notes were confiscated by the Inquisition, he addressed an eloquent appeal, his *Apologie*, to Ximenes, insisting on the central role of the grammarian in the establishment of the biblical text. Himself Grand Inquisitor after 1507, Ximenes encouraged Nebrija in his studies and in 1513 invited him to collaborate with the group of scholars at Alcalá preparing the monumental *Complutensian Polyglot*. Without doubt the finest achievement of Spanish humanism, Ximenes' bible, with its texts in the original languages along with the Vulgate and a lexicon of Hebrew, Greek and Latin terms, was issued in 1520 only after papal approval had been obtained. Consequently, although actually printed in 1514, Alcalá's edition of the New Testament was not published until four years after the appearance of Erasmus' *Novum Testamentum*. In the end, however, Nebrija participated only tangentially in the Alcalá circle of biblical scholars because he found himself unable to accept the Cardinal's rule that, while the Latin Vulgate was to be edited against the most reliable versions of the text, it was not to be compared with the Hebrew and Greek original.

In light of the resurgence of scholastic theology in Spain later in the sixteenth century, it is important to emphasize that Ximenes' second major philological enterprise was the publication of all of Aristotle's writing in the original with translation. At the cardinal's death in 1517, his secretary, the gifted Greek scholar Juan de Vergara (d. 1557), to be imprisoned in the 1530s by the Inquisition for his Erasmianism, had only completed three of Aristotle's works in Latin translation. Decades later Vergara's work would be carried on by Juan de Sepulveda (c. 1490-1573), former student of Pomponazzi, who in the atmosphere of the Counter-reform sought with these improved texts to reinforce scholasticism as a bulwark against heresy.[17]

The trials before the Inquisition of Nebrija and Vergara reveal the extent to which Spanish humanism already in the first third of the century had become a prisoner of ruling religious currents. When the brilliant young humanist, Juan de Valdés (c. 1541), passed via Erasmian humanism to a spiritualism which pursued God through an interior illumination given by divine grace, he was forced to flee Spain in 1531 to the more congenial climate of Habsburg Naples. Humanism survived in Reformation Spain largely in amalgam with scholasticism or by sacrificing the vision of the whole for the possibility of working in peace on its parts.

6. HUMANISM IN GERMANY AND THE LOW COUNTRIES

Whereas in England, France and Spain humanism found most of its adherents between 1450 and 1500 in the royal courts or the chief universities of the country (Oxford and Cambridge, Paris and Salamanca), in the highly decentralized culture of the Low Countries and Germany a number of secondary institutions and universities, imperial towns such as Augsburg, Strasbourg and Nuremberg, as well as princely courts (for example, those of Eberhard of Württemburg, Joachim of Brandenburg and Frederick III) proved themselves receptive to the new ideas coming from Italy.

By 1500 reforms along humanist lines in secondary education at schools like those of Ludwig Dringenberg (d. 1490) at Schlettstadt, Rudolf von Langen (d.1519) at Münster, Hegius (1433-98) at Deventer and Mathaeus Herbenus (1451-1538) at Maastricht prepared large numbers of students for university training. At the next level, if the universities of Cologne and Ingolstadt remained hostile to the new currents, Heidelberg, Leipzig, Tübingen, Vienna and especially Erfurt were integrating humanism into their curriculum.

Together with the predominantly philosophical and theological interests which motivated humanists in other areas of Northern Europe, German scholars also endeavored to establish their own Latin literary tradition. Already in the middle decades of the fifteenth century Peter Luder (d. 1474) and Albrecht von Eyb (1420-75) gave university lectures on the Latin poets. The Dutch scholar, Rudolph Agricola (1444-85), in his *De inventione dialectica*, completed in 1479 provided a defi-

nition of the relationship between rhetoric and logic which was to predominate in northern countries in the sixteenth century. The first
Latin drama of the Northern renaissance, *Stylpho* by Jacob
Wimpfeling (1450-1528), appeared in 1480. That Conrad Celtis
(1459-1508) received the laurel crown for poetry from emperor
Frederick III in 1487 suggests the visibility that humanism had attained
by this date.

German humanists were also the most productive editors of ancient
pagan texts in Northern Europe.[18] Celtis himself edited two tragedies
of Seneca in 1489 and Tacitus' *Germania* in 1500. An edition of
Manilius by the astronomer Johann Müller, better known as
Regiomontanus (1436-76), appeared in 1472. Among the editions of
major authors early in the next century were Avianus, Florus, Virgil
and Velleius Paterculus. German humanists such as the Alsatian humanist Thomas Wolf (1457-1509) and the Augsburg patrician Konrad
Peutinger (1465-1547), also a learned numismatist, devoted themselves to collecting ancient and medieval inscriptions.

From 1456, when an Augsburg chronicler denied the Trojan origins
of the city, German scholars eagerly worked to establish the history of
their past according to the rules of the new historiography. Celtis
sought the origins of the Germans through Tacitus' *Germania* and argued for the high level of culture of medieval Germans by publishing
the plays of the tenth-century nun Roswitha and the epic poem
Ligurinus praising the deeds of Frederick Barbarossa. Wimpheling initiated the humanist approach to German history in his *Epitome rerum
germanicarum* (1505) reinforcing Celtis' patriotic interpretation of the
German past.

Once underway humanism in England, France and Spain had for
various reasons proper to the individual areas developed a degree of
anti-Italian prejudice, but in Germany increasingly after 1500 humanists aggressively pursued a program of glorifying their homeland as
having a past at least equal to that of ancient Rome. Negatively seen as
hostility to Italian claims of cultural superiority and of a perceived subjection of the German people to the Roman Church, this deep current
in German humanism reached its height with *Arminius* of Ulrich von
Hutten (1488-1523) whose ancient German hero championed German
liberty against the tyranny of Rome.

In contrast with the multiple uses of Latin scholarship, that of Greek
was directed primarily to philosophical and theological purposes. In
the years just before his death at forty-one, Agricola had begun to ap-

ply his excellent knowledge of Greek to the writings of Dionysius. These mystical writings as well as others connected with Hermetic and cabbalistic traditions imported from Italy enjoyed an enormous popularity among the learned in the next generation. The most imminent specialist in this area was Johannes Reuchlin (1455-1522), master of Hebrew as well as Greek, who aimed at using these occult works as a means of strengthening Christian faith.

The Dominican-inspired condemnation of Reuchlin's work and the prohibition of the teaching of Hebrew at Cologne in 1509 exercised a profound effect on the German world of learning. Most humanists viewed these actions as efforts to exclude humanist learning from the schools of theology in the name of medieval ignorance. The cleft between scholasticism and the humanists grew ever wider over the next decade. Again von Hutten's writings marked the high point of the controversy. His brilliant satire *Epistolae obscurorum virorum* (c. 1515-17) enjoyed an enormous circulation, but by this time the quarrel had become part of a more profound struggle.

While the German-speaking world could be justly proud of having produced the greatest humanist of the early sixteenth century, that scholar himself was paradoxically a devoted internationalist. Of Dutch origin, Desiderius Erasmus (1469-1536) spent almost all of his adult life beyond the borders of his native land impelled by scholarly and—in the earlier days—economic concerns. Endowed with a superb wit, a limpid style, and keen insight into the sicknesses of his society, Erasmus with the help of the printing presses became the great communicator of his generation.

Sceptical as a good humanist of the capacity of reason to create elaborate theological constructs and convinced that virtuous action was the best test of true belief, Erasmus promoted what he called "the philosophy of Christ," which, actively understood, meant the grounding of the true word of Christ in the "viscera of the mind". This intimate contact transformed the human will into a creative source for acts of love within the world. While Erasmus never repudiated the authority of the Church as a second source of divine truth, his concentration on scripture suggested where his priority lay.

Just as earlier the Italian humanists had assumed that, were only the pagan texts purified from errors, the eloquence of the originals could not fail to move the hearts and minds of their readers toward virtue, so Erasmus seemed to feel that Scripture, set forth as inspired by the Holy Spirit, could not fail to have a similarly impelling effect. For this reason, at least from 1505 when he published Valla's *Annotationes in novum testamentum*, the driving ambition of his life was to prepare a Greek edition of the text according to the best manuscripts available and accompany the edition with a Latin translation, a project he accomplished in 1516. Because for him the Latin and Greek Church Fathers provided the most spiritual interpretation of Scripture, he felt the urgent need to accompany this new bible with their writings. He published a complete edition of the works of St. Jerome along with the *Novum Testamentum* in 1516 and followed this with a series of editions of patristic writings until his death.

Emphasizing the indissoluable link between inner disposition and outward act, Erasmus sharply attacked the ubiquitous reliance on ritual and ceremony as if participation in the elaborate religious protocol of the late medieval Church by itself sufficed to save souls. While he insisted that he did not criticize rituals devoutly executed, nonetheless, he clearly felt inclined to simplify outward demands so as to enhance the focus on spiritual life.

Like Valla he attacked monasticism for its claim to special favor in God's eyes. In an attack on the hierarchical conception of ways of life, Erasmus sought to bring the monastery into the world by insisting on the same level of Christian conduct for all believers. Attainment of this goal demanded lay access to the Bible and encouragement actively to study it. If he wrote only for the Latin literate, Erasmus welcomed the preparation of translations in the vernacular.

A strain of Epicurianism in Erasmus's mature work runs directly counter to the ascetic tendency of medieval Catholicism. Rather than a prison, he considered the body a partner of the soul and, within limits, natural pleasure as perfectly compatible with intense spiritual life. A valitudinarian and addicted to modest comforts such as clean sheets and well-aired rooms, Erasmus, himself celibate, saw no reason why the lay life enjoyed with spouse and children hindered one from performing works of charity.

As the theological war drew on after 1517, Erasmus found himself increasingly isolated from both Lutherans and Catholics. He could not comprehend the intensity with which supposedly learned men attacked one another over doctrinal issues difficult to determine by human reason and largely irrelevant to the core beliefs of the religion. At the same time the bickering obstructed the vital enterprise of advancing the philosophy of Christ by diverting the attention of scholars from the sources of truth to polemics.

The tolerant public stance Erasmus assumed early on toward participants in the debate became increasingly difficult to maintain by the early 1520s and in 1524 Erasmus made the final break with Luther in his *De libero arbitrio*. The truth of the matter was that like most German humanists of his generation, Erasmus wanted reform, not destruction of the Church.[19] By contast, the majority of the younger humanists, who earlier had imbibed Erasmus' teaching, were prepared to make the break and regarded Erasmus' rupture with Luther as a cowardly refusal to accept the conclusion entailed by his own arguments.

❊ ❊ ❊

By mid-century throughout northern Europe the most creative period of humanism had passed. As in Italy decades before, the reforming zeal behind the return to the ancients had lost much of its initial force. In part because of the very success of the movement in the schools, an age of unheroic specialization might have been predicted. To a large extent Western Europeans by this time had absorbed what the ancient learning had to teach and had now to pass beyond. But more important, the religious issues of reform and counterreform had by mid-century so pre-empted the attention of intellectuals that all reform attempts had to fit within a doctrinal framework. Essentially nondoctrinal, tolerant of diverse opinions and responsive to rational argument, humanism as a form of culture had no place in the new climate. Humanism henceforth existed as a group of disciplines whose search for truth operated within the limits set by the particular religious confession dominant in the area.

NOTES

1. Rüegg (1946), 1ff., and Campana (1946), 60-73, cited in Kristeller (1979), 21-22.
2. Kristeller (1979), 21-32, 85-105; Kohl, "Humanism and Education," *RHFFL*, vol. 3:5-22.
3. Baxandall (1971), 6, 8ff.
4. Greene (1982), 90.
5. The phrase belongs to Charles Trinkaus, "Italian Humanism and Scholastic Theology," *RHFFL*, vol. 3:330.
6. Baron (1966), contains his most elaborate discussion of the concept.
7. Herde (1965) and Seigel (1966) developed this approach. Baron (1967) replied directly to Seigel. See also Skinner (1978), vol. 1:23-65.
8. Grafton and Jardine (1986), esp. 3-28.
9. Camporeale (1972), esp. 278-93.
10. The following account of the development of textual criticism in the second half of the fifteenth century is based on Grafton, "Quattrocento Humanism," *RHFFL*, vol. 3:23-66.
11. Kristeller (1979), 169-81.
12. For this and the following paragraph consult Trinkaus (1970), vol. 1:171-321.
13. Camporeale (1972), 283-84.
14. R. Weiss (1947), 169.
15. R. Weiss (1957b), 108.
16. Schoeck, "Humanism in England," *RHFFL*, vol. 2:15-19.
17. Bataillon (1937), 441-42.
18. In this paragraph I follow R. Weiss (1957b), 118-19.
19. Spitz (1963), 191-92.

BIBLIOGRAPHY

For an extensive treatment of all phases of the development of humanism in Western Europe from 1300-1550 consult *Renaissance Humanism: Foundations, Forms, and Legacy*, ed. Albert Rabil, Jr., 3 vols. (Philadelphia, 1988), which is cited below as *RHFFL*. Essays frequently consulted in the above text are listed separately below by author.

Avesani, Rino. "Il preumanesimo veronese." In *Storia della cultura veneta*, 5 vols. in 8, vol. 2:111-41. Vicenza, 1976-84.

Bainton, Roland H. *Erasmus of Christendom*. New York, 1969.

Baron, Hans. *The Crisis of the Early Italian Renaissance: Civic Humanism and Republican Liberty in an Age of Classicism and Tyranny*. 2 vols. 2d ed. rev. Princeton, 1966 [1955].

Baron, Hans. "Fifteenth-Century Civilisation and the Renaissance." In *The New Cambridge Modern History*, vol. 1: *The Renaissance, 1493-1520*, ed. G.R. Potter, 50-75. Cambridge, 1957.

Baron, Hans. "Leonardo Bruni: 'Professional Rhetorician' or 'Civic Humanist?'" *PaP*, no. 36 (1967):21-37.

Bataillon, Marcel. *Erasme en Espagne. Recherches sur l'histoire spirituelle du XVIe siècle*. THR, vol. 250. Paris, 1991.

Baxandall, Michael. *Giotto and the Orators: Humanist Observers of Painting in Italy and the Discovery of Pictorial Composition, 1350-1450*. Oxford, 1971.

Bentley, Jerry H. *Humanists and Holy Writ: New Testament Scholarship in the Renaissance*. Princeton, 1983.

Billanovich, Giuseppe. *Petrarca letterato*. Vol. 1, *Lo scrittorio del Petrarca*. Rome, 1947.

Billanovich, Giuseppe. "Tra Dante e Petrarca." *IMU* 8 (1965):1-44.

Billanovich, Giuseppe. "Giovanni del Virgilio, Pietro da Moglio, Francesco da Fiano." *IMU* 6 (1963):203-34; 7 (1964):277-324.

Billanovich, Giuseppe. "Il Virgilio di Petrarca." *Studi petrarcheschi* 2 (1985):17-33.

Billanovich, Guido. "Il preumanesimo padovano." In *Storia della cultura veneta*, 5 vols.in 8, vol. 1:19-110. Vicenza, 1976-1984.

Billanovich, Guido. "*Veterum vestigia vatum* nei carmi dei preumanisti padovani: Lovato Lovati, Zambono di Andrea, Albertino Mussato e Lucrezio, Catullo, Orazio (*Carmina*), Tibullo, Properzio, Ovidio (*Ibis*), Martiale, Stazio (*Silvae*)." *IMU* 1 (1958):187-243.

Black, R. *Benedetto Accolti and the Florentine Renaissance*. Cambridge, 1985.

Bouwsma, William J. *John Calvin: a Sixteenth-Century Portrait*. Oxford, 1988.

Branca, Vittorio. *Boccaccio medievale*. Florence, 1956.

Brann, Noel L. "Humanism in Germany." In *RHFFL*, vol. 2:123-55.

Buck, August. *Italienische Dichtungslehren vom Mittelalter bis zum Ausgang der Renaissance*. Tübingen, 1952.

Bush, Douglas. *The Renaissance and English Humanism*. Toronto, 1939.

Campana, A. "The Origin of the Word Humanist." *Journal of the Warburg and Courtauld Institutes* 9 (1946):60-73.

Camporeale, S. "L. Valla, tra medioevo e rinascimento. *Encomium Sanctae Thomae*—1457." *Memorie domenicane*, n.s. 7 (1976):3-190. Also separately published (Pistoia, 1977).

Camporeale, S. *L. Valla, umanesimo e teologia.* Florence, 1972.

Camporeale, S. "Lorenzo Valla e il *De falso credita donatione*: Retorica, libertà ed ecclesiologia nel '400." *Memorie domenicane*, n.s. 19 (1988):191-293.

Camporeale, S. "Renaissance Humanism and the Origins of Humanist Theology." In *Humanity and Divinity in Renaissance and Reformation. Essays in Honor of Charles Trinkaus*, ed. John W. O'Malley, Thomas M. Izbicki, and Gerald Christianson, 101-24. SHCT, vol. 51. Leiden, 1993.

Cardini, F. *La critica del Landini.* Florence, 1973.

Chomarat, J. *Grammaire et rhetorique chez Erasme.* 2 vols. Paris, 1981.

Clavuot, O. *Biondos "Italia illustrata"-Summa oder Neuschöpfung. Über die Arbeitsmethoden eines Humanisten.* Tübingen, 1990.

D'Amico, John D. "Humanism and Pre-Reformation Theology." In *RHFFL*, vol. 3:349-79.

D'Amico, John D. "The Progress of Renaissance Latin Prose: The Case of Apuleianism." *RenQ* 37 (1984):351-92.

D'Amico, John D. *Renaissance Humanism in Papal Rome: Humanists and Churchmen on the Eve of the Reformation.* Baltimore, 1983.

Davis, Charles T. *Dante's Italy and Other Essays.* Philadelphia, 1984.

Dazzi, M. *Il Mussato preumanista, 1261-1329: l'ambiente e l'opera.* Venice, 1964.

Dazzi, M. "Il Mussato storico." *Archivio veneto* 6 (1929): 359-471.

Di Napoli, G. *Lorenzo Valla: Filosofia e religione nell'umanesimo italiano.* Rome, 1971.

Dionisotti, C. *Gli umanisti e il volgare fra Quattro e Cinquecento*, 78-130. Florence, 1968.

Dotti, U. *Vita di Petrarca.* Bari, 1987.

Fueter, Eduard. *Geschichte der neueren Historiographie.* 3d ed. Munich, 1936 [1911].

Fois, M. *Il pensiero cristiano di Lorenzo Valla nel quadro storico-culturale del suo ambiente.* Rome, 1969.

Fubini, Riccardo. *Umanesimo e secolarizzazione da Petrarca a Valla.* Rome, 1990.

Fubini, Riccardo. "Biondo, Flavio." In *Dizionario biografico degli italiani*, vol. l0:536-77. Rome, 1969.

Gaeta, Franco. *Lorenzo Valla: Filologia e storia nell'Umanesimo italiano.* Naples, 1955.

Gargan, Luciano, "Il preumanesimo a Vicenza, Treviso e Venezia." In *Storia della cultura veneta*, 5 vols. in 8; vol. 2:142-170. Vicenza, 1976-1984.

Garin, Eugenio. "La *dignitas hominis* e la letteratura patristica." *La Rinascita* 1 (1938):102-46.

Garin, Eugenio. *Italian Humanism: Philosophy and Civic Life in the Renaissance.* Trans. Peter Munz. New York, 1965.

Garin, Eugenio. *Medioevo e Rinascimento.* Bari, 1966.

Garin, Eugenio. "Poliziano e il suo ambiente." In *Ritratti di umanisti*, 131-62. Florence, 1967.

Geanakoplos, Deno J. *Greek Scholars in Venice.* Cambridge, 1962. Republished as his *Byzantium and the Renaissance* (New Haven, 1978).

Geanakoplos, Deno J. "Italian Humanism and the Byzantine Emigré Scholars." In *RHFFL*, vol. 1:350-81.

Gerl, H. B. *Rhetorik als Philosophie: Lorenzo Valla.* Munich, 1974.

Gilmore, Myron P. *Humanists and Jurists: Six Studies in the Renaissance.* Cambridge, Mass., 1963.

Grafton, Anthony. *Joseph Scaliger: A Study in the History of Classical Scholarship.* Oxford, 1983.

Grafton, Anthony. "Quattrocento Humanism and Classical Scholarship." *RHFFL*, vol. 3:23-66.

Grafton, Anthony, and Lisa Jardine. *From Humanism to the Humanities*. Princeton, 1986.

Gray, Hanna Holborn. "Renaissance Humanism: The Pursuit of Eloquence." *Journal of the History of Ideas* 24 (1963): 497-514.

Greene, Thomas M. *The Light in Troy: Imitation and Discovery in Renaissance Poetry*. New Haven and London, 1982.

Grendler, Paul F. *Schooling in Renaissance Italy: Literacy and Learning, 1300-1600*. Baltimore, 1989.

Gundersheimer, Werner L., ed. *French Humanism, 1470-1600*. New York, 1969.

Hankins, James. *Plato in the Italian Renaissance*. 2 vols. Leiden and New York, 1990.

Harbison, Elmore H. *The Christian Scholar in the Age of the Reformation*. New York, 1956.

Herde, Peter. "Politik und Rhetorik in Florenz am Vorabend der Renaissance. Die ideologische Rechtfertigung der Florentiner Aussenpolitik durch Coluccio Salutati." *AKG* 47 (1965):141-220.

Huizinga, Johan. *Erasmus and the Age of Reformation*. New York, 1957.

Hyma, Albert. *The Christian Renaissance: A History of the "Devotio moderna"*. 2d ed. Hamden, Conn., 1965.

IJsewijn, Jozef. "The Coming of Humanism to the Low Countries." In *Itinerarium Italicum: the Profile of the Italian Renaissance in the Mirror of Its European Transformations*, ed. Heiko A. Oberman and Thomas A. Brady, Jr., 191-301. SMRT, vol. 14. Leiden, 1975.

IJsewijn, Jozef. "Humanism in the Low Countries." In *RHFFL*, vol. 2:156-215.

Kelley, Donald R. *Foundations of Modern Historical Scholarship: Language, Law and History in the French Renaissance*. New York, 1970.

Kelley, Donald R. "Humanism and History." In *RHFFL*, vol. 3:236-70.

King, Margaret L. *Venetian Humanism in an Age of Patrician Dominance*. Princeton, 1986.

Kohl, Benjamin G. "The Changing Concept of the *studia humanitatis* in the Early Renaissance." *Renaissance Studies* 6 (1992):185-209.

Kohl, Benjamin G. "Humanism and Education." In *RHFFL*, vol. 3:5-22.

Kohls, Ernst-Wilhelm. *Die Theologie des Erasmus*. 2 vols. Basel, 1966.

Kristeller, Paul Oskar. "Un *Ars dictaminis* di Giovanni del Virglio." *IMU* 4 (1961):181-200.

Kristeller, Paul Oskar. *Eight Philosophers of the Italian Renaissance*. Stanford, 1964.

Kristeller, Paul Oskar. *The Philosophy of Marsilio Ficino*. Trans. V. Conant. New York, 1943.

Kristeller, Paul Oskar. *Renaissance Thought and Its Sources*, ed. M. Mooney. New York, 1979.

Kristeller, Paul Oskar. *Studies in Renaissance Thought and Letters*. 2 vols. Rome, 1956-85.

Lorch, Maristella. "Lorenzo Valla." In *RHFFL*, vol. 1:332-49.

McManamon, John M. "Innovation in Early Humanist Rhetoric. The Oratory of Pier Paolo Vergerio (the Elder)." *Rinascimento* 22 (1982): 3-32.

McManamon, John M. "Pier Paolo Vergerio (the Elder) and the Beginnings of the Humanist Cult of Jerome." *CHR* 71 (1985):353-71.

Marius, Richard. *Thomas More*. New York, 1984.

Maïer B. G. *Ange Politien: la formation d'un poète humaniste, 1469-1480*. Geneva, 1966.

Margolin, Jean-Claude. *L'umanisme en Europe en temps de la Renaissance*. Paris, 1981.

Martin, J. "Classicism and Style in Latin Literature." In *Renaissance and Renewal in the Twelfth Century*, ed. Robert L. Benson, Giles Constable and C. D. Lanham, 537-68. Cambridge, Mass., 1982.

Mercer, R. G. G. *The Teaching of Gasparino Barzizza with Special Reference to His Place in Paduan Humanism*. London, 1979.

Meuthen, Erich. "Charakter und Tendenzen der deutschen Humanisten." In *Säkulare Aspekte der Reformationszeit*, ed. Heinz Angermeier, 217-66. Munich, 1983.

Moeller, Bernd. "The German Humanists and the Reformation." In *Imperial Cities and the Reformation*, ed. H. C. E. Midelfort and Mark U. Edwards, Jr., 19-38. Philadelphia, 1972.

Monfasani, John. *George of Trebizond: a Biography and a Study of His Rhetoric and Logic.* Leiden, 1976.

Monfasani, John. "Humanism and Rhetoric." In *RHFFL*, vol. 3:131-235.

Nieto, José C. *Juan de Valdès and the Origins of the Spanish and Italian Reformation.* Geneva, 1970.

Noreña, C. G. *Juan Luis Vives.* Archives internationales d'histoire des idées, vol. 34. The Hague, 1970.

O'Malley, John W., S.J. "Egidio de Viterbo, O.S.A. e il suo tempo." *Studia augustiniana historica* 9 (1983): 68-84.

O'Malley, John W., S.J. "Grammar and Rhetoric in the *Pietas* of Erasmus." In *JMRS* 18 (1988):81-98.

O'Malley, John W., S.J. *Praise and Blame in Renaissance Rome: Rhetoric, Doctrine and Reform in the Sacred Orators of the Papal Court, ca. 1450-1521.* Durham, N.C., 1979.

Paoli, U. E. "Il latino degli umanisti." In *Storia illustrata della letteratura italiana*, vol. 1:315-28. Milan, 1942.

Percival, W. Keith. "Renaissance Grammar." In *RHFFL*, vol. 3:67-83.

Pigman, G. W. "Versions of Imitation in the Renaissance." *RenQ* 33 (1980):1-32.

Post, R. R. *The Modern Devotion: Confrontation with Reformation and Humanism.* SMRT, vol. 3. Leiden, 1968.

Renaudet, Augustin. *Erasme et l'Italie.* Geneva, 1954.

Rice, Eugene F., Jr. "Humanism in France." In *RHFFL*, vol. 2:109-22.

Rice, Eugene F., Jr. *Renaissance Philosophy of Wisdom.* Cambridge, 1958.

Rice, Eugene F., Jr. *Saint Jerome in the Renaissance.* Baltimore, 1985.

Rico, F. *Nebrija frente a los bárbaros: El canon de gramáticos nejastos en las polémicas del humanismo.* Salamanca, 1978.

Rizzo, Silvia. "Il latino nell'Umanesimo." *La letteratura italiana*, ed. A. A. Rosa, vol. 5:379-408. Turin, 1986.

Robey, D. "Humanism and Education in the Early Quattrocento: The *De ingenuis moribus* of P.P. Vergerio." *BHR* 42 (1983):27-58.

Rubinstein, Nicolai. "Municipal Progress and Decline in the Italy of the Communes." In *Fritz Saxl, 1890-1948. A Volume of Memorial Essays from his Friends in England*, ed. D.J. Gordon, 165-83. London, 1957.

Rüegg, W. *Cicero und der Humanismus.* Zurich, 1946.

Sabbadini, Remigio. *Il metodo degli umanisti.* Florence, 1922.

Sabbadini, Remigio. *Storia del ciceronianismo e di altre questioni letterarie nell'età della Rinascenza.* Torino, 1885.

Schoeck, Richard J. "Humanism in England." In *RHFFL*, vol. 2:5-38.

Seigel, Jerrold. "Civic Humanism or Ciceronian Rhetoric?" *PaP*, no. 34 (1966):3-48.

Seigel, Jerrold. *Rhetoric and Philosophy in Renaissance Humanism: The Union of Eloquence and Wisdom, Petrarch to Valla.* Princeton, 1968.

Simone, Franco. *The French Renaissance: Medieval Tradition and Italian Influence in Shaping the Renaissance in France.* Trans. H. Gaston Hall. London, 1969 [1961].

Siraisi, N. G. *Arts and Sciences at Padua: The Studium of Padua Before 1350.* Toronto, 1973.

Skinner, Q., *The Foundations of Modern Political Thought.* Vol. 1, *The Renaissance.* Cambridge, 1978.

Spitz, Lewis W. *Conrad Celtis: the German Arch-Humanist.* Cambridge, Mass., 1957.

Spitz, Lewis W. "The Course of German Humanism." In *Itinerarium Italicum: the Profile of the Italian Renaissance in the Mirror of Its European Transformations*, ed. Heiko A. Oberman and Thomas A. Brady, Jr., 371-436. SMRT, vol. 14. Leiden, 1975.

Spitz, Lewis W. *The Religious Renaissance of the German Humanists.* Cambridge, Mass., 1963.
Stinger, Charles L. *Humanism and the Church Fathers: Ambrogio Traversari (1386-1439) and Christian Antiquity in the Italian Renaissance.* Albany, N.Y., 1976.
Stinger, Charles L. "Humanism in Florence." In *RHFFL*, vol. 1:175-208.
Surtz, Edward, S. J. *The Praise of Pleasure: Philosophy, Education, and Communism in More's Utopia.* Cambridge, Mass., 1957.
Trinkaus, Charles. *In Our Image and Likeness: Humanity and Divinity in Italian Humanist Thought.* 2 vols. Chicago, 1970.
Trinkaus, Charles. "Italian Humanism and Scholastic Theology." In *RHFFL*, vol. 3:327-48.
Ullman, Berthold L. *Studies in the Italian Renaissance.* 2d ed. Rome, 1973.
Vasoli, C. "Aspetti dei rapporti culturali tra Italia e Spagna nell'età del Rinascimento." In *La cultura delle corti*, 13-37. Bologna, 1980.
Weiss, James M. "*Ecclesiastes* and Erasmus: The Mirror and the Image." *ARG 65* (1974):83-108.
Weiss, Roberto. *The Dawn of Humanism.* London, 1947.
Weiss, Roberto. *Humanism in England During the Fifteenth Century.* Oxford, 1957a.
Weiss, Roberto. "Learning and Education in Western Europe from 1470-1520." In *The New Cambridge Modern History*, vol. 1: *The Renaissance, 1493-1520*, ed. G. R. Potter, 95-126. Cambridge, 1957b.
Weiss, Roberto. "Lovato Lovati (1241-1309)." *Italian Studies* 6 (1951):3-28.
Weiss, Roberto. *Il primo secolo del umanesimo italiano.* Rome, 1949.
Wieruszowski, Helene. "Rhetoric and the Classics in Italian Education of the Thirteenth Century." In Helene Wieruszowski, *Politics and Culture in Medieval Spain and Italy*, 589-627. Rome, 1971.
Wilcox, Donald J. *The Development of Florentine Humanist Historiography in the Fifteenth Century.* Cambridge, Mass., 1969.
Witt, Ronald G. *Hercules at the Crossroads: the Life, Writings and Thought of Coluccio Salutati.* Durham, N.C., 1983.
Witt, Ronald G. "The Origins of Italian Humanist Style." In *RHFFL*, vol. 1:29-70.
Witt, Ronald G. "Petrarch and Pre-Petrarchan Humanism: Stylistic Imitation and the Origins of Italian Humanism." *Humanity and Divinity in Renaissance and Reformation. Essays in Honor of Charles Trinkaus*, ed. John W. O'Malley, Thomas M. Izbicki and Gerald Christianson, 75-100. SCHT, vol. 51. Leiden, 1993.
Witt, Ronald G. "The Rebirth of Republican Oratory." *Modern Languages Quarterly* 51 (1990):167-84.

Part 2.
Programs for Change

LUTHER'S REFORMATION

Martin Brecht
(Westfälische Wilhelms-Universität, Münster)

Following a widely shared view, this *Handbook* presents the reformation initiated by Luther as one among many. With some justice, for there were in fact several reformations, one of them definitely Lutheran, although one may not ignore the fact that almost all the other reformations grew out of Luther's and shared essential contents with it or at least owed significant impulses to it. Nor can one deny that the Protestant Reformation historically began in Wittenberg, that Luther surpassed in influence all other reformers, and that until about 1524 the Reformation largely bore his imprint. Thereafter, a specifically Lutheran reformation developed alongside others. After Luther's death in 1546, Lutheran confessional churches developed until they were more or less completed when the *Book of Concord* appeared in 1580. In 1521 Luther was already rejecting the terms "Lutheran" and "Lutherans" for the reformation movement, believing as he did that he struggled for the universal cause of Christianity.

1. LUTHER BECOMES A REFORMER

The Years of Gestation to 1518

Martin Luther was born on 10 November 1483 at Eisleben in the county of Mansfeld, and he spent his childhood in the nearby town of Mansfeld, where his father was a small businessman active in the copper mines. His education and the piety of his parents' home were perhaps average for the Late Middle Ages, and the psychohistorians' efforts to interpret Luther's thought from his early childhood development have foundered on the paucity of sources and on wrong-headed deductions. His schooling at Mansfeld, Magdeburg, and Eisenach may well have turned Luther toward a serious, socially conscious piety. In 1501 he began his studies at Erfurt, where four years later he obtained the M.A. and then turned to the study of law. At this time the fear of death and questions about the meaning of life led him into an initial religious crisis, which culminated during a thunderstorm when Luther believed that he was in danger of death from lightning and vowed to become a monk.

Luther entered the monastery of the Observant Augustinian Hermits at Erfurt, and after his novitiate he was directed to receive ordination and to study theology. Although he followed his order's rule and examined his own conscience with unusual scrupulosity, monasticism's time-tested techniques did not supply him with a certainty that he had satisfied God's demands. He felt himself unworthy to say Mass, and he saw Christ primarily as judge. Luther's "attacks [*Anfechtungen*]," which sometimes led him to doubt his own salvation—considered a mortal sin—lasted for about a decade. They form the prehistory for his later breakthrough. There is no evidence that any of the other Protestant reformers underwent such experiences.

Luther's theology at first conformed to Erfurt's nominalism, which held that God would not withhold grace from those who did their best. This presupposed, however, a contribution to one's own salvation— precisely the root of Luther's religious problem. Very early he may have expressed critical thoughts about the strongly Aristotelian character of contemporary theology, and we know that from 1505 he developed an intense interest in the Bible, with which he became familiar to an unusual degree through prayer, meditation, and theological reflection. In 1510-11 Luther was sent on his order's business to Rome, where he eagerly availed himself of the rich opportunities for graces and indulgences, and although he was aware of the religious abuses, as a true son of the church he did not take offense at them.

When Luther returned from his (unsuccessful) mission to Rome, Johann von Staupitz (d. 1524),[1] the vicar of the German Observants of the Augustinian Hermits, transferred him in 1511 to the monastery in Wittenberg. Though the city was small and its university young, Wittenberg's situation in an important territory, Electoral Saxony, was to provide Luther with a platform. His counselor and theological mentor, Staupitz, had selected Luther as his own successor in the chair of Biblical theology at Wittenberg, for which Luther was required, over his own strong protest, to qualify by obtaining a doctorate of theology in 1512. In the later conflicts he appealed to his office as a theological teacher of the church. Staupitz also appointed Luther as monastery preacher, and in 1514 he became the city preacher in Wittenberg, and accordingly for a time he called himself the "Ecclesiastes" of Wittenberg.

Luther's professorial work down to 1518 is documented by his lectures on Psalms, Romans, Galatians, and Hebrews, together with some important sets of theses prepared for disputations. These supply evidence of his development and transition to something new, still often traditional but increasingly with new insights. Initially, Luther's expositions employed the standard fourfold sense of Scripture in the conventional way, though already at this time he emphasized the literal, christological and tropological (moral) senses of Scripture. He also adopted the philological aids of Biblical humanism.

Luther's trailblazing distinction between the law and the gospel in the Word of God is first found in the lectures on Galatians, which he delivered in 1516-17. In an exegetical sense, his reformation was thus not a sudden triumph but a gradual development of scholarship. His religious "attacks [*Anfechtungen*]" came into play, leading him by 1513 to conclude that before God, man can only confess that he is a sinner and acknowledge God's judgment. He must conform to the suffering Christ. This strict theology of humility that "magnifies sin," which he expressed at the beginning of his lectures on Romans, helped Luther to endure his situation. It led him to dispute, already at this time, the view that man can contribute to his own salvation and thus threw him sharply against nominalist theology. Luther nonetheless believed—without complete warrant—that he could appeal for support to St. Augustine's anti-Pelagian writings. Moreover, his discovery of the mysticism of Johannes Tauler (1300?-61)[2] and of the treatise known as the *German Theology*[3] seemed to confirm his view about the necessary passivity of man in the process of salvation. This theology also made him aware, at least since 1516, of his differences with the moralism of Erasmus, whom he otherwise admired. Luther's attitude toward the church at this time was, despite occasional criticisms, still completely loyal.

The Turning Point

Scholars continue to debate the theology of Luther's early lectures, chiefly because the texts, which frequently contain entirely new concepts, permit widely differing interpretations. Despite his break with scholasticism, Luther had not yet achieved a stable position of his own. He did not yet achieve the certainty of salvation, though he no longer hesitated to accept insights that contradicted his own theology of humility.

By his own account in the preface to the first volume of his Latin works (1545),[4] Luther's breakthrough came somewhat later, probably in the spring of 1518. Following his lectures on Hebrews, Luther reflected anew on the revelation of God's righteousness in the gospel (Rom. 1:17), understanding it to be the righteousness that punishes the sinner, and he was offended that this should also be the gospel's content. He came to realize that, seen in terms of God's mercy, righteousness means the justification that a merciful God bestows through faith. This insight contained a new understanding of God, namely, that God does not make demands but rather acts entirely on behalf of the believer and bestows on him the benefit won by Christ. This radically new understanding of the Biblical revelation changed Luther's whole attitude, for he now felt that he had been born again and carried into Paradise. His sorrow, which flowed from his old theology of humility, gave way to joy and a certainty of salvation. The theological consequences of this turn were immense, for it undermined the traditional medieval piety based on good works and required a reconstruction of virtually all of theology, with as yet unimagined consequences for church, society, and world. The formative principle of his reconstructed theology was that faith in the gospel of Jesus Christ justifies. This message of righteousness became his primary gift to his adherents, a provocation to his opponents, and the chief mark of identify of the Lutheran Protestant Reformation. Theologians and laity, high and low, accepted it enthusiastically as a liberating message.

This appearance of Luther's discovery can be verified from his writings during the spring of 1518. It became the nucleus of Luther's reformation as a theological and religious achievement of an individual and as a paradigmatic shift almost without parallel in the history of Christendom.

In narratives of Reformation history, this shift normally (and properly) is associated with the indulgence controversy, which began shortly before. Indulgences had become the root of practices that offended many in the church. Directly at issue was a papal plenary indulgence to benefit the reconstruction of St. Peter's cathedral in Rome. Its sale in Germany depended on an agreement which allowed Albrecht of Brandenburg (1490-1545), archbishop both of Mainz and of Magdeburg, to use some of its proceeds to cover the debt he had incurred in obtaining the archbishopric of Mainz. His instructions declared that this indulgence could be acquired for both the living and the dead, from whom both the penalties and the church's punishments for sin would be remitted.[5]

Before Easter 1517, Luther, who had already criticized the sale of indulgences, became familiar through his penitents with the indulgence for St. Peter's. Believing that indulgences destroyed the seriousness of repentance, preaching, and charitable works, he took steps against them. On 31 October 1517 he sent letters to Archbishop Albrecht and to the bishop of Brandenburg, his own ordinary, in which he humbly requested that the offensive indulgence instructions be rescinded. In the letter to Albrecht he enclosed ninety-five theses "On the Power of Indulgences,"[6] which he offered for debate, since the theory of indulgences had not yet been fixed in the church's teaching. The first thesis emphasized, against current theories of indulgence, that a Christian's entire life ought to be rooted in repentance, and Luther also reiterated widespread objections to the money-making aspect of indulgences. As for posting the theses on the door of Wittenberg's Castle Church, this was first mentioned well after Luther's death by Philip Melanchthon (1497-60), who was not yet in Wittenberg in 1517. Nevertheless, although its historicity has been questioned, the posting probably did take place as preparation for an academic disputation, to which, however, nobody came. In print, by contrast, the 95 theses had a completely unexpected, sensational effect and were several times reprinted by the end of 1517. By late in the following April, Luther presented his new theology in a disputation at the chapter meeting of the Observant German Augustinian Hermits' congregation in Heidelberg. Just as he convinced most of his Wittenberg colleagues, at Heidelberg he won over Martin Bucer (1491-1550), Johannes Brenz (1499-1570), and other young, humanist-trained theologians to his side. When, in the same year, a first collected edition of his writings appeared at Basel, Luther was already on the way to becoming the leader of a school.[7]

Luther's critique of indulgences also gained him a threatening response from Rome, to which Albrecht of Mainz, sensing an attack on papal authority, had sent his writings. The issue of authority, indeed, dominated the reply to Luther by Sylvester Prierias,[8] a Curial theologian, and soon, against Luther's will, the indulgence controversy became a dispute about authority in which Luther appealed to the Holy Scriptures. The issue of the Bible gave him a second point of controversy with Rome—alongside his concept of righteousness—and helped to convince even wider circles of supporters. Indeed, for Luther and, following him, larger sectors of the Protestant Reformation, the Biblical principle became the Archimedean point that supplanted the authority of the church. Only later did it become apparent to him and his followers that this principle, being susceptible to different interpretations, could become a source of divisions.

In the summer of 1518 Luther was summoned to Rome under suspicion of heresy, and a little later he was accused of notorious heresy. At this point political interests first intervened in his fate, without which the Protestant Reformation would hardly have succeeded. It began with his prince, Elector Frederick (1463-1525) of Saxony. The Curia, wishing to prevent the election of Emperor Maximilian's grandson, Charles, to succeed him, permitted that Luther be interrogated not at Rome but at Augsburg, where the Imperial Diet met in 1518. The interrogator was Tommaso de Vio (1469-1534) of Gaeta (hence called "Cajetan"), a papal legate and learned Thomist theologian, who recognized that Luther's doctrine of the certainty of salvation through faith would result in the establishment of a new church. At Augsburg Luther, holding that indulgences had no Biblical warrant, refused to retract his views and appealed, as was the custom, from a poorly informed to a better informed pope and, a little later, to a General Council of the church. The Curia's subsequent failure to proceed energetically against Luther gave his movement an important breathing space for organization.

Meanwhile, the conflict began to dislocate the academic world, and Luther debated the Ingolstadt professor Johann Eck (1486-1543) at Leipzig in June and July 1519.[9] When Eck got Luther to admit that not only the pope, but councils also could err, he believed that he had exposed Luther as a heretic, but most of the educated public saw Luther as the victor. The Leipzig Debate become the model for numerous Reformation disputations at which the Bible served as the norm.

The Program Unfolds

Between the Diet of Augsburg in 1518 and the Diet of Worms in 1521, Luther developed programmatically the implications of his new concept with amazing theological and literary creativity. As he became the most widely published author of his age, his influence began to touch the universities. At Wittenberg scholastic theology was replaced by Biblical languages and studies in 1518, a reform which quickly spread to new or newly Protestant universities at Marburg, Tübingen, Leipzig, and Königsberg. In this work Luther's most important collaborator was the young humanist Philip Melanchthon (1497-1560), whose formation of a Protestant theological pedagogy already contained seeds, which emerged only later, of differences in accent and even concept from Luther's position. Meanwhile, Luther's commentaries on Galatians (1519)[10] and the Psalms (1519-21),[11] established him as one of the most significant exegetes of his time.

Almost all of Luther's writings between 1518 and 1520 dealt with their subject matter in a novel, often revolutionary way. Concerning confession he emphasized belief in the effectiveness of absolution, not the complete enumeration of one's sins and certainly not the satisfactions rendered for sin. Preparation for dying should consist of concentrating on the Christ who overcomes death. The practice of prayer should be made something internal and therefore the number of prayers was to be reduced. Luther denied that, in addition to Christ, the church also needed an earthly head, the pope. He was already reflecting critically on the permissibility of Christians taking interest, a problem that occupied him again and again. He also began to develop a view of marriage as of equal in religious value to celibacy. Finally, in his *Sermon on Good Works* (1520)[12] Luther presented an ethic that derived all Christian action from faith. Here he already had to address the persistent and plausible objection to teaching that righteousness secured by faith does not produce good works, which created difficulties for the Lutheran teaching on sanctification.

In his *Address to the Christian Nobility of the German Nation Concerning the Reform of the Christian Estate* of 1520,[13] Luther presented his most comprehensive statement on reform. He bolstered his call for the rulers to institute reforms with the argument that the papacy had made itself proof against reform. His theological justification for intervention, the priesthood of believers, did not represent a repudiation of clerical office but its reinterpretation in terms of service. He also took up the German *gravamina* against Rome and added reforms in church, society, and economy, making the whole an outline of the Protestant Reformation's program.

Luther's contemporaries considered his *Babylonian Captivity of the Church* (1520)[14] to be his most radical tract, because in it he attacked the sacramental basis of the church as an institution. He retained only two—Baptism and the Eucharist or Lord's Supper—of the seven sacraments, acknowledging them alone as having been instituted by Christ and provided with visible signs. Penance, which lacked a visible sign of institution, nonetheless retained great value in his eyes. In accordance with its institution, the Lord's Supper had to be distributed in both kinds, though the actual changing of the elements was left to the Divine Word's power, and Luther sharply attacked the interpretation of the Mass as a meritorious sacrifice.

The Freedom of a Christian,[15] the last of Luther's three great tracts of 1520, was dedicated to the pope in a final attempt at mediation. It dealt dialectically with the inward freedom a believing Christian enjoyed from sin, death, and the devil and with the service a Christian was simultaneously to render to his neighbor in love. The term "freedom" struck sparks, especially because it could be applied to a person's external circumstances, though to so understand it was to misunderstand Luther's meaning.

The Reaction: Banned and Outlawed

The Imperial election of Charles V in 1519 freed the Roman Curia of the need for the Saxon elector's favor and allowed it to resume legal proceedings against Luther. In the fall of 1520 Luther received a papal bull which threatened his excommunication and condemned forty-one statements from his writings. On 10 December Luther publicly burnt this bull, works of scholastic theology, and the text of the canon law. This act symbolized his rejection of the church's legal constitution, and he took little notice of the bull of early 1521 that announced his excommunication. Yet, these acts tied Luther's case to larger political concerns, and Luther now stood at the pinnacle of his fame, protected by his prince, backed by some Imperial knights, and supported by many other people. The bull of excommunication should have been followed by the Imperial ban, the Empire's decree of outlawry, but Charles V had promised to proscribe no one without the Imperial Diet's consent. This is why, over papal opposition, Luther was summoned to the Diet of Worms in 1521 to explain—and recant—his errors. There, however, he refused to recant and stated that popes and councils had erred and that his conscience was captive to the Holy Scriptures.[16] Thereupon Charles V issued the Edict of Worms, which outlawed Luther and his followers and proscribed their writings. Although this edict dogged Luther to the end of his life, the emperor lacked the power to enforce it, and the territorial rulers and urban magistrates were already divided about it. The Lutheran movement could not be entirely suppressed, and Luther himself, on his prince's orders, was kidnapped on the return trip from Worms and sequestered in Castle Wartburg near Eisenach.

The Reformation Spread, 1521-1524

Luther's months in the Wartburg produced three major things. In *The Judgment of Martin Luther on Monastic Vows*,[17] he threw his weight against monastic vows, based on the principles of justification by faith and Christian freedom, which helped to undermine monastic life in vast areas of Germany. In the Wartburg, too, he produced his first and most influential book of sermons.[18] Finally, Luther cast the New Testament into German, which was published in September 1522.[19] Its linguistic qualities far surpassed all earlier German translations and have found no competitor to this day. By 1534 he had translated the entire Bible, though he continued to revise the translation until his death in 1546. The Luther Bible, which, accompanied by his prefaces and glosses, brought the text fully into lay hands, also exerted considerable influence on the Low German, Dutch, English, and Scandinavian Protestant translations, even on the Catholic Bible translations.

Luther's disappearance in 1521-22 from public view marked a critical moment for his movement. Problems appeared at Wittenberg, where the local clergy could not agree on a new form of the Mass. Luther's colleague Andreas Bodenstein von Karlstadt (1480?-1541) nonetheless pressed ahead, and at Christmas 1521 he celebrated an Evangelical Lord's Supper for the first time. A little later came an new constitution for the church and a wave of iconoclasm, measures which lacked both a consensus in the city and the cautious elector's approval. The disturbances brought Luther back at the beginning of March 1522 to Wittenberg, where he expressed concern for the weak, who needed much more preaching, and quashed almost all of the innovations. His own reluctance to frame a new church constitution and the cautious policy of his prince, Elector Frederick, are reflected in Luther's *Temporal Authority: To What Extent it Should be Obeyed* of 1523.[20] In it he drew a distinction between the two kingdoms, that of Christ and that of the world. The latter must wield its power to preserve outward peace, a work in which Christians may participate out of love for their fellows and might even serve as soldiers. Temporal rulers, however, may not mix into the conscience's relationship to God, which has to do with salvation. In limiting government's authority, Luther, who was no absolutist, contributed to the freedom of conscience.

Down to about 1524, Luther's role in the German Reformation remained essentially a defining one. Under his influence reforms began in Electoral Saxony with little trouble, while with Luther's advice the Grand Master of the Teutonic Knights, Albrecht von Brandenburg, began to transform Prussia into a Lutheran duchy. The movement took root in a number of larger and smaller imperial cities, among them Nuremberg, Strasbourg, Augsburg, and Ulm in the south, and Bremen,

Hamburg, and Magdeburg in the north. Not only was the new order too well established in these places to be uprooted, but in some of them new church constitutions had already appeared. In this work the key figures were the preachers and pastors, prominent among them Andreas Osiander (1498-1552) and his colleagues at Nuremberg, Johannes Brenz at Schwäbish Hall, Martin Bucer and Wolfgang Capito (1472-1541) at Strasbourg, and Johannes Oecolampadius (1482-1531) in Basel, all of whom were in contact with Luther. Their sermons explicated the main themes of his theology and secured broad support among the burghers, which inspired the magistrates to caution. The urban confessions of faith prepared in anticipation of a planned national council in 1524 were almost entirely Lutheran in meaning. They document the Lutheran reformation's rootedness in the cities, many of which remained Lutheran into modern times. The Lutheran reformation also penetrated some of the territorial states, where they were tolerated, as in Brandenburg-Ansbach and Silesia, or energetically but not always successfully suppressed, as in the Hapsburg dynastic lands, Bavaria, and Ducal Saxony.

2. The Lutheran Reformation

Two circumstances, primarily explain why other reformations developed alongside Luther's. First, in 1524-25 several theological disputes emerged in the Evangelical camp. Second, the Imperial Diet of Speyer in 1526 offered the princes and magistrates the possibility for organizing church affairs in ways—necessarily various—from which they would be responsible to God and the emperor.

Unity and Fragmentation

Different conflicts affected the Reformation differently. Luther rejected the peasants' revolt in 1525 because, he believed, the peasants confused Christian freedom with political and social freedom, broke the obedience that God had commanded toward authorities, threatened chaos, and followed the promptings of a false prophet, Thomas Müntzer (1489?-1525). His partisan stand did cost him some sympathy, but it affected the Reformation only in that Luther saw himself more dependent on the authorities and that some of his peasant supporters went over to Anabaptism. The Reformation nonetheless did not cease to be a popular movement in 1525.

Luther's conflict with the Netherlandish humanist Desiderius Erasmus (1469?-1536) about free will is one of history's greatest arguments about human nature. Erasmus' distance from Luther, whom Erasmus at first thought far too impetuous, seemed a favorable neutrality that helped the young Lutheran movement, but in the long run, as Luther early realized, the difference between his own doctrine of justification, and Erasmus' moralism could not be concealed. Erasmus sympathized with the old church that Luther was trying to destroy, and in 1524 he finally declared sides in his *Dialogue on Free Will*,[21] which aimed to demonstrate exegetically that man could and must make a moral contribution to his own salvation. He thought the subject of divine election, which was hard to reconcile with this, incapable of explication, and both he and Luther recognized that this was the central point at issue. Luther's reply in his *Bondage of the Will* of 1525 analyzed the ability of man to accomplish anything and concluded that man must leave his salvation to God.[22] He did not question human freedom concerning external matters, including the organization of the world, but, unlike, Erasmus, he held that such difficult questions as election and the origin of evil had to be faced, and he trusted that God had taken the concern for his salvation away from him. The alternatives could not be reconciled. The Protestant Reformation followed Luther on this subject, though some reformers who had been influenced by humanism, Melanchthon among them, did not accept all of Luther's implication and placed a value on human moral effort. The controversy did not lead, as is sometimes alleged, to a split between the Lutheran Reformation and humanism.

Lutheran and other Evangelical churches finally split because of the sacramentarian controversy and Anabaptism, in both of which a significant role belonged to the Spiritualism that was latent in mysticism and in humanism. Spiritualism could manifest itself as a denial that God was able to enter into physical substance, as a claim of immediate possession of the Spirit, or as a demand for the separation of God's children from those of the world. Luther, who confronted spiritualism in the ideas of Thomas Müntzer and Andreas Bodenstein von Karlstadt, had in 1523 denied that the "is" in "This is My Body" was to be read as "signifies." A symbolical interpretation of the formula, he thought, would remove the trustworthiness of the Biblical Word (the foundation of Luther's theology) and reduce the Lord's Supper either to a remembrance of Christ's death or to a spiritual eating in which the receipt of salvation's gifts would depend on the recipient's action. Luther, who believed that his faith depended on an objective offer and on the real presence of Christ's body and blood, had refuted his enemies in *Against the Heavenly Prophets in the Matter of Images and Sacraments* (1524-25).[23] But the contrary views of Karlstadt, Huldrych Zwingli (1484-1531), and Oecolampadius gained support first in Switzerland and then in several southern German cities. Some early followers of Luther, such as the Strasbourgeois, began to take sides against him, while others, notably Brenz and Osiander, fought faithfully at his side. Luther himself participated in the controversy between 1526 and 1528 primarily through his writings on the Lord's Supper, in which he brought to the fore the possibility of Christ's human nature—for Luther it was as ubiquitous as His divine nature—being present in the Lord's Supper. At Marburg in the fall of 1529, Luther therefore rejected religious fellowship with his opponents. The Strasbourgeois were long active in efforts to mediate the quarrel, and in 1536 the Wittenberg Concord between the Lutherans and the Protestant free cities of southern Germany was concluded on Luther's terms. Asserting the objective Real Presence in the Lord's Supper, it restored the German Reformation's unity, though at the permanent cost of unity with the Swiss.

Luther also confronted the radical Reformation in its full spectrum of Anabaptists and spiritualists of all kinds, whose dissent forced him to formulate what became a typical Lutheran position. Against those, such as Müntzer and Caspar Schwenckfeld (1489-1561), who claimed to have received an immediate revelation, Luther insisted that revelation is contained in the external Word. He also countered the claim of Anabaptists and others to possess an immediate call from God by emphasizing the church's orderly bestowal of the ministerial office. He attacked the ethical rigor of Karlstadt and the Anabaptists as a new form of monasticism, and against all assertions of direct inspiration by the Holy Spirit, he emphasized the Spirit's close connection to the external means of grace—Word, sacrament, and ministerial office. Luther did not take very seriously the Anabaptists' theological attack on baptism, which for him was based on God's unconditional offer, so that he saw no point in requiring the recipient to possess a rational understanding of the sacrament. He had no sympathy for the separation of Christians from the world, and when the Anabaptists refused to accommodate themselves to the political community, he was quick to accuse them of revolt and to advocate their repression by force.

Shaping the Church

The Lutheran Reformation proved amazingly creative in its creation since 1523 of new orders of worship and church constitutions. Luther proceeded very conservatively: his "Order of Baptism" was largely a translation of the old baptismal liturgy to make it intelligible to parents and sponsors; and his "Formula Missae" envisioned only a purified Latin mass. The major innovation was the composition of "Evangelical" hymns, which allowed the congregation a more active role in worship. The first hymnals of 1524, which included hymns based on the Psalms, hymns for festivals, catechetical hymns, and new versions of existing hymns, formed the first stage toward Lutheranism's incomparably rich hymnology.

Luther's "German Mass," which appeared in 1526, retained the Mass as the chief worship service.[24] His conservatism aside, Luther displayed a generous breadth in liturgical questions. He allowed the Latin Mass to continue, where it was understood, and he had nothing against the simple medieval preaching service of southern Germany, which, with the Lord's Supper appended, was used in some churches in southwestern Germany and in Switzerland. The preface to the "German Mass" also mentioned the possibility of a spontaneous worship service in the home "for those who want to be Christians in earnest," though Luther himself avoided this daring form for lack of a suitable congregation. New forms for marriage and burial, in which the sermon assumed a central place, replaced the nuptial and funeral Masses.

Fearing that the schools were collapsing, in 1524 Luther called on city councils to establish schools to educate a new generation for church. He also wanted schools for girls.[25] Gradually, a system of civic Latin schools sprang up in all the areas where Protestantism prevailed, and although individual territories and cities displayed great variations in the means of support, the caliber, and the level of attendance, on the whole the new schools raised literacy and thus the independence of the individual.

Luther and his colleagues considered instruction in the faith an urgent task, and to this end they produced a rich catechetical literature. Pride of place belonged to Luther's own Small Catechism, which grew out of his sermons, and its companion piece for pastors, the Large Catechism.[26] Their structure is typically Lutheran: Ten Commandments, Apostles' Creed, Lord's Prayer, Baptism, Lord's Supper, and the Office of the Keys (absolution), all with precise explanations which highlight the essentials and maintain an impressive brevity. The only additions were a few prayers and the so-called Table of Duties, which admonished people to conduct themselves in a way that accorded with their status in society. Although they are not comparable to Luther's Small Catechism, the even briefer catechism of Johannes Brenz (1535) and the Nuremberg Children's Sermons of Andreas Osiander also circulated widely. The catechisms were supplied with pictures, for against the Spiritualists Luther maintained that images were edifying. The Lutheran churches frequently used altar paintings and other Biblical representations, based on models by Lucas Cranach the Elder (1472-1553). Although some scholars have held Lutheranism's educational and catechetical work to have been unsuccessful, in comparative perspective the contrary is nearer the truth.

Electoral Saxony

When the Catholic bishops rejected Luther's reformation, a new ecclesiastical structure larger than the congregation had to be created. Here purposes converged, for while the Saxon elector's regime aimed to supervise preaching, Luther considered it urgent that pastors be compensated and parish assets be secured. This could not happen without the ruler's collaboration, but Elector John (b. 1468, r. 1525-32) was afraid of the costs of ecclesiastical reconstruction to the state. In 1527 Luther induced him to appoint visitation commissions, composed of nobles, officials, and theologians, to regulate financial and personnel matters in the congregations. Luther, who drafted the *Instructions for the Visitors of Parish Pastors in Electoral Saxony* (1528),[27] understood visitation to be exercising the episcopal office, which the ruler assumed not to aggrandize himself but as a Christian service of love. The arrangement was to be temporary, an emergency solution, and in the long run the church's administration was to be assumed by the pastors of the larger cities. Their title, "superintendent," meant an ecclesiastical overseer, just like a bishop. Although Luther never intended to set up the territorial sovereign as a supreme bishop, he did pave the way for it. The typical Lutheran church constitutions established the office of superintendents in an episcopal sense, and, lacking presbyerial or synodical structures, remained a church run by pastors.

In time there arose a need for central institutions over the superintendents. In 1539 the function of a marriage tribunal was assigned to the Wittenberg consistory, and that body became the nucleus of the church's supreme administrative body as part of the state. The experiment of establishing Protestant bishops in Naumburg and Merseburg proved in the long run to be incompatible with the interests of the Saxon state. The ordination of pastors devolved on the Wittenberg clergy, where the theology professors examined the applicants. Procurement of pastors and schoolmasters generally took place informally, principally through the efforts of Luther and Melanchthon. One of the weak points in the Lutheran church constitution was church discipline, which was shared between the pastors and the state's officials, an arrangement which assured constant friction between church and state.

Other Lutheran Churches in the Empire

Far beyond Electoral Saxony spread the model of a church governed by superintendents and consistories, often accompanied by the Wittenberg order of worship. In Hesse it triumphed over synodical concepts. Its most important agent in North Germany was the Wittenberg city pastor, Johannes Bugenhagen (1485-1558), who wrote church constitutions for the cities of Brunswick (1528), Hamburg (1529), and Lübeck (1531). He also took an important role in organizing the Lutheran churches in the duchy of Pomerania (1535) and the Danish kingdom (1537).

Other princely territories also came under Wittenberg's influence: the Anhalt principalities (1526 and 1530), the Brunswick duchies, Ducal Saxony and Brandenburg in 1539. In the two lands Luther's influence was limited, for the regime of Ducal Saxony wanted to preserve its independence, and the Brandenburg reform was initially very conservative in liturgy. But here, too, Wittenbergs' students gained the upper hand and developed church practice along standard Lutheran lines.

In southern German the most important Lutheran city was Nuremberg, followed by Schwäbish Hall and Reutlingen. In 1528 Nuremberg and the margraviate of Brandenburg-Ansbach-Bayreuth issued a common Lutheran church order, based on superintendents. In the early years, the southern Protestant church constitutions and orders of worship displayed both Lutheran and southern influence, but following the Wittenberg Concord of 1536 the Lutheran influence became paramount in the southern free cities, especially in Augsburg. Lutheran and southern German influences competed during the Reformation in the duchy of Württemberg. Here an ecclesiastical council (Kirchenrat) grew out of the institutionalized visitation commission and became one of the central governmental bodies, which made possible a strongly centralized church administration that regulated pastoral

assignments, church property, and church discipline. The superintendents were made lesser authorities in this system, which left the congregations little independence. This model, the most effective of all the
Lutheran church constitutions, was copied in the Palatinate, Brunswick-Wolfenbüttel, and Electoral Saxony.

This (by no means complete) survey of the Lutheran territorial
churches in the Empire suggests how widely Lutheranism spread. Although the constitutions were not, and were never intended to be, uniform, a few types of worship orders and constitutions did come to prevail.   The almost universal close connection of ecclesiastical
administration with the temporal regime was not the result of a plan
but the unavoidable outcome of the political context of German Protestantism. In the building of structures, as in the course of reformation, there was no central hand, least of all of Luther, who usually took
part only when his advice and assistance was requested.

The First Lutheran Confessions

The framing of confessions as statements of faith, which came to affect
all religious parties, was begun by the Lutherans. Luther began the
process in 1528, when he appended to his "Confession Concerning
Christ's Supper" a statement designed to mark off his distance from
both Catholicism and his sacramentarian foes.[28] In 1530, after Luther
had rejected the alliance with the Zwinglians, the Protestants were
summoned by the emperor to submit their confession at the Diet of
Augsburg.   This "Augsburg Confession," presented by Electoral
Saxony, Brandenburg-Ansbach, Brunswick-Lüneburg, Hesse, Anhalt,
and the cities of Nuremberg and Reutlingen, expressed the views of a
decidedly Lutheran bloc.   The document, primarily Melanchthon's
work, aimed at the greatest possible degree of agreement with the old
church. This motive was initially criticized by Luther, who as an outlawed person could not come to Augsburg, but later he identified himself totally with the confession. It became one of the most significant
confessional writings of Protestantism and had an influence far beyond
Lutheranism. At Augsburg, too, Melanchthon drafted the first version
of the "Apology of the Augsburg Confession," a response to a critique
by the emperor's theologians. It was published, considerably enlarged,
in 1531.[29] These earliest confessional documents had profound consequence for Lutheranism, for they emphasized the forensic doctrine of
justification, that righteousness is passively received, based on the satisfaction of Christ's death. This modified Luther's view, for it did not

take into account the renewing power of faith, and although it did ensure the objective nature of justification, it did so at the price of contributing to an ethical quietism in Lutheranism.

Luther was one of the first to realize that a reconciliation with the Catholic Church was unattainable, given the insurmountable differences in theology, ecclesiology, and church law. The alternative was a coexistence, and following the Diet of Augsburg he approved the founding of the Smalkaldic League, a defensive alliance of the Protestants, even though its legality was questionable and could hardly be reconciled with the obedience owed to the emperor. Indeed, these events stimulated the development of a theory of resistance within Lutheranism, which some Lutherans later put into practice. This tradition is as genuinely Lutheran as that of obedience to authority, though the latter is certainly stronger. Luther's real interests, nevertheless, were in a peaceful political solution, which was secured in the Truce of Nuremberg (1532) and the Truce of Frankfurt (1539), temporary concessions until a general council of the church should meet.

Luther believed that no acceptable council would meet, and that if one did, no understanding would be possible. He stated so in his "Smalkaldic Articles," which he composed after a general council was announced for Mantua in 1537,[30] and in which he declared the doctrine of justification to be "the article on which the church stands or falls" and the central point of issue with the papacy. This reflected the placement of justification at the theological center in his second course of lectures on Galatians in 1531 and in a large commentary of 1535.[31] His lecture on Psalm 51 (1532) declared that the subject matter of theology was guilty and lost humankind and the justifying or saving God.[32] It came as no surprise, therefore, that Luther had no use for the religious colloquies held at Hagenau, Worms, and Regensburg (1540-41), and their failures confirmed his opinion. During these years he mounted a great effort to show the distinction between the true and the false church. In 1539 in *On the Councils and the Church*[33] he relativized the importance of church councils and their authority. The true church, he taught, can be recognized by certain marks: the proclamation of God's Word, baptism, the Lord's Supper, the office of the keys (Penance), prayer, and the cross (understood as tribulation or persecution). Luther's polemics against the pope reached their climax when he learned in 1545 that the emperor was planning a war against the true (i.e., the Protestant) church, and in *Against the Roman Papacy, an Institution of the Devil* he denounced this perverse, anti-Christian action.[34]

The aging Luther entertained a similarly harsh attitude toward the Jews, for whom in earlier years he had advocated legal equality. Now he had come to the view that the Jews were perverting the Bible and blaspheming Christ and the Virgin Mary to such an extent that Christians could not coexist with them.[35] With few exceptions, Lutheran governments and churches have not followed his extreme position.

Luther did not idealize the conditions in his own church. He sharply and ultimately ineffectively criticized moral derelictions, particularly the lack of love among peasants, burghers, and nobles, and warned that God would use the Turks as an instrument of His punishment. Moreover, the political situation of the Protestants in the Empire was deteriorating noticeably. Luther anticipated that the Last Day was close at hand and believed that he could already see its evil messengers. He hardly considered himself the victor in the conflict that he had initiated. His experience of the Devil's machinations made him, as he said, a beggar, ultimately and utterly dependent on God. Gradually, as his health waned, he grew tired of living. On 18 February 1546, during a trip at which he was to restore peace among the feuding counts of Mansfeld, he died in his hometown of Eisleben. At Wittenberg—and in all Lutheran churches—people knew that they had lost the "charioteer of Israel" in a critical hour.

The European Luther

Luther's Reformation was not limited to the Empire, though elsewhere his influence vied with others'. Zwingli, Oecolampadius, and not a few other agents of the Swiss Reformation were initially affected by him—to what degree is debated by scholars—though in their case the impact of humanism was stronger than with Luther. The leaders of the radical Reformation, too, such as Thomas Müntzer, Caspar Schwenckfeld, Balthasar Hubmaier, and Sebastian Franck, owed essential impulses to Luther, though they later turned away from him in disappointment. John Calvin, the chief of the second generation of Protestant reformers, showed Luther's impact in every stage of his theological development. Luther's influence also spread via members of his own order of Augustinian Hermits to the Netherlands, though it touched only a small minority there, far fewer than Anabaptism and (later) Calvinism. His touch was also felt in the early English Reformation by William Tyndale, Thomas Cranmer, Robert Barnes, and others, though here he had no lasting influence.

Outside the Empire, the Lutheran Reformation established itself permanently only in Scandinavia.[36] In these kingdoms, perhaps even more strongly than in the Empire, the Lutheran church was subordinated to the state, a development sanctioned by the Wittenbergers. The lasting contribution of Bugenhagen and the Wittenbergers to Denmark's Reformation has already been mentioned. In Norway, which was politically united to Denmark, a Lutheran church order was introduced in 1539, though it gained but slow acceptance from the people. Sweden, which had become politically independent from Denmark in 1523, also subjected the ecclesiastical hierarchy to the Crown and, following the break with Rome in 1527, developed its own connections with Wittenberg in competition with Denmark. Its ecclesiastical constitution, however, followed German rather than Danish lines. The episcopal system was preserved, and the order of worship remained relatively conservative. The connection of King John III (1569-92) with Poland brought with it efforts at re-Catholicizing the country, which, however, were met with successful resistance. The Reformation in Finland, which was politically a part of Sweden, depended on the Swedish Reformation. It was initiated by Bishop Martin Skytte, then still a Catholic, but its form came from Michael Agricola (1508-57), who had been educated in Wittenberg. The Counterreformation was also unable to establish itself in Finland. In the long run the various Lutheran churches of Scandinavia became thoroughly independent representatives of Lutheranism.

On the other shore of the Baltic Sea, the Lutheran Reformation took hold in the cities of Livonia after 1523, and later the nobility also joined it. The Latvian populace was reached relatively late, and under Polish sovereignty there was a partial re-Catholicization after 1566. In Poland the Reformation led to confessional fragmentation, and Lutheranism established itself only among the German population in the cities. In Bohemia and Moravia Luther was since 1519 in contact with the Utraquists, the Bohemian Brethren, and the German population. In 1533 the Bohemian Brethren sent their *Apologia* to Luther for approval, but they maintained their independence and later became receptive to Calvinism. In Hungary and Transylvania the Lutheran Reformation was spreading since 1526, and soon it was competing with Swiss-style Protestants, anti-Trinitarians, and reformed Catholicism. In Austria, despite Hapsburg religious policy, Lutheranism took root among the nobility and in the cities, but by the Thirty Years' War it had almost completely, if not totally, fallen victim to the Counterreformation. Finally, we should mention the efforts at a Lutheran Reformation among the Slovenes and Croats, the legacy of which comprised chiefly the creation of a literature in their vernaculars.

This brief survey of the Lutheran reformations in western, northern, and eastern Europe shows that everywhere the beginnings stemmed from Luther's influence. Although it often failed to triumph over competition from the Catholics and from other forms of Protestantism, Lutheranism nonetheless became numerically the strongest of the Protestant confessions.

3. LUTHERAN CHURCHES IN THE EMPIRE

The Peace of Augsburg and Beyond

Although the Smalkaldic War's (1546-47) unhappy outcome seemed to place the Lutheran Reformation in grave danger, it soon became clear that Charles V was politically unable to undertake a Catholic restoration in the Empire. The Interim, which he issued at the Diet of Augsburg in 1548, was intended as a temporary settlement, until a general council should settle the schism, but it was not really accepted by either side and was thus doomed to failure. Electoral Saxony and the Lutherans in southwestern Germany under Württemberg's leadership were still prepared to state their opinions to the Council of Trent, but there were not even any serious negotiations to that end. All that was left, therefore, was a political solution of the religious conflict, which was achieved by the Religious Peace of Augsburg of 1555. The estates of the Empire "espousing the Augsburg Confession," i.e., the Lutheran territorial churches, thereby gained the same legal protection as the Catholics.

The determination of a church's confession now became a prerogative of the state and its ruler, who were obliged to maintain its confessional character. This consumed valuable efforts in drawing distinctions over against rival confessions (Catholics or Calvinists), and it limited the sphere of a church's activity to its own territory. The Lutheran Reformation enjoined on the territorial rulers their responsibility for the protection and welfare of the church. Many Lutheran churches acquired their definitive form only after the Interim, by which time the Religious Peace of 1555 satisfied the interests of most Lutheran princes. They therefore tended to back the emperor to defend the Peace, which accounts for their political passivity in contrast to

Calvinists. One may criticize this attitude as naive, but we should not overlook the fact that preserving the peace also deserves respect.

The cities, by contrast, clearly were losing influence. In some the Religious Peace obligated a Protestant majority to co-exist with a Catholic minority. Often they at least had to tolerate Catholic institutions within their walls. Some of them, like Nuremberg or Strasbourg and their higher schools, or also Brunswick and the three united cities of Hamburg, Lübeck, and Lüneburg in the north, remained significant ecclesiastical and intellectual centers, important also for the publication of religious books, and their churches rivaled the princes' consistories in intellectual influence. There were conflicts, of course, on such issues as church discipline or social justice, as the watchful magistrates jealously guarded their authority over the church. The Lutheran pastors, for their part, were by no means subservient to their governments, whose new "caesaropapism" they frequently resisted. In this respect, future research will certainly have to present a picture of the Lutheran state church at odds with the traditional one.

Conflict and Resolution

Luther's death in February 1546 left German Lutheranism in a state of theological desolation. Even while he lived, it had become apparent that Melanchthon and his disciples had not totally agreed with Luther, something the other Wittenberg theologians viewed with suspicion. The first real conflict erupted over the Interim, when many southern and northern Lutherans chose exile rather than accept it. Melanchthon and Bugenhagen, however, approved a weakened version, the "Leipzig Interim," declaring that its concessions on worship ceremonies were "indifferent matters [adiaphora]," which did not affect pure doctrine. This brought upon them the sharp critique of the former Wittenbergers Matthias Flacius Illyricus (1520-75) and Nicholas von Amsdorf (1483-1565), who, together with others, now understood themselves to be the true Lutherans (Gnesio-Lutherans). Melanchthon's halting attitude seriously damaged his authority.

Further arguments arose over the doctrine of justification. In order to preserve sanctification alongside the declaration of justification, Georg Major (1502-74), a pupil of Melanchthon, defended the sentence, "Good works are necessary for salvation." In opposition to this, Amsdorf exaggeratedly labeled good works injurious to salvation. A similar problem, disputed among the Gnesio-Lutherans themselves, was the question of whether the law only reveals sin or whether it is also a rule of life for those who are justified. Melanchthon and his disciples, along with even a few Gnesio-Lutherans, taught that in repentance the human will plays a part (synergism), which appeared to jeopardize God's omnipotence. In contrast, Flacius exaggeratedly posited a sinner's complete inability to contribute to his salvation, thus maneuvering himself to the periphery.

Andreas Osiander, who had moved from Nuremberg to Königsberg in Prussia in 1548 as a result of the Interim, taught a unique doctrine of justification, holding that justification consisted not merely in the imputation of Christ's righteousness, but rather in Christ's indwelling in the believer. This threatened to displace forgiveness of sins as the center of justification from its central position in favor of an unverifiable, essential righteousness of the individual. The controversy severely disturbed the church, particularly in Prussia. All the conflicts about the doctrine of justification show how difficult it already was for the emerging Lutheran scholasticism to articulate its central doctrine both comprehensively and sufficiently, yet without one-sidedness.

The Lutherans also experienced a reprise of the old controversy with the Zwinglians about the Lord's Supper and christology, as Calvinism spread in the Empire and "crypto-Calvinist" tendencies surfaced even within the Melanchthonian camp itself. Melanchthon himself was more interested in the presence of Christ's person than of Christ's body and blood in the Lord's Supper. In contrast, Luther's doctrine of the participation of Christ's human nature in the divine nature and thus of ubiquity was impressively developed by Johannes Brenz, but it encountered more or less strong reservations among most of the other Lutherans.

For the quarreling Lutherans it was a theological, ecclesiastical, and not least a political necessity to restore their confessional unity in the face of the threats from both Catholicism and Calvinism. As a first step, the leaders of individual territorial churches, such as Ducal Saxony, Electoral Saxony, Brunswick, Pomerania, and Württemberg, took the lead in compiling collections of confessions (*corpora doctrinae*) or individual confessions. From 1567 onward the principal role in unifying the Lutherans was played by the duchy of Württemberg, which at that time was politically and ecclesiastically well organized. Jacob Andreae (1529-90), professor of theology and chancellor of the University of Tübingen, was the energetic and not uncontroversial agent of this work of unity. In 1568 he helped reorganize the church in Brunswick-Wolfenbüttel. Next to Andreae, the Brunswick superintendent Martin Chemnitz (1522-86) made the most important contribution to unity.

A first attempt collapsed because of the resistance of the quarreling theologians of the two Saxon territories (and the universities of Wittenberg and Jena). A second attempt, begun in 1573, in which Nicholas Selnecker (1530-92), who was now active in the church administration of Brunswick-Wolfenbüttel, participated, achieved success. From sermons on the controverted questions, Andreae first developed a "Swabian Concord," which then was revised chiefly by Chemnitz into a "Swabian-(Lower) Saxon Concord." The work of unity was favored by the fact that in 1574 Melanchthonian crypto-Calvinism in Electoral Saxony had collapsed—Andreae was entrusted with reregulating the situation—and thereafter this important territory participated, as did Electoral Brandenburg. At theological conferences in Torgau and at the Bergen monastery near Magdeburg, the Formula of Concord was finally completed in 1577. The rulers of Hesse, Anhalt, Pomerania, Bremen, Holstein, and Denmark nonetheless did not adopt the agreement, and its adoption by the Palatinate, which was briefly re-Lutheranized in 1576 under Louis VI, was only temporary. Unity of all of German Lutheranism was therefore not attained, though the majority was won back. At the same time the boundary to Calvinism was sharply drawn, a move which touched off severe reactions by the opposing side, e.g., in England. Admittedly, subscription by clerics in the territories that adopted the Formula of Concord was obtained in part by threatening them with dismissal. In the future also, civil officials of territories in which the Formula of Concord was in force were pledged to it, an imposing manifestation of the Lutheran confessional church.

The Formula of Concord was intended to be nothing else than a restatement of the Augsburg Confession. As a matter of fact, it emphasized the responsibility of the Lutheran princes and estates for the salvation of their subjects' souls. In the twelve chapters of the Formula of Concord the controversies concerning the doctrine of justification were treated first. Mediating solutions between the extreme positions were stated. The fathers of the Concord could not deny that almost all of them had been pupils of Melanchthon. His schemata, which were more limited than Luther's and inferior to them, can often be recognized. In the doctrine of the Lord's Supper and in christology Luther's positions were adopted with certain qualifications. In regard to adiaphora it sought to clarify the term and thereby essentially accommodated the Gnesio-Lutherans. In the doctrine of predestination it did hold to the universality of God's offer of salvation, but it did not adopt Luther's exaggerated statements. The final article expressly distanced itself from the Anabaptists, Schwenckfelders, and anti-Trinitarians, thus from the radicals who were still continuing to cause trouble for Lutheranism.

In 1580, fifty years after the Augsburg Confession, when the *Book of Concord* appeared, which contained the Lutheran confessional writings including the Formula of Concord,[37] the confessional development in Lutheranism essentially came to an end. No great feeling of excitement over what had been achieved can really be documented. The later Lutheran reformers had painstakingly attempted as best they could to preserve the legacy they had received; however, no new beginning was associated with it. There were strong threats posed by the Counterreformation and by Calvinism, which was spreading in the western part of the Empire, and the Lutherans felt compelled to engage in polemical defense. Not a few people already felt that the spiritual situation in the Lutheran territorial churches was unsatisfactory. The doctrine of imputed righteousness provided very little moral motivation and encouraged a routine Christianity. Its close connection with the state could become a burden for the church and restrict it in the perception of its own interests, e.g., regarding church discipline. Moreover, the state church left little room for individual responsibility and initiative among its members. The only way those who bore the responsibility knew how to meet the persistent underground criticism from the Schwenckfelders, Paracelsians, and other dissenters, was with doctrine or with force. In contrast, even in the sixteenth century, efforts began at intensifying or verifying individual piety, which then also touched off within Lutheranism a new movement of piety, primarily through Johann Arndt (1555-1621). Appealing in part to Luther, people returned again to the tradition of mysticism, something that could lead, along with a revival, to a spiritualizing or moralizing transformation of the Lutheran heritage.

When we review what has become of Luther's Reformation, what we see is an undisputed historical achievement and organization, as well as a failure to achieve what was intended. The Reformation of the entire church was not achieved, and not even the unity of Protestantism could be maintained. To be sure, Luther was able for a time to get a significant portion of the reforming forces on his side, but these also inevitably developed their own virulence, even within the Lutheran camp. Without the participation of the authorities the Reformation would hardly have materialized to the extent it did. However, this undoubtedly brought the church into a problematic dependence. Not even Luther himself was able optimally to communicate life on the basis of justification and the practice of the priesthood of all believers in such a way that it really accorded with his own concepts. Luther himself had no illusions about the inadequacies in his church. With the proclamation of the pure Word of God, the right administration of the sacraments, and the practice of forgiveness he saw that it was set on the right foundation, from which corrections were also possible. For Lutheran Christians, it was a certainty that in this church one could live in this faith and also confidently die in it.

Translated by James L. Schaaf

NOTES

Abbreviations (see Bibliography):
BC = *Book of Concord; DB = Deutsche Bible;*
LW = *Luther's Works;* WA = *Luthers Werke. Kritische Gesamtausgabe.*

1. Johann von Staupitz, *Sämtliche Schriften. Abhandlungen, Predigten, Zeugnisse*, vol. 1: *Lateinische Schriften. Tübinger Predigten*; vol. 2: *Lateinische Schriften. Libellus de executione aeternae praedestinationis*, ed. by Lothar Graf zu Dohna and Richard Wetzel (Berlin and New York, 1987-89).

2. See Luther's marginal comments on Tauler's sermons. *WA*, vol. 9:(95) 97-104.

3. See Luther's preface to the incomplete edition of the *German Theology*, in *WA*, vol 1:(152) 153, and Luther's preface to the complete edition of the *German Theology*, in *WA* 1:(375) 378-79 = *LW*, vol. 31:71-76.

4. *WA*, vol. 54:(176) 179-87 = *LW*, vol. 34:323-38.

5. Fabisch and Iserloh (1988-91), vol. 1:224-46, 246-93.

6. "Disputatio pro declaratione virtutis indulgentiarum," *WA*, vol. 1:(229) 233-38 = *LW*, vol. 31:17-33.

7. *Ad Leonem X. Pontificem Maximum, Resolutiones disputationum de uirtute indulgentiarum . . . reuerendi patris ac sacrae Theologiae doctoris Martini Luther Augustiniani Vuittenbergensis.* On this imprint, which contains a number of other works by Luther and others, see Hans Volz, "Erste Sammelausgaben von Lutherschriften und ihre Drucker," *Gutenberg-Jahrbuch* (1960):185-204.

8. Fabisch and Iserloh (1988-91), vol. 1:33-107

9. "Disputatio inter Ioannem Eccium et P. Martinum Lutherum," *WA*, vol. 59:433-605.

10. "In epistolam Pauli ad Galatas M. Lutheri commentarius," *WA*, vol. 2:433-618 = *LW*, vol. 27:151-410.

11. "Operationes in psalmos," *Archiv des Weimarer Ausgabe* $1^{1,2}$ (Cologne and Vienna, 1981-91).

12. *WA*, vol. 6:202-76 = *LW*, vol. 44:15-114.

13. *WA*, vol. 6:404-69 = *LW*, vol. 44:115-217.

14. *WA*, vol. 6:497-573 = *LW*, vol. 36:3-126.

15. *WA*, vol. 7:20-38 = *LW*, vol. 31:327-77.

16. "Verhandlungen mit D. Martin Luther auf dem Reichstage zu Worms," in *WA*, vol. 7:825-87 = *LW*, vol. 32:101-31.

17. *WA*, vol. 8:573-669 = *LW*, vol. 44:243-400.

18. *WA*, vol. 10, part 1, 1st half:1-728, and *WA*, vol. 10,1,2nd half:1-208).

19. *WA DB*, vols. 6-7.

20. *WA*, vol. 11:245-81 = *LW*, vol. 45:75-129.
21. Erasmus of Rotterdam, *Ausgewählte Schriften,* ed. Werner Welzig, vol. 4 (Darmstadt, 1969):2-195.
22. *WA*, vol. 18:600-787 = *LW*, vol. 33:3-295
23. *WA*, vol. 18:62-125 and (126) 134-214 = *LW*, vol. 40:73-223.
24. *WA*, vol. 19:72-113 = *LW*, vol. 53:51-90.
25. "An die Ratherren aller Städte deutsches Lands, daß sie christliche Schulen aufrichten und halten sollen," *WA*, vol. 15: (9) 27-53 = *LW*, vol. 45:339-78.
26. *WA*, vol. 30, pt. 1:125-238 = *BC*, 357-461.
27. *WA*, vol. 26:195-240 = *LW*, vol. 40:263-320.
28. *WA*, vol. 26:499-509 = *LW*, vol. 37:360-72.
29. *Die Bekenntnisschriften der evangelisch-lutherischen Kirche* 2d ed. (Göttingen, 1952), (xxii-xxiii) 141-404 = *BC*, 97-285.
30. *WA*, vol. 50:192-254 = *BC*, 287-318.
31. *WA*, vol. 40, pt. 1:15-688, and *WA*, vol. 40, pt. 2: 1-184.
32. *WA*, vol. 40, pt. 2:315-470 = *LW*, vol. 12:301-410.
33. *WA*, vol. 50:509-653 = *LW*, vol. 41:3-178.
34. *WA*, vol. 54:206-99 = *LW*, vol. 41:257-376.
35. "Von den Juden und ihren Lügen," *WA*, vol. 53:417-552 = *LW*, vol. 47:121-306.
36. See Michael Metcalf, in this *Handbook*, vol. 2:523-50.
37. *Bekenntnisschriften*, (xxxii-xliv) 739-1100 = *BC*, 463-636.

BIBLIOGRAPHY

Sources

Brenz, Johannes. *Werke.* Ed. Martin Brecht and Gerhard Schäfer. Vol. 1- . Tübingen, 1970- .
Die Bekenntnisschriften der evangelisch-lutherischen Kirche. 2d ed. Göttingen, 1952.
Luther, Martin. *D. Martin Luthers Werke. Kritische Gesamtausgabe.*
— *Werke.* 61 vols. Weimar, 1883-1983.
— *Briefwechsel.* 18 vols. Weimar, 1930-85.
— *Deutsche Bibel.* 12 vols. Weimar, 1906-61.
— *Tischreden.* 6 vols. Weimar, 1912-21.
Luther, Martin. *Luther's Works.* Ed. Jaroslav Pelikan and Helmut T. Lehmann. 55 vols. St. Louis and Philadelphia, 1955-86.
Melanchthon, Philipp. *Melanchthons Briefwechsel.* Ed. Heinz Scheible. Vol. 1-. Stuttgart-Bad Cannstatt, 1977- .
Melanchthon, Philipp. *Melanchthons Werke in Auswahl.* Ed. Robert Stupperich. 7 vols. Gütersloh, 1951-75.
Melanchthon, Philipp. *Philippi Melanchthonis Opera.* Ed. Carolus Gottlieb Bretschneider. Corpus Reformatorum, vols. 1-29. Halle, 1834-60.
Melanchthon, Philipp. *Supplementa Melanchthoniana.* 5 vols. Leipzig, 1910-29.
Sehling, Emil, ed. *Die Evangelischen Kirchenordnungen des XVI. Jahrhunderts.* Vol. 1-. Leipzig and Tübingen, 1902- .
Tappert, Theodore G., ed. *The Book of Concord. The Confessions of the Evangelical Lutheran Church.* Philadelphia, 1959.
Tjernagel, Neelak S., ed. *The Lutheran Confessions. A Harmony and Resource Book.* Mankato, Minn., 1979.

Reference Works

Aland, Kurt. *Hilfsbuch zum Lutherstudium.* 3d ed. Bielefeld, 1970.
Benzing, Josef. *Lutherbibliographie. Verzeichnis der gedruckten Schriften Martin Luthers bis zu dessen Tod.* Bibliotheca Bibliographica Aureliana, vols. 10, 16, and 19. Baden-Baden, 1966.
Lutherjahrbuch. Vol. 1- (1926-). Contains the most extensive running bibliography of Luther Studies.

Literature

General Literature on Luther
Althaus, Paul. *The Ethics of Martin Luther.* Trans. Robert C. Schultz. Philadelphia, 1972.
Althaus, Paul. *The Theology of Martin Luther.* Trans. Robert C. Schultz. Philadelphia, 1966.
Bainton, Roland H. *Here I Stand: a Life of Martin Luther.* New York, 1961.
Bornkamm, Heinrich. *Luther in Mid-Career, 1521-1530.* Trans. E. Theodore Bachman. Philadelphia, 1983.
Brecht, Martin. *Luther als Schriftsteller.* Stuttgart, 1990.

Brecht, Martin. *Martin Luther.* 3 vols. Trans. James L. Schaaf. Philadelphia and Minneapolis, 1985-92.

Ebeling, Gerhard. *Luther: an Introduction to His Thought.* Trans. R. A. Wilson. Philadelphia, 1970.

Gritsch, Eric W. *Martin - God's Court Jester. Luther in Retrospect.* Philadelphia, 1983.

Junghans, Helmar, ed. *Leben und Werk Martin Luthers von 1526-1546.* 2 vols. Göttingen, 1983.

Kittelson, James M. *Luther the Reformer: the Story of the Man and His Career.* Minneapolis, 1986.

Loewenich, Walther von. *Martin Luther: the Man and His Work.* Minneapolis, 1983.

Lohse, Bernhard. *Martin Luther: an Introduction to His Life and Work.* Trans. Robert C. Schultz. Philadelphia, 1987.

Manns, Peter. *Martin Luther: an Illustrated Biography.* Trans. Michael Shaw. New York, 1982.

Oberman, Heiko A. *Luther: Man between God and Devil.* Trans. Eileen Walliser-Schwarzbart. New Haven, 1986.

Olivier, Daniel. *Luther's Faith: the Cause of the Gospel in the Church.* St. Louis, 1982.

Todd, John M. *Martin Luther: a Biographical Study.* New York, 1982.

Luther's Development and Program to 1524

Aland, Kurt. *Martin Luther's 95 Theses.* Trans. P. J. Schroeder. St. Louis and London, 1967.

Bayer, Oswald. *Promissio. Die Geschichte der reformatorischen Wende in Luthers Theologie.* Göttingen, 1971.

Baylor, Michael G. *Action and Person: Conscience in Scholasticism and the Young Luther.* SMRT, vol. 20. Leiden, 1977.

Bizer, Ernst. *Fides ex auditu. Eine Untersuchung über die Entdeckung der Gerechtigkeit Gottes durch Martin Luther.* 3d ed. Neukirchen, 1966 [1958].

Bluhm, Heinz. *Martin Luther, Creative Translator.* St. Louis, 1965.

Borth, Wilhelm. *Die Luthersache.* Historische Studien, vol. 414. Lübeck and Hamburg, 1970.

Fabisch, Peter, and Erwin Iserloh, eds. *Dokumente zur Causa Lutheri (1517-1521).* 2 vols. Corpus Catholicorum, vols. 41-42. Münster, 1988-91.

Gänssler, Hans-Joachim. *Evangelium und weltliches Schwert. Hintergrund, Entstehungsgeschichte und Anlass von Luthers Scheidung zweier Reiche oder Regimente.* VIEG, vol. 109. Wiesbaden, 1983.

Grane, Leif. *Contra Gabrielem. Luthers Auseinandersetzung mit Gabriel Biel in der Disputatio Contra Scholasticam Theologiam 1517.* Trans. Elfriede Pump. Copenhagen, 1962.

Hendrix, Scott H. *Ecclesia in Via: Ecclesiological Developments in the Medieval Psalms Exegesis and the Dictata super Psalterium (1513-1515).* SMRT, vol. 8. Leiden, 1974.

Junghans, Helmar. *Der junge Luther und die Humanisten.* Göttingen, 1984.

Loewenich, Walther von. *Luther's Theology of the Cross.* Minneapolis, 1976.

Lohse, Bernhard, ed. *Der Durchbruch der reformatorischen Erkenntnis bei Luther.* WdF, vol. 123. Darmstadt, 1968.

Lohse, Bernhard, ed. *Der Durchbruch der reformatorischen Erkenntnis bei Luther. Neuere Untersuchungen.* VIEG, suppl. vol. 25. Stuttgart, 1988.

Oberman, Heiko A. *The Dawn of the Reformation. Essays in Late Medieval and Early Reformation Thought.* Edinburgh, 1986.

Olivier, Daniel. *The Trial of Luther.* St. Louis, 1978.

Ozment, Steven. *Homo Spiritualis: a Comparative Study of the Anthropology of Tauler, Gerson, and Martin Luther (1509-1516).* SMRT, vol. 6. Leiden, 1968.

Prien, Hans-Jürgen. *Luthers Wirtschaftsethik.* Göttingen, 1992.

Reuter, Fritz, ed. *Der Reichstag zu Worms von 1521. Reichspolitik und Luthersache.* Worms, 1971.
Rupp, Gordon. *The Righteousness of God. Luther Studies.* 3d ed. London, 1953.
Schwab, Wolfgang. *Entwicklung und Gestalt der Sakramententheologie bei Martin Luther.* Frankfurt am Main and Bern, 1977.
Schwarz, Reinhard. *Fides, Spes und Caritas beim jungen Luther.* Berlin, 1962.
Stamm, Heinz Meinolf. *Luthers Stellung zum Ordensleben.* VIEG, vol. 101. Wiesbaden, 1980.
Steinmetz, David. *Luther and Staupitz.* Durham, N.C., 1980.
Wicks, Jared, S.J. *Man Yearning for Grace: Luther's Early Spiritual Teaching.* Washington D.C., 1968.
Wriedt, Markus. *Gnade und Erwählung. Eine Untersuchung zu Johann von Staupitz und Martin Luther.* VIEG, vol. 141. Mainz, 1991.

The Lutheran Church in Luther's Later Years
Barton, Peter F. *Die Geschichte der Evangelischen in Österreich und Südostmitteleuropa.* Vol. 1. *Im Schatten der Bauernkriege. Die Frühzeit der Reformation.* Jahrbuch für die Geschichte des Protestantismus in Österreich, vol. 101. Vienna, 1985.
Bizer, Ernst. *Studien zur Geschichte des Abendmahlsstreits im 16. Jahrhundert.* 2d ed. Darmstadt, 1962.
Brecht, Martin. *Die frühe Theologie des Johannes Brenz.* Beiträge zur Historischen Theologie, vol. 36. Tübingen, 1966.
Brecht, Martin and Ehmer, Hermann. *Südwestdeutsche Reformationsgeschichte.* Stuttgart, 1984.
Ebeling, Gerhard. *Lutherstudien.* Part 2, *Disputatio de Homine.* 3 vols. Tübingen, 1977-89.
Edwards, Mark U., Jr. *Luther and the False Brethren.* Stanford, 1975.
Edwards, Mark U., Jr. *Luther's Last Battles. Politics and Polemics, 1531-1546.* Ithaca, 1983.
Garstein, Oskar. *Rome and the Counter-Reformation in Scandinavia.* Vol. 1, *1539-1583.* Copenhagen, 1963.
Gaßmann, Günther. "Lutherische Kirchen." In *TRE*, vol. 21:599-616. Berlin, 1991.
Grane, Leif. *The Augsburg Confession. A Commentary.* Trans. John H. Rasmussen. Minneapolis, 1987.
Greschat, Martin. *Melanchthon neben Luther. Studien zur Gestalt der Rechtfertigungslehre zwischen 1528 und 1537.* Witten, 1965.
Grimm, Harold J. *Lazarus Spengler. A Lay Leader of the Reformation.* Columbus, Ohio, 1978.
Hahn, Gerhard. *Evangelium als literarischen Anweisung. Zu Luthers Stellung in der Geschichte des deutschen kirchlichen Liedes.* Munich and Zurich, 1981.
Junghans, Helmar, ed. *Das Jahrhundert der Reformation in Sachsen.* Berlin, 1988.
Köhler, Walther. *Zwingli und Luther. Ihr Streit über das Abendmahl nach seinen politischen und religiösen Beziehungen.* 2 vols. QFRG, vols. 6-7. Leipzig, 1924; Gütersloh, 1953.
Krumwiede, Hans-Walter. *Zur Entstehung des landesherrlichen Kirchenregiments in Kursachsen und Braunschweig-Wolfenbüttel.* Göttingen, 1967.
Leder, Hans-Günter and Norbert Buske. *Reform und Ordnung aus dem Wort. Johannes Bugenhagen und die Reformation im Herzogtum Pommern.* Berlin, 1985.
Lehmann, Martin. *Justus Jonas, Loyal Reformer.* Minneapolis, 1963.
Lienhard, Marc. *Luther, Witness to Jesus Christ. Stages and Themes of the Reformer's Christology.* Minneapolis, 1982.
Lindhardt, Poul Georg. "Skandinavische Kirchengeschichte seit dem 16. Jahrhundert." *Die Kirche in ihrer Geschichte,* vol. 3:235-314. Göttingen, 1982.
Lohff, Wenzel, ed. *450 Jahre Reformation in Hamburg.* Hamburg, 1980.

Lutheranism in the Holy Roman Empire and in Europe

Barton, Peter F. *Um Luthers Erbe. Studien und Texte zur Spätreformation.* Untersuchungen zur Kirchengeschichte, vol. 6. Witten, 1972.

Brecht, Martin, and Reinhard Schwarz, eds. *Bekenntnis und Einheit der Kirche. Studien zum Konkordienbuch.* Stuttgart, 1980.

Heckel, Martin. *Gesammelte Schriften.* Vol. 1. Tübingen, 1989.

Kolb, Robert. *Nikolaus von Amsdorf (1483-1565).* Bibliotheca Humanistica et Reformatorica, vol. 24. Nieuwkoop, 1978.

Mahlmann, Theodor. *Das neue Dogma der lutherischen Christologie.* Gütersloh, 1969.

Maurer, Wilhelm. *Historischer Kommentar zur Confessio Augustana.* 2 vols. Gütersloh, 1976-78.

Oberman, Heiko A. *The Roots of Antisemitism in the Age of the Renaissance and Reformation.* Trans. James Porter. Philadelphia, 1983.

Peters, Albrecht. *Kommentar zu Luthers Katechismen.* Vol. 1, *Die Zehn Gebote.* Göttingen, 1990.

Preus, Robert D. *The Theology of Post-Reformation Lutheranism.* St. Louis, 1970.

Rublack, Hans-Christoph, ed. *Die lutherische Konfessionalisierung in Deutschland.* SVRG, no. 197. Gütersloh, 1992.

Schwarz Lausten, Martin. "Dänemark I." *TRE*, vol. 8:304-6. Berlin, 1981.

Schwarz, Reinhard, ed. *Die Augsburger Kirchenordnung und ihr Umfeld.* SVRG, no. 196. Gütersloh, 1988.

Seebaß, Gottfried. "The Reformation in Nuremberg." In *The Social History of the Reformation*, ed. Lawrence P. Buck und Jonathan W. Zophy, 17-40. Columbus, Ohio, 1972.

Spitz, Lewis W., and Wenzel Lohff, eds. *Discord, Dialogue and Concord. Studies in the Lutheran Reformation's Formula of Concord.* Philadelphia, 1977.

Steitz, Heinrich. *Geschichte der Evangelischen Kirche in Hessen und Nassau.* Vol. 1, *Reformatorische Bewegungen, Reformationen, Nachreformationen.* Marburg, 1961.

Strauss, Gerald. *Luther's House of Learning: Indoctrination of the Young in German Reformation.* Baltimore, 1978.

Wartenberg, Günther. *Landesherrschaft und Reformation. Moritz von Sachsen und die albertinische Kirchenpolitik bis 1546.* Gütersloh, 1988.

Wolgast, Eike. *Die Wittenberger Theologie und die Politik der evangelischen Stände. Studien zu Luthers Gutachten in politischen Fragen.* QFRG, vol. 47. Gütersloh, 1977.

THE POPULAR REFORMATION

Peter Blickle
(Universität Bern)

Throughout Europe in the early 1520s, the name of Martin Luther was on many lips, if not on all. The Spanish Inquisition prohibited the importation of his writings, while in Sweden they were read avidly. At Meaux in France, dissidents and heretics were vilified as Lutherans, while in the mining regions of Hungary people were already familiar with Luther's principal writings by 1522. Luther polarized people, yet both friend and foe associated a new kind of Christianity with his name, which they referred to as the "Lutheran doctrine" or "Lutheran sect." How did the common people conceive of Luther?

1. THE REFORMATION MESSAGE

Martin Luther was formed by his personal experiences as a monk and his academic studies of the Holy Scriptures as Professor of Exegesis at Wittenberg.[1] His painful experience, that the Church's methods of obtaining grace had absolutely no effect on him despite his strict observance of the monastic vows, made him skeptical of the doctrine of grace then prevailing in the Church. According to this doctrine, God had mercy on whoever strove to realize the abilities God had imparted to them through the divine act of creation: "If man does what he can, God will grant him grace [*Facientibus, quod in se est, Deus dat gratiam*]." Yet Luther's own experience was that human strivings could only be sinful. His problem was how to find a merciful God, and because this question deeply concerned everyone in the West, his answer had the potential of becoming universally accepted.

Luther found a relatively simple answer to his question: God makes the sinner righteous when the sinner is justified before God, that is, when the sinner believes. Belief and grace as mutually dependent categories are central to Luther's doctrine of "justification by faith," which is the centerpiece of his theology. The experience of wickedness in thought and deed is reconciled with grace by arguing that the person is "at the same time righteous and a sinner [*simul iustus et peccator*]," that the sinner while sinner is justified before God and man. The path towards belief is the "Word," Christ, the revealed word of God in the form of the gospel. Around grace, belief, and the Bible, Luther organized his theology.

Luther's teaching on grace had devastating consequences for the Roman Church. The central role played by the sacraments in salvation was made unnecessary, and with them the priests who administered them. This the first threat to the Church, an institution which derived its understanding of itself from precisely this administration of salvation through its dispensation of the sacraments. The second threat to the old Church was to deprive it of its doctrinal authority. "The Bible alone [*sola scriptura*]," Luther's norm for dealing with revelation, was intended to mean that scripture "interpreted itself [*sui ipsius interpres*]" for the believer. With this one blow, the exegetical functions claimed by the papacy and the general councils were eliminated.

The practical consequences of this theological approach are that the parish replaces the hierarchically organized Church as a community of believers, and within it each believer has the potential to interpret the word of God, that is, to be a priest. Good works, and therefore the Mass as the central rite of Catholicism, are made irrelevant to salvation. All interpretations and codicils added by the Roman Church amount to restrictions on "Christian freedom" and must thus be eliminated, along with the Church's unjust canon law. Monks are now seen as men who selfishly seek their own salvation and thereby make themselves burdensome to other people. Truly Christian, by contrast, is the conscientious fulfillment of one's calling, because in this calling the basic Christian tenet of brotherly love can and must ultimately express itself. Max Weber's assessment of this position was that this moral qualification of the worldly vocational pursuit was one of the Reformation's most significant achievements.[2]

All of the reformers essentially shared these basic convictions. What Ulrich (Huldrych) Zwingli and John Calvin added lies principally in the area of ethics and in the related sphere of political theory. For Luther, worldly rule is, from a historical point of view, the result of the Fall of Adam and Eve. Since people tend towards evil and anarchy because of Original Sin, power must be wielded in the world in order to preserve the creation from destruction. Because the primary authority attested to by the Old Testament is the father's rule over the home, the family becomes both the origin of and model for legitimate political authority. The consequences are clear: temporal rule must be accepted as divinely established and preferably, as the paternal comparison suggests, in patriarchal, that is, monarchical, form. Zwingli and Calvin viewed the matter similarly, though both made an exception for the extreme case of tyrannical rule. Resistance to a tyrant, who demonstrates his illegitimacy primarily through godlessness, is possible, but it must take place within the strict confines of the legitimate exercise of authority. In other words, the exercise of power is not the province of individuals, but is reserved to subordinate authorities: noble lords, urban magistrates or their leagues, parliaments and estates.

These introductory comments about the basic positions of reformed theologies and political ideas, brief as they must be, are essential to any understanding of the "popular Reformation" in Europe. The phrase "popular Reformation" here describes the phase of the complicated process of reform that was shaped by the burghers and peasants, that is, by the people, as contrasted with the political, social, and intellectual elites.

2. THE FIRST PHASE: THE HOLY ROMAN EMPIRE

The Reformation first unfolded in Luther's immediate sphere of influence—the Holy Roman Empire of the German Nation—mainly because Luther primarily employed the German language to convey his teachings. The Reformation in Central Europe is difficult to periodize, though there is some agreement that an initial phase of activity, in which broad groups of society took part, was followed by a phase of consolidation under the aegis of the German princes.[3] The year 1525 represents a watershed, and not only for the history of the Reformation. For Otto von Gierke, the jurist who accomplished for the thematization of European legal history what Max Weber did for sociology, it was a pivotal year because thereafter authoritarian forms of government supplanted corporative ones for the next 300 years.[4] The most recent research in urban history, however, has pushed forward into the 1530s the end of the phase during which the Reformation was spread by the people.[5]

The Reception of Reformation Thought, 1521-1525
In the Empire, burghers and peasants were separate groups distilled out of the originally undifferentiated estate of the "those who work

[*laboratores*]." These two major social groups were first differentiated
by the progressive division of labor between agriculture and the crafts
during the late Middle Ages and by the difference of scale between
towns and villages. For this reason, it may make sense to present separately the reactions of two sectors of the people, burghers and peasants, to the reformers' appeals.

The Burghers' Reformation

Despite what appears at first glance to be the varied development of
the Reformation in the cities, recent analyses have worked out a single
generalized developmental model which accounts for both the actors
and their motives. We will first describe the process paradigmatically,
using the Imperial free city of Memmingen, and then from this model
offer some general insights into the process.

Memmingen as Paradigm

Memmingen lies in South Germany between the Danube and the Alps,
halfway between Lake Constance and Munich. At the time of the Reformation, it was a medium-sized city. Its constitution was strongly influenced by the guilds, and economically the city prospered from a
solid crafts sector and a long-distance trade dominated by old patrician
families.

According to an entry in the council's minutes for 21 August 1524,
"the preacher at St. Martin's gave a wicked sermon on the street fourteen days ago, saying that the rich are not punished as much as the
poor, . . . and he added that he wanted to make the community aware
of this."[6] The city council was in an uproar. A delegation was sent to
the preacher, Dr. Christoph Schappeler, to warn him against inciting
the community against the council.

Schappeler's sermons were also responsible for causing unrest in the
following years. He preached that Masses were pointless, and that the
priests were unfit for their office because of their ignorance of theology
and the bad examples they set. Canon law was nothing other than a
huge pile of unchristian papal regulations. These charges created tensions and conflicts in the city, for the burghers had endowed numerous
Masses, and from these funds and from forty-four chaplaincies, about
130 priests drew their livings. In 1523, Schappeler's tone turned
sharper:

> It will come to pass, that the clergy will be forced to confess their
> sins to the laity; . . . that, God be praised, the laity of both sexes are
> more learned than the clergy and can preach the Word of God.
> There is no priest who knows what the word "gospel" means in
> German.[7]

Such invective may have reflected existing hostilities between the
burghers and city council, on the one hand, and the clergy, on the
other. In 1494 Memmingen's council had lodged a complaint against
the city's priests with the papal legate to the Empire that the priests
flouted the council's authority, marched armed through the streets at
night, and "did violence to the burghers now and then." They adorned
themselves with fringed garments instead of cassocks and started
drunken brawls with burghers instead of leading exemplary lives, for
they were often drunk. Two decades later, the town turned to the
archbishop of Mainz with the accusation that

> the priests here dismiss, do not obey, and disgracefully insult our
> lawful and honorable edict, statute, and law, which we passed in our
> city because of the games, cards, long knives, and other things, and
> which our burghers and residents are obliged to observe upon pain
> of fines and punishments. The clergy's behavior gives cause to our
> common man to disregard our edicts and laws, although the priests
> really ought to set a good example for the people rather than
> encourage our common man to be recalcitrant.[8]

Sermons such as Schappeler's involved the bishop (of Augsburg), who
eventually demanded that Schappeler be handed over to the clerical
courts. This had the effect of mobilizing Schappeler's supporters, who
may be described as a "conventicle"—middling burghers and some intellectuals, but few of the poor and only one patrician.[9] The council
was undecided, split down the middle between those supporting reform and those supporting the Roman Church, and declined to deliver
Schappeler up.

Things deteriorated dramatically in 1523, when Schappeler
preached that there were no theological reasons to pay tithes. Immediately after the next harvest, in the summer of 1524, many burghers and
the peasants from the villages surrounding the city stopped paying
tithes. The city council, concerned about the continued operation of
the hospital, which received the lion's share of the tithes, insisted energetically and successfully that the tithes be paid, and one recalcitrant
burgher was imprisoned. The burghers gathered spontaneously in the
marketplace, organized a committee to represent the guilds, secured

the release of the arrested man, and demanded, among other things, a doctrinal debate with the council.

Now the pace of events accelerated. On 5 December 1524 Schappeler for the first time administered communion with both elements in the parish Church of St. Martin. In another parish, the Church of Our Lady, which was located where the poor lived, people demanded that the "pure gospel" be preached. The women were especially vociferous. On Christmas Day there was a riot in the Church of Our Lady: windows and pictures were smashed, the tips of candles chopped off, altars overturned, and objects thrown at the priest. Beaten and driven into the sacristy for refuge, the priest was finally taken into protective custody by the mayor and the city council members present. Without their help, averred the priest, "I would have been beaten to death in the sacristy," which was confirmed by the council members.[10]

Peace urgently needed to be established again in the city, and apparently the council felt that having the debate which had been demanded for some time was the only way to restore it. It was scheduled immediately and convened on 2 January 1525 in the presence of all of the city's clergymen, all of the council members, as well as "a person from each guild to represent the community," elected by the guilds themselves.[11]

Schappeler had prepared seven theses, but the clergymen who held to the old faith did not defend themselves and clearly did not want to, as demonstrated by their argument that disputation belonged in ecclesiastical councils or in the lecture halls of universities. The city council came up with a truly euphemistic description for the whole enterprise's outcome: everyone "agreed upon the matter at hand."[12] Now the Reformation cause was able to set up house in the city: the rites of the old faith were suppressed, the clergy required to take citizenship, the monasteries in the city confiscated by the city council, and a new church ordinance drafted.

The Urban Reformation

The case of Memmingen can be generalized on the basis of the rich literature on the urban Reformation. The cities took up the reform impulse with astonishingly near unanimity. A crude rule of thumb, allowing for exceptions,[13] might be that those cities in which the civic regime was weak went over to the side of the Reformation.[14] The imperial cities[15] confirm this rule, as do territorial cities such as Erfurt[16] and Kitzingen.[17] This given, one can easily correlate 1) the social basis of the urban reform, 2) the course of the reforming process, and 3) the movement's goals, if one is willing to accept a certain degree of abstraction.

The judgment that the "people" participated considerably in the urban Reformation has been accepted since Kurt Kaser's work at the turn of the century.[18] "The people," however, is a vague expression, too little analytical to be used as a technical term. Historians used it for quite a while,[19] before it was superseded in the 1970s by the phrase "Reformation from below." Underlying this concept is the idea that different social groups or classes absorb ideas quite differently. The social history of the Reformation in this stricter sense began with the work of Robert Scribner[20] and Thomas A. Brady, whose work on Strasbourg, thanks to its empirical breadth, unleashed an extensive debate.[21] Brady argues that the Protestant attacks on the Mass and the religious icons endangered the chapels, altars, and Mass funds, which had been endowed by the political and economic elite. The refusal to pay tithes and interest hit the patricians as receivers of such incomes hard, while the dissolution of the monasteries and convents threatened the welfare of their sons and daughters. Strasbourg's elites ultimately carried out reform only because they could not otherwise have maintained their positions. In reality, the Reformation was "a story of attack and threat from below."[22]

Brady's arguments rest on a collective biography, or prosopography, of Strasbourg's magistrates, a methodological approach that has since become established and even today is viewed as the ideal method for researching the urban Reformation.[23] Objections have been raised to his interpretation, however, and have found their way into current German surveys in the form of such claims as the following: "in general it may be said that the upper classes, including the political elite, were open to the new thought to essentially the same degree as the guilds and less well-to-do burghers."[24] This statement is difficult to square with the fact that in almost all cities the beginning of the Reformation was accompanied by revolts.[25]

Our interpretative ability may be enhanced by a structural approach to the course of the Reformation. The reform movement began in small, socially heterogeneous circles—often referred to as "conventicles"—which sometimes received a strong impetus from the poorer and lower classes, either the weavers or suburban residents,[26] but divisions quickly surfaced between the commune and the city council. In confrontational situations, the burghers established a committee, which negotiated with the city council reforms. Depending on the specific constitutional structure of the city, the committee might be recruited by guilds, parishes, or the residential districts.[27] It was often the committees which, by means of religious debates—since Zurich's in 1523 called "disputations"—brought about religious unity by acting as a representative body for the commune and deciding in judicial fashion, along with the city council, what was correct doctrine.[28] The old scholarly debate over whether the urban Reformation was a "magisterial reformation" or was shaped by the people or the citizens, can be settled by the finding that "the community" was the engine for the Reformation's introduction.[29]

From this starting point, strongly grounded in constitutional and political history, we can also explain the reception of reformed theology and ethics. The urban Reformation always involved making the urban clergy—both the priests and religious orders—equal to the burghers by giving them the same rights and duties.[30] Equal duties meant paying taxes, helping to defray the costs of the constabulary, and the loss of benefit of clergy for the sale of things produced by ecclesiastical institutions. Equal rights meant being subject to the municipal courts and, therefore, the loss of the clergy's legal privilege of being subject only to ecclesiastical courts.[31] Ultimately, such an egalitarian move raised the question of equal rights for all residents of the city.

The urban reformation's theological dimension was encapsulated in the word "gospel," which developed into an extremely emotional and very effective popular slogan. "Gospel" became the irreducible abbreviation for "pure gospel," which, as shorthand for "gospel without human teachings," referred to the repudiation of the doctrinal tradition of the Church, both dogmas and canon law. The urban reformation thus based itself strongly on the proclamation of the "gospel," and in order to guarantee the correct content of sermons, the city community logically demanded the right to appoint priests and to decide on doctrinal matters in the case of disagreement, as the many disputations amply demonstrate. Once these demands had finally been accepted, lay jurisdiction in religious matters was returned to the city council. All of the attempts to frame church ordinances (*Kirchordnungen*) had the character of law.

At the present time, research on the urban Reformation seems to have exhausted all possible interpretations. The most recent historiographical phase began with the work of Bernd Moeller,[32] who combines constitutional with theological themes. His thesis holds that the city, which understood itself as "Christian body [*corpus christianum*]," responded to the appeal for reform with the desire to christianize the communal polity. This general concern could lead to various manifestations of reform, depending on the constitutional structure of the city: "the more corporative structured and corporatively committed communes" of South Germany "fell to Zwingli and Bucer,"[33] while the Franconian cities, with their patrician constitutions (e.g., Nuremberg) opted for Luther. The analytical rigor with which Moeller divided the South German from the Lutheran Reformation and the synthetic power with which he cast constitutional structure and theology as mutually dependent, have made his book extremely influential.[34]

Moeller has opposed the newer interpretation, which Thomas A. Brady's social approach brought to the debate,[35] with increasing force, despite the empirical progress this approach has made. Moeller fears the "specter of 'sociologism,'"[36] against which Brady has noted that the historian must explain what can be explained with the methods that lie to hand.[37] Possibly, in his view, religious conviction and confessional choices cannot be explained historically.[38]

Other methods have been explored. Heinrich Richard Schmidt has used the records of the free cities' assemblies, called "urban diets [*Städtetage*]," a previously neglected source, to show that the urban reformation began on the basis of Luther's doctrine of justification, which, with its appeal to the "gospel," did not at first polarize urban society. Under the leadership of Zwingli and the South German urban reformers, however, the movement soon began to seek political changes. The "common man" expressed himself in the pressure for change, which in Schmidt's interpretation made him the "patron" of the Reformation. The city councils, responsible for law and order inside the city, merely carried out the wishes of the majority of the commune by "introducing" the Reformation through the reorganization of the church, thereby becoming the reform movement's heirs.[39]

The Peasants' Reformation

For a long time the Reformation was interpreted as an exclusively intellectual event, which effectively excluded rural society.[40] Even in recent works, the burghers are sometimes sharply contrasted to the peasants. "The magical incantations for the blessing of the harvest," writes one historian, "and the peal of the bells against hail and lightning were

more important to the peasants than acquiring an understanding of
God's grace."[41] The peasant who read and discussed the Bible, the
peasant "who knows his own mind [*wird witzig*]," as pamphlets often
referred to him, was long considered an invention of Reformation
propaganda, a foil used to denounce more effectively the theological
ignorance of the priests and monks.[42] Such views may now be considered obsolete.[43] Indisputably, the Reformation in the early 1520s was
a movement both of burghers and peasants.[44]

Wendelstein as Paradigm

We can approach the peasants' reformation as we did the burghers'
reformation, beginning with a single community, the Franconian village of Wendelstein.[45] It was a typical South German village, in that it
possessed its own administration. Wendelstein's commune admitted
new members, elected the two mayors (*Dorfmeister*) and the eight jurors (*Dorfpfleger*), managed the village's property, and regulated the
economy of the village and its lands.

Wendelstein also possessed a parish church, to which the margrave
of Ansbach had held the right of pastoral presentation since 1464. Piety in Wendelstein apparently flourished. There was a confraternity,
many endowed anniversaries (*Jahrtage*) and votive commemorations
(*Gedenktage*), and most importantly an endowed early Mass which
brought in enough—52 florins (*Gulden*) per year—to fund a benefice.
Two important altarpieces were built for this church just before the
Reformation. Three churchwardens (*Kirchpröpste*), elected by the
parish assembly each Ascension Day, managed the church's assets.

The villagers' devotion, however, was not matched by the quality of
its pastoral care. Their priest, Hieronymus von Ansbach, neglected his
duties so much that his patron, the margrave, had to force him to resign. His vicar, Friedrich Santner, a native Wendelsteiner, was at first
very popular, and his kinsfolk helped him to renovate the dilapidated
presbytery. Soon, he ran into difficulties, however, because his income
was little more than a mere thirty florins. Despite the fact that he received a third of the large and of the small tithe, pension payments to
the retired pastor seriously reduced his regular income. Santner therefore introduced a new fee for the sacraments, based on an old register
the legality of which the villagers denied. The ensuing fruitless dispute
between him and his flock dragged on for years through every court in
the land, until it landed in the episcopal court at Eichstätt. During this
tension-filled time, priests sometimes came from Nuremberg to

Wendelstein, baptized children in German in the houses, and spoke contemptuously of the Mass. Anyone interested merely in sensational novelty attended services in nearby Nuremberg.

Apparently, the peasants of Wendelstein began to demand the preaching of the pure gospel, just like the burghers. In 1523 they hired a "Christian preacher," whom they paid by splitting the cost themselves. People spoke of a "schism" in the village, violence was done to the priest who followed the old teaching, causing him to ask repeatedly to be transferred. Finally, the margrave of Ansbach agreed to the investiture of a new priest. On 19 October 1524 his official (*Amtmann*) at Schwabach installed Kaspar Krantz in his pastoral duties, on which occasion a representative of Wendelstein made a speech that became famous when it was printed as a pamphlet in the same year. "We will not recognize you as a lord," he told Krantz, "but only as a servant of the community. We will command you, not you us, and we order you to preach the gospel and the word of God purely, clearly, and truthfully—without any human teachings [*Menschenlehre*]—faithfully and conscientiously."[46] The representative did not conceal that the village commune was determined to be boss. The new priest was required to live in exemplary fashion, to "live the gospel in your deeds as a faithful servant of Jesus Christ in the community and in the church." Endowment and tithes would guarantee an income befitting his social rank, so that the village would no longer have to pay for all supplementary expenditures "with collections, Masses for the dead, venerations, and other made up things that make for us a lot of expense." They even wanted to put a halt to the endless lawsuits, for should Krantz make demands on the villagers, he would have to use the local courts and not that of the bishop (at Eichstätt).

Krantz, as time would tell, was not prepared to submit unconditionally to the communal will, he even came into conflict with the preacher who had already been hired by the community. Yet later events do not help us clarify the peasants' religious understanding, because in 1525 the conflicts over the parish at Wendelstein were resolved by the Imperial free city of Nuremberg and the margrave of Ansbach. After the crushing of the Peasants' War in 1525, the village community no longer had a voice.

The Rural Reformation
The shapes of a rural reformation can be detected since 1523,[47] beginning in the territory of the Imperial city of Zurich.[48] It quickly spread

during the next two years, extending in the east to Salzburg,[49] in the west to Alsace,[50] in the south down to Trent, and in the north to the border between Thuringia and Saxony. The demands now made by the peasants on the Church were comparatively uniform and may be summarized as follows. Theologically, the peasants' understanding of reformation expressed itself in the demand for: 1) preaching of the "pure gospel;" 2) appointment of the priest by the community; and 3) the right to enjoy doctrinal authority. Organizationally, the peasants' understanding of the Reformation manifested itself in the desire for: 1) the priest to reside in the village; 2) a less expensive church; and 3) the abolition or reduction of the ecclesiastical courts' jurisdictions.

At first, the term "pure gospel" as used by the peasants had the same meaning as it did in the cities. The concern was that sermons be drawn from the gospel without being seriously changed by ecclesiastical tradition. The peasants repeatedly emphasized that they could not be saved without the preaching of the gospel. They also drew practical consequences for their life in this world: the pure gospel encourages the common good (*gemeiner Nutzen*) and the practice of "brotherly love," promotes equality, and aims at a christianization of society.[51] In this sense, the pure gospel, functioning as a kind of law (*lex*), was supposed to guide political and judicial affairs. This understanding of the gospel, expressed by the phrase "godly law," was of great significance in the Peasants' War.

After the "pure gospel," the election of priests played a prominent role. Control over appointments alone guaranteed that sermons would be faithful to scripture, for the community would decide in borderline cases whether a priest was true to the Word. The conviction of the village communes, that a schism can be ironed out through disputation, was not shared by the cities.

If salvation required access to the Word of God, it was essential that the priest live in the village. If he was paid sufficiently out of endowment and tithes, then fees and taxes for baptisms, weddings, burials, and other rituals were entirely unnecessary. If canon law made no sense whatsoever, then it seemed reasonable to transfer the jurisdiction of the ecclesiastical courts to the local and village courts. Just like the cities, the villages attempted to communalize the Church.

Political Consequences: The Peasants' War
Popular pressure for fundamental changes was stronger in the Reformation than ever before and thereafter in German history. Hundreds

of thousands took part in it. The change from the Old Regime to a modern constitutional monarchy and to industrialism was, by comparison, an elite undertaking, in which some hundreds of enlightened burghers took part. To a certain degree, the Peasants' War can be seen as an escalation of the peasants' (and the burghers') reformation—though the Reformation alone does not explain it fully—while the ensuing magisterial reformation of the princes was a reaction to the popular reformation.

"Anno Domini 1525. At the beginning of this year there was a large, unheard of revolt of the common man everywhere in the whole of *Germania*," wrote a contemporary observer.[52] "The whole of *Germania*" meant both more and less than Germany—the area of rebellion ran from Leipzig to Trent, and from the border of Lorraine to the border of Upper Austria. It included large parts of Switzerland, but large areas of northern and western Germany were not involved at all. Contemporaries were of the opinion that "such rebellion is both caused and defeated by tyranny; tyranny and rebellion go hand in hand, as the lid goes with the pot."[53]

The uprising began between Basel and Lake Constance in the summer of 1524, accompanied by iconoclasm and the refusal to pay feudal dues.[54] At first, the peasants sought legal compensation. Those of the county of Stühlingen near Lake Constance filed a massive list of grievances numbering 62 articles with the Imperial Chamber Court (*Reichskammergericht*), criticizing the hardships of serfdom, unjustly high taxes, and serious abuses in the administration of justice.

The unrest spread quickly, reaching in January 1525 the region of Upper Swabia, where tens of thousands of peasants assembled in three large encampments (*Haufen*). Since their lords wanted to negotiate, they drew up lists of grievances. Admittedly, the peasants no longer cared about legal proceedings, demanding instead that "the godly law that tells every estate what it is proper to do or not to do" be used as a standard of judgment.[55] This meant nothing else than using the "gospel" to measure the justice of civil agreements, which meant transforming theologians into judicial arbiters. The most famous list of grievances from the Peasants' War, the "Twelve Articles of the Upper Swabian Peasants," was adopted at a peasants' parliament at Memmingen in March of 1525. In it the peasants pleaded for a reduction of dues, the introduction of the reformation, the abolition of serfdom, the freedom to hunt and fish, and the extension of communal rights. The

"Twelve Articles" acknowledged the implications of using the "gospel" as a standard of justice by referring to Luther, Zwingli, and other well-known reformers as "judges."[56]

At the same time when these grievances were formulated, the Upper Swabians worked out a "federal ordinance [*Bundesordnung*]" for the "Christian Association [*Christliche Vereinigung*]," as they called their alliance. Each of the three troops (*Haufen*) elected four councilors and a chief (*Oberst*) to act as representatives of the community. The three chiefs were to serve as the rulers and the twelve councilors as the parliamentary body. It was truly only a small step away from becoming a republic.

The reformers either failed entirely to react to the peasants' wishes, or they attacked them, while the princes armed themselves and prepared to move on the peasant encampments. And so it came to war. Already by the end of March, twenty-three monasteries and twenty-four castles had been either "burned" or "plundered," according to a rather sensationalist pamphlet.

Now the rebellion expanded in all directions. The "Twelve Articles" delivered the demands, the "federal ordinance" served as a framework for the organization. The peasants from the Franconian and Swabian border country around Rothenburg ob der Tauber and around Heilbronn forced those further west and north to join them. The adoption of the "Twelve Articles" in the archbishopric of Mainz in May of 1525 was a spectacular event, which was soon followed by numerous urban riots, beginning in Mainz and Frankfurt and extending to Cologne, plus equally spectacular seizures, against token resistance, of the monasteries all the way to Saxony. The residents of Bamberg declared that they did not want "to leave any castle, any monastery in the country standing," and they burnt 200 castles in three days. Accompanying these events there was always talk of a "Reformation," which now had to be addressed because of the peasants' and burghers' demands. The term referred to Imperial reform, and in modern parlance they had in mind a constitutional assembly in which not only peasants and burghers, but also nobles and above all theologians, would participate.

From Upper Swabia the revolt spread to the Alpine countries, where Tyrol, Salzburg, and the Graubünden (Grisons) became strongholds of the rebellion. The Salzburgers won a spectacular victory against the nobles at Schladming; the Tyrolean parliament (*Landtag*) forced Archduke Ferdinand to have drafted a provincial constitution (*Landesord-*

nung) that remained in force for a century; and the Graubündners gained their independence from their lord, the prince-bishop of Chur.

Meanwhile, the prelates, nobles, and princes looked on, paralyzed by the peasants' triumphs. Monks fled their monasteries and hid their habits, so as not to be recognized. Nobles fled their castles, in which they no longer felt safe. And Princes left their residences to seek refuge in the imperial cities. Elector Frederick the Wise (d. 1525) of Saxony said resignedly that "if God so desires it, then so it will come to pass that the common man will reign."[57] It was above all the Catholic princes of Bavaria, Lorraine, and Saxony who energetically drove off the nightmare. The charismatic Thomas Müntzer (d. 1525) stood preaching in the peasant encampment near Frankenhausen when the first cannonballs of the unified princes' army struck on May 15. Panic broke out among the peasants, who had confidently expected God's judgment in their favor. It cannot really be called a battle: out of 6,000 peasants, 5,000 were killed. The Battle of Frankenhausen was nearly contemporary with a battle in Alsace near Zabern/Saverne and another near Böblingen in Württemberg, which sealed the defeat of the peasants.

Today, the causes, goals, and consequences of the Peasants' War are interpreted in a relatively coherent fashion.[58] Earlier interpretations viewed the Peasants' War as an insurrection that was difficult to explain in the wake of the Reformation, a view which found classical expression in Leopold von Ranke's dictum that it was a "natural event." Another interpretation, which was authoritative for decades, came from Günther Franz in 1933.[59] For him the Peasants' War was a consequence of the development of the territorial state at the expense of the old rights of the villages. Its goal was therefore to remove princely rule and replace it with the emperor; its failure necessarily led to a victory of the princes and thus prepared the way for the early modern, princely territorial state.

Causes

The causes of the Peasants' War were, at first, economic. A slowly rising population brought with it relative poverty, especially since the use of common land was being restricted and the state's burden of taxation increased. This situation promoted social tensions in the villages, as the gap between rich and poor grew, and the lords reactivated serfdom in order to prevent their subjects from migrating to the city.[60] The enormous growth in the peasants' political expectations, however,

must also be counted among the causes of the insurrection. The villages had in the recent past noticeably expanded their administrative
competences, and they were widely represented in the territorial parliaments or other corporate bodies.[61] That the Peasants' War did not
erupt earlier is clearly related to problems of legitimacy and legality of
direct action. The legitimizing principle of "the old law [*das Alte
Recht*]" was closely tied to the specific lordships and not, therefore, a
general principle, and as a law transmitted by oral tradition alone it
was highly vulnerable to being used by the lords for their own purposes.[62] The Reformation may be said to have performed the service of
placing the peasants in a position to interpret the "pure gospel" in legal
terms as a guideline for developing positive legal code by means of the
category of "godly law." Zwingli's influence, most likely, was at work
here. Unlike "the old law," "godly law" by nature recognized no territorial boundaries, so it enabled solidarity between peasants across
large distances. The coming of "godly law" also unleashed a fundamentally new debate about the proper structure of society and so became at least potentially revolutionary.[63]

Goals

The peasants' demanded of the elites that they make the "gospel" and
"godly law" a reality. To the extent that the "gospel" was also native
to the urban Reformation, it made possible alliances across the social
boundaries between estates. Cooperation between peasants and
burghers developed with little difficulty in all the larger territories,
wherever territorial (i.e, not Imperial free) cities and villages worked
together. This was the case notably in Württemberg, Franconia,
Thuringia, and Tyrol. Such alliances were also formed with the suburban populations and the poor classes of Imperial free cities, such as
Heilbronn, Rothenburg ob der Tauber, and Wissembourg, as well as
with the miners in Tyrol and Salzburg.

Wherever the rebels came to hold sway, their actions created a governmental vacuum that had to be filled in both theory and practice.
Conceptually, this occurred in one of two distinct ways, depending on
the existing constitutional structures in the areas of rebellion.[64] The
first way, following the Upper Swabian "federal ordinance [*Bundesordnung*]," based a republican constitution on the communes and on
representative organs (councils and military committees). This form
appeared in Franconia and in the Southwest. The other way, in territories which already had territorial corporate institutions, altered the ex-

isting constitution by merely excluding the prelates, reducing noble influence, and enhancing greatly the roles of the urban, market town, rural, village, and mountain communes. This form appeared in Württemberg, Tyrol, Salzburg and, with modifications, in other ecclesiastical states. The communes elected their representatives to the territorial parliament, and this assembly elected a regime (*Regiment*) which ruled with or without the territorial prince.

Consequences

The Peasant War's military defeat led to brutal acts of vengeance here and there, but conditions for the peasants did not worsen fundamentally, and in some parts of the Empire they were even improved by contractual agreements and newly drafted territorial constitutions (*Landesordnungen*). Wherever treaties were signed, they were legally binding and, down to the eighteenth century, were often used as grounds for suits precedents before the highest Imperial courts. What Winfried Schulze has called the "judicialization [*Verrechtlichung*]" of social conflicts" is related to this phenomenon.[65] His thesis rests on the observation that, to an increasing degree between the sixteenth and the eighteenth century, the peasants turned to the courts to defend their rights and assert their interests. In general, the treaties and the territorial constitutions led to a reduction of feudal dues and greater legal security, chiefly by fixing peasant and lordly demands.

As a revolution, the German Peasants' War never had a chance to succeed. The debate launched about "godly law," which was nothing less than a debate in Christian language about the basic principle of natural rights, was broken off without any results, and the princes energetically took over the reform movement and made it their own.

The Territorial Reformation

We know today that during the century before the Reformation, the princes had striven to improve morals and piety, to undertake a reform of the monasteries and pastoral care, and to reduce the power of the ecclesiastical courts and gain more control over them.[66] To this extent, the concerns of the princes overlapped with other desires for reform, though they displayed little obvious commitment to the Reformation before 1525. After the Peasants' War, however, the traditional elites became more energetic in pursuing reform at the territorial as well as at the Imperial level. As Bernd Moeller has written, "another ecclesiastical hierarchy" sprang up everywhere, and the newly emerging church governments "impressed an official and bureaucratic character upon the entire ecclesiastical apparatus."[67] Heiko A. Oberman agrees:

> The enormous disadvantages of this princely Reformation via bureaucratization, which assumed increasing influence over appointments and doctrine, . . . meant above all a disappearance of communal autonomy and the increasing readiness, based on the "right to reform [*ius reformandi*]," to accord to the prince a political power unrestrained by church or theology. This occurred under the sign of a false interpretation of Luther's doctrine of the "Two Kingdoms." From an emergency bishop the prince became a "territorial patriarch [*Landesvater*]" ordained by God.[68]

Rainer Wohlfeil believes that since the Imperial Diet at Speyer in 1526, "the Imperial estates [*Reichsstände*] strove not to include the 'Common Man' in, but to exclude him from, the process of social communication."[69]

The popular Reformation continued in the Imperial free cities and in a few territorial cities whose ruling princes were weak,[70] but these were admittedly isolated developments that lacked the local integration of effort that characterized the burghers' and peasants' reformations in South Germany. The movement called "Anabaptists [*Täufer*]" drew its own consequences from these events and undertook a kind of radical Reformation, based on the community as a voluntary association of individuals, a kind of "free church" beyond the state's power.[71]

3. The Spread of the Reformation

It is a historiographical commonplace that the "popular Reformation" was limited to Germany, Switzerland, and part of Austria.[72] The insurmountable difficulties encountered by the "evangelicals outside Germany in converting the initial enthusiasm for church reform into a viable popular movement"[73] is indisputable. Andrew Pettegree recently explained this by means of three factors: the quantity and quality of the German pamphlets; the very great number of cities; and the uniquely severe condition of conflict between the Empire and the Roman Curia.

The truth is, however, that impulses toward a popular Reformation appeared in many parts of Europe, principally in the cities. Only France, where the movement developed in the countryside as well, supplies (at best a weak) parallel to developments in Central Europe.

Popular Reformation and the Cities

Because of the number and wealth of its cities, it makes sense to begin this brief survey with the Netherlands. Although the reform movement began at about the same time in the Netherlands as in the other parts of the Holy Roman Empire, it made little progress in the first half of the sixteenth century, mainly because of harsh government repression. Between 1523 and 1555, the government had executed some 53 heretics in the Walloon states, 100 in Flanders, and 384 in the county of Holland.[74] As in the German cities, the partisans of the Reformation organized conventicles recruited from the better-off artisans, particularly those in the luxury trades. They devoted themselves to the study of the Bible and developed a lively communal life, though always as an underground movement. There are no signs that a broader movement in the community would have developed out of the conventicles, as it did in the German cities. Under such conditions, the division between Evangelicals and the Anabaptists was not sharp,[75] though the Lutherans in particular did not seek an institutional break with the church.

In Italy, the original center of Europe's urban belt, the Reformation failed despite auspicious beginnings at Lucca, Piedmont, Bologna, Modena, and Veneto because "it was not firmly rooted in the people."[76] It has been said of Italy that there were "numerous Protestant cells composed of artisans, craftsmen, and other burghers."[77] This comment must be judged, however, against the general social character of the movement in the northern and central Italian cities,[78] which secured its first adherents among the clerical and academic elites, then in noble circles, and finally in the bourgeoisie—above all the patriciates.[79] Before the Reformation developed a broader social basis came the establishment in early 1542 of the Roman Inquisition, which set in motion the numerous waves of expulsions during the remainder of the sixteenth century. Protestantism, the city, and the countryside entered into an enduring alliance only in Piedmont, where the Reformation converged with deeply rooted Waldensians. In 1532 the Piedmontese communities sided with the Protestant movement by means of a written confession of faith. In 1602 about 12,000 families of them were expelled from the country.

Italy demonstrates that reform could be successfully stifled through decisive action by ecclesiastical and political institutions. This also explains the limited success of the Reformation in Spain, which had at its disposal a royal ecclesiastical tribunal since the establishment of the Inquisition in 1478.[80] The Inquisition was as successful in preventing the importation of Luther's writings as it was in suppressing the few academic and noble conventicles that came to light around 1560 at Seville and Valladolid and in Aragon.

Sometimes parliaments played an important role in the progress of the Reformation. This is well known from the case of England, and is valid for other countries, too, but wherever the estates or parliament opted for reform, the concept of a popular Reformation is inapplicable, because such bodies were usually dominated by the nobility, even when the cities had seats and the right to vote in the local or national assembly. In Bohemia, Moravia, Silesia, and the lower Austrian territories, the cities played a role only within the framework of the estates. Hungary is an exception because of Transylvania, a region which supported reform, similar to Piedmont in Catholic southern Europe.[81]

In the three Scandinavian states, the unified duchies of Schleswig and Holstein, on the one hand, and the kingdom of Sweden, on the other, can be entirely ignored in discussing a popular Reformation, since both cases represent "a purely princely Reformation."[82] In Denmark, King Frederick I was obliged in his election agreement to swear "not to allow any heretics, disciples of Luther or others to preach and teach,"[83] which implies that there was a latent reform movement. Proof of such a movement can be established only for Viborg, Malmö, and Copenhagen, however, and even in these centers it was restricted to the preaching of the gospel under the protection of the city councils. The relationship between the many peasant revolts of the 1530s and the Reformation is rather unclear, given the lack of peasant pronouncements.[84]

The political establishment of the Reformation in Lutheran form ultimately succeeded in Denmark—after the preparatory "Herrendagen" in 1526—because of the massive pressure brought to bear by the king on the diet of October 1536, in which the nobility, the burghers, and the peasantry participated in large numbers.[85]

In England, the Reformation was "a creation of the English monarchy, more an act of state than in any other part of Europe apart from Scandinavia."[86] The fact that the people came out against all changes in theology and liturgy[87] during the revolts of 1549 makes unnecessary a broader discussion of the course of reform in England.

France

In three synods between 1559 (Paris) and 1562 (Orléans), French Protestantism confessed its Calvinist confessional orientation and its communal-aristocratic ecclesiastical organization.[88] It was at this time that Calvinism reached the height of its expansion, with a clear preponderance in southern France, reaching from La Rochelle to the Dauphiné, but with large Protestant minorities elsewhere (for example, in the larger cities of Normandy).

The point of departure for the movement in the 1520s was the diocese of Meaux, which has been referred to as "a springboard of Reformation,"[89] because its great proximity to Paris, to the court, and to the university helped launch the intellectual debate on the Reformation. Under the protection of its bishop, Guillaume Briçonnet, around whom gathered an extraordinary circle that included Jacques Lefèvre d'Etaples and Guillaume Farel, a well-organized preaching movement sprang up and was quickly denounced as a "Lutheran plague." Socially, the movement was composed of "bourgeois ruling groups of the towns and well-off artisans, some of whom still had a voice in urban politics."[90]

Since the 1540s, Protestantism in France attained a dogmatic unity to the extent that it followed the teaching of Calvin, whose *Institutio* was available for purchase since 1542.[91] This was preceded by a perceptible turning away from the Mass in the 1530s, which led to the first massive persecutions and so acted as an integrating force.[92] The high point of the development was the foundation of Calvinist churches beginning in 1555 and the emergence of a respectable Calvinist political party on a national, regional, and local basis,[93] in some places even under the protection of the French upper nobility. "The years from around 1555 to 1562 saw an explosion of Calvinist conversions."[94]

Although it was "primarily urban,"[95] the desire for renewal of the church can be termed a popular Reformation in France, for even "rural folk were not immune to Protestantism."[96] Together with the artisans, the largest group of urban Huguenots,[97] came peasants, particularly in the Cévennes, but sometimes elsewhere as well, such as in the Dauphiné, the Midi, and Normandy.[98] The movement radiated from the cities into the villages, and the Huguenot seigniories became its strongholds.[99]

There are no convincing explanations for Calvin's success in France. Whether the social and political position of the Huguenots can be employed to interpret the history of theological reception, remains a subject of debate.[100] Case studies seem to demonstrate that here and there the poor and the surburbanites joined the reform movement, as in Germany. But the elitist implications of the Calvinist doctrine of predestination fascinated the upper classes in the cities as well. "No class analysis," Nicholls insists, "can do justice to the urban atmosphere in which Protestantism spread."[101]

4. EXPLANATIONS

The German historiography of the Reformation has long spoken in terms of "wild growth [*Wildwuchs*]" and the "storm years [*Sturmjahren*]" of the Reformation in years preceding Luther's cooperation with the princes. The rich images captured in these two phrases need not defy analysis.

People's Reformation or Early Bourgeois Revolution?
In 1947 the Soviet historian Moisei M. Smirin introduced the analytical term "People's Reformation [*Volksreformation*]."[102] Smirin sought to describe a type of reformation that was distinguished by its abstraction from popular ideas and was sharpened into a theory by means of theological language that could be employed for agitational purposes. The popular demand for an end to serfdom, for the improvement of property rights, and for the expansion of communal rights—all of which were rooted in the "ideal of equality"—were understood by Thomas Müntzer as "a moral concept entailing the subordination of private to common and general interests." According to Smirin's interpretation of Müntzer's theology, the "true understanding of God" requires the uncompromising "realization of the basic principles of human morality and human reason," by means of revolution if necessary. Müntzer's conception of Christ's temporal rule is nothing less than the theologically articulated theory of a "transfer of rule [*translatio imperii*]" to the common people.[103]

Around 1970 the "people's Reformation" gave way—whether deliberately or because of a superficial appreciation of Smirin's analytic and synthetic achievement—to the term "early bourgeois revolution." Even if "explaining the explanation [of the Reformation as revolution] takes more energy than accepting the accepted explanation,"[104] (to use Otto Hermann Pesch's nice turn of phrase), the concept should be briefly explored.

Taking up a phrase of Friedrich Engels, Marxist historians in Germany have united the Reformation and the Peasants' War under the idea of an "early bourgeois revolution."[105] The class contradictions inherent in feudalism between the nobility and peasants, as well as the eclipse of feudalism by capitalism, provoked a general social crisis. Because capitalism follows feudalism, the nobility is supplanted by the bourgeoisie as ruling class in Marxian theory, and the transition from one social formation to the next takes place by means of revolution, the uprising necessarily had to be conceived in terms of a "bourgeois revolution." Marxist historians remain faithful to the basis-superstructure paradigm of historical materialism by reducing Martin Luther's theology to his criticism of the Church. Luther is thereby transformed into a theoretician who launched a fundamental attack, radicalized by Müntzer, on the papacy, a feudal institution belonging to the social superstructure. The revolution was termed "early" bourgeois because capitalism and the theology that accompanied it were not yet mature enough to ensure the revolution's success.

Communal Reformation or Revolution of the Common Man

The suggestion that we refer to the reform movement in South Germany before the mid-1520s—that is, until its appropriation by the princes—as a "communal Reformation" is based on the observation that the peasants and burghers made the same demands of the Church and of religion: the "pure gospel" must be preached because it is the exclusively necessary path to salvation; priests should be appointed by the community, which has the right to decide on doctrine and its correctness in disputed situations.[106] The communalization of the Church, as we might call these intentions, logically implied that the clergy must be stripped of its privileges and made equal to the other members of the community in their rights and duties, in order that the legal rights of cities and villages be strengthened by eliminating the ecclesiastical courts.

Furthermore, this phase of the Reformation is called "the communal Reformation" because the reformers themselves demanded the free preaching of the "pure gospel," the election of priests, the community's right to decide doctrine, the elimination of clerical privilege, and the abolition of ecclesiastical courts. Only after the Reformation fell into the hands of the lords were confessions of faith drafted, the territorial organization of the church codified, priests ordained, and new ecclesiastical courts (*Kirchenkonvente*, *Chorgerichte*) established.

The participation of hundreds of thousands of people in upper Germany, Switzerland, and Austria is probably best explained by the fact that communes, rural as well as urban, made enormous progress in self-administration during the fourteenth and fifteenth centuries. The communes became the primary political form of organization for both burghers and peasants. The Reformation brought with it the theory and ideology for the revitalization of communal Christianity.

This explains, too, the alignment of the communal Reformation with the revolution of the common man.[107] Geographically, the two movements occupied nearly identical space.[108] Independently of its mass support and recourse to violence, the Peasants' War took on a revolutionary quality, when it drafted a completely new political order on the basis of the community. The shape of the new state was derived from the village, town, and mountain communes. The descriptive phrase "common man"[109] is empirically grounded in evidence that the Peasants' War was not waged exclusively by the peasantry, but also by the burghers and the miners, who were possibly overrepresented in proportion to the percentage each group comprised of the total population. It is therefore incorrect to call it merely a "Peasants' War."

The Reformation as a Movement

The concept of a "reform movement" was developed by Hans-Jürgen Goertz. "The sudden appearance of different reform movements," he writes, was

> characteristic of the early years of the Reformation, so much so that one can speak of a significant variety of movements in the second decade of the sixteenth century: anti-clerical, humanist, reformist, radical reformist movements, as well as those in which the Imperial knights, the peasantry, and the cities took part.[110]

These movements possessed two focal points: on the one hand, "anti-clericalism" and, on the other, the gospel with its "relentless normalization of clerical and secular life." The late medieval attempts at reform received their "energetic concentration" through recourse to the gospel, while the traditional "hatred of clerics [Pfaffenhass]" derived its theological authority from the idea of the priesthood of all believers. In his assessment of both focal points of the "movements" of the 1520s, Goertz ultimately seems to grant primary importance to anti-clericalism. The title of his book, "hatred of priests [Pfaffenhass]," makes this clear, as does his conviction that "anti-clericalism became the point of crystallization for a religious and social movement." "The 'revolt against the priests' was the beginning of the Reformation in Germany," he argues.[111] The advantage of Goertz's interpretation is that it accounts for all the various strands of the Reformation, including those that arose in both urban and rural social milieux, and does not rank them hierarchically, so that the burghers' and peasants' reformation did not become merely two streams among many others.

The Popular Reformation as a European Event

Convincing interpretations of how reformed theology and ethics were received by "the people" have necessarily employed Central European sources, because elsewhere, except in France, there was no broad social response to the Reformation. The real if limited commensurability of Germany and France on this point still awaits an adequate evaluation. Robert M. Kingdon has assigned to French Calvinism the character of "democratic centralization," implying that the anti-absolutist forces were able to rally behind it.[112] Where the popular elements of the French Reformation have been examined in greater detail, they have been represented as "early bourgeois," notably in the recent work of Henry Heller. In summarizing extremely detailed studies of Rouen, Meaux, Troyes, Tours, Poitiers, Agen, and Valence, he writes that "we are forced to the conclusion that the wars [the French religious wars] were an abortive form of what Marxists after Engels refer to as an early bourgeois revolution."[113] Heller defends this statement by noting that those artisans whose social ascent in the 1540s was abruptly ended by enormous price increases and tax burdens paved the way for the Reformation. The initially latent sympathies of "merchants, notables and nobles" for Calvin became important beginning in the 1550s, once the bankruptcy of the state noticeably increased their burdens. That the "bourgeois" movement ultimately subordinated itself to aristocratic leadership may be explained by the marked feudal and patrimonial conditions in France. Heller is prudent enough not to make absolute the correlations between economic and political structures and developments, on the one hand, and confessional choices, on the other. Education, age, and professional independence play a role in explaining pro-Calvinist attitudes. This makes clear that the model of an "early bourgeois revolution" is as unsatisfactory an explanation of French as it is of German conditions. A historiography that is increasingly outgrowing national limitations will continue to seek new interpretations.

Translated by Jonathan Zatlin

NOTES

1. See Martin Brecht, in this *Handbook,* vol. 2:129-59; for details, Martin Brecht, *Martin Luther,* 3 vols. (Stuttgart, 1981-87).
2. Max Weber, *The Protestant Ethic and the Spirit of Capitalism.*
3. Moeller (1988), 115.
4. Otto Gierke, *Rechtsgeschichte der deutschen Genossenschaft* (Berlin, 1868), 633.
5. Schilling (1979).
6. Kroemer (1981), 70. The description is based, in addition to Kroemer's study, on the work of Brecht (1974), 174-208; Friedrich Dobel, *Memmingen im Reformationszeitalter,* vol. 1, 2d ed. (Memmingen, 1877); Rolf Kießling, *Die Stadt und ihr Umland. Bürgerbesitz und Wirtschaftsgefüge in Ostschwaben vom 14. bis ins 16. Jahrhundert* (Cologne and Vienna, 1989); Wolfgang Schlenk, "Die Reichsstadt Memmingen und die Reformation," *Memminger Geschichtsblätter* (1968).
7. Franz Ludwig Baumann, ed., *Akten zur Geschichte des Bauernkrieges aus Oberschwaben* (Freiburg im Breisgau, 1877), 1f. no. 2.
8. Kroemer (1981), 36.
9. Careful sociological investigation of the group around Kroemer (1981), 76ff.
10. Ibid., 103.
11. Evangelisches Kirchenarchiv Kaufbeuren, Anlage 102/7.
12. Ibid.
13. Wilfried Enderle, *Konfessionsbildung und Ratsregiment in der katholischen Reichsstadt Überlingen (1500-1618)* (Stuttgart, 1990).
14. Schilling (1993), 94-97.
15. Moeller (1987), 70-96 (afterword to 1985 edition).
16. Ulman Weiss, *Die frommen Bürger von Erfurt* (Weimar, 1988).
17. Klaus Arnold, "Die Stadt Kitzingen im Bauernkrieg," *Mainfränkisches Jahrbuch für Geschichte und Kunst* 27 (1975):11-50.
18. Kurt Kaser, *Politische und soziale Bewegungen im deutschen Bürgertum zu Beginn des 16. Jahrhunderts* (Stuttgart, 1899), 194.
19. See Blickle (1992), 82f.
20. The most important contributions are now found in Scribner (1987), 145-241.
21. Brady (1978), 234f., 291ff.
22. Ibid., 292.
23. See, for example, Ingrid Bátori and Erdmann Weyrauch, *Die bürgliche Elite der Stadt Kitzingen* (Stuttgart, 1982); Olaf Mörke, *Rat und Bürger in der Reformation. Soziale Gruppen und kirchlicher Wandel in den welfischen Hansestädten Lüneburg, Braunschweig und Göttingen* (Hildesheim, 1981). A survey of the literature can be found in Kaspar von Greyerz, "Stadt und Reformation: Stand und Aufgaben der Forschung," *ARG* 76 (1985):6-63. See also Schilling (1993), 130-34.

24. Schilling (1993), 97.
25. Erich Maschke, "Deutsche Städte am Ausgang des Mittelalters," in *Die Stadt am Ausgang des Mittelalters*, ed. Heinz Rausch (Linz, 1974), 1-44.
26. Czok (1975), 53-68.
27. Rammstedt (1975), 239-76.
28. Heiko A. Oberman, *Werden und Wertung der Reformation*, 2d ed. (Tübingen, 1979), 241-50; Moeller (1970) and (1974).
29. Important to this debate is Schmidt (1986), though it should be mentioned that there was no Reformation in Nuremberg's city council. See also Günter Vogler, *Nürnberg 1524/5* (Berlin, 1982); Moeller (1987), 29; Blickle (1992), 82-86.
30. Bernd Moeller, "Kleriker als Bürger," in *Festschrift für Hermann Heimpel zum 75. Geburtstag* (Göttingen, 1972), vol. 2:195-224.
31. Peter A. Dykema and Heiko A. Oberman (eds.), *Anticlericalism in Late Medieval and Early Modern Europe* (Leiden, 1993) contains rich data.
32. Moeller (1987).
33. Ibid., 58.
34. In the 1987 edition, Moeller judges Luther's importance higher. The difference between two Reformations (an upper German and a Wittenberg one) is relinquished in favor of Luther's overwhelming influence.
35. Brady (1978). The approach is ably employed for a political history of the Reformation in Brady (1985).
36. Bernd Moeller, "Stadt und Buch," in Mommsen (1979), 25-39.
37. Thomas A. Brady, Jr., "The Social History of Reformation between 'Romantic Idealism' and 'Sociologism:' A Reply," in Mommsen (1979), 40-43.
38. See Thomas A. Brady, Jr., "In Search of the Godly City: The Domestication of Religion in the German Urban Reformation," in R. Po-Chia Hsia, ed., *The German People and the Reformation* (Ithaca, 1988), 14-31.
39. Schmidt (1986), 330-37.
40. Bernd Moeller (1988), 91. "The peasants . . . seemed to remain in the history-lessness of their local and natural context in the face of the Reformation, as if they had simply not heard of the new doctrine—after all, they contribute little to its articulation." The sentence remains in all later editions.
41. Heinz Schilling, "Die deutsche Gemeindereformation. Ein oberdeutsch-zwinglianisches Ereignis vor der 'reformatorischen Wende' des Jahres 1525," *ZHF* 14 (1987):329.
42. See Hans-Joachim Köhler, "'Der Bauer wird witzig!': Der Bauer in den Flugschriften der Reformationszeit," in Blickle (1987), 187-218.
43. See Thomas A. Brady, Jr., "From the Sacral Community to the Common Man: Reflections on German Reformation Studies," *CEH* 20 (1987):229-45.
44. Conrad (1984); Blickle (1992) and (1987); v. Rütte (1988); Bierbrauer (1993); Kamber (1994).
45. Endres (1987), 127-46.
46. The text is easily accessible in Franz (1963), 315f., no. 97.
47. Blickle (1992), 11-62.
48. See Kamber (1994); Christian Dietrich, *Die Stadt Zürich und ihre Landgemeinden während der Bauernunruhen von 1489 bis 1525* (Frankfurt am Main, 1985), 125-203.

49. See the case study in Bierbrauer (1993).
50. See the case study in Conrad (1984).
51. See Frank Ganseuer, *Der Staat des "gemeinen Mannes". Gattungstypologie und Programmatik des politischen Schrifttums von Reformation und Bauernkrieg* (Frankfurt am Main, 1985).
52. Ernst Gagliardi, et al., eds., *Johannes Stumpfs Schweizer und Reformationschronik*, part 1 (Basel, 1952), 261f.
53. Ibid.
54. See Franz (1933).
55. Franz (1963), 146f., Nr. 31.
56. The most important documents translated into English can be found in Scott and Scribner (1991).
57. Blickle, (1981), 194.
58. Compare the interpretations in the essays in Buszello (1969) with Blickle (1981).
59. Franz (1933).
60. David Sabean, *Landbesitz und Gesellschaft am Vorabend des Bauernkrieges* (Stuttgart, 1972); Franz Irsigler, "Zu den wirtschaftlichen Ursachen des Bauernkriegs von 1525/6," in Kurt Löcher, ed., *Martin Luther und die Reformation in Deutschland* (Schweinfurt, n.d.), 95-120.
61. Peter Bierbrauer, *Freiheit und Gemeinde im Berner Oberland* (Bern, 1991), 65-82; Peter Blickle, *Landschaften im Alten Reich* (Munich, 1973); also the essays in Peter Blickle, ed., *Landgemeinde und Stadtgemeinde in Mitteleuropa* (Munich, 1991).
62. Karl Heinz Burmeister, "Genossenschaftliche Rechtsfindung und herrschaftliche Rechtssetzung. Auf dem Weg zum Territorialstaat," HZ, Beiheft 4 (Munich, 1974):171-85.
63. Peter Bierbrauer, "Das Göttliche Recht und die naturrechtliche Tradition," in Peter Blickle, ed., *Bauer, Reich und Reformation. Festschrift für Günther Franz* (Stuttgart, 1982), 210-34.
64. See Buszello (1969), 19-91.
65. Schulze (1975). See also Hermann Rebel, *Peasant Classes: The Bureaucratization of Property and Family Relations under Early Habsburg Absolutism 1511-1636* (Princeton, 1983).
66. Manfred Schulze, *Fürsten und Reformation. Geistliche Reformpolitik weltlicher Fürsten vor der Reformation* (Tübingen, 1991).
67. Moeller (1988), 115.
68. Heiko A. Oberman, "Stadtreformation und Fürstenreformation," in *Humanismus und Reformation als kulturelle Kräfte in der deutschen Geschichte*, ed. Lewis W. Spitz (Berlin, 1981), 88.
69. Wohlfeil (1976), 19.
70. Heinz Schilling, *Aufbruch und Krise. Deutschland 1517-1648* (Berlin, 1988), 162-83.
71. Hans-Jürgen Goertz, *Die Täufer. Geschichte und Deutung*, 2d ed. (Munich, 1988). The continuities between rebellious peasants and Anabaptists are worked out in Stayer (1991).
72. Cameron (1991), 197-263; Pettegree (1992), 1-22.
73. Pettegree (1992), 9.
74. See Alastair Duke, "The Netherlands," in Pettegree (1992), 142-65; and id., *Reformation and Revolt in the Low Countries* (London, 1990), 29-59.

75. See James Stayer, in this *Handbook,* volume 2:249-82.
76. Welti (1985), 139.
77. Cameron (1992), 188-214.
78. See Welti (1985), 28-84 for an overview.
79. Cameron (1992), 196-98; 207.
80. A. Gordon Kinder, "Spain," in Pettegree (1992), 215-37.
81. Winfried Eberhard, "Bohemia, Moravia and Austria" in Pettegree (1992), 23-48; David P. Daniel, "Hungary" in ibid., 49-69.
82. Grell (1992), 97f.
83. Ibid., 104.
84. Alex Wittendorff, "Popular Mentalities and the Danish Reformation", in Grane and Hørby (1990), 211-22.
85. Grell (1992), 111.
86. Diarmaid MacCullough, "England," in Pettegree (1992); and in general Geoffrey E. Elton, *Reform and Reformation in England 1509-1558* (London, 1977). See W. Ian P. Hazlett, in this *Handbook,* vol. 2:455-90.
87. Julian Cornwall, *Revolt of the Peasantry 1549* (London, 1977).
88. Introduction in Greengrass (1987); a short overview in Nicholls (1992), 120-41; a broad narrative rich in detail in Imbart de La Tour (1914/35); see also Philip Benedict, in this *Handbook,* vol. 2:417-54.
89. Nicholls (1992), 123; Sutherland (1980), 10-30.
90. Nicholls (1992), 121.
91. Easily accessible in *Calvinism in Europe, 1540-1610,* ed. Alastair Duke, Gillian Lewis, Andrew Pettegree (Manchester, 1992), 60-128.
92. Sutherland (1980), 30-36.
93. On the organization of the church see Robert M. Kingdon, *Geneva and the Consolidation of the French Protestant Movement 1564-1572* (Geneva, 1972), 37-148.
94. Prestwich (1985), 71.
95. Nicholls (1992), 121.
96. Ibid., 129.
97. Heller (1986), 234.
98. For a skeptical view on the participation of the peasants in the Reformation, see Garrisson (1991).
99. Nicholls (1992), 130; Greengrass (1987), 42-62; for a detailed case study, see Garrisson (1991).
100. Nicholls (1992), 132.
101. Ibid., 132.
102. Smirin (1956).
103. Citations from Smirin (1956), 96-97, 164, 294, 653, 660.
104. Otto Herrmann Pesch, *Hinführung zu Luther* (Mainz, 1982), 305.
105. Compare Vogler (1969); Vogler (1974); Laube (1978).
106. Blickle (1992), 98-110.
107. Blickle (1981).
108. For a different view, see Berndt Hamm, in this *Handbook,* vol. 2:193-227.
109. On the history of concepts, see Lutz (1979).
110. Goertz (1987), 244.
111. Ibid., 244f.
112. Kingdon (1956), 128f.
113. Heller (1986), 258.

BIBLIOGRAPHY

Abray, Lorna Jane. *The People's Reformation. Magistrates, Clergy, and Commons in Strasbourg 1500-1598.* Oxford, 1985.

Bierbrauer, Peter. "Die Reformation in den Schaffhauser Gemeinden Hallau und Thayngen." In Blickle (1987), 21-53.

Bierbrauer, Peter. *Die unterdrückte Reformation. Der Kampf der Tiroler um eine neue Kirche.* Bauer und Reformation, vol. 2. Zurich, 1993.

Blickle, Peter. *Communal Reformation: the Quest for Salvation in Sixteenth Century Germany.* Trans. Thomas Dunlap. Studies in German Histories. Atlantic Highlands, N.J., 1992.

Blickle, Peter. *The Revolution of 1525: the German Peasants' War from a New Perspective.* Trans. Thomas A. Brady, Jr., and H. C. Erik Midelfort. Baltimore, 1981.

Blickle, Peter, ed. *Zugänge zur bäuerlichen Reformation.* Bauer und Reformation, vol. 1. Zurich, 1987.

Blickle, Peter, and Johannes Kunisch, eds. *Kommunalisierung und Christianisierung. Voraussetzungen und Folgen der Reformation 1400-1600.* ZHF, Beiheft 9. Berlin, 1989.

Brady, Thomas A., Jr. *Ruling Class, Regime and Reformation at Strasbourg 1520-1550.* SMRT, vol. 22. Leiden, 1978.

Brady, Thomas A., Jr. *Turning Swiss. Cities and Empire, 1450-1550.* Cambridge, 1985.

Brecht, Martin. "Der theologische Hintergrund der Zwölf Artikel der Bauernschaft in Schwaben von 1525. Christoph Schappelers und Sebastian Lotzers Beitrag zum Bauernkrieg." *ZKiG* 85 (1974):174-208.

Brendler, Gerhard, and Adolf Laube. *Der deutsche Bauernkrieg 1524/25. Geschichte-Traditionen-Lehren.* Berlin, 1977.

Buszello, Horst. *Der deutsche Bauernkrieg als politische Bewegung mit besonderer Berücksichtigung der anonymen Flugschrift an die Versammlung gemayner Pawerschafft.* Studien zur europäischen Geschichte, vol. 8. Berlin, 1969.

Buszello, Horst, Peter Blickle, and Rudolf Endres, eds. *Der deutsche Bauernkrieg.* Paderborn, 1991 [1984].

Cameron, Euan. *The European Reformation.* Oxford, 1991.

Cameron, Euan. "Italy." In Pettegree (1992), 188-214.

Chaunu, Pierre. *Eglise, culte et société. Essais sur Réforme et Contre-Réforme (1517-1620).* Paris, 1981.

Conrad, Franziska. *Reformation in der bäuerlichen Gesellschaft. Zur Rezeption reformatorischer Theologie im Elsaß.* VIEG, vol. 116. Stuttgart, 1984.

Czok, Karl. "Zur sozialökonomischen Struktur und politischen Rolle der Vorstädte in Sachsen und Thüringen im Zeitalter der deutschen frühbürgerlichen Revolution." *Wissenschaftliche Zeitschrift der Karl-Marx-Universität, Gesellschafts- und Sprachwissenschaftliche Reihe* 24 (1975):53-68.

Delumeau, Jean. *Naissance et affirmation de la Réforme.* Nouvelle Clio, vol. 30. Paris, 1968.

Dörrer, Fridolin, ed. *Die Bauernkriege und Michael Gaismair. Protokoll des internationalen Symposiums vom 15. bis 19. November 1976 in Innsbruck-Vill.* Veröffentlichungen des Tiroler Landesarchivs, vol. 2. Innsbruck, 1982.

Edwards, Mark U., Jr. *Luther and the False Brethern.* Stanford, 1975.

Endres, Rudolf. "Die Reformation im fränkischen Wendelstein." In Blickle (1987).

Endres, Rudolf. "Ursachen." In Buszello, Blickle, and Endres (1991), 217-53.

Franz, Günther. *Der deutsche Bauernkrieg.* Munich and Berlin, 1933.

Franz, Günther, ed. *Quellen zur Geschichte des Bauernkriegs.* Darmstadt, 1963.

Fuhrmann, Rosi. "Dorfgemeinde und Pfründstiftung vor der Reformation. Kommunale Selbstbestimmungschancen zwischen Religion und Recht." In Blickle and Kunisch (1989), 77-112.

Gäbler, Ulrich. *Huldrych Zwingli. Eine Einführung in sein Leben und sein Werk.* Munich, 1983.

Ganseuer, Frank. *Der Staat des "gemeinen Mannes". Gattungstypologie und Programmatik des politischen Schrifttums von Reformation und Bauernkrieg.* Europäische Hochschulschriften, ser. 3, vol. 228. Frankfurt am Main and Bern, 1985.

Garrisson, Janine. *Protestants du Midi 1559-1598.* Toulouse, 1991.

Goertz, Hans-Jürgen. *Pfaffenhaß und groß Geschrei. Die reformatorischen Bewegungen in Deutschland 1517-1529.* Munich, 1987.

Grane, Leif, and Kai Hørby, eds. *The Danish Reformation against its International Background.* Forschungen zur Kirchen- und Dogmengeschichte, vol. 46. Göttingen, 1990.

Greengrass, Mark. *The French Reformation.* Oxford and New York, 1987.

Grell, Ole Peter. "Scandinavia." In Pettegree (1992), 94-119.

Heller, Henry. *The Conquest of Poverty: the Calvinist Revolt in Sixteenth Century France.* SMRT, vol. 35. Leiden, 1986.

Imbart de la Tour, Pierre. *Les origines de la Réforme.* Vols. 3-4. Paris, 1914-35.

Kamber, Peter. *Bauern, Reformation und Revolten in Zürich. Versuch einer Ereignisgeschichte von unten.* Bauer und Reformation, vol. 3. Zurich, forthcoming 1995.

Kingdon, Robert M. *Geneva and the Coming of the Wars of Religion in France 1555-1563.* THR, vol. 22. Geneva, 1956.

Köhler, Hans-Joachim. "Erste Schritte zu einem Meinungsprofil der frühen Reformationszeit." In *Martin Luther. Probleme seiner Zeit,* ed. Volker Press and Dieter Stievermann, 244-81. SFN, vol. 16. Stuttgart, 1986.

Kroemer, Barbara. *Die Einführung der Reformation in Memmingen. Über die Bedeutung ihrer sozialen, wirtschaftlichen und politischen Faktoren.* Memminger Geschichtsblätter, Jahresheft 1980. Memmingen, 1981.

Lau, Franz. "Der Bauernkrieg und das angebliche Ende der lutherischen Reformation als spontaner Volkserhebung." *Luther-Jahrbuch* 26 (1959):109-34.

Laube, Adolf. "Bemerkungen zur These von der Revolution des gemeinen Mannes." *ZfG* 26 (1978):607-14.

Locher, Gottfried W. *Die Zwinglische Reformation im Rahmen der europäischen Kirchengeschichte.* Göttingen and Zurich, 1979.

Lutz, Robert H. *Wer war der gemeine Mann? Der dritte Stand in der Krise des Spätmittelalters.* Munich and Vienna, 1979.

Moeller, Bernd. *Deutschland im Zeitalter der Reformation.* Deutsche Geschichte, vol. 4. Göttingen, 1988 [1977].

Moeller, Bernd. *Reichsstadt und Reformation.* Rev. ed. Berlin, 1987 [1962]).

Moeller, Bernd. "Zwinglis Disputationen. Studien zu den Anfängen der Kirchenbildung und des Synodalwesens im Protestantismus." *ZSRG, KA* 56 (1970):274-324; 60 (1974):213-364.

Mommsen, Wolfgang J., ed. *Stadtbürgertum und Adel in der Reformation. Studien zur Sozialgeschichte der Reformation in England und Deutschland.* Veröffentlichungen des Deutschen Historischen Instituts London, vol. 5. Stuttgart, 1979.

Nicholls, David. "France." In Pettegree (1992), 120-141.

Nipperdey, Thomas. "Theologie und Revolution bei Thomas Müntzer." *ARG* 54 (1963):145-181.

Oberman, Heiko A. *Die Reformation. Von Wittenberg nach Genf.* Tübingen, 1986.

Ozment, Steven E. *The Reformation in the Cities: the Appeal of Protestantism to Sixteenth-Century Germany and Switzerland.* New Haven, 1975.

Pettegree, Andrew, ed. *The Early Reformation in Europe.* Cambridge, 1992.

Prestwich, Menna. "Calvinism in France, 1559-1629." In *International Calvinism 1541-1715*, ed. Menna Prestwich, 71-107. Oxford, 1985.

Rammstedt, Otthein. "Stadtunruhen 1525." In *Der Deutsche Bauernkrieg 1524-1526*, ed. Hans-Ulrich Wehler, 239-76. GG, Sonderheft 1. Göttingen, 1975.

Rich, Arthur. "Zwingli als sozialpolitischer Denker." *Zwingliana* 13 (1969-73):67-89.

Rütte, Hans von. "Von der spätmittelalterlichen Frömmigkeit zum reformierten Glauben. Kontinuität und Bruch in der Religionspraxis der Bauern." *Itinera* 8 (1988):33-44.

Sabean, David. *Landbesitz und Gesellschaft am Vorabend des Bauernkriegs. Eine Studie der sozialen Verhältnisse im südlichen Oberschwaben in den Jahren vor 1525*. Quellen und Forschungen zur Agrargeschichte, vol. 26. Stuttgart, 1972.

Schilling, Heinz. *Konfessionskonflikt und Staatsbildung. Eine Fallstudie über das Verhältnis von religiösem und sozialem Wandel in der Frühneuzeit am Beispiel der Grafschaft Lippe*. QFRG, vol. 48. Göttingen, 1982.

Schilling, Heinz. "Die politische Elite nordwestdeutscher Städte in den religiösen Auseinandersetzungen des 16.Jahrhunderts." In Mommsen (1979), 235-307.

Schilling, Heinz. *Die Stadt in der Frühen Neuzeit*. Enzyklopädie Deutscher Geschichte, vol. 24. Munich, 1993.

Schmidt, Heinrich Richard. *Reichstädte, Reich und Reformation. Korporative Reichspolitik 1521-1529/30*. VIEG, vol. 122. Stuttgart, 1986.

Schulze, Winfried. "Die veränderte Bedeutung sozialer Konflikte im 16. und 17. Jahrhundert." In *Der deutsche Bauernkrieg 1524-1526*, ed. Hans-Ulrich Wehler, 277-302. GG, Sonderheft 1. Göttingen, 1975.

Scott, Tom, and Robert W. Scribner, eds. *The German Peasants' War. A History in Documents*. Atlantic Highlands, N.J., 1991.

Scribner, Robert W. *For the Sake of the Simple Folks. Popular Propaganda for the German Reformation*. Cambridge Studies in Oral and Literatur Culture, vol. 2. Cambridge, 1981.

Scribner, Robert W. *The German Reformation*. London, 1986.

Scribner, Robert W. *Popular Culture and Popular Movements in Reformation Germany*. London, 1987.

Smirin, Moisej M. *Die Volksreformation des Thomas Münzer und der große Bauernkrieg*. Trans. Hans Nichtweiß. Berlin, 1956 [1947].

Stayer, James M. *The German Peasants' War and Anabaptist Community of Goods*. Montreal, 1991.

Steinmetz, Max. "Die frühbürgerliche Revolution in Deutschland (1476-1535). Thesen zur Vorbereitung der wissenschaftlichen Konferenz in Wernigerode vom 20. bis 24. Januar 1960." *ZfG* 8 (1960):113-24.

Sutherland, N. M. *The Huguenot Struggle for Recognition*. New Haven, 1980.

Vogler, Günter. "Marx, Engels und die Konzeption einer frühbürgerlichen Revolution in Deutschland." *ZfG* 17 (1969):704-17.

Vogler, Günter. "Revolutionäre Bewegungen und frühbürgerliche Revolution." *ZfG* 22 (1974):394-411.

Welti, Manfred E. *Kleine Geschichte der italienischen Reformation*. SVRG, vol. 193. Gütersloh, 1985.

Wohlfeil, Rainer. "Der Speyerer Reichstag von 1526." *Blätter für pfälzische Kirchengeschichte und religiöse Volkskunde* 43 (1976):5-20.

THE URBAN REFORMATION
IN THE HOLY ROMAN EMPIRE

Berndt Hamm

(Universität Erlangen)

1. PRELIMINARY CONSIDERATIONS

The term "urban reformation" is used here to describe the cities' role in the predominantly urban phase, plus the burghers' role in the larger process of the Protestant reformation, the sixteenth-century rupture with the medieval system of church, theology, and piety.[1] Rooted in Martin Luther's theology, the urban reformation brought a new way of believing and confessing faith, a new liturgy and church governance, and the beginnings of new forms of piety, all legitimized by Biblical norms. This initial reformation lasted only a few decades, in some places a few years, before it gave way to the long process called "confessionalization," in which the various church systems consolidated their dogma, law, and constitution and formed distinctive ways of life, mentality, and culture, both high and low.[2]

In both social place and actors, the burghers' reformation confronts us with a face quite different from those of the reformations associated with the princes, the nobles, and the peasants. The contrasts raise several important questions. Did a special affinity of the reformation for the city make it especially effective in urban contexts? How did the cities' reformation influence the course and character of the larger reformation? To what degree is it true that the Protestant reformation was, as alleged, an "urban event"?[3]

A brief overview such as this must emphasize not details but dominant and coherent features. If this constraint privileges the urban landscape of South Germany, it is both because of these cities' pioneering role in the spread of the reformation and their leadership of the cities' engagement in reformation on the Imperial level. Yet past scholarship has excessively privileged the southern cities and relatively neglected those of central and northern Germany.[4] This chapter tries to rectify that situation, though it has, alas, no space for cities outside the Empire.

We start from the viewpoint of "religion and society," wherein "re-

ligion" refers to belief, piety, theology, ecclesiastical practice, and religiosity—humanity's transcendent connections—and "society" stands
for politics, the state, social position, economy, and law, respectively
humanity's horizontal and secular connections.[5] The reformation as a
whole represents an encounter of religion's claims to truth with society's forces, which occurred most intensely and fruitfully in the city.
Here, where many people lived close together, the practice of religion
was most effectively shaped by ecclesiastical institutions, and religion
was most vulnerable to the heightened aims of the state, to social tensions, to the production, distribution, and consumption of goods, and
to the powers of finance.

The presentation of the urban reformation as a paradigm of the
Protestant reformation depends on this view of the city as an integrated
nexus of religion and society, in which the socio-political and cultural
framework of religious and theological forces is meant to be taken just
as seriously as the religious and theological embeddedness of political,
economic, and cultural factors.[6] This principle yields a two-step rule
for studying societies of the reformation era. First, the ways in which
people felt themselves to be menaced and their need to have things put
right—in their consciences, social roles, economic activities, and physical health—directly shaped how they believed, their understanding of
theology, and thus the character of the religious reformation. This is
not to say, however, that their faith and the ecclesiastical changes were
simply caused by their social context. Secondly and reciprocally, the
new faith and the reformation's transformation of the church influenced how people dealt with these threats, with insecurity, and loss of
legitimacy, which did not derive from the new theology and the new
ecclesiastical practice.

2. PIETY AND CHURCH LIFE

The late medieval cities' intense piety and lively ecclesiastical life can be
measured by proliferations: buildings, pious foundations, altars, endowed Masses, religious images, collections of relics, processions, indulgence campaigns, and confraternities.[7] They can also be comprehended in terms of an intensified, internalized urban spirituality among
groups of both secular and regular clergy and laity, some of them influenced by humanism. This enhanced piety, religious sensitivity, and devotion fed the urban ideal of sacral communalism, that a vital connec-

tion existed between devotion to the temporal "common good" and concern for eternal salvation.[8] According to Bernd Moeller's well-known dictum, "the late medieval German city inclined to understand itself as a "Christian body [corpus christianum]" in miniature."[9] This social side of urban religiosity was complemented by an individual side, for many burghers, male and female, cultivated a personal, private penitential piety focused on the sufferings of Christ and employing the practice of meditation. This tendency produced some odd shifts, notably in the image of St. Jerome who was transformed from a paragon of ascetic retreat from the world into a model of burgher piety of conscience and individual improvement.[10] The dual character of urban piety, social and personal, helps to explain why Luther, too, addressed the burghers with a combination of communal values and extremely individualistic features.

The accumulation of good works to assure eternal salvation and avoid the fires of Hell was not peculiar to cities, of course, but the proliferation of its traces in urban images and documents make it appear to have been especially intense. The burghers thus appear to have been fired by a concern for salvation, anxious about God's justice, and fearful of His judgment, and perhaps they, more than others, were also inspired by acquisitiveness and calculation. As if to balance this concern, they also supply rich evidence for religious trust in God's mercy in the form of devotion to the sufferings of Christ, the benignity of Mary, the intercession of the saints, and the mercifulness of a divine Judge Who throws His Son's sufferings onto the scales.[11] Well before the reformation, we find these two tendencies side-by-side in urban piety: the turn to "mercy alone [sola misericordia]" and a desire for spiritual freedom from the need to achieve. We find there, too, another dyad, an intense anticlericalism and a strong sense of responsibility for the burghers' own communal church.[12]

These dualities of the civic mentality may be understood in terms of convergence and conflict. With "convergence" we mean both the identification of the urban political community with the urban church and the corresponding desire to unite political and ecclesiastical jurisdiction in magisterial hands.[13] These values validated the magistrates' claim to supervise the church's institutions, buildings, and personnel, which they understood to belong to *their* church, that is, to the religious community understood as a burghers' association.[14] In practice this meant the right to administer ecclesiastical properties, influence the appointments of pastors and other offices, establish preacherships, supervise the convents, and control clerical personal and civic behavior—for example, requiring them to become citizens and pay taxes. As the burghers moved into the church's sacral and clerical space, their magistrates tried to wrest from the hierarchy's jurisdiction certain institutions that particularly concerned the laity: schools, poorhouses, hospitals, marriage litigation, wills, and other legal matters. On the eve of the reformation, therefore, the tide was running strongly toward an amalgamation of temporal and spiritual jurisdictions in the hands of the burgher, validated by the magistrates' perceived responsibility—as they continuously proclaimed—for both the burgers' temporal welfare and the salvation of their souls.[15] The urban reformation would greatly intensify this belief.

Under the term "conflict" we may comprehend the strife between burghers and clergy. Two motives characterized urban anticlericalism. First, there was competition or rivalry between urban political principles—communal association and magisterial authority—and the hierarchy's claims to jurisdiction and obedience. The burghers resented the fact that their church, its properties and incomes, jurisdiction, benefices, convents, and the right to institute reform lay in alien, i.e., nonburgher, hands. Secondly, the laity were escalating their religious demands on the urban clergy. The concerns of women and men for a more intensive piety, better education, and better pastoral care placed correspondingly greater demands on the monks, nuns, and secular priests. They also stigmatized those who were thought to be immoral, neglectful, ignorant, or greedy.[16]

Thus, both convergence and conflict stimulated criticism of the clergy from top to bottom, though rarely a fundamental hostility to the church or religion as such. On the contrary, these critical attitudes reveal a heightened sense of church involvement, piety, and pastoral care. Such tendencies also existed outside the cities, of course, but the extreme density of urban religious practice and intensity of urban political authority made both political-ecclesiastical convergence and anticlerical conflict most intense in the cities.

3. THE "CONCENTRATION OF NORMS" IN RELIGION AND SOCIETY

From the processes of convergence and conflict[17] arose what may be described as "the concentration of norms [*normative Zentrierung*],"[18] which means a shift of all of a city's normative, legitimizing, and regulating forces to a single center. This shift characterized the theological, social, and political changes of the Reformation and confessional eras, though impulses in this direction also appear in all of the late medieval ideas of reform, especially in the promotion of simplicity, unity, truth, peace, and law as components of an all-embracing and radically reformed social order. This drive to concentrate norms responded both to the shocking urban experience of social competition and division and to the escalating religious insecurity about sin, dying, and final judgment. It had considerable impact on both urban religion and urban politics. On the one hand, the burghers' piety merged with reform impulses in humanism to shape an ideal of Christian life based on simplicity and a theology based on penitence and the love of God. On the other hand, the early modern state, both in the territories and in the cities, sought to bring all areas of public and private life under its regulating discipline. The cities, with their special type of rationality, pioneered this development during the fifteenth century. Assisted by their lawyers and secretaries, the magistrates formed ideas of an integrated and rigidly ordered society, which was expressed in legal reform, a new interest in record-keeping, and in the official promotion of a pious and honorable way of life.[19] There came a flood of new disciplinary and police measures—sumptuary laws, poorlaws, laws on begging, hospitals, dancing, schools, and economic life—regulating everything from the size and price of buns to bedcovers in the civic whorehouse. On the eve of the Reformation the urban ruling classes became the pioneers of early modern "social discipline."

We can see the magistrates' desire to shape urban society—it later spread to the princely regimes in the territories—combined with and intensified the new religious piety and the new socio-political regulation. Its most obvious sign is the unification of political and religious jurisdictions, based on the magistrates' and religious reformers' belief that religious discipline and civic regulation [policey] could not be separated from one another. As the magistrates moved to reform the clergy and the monasteries and to improve worship, preaching, pastoral care, and Christian behavior, reform-minded theologians, preachers, and pastors strove to influence the sensibilities and consciences of the political, social, and economic elites. Building on late medieval achievements, the urban reformation thus concentrated norms by uniting socio-political discipline with a renewal of theology, faith, and piety.

The connection made between the "common good" and eternal salvation was by no means the monopoly of the urban elites, although, because their training in the law and in humanism allowed them to monopolize formal thinking and writing about values, the written record does privilege their desire to impose norms "from above."[20] The hunger for clear, fixed norms, however, was general. This is shown by the peasants' appeal in 1525 to divine justice and the godly law,[21] and even more by the evangelical communal movements in the cities. The appeals demonstrate how the will to concentrate the norm on the Bible alone also pressed upward from below. It is nevertheless true that in the mentality and language of the "Common Man," the reorientation of norms toward faith in Christ, Biblical law, and evangelical faith bore other features than they did in the more strongly authoritarian mentality of the magistrates.[22]

4. FOUNDATIONS OF THE URBAN REFORMATION

The characteristics of the late medieval and early modern city, which mutatis mutandis largely apply to the non-urban world as well, shaped and were shaped by the urban reformation, which though it gave a new quality to relations between church and city, did not disrupt the main lines of urban life. It remains to ask how the urban reformations differed from those that occurred under the rule of nobles and princes, and how this difference gave the cities a special prominence in the Reformation as a whole. At least seven significant characteristics of the urban reformations bear mentioning.

In the first place, the spiritual mobility within the cities—the large southern cities more than the others—predestined them to form both the vanguard and part of the main body of the Reformation movement. As the centers of literary and artistic production, of printing and humanism, they were the ideal soil for a movement which spread by means of the avalanche of print that poured over the land since about 1518:[23] Biblical translations, pamphlets and broadsides, mass-produced woodcuts and copper engravings of agitational and pedagogical content.[24] Without the specifically urban culture of print and humanism, without the presence of many multipliers of ideas, the Reformation is unthinkable.[25]

Secondly, the Reformation is inconceivable without the urban preachers and their sermons. Not only did preaching's direct and public impact magnify that of pamphlets and illustrated broadsides, but it was the chief medium through which evangelical theology reached the illiterate people and drew them into reasoned discussion. Some preaching occurred in the villages,[26] but the rural folk also streamed in to hear famous urban preachers, such as Matthäus Alber in Reutlingen's Church of Our Lady[27] and Christoph Schappeler at Memmingen.[28] From 1521 on, the urban preachers took the leadership of what was becoming a broadly communal movement. They often took up the pen as well, and a great many of the pamphlets derive from sermons.[29] The late medieval cities had been the chief centers of preaching, and the urban reformation swiftly became a preaching event in the cities and moved outward into the countryside.[30]

Thirdly, the mendicant orders and their preachers were vital to the urban reformation. The Dominicans, Franciscans, and Augustinian Hermits had done most of the late medieval preaching and composed most of the devotional literature, and their houses, especially those of the reform known as the "Observance," were centers of religious influence on the laity. This religious symbiosis of mendicant orders and cities[31] explains why so many of the reformers, evangelical preachers, and writers of pamphlets were former mendicant friars.[32] During the "quiet years," when the Reformation movement was spreading unofficially through reading and preaching,[33] its cells were the convents and humanist circles, in which the works of Luther, an Augustinian Hermit, were avidly read. His words fell on soil long prepared by the Observance, which had promoted a full, strict, and closely supervised obedience to God, based on the orders' original rules,[34] while to the laity it had taught the idea of a "Christian Order" with the Bible as its "rule" of faith and love. Erasmus of Rotterdam, writing in 1518, referred to the "vows" taken to Christ in every Christian's baptism, and asked, "What is the city but a great convent?"[35]

Fourthly, the late medieval burghers had come to treat their city as an intensely sacral community, in which all areas of life were progressively sacralized. This tendency merged with the urban reformation's ideals of the centrality and sovereignty of faith,[36] obedience to God's Biblical commands, and the need for "true" worship and renewed religious discipline for all the burghers. Against the background of late medieval pressure for greater regulation, we can understand why it fell to the cities to lead in the creation of specific institutional forms before the Reformation, notably for regulation of the poor, of baptism, of public worship, and of marriage. This entire process found its capstone in the comprehensive church constitutions created by the urban reformation.

Fifthly, the burghers' drive for holiness absorbed the objectively desacralizing impulses present in the late medieval city, such as a greater use of writing in education, administration, and economic life, a more rationalized organization of life, a movement away from legal ritual, and a general pressure for new and more credible forms of explanation, justification, reflection, and discussion. All these changes weakened the traditional forms of religiosity, which had been unreflective, popular, and suited to a rural way of life. This older religiosity had roots in an archaic, animistic, and magical worldview, which marked off specific sacred places, times, objects, persons, and actions from the mundane world. Late medieval worship and devotion had always both participated in this visibly and palpably sacral religion and diverted it onto supervised paths.[37] The Protestant reformation completed this process, opposing to the old sacrality its own principles of sacral legitimization and desacralizing liberation based on the Holy Scriptures. Its aim was to desacralize in the sense of overcoming paganism, and its weapons were the written word, images, and actions—often deliberate and provocative acts of profanation—against holy spaces, times of the year, sacramentals, relics, hosts, images, lamps, rosaries, liturgical vessels, vestments, processions, and pilgrimages, but especially against the sacral character of the clergy itself.[38] This deconstruction of a deep, complex sacrality, and this reflective and argumentative employment of the Holy Scriptures, especially the principle of "clarity [claritas scripturae]," against rituals rooted in the power of custom, spoke in a special voice to the burgher's mentality. When, however, the burghers' profanation of the sacral and the mundanization of the holy spread out into the countryside, they evoked a much stronger resistance—the reformers called it "ignorant stubbornness against God's Word"—than in the cities. "Village folk," wrote a theologian of Brandenburg-Ansbach in 1527, "who understand very little of the Word of God, are stiff-necked and hard to pry from their accustomed abuses."[39]

Sixthly, the cities' social and legal structures especially favored the Reformation. The strong social tensions created both a strong will from below for change and a strong desire from above for stability and moderation. In an atmosphere shot through with anticlericalism, the Reformation's mobilizing and stabilizing impulses brought the essential questions—eternal salvation, church reform, and the struggle "for a form of religion and of the church adequate to the city and its burghers"—onto the political community's agenda.[40] The consensus, on the one hand, which was vital to the urban community, came to depend on the clarification of such questions, which if unresolved could lead to unrest, revolution, and repression. For the first time in the German-speaking lands, thanks to the Reformation, issues of theology and church reform came to shape and become a central force in the social and political tensions in the cities and, shortly thereafter, on the land. The convergence, on the other hand, of pre-existing political, social, and economic unrest with the new religious question produced by 1525 a readiness for revolution unique in the Empire's urban history, as the Reformation's initial empowerment of the Christian community briefly bolstered the burghers' communal traditions against the long-dominant oligarchy of the magistrates.[41] Since the urban constitutions—unlike those of the territories—made the regimes susceptible to pressure from below, large groups of citizens could press successfully for religious changes and, for a time, influence the magistrates' will. Containing this force within established lines meant that the Reformation's victory produced a transformation of the urban church, as the magistrates, pushed forward by the communal reformation,[42] became the Empire's first rulers to evolve a deliberate policy of reform. In the years between 1522 and 1525, therefore, the official urban reformation began as a magisterial reform in a number of leading autonomous cities. The pioneers were Zurich, Nuremberg, Strasbourg, Memmingen, Reutlingen, and other free cities in the South, and in the North chiefly Bremen, Magdeburg, and Stralsund. Before any of these, however, came the reform ordinances issued at Wittenberg on 24 January 1522 and at Leisnig in early 1523 under the influence of Karlstadt and Luther respectively, of which the latter became a model for church ordinances in other communities.[43]

Seventhly and finally, the cities' pioneering reforms had a dramatic impact on the reformations outside their own territories, not least because the magistrates aggressively supported collaboration between cities and territorial princes. The peak of this development came in the far-reaching religious policies of Zurich, Bern, Strasbourg, Nuremberg, and Ulm. Most of the smaller cities, which lay in princely or noble territories—not to speak of the villages—lacked just this capability to choose their own course of reform and defend it against powerful external resistance, though the territorial towns could try to influence the religious policies of a prince who was friendly to the Reformation.

The importance of the larger free cities to the Reformation lay not in their autonomy, which was more vulnerable than that of the great princes, such as the Saxon elector, the Hessian landgrave, and the margrave of Brandenburg-Ansbach. Rather, their role in the Reformation's advance depended on the unique combination of political autonomy and internal religious conditions, and not on clever, efficient diplomacy alone. Among the cities' strengths were the complex religious and social impulses emitted by the communal reformation; the concentrated theological and political skills of educated preachers, writers of pamphlets, lawyers, secretaries, and humanists; and an aggressive partisanship for the Reformation during its decisive phase in the years 1524 to 1530—more precisely between the cities' assembly at Ulm in December 1524 through the protest at the Imperial Diet of Speyer in 1529 to the signing of the two Protestant confessions at Augsburg in 1530. The cities' entire economic and political configuration, plus their precocity in religious reform, thus made them for a few years the major voices of the Protestant party. Among the territorial states only Electoral Saxony and Hesse kept pace, whereas the special dynamism of the peasants' reformation, which depended on impulses from the cities,[44]was crushed in 1525-26 with the collaboration of the leading reformers and urban politicians.

5. THE CITIES AS VANGUARD OF THE REFORMATION

The course of the Reformation lends itself to hyperbolic formulae: without Luther and the cities, there would have been no Reformation;[45] without the knights and the peasants, the Reformation's course would have been quite different; without friendly princes, the Reformation would have been defeated. The connections between the cities and the Reformation can be expressed as well by the formula: the cities, free and territorial, were "the avant-garde of the Reformation."[46] They were its initiators and most influential agents, at least during the earliest and most popular phase, and its resonant centers of communications. They were also concentrations of theological ability, and the careers of the most important reformers were closely connected to specific cities: Huldrych Zwingli with Zurich; Johannes Oecolampadius with Basel; Martin Bucer with Strasbourg; Johannes Brenz with Schwäbisch Hall; Andreas Osiander with Nuremberg; Philip Melanchthon with Wittenberg; Andreas Bodenstein von Karlstadt with Wittenberg and Orlamünde; Thomas Müntzer with Zwickau, Allstedt, and Mühlhausen; Balthasar Hubmaier with Regensburg and

Waldshut; and John Calvin with Geneva. Luther's career, too, can be thought of in terms of such typically urban settings: the Augustinian convent, the university, the pulpit and services in a parish church, and the printshops.[47] Yet, the interplay between Luther and Wittenberg also shows how the Reformation depended from the very first on princely protection.

The urban reformations had a profound impact in many areas, notably in communications and scholarship. Luther's writings mobilized the literary, theological, legal, and political elites who were educated in Latin and humanist values. In the persons of theologians and educated councilors, this impact resonated into the princely residences and chancelleries, where it became a moving force. One famous example is Georg Spalatin, a tanner's son from Spalt, a town located near Nuremberg and in the diocese of Eichstätt. His legal, humanist, and theological training enabled him to secure an influential position in the Electoral Saxon chancellery and won him the confidence of Elector Frederick II (1463-1525), called "the Wise" (r. 1486-1525). From this power base Spalatin was able to supply Luther with his sovereign's protection and pave the way for a genuinely Protestant policy under Frederick's brother and successor, Elector John (1468-1532), called "the Constant" (r. 1525-32).[48]

Another such figure was Georg Vogler, who rose from the Latin school at Kulmbach to become secretary to Margrave Casimir and since 1521 the driving force for the introduction of the Reformation into the margraviates of Brandenburg-Ansbach-Kulmbach.[49] As chancellor of Margrave George (b. 1484, r. 1527-34), called "the Pious," Vogler collaborated with his good friend Lazarus Spengler, town secretary of Nuremberg, to promote the lands' conversion to Protestantism.[50] The names of Spalatin and Vogler may stand for the entire stratum of educated burghers who since around 1500 had moved into princely service, and who decisively influenced the decisions in favor of Protestantism.

The second effect of the urban reformation involved what may be collectively called "propaganda" for the Reformation. Its chief agents included 1) reformers of supra-local, even supra-regional stature, whose work in both local and broader contexts gave the larger Reformation a high measure of coherence; 2) the many theologically educated preachers, who through sermons and pamphlets unleashed the popular movement; 3) educated laymen (and a few women) whose pamphlets influenced the opinions of both the "Common Man" and

the magistrates;[51] 4) artisans and other middling folk who possessed
enough education to be able to write pamphlets or other documents
and, occasionally, to preach; and 5) agitators—among them assertive
women—who by word and deed built the movement's pressure
through the threat of violent disturbance and revolution. Groups of
partisans sometimes combined to disrupt divine services and processions, attack the clergy, invade the convents, destroy images and sacred
objects, organize demonstrations, sing provocative songs in public,
refuse to pay tithes, and even challenge the magistrates. This new, at
first typically urban combination of mass communications and the formation of public opinion brought the questions of salvation and reform of the Church out of the churches and into the streets and
squares, the inns and town halls, soon spreading beyond the walls to
the smaller territorial cities and the villages. It touched off the peasants' reformation and movements of radical social protest against the
lords, of spiritualist criticism of the "scholars of the [written] word,"
and of sectarian purity against the mixing of church with social "detri-
tus." Finally, the urban reformation's potential for disruption and violence influenced both the politics of the free cities ensemble and the Imperial Diet. Fear of revolt by the "Common Man" beset the civic and
princely authorities.[52] It played an essential role in preventing enforcement of the Edict of Worms of 1521, encouraging a policy of lax opportunism, and eventually mobilizing magisterial support for the Reformation.[53] The mass basis and the religious intensity of the early
urban reformation movement thus made the Reformation an irreversible event.

A third effect of the urban reformation was the powerful radiation
of reform into the princely reformations. The late medieval city possessed greater power to regulate local life than the princely regimes did,
and this power and their autonomy gave them the lead in forming new
churches. Essentially ahead of the princes, between 1525 and 1535
this step was taken at Zurich, Nuremberg, Strasbourg, Ulm, Memmingen, Reutlingen, Schwäbisch Hall, Constance, Basel, Magdeburg,
Bremen, Stralsund, Celle, Goslar, Brunswick, Göttingen, Hamburg,
Lübeck, Rostock, Greifswald, Hanover, and Breslau. The very few
princes who did reform in these early years—Prussia, Electoral Saxony,
Hesse, and Brandenburg-Ansbach-Kulmbach—took the cities as their
models.[54] From the cities they learned how to ensure uniform content
in the preaching of the gospel by means of edicts, inspections, and appointment policies; how to integrate the clergy as citizens or subjects;

how to dissolve the convents and secularize ecclesiastical property; how to redeploy ecclesiastical foundations and endowments into Protestant poorhouses, hospitals, and schools; how to suppress the Catholic Mass and establish a Protestant form of worship; how to get rid of excommunication and assume jurisdiction over marriage; how to get rid of dissidents; and how to establish regular visitations and regular catechetical instruction.[55] In these actions in the cities, late medieval "convergence" culminated in Reformation "congruence," as political responsibility for the citizenry and ecclesiastical responsibility for the parish converged in the hands of the Christian magistrates. The magistrates now claimed sovereignty not only over the ecclesiastical order and morals, but also over doctrine, which had formerly been strictly reserved to the church.[56] From the cities, where this new integrated church was created, the model passed beyond their walls and into the new territorial churches of the princes.

The urban reformation's fourth effect was to expand greatly the role of professional officials of bourgeois origin in the reformation and the confessionalization of the territories.[57] Urban influence was especially strong in the princes' corps of officials, which gave them a new quality of grip on their lands, and the Reformation's laicizing tendencies brought into these administrative posts ever larger cohorts of burghers, who replaced the clergy as partners of the nobles. It was precisely this stratum in the territories, too, which identified most closely with Protestantism and became, along with the Protestant clergy, the chief agents of the new Protestant confessions. Their presence formed a principal part, Volker Press wrote, of changes "which make the sixteenth a relatively 'bourgeois' century in the era of Old European status society."[58] The urban reformation's impact on the territories' reformations, was one aspect of what Schilling has called the "spread of urban behavior, sensibility, thought, and action, regardless of whether people lived in cities."[59]

Cities and princes were also old foes, of course, for in the late Middle Ages the former had to struggle to preserve their autonomy from the latter. The Reformation did not end this conflict, but it did promote a remarkable convergence of urban and territorial reformations, both in the confessionally based Smalkaldic League and through urban influence on territorial reformations. Although the Reformation's center of gravity did shift from the cities to the territories, it is nonetheless short-sighted to see the princes and the cities as rivals for the leadership of the Reformation or the Reformation as promoting the rise of one and the decline of the other. Our recognition of the territorial reformation's deep dependence on the urban communal reformation and on bourgeois officialdom warns us to avoid both exaggerated contrasts and schemes of periodization based on contrasts between urban and princely reformations.[60] Indeed, we should view the era from 1521 to 1555 in terms of a double movement: an embourgeoisement connected with the general urbanization; and expansionism of the princes in the context of early absolutism. The result was to diminish the space for an independent religious policy of the cities and to curb the urban reformation's communal element in favor of princely centralism.

6. The Urban Reformation and the Holy Roman Empire

It is correct to see the cities as leaders of the Reformation, but a view of the Reformation as "urban event" is exaggerated.[61] The Reformation's leadership also came from non-burghers—peasants, lesser nobles, and princes—and the cooperation between and amalgamation of urban and princely reformations shows that we must see the question of leadership in terms of social exchange rather than social rivalry. The cities did lead the Reformation, but only briefly and only in certain respects.

The limits on the urban reformation emerge clearly when we look at the religious policies of the Imperial estates in terms of the Reformation's ability to establish itself at the Imperial level. Its fate at the local level, of course, depended not only on its attractive power but also on external politics. While for a territorial city this meant its relationship to its territorial lord, for a free city it meant those to the emperor and the other Imperial estates represented in the Imperial Diet. What role could the Protestant free cities play on this stage? Or, to put it more generally, what importance did the cities have in the Reformation's success at the Imperial level?[62]

At the Imperial level, the free cities combined economic and cultural eminence with political dependence, so that the favor of even a weakened emperor meant more to them as princely power grew. Cities and princes did sometimes act together, for example, in the Swabian League's campaigns against noble banditry, but between them wariness or even hostility was the rule. The situation changed with the coming of the Reformation, notably in that the major free cities played an important Imperial role between the Diet of Worms in 1521 and that of Speyer in 1529 and a leading one in the Reformation movement from 1524 to 1526. The three leading southern free cities—Nuremberg, Strasbourg, and (to a lesser degree) Ulm—towed the smaller free cities in their wake toward an Imperial policy favoring the Reformation.

The free cities became the first "protestants" in the Reformation's history. On 6 April 1524 their envoys to the Imperial Diet of Nuremberg protested against the electors' and princes decision that the estates would enforce the Edict of Worms against Luther and his followers "to the degree that they can," and they named the Bible as the sole norm for all future proposals concerning religion.[63] This was the first occasion on which any Imperial estates took a public stand for the Reformation. And they maintained it. After learning that the Emperor Charles V had forbidden (on 15 July 1524) the proposed "national council" and called for enforcement of the Edict of Worms, the cities' envoys met in December 1524 at Ulm. Here they advanced from maneuver to affirmation, and their letter to Charles of 12 December may be regarded as the Reformation's first public confession on the Imperial level. The signatories, led by Nuremberg, both announced their obedient loyalty and confessed they would hold to the Word and to Christ's gospel to the last breath. Invoking Luther's doctrine of the Two Kingdoms, they acknowledged that in temporal matters ("as concerns ourselves and our property") they would obey the emperor and cling to their tradition of loyalty to the throne. In what concerned "the salvation of our souls," however, the civic regimes would defend the Reformation position even against the emperor and his edicts. The free cities maintained this position at the Imperial Diet of Speyer in 1526, where they retained the initiative in religious politics. With Saxon and Hessian support, their religious solidarity, political good judgment, and creativity in the religious question led to a partial success.

In the following years active leadership of the Reformation shifted to the Protestant princes, a change already visible at the Imperial Diet of Speyer in 1529. While fourteen free cities did sign the protest against the Diet's recess (19 April),[64] the free cities as a whole split into a Protestant, a Catholic, and an undecided group.[65] The initiative seized by the Protestant princes thereafter made the cities more and more into an appendage of their own confessional and alliance policy. This became clear at the Imperial Diet of Augsburg in 1530, when only two free cities—Nuremberg and Reutlingen—signed the princes' Confession of Augsburg. Thereafter, from 1531 on, the free cities played a subordinate role in the Protestant alliance called the "Smalkaldic

League."[66] With this shift the Protestant party began to mirror the Empire's own balance-of-power, following a brief interruption of princely dominance from which others—the Imperial knights and the peasants—benefited along with the cities.

The free cities' brief, episodic leadership of the Reformation movement can be explained by several things. First, the strongly popular nature of the urban communal reformation, which forced magistrates to adopt an Imperial policy favorable to change, also impressed some other Imperial rulers. A second reason was that the leading urban politicians united their diplomatic skills with a clear religious policy based on Protestant conviction.[67] Thirdly, during the years from 1521 to 1529 the highly competent urban theologians, who advised the politicians, brought the religious question to the fore against competing motives of political caution and economic opportunism.[68] Fourthly, the cities maintained a relative solidarity behind their religious policy. Finally, the emperor's absence and the princes' quiescence temporarily enhanced urban power, though their successes were made possible with Saxon (in 1524) and later (in 1526) also Hessian support.

The subsequent decline[69] of urban leadership mirrored the drift of events during the 1540s and 1550s: the bitter defeat in the Smalkaldic War (1546-47), the dangerous test posed by the Interim of Augsburg (1548),[70] and the Religious Peace of Augsburg, which denied them the full right of reformation (*jus reformandi*).[71] But the roots lay deeper, for after the Peasant War's failure neutralized the popular urban reformation, the initiative seized by the magistrates led the urban reformation to make a major step toward absorption in the princes' reformation.[72] Then, too, in the late 1520s the cities' solidarity collapsed, as the Catholic free cities gathered under Überlingen's leadership,[73] while others—Augsburg and Frankfurt—remained indecisive.[74] The eucharistic dispute, which split the Protestant cities into Lutheran and Swiss-South German parties, further weakened the cities' political position, and so did the debate on resistance to the emperor, which encouraged powerful Nuremberg to shun the Smalkaldic League for a path which was politically moderate and theologically punctilious.[75]

Nuremberg's policy illustrates how neuralgic their relationship to the emperor remained for the Protestant free cities, for religious resistance robbed them of their natural protector against the princes, while the war of 1546-47 turned their natural protector into their military opponent and conqueror. To be sure, the Protestant cause brought cities and princes, natural rivals, together as allies, showing the Reformation's power to disrupt old political loyalties and bridge traditional hostilities. In the longer run, however, this merely accelerated the free cities' political disfranchisement, for the only possible alternative—alliance with the free city-states of Switzerland—[76] was of dubious utility in Imperial politics. Some, notably Constance, Strasbourg, and Memmingen, did temporarily form close ties to Zurich,[77] but Zurich's defeat and Zwingli's death closed this door for good. The year 1531 witnessed the final shift of Protestant leadership from the free cities to the princes, as the split with the Swiss removed the most important religious counterweight to Lutheranism and the major political counterweight to the princes' reformation. At the same time, the renewal of the Edict of Worms by emperor and Diet in 1530 forced the Protestant cities to give up their Imperial loyalism and enter the Smalkaldic League, in which they became—as the Nurembergers correctly predicted—pawns of the princes' politics. The new order of things—Hessian political and Saxon theological leadership—restored the natural arrangement of Imperial politics after a brief period in which the cities' cultural creativity and communications had outweighed their political weakness.

We are now in a position to sum up the place of the urban reformations in the larger event of the German Reformation. So long as the movement's fate lay in the hands of educated men and the popular classes aroused by their sermons and pamphlets, and so long as the forces of a spontaneous mobilized, communally-minded Christian people bent on social and religious reform worked in a climate marked by political and military caution, the Reformation was overwhelmingly an urban affair—and briefly, too, a rural one. When, however, the Reformation became an irreversible political event of the first rank, and when the princes abandoned their caution, appropriated the Reformation and formed a military alliance, the Reformation was thenceforward a princely event.[78] Down to the beginning of the 1530s, the urban elites and their reformation enjoyed a certain political lead, but thereafter the princes absorbed this advantage into their own territorial reformations. At this point the modernity of the centralizing princely state overcame the corporate medieval governance of the magistrates, and the urban reformation was absorbed into the process of territorial confessionalization. Islands of communal, corporate reformation—too long ignored by research—long survived in the Empire's northern and western regions,[79] but such survivals little disturbed the hegemony of the princely reformation, now armed with the tools of a subordinated urban reformation.

Some other themes of current research on the urban reformation should at least be mentioned here:
1. the reasons for the success, delay, alteration, or failure of a particular city's reformation, including the intervention of external powers;[80]
2. the reformation's concrete effects on the burghers' everyday lives;[81]
3. the typology of urban reformation;[82]
4. the phases of urban reformations;[83]
5. possible correspondences between certain courses of reformation and specific types of cities and of outcomes;[84]
6. women's role in, and losses and gains from, the urban reformations (currently there is much interest in this subject);[85]
7. ecclesiastical discipline and especially the use of excommunication;[86]
8. the relationships among clergy, magistrates, and burghers, the formation of a new clergy and a new anticlericalism;[87]
9. a great deal has been written on the treatment of urban religious minorities and dissenters;[88] and
10. he specifically urban and bourgeois quality of the urban reformations.[89]

These and other open questions remain on the agenda of researchers of the urban reformations in the Empire. One other, vitally important subject, however, has been relatively neglected: the urban reformation as a theological event.

7. THE URBAN REFORMATION AS A THEOLOGICAL EVENT

The central thread of "religion and society," which runs through all of the questions named above, points us toward considering the urban reformation as a religious, ecclesiastical, and theological event. What the Reformation did, after all, was to put the central issues—the nature of true religion and the true form of the Church—at the center of public discussion, where it combined with burning social and political issues. That it served to mask quite mundane interests, which has happened in all eras of Christian history, is less interesting than how very intensely religious passion, theological understanding, and readiness to profess faith publicly invigorated and illuminated their social, economic, legal, cultural, and political contexts, either to make common cause with worldly calculations or—driven by the claims of truth and the promise of salvation—to oppose them.[90]

Contemporary observers were impressed by theology's extraordinarily forceful presence among the ordinary burghers and in high politics. If the fifteenth century had been an age of piety, the Reformation era was an age of theology. The shift is to be explained, first of all, by the discovery of a new religious security and law, not in a more intense piety but in a theological revolution. Secondly the shift arose from Luther's anchoring of ultimate truth in the purity of doctrine, not in the purity of life. Finally, the public clash of opinion, heated by propaganda, made theological truth the object of general debate, social demands, social conflict, and magisterial intervention. It is not easy for modern historians to grasp that the understanding of sin, justification, christology, and the sacraments—as Luther had conceived them—not only belonged to the educated elites but migrated also to the Common Man by means of the avalanche of pamphlets and sermons, Bible translations, songs, and catechisms. Ordinary people, even simple artisans, sought to learn them and absorbed them with great understanding.[91]

Theology's great impact meant the inclusion of much in the urban reformation that had nothing specifically to do with cities and burghers. The theology of a Luther or a Zwingli did possess a certain social embeddedness, to be sure, but it was not derived from a particular social or political constellation, nor was it exhausted by the reformers' social environments or those of their audiences.[92] Rather, they touched a common and fundamental level of the personality—what was called "conscience [Gewissen]" and awakened commitment on the part of individuals who felt called and liberated by God's Word. This effect went quite beyond the individual's social place and cannot be comprehended or explained in terms of it.

Hence, theology could cross all social boundaries, speaking to princes, nobles, and officials as well as artisans and peasants, and it could bind together different sorts of people in a common faith, theological reflection, confession, and ecclesiastical agenda. Compared to late medieval notions of solidarity, Reformation theology contained a new kind of penetration, which worked to unite as well as to divide. In the 1520s it split the Imperial estates of the free cities and the princes, recombining them into two socially dissimilar but confessionally similar blocks, producing what may be called a "similarity of the structurally dissimilar."[93]

Why did Luther and other Protestant reformers manage to engage specific groups of readers and listeners and speak to their specific conditions of life? First of all, because their theologies penetrated the burghers' world, adapting to the social, political, and legal situations of particular urban groups, but they were not swallowed up by it. Adaptation happened through hearing and reading, although content analysis of pamphlets by urban writers shows that most of their content is not peculiarly or typically "urban" in any sense but is informed by the existentially general character of the reformers' message and the religious situation. This well-attested fact raises questions about a specifically urban theology and the reformers' particular attraction for city folk. The central point in trying to answer these difficult questions is to limit the concept of "urban" to those aspects of theology framed especially to speak to the needs of urban people, without being exclusive to them. Such an "urban" theology could also become effective in the rural communal reformation or in the hands of a territorial reformer.

The burghers found especially attractive a theology which not only relieved them of clerical lordship and the pressure for religious accomplishment, but also provided for personal assurance of salvation and a good conscience, on the one hand, and strengthened "communal" values against the tyranny of "selfishness," on the other. This theology revitalized the communal idea and promoted collective moral renewal within the repristinated urban community. Its freely offered salvation liberated the believer from the religious egoism of a piety based on merit and satisfaction through good works, and it promoted brotherly love and an orientation to welfare of the neighbor and thus of the whole city. The doctrines of Christian community and believers' priesthood not only supplied a spiritual content to the urban values of the "common good," justice, civic equality, peace, and harmony, it also justified attacks on the "anti-communal" hierarchy of the old church. The result was a remarkable affinity of the new theology to the burghers' sacrally understood idea of community.[94] Finally, the slogan of "the Bible alone [sola scriptura]" offered the burghers a plausible, simple, comprehensible principle of emancipation and order, which could be extended to all areas of life and be employed to order them and to supply the civic community with a moral holism. The urban reformation's concentration of values preserved and escalated the late medieval ideals of the sanctification and purification of urban space and promised to elevate the burghers' city into a city of God, a new Jerusalem.

The power of Reformation theology in an urban context is represented by such figures as Jörg Vögeli[95] of Constance and Lazarus Spengler of Nuremberg, educated town secretaries whose pamphlets merged the theology of Luther or Zwingli with the heritage of urban values. The same could be said of those urban reformers who worked in the zone in which Luther's and Zwingli's influences overlapped: Ambrosius Blarer, Johannes Zwick, and Johannes Wanner at Constance[96] and Martin Bucer at Strasbourg.[97] The core of the paradigm, which these men created during the early 1520s, is present in both Zwingli and in Bucer, and its basic principle—the more Christian, the more social—is expressed by the title of Bucer's first pamphlet, *That None Should Live for Himself, But Only for Others, and How That is to be Done* of 1523.[98] Zwingli and Spengler cast this ethical formulation of the reformers' message into a thesis: Christian believers are the best citizens, the best rulers, and the best subjects.[99] This urban theology, of course, could be interpreted from below, based on the Common Man's needs, or from above, based on the elites' interests. The urban artisan-theologians, such as Sebastian Lotzer and Hans Sachs, turned their guns on wealth and learning, employing this theology differently from Zwingli and Bucer, not to speak of Osiander and Spengler.[100] Yet all of them shared a common theology developed in an urban context.

This foregoing places us in a position to summarize the chief characteristics of this "urban theology":

1. it was strongly weighted toward social ethics and tended to give equal standing to faith and love;[101]
2. it incorporated—unlike Luther's dialectic of law and gospel—the law into the gospel's domain;
3. it emphasized simultaneously individual and communal sanctification through obedience to divine law;
4. it regarded the religious and political communities as a Christian body (*corpus christianum*) and the kingdom of Christ, which existed simultaneously under the gospel (which frees for love), the law of Christ (which teaches love), and the spirit of Christ (which grants love);
5. it contained a strong emphasis on the union of the law with the Holy Spirit;

6. it tended to merge the natural law of creation with the "godly law" of salvation history, to which it subordinated human laws and norms;

7. it weakened, reinterpreted, or even rejected Luther's doctrine of the Two Kingdoms in favor of corporate ideal of a closed urban community and the fusion of spiritual with civic discipline;

8. it promoted order and discipline in a church purified of idolatry, in which special attention was paid to visual (images) and aural (music) aspects of worship; and

9. it united the honor of God with the "common good," the latter understood both personally as a good conscience and socially as civic peace.

This portrait of the urban theology largely agrees with the profile of the South German-Swiss urban reformation projected more than three decades ago by Wilhelm Bofinger and Bernd Moeller.[102] In the hands of Zwingli, Bucer, and Blarer, they found, the Reformation theology proved strongly adaptable to specifically communal patterns of thought and experience in this milieu. Not exclusively, of course, because some of its features are found as well both in both free and territorial cities in more northern regions. Their presence has also been detected in the South German rural reformation and in places where Luther's influence was dominant and Zwingli's weak or absent.[103] This suggests that we need not distinguish sharply between Luther's influence and that of Zwingli. Luther's writings predominated in the South German free cities until the beginning of the eucharistic dispute, while Zwingli had hardly any impact until April 1522. Luther's writings, therefore, formed the chief early source of the theology of the urban reformation, and the burghers understood him remarkably well, though after their own fashion and in a communally colored sense.[104] Somewhat later, the influence of Zwingli and other urban reformers strengthened and modified that of Luther.[105]

The evidence thus confirms that despite their different theological starting points, Luther and Zwingli stood closer to one another on the central theological points, notably on justification, than was traditionally recognized.[106] At least until the eucharistic dispute burst forth in 1525, their urban audiences considered them to be mutually supportive witnesses to the same evangelical truth.[107] Thereafter, tensions and polarizations emerged both within the cities and between cities, especially in the Southwest.[108] Parties then formed, and eventually the situation in the Southwest shifted in Luther's favor, making Zwinglianism a mere episode between the initial reception of Luther around 1520 and the eventual victory of the Lutheran confession since the mid-1530s.

This picture can be made more precise. Zwingli's impact seems to have been especially strong in the southern cities that possessed strong guilds, while Luther's was stronger in those that were ruled by patrician elites.[109] Then, too, during the eucharistic quarrel Zwingli spoke especially to the less educated folk of the middling and lower classes, while Luther was heard more in better-off circles.[110] Why should this have been so? Perhaps because Zwingli's view was simpler and easier to understand than Luther's more complex doctrine.[111] Possibly, too, to simpler folk Zwingli's more radical rejection of the Mass, images, and holy objects may have seemed *the* clear, logical, and unambiguous break with the old Church and its priests. Ultimately, however, the "Common Man's" preference for Zwingli probably depended on an understanding of reformation as the renewal of both Church *and* society. Both during and after the Peasants' War, the strong orientation of his theology toward social ethics and toward communal values[112] appealed more strongly to the little people than did Luther's teaching that the political, social, and economic realms cannot be judged according to an understanding of Christianity which unifies the political and the religious communities under the norm of "godly law."

These speculations should be regarded with healthy skepticism, so long as they cannot be documented unambiguously from the sources. Other findings also suggest the need for caution. We know, for example, that in northwestern Germany Lutheranism combined strongly with movements of social revolt in the cities,[113] and that Swiss Zwinglianism strongly supported the magistrates' oligarchical rule over the church. Further, the social transcendence of Reformation theology's impact and reception, described above, makes the brief alliances between a particular version of it and specific social groups very difficult to evaluate. The most we can state with certainty at this time is that in this theological age people chose to grapple with their social insecurity, loss of rights, and anxiety in religious and theological terms, and, further, that the position of a specific theologian—Luther, Zwingli, Bucer, Karlstadt, or Müntzer—could fuse either with specific social demands for change or with specific needs for stability, authority, and subordination. Whether the goal was emancipation or stability, all chose theology as their proper mode of expression. We must grasp this fact in all its complexity and recognize the autonomous dynamics of theology, piety, and reform, which frequently ran counter to the interests and mentalities of social groups. Such is the future task of research on the theme "religion and society" in the Reformation era.[114]

Translated by Thomas A. Brady, Jr.

NOTES

1. On the continuities between the Reformation and late medieval reform of church, theology, and piety, see Oberman (1977; English [1981]); Hamm (1993c).
2. For the literature on the urban reformation, see Rublack (1978a); Greyerz (1985); Rüth (1991), 198 note 3; H. Schilling (1993).
3. Dickens (1976), 182.
4. Lau (1959), 109-34, already criticized this neglect; see more recently the writings of Wilfried Ehbrecht, Rainer Postel, Heinz Schilling und Olaf Mörke.
5. See Mommsen (1979); Bátori (1980); Ehbrecht (1980); Greyerz (1984a) and (1984b).
6. Hamm (1992a), 179-81.
7. Isenmann (1988), 210-30; Boockmann (1986), 179-282; Meuthen (1984), 147-55, 197-203.
8. See Hamm (1992a), 184f.
9. Moeller (1987), 15.
10. See Hamm (1990).
11. Hamm (1989), 136, and (1993c), 24-41.
12. Dykema and Oberman (1993); Goertz (1987).
13. Pfeiffer (1966).
14. See esp. Kießling (1971).
15. Hamm (1993c), 68; and the argument by Constance's city council, 1526, in Dobras (1993), 113.
16. Rublack (1991), 9-14.
17. Hamm (1992a).
18. Hamm (1992b).
19. H. Schilling (1993), 38-39; Hamm (1992b), 256-57.
20. Examples in Hamm (1993c), 46-47, 59.
21. Bierbrauer (1982); Blickle (1986).
22. Arnold (1990); Russell (1986).
23. Köhler (1981) and (1986); Hohenberger (1994), 143-76; Edwards (1994).
24. See Scribner (1981a) and (1981b); Oelke (1992).
25. My variations on Moeller "No humanism, no Reformation," and "No printing, no Reformation." Moeller (1991), 109 and 115.
26. Maurer (1979), 325-61.
27. Rublack (1991), 64-65.
28. On Schappeler, see Maurer (1979), 67-69, 386-99.
29. Moeller (1981) and (1984); Hohenberger (1994), 296-302.
30. Ozment (1975), 38-42.
31. Berg (1992), xv-xxxiv.

32. J. Schilling (1990), 32-33, who declares, "No monks, no Reformation."
33. Oberman (1977), 347.
34. Elm (1989); Weinbrenner (1994).
35. Erasmus of Rotterdam (1968), 48.
36. See Hamm (1992b), 261-64.
37. See essays by Christoph Burger and R. W. Scribner, in Dinzelbacher and Bauer (1990).
38. On desacralization of things, see Rublack (1991), 84-99; Scribner (1985) and (1987), 95-97, 103-22. On desacralization of persons, see Goertz (1987), 56-57; Cohn in Mommsen (1979); Scribner (1987), 243-56; Dobras (1993), 101.
39. Muck (1879), 323 (my thanks to Martin Gernot Meier of Erlangen for this reference).
40. H. Schilling (1979), 239.
41. Examples in Schramm (1977), 139-41, 145-46, 152 (Danzig/Gdansk); Lau (1959), 131.
42. Blickle (1992), though Lau (1959) pointed in this direction.
43. Hamm (1993b), 270, 276.
44. For example, see Conrad (1984), 49-76.
45. Moeller (1983), 16.
46. Rüth (1991), 200.
47. Schwarz (1986), 123-31; Brecht (1987), vol. 2:64-66, 277-81, 415-21, and vol. 3:248-63.
48. Höß (1989). On this social type, see Stievermann (1986), 148-51.
49. Schuhmann (1980), 537-38.
50. Grimm (1978).
51. In Nuremberg especially the town secretary, Lazarus Spengler, who published his first evangelical pamphlet in 1519. H. von Schubert (1971); Grimm (1978); Hamm (1986) and (1993b), 269-70.
52. *Deutsche Reichstagsakten* (1963), vol. 4:507 line 16-508 line 2, no. 113.
53. Seebaß (1978), 74-75.
54. Blaschke (1978); Meier (1993), 10-12; Spitz (1981), 177, 179-80; H. Schilling (1981), 138-39, 145-46.
55. See, for illustrations, the themes of the opinions and ordinances concerning Nuremberg's reformation in Osiander (1975-90).
56. Moeller (1970) and (1974); Dobras (1993), 111.
57. Press (1980), 295, and his chapter in this *Handbook*, vol. 1, 437-66.
58. Press (1980), 283.
59. H. Schilling (1993), 58.
60. Hamm (1993b), 259-60, 289-93.
61. A. G. Dickens; as above note 3. Cf. the critique by Rublack (1978a), 22.
62. Baron (1937); Brecht (1977); G. Schmidt (1984); Brady (1985a); H. R. Schmidt (1986).
63. *Deutsche Reichstagsakten* (1963), vol. 4:500, 508 lines 28-33. See Brecht (1977), 189-202, 220-29; H. R. Schmidt (1986), 133-36, 145-49. 227-34, 268-74; Pfeiffer (1968), 308-10.
64. Brecht (1977), 233-41; Eger (1990), who lists the signatories at 60.
65. H. R. Schmidt (1986), 298-303.
66. G. Schmidt (1984); Brady (1994).
67. For example, the Strasbourg stettmeister Jacob Sturm. Brady (1995).
68. Pfeiffer (1968), 168-77; Brecht (1977), 197-200.

69. Moeller (1987), 59-67, 94-96; Dickens (1976), 177-99; Oberman (1977), 342-47.
70. See the example of Strasbourg in Weyrauch (1978) and Brady (1978).
71. Pfeiffer (1955); Warmbrunn (1983).
72. Except in the north, where the urban reformation continued as a spontaneous popular movement. Lau (1959). For the term "domestication, see Brady (1985a) and (1985b).
73. Brecht (1977), 231; and see H. R. Schmidt (1986), 299-303.
74. H. R. Schmidt (1986), 204-7; Jahns (1976) and (1991).
75. G. Schmidt (1984); and for a correct judgment on Nuremberg's policy, see Seebaß (1991), 123-26.
76. On the possibilities for and hindrances to such a constellation, see Brady (1985a).
77. Rublack (1971), 120-128; Bender (1970), 112-13, 170-72; Locher (1979), 344-45, 452-501.
78. Fabian (1962), 28.
79. Argued in a contrary sense by H. Schilling (1988a), (1988b), 181-83, and (1993), 87-93.
80. Such as a bishop or the Swabian League. Rublack (1978b); Mörke (1991).
81. On these three questions, see Greyerz (1980) on Colmar; Rublack (1982b) on Nördlingen; Mörke (1983) on Lüneburg, Brunswick and Göttingen; Abray (1985) on Strasbourg; Postel (1986) on Hamburg; Schröder (1987) on Esslingen; Weiß (1988) on Erfurt; Dobras (1993) on Constance; and Kaster and Steinwascher (1993) on Osnabrück.
82. Rüth (1991), 248-51; Moeller (1987), esp. 50-59, (1964), and (1987), 90-93.
83. Rublack (1980), whose plausible scheme identifies an "incubation phase" (entry and wakening of public interest), a "conflict phase" (formation of parties), an "interval phase" (first official changes), and a final "institutionalizing phase" (transformation of the local church). See also Rüth (1991), 247-48.
84. See Greyerz (1985), 46-48, and Rüth (1991), 248-51, for the literature.
85. Davis (1975), chaps. 3, 5; Roper (1990); Nowicki-Pastuschka (1990); Wunder (1992); Kobelt-Groch (1993); Dobras (1993).
86. W. Köhler (1932-42); Hamm (1984), 718-21.
87. On the new anticlericalism, which charged the "new popes" not with laxity but rigidity, see Dykema and Oberman (1993), esp. part 4.
88. Schneider (1970); Lienhard (1981).
89. Oberman (1977), 358-61.
90. See, for example, Dobras (1993), 53-109.
91. Zimmermann (1989); Arnold (1990).
92. On Luther, see Press (1984); on Zwingli, Hamm (1988).
93. Press (1989), 243.
94. H. Schilling (1988b), 164; Hamm (1988), 123.
95. Dobras (1993), 104.
96. Moeller (1961) and (1964).
97. Krieger and Lienhard (1993).
98. Bucer (1960), 59 lines 17-20.
99. Hamm (1988), 117, and (1984), 716 and note 67.
100. Arnold (1990), 56-105, 145-93; Hamm (1993a), 399-416; H. R. Schmidt (1986), 254-63.

101. Hamm (1978), 284.

102. Moeller (1987), esp. 31-59, 87-94.

103. H. Schilling (1987), esp. 327-28, 330-32, makes this point against Peter Blickle.

104. Hohenberger (1994). On Lazarus Spengler's communal understanding of Luther, see Hamm (1984).

105. Hamm (1978).

106. Hamm (1986) and (1988).

107. Hamm (1978); H. R. Schmidt (1986), 262.

108. Brecht and Ehmer (1984), 151-86.

109. H. R. Schmidt (1986), 262.

110. Moeller (1987), 52-53.

111. Zwingli taught a clear, one-dimensional desacralization of the eucharistic elements, while Luther's doctrine, although rejecting a magical, physical belief in the host, argued for a real presence of Christ. The latter presumes a higher degree of differentiation and abstraction, and it could easily be charged with only half-heartedly rejecting the materialistic and sacerdotal sacramental magic of the late Middle Ages. I owe this idea to Petra Seegets.

112. This is the basis for Zwingli's strong emphasis on the eucharist as a communal meal. Moeller (1987), 48 note 96.

113. Lau (1959); H. Schilling (1975); Moeller (1987) for literature; Ehbrecht (1980); Rotz (1985); Blickle (1988), 7-12, 25-28, 114-16, 120-21.

114. For their criticisms I am grateful to Heiko A. Oberman, Wolfgang Huber, Petra Seegets, and Martin Gölkel.

BIBLIOGRAPHY

Abray, Lorna Jane. *The People's Reformation, Magistrates, Clergy, and Commons in Strasbourg, 1500-1598.* Oxford, 1985.

Arnold, Martin. *Handwerker als theologische Schriftsteller. Studien zu Flugschriften der frühen Reformation (1523-1525).* Göttinger theologische Arbeiten, vol. 42. Göttingen, 1990.

Baron, Hans. "Religion and Politics in the German Imperial Cities during the Reformation." *English Historical Review* 52 (1937): 405-27, 614-33.

Bátori, Ingrid, ed. *Städtische Gesellschaft und Reformation. Kleine Schriften, 2.* SFN, vol. 12. Stuttgart, 1980.

Bender, Wilhelm. *Zwinglis Reformationsbündnisse. Untersuchungen zur Rechts- und Sozialgeschichte der Bürgerrechtsverträge eidgenössischer und oberdeutscher Städte zur Ausbreitung und Sicherung der Reformation Huldrych Zwinglis.* Zurich, 1970.

Berg, Dieter. *Bettelorden und Stadt. Bettelorden und städtisches Leben im Mittelalter und in der Neuzeit.* Saxonia Franciscana, vol. 1. Werl, 1992.

Bierbrauer, Peter. "Das Göttliche Recht und die naturrechtliche Tradition." In *Bauer, Reich und Reformation. Festschrift für Günther Franz,* ed. Peter Blickle, 210-34. Stuttgart, 1982.

Blaschke, Karlheinz. "Die Auswirkungen der Reformation auf die städtische Kirchenverfassung in Sachsen," in Moeller (1978), 162-67.

Blickle, Peter. *Communal Reformation: the Quest for Salvation in Sixteenth-Century Germany.* Trans. Thomas Dunlap. Studies in German Histories. Atlantic Highlands, N.J., 1992.

Blickle, Peter. "Das göttliche Recht der Bauern und die göttliche Gerechtigkeit der Reformatoren." *Archiv für Kulturgeschichte* 68 (1986):351-69.

Blickle, Peter. *Unruhen in der ständischen Gesellschaft 1300-1800.* Enzyklopädie deutscher Geschichte, vol. 1. Munich, 1988.

Boockmann, Hartmut. *Die Stadt im späten Mittelalter.* Munich, 1986.

Brady, Thomas A., Jr. "Göttliche Republiken: die Domestizierung der Religion in der deutschen Stadtreformation." In *Zwingli und Europa,* ed. Peter Blickle, Andreas Lindt and Alfred Schindler, 109-36. Zurich, 1985b.

Brady, Thomas A., Jr. *Protestant Politics: Jacob Sturm (1489-1553) and the German Reformation.* Studies in German Histories. Atlantic Highlands, N.J., 1995.

Brady, Thomas A., Jr. *Ruling Class, Regime and Reformation at Strasbourg, 1520-1555.* SMRT, vol. 23. Leiden 1978.

Brady, Thomas A., Jr. *Turning Swiss. Cities and Empire, 1450-1550.* Cambridge, 1985a.

Brecht, Martin. "Die gemeinsame Politik der Reichsstädte und die Reformation." *ZSRG, KA* 94 (1977):180-263.

Brecht, Martin. *Martin Luther.* Vol. 2, *Ordnung und Abgrenzung der Reformation, 1521-1532.* Vol. 3, *Die Erhaltung der Kirche, 1532-1546.* Stuttgart, 1987.

Brecht, Martin, and Hermann Ehmer. *Südwestdeutsche Reformationsgeschichte. Zur Einführung der Reformation im Herzogtum Württemberg 1534.* Stuttgart, 1984.

Bucer, Martin. *Deutsche Schriften.* Vol. 1, *Frühschriften 1520-1524,* ed. Robert Stupperich. Gütersloh, 1960.

Cohn, Henry J. "Reformatorische Bewegung und Antiklerikalismus in Deutschland und England," In Mommsen (1979), 309-29.

Conrad, Franziska. *Reformation in der bäuerlichen Gesellschaft. Zur Rezeption reformatorischer Theologie im Elsaß.* VIEG, vol. 116. Wiesbaden, 1984.

Davis, Natalie Zemon. *Humanismus, Narrenherrschaft und die Riten der Gewalt. Gesellschaft und Kultur im frühneuzeitlichen Frankreich.* Frankfurt am Main, 1987.

Deutsche Reichstagsakten, Jüngere Reihe. Edited by Historische Kommission bei der Bayerischen Akademie der Wissenschaften. Vol. 4. 2d ed. Göttingen, 1963.

Dickens, Arthur Geoffrey. *The German Nation and Martin Luther.* London, 1976 [1974].

Dinzelbacher, Peter, and Dieter R. Bauer, eds. *Volksreligion im hohen und späten Mittelalter.* Quellen und Forschungen aus dem Gebiet der Geschichte, n.s., vol. 13. Paderborn, 1990.

Dobras, Wolfgang. *Ratsregiment, Sittenpolizei und Kirchenzucht in der Reichsstadt Konstanz 1531-1548. Ein Beitrag zur Geschichte der oberdeutsch-schweizerischen Reformation.* QFRG, vol. 59. Gütersloh, 1993.

Dykema, Peter A., and Heiko A. Oberman, eds. *Anticlericalism in Late Medieval and Early Modern Europe.* SMRT, vol. 51. Leiden, 1993.

Edwards, Mark U., Jr. *Printing, Propaganda, and Martin Luther.* Berkeley and Los Angeles, 1994.

Eger, Wolfgang, ed. *Reformation und Protestation in Speyer. Quellen zur Reformationsgeschichte.* Veröffentlichungen des Vereins für pfälzische Kirchengeschichte, vol. 16. Speyer, 1990.

Ehbrecht, Wilfried. "Form und Bedeutung innerstädtischer Kämpfe am Übergang vom Mittelalter zur Neuzeit: Minden 1405-1535." In *Städtische Führungsgruppe und Gemeinde in der werdenden Neuzeit,* ed. Wilfried Ehbrecht, Städteforschung, ser. A, vol. 9, 115-52. Cologne and Vienna, 1980.

Elm, Kaspar. *Reformbemühungen und Observanzbestrebungen im spätmittelalterlichen Ordenswesen.* Berliner Historische Studien, vol. 14 = Ordensstudien, vol. 6. Berlin, 1989.

Erasmus of Rotterdam. "Epistola ad Paulum Volzium." In Erasmus of Rotterdam, *Ausgewählte Schriften,* ed. Werner Welzig, vol. 1:1-53. Darmstadt, 1968.

Fabian, Ekkehart. *Die Entstehung des Schmalkaldischen Bundes und seiner Verfassung 1524/29 - 1531/35. Brück, Philipp von Hessen und Jakob Sturm.* SKRG, vol. 1. 2d ed. Tübingen, 1962.

Goertz, Hans-Jürgen. *Pfaffenhaß und groß Geschrei. Die reformatorischen Bewegungen in Deutschland 1517-1529.* Munich, 1987.

Greyerz, Kaspar von. *The Late City Reformation in Germany. The Case of Colmar, 1522-1628.* VIEG, vol. 98. Wiesbaden, 1980.

Greyerz, Kaspar von, ed. *Religion and Society in Early Modern Europe 1500-1800.* London, 1984a.

Greyerz, Kaspar von, ed. *Religion, Politics and Social Protest. Three Studies on Early Modern Germany.* London, 1984b.

Greyerz, Kaspar von. "Stadt und Reformation: Stand und Aufgabe der Forschung." *ARG* 76 (1985):6-63.

Grimm, Harold J. *Lazarus Spengler: a Lay Leader of the Reformation.* Columbus, Ohio, 1978.

Guggisberg, Hans R., Gottfried G. Krodel, and Hans Füglister, eds. *The Reformation in Germany and Europe: Interpretations and Issues.* Gütersloh, 1993.

Hamm, Berndt. "Geistbegabte gegen Geistlose: Typen des pneumatologischen Antiklerikalismus - zur Vielfalt der Luther-Rezeption in der frühen Reformationsbewegung (vor 1525)." In Dykema and Oberman (1993), 379-440. [= 1993a]

Hamm, Berndt. "Das Gewicht von Religion, Glaube, Frömmigkeit und Theologie innerhalb der Verdichtungsvorgänge des ausgehenden Mittelalters und der frühen Neuzeit." In *Krisenbewußtsein und Krisenbewältigung in der Frühen Neuzeit - Crisis in Early Modern Europe. Festschrift für Hans-Christoph Rublack,* ed. Monika Hagenmaier and Sabine Holtz, 163-96. Frankfurt am Main, 1992a.

Hamm, Berndt. "Hieronymus-Begeisterung und Augustinismus vor der Reformation. Beobachtungen zur Beziehung zwischen Humanismus und Frömmigkeitstheologie

(am Beispiel Nürnbergs)." In *Augustine, the Harvest, and Theology (1300-1650).*
Festschrift für Heiko A. Oberman, ed. Kenneth Hagen, 127-235. Leiden, 1990.

Hamm, Berndt. "Humanistische Ethik und reichsstädtische Ehrbarkeit in Nürnberg."
Mitteilungen des Vereins für Geschichte der Stadt Nürnberg 76 (1989):65-147.

Hamm, Berndt. "Laientheologie zwischen Luther und Zwingli: Das reformatorische
Anliegen des Konstanzer Stadtschreibers Jörg Vögeli aufgrund seiner Schriften von
1523/24." In *Kontinuität und Umbruch. Theologie und Frömmigkeit in Flugschriften und Kleinliteratur an der Wende vom 15. zum 16. Jahrhundert*, ed. Josef Nolte,
Hella Tompert and Christof Windhorst, 222-95. SFN, vol. 2. Stuttgart, 1978.

Hamm, Berndt. "Reformation als normative Zentrierung von Religion und Gesellschaft." *Jahrbuch für Biblische Theologie* 7 (1992b):241-79.

Hamm, Berndt. "Reformation 'von unten' und Reformation 'von oben'. Zur Problematik reformatorischer Klassifizierungen." In Guggisberg, Krodel and Füglister
(1993), 256-93. [= 1993b]

Hamm, Berndt. "Stadt und Kirche unter dem Wort Gottes: das reformatorische
Einheitsmodell des Nürnberger Ratsschreibers Lazarus Spengler (1479-1534)." In
Literatur und Laienbildung im Spätmittelalter und in der Reformationszeit, ed. Lud-
ger Grenzmann and Karl Stackmann, 710-31. Stuttgart, 1984.

Hamm, Berndt. "Von der spätmittelalterlichen reformatio zur Reformation: der Prozeß
normativer Zentrierung von Religion und Gesellschaft in Deutschland." *ARG* 84
(1993c):7-82.

Hamm, Berndt. "Was ist reformatorische Rechtfertigungslehre?" *Zeitschrift für Theologie und Kirche* 83 (1986):1-38.

Hamm, Berndt. *Zwinglis Reformation der Freiheit.* Neukirchen-Vluyn, 1988.

Hohenberger, Thomas. *Evangeliumstreue und Christusglaube. Die Rezeption der lutherischen Rechtfertigungslehre in den reformatorischen Flugschriften der Jahre um
Worms 1521/22.* Unpublished Theological Dissertation, Erlangen, 1994.

Höß, Irmgard. *Georg Spalatin 1484-1545. Ein Leben in der Zeit des Humanismus und
der Reformation.* 2d ed. Weimar, 1989.

Isenmann, Eberhard. *Die deutsche Stadt im Spätmittelalter: 1250-1500. Stadtgestalt,
Recht, Stadtregiment, Kirche, Gesellschaft, Wirtschaft.* Stuttgart, 1988.

Jahns, Sigrid. "Frankfurt am Main im Zeitalter der Reformation (um 1500-1555)." In
Frankfurt am Main. Die Geschichte der Stadt in neun Beiträgen, 151-204. Veröffentlichungen der Frankfurter Historischen Kommission, vol. 17. Sigmaringen,
1991.

Jahns, Sigrid. *Frankfurt, Reformation und Schmalkaldischer Bund.* Studien zur Frankfurter Geschichte, vol. 9. Frankfurt am Main, 1976.

Kaster, Karl Georg, and Gerd Steinwascher, eds. In *450 Jahre Reformation in Osnabrück. Ein Ausstellungskatalog*, 267-69. Osnabrücker Kulturdenkmäler, vol. 6.
Bramsche, 1993.

Kießling, Rolf. *Bürgerliche Gesellschaft und Kirche in Augsburg im Spätmittelalter. Ein
Beitrag zur Strukturanalyse der oberdeutschen Reichsstadt.* Abhandlungen zur Geschichte der Stadt Augsburg, vol. 19. Augsburg, 1971.

Kobelt-Groch, Marion. *Aufsässige Töchter Gottes. Frauen im Bauernkrieg und in den
Täuferbewegungen.* Geschichte und Geschlechter, vol. 4. Frankfurt am Main and
New York, 1993.

Köhler, Hans-Joachim. "Erste Schritte zu einem Meinungsprofil der frühen Reformationszeit." In *Martin Luther: Probleme seiner Zeit*, ed. Volker Press, Dieter
Stievermann, 244-81. SFN, vol. 16. Stuttgart, 1986.

Köhler, Hans-Joachim. *Flugschriften als Massenmedium der Reformationszeit.* SFN,
vol. 13. Stuttgart, 1981.

Köhler, Walther. *Zürcher Ehegericht und Genfer Konsistorium.* 2 vols. Quellen und
Abhandlungen zur schweizerischen Reformationsgeschichte, vols. 7, 10. Leipzig,
1932-42.

Krieger, Christian, and Marc Lienhard, eds. *Martin Bucer and Sixteenth Century
Europe.* 2 vols. SMRT, vols. 52-53. Leiden, 1993.

Lau, Franz. "Der Bauernkrieg und das angebliche Ende der lutherischen Reformation
als spontaner Volksbewegung." *Luther-Jahrbuch* 26 (1959):109-134.

Lienhard, Marc. *Croyants et sceptiques au XVIe siècle. Le dossier des épicuriens.* Société savante d'Alsace et des régions de l'Est, ser. "Recherches et Documents," vol. 30. Strasbourg, 1981.

Locher, Gottfried W. *Die Zwinglische Reformation im Rahmen der europäischen Kirchengeschichte.* Göttingen and Zurich, 1979.

Maurer, Justus. *Prediger im Bauernkrieg.* Calwer Theologische Monographien, vol. 5. Stuttgart, 1979.

Meier, Martin Gernot. *Die Einführung der Reformation in der Markgrafschaft Ansbach - Bayreuth - Kulmbach in den Jahren 1526-1533.* Unpublished. M.A. Thesis, Erlangen, 1993.

Meuthen, Erich. *Das 15. Jahrhundert.* Oldenbourg Grundriß der Geschichte, vol. 9. 2d ed. Munich, 1984.

Moeller, Bernd. "Einige Bemerkungen zum Thema: Predigten in reformatorischen Flugschriften." In Köhler (1981), 261-68.

Moeller, Bernd. *Johannes Zwick und die Reformation in Konstanz.* QFRG, vol. 28. Gütersloh, 1961.

Moeller, Bernd, ed. *Der Konstanzer Reformator Ambrosius Blarer 1492-1564. Gedenkschrift zu seinem 400. Todestag.* Constance, 1964.

Moeller, Bernd. "Luther und die Städte." In *Aus der Lutherforschung. Drei Vorträge,* ed. gemeinsame Kommission der Rheinisch-Westfäl. Akademie der Wissenschaften und der Gerda Henkel Stiftung, 9-26. N. p., 1983.

Moeller, Bernd. *Die Reformation und das Mittelalter. Kirchenhistorische Aufsätze.* Ed. Johannes Schilling. Göttingen, 1991.

Moeller, Bernd. *Reichsstadt und Reformation. Bearbeitete Neuausgabe.* Berlin, 1987 [1962].

Moeller, Bernd, ed. *Stadt und Kirche im 16. Jahrhundert.* SVRG, no. 190. Gütersloh, 1978.

Moeller, Bernd. "Was wurde in der Frühzeit der Reformation in den deutschen Städten gepredigt?" *ARG* 75 (1984):176-93.

Moeller, Bernd. "Zwinglis Disputationen. Studien zu den Anfängen der Kirchenbildung und des Synodalwesens im Protestantismus, part 2." *ZSRG, KA* 56 (1970): 275-324; 60 (1974):213-364.

Mommsen, Wolfgang J., ed. *Stadtbürgertum und Adel in der Reformation / The Urban Classes, the Nobility and the Reformation.* Publications of the German Historical Institute London, vol. 5. Stuttgart, 1979.

Mörke, Olaf. *Rat und Bürger in der Reformation. Soziale Gruppen und kirchlicher Wandel in den welfischen Hansestädten Lüneburg, Braunschweig und Göttingen.* Veröffentlichungen des Instituts für historische Landesforschungen der Universität Göttingen, vol. 19. Hildesheim, 1983.

Mörke, Olaf. *Die Ruhe im Sturm. Die katholische Landstadt Mindelheim unter der Herrschaft der Frundsberg im Zeitalter der Reformation.* Studien zur Geschichte des Bayerischen Schwabens, vol. 19. Augsburg, 1991.

Muck, Georg. *Geschichte von Kloster Heilsbronn von der Urzeit bis zur Neuzeit,* Vol. 1. Nördlingen, 1879.

Nowicki-Pastuschka, Angelika. *Frauen in der Reformation. Untersuchungen zum Verhalten von Frauen in den Reichsstädten Augsburg und Nürnberg zur reformatorischen Bewegung zwischen 1517 und 1537.* Pfaffenweiler, 1990.

Oberman, Heiko A. *Werden und Wertung der Reformation. Vom Wegestreit zum Glaubenskampf.* Tübingen, 1977 (English: *Masters of the Reformation.* Cambridge, 1981).

Oelke, Harry. *Die Konfessionsbildung des 16. Jahrhunderts im Spiegel illustrierter Flugblätter.* Arbeiten zur Kirchengeschichte, vol. 57. Berlin - New York, 1992.

Osiander d. Ä., Andreas. *Gesamtausgabe.* 8 vols. Ed. Gerhard Müller and Gottfried Seebaß. Gütersloh, 1975-1990.

Ozment, Steven E. *The Reformation in the Cities. The Appeal of Protestantism to Sixteenth-Century Germany and Switzerland.* New Haven and London, 1975.

Petri, Franz, ed. *Kirche und gesellschaftlicher Wandel in deutschen und niederländischen Städten der werdenden Neuzeit.* Städteforschung, ser. A, vol. 10. Cologne and Vienna, 1980.

Pfeiffer, Gerhard. "Der Augsburger Religionsfrieden und die Reichsstädte." *Zeitschrift des Historischen Vereins für Schwaben* 61 (1955):213-321.

Pfeiffer, Gerhard, ed. *Quellen zur Nürnberger Reformationsgeschichte. Von der Duldung liturgischer Änderungen bis zur Ausübung des Kirchenregiments durch den Rat (Juni 1524 bis Juni 1525).* Einzelarbeiten aus der Kirchengeschichte Bayerns, vol. 45. Nuremberg, 1968.

Pfeiffer, Gerhard. "Das Verhältnis von politischer und kirchlicher Gemeinde in den deutschen Reichsstädten." In *Staat und Kirche im Wandel der Jahrhunderte,* ed. Walther Peter Fuchs, 79-99. Stuttgart, 1966.

Postel, Rainer. *Die Reformation in Hamburg 1517-1528.* QFRG, vol. 52. Gütersloh, 1986.

Press, Volker. "Martin Luther und die sozialen Kräfte seiner Zeit." In *Luther und die politische Welt,* ed. Erwin Iserloh and Gerhard Müller, 189-217. Historische Forschungen, vol. 9. Stuttgart, 1984.

Press, Volker. "Stadt und territoriale Konfessionsbildung." In Petri (1980), 251-96.

Press, Volker. "Die Territorialstruktur des Reiches und die Reformation." In *Reformation und Revolution. Beiträge zum politischen Wandel und den sozialen Kräften am Beginn der Neuzeit. Festschrift für Rainer Wohlfeil,* 239-68. Stuttgart, 1989.

Roper, Lyndal. *The Holy Household. Women and Morals in Reformation Augsburg.* Oxford, 1990.

Rotz, Rhiman A. "'Social Struggles' or the Price of Power? German Urban Uprisings in the Late Middle Ages." *ARG* 76 (1985):64-95.

Rublack, Hans-Christoph. *Eine bürgerliche Reformation. Nördlingen.* QFRG, vol. 51. Gütersloh, 1982b.

Rublack, Hans-Christoph. *Die Einführung der Reformation in Konstanz von den Anfängen bis zum Abschluß 1531.* QFRG, vol. 40. Gütersloh and Karlsruhe, 1971.

Rublack, Hans-Christoph. "Forschungsbericht Stadt und Reformation." In Moeller (1978), 9-26. [= 1978a]

Rublack, Hans-Christoph. *Gescheiterte Reformation. Frühreformatorische und protestantische Bewegungen in süd- und westdeutschen geistlichen Residenzen.* SFN, vol. 4. Stuttgart, 1978b.

Rublack, Hans-Christoph. "Grundwerte in der Reichsstadt im Spätmittelalter und in der frühen Neuzeit." In *Literatur in der Stadt. Bedingungen und Beispiele städtischer Literatur des 15. bis 17. Jahrhunderts,* ed. Horst Brunner, 9-36. Göppinger Arbeiten zur Germanistik, vol. 343. Göppingen, 1982a.

Rublack, Hans-Christoph. *... hat die Nonne den Pfarrer geküßt? Aus dem Alltag der Reformationszeit.* Gütersloh, 1991.

Rublack, Hans-Christoph. "Reformatorische Bewegung und städtische Kirchenpolitik in Esslingen." In Bátori (1980), 191-220.

Russell, Paul A. *Lay Theology in the Reformation. Popular Pamphleteers in Southwest Germany 1521-1525.* Cambridge 1986.

Rüth, Bernhard. "Reformation und Konfessionsbildung im städtischen Bereich. Perspektiven der Forschung." *ZSRG, KA,* 77 (1991):197-282.

Schilling, Heinz. *Aufbruch und Krise: Deutschland 1517-1648.* Berlin, 1988b.

Schilling, Heinz. "Aufstandsbewegungen in der Stadtbürgerlichen Gesellschaft des Alten Reiches. Die Vorgeschichte des Münsteraner Täuferreichs, 1525-1534." In *Der Deutsche Bauernkrieg 1524-1526,* ed. Hans-Ulrich Wehler, 193-238. Geschichte und Gesellschaft, Sonderheft 1. Göttingen, 1975.

Schilling, Heinz. "Die deutsche Gemeindereformation - ein oberdeutsch-zwinglianisches Ereignis vor der 'reformatorischen Wende' des Jahres 1525?" *ZHF* 14 (1987):325-33.

Schilling, Heinz. "Gab es im späten Mittelalter und zu Beginn der Neuzeit in Deutschland einen städtischen 'Republikanismus'? Zur politischen Kultur des alteuropäischen Stadtbürgertums." In *Republiken und Republikanismus im Europa der Frühen Neuzeit*, ed. Helmut Koenigsberger, 101-143. Schriften des Historischen Kollegs. Kolloquien 11. Munich, 1988a.

Schilling, Heinz. *Konfessionskonflikt und Staatsbildung. Eine Fallstudie über das Verhältnis von religiösem und sozialem Wandel in der Frühneuzeit am Beispiel der Grafschaft Lippe.* Quellen und Forschungen zur Reformationsgeschichte, vol. 48. Gütersloh, 1981.

Schilling, Heinz. "Die politische Elite nordwestdeutscher Städte in den religiösen Auseinandersetzungen des 16. Jahrhunderts." In Mommsen (1979), 235-308.

Schilling, Heinz. *Die Stadt in der frühen Neuzeit.* Enzyklopädie deutscher Geschichte 24. Munich, 1993.

Schilling, Johannes. *Gewesene Mönche. Lebensgeschichten in der Reformation.* Schriften des Historischen Kollegs, Vorträge, vol. 26. Munich, 1990.

Schmidt, Georg. *Der Städtetag in der Reichsverfassung. Eine Untersuchung zur korporativen Politik der Freien und Reichsstädte in der ersten Hälfte des 16. Jahrhunderts.* VIEG, vol. 113. Wiesbaden 1984.

Schmidt, Heinrich Richard. *Reichsstädte, Reich und Reformation. Korporative Religionspolitik 1521-1529/30.* VIEG, vol. 122. Wiesbaden, 1986.

Schneider, Gerhard. *Der Libertin. Zur Geistes- und Sozialgeschichte des Bürgertums im 16. und 17. Jahrhundert.* Studien zur Allgemeinen und Vergleichenden Literaturwissenschaft, vol. 4. Stuttgart, 1970.

Schramm, Gottfried. "Danzig, Elbing und Thorn als Beispiele städtischer Reformation (1517-1518)." In *Historia Integra. Festschrift für Erich Hassinger,* ed. Hans Fenske, Wolfgang Reinhard, and Ernst Schulin, 125-54. Berlin, 1977.

Schröder, Tilman Matthias. *Das Kirchenregiment der Reichsstadt Esslingen. Grundlagen - Geschichte - Organisation.* Esslinger Studien vol. 8. Esslingen, 1987.

Schubert, Hans von. *Lazarus Spengler und die Reformation in Nürnberg.* QFRG, vol. 17. New York and London 1971 [1934].

Schuhmann, Günther. "Die Markgrafen von Brandenburg-Ansbach. Eine Bilddokumentation zur Geschichte der Hohenzollern in Franken." *Jahrbuch des Historischen Vereins für Mittelfranken* 90 (1980).

Schwarz, Reinhard. *Luther.* Die Kirche in ihrer Geschichte, vol. 3, part I. Göttingen, 1986.

Scribner, Robert W. "Flugblatt und Analphabetentum. Wie kam der gemeine Mann zu reformatorischen Ideen?" In H.-J. Köhler (1981), 65-76. [= 1981a]

Scribner, Robert W. *For the Sake of Simple Folk. Popular Propaganda for the German Reformation.* Cambridge Studies in Oral and Literate Culture, vol. 2. Cambridge, 1981b.

Scribner, Robert W. *Popular Culture and Popular Movements in Reformation Germany.* London, 1987.

Scribner, Robert W. "Volkskultur und Volksreligion. Zur Rezeption evangelischer Ideen." In *Zwingli und Europa,* ed. Peter Blickle, Andreas Lindt, and Alfred Schindler, 151-61. Zurich, 1985.

Seebaß, Gottfried. "The Importance of the Imperial City of Nuremberg in the Reformation." *Humanism and Reform: the Church in Europe, England, and Scotland, 1400-1643. Essays in Honour of James K. Cameron,* ed. James Kirk, 113-27. Studies in Church History, Subsidia 8. Oxford, 1991.

Seebaß, Gottfried. "Stadt und Kirche in Nürnberg im Zeitalter der Reformation." In Moeller (1978), 66-86.

Spitz, Lewis W., ed. *Humanismus und Reformation als kulturelle Kräfte in der deutschen Geschichte. Ein Tagungsbericht.* Veröffentlichungen der Historischen Kommission zu Berlin, vol. 51. Berlin and New York, 1981.

Stievermann, Dieter. "Sozial- und verfassungsgeschichtliche Voraussetzungen Martin Luthers und der Reformation - der landesherrliche Rat in Kursachsen, Kurmainz und Mansfeld." In *Martin Luther: Probleme seiner Zeit,* ed. Volker Press and Dieter Stievermann, 137-76. SFN, vol. 16. Stuttgart, 1986.

Warmbrunn, Paul. *Zwei Konfessionen in einer Stadt. Das Zusammenleben von Katholiken und Protestanten in den paritätischen Reichsstädten Augsburg, Biberach, Ravensburg und Dinkelsbühl von 1548-1648.* VIEG, vol. 111. Wiesbaden, 1983.

Weinbrenner, Ralph. *Observanz und Privileg. Observanzideal und Reformpraxis im 15. Jahrhundert, dargestellt am Beispiel des Augustinervikars Andreas Proles.* Unpublished dissertation, Erlangen, 1994.

Weiß, Ulman. *Die frommen Bürger von Erfurt. Die Stadt und ihre Kirche im Spätmittelalter und in der Reformationszeit.* Weimar, 1988.

Weyrauch, Erdmann. *Konfessionelle Krise und soziale Stabilität. Das Interim in Straßburg (1548-1562).* SFN, vol. 7. Stuttgart, 1978.

Wunder, Heide. *"Er ist die Sonn', sie ist der Mond". Frauen in der Frühen Neuzeit.* Munich, 1992.

Zimmermann, Gunter. "Die Rezeption der reformatorischen Botschaft: Laienaussagen zu Predigten des Franziskanerpaters Jeremias Mülich in der Fastenzeit 1524." *ZBLG 58* (1989):51-70.

INTERNATIONAL CALVINISM

Robert M. Kingdon
(University of Wisconsin-Madison)

Calvinism was from the beginning an international form of Protestantism. It never had the ethnic rootings in a single culture so evident in Germanic Lutheranism and in many forms of Germanic or Dutch religious radicalism. It became the form of Protestantism most widespread in Switzerland, France, the Netherlands, Poland, Hungary, Scotland, England, and elsewhere. It made brief if unsuccessful attempts to penetrate Italy and Spain. It won over significant parts of the German homeland of the Reformation, providing an alternative to Lutheranism that many local governments found attractive, leading in the end to the "united" Lutheran-Calvinist churches which are such a prominent part of the German ecclesiastical scene today.

The international character of Calvinism was built into its structure at its very beginning. Calvinism was created within colonies of religious refugees, sometimes powerful enough to take over effective control of their host communities. These refugees had particularly strong attachments to a new form of religion, had often suffered considerably because of their commitment to it. They were particularly determined to make it strong and effective, free of any contamination from the forms of religion against which they were in revolt. Yet these refugees were often not fully at home in their host communities, regularly dreamed of returning to their homelands, in many cases did. The constant coming and going associated with these colonies of refugees necessarily made them more internationally-minded than other groups of Protestants. They kept more informed of religious developments in other areas, most prominently in their home countries. They remained more determined to share their beliefs with others, again most obviously in their home countries. These factors explain the institutional dynamics that made of Calvinism a peculiarly international form of Protestantism.

1. Geneva: Foundation

It was in the city-state of Geneva that the international character of Calvinism first became evident. Its newly reformed church served as a "mother-church" to the many congregations all over Europe and even beyond that adopted its form of Protestantism. It provided a set of institutional models that these other churches imitated in many details. It is thus with Geneva that we must begin our analysis.

Before the Reformation, Geneva was the capital of an ecclesiastical state, governed by a prince-bishop, in close collaboration with the neighboring duchy of Savoy, a relatively large state controlling much of what is now southeastern France and northwestern Italy. If developments had followed the course usual in most of Europe, the Genevan state would have been gradually absorbed into Savoy. Instead the citizens of Geneva staged a revolution against both the temporal and ecclesiastical authority of their prince-bishop. They made of their city an entirely independent state. They took with them only a small part of the hinterland around their city. The greater part of the diocese of Geneva remained Catholic and under strong Savoyard influence. The citizens of Geneva were able to succeed in this revolution only because they won the support of Swiss neighbors, most importantly the republic of Bern which was then a formidable military power and which had recently adopted a Zwinglian form of Protestantism. Bernese armies swarmed south around Geneva, conquering sections of Savoyard territory for their own use, effectively shielding Geneva from Savoyard military retaliation.

The revolution by which Geneva became Protestant was unusually radical. It involved the ejection not only of the bishop, but also of practically all the priests, monks and friars, nuns and sisters, and others employed by the episcopal establishment. An entire social class, the clergy, was destroyed. It included many of the richest, most powerful, and best educated people in the city.[1] To fill the resulting social vacuum, religious refugees were invited into Geneva. Most of them came from France, where Protestantism coincidentally was rapidly spreading. Many refugees also came from Italy, with one particularly influential group from the town of Lucca. Other groups came from Britain, the Netherlands, and Germany. Individuals came from eastern Europe. Geneva became the cosmopolitan center it remains to this day.

Of these refugees, the most prominent was John Calvin (1509-64).

During a casual visit to Geneva in 1536, he was invited by William Farel (1489-1565), the founder of Protestantism in Geneva, to become a public lecturer. The two were both ejected in 1538, for demanding reforms more radical than the local government was then prepared to accept. Calvin moved on to Strasbourg, where he became minister of a congregation of French refugees. There he found a group of enthusiastic and dedicated converts who provided an ideal laboratory for creating a more tightly disciplined religious community than had been common among Protestants to that date. When he was called back to Geneva in 1541, he was prepared to establish this new form of Protestantism. To this end he immediately began deploying the formidable skills he had acquired not only in the ministry but also in advanced legal training. A set of laws he drafted for the city created four orders of ministry: pastors who were to preach the Word of God; doctors who were to do scholarly research on the Word of God; elders who were to maintain Christian discipline by controlling the behavior of the population; deacons who were to administer charity.[2] Each of these groups of ministers was to be governed collectively. All traces of the one-man rule associated with the Catholic institution of bishop were to be abolished. The pastors alone met as the Company, over which Calvin presided as Moderator, to govern the local church. The pastors and elders together met as the Consistory, to control all behavior in the community.[3] The supervisors of the new General Hospital, who were responsible for supervising all local charity, found their position sacralized when Calvin supplied them with the title of deacon. Additional sets of foreign deacons were chosen at Calvin's suggestion to handle charity among the groups of refugees pouring into the city. These institutions became characteristic of Calvinism, and were replicated in one way or another in the many communities that followed Calvin's lead. The functions of the Consistory were particularly distinctive. Ecclesiastical control of behavior became a defining characteristic of Calvinism. Other magisterial Protestants agreed that there should be control of behavior, but believed that it should be left to the state. Radical Protestants believed in tight discipline, but as independent and often illegal congregations did not control secular tools of enforcement. Only an occasional Catholic reforming bishop built a program of discipline as thoroughgoing as the Calvinist one.

The authority of these new ecclesiastical institutions, to be sure, was not fully recognized at the beginning of Calvin's ministry in Geneva. Many local citizens found in the Consistory, in particular, a return to

ecclesiastical repression of a kind they had disliked under the Catholic
bishop. They were quite prepared to accept Calvin's theology, but they
resented his discipline. This faction of the population was roundly defeated by a faction supported by ever-growing numbers of refugees,
mostly from France. In what amounted to a second ecclesiastical revolution, the pro-French faction took over control of the city in 1555.[4]
Now even larger groups of refugees poured into Geneva, not only from
France but from other countries. Significant groups of Italians and
English organized refugee churches. By 1560, nearly half the population was made up of refugees. From 1555 on Calvin's power was without challenge. He was in effective charge of the entire city. The city of
Geneva had been taken over by refugees as effectively as the German
episcopal city of Münster had earlier been taken over by refugees, most
of them radicals from the Netherlands. The difference is that in Geneva the refugees remained in power.

It was at this point, in 1555, that Geneva became the most important center for the international spread of a new type of Protestantism.
Its influence was so great that it even came to be called the Protestant
Rome. At the institutional center of this activity was the Geneva Company of Pastors. It was now made up almost entirely of French refugee
pastors chosen by Calvin, men of advanced education and often of
high social standing, many of them sons of noblemen. There were almost no local people within it. There were comparatively few with
previous experience in the priesthood or in religious orders. This made
them quite different from groups of Protestant clergymen in other mu-
nicipalities. The Italian and English churches organizing within Geneva in these years were of a similar social composition. Prominent
among their leaders were refugee noblemen. Because of differing developments within their native countries, the Italians stayed and the
English went home.

These years of Calvinist triumph in Geneva coincided with a rapid
spread of Protestantism in France. The movement was now spreading
like wildfire, overwhelming all the many strenuous attempts by the Roman Catholic Church and the French monarchy to contain it. Dozens,
hundreds, finally thousands of Protestant congregations were organized. In many cities, including most of the major ones outside of the
Paris, the capital, Protestant factions became so strong that they seized
control of city governments, although usually for only a short period of
time. A substantial percentage of the nobility, including high aristocrats, most prominently the Bourbon princes of the blood royal, be-

came Protestant, and mobilized armies designed to defend the Reformed cause. The spread of Protestantism in France was finally checked only when Catholic aristocrats gained support of the royal armies and, in addition, organized armies of their own, to resist with force the Protestant advance. This provoked religious wars which began in 1562, and were punctuated by appalling massacres and systematic devastation of the entire country. They ended in 1598 when the royal Edict of Nantes granted a degree of temporary toleration to the Reformed. When peace returned Protestantism had survived in France, but only as a thoroughly humbled minority, whose worship and discipline were closely regulated by royal law.

In the period of Protestant spread within France before 1562, and to a more limited degree thereafter, Geneva and its Company of Pastors played a central role. It was at this time that Geneva's role as a "mother-church" became most obvious. Dozens of French Protestant churches organizing for the first time appealed to the Geneva Company for pastoral leadership. The Company responding by creating institutions of education, including rounds of sermons from the city pulpits, a series of lectures outside of church services undertaken by Calvin himself, and "congregations" or adult Bible classes for laymen with leadership provided by pastors. Finally in 1559 the Academy of Geneva (a forerunner to the present University of Geneva) was created, primarily to train Protestant pastors. From the pool of men introduced by these institutions to the Calvinist version of Christianity, the Company selected pastors for new churches, primarily in France. Some of Geneva's own pastors joined this pool, including several of the more prominent. Thus François de Morel, sieur de Collonges, was sent to Paris as a pastor. And Nicolas des Gallars, sieur de Saules (c. 1520-c. 80), was sent to London to a church of French refugees, later to Orleans where he created another Academy as well as leading a Reformed church in a community which for a time had housed the headquarters of the French Huguenot army.

Within France itself, these new churches created for themselves a number of supervisory and coordinating bodies. Within localities these bodies were called colloquies. Within provinces they were called synods. Within the nation as a whole they were called national synods. Each of these bodies represented all of the churches under its jurisdiction, including among its members both ordained pastors and lay elders. Each of them resolutely followed the principle of collective leadership, going to considerable lengths to avoid any appearance of

one-man rule. Even the presiding officer of a national synod was not
elected until the synod began and maintained his authority only until
the synod ended. The national synod had the special duty of creating
an official Confession of Faith, defining the belief of the entire body of
French Reformed Churches. It also drew up a general Discipline, or
constitution, for these churches, and then supervised its use in maintaining order among them. A first Confession and Discipline were
drawn up in the constituting synod of the French Reformed Churches,
meeting secretly in Paris in 1559. More official versions were drawn
up in the synod of La Rochelle in 1572, meeting openly under the protection of Huguenot military commanders. In both of these national
synods, representatives from Geneva played a prominent role.[5]

In theory these bodies created a hierarchy, with local congregations
responsible to colloquies, colloquies responsible to provincial synods,
and provincial synods responsible to national synods. In practice it
was impossible to create and maintain a hierarchy that neat. The
spread of Protestantism within France had been very uneven. And the
continuing chaos generated by waves of persecution and then sporadic
warfare, made it impossible to maintain regular communications, let
alone an orderly ecclesiastical hierarchy.

This fact created for the Geneva Company of Pastors a new function. It came to act as a continuing source of advice and as a court of
appeals, to iron out disputes within local churches, colloquies, and
even synods. If a problem could not be resolved through normal channels, perhaps because a local colloquy or synod could not meet, the
problem would often be referred to Geneva for resolution. This became so widely known as an important part of its work, that the Geneva Company even came to act as a court of appeals for other countries. Sticky problems that had developed in places like London and
Frankfurt could and were referred to Geneva for resolution. In this the
Company did indeed function in some ways as a Protestant Rome. It
never gained, however, the general and continuing recognition that the
appellate courts in Rome held for the international Catholic community. As peace returned to France and to other countries containing
Calvinist congregations, local and national synods, or equivalent bodies, took over these functions.

Not only did Geneva provide leaders and supervision for new Calvinist congregations in France. It also provided printed matter, most
importantly Calvinist service books and catechisms, in significant addition works of theology and polemic. Among the many refugees flood-

ing into Geneva were printers, including some of the most illustrious from France's largest printing centers, men like Robert Estienne of Paris (1499-1559), the king's own printer, and Antoine Vincent of Lyons (d. 1568). They made of Geneva a major center of publication, second only to Paris and Lyons for the French-speaking world, of some significance to other countries as well. Large quantities of works in Latin produced in Geneva, for example, sold in such outlets outside of France as the semi-annual Frankfurt book fairs. In Frankfurt they would be purchased by buyers primarily from Germany, of course, but they would also reach buyers there from many other countries. The fact that one finds significant numbers of these books even today in libraries as far away as eastern Hungary indicates the range of the market to which they appealed. In addition to their voluminous printings of works in Latin and French, the presses of Geneva produced as well works in such other vernacular languages as English, Italian, and Spanish. Networks of colporteurs, book peddlers, fanned out from Geneva to distribute these books, primarily within France, but to a degree throughout the Protestant world.[6] Some of these networks were directed by publishers, some were assisted by ecclesiastical institutions. The *bourse française*, for example, nominally an institution of charity designed to help poor French refugees, also got involved in the business of producing and peddling books.[7]

The degree to which Geneva provided leadership for the international Calvinist movement was most pronounced at the beginning, between 1555 and 1564, in the period of Calvin's personal leadership. This, indeed, may explain why his name is so often attached to the movement. Strong leadership continued under his immediate successor, Theodore Beza (1519-1605), who had the same high-powered education and many of the same personal skills, with the useful addition of noble blood. But it began to fade in the later years of Beza's career, particularly after 1580, when he stepped down as Moderator of the Company of Pastors. As local Calvinist churches established themselves, they saw less and less reason to resort to Geneva for leaders and books, or to appeal to Geneva to resolve disputes. Geneva's role diminished particularly after relative peace returned to France with the Edict of Nantes in 1598, and newly militant dukes of Savoy threatened to reconquer Geneva, climaxing in an armed attack on the city in 1602, known as the Escalade. New centers of education began training Calvinist leaders, including academies like Saumur and Sedan in France, including a particularly well-endowed new university of the Netherlands in Leiden, including such German institutions as the University of Heidelberg and an Academy in Herborn. New centers of publishing began producing Calvinist books, especially in Germany, in the Netherlands, and in England. Disputes were now usually referred to synods for resolution, including both provincial and national synods, climaxing in the international Synod of Dordrecht that met between 1618 and 1620 to hammer out a definitive statement on the details of the key Calvinist doctrine of predestination. Geneva retained the affection and respect of the international Calvinist community. But in the late sixteenth and early seventeenth centuries it was reduced to begging other Calvinist centers for money to keep its own activities going. Only in the late seventeenth century did it regain some of its earlier prestige and power. By this time the duchy of Savoy had given up its dreams of reconquering Geneva. And the persecution of Protestantism within France, climaxing in the revocation of the Edict of Nantes by King Louis XIV in 1689, led to a collapse of French Protestant ecclesiastical institutions and an urgent need for men in Geneva and elsewhere to step into a resulting vacuum in leadership.

2. EMDEN: GATHERING

Of the other centers that joined Geneva in providing leadership to international Calvinism, one which became particularly prominent was Emden, in northwestern Germany, close to the border with the Netherlands. For a time in the later sixteenth century it was called, with good reason, the "Geneva of the North." It acted as a "mother-church" to many communities in that part of Europe, particularly in the Netherlands. Its contributions to the Dutch Reformation are strikingly similar to those of Geneva's contributions to the French Reformation. It did not import its Calvinism directly from Geneva, but it moved in a strikingly similar way to a position that in the end was formally labeled Calvinist.

The Reformation had begun in the parts of northern Germany around Emden in the usual Lutheran way, with the main initiatives coming from secular governments and their advisers. The counts who controlled East Friesland and its most important city, the port of Emden, joined princes all over the Holy Roman Empire in moving in this direction. The key figure in the early reformation of Emden was Countess Anna (1501-75), who assumed power in 1540. She hired as a superintendent for the churches that were being reformed in her area a Polish nobleman named John a Lasco (1499-1560). Lasco, however, was not an orthodox Lutheran trained in Wittenberg of the sort then reforming most north German cities. He was a highly educated humanist who displayed many sympathies for the Zwinglian variety of Protestantism then being embraced in parts of southern Germany, usually within free imperial cities. He displayed an additional sympathy for the Calvinist concern for strict discipline, superintended by the church. He created a rudimentary disciplinary committee within the Great Church of Emden, the most important church in the area. It was not as yet a disciplinary institution of the Calvinist type, like the Genevan Consistory, since its lay members were chosen by the local countess rather than from within the church.

Lasco's work in East Friesland was interrupted by the imperial Interim of 1548, which forced Protestants throughout the Holy Roman Empire either to compromise with Catholics or give up. Lasco, like many of the more committed Protestants, decided to leave. He moved to England, then turning in a solidly Protestant direction under the government of Edward VI. He was given responsibility for directing a large congregation of religious refugees in London, most of them Dutch. He was thus in a position quite like Calvin's in Strasbourg. In London he, too, found a group of enthusiastic and dedicated converts who provided him with an ideal laboratory for creating a more tightly disciplined religious community than had been common among Protestants. When England's return to Catholicism forced Lasco and most of his congregation to leave London, they returned to the continent, finally settling in Emden in 1554. They brought with them an experience of ecclesiastical discipline under their own supervision and a real enthusiasm for its use. They were already a community much like the ones that Calvin had created out of French refugees, at first in Strasbourg and later in Geneva. Lasco soon left Emden to return to his native Poland. His followers in Emden, however, were determined to implement his program of ecclesiastical discipline. They were supported in this by thousands of Dutch religious refugees fleeing their native Netherlands, in reaction to the bitter persecution launched by their Spanish suzerains. These refugees together, both those who had come directly from the Netherlands and those who came via London, effectively took over control of the Church in Emden. They made of Emden a Calvinist republic in many ways similar to Geneva. Just as the Geneva church had been taken over by French refugees, so was the Emden church taken over by Dutch refugees.

The Reformed Church of Emden adopted a characteristically Calvinist organization in developing three orders of the ministry: pastors to preach the Word of God, elders to control behavior, and deacons to administer charity. Like many of the churches following in Geneva's footsteps, it omitted the order of doctors, in effect combining it with the order of pastors. The activities of these ministers were coordinated not by several institutions as in Geneva, but by one body, a Church Council made up of all the pastors and elders in the city, commonly called either the "presbyterium" or the "consistorium." This Council exercised all the supervisory functions of the Geneva Company of Pastors and all the disciplinary functions of the Geneva Consistory. In addition all the deacons in the community reported to it, including both those who operated the "Gasthaus" for the local poor and those who ministered to the needs of the foreign poor.

This Reformed Church belonged to the *classis* of East Friesland, a representative body coordinating the work of all Protestant churches within the county. It was thus subject to a degree of external supervision that one does not find in Geneva. Emden, however, was by any standard the most powerful and most influential church in the area. The *classis*, thus, was generally likely to follow Emden's lead. Both in submitting to this exterior control and in governing itself with a single ecclesiastical body, Emden was far more typical than Geneva of most of the communities that came to call themselves Calvinist.

Emden's Reformed Church was an established one, with a legal monopoly of all forms of worship. That monopoly was not as absolute, however, as that of Geneva's Reformed Church. It had to face a certain amount of internal competition. There was a Lutheran church that first won official encouragement from Count Edzard II (1532-99) in 1568, and became a positive threat to the Reformed in the 1590's, when, after a period of joint rule with his brother John II (1538-91), Edzard took over full control of the government. There was a large community of Mennonites that bothered the established Calvinists by competing successfully for the allegiance of many local people of the lower classes. There were occasional groups of other radicals, including followers of David Joris. There were a few Catholics. There was even a Jewish congregation. Only after the Emden "revolution" of 1595, in which the Church, with the help of Dutch military intervention, won complete independence from the secular government of Edzard II, were the Calvinists in full control. It was as a result of this process, in fact, that the Reformed Church became formally and self-consciously Calvinist. Menso Alting (1541-1612), who became the leading pastor of Emden in 1575, after a period of service in Heidelberg, was an enthusiastic exponent of Calvinist theology in all its nuances. More than any other person, he directed the process that made of Emden a republic that was proud to call itself Calvinist.

Long before that happened, however, Emden had served as a "mother-church" to communities all over northern Europe that were to join it in becoming formally Calvinist. The development of a characteristically Calvinist ecclesiastical discipline in Emden had coincided with the rapid spread of Calvinism in the Netherlands, which began a few years after the spread of Calvinism in France. To a degree it was stimulated by the development of French Protestantism, entering the Netherlands at first in its southern French-speaking provinces. In the "wonderyear" of 1566, Calvinism had raced throughout the provinces, winning control of entire cities, often accompanied by iconoclastic riots. It had won to its support many of the most prominent members of the Dutch nobility, most importantly from the House of Orange. These initial Calvinist successes had provoked savage persecution from the Spanish authorities who claimed supreme control over all the seventeen provinces that then made up the Netherlands. This persecution drove thousands of committed Protestants from their homes, creating large refugee communities, at first in such Netherlandish cities as Antwerp, then in Emden, in England, and in many parts of Germany. This persecution also, however, helped provoke the political revolt of the Netherlands, which first began to take shape in 1572 under the leadership of the Prince of Orange, which soon won control of the northern provinces of Holland and Zealand, and which was ultimately to create an independent Dutch republic entirely free of Spanish control. Everywhere the Dutch won control they established Calvinist churches. And in this process Emden played a crucial role.

Like Geneva, Emden served as a recruiting point for Reformed pastors to serve a much larger neighboring country, this time the Netherlands. Many of them were refugees simply waiting for an opportunity to return to their home areas. Requests for their services as pastors poured into the Emden Church Council, throughout the late 1560s and early 1570s. The Council took over much of the responsibility for matching candidates and congregations. In this it was acting much like the Geneva Company of Pastors, faced with a similar opportunity in France, in the late 1550s and early 1560s. Like Geneva, Emden also served as center of Protestant publication. For a time a high percentage of all the Reformed books printed for distribution in the Netherlands were products of presses in Emden, most of them moved there from the south.[8] Like Geneva, Emden also helped the Dutch Reformed in creating an institutional framework for their churches. The constituting synod of the Dutch Reformed Church, which adopted the Belgic Confession designed to define the faith of Dutch Calvinists, and which created its first written Discipline, actually met in Emden, in 1571.[9] It was almost entirely the work of refugees rather than of Emden natives, including, to be sure, some who had been in the city for a considerable period of time. The local Church Council was not formally involved in the work of this synod in any significant way, although its members must have followed the synod's deliberations with interest. As in France, the hierarchical structure created by this synod could not begin to function freely for some time. The Emden Church Council, as a result, was often called upon to imitate Geneva in supplying advice and in mediating conflicts within Dutch churches all over northern Europe. An inordinate amount of its time went into mediating conflicts within the Dutch Church in London and within the French-speaking Church made up of refugees from the southern Netherlands that was housed in Emden itself.

The big difference between Emden and Geneva is that the Reformation directed from Emden succeeded whereas the one directed from Geneva failed. The northern provinces of the Netherlands did become Calvinist. France never did. This meant that a high percentage of the refugees who had fled to Emden and who for a time controlled its church went home again. It meant that the training of new generations of Dutch Reformed ministers was entrusted to institutions within the Netherlands itself, most prominently the new university in Leiden. It meant that practically all the printers who had made of Emden a flourishing center for publication either retired or moved south again. It even meant that the port of Emden, which at the height of the Dutch refuge had been arguably the most prosperous along the entire north Atlantic seacoast, lost most of its business and shrank once more into a relatively insignificant backwater. It has also meant that modern historians, well aware of Geneva's role in organizing international Calvinism, have overlooked Emden's. For a time, however, Emden made contributions to the spread of international Calvinism that were of crucial importance.

3. Branching Out

The pattern we have observed in Geneva and Emden can be found in many other areas. The process of turning to Calvinism often began within a group of dedicated religious refugees, who created abroad communities characterized by tight social discipline to which all their members became intensely committed, and then brought that disciplined form of religion home. This happened not only in France and the Netherlands. It also happened in Britain. The Marian exiles, groups of committed Protestants who left Britain during the reign of Mary Tudor because they were offended by her strenuous attempts to return all of England to the Roman Catholic Church and frightened by the savage persecution with which she implemented this program, returned to Britain to make it Calvinist. Calvinism in its most complete form was brought to Scotland directly from Geneva by John Knox (c. 1513-72). In a rather short period of exile there, Knox had discovered a purer form of religion than he had seen in any other community, the purest, he was convinced, that the world had seen since the time of the apostles. In other towns he had found religion truly preached but nowhere else had he found it so truly lived.[10] When Knox returned to Scotland he led in the creation of a Reformed Church that adopted a typically Calvinist Confession of Faith and Book of Discipline in its constituting General Assembly of 1558. The further work of building in Scotland such typically Calvinist institutions as the coordinating presbytery, the Scottish equivalent to the French colloquy or the Dutch *classis*, was the work of a successor to Knox, Andrew Melville (1545-1622), who also spent a period of time in Geneva.

Calvinism was also brought to England at the same time, again by religious refugees returning from the continent. It developed in England, however, in a diluted way. Under Elizabeth I (1533-1603), the Church of England became Calvinist in theology but not in church organization or liturgy. Elizabeth had no use for institutions of collective leadership and was determined to maintain an episcopal organization for her newly Reformed church. In this she was helped by such returning refugees as John Jewel (1522-71), who returned from Zurich to become her Bishop of Salisbury, and Edmund Grindal (c. 1519-83), who returned from Strasbourg to become her bishop of London, then her Archbishop of York, finally her second primate, succeeding Matthew Parker (who had not gone into exile) as Archbishop of Canterbury. Calvinists who wanted to push the Elizabethan Reformation further,

to "purify" the Church of England of remnants of Catholic practice
and ritual, created the Puritan party in both church and state. It became increasingly militant in the succeeding decades, and England became increasingly polarized between militant Calvinist Puritans and
moderate Calvinist Anglicans. In the seventeenth century the Anglicans became less Calvinist, with many of them adopting the modifications of Calvinist theology worked out by Arminius and his followers.
The controversy between Puritans and Anglicans pushed England into
a civil war, beginning in 1640 and ending in 1660. That war resulted
in an initial triumph of Calvinist Puritans, in alliance with their brethren from Scotland. But in the end it resulted in an Anglican resurgence
that left only dissenting minorities faithful to a fully developed version
of Calvinism.

4. The Palatinate and Germany

Calvinism penetrated other areas in a somewhat different way. In a
number of principalities within the Holy Roman Empire of the German
Nation, Calvinism was introduced from above by existing governments, in much the same way that Lutheranism was normally introduced, not from below by groups of militant refugees in full revolt
against an established regime. From the beginning Calvinism had
proved itself attractive to the nobility in the many of the parts of Europe in which it had first spread. Aristocrats from the French House of
Bourbon had been crucial in winning its limited toehold in France.
Aristocrats from the Dutch House of Orange had made possible its triumph in the Netherlands. Aristocrats assembled into a group called
the Lords of the Congregation had made possible its victory in Scotland. These noblemen had all found Calvinism a useful tool in revolts
against central governments.

Aristocrats in other parts of Europe, who were already in control of
local governments, now also saw advantages in adopting Calvinism.
They may have been attracted by its evident internationalism, hoping it
would make it easier for them to attract allies from other countries.
They may have hoped to find in Calvinist ecclesiastical discipline a way
of increasing control over their subjects to a greater degree than would
have been possible with such alternative religions as Lutheranism and
Catholicism. The pattern for this type of Calvinism was established for
Germany in the County Palatine of the Rhine, with its headquarters in
Heidelberg.

The Palatinate was one of the seven great electoral principalities that provided an important level of political leadership for much of the Holy Roman Empire. While the chief executive of the imperial government was provided by the imperial household controlled by the Hapsburg family, with its headquarters in Vienna, an important secondary level of leadership came from the seven electoral princes. They not only controlled directly their own substantial territories. They also shared considerable responsibilities in the imperial administration. It was the support of one of these princes, the Elector of Saxony, which had made the initial Reformation led by Luther possible. It was the support of other electors and their princely allies that helped make the further spread of Protestantism throughout Germany possible. The County Palatine of the Rhine had first adopted a form of Lutheran Protestantism. But it moved in a Calvinist direction under Frederick III (1515-76), who ruled from 1559. Hard-line Lutherans were expelled from the leadership of the Church of the Palatinate and from the University of Heidelberg, its most important educational institution. In their place a number of moderates were appointed, including moderate Lutherans influenced by Melancthon, including Zwinglians influenced by Zurich, including finally Calvinists influenced by Geneva. They were an unusually cosmopolitan group, with Italian and French intellectuals joining Germans. The two most influential were Zacharias Ursinus (1534-83), who had been trained by Melancthon in Wittenberg, and Kaspar Olevianus (1536-87), who had received a part of his training from Calvin in Geneva. They prepared an instrument for instruction in the Reformed faith, the Heidelberg Catechism, which became another of the great defining documents of Calvinist belief. It was drafted in 1562, approved by a local synod, and issued in 1563. It was issued in the name of the Prince Elector with a preface he had written himself. It thus had a very different character from the confessions issued by the French, the Dutch, and the Scots, entirely on the authority of their constituting synods.

Several years later, in 1570, at the urging of Olevianus and others, the Prince Elector established within the Reformed Church of the Palatinate social discipline of a Calvinist kind. This introduction of consistorial discipline had to overcome suspicion from many among the nobility and considerable formal opposition from theologians, mostly from a party of Zwinglians led by Thomas Erastus. But in the end the Calvinists triumphed and established their form of religion in the Palatinate. That establishment was soon overturned following the death of Frederick III in 1576, by his son Ludwig VI (1539-83), who was determined to restore pure Lutheranism in the principality. The men who had created Calvinism in the Palatinate were then forced to move to such other principalities as Herborn and Nassau, where they once again turned churches in a Calvinist direction. But Ludwig was in turn succeeded by John-Casimir (1543-92), who brought Calvinism back. By the early seventeenth century the Palatinate and its capital Heidelberg were unquestioned centers of German Calvinism.

Calvinism in the Palatinate displayed a strikingly international character. This character was particularly obvious in its university in Heidelberg, which became one of the most important training centers for Calvinist pastors in all of Europe. Among its faculty members one finds the great Italian Hebraist Emmanuel Tremellio (1510-80) and the great Italian systematic theologian Jerome Zanchi (1516-90). Among its students one finds many who became leaders in the Dutch Reformed Church. This work of training was supported by several publishing houses, some of them local, some of which had moved to Heidelberg from other countries, like Jean Mareschal of Lyons in France.

The government of the Palatinate involved itself deeply in international Calvinist politics. Electors during the sixteenth century sent substantial military detachments to France in support of the Huguenot revolt against the royal government. A seventeenth-century Elector, Frederick V (1596-1632), pushed this international policy to a length that proved catastrophic, provoking the disaster that historians call the Thirty Years War.

This pattern of a Calvinism imposed from above by a princely government was replicated in many German principalities, most of them relatively small ones in the west, not far from the frontiers with France and the Netherlands. Toward the end of the sixteenth century, however, the Margraves of Brandenburg, another of the seven great electoral houses, began toying with the Calvinist option. They eventually made of Calvinism a court religion at their capital in Berlin, but they never could carry the bulk of their Lutheran population with them. In the end, centuries later, they imposed a Calvinist-Lutheran union on Brandenburg and Prussia.

Calvinism was also carried to Poland and Hungary by powerful aristocrats. Even though a substantial percentage of the Polish nobility for a time adopted Calvinism, that adoption turned out to be relatively ephemeral. By the end of the sixteenth century Poland was being restored to pure Catholicism by forces of the Catholic Counter Reformation, spearheaded by Jesuits. Its politico-religious history resembles that of France. In Hungary Calvinism won a somewhat more enduring success. Hungarian magnates established a number of important Calvinist centers in the eastern part of their country, which survived a long period of Turkish occupation, emerging with a Calvinist church structure led by bishops, in some ways reminiscent of the Church of England.

Whether led by groups of religious refugees as at the beginning or by ambitious aristocrats as in later times, Calvinism remained a peculiarly international form of Protestantism. That remained true throughout the sixteenth century. It remains true to this day.

NOTES

1. For further development of this argument, see Robert M. Kingdon, "Was the Protestant Reformation a Revolution? the Case of Geneva," in Robert M. Kingdon, ed., *Transition and Revolution: Problems and Issues of European Renaissance and Reformation History* (Minneapolis, 1974), 53-107.

2. There are many editions of these laws. One good one can be found in Jean-François Bergier, ed., *Registres de la Compagnie des Pasteurs de Genève au temps de Calvin*, vol. 1 (Geneva, 1964): 1-13.

3. For a report on recent research on this institution, see Robert M. Kingdon, "Calvin and the Establishment of Consistory Discipline in Geneva: the institution and the men who directed it," *Nederlands Archief voor Kerkgeschiedenis* 70 (1990): 158-72.

4. For a good recent account of this revolution, see William G. Naphy, *Calvin and the Consolidation of the Genevan Reformation*. Manchester, 1994.

5. A team of scholars directed by Bernard Roussel of the Ecole des Hautes Études in Paris is working intensively on these institutions, with a view to preparing a critical edition of the acts of the French national synods. For a useful preliminary report on their work, see Glenn Sunshine, "From French Protestantism to the French Reformed Churches: the development of Huguenot ecclesiastical institutions, 1559-1598," unpublished Ph.D. diss., University of Wisconsin, Madison, 1992.

6. For the history of Calvinist printing in Geneva, see, i. a., Eugénie Droz, ed., *Aspects de la propagande religieuse* (Geneva, 1957); Paul Chaix, *Recherches sur l'imprimerie à Genève de 1550 à 1564* (Geneva, 1954); Hans Joachim Bremme, *Buchdrucker und Buchhändler zur Zeit der Glaubenskämpfe: Studien zur Genfer Druckgeschichte, 1565-1580* (Geneva, 1969).

7. Jeannine E. Olson, *Calvin and Social Welfare: Deacons and the Bourse Française* (London and Toronto, 1989), 50-69.

8. On Calvinist printing in Emden, see Andrew Pettegree, *Emden and the Dutch Revolt: Exile and the Development of Reformed Protestantism* (Oxford, 1992), 87-108, 252-311.

9. J. F. Gerhard Goeters, ed., *Die Akten der Synode der Niederländischen Kirchen zu Emden vom 4.-13. Oktober 1571* (Neukirchen-Vluyn, 1971).

10. John Knox to Mrs. Locke, December 9, 1556, in David Laing, ed., *The Works of John Knox*, vol. 4 (Edinburgh, 1855): 240.

BIBLIOGRAPHY

For a useful and recent general introduction to the growth and spread of international Calvinism, see Menna Prestwich, ed., *International Calvinism, 1541-1715* (Oxford, 1985), a compilation of essays by a number of authors who are specialists on Calvinism in specific countries. It may be criticized for tending to lose sight of the connections between these countries, and thus of the international character of the movement, but it could be argued in reply that there was some tendency for national Calvinist churches to go their own way once they were firmly established.

For the contribution of Geneva to the early creation and spread of international Calvinism, see Robert M. Kingdon, *Geneva and the Coming of the Wars of Religion in France, 1555-1563*, THR, vol. 22 (Geneva, 1956), and *Geneva and the Consolidation of the French Protestant Movement, 1564-1572*, THR, vol. 92 (Geneva, 1967). For the records of the institution primarily responsible for this spread, see Jean-François Bergier, Robert M. Kingdon, Olivier Fatio, Olivier Labarthe, Bernard Lescaze, Micheline Tripet, Sabine Citron, Marie-Claude Junod, Gabriella Cahier, and Michel Grandjean, eds., *Registres de la Compagnie des Pasteurs de Genève*, THR, vols. 55, 107, 137, 153, 180, 198 (Geneva, 1962-84). These seven volumes cover the period from 1546 to 1599. Other scholars are carrying the edition forward into the seventeenth century.

For Emden's contribution to the spread of international Calvinism, see Andrew Pettegree, *Emden and the Dutch Revolt: Exile and the Development of Reformed Protestantism* (Oxford, 1992). For the records of the institution primarily responsible for this spread, see Heinz Schilling and Klaus-Dieter Schreiber, eds., *Die Kirchenratsprotokolle der Reformierten Gemeinde Emden, 1557-1620*, Städteforschung. Veröffentlichungen des Instituts für vergleichende Städtegeschichte (Cologne, Vienna, and Weimar, 1989-1992). See also, J. F. Gerhard Goeters, ed., *Die Akten der Synode der Niederländischen Kirchen zu Emden vom 4.-13 Oktober 1571* (Neukirchen/Vluyn, 1971); Menno Smid, *Ostfriesische Kirchengeschichte*, Ostfriesland im Schutz des Deiches, vol. 6 (Pewsum, 1974).

For studies of other groups of refugees within which Calvinist churches developed and from which Calvinism spread, see Philippe Denis, *Les églises d'étrangers en pays rhénans 1538-1564* (Paris, 1984); Christina Hallowell Garrett, *The Marian Exiles: a Study in the Origins of Elizabethan Puritanism* (Cambridge, 1938 [1966]); Charles Martin, *Les protestants anglais réfugiés à Genève au temps de Calvin, 1555-1560* (Geneva, 1915); Andrew Pettegree, *Foreign Protestant Communities in sixteenth-century London* (Oxford, 1986).

For the Palatinate, see Volker Press, *Calvinismus und Territorialstaat: Regierung und Zentralbehörden der Kurpfalz, 1559-1619* (Stuttgart, 1970). For the process in Germany as a whole, see Heinz Schilling, ed., *Die reformierte Konfessionalisierung in Deutschland: das Problem der 'Zweiten Reformation.' Wissenschaftliches Symposion des Vereins für Reformationsgeschichte 1985*, SVRG, no. 195 (Gütersloh, 1986).

THE RADICAL REFORMATION

James M. Stayer
(Queen's University)

1. From Theology to History

The conception of a Radical Reformation has undergone continual re-definition since it was introduced by George Huntston Williams in 1962. From its introduction onward it had evident attractions as an alternative to "Anabaptists," the conventional English term, which signifies the groups organized around the principle of the baptism of adult believers. For Williams, Anabaptists, Spiritualists and Evangelical Rationalists had distinct identities but shared a certain "implicit sectarian ecumenicity." Williams' criteria for the definition of the Radical Reformation were explicitly theological: the "widely held" theological beliefs of believers' baptism, the sleep of the soul pending the resurrection, the separation of church and state, and a commitment to missions. A general insistence on free will as opposed to predestination was also frequently mentioned. Critics were quick to point out, however, that not a single one of these beliefs was held by all radicals. Williams was particularly concerned to project the Radical Reformation on a European stage comparable to Humanism, the "Magisterial Reformation" (as he named the Lutheran, Reformed and Anglican traditions) and the Counterreformation, "topographically and topically complete from Spain to the Ukraine, from Anglia to Livonia."[1]

This chapter will not present the Radical Reformation on so broad a scale, because I am sympathetic to Williams' critics, particularly the social historian Hans-Jürgen Goertz and the Marxist historian Adolf Laube. In a converging critical analysis they have accepted the notion of a Radical Reformation but drastically pruned and refocused it. Lutheran church historians and theologians had argued cogently that if the criterion of Reformation radicalism was to be far-reaching theological innovation, then Luther was by far the most radical reformer[2] and the figures of Williams' Radical Reformation stood much closer to medieval tradition, making them a sort of "right wing of the Reformation." Aware of the force of this standpoint from his early studies of

Thomas Müntzer's mystical theology, Hans-Jürgen Goertz rejected a merely intellectual criterion for Reformation radicalism: "radicalness cannot be measured by the criterion of rupture with the intellectual tradition of the immediate past, but only by the break with the society of the present."[3] Sharpening a position merely implied by Williams and rejected by most Lutheran church historians, Goertz stressed that the Reformation was not to be regarded as originally moderate and then subjected to radicalization. Instead the Reformation began with Luther's radical rupture with tradition and later moderated in the process of being institutionalized and established. The Reformation radicals par excellence were those who maintained the original radical impulse, which Goertz thought to be laicism or anticlericalism, against the partial reclericalisation undertaken by established Protestant churches.[4]

Goertz's positions were refined and extended in 1988 in Adolf Laube's seminal essay, "Radicalism as a Research Problem in the History of Early Reformation."[5] Laube was unenthusiastic about Williams' desire to transcend Germanocentric Reformation history. In order to determine the character of the Reformation "it is necessary to proceed from the conditions and events in the country of origin of the Reformation, i.e. from the events in Germany." Outside Germany, he implied, the Reformation appeared in diluted forms, its ideas often detached from their original social grounding. In Germany particularly, "the notion of Reformation was associated with the expectation of a fundamental change in church and society." Here, "Reformation was radical to the extent to which it resulted in a revolutionary upheaval or awakening." Luther was radical until the time of his exile in the Wartburg and the outbreak of the Wittenberg Movement of 1521-1522. The substance of the Radical Reformation was for Laube, like Goertz, the social movement that refused to countenance the moderation and consolidation of the Reformation in Saxony and in south Germany and Switzerland.

The present essay employs a concept of Reformation radicalism similar to that of Goertz and Laube and differing considerably from the one Williams originated. With its pan-European extension and its inclusion of seventeenth-century eastern European unitarianism, Williams' Radical Reformation is not socially radical. Moreover, in becoming an encyclopedia of certain types of religious and theological phenomena, it loses all sense of unified narrative. But if we drop the "Evangelical Rationalists" and focus on greater Central Europe ("the

Germanies" including Bohemia-Moravia, Switzerland and the Netherlands) the Radical Reformation yields a coherent historical narrative,
beginning with the Wittenberg Movement of 1521-22 and ending with
the fading of Reformation radicalism into semi-legitimate religious
nonconformity as practiced in the late sixteenth century by Mennonite
groups in the Dutch Republic and by the Hutterites in Moravia.

2. LUTHER AND THE SPIRITUALISTS

According to Philip Melanchthon all the fanatics and Anabaptists of
his day were delivered into the world by a single stork—Nicholas
Storch, the Zwickau weaver, who appeared in Wittenberg in December
1521, claiming the highest Christian authority, that conferred by direct
conversations with the Holy Spirit. In this sense the Radical Reformation began in a figment, because Storch and his Zwickau Prophets were
a lot more important in Melanchthon's disturbed imagination and subsequent polemic than they ever were in Zwickau or Wittenberg.[6] But
no matter how unimportant and unrepresentative the Zwickau Prophets were, the winter of 1521-22 in Wittenberg witnessed the birth of a
distinct Radical Reformation. The early Reformation was radical in its
entirety but as it "moderated" a Radical Reformation became distin-
guishable from it. While Luther brooded in exile in the Wartburg from
May 1521 to March 1522, he came to theological decisions rich in implications for church and government. He rallied to his side figures
who were to become the leading lights of the Lutheran Reformation as
a confessional force, men such as Philip Melanchthon, Nicholas
Amsdorf, Justus Jonas, and Johannes Bugenhagen. But a wide assem-
blage of pastors and literate laity could not accept the direction of the
Reformation laid down when Luther returned to Wittenberg and
preached his *Invocavit* sermons of March 1522. They fought to maintain Reformation radicalism. The division of spirits about the
Wittenberg Movement of 1521-22 was a battle over the character and
direction of the Reformation.[7]

Luther always insisted that the decisions he reached at the Wartburg
and upon his return to Wittenberg were purely theological. Theology
was the language of the Reformation, and theological positions were
not calculatedly taken to serve ulterior purposes; nevertheless they
were saturated with implications for church and society, of which the
theologians were, to different degrees, aware. During this period

Luther brought three of his characteristic, mature theological positions into focus: 1) he insisted upon the liberty of the gospel against any coercive legalism "under the pretext of the gospel," 2) he placed explicit value upon the objective function of the Lord's Supper and baptism and upon the preaching of the Word of God, and 3) he insisted upon the authority of the Bible in its literal meaning, as opposed to any notions of the freedom of the Holy Spirit. These positions underlay the "moderate" or "magisterial" Lutheran Reformation. If the gospel was not a law, all matters of outward practice, including the exterior religious cult, could be left to the ultimate discretion of friendly temporal authorities. Luther had never countenanced direct popular action in affairs of church and state, but from the *Address to the Nobility* (1520) to *On Temporal Authority* (1523) he narrowed his call for external reform initiatives from an appeal to the whole political class, the aristocracy, to one directed specifically at the magistracy, that is, ruling princes and city councils. The original theme in Reformation discourse on the sacraments, that they must not be allowed to replace Christ's unique sacrifice, emphasized their subjective appropriation through faith. Stress upon their objective importance and upon the preached word as an intermediary between Christ and the believer enhanced the importance of the ministry of the newly reformed churches and blunted the initial, laicist anticlerical message of the early Reformation. The Bible in its original Hebrew and Greek texts was in this era of biblical humanism above all the working area of competent scholars (a second "magisterial" authority) inside and outside of universities. Anticlerical laymen, who suspected that professional pride and partisan bias more than overbalanced the value of learning, sometimes appealed from the Bible to the Holy Spirit, who after all inspired the authors of the canonical books. Luther had at first been quite receptive to the mystical piety of the *German Theology*, but in the early twenties he attacked mystical and spiritualist language such as appeared in some writings by Reformation supporters as a pretentious, unbiblical jargon and its spokesmen as "heavenly prophets."

Luther's focusing of Reformation theology was unacceptable to a wide group of early Reformation partisans, most prominently Andreas Karlstadt, who had annoyed the Electoral Saxon court by his efforts to put the Reformation into practice while Luther remained at the Wartburg. Beyond him were circles of Reformation leaders who objected to what they regarded as Luther's "truncating" of the movement. Thomas Müntzer, erstwhile "Martinian" pastor at Zwickau,

Jakob Strauss, pastor at Eisenach, Wolfgang Stein, court preacher at Weimar, Melchior Rinck, pastor at Eckhardshausen, Heinrich Pfeiffer at Mühlhausen; laymen such as the schoolmaster Hans Denck in Nuremberg, the book pedlar Hans Hut from Bibra, even the furrier-missionary Melchior Hoffman in the Baltic lands, were all radicals with ties to Wittenberg who tended to take umbrage at some or all of the theological positions that Luther pronounced in the years from 1521 to 1524. They did not agree on all points among themselves, but Luther was not incorrect in seeing them as a coalescing front of his opponents, as he told Karlstadt about his common spirit with Müntzer in a famous encounter between Luther and Karlstadt at the Inn of the Black Bear in Jena in 1524.[8]

These persons were Spiritualists, in Williams' terminology, and they tended to be "sacramentarians" in the language of their own day. They did not replace the Bible with the Spirit; indeed they attributed more authority to the Old Testament and its law than did Luther. But Karlstadt abandoned his academic costume and worked with his hands in his parish at Orlamünde; Müntzer denounced the "scribes" at Wittenberg with their Scriptural learning, accusing them of wanting "to have the testimony to the spirit of Jesus brought within the walls of the university."[9] Their difference from Luther over applying biblical authority was their assertion that ordinary people inspired by the Spirit need not defer to professors and humanists. Luther, who derived so much of his sense of worth from his calling as professor of the Bible, found that totally unacceptable. The decisive split between Luther and Karlstadt in 1523 was over the real presence of Christ in the elements of the Lord's Supper.[10] Karlstadt's advocacy of a symbolic Lord's Supper was related to his ministry as a "new layman" at Orlamünde, while Luther's evolving doctrine of consubstantiation was connected with his concern to bolster the ministerial office. From his new parish at Allstedt Thomas Müntzer joined Jakob Strauss and Karlstadt in criticizing pedobaptism, which Luther based upon the "implicit faith" of the infant and the pledge of the godparent. According to Müntzer's current analysis of church history, the degeneration of the church had begun in the second century when sterile quarrels about ceremonies replaced receptivity to the Holy Spirit.[11] This very spiritualist notion of the fall of the church went far beyond the humanist-Lutheran consensus (to which Müntzer had earlier adhered) that the trouble had begun about four hundred years ago with the emergence of scholasticism, canon law and the papal monarchy.

The idea that the Reformation should bring justice to the world by implementing the divine law preceded the Peasants' War. Luther foretold in his denunciations of Müntzer that such beliefs would lead to violence. Jakob Strauss and Müntzer upheld apostolic community of goods as described in Acts 2 and 4. Karlstadt and the congregation at Orlamünde warned Müntzer against his drift towards violence in 1524, and Strauss turned against him just in time to avoid punishment as an inciter of the Peasants' War. Still, Müntzer, too, addressed repeated warnings against rebellion to his followers while pastor at Allstedt.[12] The point of his famous sermon to the Saxon princes in 1524 was not so much that the elect should launch a bloody crusade against the godless as that the Electoral Saxon rulers must do their duty and protect Müntzer's reformed flock against the violence of neighboring Catholic rulers. If the rulers did not properly wield the sword of justice, to be sure, it reverted to the common people, something Luther, who ultimately turned for his defence to the princes and cities of the Smalkaldic League, would never have allowed. In the crisis of the Peasants' War, which had the most intimate connections with the Reformation, prominent radical pastors like Müntzer and Balthasar Hubmaier joined the rebels, as did the future Anabaptists Hans Hut and Melchior Rinck, while others like Strauss, Karlstadt and Hans Denck had murky, impenetrable connections with the uprising (something they later treated either with silence or unconvincing explanations). In the immediate aftermath of the debacle of the Peasants' War, which victors and vanquished alike accepted as a judgement of God, many of the anti-Lutheran spiritualists joined the new covenant of Anabaptism spreading from Switzerland, and thereby immediately complicated its character.

3. CONSTRUCTIVE MISUNDERSTANDING: FROM SPIRITUALISTS TO ANABAPTISTS

Zurich, Basel, and Bern were Swiss cities where in the course of the 1520s the externalities of the old faith—the altars, the images, the crucifixes, the painted glass, and the music—were swept away much more thoroughly than in Lutheran Germany. Here the symbolic interpretation of the Lord's Supper as taught by Karlstadt found both popular support and learned champions in Zurich's Ulrich Zwingli and Basel's Johannes Oecolampadius. Zwingli gave a similar symbolic interpretation to pedobaptism, likening it to circumcision under the old covenant of the Jews. Zwingli swam skillfully in the treacherous waters of Swiss urban politics since his call to Zurich in 1518, and he never imagined reformation by any other means than the ultimate endorsement of the temporal authorities.[13]   The radicals in Zurich, a combination of urbanites such as the patrician Conrad Grebel and the bookseller Andreas Castelberger and radical priests from dependent villages like Wilhelm Reublin from Witikon and Johannes Brötli from Zollikon, at first in 1523 objected to the cozy manner in which Zwingli and the government transferred the tithes of the old religious order to the support of the new Reformed establishment.   Then in 1524 they turned against pedobaptism (i.e., infant baptism), reaching out for ties with Strauss, Karlstadt and Müntzer, whose opposition to Lutheran pedobaptism they imagined to be like their problem with Zwingli. The constructive misunderstanding between the Swiss proto-Anabaptists and the anti-Lutheran Spiritualists was that, although they said some of the same things about infant baptism, their religious and theological meanings were fundamentally different. The Swiss radicals were not Spiritualists like Karlstadt and Müntzer, they were New Testament biblical literalists committed to restoring the practice of the two ceremonies endorsed by Christ in the same form they had been practiced by Christ and the apostles. While the Saxon anti-pedobaptists attacked the baptism of infants because they opposed Luther's new bent towards ceremonialism, the Swiss wanted to replace pedobaptism with the long-obscured correct ceremony.[14] The fact that only the New Testament was available in Swiss German for their lay-dominated study groups likely contributed to their New Testament hermeneutic,[15] something quite foreign to Karlstadt and Müntzer, who held that the Old and New Testaments were of equal authority, and that they were harmonized by the Spirit. Contrary to the Saxon mystical piety of *Gelassenheit* (yieldedness) and mortification, the Swiss radicals focused upon the fruits of sanctification, "improvement of life,"[16] very much in the spirit of Zwingli's preaching, which in turn owed much to the Erasmian notion of *philosophia Christi*.

The initiation of believers' baptism in Zurich at the home of Grebel's close associate Felix Mantz, likely on 21 January 1525, was a defiant response to action by the Zurich government to suppress anti-pedobaptist agitation.[17] Its immediate objective was not to begin the creation of a network of separatist conventicles but to turn the Swiss Reformed in the direction of a more radical sacramentarianism.

Zwingli had toyed with the idea of complementing his sacramentarian approach to the Lord's Supper with the baptism of adult believers, but he turned away from it in the name of a more inclusive civic covenant parallel to Old Testament circumcision. Although it had been his slogan at the outbreak of the Zurich Reformation in 1522 that ordinary laymen guided by the Spirit could interpret the Bible, he now scorned the radicals as undereducated persons who failed to grasp that the Old Testament was the Bible of the apostles and who lacked all competence in Scriptural exegesis.[18] His opponents prided themselves on their non-scholarly vernacular biblicism, and the Latin-educated and former clerics among them made it a virtue to be equal to those who could read only German and to the illiterate in clarifying biblical meanings. This struggle was at first, like the one in Saxony, a battle over the character of the Reformation, not a secession from it. However, Zwingli from the beginning of the new baptisms denounced them as a separation within the ranks of Reformation sympathizers. This became a self-fulfilling curse; the persecution of the dissidents by the Swiss Reformed governments soon forced them to meet in semi-secret conventicles. Before that happened, however, the Peasants' War swept over northeastern Switzerland and further complicated the Anabaptists' plight.

In early 1525 rural unrest erupted in the territories of Zurich, Schaffhausen and St. Gallen, and Swiss rebels established connections with rebellious Austrian subjects in the Black Forest, centred on the newly reformed town of Waldshut and its radical pastor Balthasar Hubmaier. Grebel and Mantz, possibly inspired by their Erasmian background, spoke out decisively against defense of the gospel by violent means when they wrote to Müntzer in 1524. But in 1525 Anabaptism spread in northeastern Switzerland and the Black Forest in close connection with the Peasants' War. Hubmaier joined the rebellion and then adopted Anabaptism; Reublin and Brötli won converts in the territories of rural Schaffhausen under the protection of peasant rebels; and Grebel and Mantz won support for Anabaptism from Zurich subjects who believed that their Zwinglian pastors had left them in the lurch during the uprising.

Besides resisting the magistrates' power over religious observance and becoming entangled in the Peasants' War, the early Swiss Anabaptists made themselves notorious as advocates of community of goods. A congregational ordinance of 1527 appealed to Acts 2 and 4 and the practice of the early church at Jerusalem. By this they seem to have meant that everyone should live by his own work and that persons of property should sell it and give the proceeds to a common chest for distribution among the baptized poor. In disputations between Anabaptists and Reformed pastors in Switzerland, the Anabaptists opposed the pastors' flexible acceptance of taking of interest on loans. Although the early Swiss Anabaptists continued to live in single family households as the center of their workaday lives, and their attempts to model their behavior on Acts 2 and 4 were voluntary and inconsistent, their raising the slogan of Christian communism was a red flag for the authorities and another pretext for their persecution and suppression.[19]

The escalation of punishments of Anabaptism in Zurich, from exile to imprisonment to execution, was a major factor in the dispersion of the original group throughout northern Switzerland and into neighboring areas of the Empire: Alsace, Swabia and the South Tyrol. For instance, Wilhelm Reublin was active in 1526 and 1527 in the Imperial free cities of Strasbourg and Esslingen and George Blaurock worked in 1527 in the South Tyrol, appealing to the discontent with church and government in the aftermath of the 1525-26 rebellion led by Michael Gaismair. These wandering Anabaptists thought of themselves as obeying Christ's command in Mark 16 to go into "all the world," preaching the gospel and baptizing believers. Their revivalistic preaching was a call to repentance in the last days before Christ returned. By accepting baptism in this first wave of Anabaptist missions thousands of ordinary laymen committed themselves to a sanctified life and to sharing their goods; at the same time they defied their established churches and governments. The principles of early Swiss-generated Anabaptism were formalized in the Seven Articles of Schleitheim, a village near Schaffhausen. The articles were drawn up in February 1527 by a group including Reublin and led by an ex-monk from the Black Forest, Michael Sattler.[20]

In form the Seven Articles of Schleitheim recall the programs of the recently concluded Peasants' War. They suggest a disciplining and focusing of the Anabaptists just after their compromising entanglement with the rebellion; but at the same time they voice a repudiation of "the world," all structures of authority with traditional claims to deference, that was more radical than any of the Peasants' War programs. The topics of the particular articles were the two sacraments, baptism and the Lord's Supper, congregational leadership, excommunication through "shunning" as a means of congregational discipline, refusal to swear oaths, bear arms or hold governmental office, and separation from the world. The article on separation, which called civic affairs and the church services of the pope and the "new popes" abominations which must be shunned and fled from, trumpeted forth the document's total rejection of the world: "Truly all creatures are in but two classes, good and bad, believing and unbelieving, darkness and light, the world and those who have come out of the world, God's temple and idols, Christ and Belial; and none can have part with the other."[21]   The Anabaptists of Schleitheim renounced the violence of the peasant rebels but they surpassed them in defiance. When Sattler faced a death sentence from Catholic authorities at Rottenburg am Neckar he said that he would not fight because God forbade it, but that if fighting were right he would rather take arms against so-called Christian governments than against the Turks: the persecuting Christian rulers were, he said, "Turks according to the spirit."

The Spiritualists of Lutheran territories frequently, if not invariably, adopted the new covenant of adult baptism. Thomas Müntzer at Allstedt and Mühlhausen had initiated covenants among his followers, first for purposes of self-defence against Catholic rulers, but later apparently to single out the end-time elect.[22] One of Müntzer's covenanters was the book pedlar Hans Hut from Bibra, who had supervised the publication of a major pamphlet by Müntzer in 1524. Another, very likely, was Hans Denck, schoolmaster at Mühlhausen during the rebellion. Denck escaped to Switzerland after the Peasants' War and came into contact with Anabaptists in the St. Gallen area. He and Hut had known each other before the Peasants' War in Nuremberg, drawn together by their interest in the writings of Müntzer and Karlstadt. Now they met again in Augsburg on the Day of Pentecost, 1526, and Denck baptized Hut. Hut became the major south German Anabaptist missionary, in the next year and a half constantly on the move from his home territory in Franconia through Austria and as far as Moravia. Everywhere he went he dispensed adult baptism as the seal of the covenant, an apocalyptic assembling of elect believers before Christ's second coming, which he predicted for 1528. In Franconia particularly, he appealed to fugitive veterans of the rebellion, telling them to keep their swords sheathed for the time being, but only until the final tribulations began. At that time the Turk would invade, and then the little band of Anabaptist covenanters would complete the punishment of the godless, ruthlessly wielding the sword of Gideon in accord with Müntzer's most bloodthirsty rhetoric.[23]

This was a different Anabaptism from the one spreading from Switzerland, but in the south German imperial cities, especially Augsburg,

Esslingen and Strasbourg, the Spiritualists mingled with the New Testament biblicists, not without friction, but without immediately separating into opposing groups. The Strasbourg reformers commented that, if Michael Sattler was a schismatic, he was at least not a heretic like Denck. And a major meeting of Anabaptist leaders of various backgrounds in Augsburg in the summer of 1527 convinced Hut to treat his apocalyptic predictions as an esoteric teaching, only to be shared with select followers in private. Later, when in prison in Augsburg, Hut commented that Anabaptists in Switzerland had made some rules (obviously the Schleitheim Articles) but that he did not feel himself bound by them. The Spiritualist recruits had one major belief in common with Anabaptists of the Swiss type. They advocated community of goods, which they regarded in Müntzer's sense as a supreme example of *Gelassenheit*, in this case meaning the renunciation of creaturely attachments.[24] Above all, the common experience of persecution united Swiss-type Anabaptists with the Spiritualists. These new adherents adopted believers' baptism, in Denck's phrase, as "the covenant of a good conscience with Christ," but they maintained the mystical piety of Müntzer and Karlstadt. Rather than regarding these persons as converts from the religion of Thomas Müntzer to that of Conrad Grebel, we should give more credence to Sebastian Franck's observation that, had Müntzer survived the Peasants' War, he would have become an Anabaptist (and likely thought and acted very much like Hans Hut).

4. The Primacy of Moravia in Swiss-South German Anabaptism

Severe persecution went far in the direction of displacing the Anabaptists of Switzerland and south Germany to a "refuge in the wilderness" in Moravia. Before the research of Claus-Peter Clasen introduced empirical sobriety into the discussion, both the numbers of early Anabaptists and the numbers of their martyrs were greatly exaggerated. Only a small number of persons in sixteenth-century Central Europe were willing to adopt a religion in defiance of their rulers; Anabaptist numbers become much greater at the end of the century in conditions of partial toleration. Rufus Jones once wrote that "no other movement for spiritual freedom in the history of the church has such an enormous martyrology."[25] In fact, relying on the most recent reliable scholarship, that of Clasen for Switzerland and south Germany and Alastair Duke for the Netherlands, the sixteenth-century total number of executions could be as low as 2,000.[26] In Switzerland and south Germany the executions of Anabaptists were most numerous in the late 1520s. Clasen's census of Anabaptists names or otherwise identifies ca. 4,400 in the years 1525-29 in Switzerland and south Germany, as many as he can find in the twenty years following 1529. According to him the persecution reached its height with 352 executions in 1528 and 1529; and of the 845 Anabaptist executions that he has documented for his areas of study, 80 percent took place in the years 1525-33. In the middle of this period, the Imperial Diet of Speyer in 1529 decreed the death penalty for Anabaptists. The overwhelming majority of these executions (85 percent of them) took place at the hands of Catholic authorities, principally the Habsburgs, the Swabian League and the dukes of Bavaria. Although Anabaptism began as a quarrel among supporters of the Reformation, Catholic rulers treated them much more ruthlessly and brutally. In Bavaria and the Habsburg lands, where no official Reformation was tolerated, these dissidents were almost the only overt opponents of the old faith and they paid a high price for it. Only Catholic governments practiced the cruel death by fire; only Catholic governments executed recanters. Protestant authorities, although they frequently evaded the death penalty called for in Imperial law, applied lengthy imprisonment and exile, as well as various forms of indoctrination, to enforce religious conformity upon Anabaptists.

Moravia, like Bohemia, was a land unique in Europe for its legal guarantees of confessional pluralism, left over from the inconclusive ending of the Hussite Wars a century earlier. Although Ferdinand of Austria acquired the crowns of Bohemia and Moravia in 1526, the aristocracy retained a strong constitutional position against the monarchy. Among the Moravian nobility particularly, Catholics were a weak minority, and religious persecutions in neighboring lands could be taken advantage of without confessional scruple to attract economically valuable settlers. The first Anabaptist leader of note to come to the area of southeastern Moravia that became the center of Anabaptist settlement was Balthasar Hubmaier, who had led the rebellion of Waldshut against the Habsburgs during the Peasants' War. He arrived in Nikolsburg (now Mikulov) in the late spring or summer of 1526; here he won church leaders and the lord of the town to believers' baptism and began a unique experiment in a socially conservative, "moderate" Anabaptist reformation explicitly based upon the patronage of the Moravian nobility.[27] Although this approach was successful with the German-speaking, settled population of the area, Hubmaier soon found his new religious establishment threatened by large numbers of propertyless Anabaptist refugees from all parts of south Germany and Switzerland. They rallied around the travelling missionary Hans Hut, who visited Nikolsburg in 1527 to proclaim a message of apocalyptic violence and community of goods. In this case the most conservative fellow traveller of Conrad Grebel and the disciple of Thomas Müntzer saw very clearly what different Anabaptisms they represented. Hubmaier said that his baptism was the very opposite of Hut's baptism—the two were as different as heaven and hell, Orient and Occident, Christ and Belial.[28] Although Hubmaier's noble patron expelled Hut from Moravia, Hut's kind of Anabaptism prevailed there. Moravian Anabaptism was to be above all a refugee community experimenting with, and endlessly quarreling about, the community of goods that Acts 2 and 4 seemed to prescribe for New Testament Christians.

While previous scholarship has tended to regard Moravian Anabaptism as an episode peripheral to Swiss and south German Anabaptism, it was in fact the main Anabaptist center in the southern Germanic lands after the major persecutions at the time of the Imperial mandate of Speyer (1529).[29] Moravia was a place of relative safety and, while many Moravian Anabaptist leaders lost their lives in 1535-37, what occurred then was that the Habsburg government, emboldened by its temporary success in the Turkish wars, compelled their aristocratic landlords to expel them, after which they were tracked down and executed outside the borders of Moravia. Before that disaster, which ended the first period of Moravian Anabaptism, the various groups numbered about 5,000, comparable to Clasen's figure for the whole of Swiss-south German Anabaptism in the 1520s. In Moravia better than anywhere else, the piety of the first Swiss Anabaptists was successfully amalgamated with that of anti-Lutheran Spiritualists like Hut and Denck. Moravia was the melting pot of early Anabaptism. All of the major Anabaptist leaders in Moravia in this period came from elsewhere: Jakob Hutter (South Tyrol), Jakob Wiedemann (Swabia), Philip Plener (the Palatinate), Gabriel Ascherham (Nuremberg and Silesia). Besides Hubmaier and Hut, already mentioned, many other early Anabaptist leaders found their way to Moravia. One prominent figure was the south German group leader and patrician lay theologian Pilgram Marpeck; the spiritualist Anabaptists whom

Marpeck wrote against, Johannes Bünderlin and Christian Entfelder, were also for a time in Moravia. The leaders of the most important early congregations in northeastern Switzerland, Johannes Brötli, Wilhelm Reublin and Wolfgang Ulimann, also came there with numbers of followers. Important parts of the tradition of Swiss Anabaptism were preserved in Moravia: the Schleitheim Articles, a revised version of the earliest Swiss congregational ordinance, and, most strikingly of all, the only independent account of the first believers' baptisms in Zurich.

The project uniting Swiss and south German Anabaptists was the restoration of the community of goods practiced by the apostles in Jerusalem after Pentecost. In the name of this goal two hundred persons split from the Nikolsburg church in March 1528 and established a new congregation at Austerlitz, the first Anabaptist settlement in which implementation of Acts 2 and 4 became the primary "sectarian distinctive." The Philipite, Gabrielite and Hutterite communities were established soon afterward for Anabaptist refugees from the Rhine-Neckar area, Silesia and the Tyrol respectively. Individual households were not at first abandoned, much emphasis was placed upon the loving, voluntary character of community of goods and there was no uniformity of practice among the groups, let alone equality of condition among their members. What had been secured was an area of common disagreement. Following the disappointment of Hans Hut's apocalyptic hopes centered on 1528, for a number of years the Moravian experiment became the Anabaptist norm in wide areas of south Germany. Conversion to Anabaptism in Austria and the Tyrol, and the hunted life that resulted for the faithful, was regarded as provisional pending the journey to Moravia, where alone the true Christian life in community of goods could be practiced. Wolfgang Lassmann introduces the illuminating parallel to the mentality of the Bolsheviks after their revolution succeeded only in the Russian Empire; just as they hoped for the possibility of "socialism in one country," "Christianity in one country" was the hope of many south German Anabaptists looking to a promised refuge in Moravia.[30] Pilgram Marpeck, working in the areas of Strasbourg and Speyer in the early 1530s, baptized as a minister commissioned by "the church in the land of Moravia," in his case the Austerlitz brethren. Most scholars now agree that in this period Marpeck authored the anonymous *Exposure of the Babylonian Whore*, a pamphlet advocating both community of goods and nonresistance.[31] The tenet of nonresistance, foreshadowed in the Schleitheim

Articles, had received its first substantial discussion in Moravia in 1529 from the Silesian Spiritualist Clement Adler, probably a member of the Gabrielite community.[32] Until its partial suppression in 1535 Moravian Anabaptism was a lively pluralist ferment and its goal of community of goods according to Acts 2 and 4 was accepted as the Anabaptist norm, also by many Anabaptists outside Moravia.

Although the Moravian Anabaptists and their fractious experiment with community of goods held center stage, the southern German Anabaptist movement produced a colorful variety of Anabaptist or post-Anabaptist sects in the early 1530s. New Testament literalism could be invoked just as easily on behalf of Saturday-Sabbath observance as in support of adult baptism. The remnants of Hubmaier's Nikolsburg congregation fell under the leadership of the Silesian Sabbatarian Andreas Fischer.[33] Hut's following produced the bizarre apocalyptic cult of Augustine Bader (executed in 1530)[34] and the antinomian sexuality of the Uttenreuth Dreamers (suppressed in 1531).[35] Both of these latter groups thought of themselves as having "gone beyond" Anabaptism.

5. STRASBOURG SPIRITUALISTS AGAINST ANABAPTISM

In the early 1530s besides Moravia the imperial city of Strasbourg was the major Anabaptist center. Until the firming up of the Protestant order under Bucer's leadership in 1533 it was a safe haven and debating forum for Reformation dissenters of all types. A refuge for the dispersed Anabaptists of Augsburg and Esslingen and in lively contact with Moravia, Strasbourg was the main place where Spiritualists who had submerged themselves in Anabaptism in the 1520s began to subject the movement to criticism. Hans Denck was first, expressing regrets for his fixation on renewing baptism as a ceremony instead of concentrating on the inner word of God, when he took refuge in Basel just before his death in 1527. Even earlier in 1526 in Liegnitz in Silesia Caspar Schwenckfeld and Valentin Crautwald had pronounced the first suspension of the sacrament (in this case, the Lord's Supper only) as their response to the hostility and confusion caused by the various conflicting doctrines on the subject.[36] The Moravian Anabaptists Johannes Bünderlin and Christian Entfelder came to Strasbourg in 1530 to publish tracts that called the entire Anabaptist venture into fundamental question. Bünderlin challenged the attempt to restore the

New Testament ceremony of baptism, arguing that baptism was a special commandment given to the apostles as a concession to Jewish ceremonialism. The ceremony had degenerated in the hands of the later church and, rather than setting up a new baptismal ceremony, the Reformation should do away with ceremonies and open its adherents to the Spirit. Entfelder, from a similar Spiritualist standpoint, argued that the biblicism of the "new scribes" who prided themselves on their lack of education was even worse than that of the humanists and professors, puffed up with their Hebrew and Greek.[37] Jakob Wiedemann of Austerlitz was said to have made a quick visit to Strasbourg at this time, and it was likely as a spokesman for Austerlitz that Pilgram Marpeck first went into print in Strasbourg in 1531 to defend the New Testament and its ceremonies against these one-time spiritualist Anabaptists, who now found Anabaptism incompatible with their Spiritualism.[38]

Weightier Spiritualist presences than Bünderlin and Entfelder, also residing in Strasbourg at that time, were Sebastian Franck, newly arrived from the Nuremberg area, and the nobleman Caspar Schwenckfeld, exiled from Silesia in 1529. Each had had sympathetic contact with Anabaptists before coming to Strasbourg and both deplored the persecution of Anabaptists, then at its height, and aspired to assume a mediating position between the Anabaptists and the Strasbourg pastors. Each involuntarily made an indirect contribution to the new Anabaptism transplanted by Melchior Hoffman from Strasbourg to north Germany and the Netherlands: Franck through his chronicles by orienting the Dutch Anabaptists into the history of the south German movement and Schwenckfeld by stimulating Hoffman's idiosyncratic Christology through his own preoccupation with the glorified Christ. Franck, too, believed that after the death of Christ and the apostles the external church and the sacraments disappeared from earth. He thought that God's revelation continued, not in propositions and doctrines, but, as he expressed it in his *World Chronicle* (Strasbourg, 1531), in the historical suffering of a tradition of heretics. Institutional success was the mark of the beast, the Spirit spoke only through individual dissenters. The suffering of heretics like Müntzer or the Anabaptists put them close to God, but Franck would identify himself no more with the small conventicles than with the big churches; to him they were all "sects."[39] Schwenckfeld strengthened the resistance of "politiques" in the Strasbourg city Council against the "new Judaism" that he saw emerging in Bucer's Reformed establishment. At first Pilgram Marpeck learned from him a proper distinction between the revelations of the Old and New Testaments. But if Franck was a radical's radical pillorying worldly success in all its forms, Schwenckfeld pioneered a modern-sounding separation of religion and politics that was hardly radical at all. He was absolutely deferential and respectful to worldly rulers, only warning them not to throw their weight around in religion. On matters such as adult baptism the Anabaptists were correct, or at least much closer to the truth than all pedobaptists, but it was wrong to disrupt Christian unity over external ceremonies. Instead all sacraments should be suspended until God led Christians to consensus on their proper form and interpretation.[40] Marpeck, competing with Schwenckfeld for the patronage of some noble ladies, eventually in the 1540s conducted polemics against what he considered Schwenckfeld's subversion of the external Christian church.

6. MARPECK, SWISS BRETHREN, HUTTERITES

Marpeck shared with the remnants of the Gabrielites and Philipites a shifting away from the goal of Christian community of goods that had dominated Anabaptism more or less from its inception to 1535. In 1535, of course, the notoriety of the Münsterite experiment with community of goods associated Christian communism with polygamy and apocalyptic megalomania. The Swiss, south German and Moravian Anabaptists were made aware of Münster by the way it confirmed all the hostile stereotypes of their persecutors. Even more important was the effective persecution of Moravian Anabaptism in 1535, which destroyed the Austerlitz community and drove the Gabrielites and Philipites back to their former homes in Silesia and the Rhineland. Outside of Moravia conditions were less propitious for putting Acts 2 and 4 into practice. The former communitarians now identified themselves with the early Christians after their dispersion from Jerusalem and affirmed private property, so long as it was held in a spirit of mutual aid.[41] In the aftermath of the 1535-37 persecutions the Hutterites, who had dispersed into small groups and remained in Moravia, were alone able to revive the Anabaptist life in community of goods; they subsequently attracted fragments of the other congregations. They survived a second major persecution in 1547 at the time of the Smalkaldic War, then expanded into a large prosperous community in

their "golden years" in the late sixteenth century. Beginning in the
1540s Anabaptists living in scattered individual households and holding private property were usually called "Swiss Brethren," whether
they lived in Switzerland, south Germany or Moravia. The divisions of
the southern Anabaptists were further complicated, however, by a distinct Marpeck congregation, also spread from Switzerland across
south Germany to Moravia, which denounced the Swiss Brethren for
wooden biblicism and excessive legalism just as it condemned the
Hutterites for making community of temporal goods into the way of
salvation.

The Hutterites in Moravia and Slovakia were without doubt the
great Anabaptist success in the southern Germanic lands in the second
half of the sixteenth century. Their highly disciplined communism of
production and consumption transcended the economics of single family households, which had impeded the realization of apostolic community of goods among early Swiss, south German and Moravian
Anabaptists. Living in multi-family dwellings and tightly organized
under "servants of the word" (preachers) and "servants of temporal
needs" (economic managers) into settlements of about 500, they
practiced a mainly craft economy. The profits of their excellent crafts-
manship enabled them to purchase agricultural goods beyond their
own production and to achieve their stated goal of *Nahrung* ("modest
sufficiency") in such a way as to attract "economic immigrants" to
Moravia during hard times in south Germany. Normally their presiding elders were craftsmen, and craftsmen enjoyed a higher prestige
among them than agricultural workers. Their copyists preserved the
writings, ordinances and history of the Swiss-south German
Anabaptist tradition from which they came, which appears to later
scholarship as an eclectic amalgam of the New Testament biblical literalism of the Swiss Anabaptists and the spiritualist theology of Luther's
early opponents. By the end of the century a minimum of 20,000
Hutterites lived in seventy settlements in Moravia and Slovakia under a
sort of theocratic oligarchy selected from the ranks of the brotherhood.
By this time, however, the Radical Reformation was more a cherished
historical memory than an ongoing reality. After the religious peace of
Augsburg (1555) and even more after the accession of Emperor
Maximilian II (1564), Hutterites enjoyed *de facto* toleration by com-
mon consent of the Moravian aristocracy and the court at Vienna.
One of the reasons for the relative success of their missions to win over
Anabaptists in Switzerland to emigrate to Moravia, where "true Chris-

tian order" prevailed, was that fierce persecution with threats of execution continued among the Swiss. In southeastern Moravia, although the Hutterites continued their ritual denunciations of the world, their nonconformity had become semi-legitimate and their relations with the protecting Moravian nobility were mutually profitable and often friendly. This state of affairs was described and denounced by Jesuit observers at the end of the century.[42]

7. THE MELCHIORITE KINGDOM OF MÜNSTER AND ITS RADIANCE

In the hothouse of Protestant dissent in Strasbourg, 1529-33, a new mutation of the Radical Reformation arose, Melchioritism, named for Melchior Hoffman. Hoffman, a furrier, had been a lay preacher of the Reformation in the Baltic and Scandinavian lands from 1522 to 1529, when his quarrels with the educated Lutheran pastorate and his adoption of Karlstadtian sacramentarianism resulted in his being exiled to south Germany. The Strasbourg pastors at first welcomed him but soon suggested that he go back to being a furrier, while he moved into the radical circles of Anabaptists and Spiritualists. Hoffman was already an apocalyptic sacramentarian when he came to Strasbourg; while there he accepted believers' baptism as a sign of God's covenant and first articulated a unique Christology, according to which Christ's flesh descended from heaven and passed through Mary like water through a funnel. This variation on Schwenckfeld's theme of spiritualizing the body of Christ became a litmus test for Melchioritism in its various forms. Travelling from his Strasbourg base Hoffman began baptizing adults in Emden in East Frisia in 1530, whence his sect soon spread into the Habsburg Netherlands. Here it won adherents among some Reformation sympathizers, especially figures like Jan Matthijs, a baker from Haarlem, and David Joris, a glasspainter from Delft, both of whom had already received legal punishments for sacramentarian views. Even more essential to Melchioritism than its Christology was its strident proclamation of the end of the world, to occur in 1533.[43] Wherever it appeared Melchioritism glided back and forth between Anabaptism and Spiritualism. Hoffman himself called for a spiritualist truce on believer's baptism when it led to the execution of some of his prominent followers in 1531. Melchioritism, which became the major tradition of the Radical Reformation in north Germany and the Netherlands, contained an unstable amalgam of

Anabaptism and Spiritualism, so that its groupings were sometimes "baptist" (Münsterites, Mennonites), sometimes not (Jorists, Batenburgers). Among its Mennonite survivors, too, baptizing, congregation-building currents always had to contend with spiritualistic, individualistic countercurrents.

Probably Melchioritism would never have become more than a sect on the margins of Dutch Reformation sentiment were it not for its fateful union with the civic Reformation in Münster in Westphalia. For this reason Münster cannot be regarded as a mere aberration from the normal course of the Radical Reformation in the northern Germanic lands. It not only fascinated Christian Europe with the horrific potentials of Reformation radicalism, it also attracted the initial reservoir of radical supporters in the Netherlands, who were drawn not merely by Melchiorite apocalyptic preaching but by its apparently miraculous political success, when the Anabaptists took power in Münster in February 1534. That such a thing could happen convinced many contemporaries that the end was indeed at hand. As Tiara Kuratsuka observed, taking power in Münster was for the Melchiorites what the Red Sea crossing was for the Israelites, God's hand made visible in history.[44]

The reformation of Münster was confirmed by the Treaty of Dülmen of February 1533 between the town and its prince-bishop, with Landgrave Philip of Hesse as its guarantor. It was like a Reformed civic reformation torn out of its proper time and place. Münster's reformer Bernhard Rothmann was interested in south German and Swiss theologies and church ordinances, a strong advocate of lay selection of pastors.[45] The city elite went through a typical transition in which the old ruling families of the Council were replaced by a new group of notables from the guilds, just as wealthy as the persons they pushed aside. Aside from a weak group of politiques on the Council, Lutheranism had little support in Münster; ministers sent from Hesse were unable to prevail over Rothmann's local following. He welcomed some preachers from Wassenburg in Jülich led by Heinrich Roll, who was definitely a sacramentarian and probably a Melchiorite when he came to Münster. The history written by the erstwhile Melchiorite, Nicholas Blesdijk,[46] asserts that Roll convinced Rothmann of an anti-pedobaptist theology, and that the *Confession of the Two Sacraments*, a statement of Anabaptist sacramental theology co-authored by Rothmann and the Wassenberger preachers in November 1533, was the stimulus behind the beginning of a new, more powerful phase of Anabaptism in the Netherlands. There Jan Matthijs, a baker from Haarlem, and his close supporter Jan Beukelsz, a journeyman tailor from Leiden who had just returned from Rothmann's Münster, declared that the end of the world was at hand and that it was time to lift Hoffman's truce and to renew the practice of adult baptism. Melchior Hoffman had been imprisoned in Strasbourg in 1533; thus the prediction of the Dutch prophets that Münster, not Strasbourg, was to be the promised heavenly Jerusalem had no Anabaptist of authority to contradict it.

In January 1534 emissaries of Jan Matthijs baptized Rothmann and his leading followers in Münster. Because of its defiance of Imperial law, which mandated the death penalty for Anabaptism, this act led to a split down the middle of Münster's political elite. In the crisis of 9-11 February, Rothmann's followers claimed miraculous and prophetic sanction to abandon their previous non-violence and to take arms to defend themselves. The outcome was that notables opposed to Rothmann left the town and that the new Council elected in late February consisted mostly of Anabaptists led by Bernhard Knipperdolling as burgomaster. The bishop of Münster immediately began a siege of the town. In the course of the sixteenth-month siege he was able to gain military and financial support from the Empire, invoking legislation enacted in 1526 after the Peasants' War for the purpose of suppressing any future commoners' rebellion.

March 1534 was the high point of Anabaptist credibility in the Netherlands. That the despised and proscribed Anabaptists had come to power in Münster was seen as a sign of the last days by a population that had in recent years experienced more than its share of war, pestilence and economic hard times. Jan Matthijs declared that all Christian believers should seek refuge in Münster before the end of the world, 5 April 1534, Easter Sunday. Thousands of trekkers set out, particularly in boats on the Zuider Zee, only to be apprehended, then sent home after their arms and money had been confiscated. The magistrates had no stomach for mass executions of persons they thought of as deluded apocalyptic zealots. These people, however, became the initial recruiting pool for the future Dutch Anabaptist sects.[47] Apparently about 2,500 persons from Westphalia and the Netherlands did reach Münster. The social composition of this group is disputed. Contemporary art shows some of them selling jewels and landed property, so they were probably not a "poor people's crusade."[48] Karl-Heinz Kirchhoff studied the property-holders among the native Münster

Anabaptists and found them a surprisingly normal group, not different in wealth from the Catholics or Lutherans.[49] What was unusual about besieged Anabaptist Münster was a preponderance of women over men (ca. 5,000 to 2,000). This went together oddly with a misogynist theology stressing the lordship of men and with the apparent zeal with which these women supported the defense of the town.

When Easter 1534 arrived without divine deliverance Jan Matthijs died in a suicidal attack on the besieging army. Much less is known about him than about his successor, Jan Beukelsz, who assumed the leadership and directed the resistance for fourteen months until Münster was finally subdued in June 1535. It is clear that Jan Beukelsz had less prophetic authority among Anabaptists in the Netherlands than his predecessor. This accounts for the pathetic failures of his attempts to raise supporting uprisings at Oldeklooster in Frisia and in Amsterdam in the spring of 1535. Furthermore the retreat from the community of goods which had been proclaimed by Rothmann and Jan Matthijs at the beginning of Anabaptist rule in Münster suggests the weakness of Jan Beukelsz' power. A redistribution of houses and landed property, proposed but not carried out, shows how his authority was checked by resident notables who had helped bring the Anabaptists to power in Münster to begin with. Kirchhoff's studies demonstrate how powerful this group continued to be, so that the institutions of government established by Jan Beukelsz, the Twelve Elders (April-September 1534) and the Davidic Kingship (September 1534-June 1535), were careful power-sharing arrangements between the resident notables and the newcomers from the Netherlands. King Jan had once acted in the Dutch chambers of rhetoric and it is important not to confuse the pageantry of his rule with real personal power.[50] His personal stamp appears in the notorious institution of polygamy in the summer of 1534, which provoked an internal uprising among the Münster Anabaptists. This seems to have been acceptable to the collective leadership behind Bokelson as an attempt to officer the numerous women by dividing them into patriarchal households. The highly touted community of goods in the end became little more than wartime rationing, a facade behind which great disparities of condition continued, ranging from the excess of the royal court to near starvation in the final days of the siege.[51] In assessments of Anabaptist Münster the continuing power of the notables must not be forgotten. Behind its radical trappings it was a much more traditional society than that created in Anabaptist Moravia.

8. BATENBURGERS, JORISTS, AND MENNONITES

Still another sign of King Jan's low prestige in the Netherlands was that in April 1535 a group of militant Melchiorites, having lost all faith in his prophetic credentials, approached the noble bastard Jan van Batenburg and asked him to be their new messianic David. This group abandoned baptism, declaring that the time of grace had now given way to the time of wrath. They continued polygamy and conducted a sort of guerilla warfare against religious and temporal powers by means of church robberies, crop burnings and murders. Batenburg's execution in 1538 did not still them. They continued for several decades longer.[52]

When apprehended, Jan van Batenburg referred to David Joris of Delft as "the chief Anabaptist" in north Germany and the Netherlands. Contemporary scholarship confirms him[53] after a long period of ignoring David to concentrate on Menno Simons. David catapulted himself to prominence by acting as mediator at a meeting of various Melchiorite groups at Bocholt in Westphalia in August 1536. Here militant and non-militant Melchiorites tried to come to terms with the distinctive beliefs of Münster Anabaptism. David's proposal was to spiritualize the apocalyptic vengeance on the wicked world which had been proclaimed in the writings of Bernhard Rothmann. Later that year he underwent ecstatic experiences that convinced him that, in a spiritual sense, he was the messianic David, a humbler, lesser successor of Christ, the second David. He maintained the characteristic Melchiorite Christology and believers' baptism, but allowed his followers to feign conformity to the official Catholicism of the Netherlands. His following was geographically concentrated in the towns of Holland. It consisted mainly of artisans, with a significant minority of persons of high social standing. Continually hunted and fugitive, David tirelessly sought recognition among the various Melchiorite sects. Jan van Batenburg tried to have him murdered and pronounced that either he or David would soon die, and that the survivor would be the true prophet. When Jan was arrested and executed soon afterward, David gained the adherence of a number of openly polygamous ex-Batenburgers. Less successful was David's journey to Strasbourg in 1538 to win the allegiance of the inner circle of the still-imprisoned Melchior Hoffman. These Strasbourg Melchiorites insisted on biblical verification of David's authority. They soon afterward expressed their own form of Melchiorite spiritualization by abandoning believers'

baptism and making their reconciliation with Bucer's Reformed church
in exchange for promises of a greater stress on the ban and holy living.[54] Wearying of his life on the run, in 1539 David took refuge with a
wealthy supporter in Antwerp and devoted himself to a primarily literary career. His more than 200 titles, including the two editions of the
massive *Wonder Book*, were the largest, if far from the most distinguished, publishing venture of the Radical Reformation. These form-
less writings supposedly were put down by David just as the Spirit dictated them; and they represented a large financial outlay by his
supporters. In his Antwerp refuge he abandoned adult baptism, made
the return of the Lord something that occurred in people's hearts and
came to regard his own messianic claims in an increasingly metaphori-
cal light. In 1544 David, his household and his patrons moved from
Antwerp to Basel, where they carried on their activities in secret, outwardly conforming to the Reformed church until David's death in
1556.

Following David's departure for Switzerland, from the late 1540s
onward the great majority of Anabaptists executed for their faith in the
Habsburg Netherlands were followers of Menno Simons.[55] Menno
was a Frisian, a Catholic priest until 1536. Some of his writings dis-
play a good humanist Latin education, but as an Anabaptist leader he
wrote in Dutch for followers with vernacular literacy. His Dutch publications, starting with the *Foundation Book* of 1539, established his
authority within the Melchiorite remnant. Menno was an archetypi-
cally anti-spiritualist Anabaptist. He insisted that Christ was the only
David of promise and that the Münsterite leaders were deceivers, succeeded after 1535 by "corrupt sects." Still, he upheld the believers'
baptism that Jan Matthijs had reinstituted in 1533. Indeed he fell heir
to the followers of the Frisian Melchiorite Obbe Philips when in 1540
this leader renounced Anabaptism, announcing Spiritualist scruples
about whether he or anyone else had received a valid divine calling to
restore the baptism of the New Testament. David Joris' feigned conformity to other rites and his eventual abandonment of baptism confirmed Menno in denouncing him as a corrupt hypocrite. The earliest
congregations under Menno's direct influence formed outside the
Habsburg Netherlands near centers like Danzig and Oldesloe where
persecution was less intense and where David Joris held less sway. In
the second half of the sixteenth century Mennonites became the dominant heirs to the radical tradition throughout north-central continental
Europe. Menno was authentically Melchiorite in respect to Christol-

ogy. Although Mennonite elders lacked the prophetic charisma of the leaders of earlier Melchiorite sects, they had much more authority, say, than Swiss Brethren leaders. This was expressed especially in their power of pronouncing the ban, which called for the shunning of the excluded, even one's own children, parents or spouse. The aspiration for congregations "without spot or wrinkle" unfortunately soon led zealous Mennonite elders to ban one another. This was more the fault of Menno's fellow elders Leonard Bowens and Dirk Philips than of Menno himself, but he did not effectively stand in their way. Not only did the Mennonites ban the Swiss Brethren congregations of the south with which they had much in common, they soon began to splinter internally. A number of congregations from the Waterland area of Holland split away before Menno's death, and shortly afterward there occurred the far more damaging schism between the Frisians and the Flemish refugee congregations. Still, by the time of Menno's death in 1561 on the estate of a noble supporter in Schleswig-Holstein, he had moved the remnants of the Melchiorite movement far in the direction of nonconformist respectability. Not only did he denounce Münster but he opposed war and violence of all sorts, without copying the Schleitheim Articles in denying all possibilities of Christian rulership. Community of goods, he said, had been practiced only for a short time in the history of the early church and that was, no doubt, God's will. Mennonites concentrated on mutual assistance with no pretensions of reviving the church of Acts 2 and 4.

The end of the Radical Reformation came with the Revolt of the Netherlands against Philip of Spain. Although God commanded them not to fight, the Mennonites, who had witnessed the suffering at Catholic hands of about one thousand of their martyrs in the two preceding decades, could not be neutral when militant Calvinists arose for the Protestant cause. The Waterlanders, the most flexible of the baptist groups, took up a collection for William of Orange. He in his turn decreed toleration for Mennonites in the 1570s. For the rest of the century the Dutch Reformed church, which constituted itself as a believers' church and comprised only about 10 percent of the population of the United Netherlands, barely surpassed the Mennonites in numbers.[56] It, of course, enjoyed patronage and respectability, and the Mennonites suffered the disgrace of being divided into a half dozen competing factions. Nevertheless, the Mennonites of the late sixteenth century in the Netherlands, according to their historian Karel Vos, numbered 100,000 in hundreds of congregations.[57] They were on their

way to full participation in the life of the "golden" seventeenth-century
Netherlands, quarreling internally about whether or not to arm their
boats in the profitable herring and whale catch, engaging in international philanthropy not only to Anabaptist cousins but also to
Schwenckfelders and Huguenots. They enjoyed exemption from military service and the swearing of oaths as privileges of a legitimate nonconformity, despite the protests of Reformed pastors. Some of their
own conservatives well understood how much the world had accommodated itself to them and they to the world. A conservative
Mennonite pastor, Thieleman van Braght, in 1660 produced the *Martyr's Mirror* to recall for them the sufferings of their ancestors a hundred years previously. The *Martyr's Mirror* became the beloved book
of Mennonites, enjoying an authority that rivaled the Bible, but it celebrated a Radical Reformation that was a concluded chapter of history.

9. THE RADICALISM OF THE RADICAL REFORMATION

The Radical Reformation did involve an intrusion of people of low estate into religious and social affairs previously reserved to holders of
traditional authority in church and government. But this is a point that
must not be exaggerated. Anabaptism and the Peasants' War brought
only a limited and temporary opportunity, for instance, for the self-ex-
pression of "uppity women."[58] Claus-Peter Clasen's finding that "only
about one-third of the Anabaptists were women"[59] is no longer credible. Anecdotal evidence from Münster and the Netherlands points
rather to instances when women were more numerous than men. But
the reasons why Clasen's statistics may be discounted—that
Anabaptist women appear less often in judicial records because they
were not permitted to come to the fore in Anabaptist congregations
and were not considered fully responsible by magistrates—show the
limits of the movement as a vehicle for greater gender equality. Nor do
the Reformation's radicals lend themselves to straightforward class
analysis. Clasen's work on the Swiss-south German Anabaptists is
very useful here. In the areas studied he finds a religion of commoners,
including only 2 percent who were persons of aristocratic birth or
higher education (and many of them perished at the very beginning of
Anabaptism in the 1520s). The majority of Swiss-south German
Anabaptists came from small towns, villages and farms—at least 60

percent at the start and eleven out of twelve at the end of the sixteenth
century. The most characteristic Swiss-south German Anabaptist
leader was the village craftsman.[60] But in north Germany and the
Netherlands, where the movement was more numerous, it centered, according to current preliminary studies,[61] in the towns and attracted a
greater following than in the south of notables and persons of wealth.
The prominence of notables in Anabaptist Münster was not a total
anomaly. Commoners were assuredly more prominent in the Radical
Reformation than in institutional Protestantism, but their predominance was not absolute—it is easy to think of a Marpeck or a
Schwenckfeld. Nor should too much be made of Clasen's finding that
there were only 30,000 Anabaptists in Switzerland and south Germany
in the sixteenth century.[62] He did not enumerate Anabaptists in the regions where they congregated most heavily, Moravia and the Netherlands. The recent study of Alastair Duke states that in parts of the
Netherlands Mennonites outnumbered Reformed Christians in the late
sixteenth century.[63] Anabaptist numbers swelled when the groups began to experience toleration, and we should probably not hold unreal-
istic expectations about how many sixteenth-century central Europeans were willing to adopt a religion proscribed by their rulers. Robert
Scribner's guess that "involuntary Protestants" may have numbered up
to 90 percent[64] make Clasen's conclusions about the small number of
Anabaptists less impressive than they seemed twenty years ago. Aside
from the special situation at Münster, there were no "involuntary
Anabaptists."

The radicalism of the Radical Reformation, the reason its adherents
and opponents repudiated each other with such vehemence, lay in its
program. First of all, it clung fiercely to anticlericalism, to the early
Reformation slogan of "the priesthood of all believers," when the major reformers began to "moderate" and rescind it. Both the Anabaptist
hermeneutic community, in which religious authority was centered in
the vernacular translation of the New Testament as commonly understood, and the Spiritualist belief that the Spirit was revealed in the
mortifications of ordinary people, and that the Bible was there only as
a safeguard against charlatans and eccentrics, had as a common denominator the ringing insistence that Christianity was too important to
be monopolized by priests, professors and humanists. Second, Roland
Bainton's idea that the Reformation had a "left wing" that "rejected
the civil arm in matters of religion"[65] also has continuing worth, even
though the generalization is not applicable to all radicals and although

separation of church and state was not a sixteenth-century conception.
It was very radical in the sixteenth-century Holy Roman Empire to tell
the civil arm to keep out of the manipulation of religion, even when it
was presented so respectfully as by Caspar Schwenckfeld, as a way of
keeping the new Protestant preachers at arm's length and in their place.
Schwenckfeld, Franck, Balthasar Hubmaier and David Joris may have
been pleading their own cases when they argued for toleration of religious dissent, but they were also violating the sixteenth-century truism
that only religious uniformity rendered a polity governable. Third, and
by no means least important, anti-Lutheran Spiritualists and all
Anabaptists until 1535, the first expulsion of the Anabaptists from
Moravia and the fall of Münster, fretted, brooded and experimented
with the grandest social vision of all, that *omnia sunt communia*, that
everything belongs to everyone, just as in the Jerusalem church described in Acts 2 and 4. They didn't mean exactly the same thing, indeed they didn't know exactly what they meant, but in the aftermath of
the Peasants' War in its very indefiniteness this was a frightening notion indeed; more so then than in the Hutterite "golden age" when it
was demonstrated that Christian community of goods could be a
means of yielding windfall profits for the Moravian aristocracy. In
short, the sixteenth-century Germanies produced a Radical Reformation that repudiated and enraged the clergy of the old and new established churches, the traditionally legitimate magistracies and the com-
fortably wealthy. They responded with persecutions and defamation
that marginalized but failed to destroy these critics and dissenters.
When the suffering stopped, when the mutual de-legitimation abated,
the Radical Reformation had passed.[66]

NOTES

1. Williams (1992), 1241-1311.
2. Lindberg (1976).
3. Goertz (1982), 21.
4. Goertz (1987).
5. Laube (1988).
6. Steinmetz (1971), 60-62.
7. Preus (1974).
8. Sider (1978), 36-48.
9. Müntzer Collected Works (1988), 264.
10. Williams (1992), 117-20.
11. Friesen (1990), 33-52.
12. Laube (1990).
13. Gäbler (1986), 43-90.
14. Stayer (1993).
15. Packull (1993).
16. Goertz (1988), 67-75.
17. Bender (1950), 136-38.
18. Snyder (1990).
19. Stayer (1991), 95-106.
20. Snyder (1984).
21. Wenger (1945), 249-50.
22. Scott (1989), 47-100.
23. Packull (1977), 35-117; Seebass (1980).
24. Stayer (1991), 107-22.
25. Jones (1923), 392.
26. Clasen (1978), 9; Clasen (1972), 370-86, 419-22; Duke (1990), 108.
27. Zeman (1969), 130-32; Packull (1991), 41-58.
28. Packull (1977), 99-106.
29. Packull (1993).
30. Lassmann (1987).
31. Klaassen (1987).
32. Packull (1993).
33. Liechty (1988).
34. Packull (1977), 130-38.
35. Clasen (1972), 131-34.
36. McLaughlin (1986), 74-76, 83-84.
37. Packull (1977), 155-75.
38. Klassen (1968); Boyd (1992).
39. Dejung (1980).
40. McLaughlin (1986), 123-59.
41. Packull (1993).

42. Stayer (1991), 139-59.
43. Deppermann (1987).
44. Kuratsuka (1985), 261.
45. Brecht (1985).
46. Zijlstra (1983).
47. Jansma (1979).
48. Kühler (1980), 99.
49. Kirchhoff (1973).
50. *Pro* Rammstedt (1966); *contra* Klötzer (1992).
51. Stayer (1991), 123-38.
52. Stayer (1976), 284-97.
53. Zijlstra (1983); Waite (1990).
54. Packull (1992).
55. Bornhäuser (1973); Krahn (1968), 169-237.
56. Duke (1990).
57. Vos (1980), 91.
58. Kobelt-Groch (1993).
59. Clasen (1972), 335.
60. Ibid, 305-34; and see Stayer (1991), 5.
61. Waite (1990), 28-36.
62. Clasen (1972), 15-29.
63. Duke (1990), 240.
64. Scribner (1986), 34.
65. Bainton (1980), 41.
66. The author expresses his gratitude to Professor Werner O. Packull, Conrad Grebel College, for sharing his unpublished research on the beginnings of Moravian Anabaptism.

BIBLIOGRAPHY

Topical Bibliography
Hillerbrand, Hans J., ed. *Anabaptist Bibliography 1520-1630*. St. Louis, 1991.

Source Editions
Älteste Chronik der Hutterischen Brüder. Ed. A. J. F. Zieglschmid. Ithaca, 1943.
Bibliotheca Reformatoria Neerlandica—Geschriften uit den tijd der Hervorming in de Nederlanden. Ed. Samuel Cramer and Fredrik Pijper. 10 vols. The Hague, 1904-10.
Corpus Schwenckfeldianorum. Ed. Selina G. Schultz, et al. 19 vols. Leipzig, 1907-61.
Documenta Anabaptistica Neerlandica. 4 vols. Leiden, 1975- .
Flugschriften vom Bauernkrieg zum Täuferreich (1526-1535). Ed. Adolf Laube, et al. 2 vols. Berlin, 1992.
Müntzer, Thomas. *Schriften und Briefe*. Ed. Günther Franz. Gütersloh, 1968.
Quellen zur Geschichte der (Wieder)Täufer. 16 vols. Leipzig and Gütersloh, 1930- .
Quellen zur Geschichte der Täufer in der Schweiz. 3 vols. Zurich, 1952- .
Schriften der Münsterischen Täufer und ihrer Gegner. Ed. Robert Stupperich. 3 vols. Münster, 1970-83.

Sources in Translation
Chronicle of the Hutterian Brethren. Vol. 1, *Das grosse Geschichtbuch der Hutterischen Brüder*. Trans/ed. Hutterian Brethren. Rifton, N.Y., 1987.
Denck, Hans. *Selected Writings*. Trans./ed. Edward J. Furcha. Pittsburgh, 1975.
Durnbaugh, Donald F., ed. *Every Need Supplied: Mutual Aid and Christian Community of Goods in the Free Churches, 1525-1675*. Documents in Free Church History, vol. 1. Philadelphia, 1974.
Grebel, Conrad. *Swiss Anabaptism, Sources of: the Grebel Letters and Related Documents*. Ed. Leland Harder. CRR, vol. 4. Scottdale, Pa., 1985.
Hubmaier, Balthasar. *Theologian of Anabaptism*. Trans./ed. H. Wayne Pipkin and John H. Yoder. CRR, vol. 5. Scottdale, Pa., 1989.
Irwin, Joyce L., ed. *Womanhood in Radical Protestantism, 1525-1675*. New York, 1979.
Marpeck, Pilgram. *Writings*. Trans./ed. William Klassen and Walter Klaassen. CRR, vol. 2. Scottdale, Pa., 1978.
Müntzer, Thomas. *Collected Works*. Trans./ed. Peter Matheson. Edinburgh, 1988.
Sattler, Michael. *Legacy*. Trans./ed. John H. Yoder. CRR, vol. 1. Scottdale, Pa., 1973.
Sider, Ronald J., ed. *Karlstadt's Battle with Luther. Documents in a Liberal-Radical Debate*. Philadelphia, 1978.
Simons, Menno. *Complete Writings*. Ed. John C. Wenger. Trans. Leonard Verduin. Scottdale, Pa., 1956.
Williams, George Huntston, and Angel M. Mergal, eds. *Spiritual and Anabaptist Writers*. The Library of Christian Classics. Philadelphia, 1957.

Literature
Armour, Rollin Stely. *Anabaptist Baptism: a Representative Study.* SAMH, vol. 11. Scottdale, Pa., 1966.
Bainton, Roland H. "The Left Wing of the Reformation." In *The Anabaptists and Thomas Müntzer,* ed. Werner O. Packull and James M. Stayer, 41-45. Dubuque, Iowa, 1980.
Bender, Harold S. *Conrad Grebel, Founder of the Swiss Brethren.* SAMH, vol. 6. Goshen, Ind., 1950.
Bornhäuser, Christoph. *Leben und Lehre Menno Simons'.* Neukirchen-Vluyn, 1973.
Boyd, Stephen B. *Pilgram Marpeck. His Life and Social Theology.* Durham, N. C., 1992.
Bräuer, Siegfried, and Helmar Junghans, eds. *Der Theologe Thomas Müntzer. Untersuchungen zu seiner Entwicklung und Lehre.* Göttingen, 1989.
Brecht, Martin. "Die Theologie Bernhard Rothmanns." *Jahrbuch für Westfälische Kirchengeschichte* 78 (1985): 49-85.
Bubenheimer, Ulrich. *Thomas Müntzer. Herkunft und Bildung.* SMRT, vol. 46. Leiden, 1989.
Clasen, Claus-Peter. *Anabaptism: a Social History, 1525-1618. Switzerland, Austria, Moravia and South and Central Germany.* Ithaca, 1972.
Clasen, Claus-Peter. *The Anabaptists in South and Central Germany, Switzerland and Austria: Their Names, Occupations, Places of Residence and Dates of Conversion, 1525-1618.* Ann Arbor, 1978.
Davis, Kenneth R. *Anabaptism and Asceticism.* SAMH, vol. 16. Scottdale, Pa., 1974.
Dejung, Christoph. *Warheit und Häresie. Eine Untersuchung zur Geschichtsphilosophie bei Sebastian Franck.* Zurich, 1980.
Deppermann, Klaus. *Melchior Hoffman. Social Unrest and Apocalyptic Visions in the Age of Reformation.* Trans. Malcolm Wren. Edinburgh, 1987.
Deppermann, Klaus, Werner O. Packull, James M. Stayer. "From Monogenesis to Polygenesis. The Historical Discussion of Anabaptist Origins." *MQR* 49 (1975): 83-122.
Duke, Alastair. *Reformation and Revolt in the Low Countries.* London, 1990.
Erb, Peter C., ed. *Schwenckfeld and Early Schwenckfeldianism.* Pennsburg, Pa., 1986.
Friedmann, Robert. *The Theology of Anabaptism.* SAMH, vol. 15. Scottdale, Pa., 1973.
Friesen, Abraham. *Thomas Muentzer, a Destroyer of the Godless: the Making of a Sixteenth-Century Religious Revolutionary.* Berkeley and Los Angeles, 1990.
Gäbler, Ulrich. *Huldrych Zwingli. His Life and Work.* Trans. Ruth C. L. Gritsch. Philadelphia, 1986.
Goertz, Hans-Jürgen. *Innere und äussere Ordnung in der Theologie Thomas Müntzers.* SHCT, vol. 2. Leiden, 1967.
Goertz, Hans-Jürgen. *Pfaffenhass und gross Geschrei. Die reformatorischen Bewegungen in Deutschland, 1517-1529.* Munich, 1987.
Goertz, Hans-Jürgen, ed. *Profiles of Radical Reformers.* 2d ed. Scottdale, Pa., 1982.
Goertz, Hans-Jürgen. *Religiöse Bewegungen in der frühen Neuzeit.* Enzyklopädie deutscher Geschichte, vol. 20. Munich, 1993a.
Goertz, Hans-Jürgen. *Die Täufer. Geschichte und Deutung.* Munich, 1988. 2d ed.
Goertz, Hans-Jürgen. *Thomas Müntzer. Apocalyptic Mystic and Revolutionary,* trans. Jocelyn Jaquiery. Edinburgh, 1993b.
Goertz, Hans-Jürgen, ed. *Umstrittenes Täufertum, 1525-1975. Neue Forschungen.* Göttingen, 1975.
Hoyer, Siegfried. "Die Zwickauer Storchianer—Vorläufer der Täufer?" *Jahrbuch für Regionalgeschichte* 13 (1986):60-78.
Jansma, Lammert G. "De chiliastische beweging der Wederdopers (1530-1535)." *DB,* n.s. 5 (1979): 41-55.
Jones, Rufus. *Studies in Mystical Religion.* London, 1923.
Kirchhoff, Karl-Heinz. *Die Täufer in Münster 1534/35.* Münster, 1973.

Klaassen, Walter. "Investigation into the Authorship and the Historical Background of the Anabaptist Tract *Aufdeckung der Babylonischen Hurn.*" *MQR* 61 (1987): 251-61.

Klaassen, Walter. *Living at the End of the Ages. Apocalyptic Expectation in the Radical Reformation.* Lanham, Md., 1992.

Klassen, William. *Covenant and Community.* Grand Rapids, 1968.

Klötzer, Ralf. *Die Täuferherrschaft von Münster. Stadtreformation und Welterneuerung.* Münster, 1992.

Kobelt-Groch, Marion. *Aufsässige Töchter Gottes. Frauen im Bauernkrieg und in den Täuferbewegungen.* Frankfurt, 1993.

Krahn, Cornelius. *Dutch Anabaptism: Origin, Spread, Life and Thought.* The Hague, 1968.

Kühler, W. J. "Anabaptism in the Netherlands." In *The Anabaptists and Thomas Müntzer,* ed. Werner O. Packull and James M. Stayer, 92-103. Dubuque, Iowa, 1980.

Kuratsuka, Taira. "Gesamtgilde und Täufer. Der Radikalisierungsprozess in der Reformation Münsters: Von der reformatorischen Bewegung zum Täuferreich 1533/34." *ARG* 76 (1985): 231-70.

Lassmann, Wolfgang. "Möglichkeiten einer Modellbildung zur Verlaufsstruktur des tirolischen Anabaptismus." In *Anabaptistes et dissidents au XVIe siècle,* ed. Jean-Georges Rott and Simon L. Verheus, 297-309. Baden-Baden and Bouxwiller, 1987.

Laube, Adolf. "Radicalism as a Research Problem in the History of Early Reformation." In *Radical Tendencies in the Reformation: Divergent Perspectives,* ed. Hans J. Hillerbrand, 9-23. SCES, vol. 9. Kirksville, Mo., 1988.

Laube, Adolf. "Thomas Müntzer und die frühburgerliche Revolution." *ZfG* 38 (1990): 128-41.

Liechty, Daniel. *Andreas Fischer and the Sabbatarian Anabaptists. An Early Reformation Episode in East Central Europe.* SAMH, vol. 29. Scottdale, Pa., 1988.

Lindberg, Carter. "Theology and Politics: Luther the Radical and Müntzer the Reactionary." *Encounter* 37 (1976): 356-71.

McLaughlin, R. Emmet. *Caspar Schwenckfeld Reluctant Radical. His Life to 1540.* New Haven, 1986.

Mullett, Michael. *Radical Religious Movements in Early Modern Europe.* London, 1980.

Oyer, John S. *Lutheran Reformers Against the Anabaptists: Luther, Melanchthon and Menius and the Anabaptists of Central Germany.* The Hague, 1964.

Packull, Werner O. "The Beginnings of the Hutterian Brethren." Unpublished manuscript, 1993.

Packull, Werner O. "The Melchiorites and the Ziegenhain Order of Discipline, 1538-39." In *Anabaptism Revisited. Essays on Anabaptist/Mennonite Studies in Honour of C. J. Dyck,* ed. Walter Klaassen, 11-23. Scottdale, Pa., 1992.

Packull, Werner O. *Mysticism and the Early South German-Austrian Anabaptist Movement, 1525-1531.* SAMH, vol. 19. Scottdale, Pa., 1977.

Packull, Werner O. *Rereading Anabaptist Beginnings. The 1990 J.J. Thiessen Lectures.* Winnipeg, 1991.

Pater, Calvin A. *Karlstadt as the Father of the Baptist Movements: the Emergence of Lay Protestantism.* Toronto, 1984.

Preus, James S. *Carlstadt's "Ordinaciones" and Luther's "Liberty": a Study of the Wittenberg Movement 1521-1522.* Cambridge, 1974.

Rammstedt, Otthein. *Sekte und soziale Bewegung. Soziologische Analyse der Täufer in Münster.* Cologne and Opladen, 1966.

Scott, Tom. *Thomas Müntzer. Theology and Revolution in the German Reformation.* New York, 1989.

Scribner, Robert W. *The German Reformation.* London, 1986.

Seebass, Gottfried. "Peasants' War and Anabaptism in Franconia." In *The Anabaptists and Thomas Müntzer,* ed. Werner O. Packull and James M. Stayer, 154-63. Dubuque, Iowa, 1980.

Sider, Ronald. *Andreas Bodenstein von Karlstadt: the Development of his Thought.* SMRT, vol. 11. Leiden, 1974.

Snyder, C. Arnold. *The Life and Thought of Michael Sattler.* SAMH, vol. 26. Scottdale, Pa., 1984.

Snyder, C. Arnold. "Word and Power in Reformation Zurich." *ARG* 81 (1990): 263-85.

Stayer, James M. *Anabaptists and the Sword.* 2d ed. Lawrence, 1976.

Stayer, James M. *The German Peasants' War and Anabaptist Community of Goods.* Montreal, 1991.

Stayer, James M. "Saxon Radicalism and Swiss Anabaptism: the Return of the Repressed." *MQR* 67 (1993): 5-30.

Steinmetz, Max. *Das Müntzerbild von Martin Luther bis Friedrich Engels.* Berlin, 1971.

Vogler, Günter. *Thomas Müntzer.* Berlin, 1989.

Vos, Karel. "Revolutionary Reformation." In *The Anabaptists and Thomas Müntzer,* ed. Werner O. Packull and James M. Stayer, 85-91. Dubuque, Iowa, 1980.

Waite, Gary K. *David Joris and Dutch Anabaptism, 1524-1543.* Waterloo, 1990.

Wenger, John C. "Schleitheim Confession of Faith." *MQR* 19 (1945): 243-53.

Williams, George Huntston. *The Radical Reformation.* 3d ed. SCES, vol. 15. Kirksville, Mo., 1992 [1962].

Zeman, Jarold K. *The Anabaptists and the Czech Brethren in Moravia, 1526-1628.* The Hague, 1969.

Zijlstra, Samme. *Nicolaas Meyndertz van Bleskijk. Een bijdrage tot de geschiedenis van het Davidjorisme.* Assen, 1983.

THE NEW RELIGIOUS ORDERS, 1517-1648

John Patrick Donnelly, S.J.[1]
(Marquette University)

This chapter is divided into seven sections. The first presents an overview of the thirty new religious orders and congregations founded in the Reformation era and indicates their impact on church and society. The second section discusses the small Italian orders of clerks regular which engaged in active ministry. Several had female branches. Because of their importance the Jesuits receive the third section to themselves. The fourth section takes up Capuchins and the Discalced Carmelites, both of which had female branches, and argues that they should be seen as new orders despite their medieval roots. The fifth section examines six active congregations of priests, mainly in France, who lived in community but took only simple vows or no vows at all. The sixth section examines nine new orders or congregations of women which tried with varying success to escape cloister and engage in active ministry. The last section suggests some new directions for research.

1. NEW ORDERS: SHAPES OF THE SUBJECT

The foundation of new religious orders and congregations is usually an index of Catholic vitality since they begin as a response to religious needs on the local level, usually by lay men and women or by priests, rarely by the hierarchy, never by the papacy. None of the male orders began as a response to the Protestant challenge. Significantly, none of the new orders began in Germany, the Netherlands, or eastern Europe where the Protestant challenge was strongest. Italy took the lead, then Spain, followed by France in the seventeenth century. In their early years the new orders discussed various merger schemes, and some short-lived mergers did take place, but these came to naught since each group had its own identity and purpose. Several new orders added a fourth vow to the traditional ones of poverty, chastity and obedience.

All the new male orders except the Discalced Carmelites stressed ac-

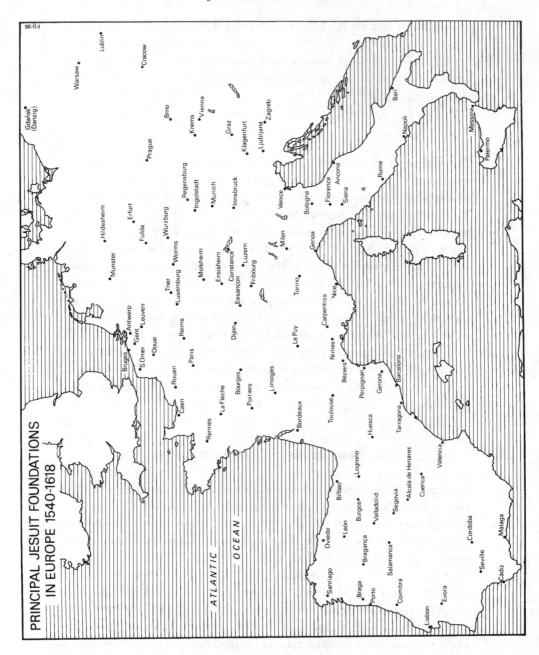

PRINCIPAL JESUIT FOUNDATIONS
IN EUROPE 1540-1618

tive ministry to an unprecedented degree, if one excepts the crusading military religious orders. The new orders were a creative response to the challenges of a new and dynamic age. Other religious groups with strong monastic traditions, such as the Eastern Orthodox and Buddhists, never developed the equivalents of the Jesuits or Capuchins. The greatest achievement of the new orders were in education, missionary work, and preaching in rural missions. Some of the new orders wore distinctive habits; others, notably the Jesuits, did not. Some were highly centralized, others radically decentralized. Some orders sharply restricted their ministry (for example to teaching or helping the sick or conducting parish missions), but others such as the Jesuits and Capuchins engaged in a wide range of ministries. The new orders generally encouraged frequent confession and communion; they preached, taught catechism and administered the sacraments. Many sent missionaries to Asia and the Americas. They served as chaplains in Catholic armies and in the thousands of confraternities which characterized baroque Catholicism. A few served as papal nuncios or royal confessors or reformers of lax convents. Some orders opened hospitals and orphanages and staffed schools and seminaries. The members of the new orders published a flood of books—devotional works, theological tracts, textbooks for their schools, books for the common folk, works of erudition for scholars. The new orders generally followed the scholastic theology of the thirteenth century and ignored the *via moderna*.

All the same, we should not exaggerate the contribution of the new orders. Except for the Capuchins and Jesuits, membership in the new active male orders remained small. Reform movements among the friars was far more important for the Catholic Reformation than were the smaller new orders. Even though religious orders were largely driven from Protestant lands, their total membership was at least as large in 1600 as in 1500 and continued to outstrip population growth during the next century. Male religious seem to have outnumbered female religious roughly three to two.[2]

2. SMALL ORDERS OF CLERKS REGULAR IN ITALY

On 14 September 1524 four men took the traditional solemn vows of poverty, chastity, and obedience at the main altar in St. Peter's Basilica and began a new kind of religious order, the clerks regular (from *regula* or rule), whose life and goals differed from the earlier monks and friars. The new Theatine order (CRT, OT, OTheat) had two very different early leaders or founders: Gaetano Thiene (1480-1547) and Gian Pietro Carafa (1479-1559). The first became a canonized saint (St. Cajetan), the second became Pope Paul IV, (1555-59). Both came from wealthy noble families and were well educated; both belonged to the Roman Oratory of Divine Love, which stressed personal sanctification and church reform. Thiene was ordained in 1516 and traveled for several years through the northern Italian cities setting up confraternities, encouraging frequent confession and communion, and establishing hospitals for the incurables (mostly syphilitics). All three of these activities characterized the new orders in Italy. Thiene determined to return to Rome and establish a community of reformed priests to inspire lay Christians. There he was joined by two priests and Carafa, who was already bishop of Chieto (or Theate in Latin, whence Theatines) and an accomplished humanist. Gradually Carafa turned against Erasmian ideas of reform. Later as head of the Roman Inquisition and pope Carafa felt that he had the solutions to the Church's problems, and his solutions allowed no compromise with human weakness, clerical abuse, or Protestant ideas. Thiene was more interested in helping the poor and neglected.

The Apostolic letter of 1524 authorized the new order and put its members directly under the pope, but a superior general actually governed the Theatines. After a year's novitiate priests and brothers took the traditional vows. Distinctive was their commitment to poverty, which forbade them to beg; the community was to live from the spontaneous offerings of the people. Distinctive too was their recitation of the office in common without singing. They wore no special habit, only the ordinary garb of local priests. Carafa resigned his benefices and was elected first superior; he drew up a letter of regulations, which with some additions governed the Theatines until the publication of their *Constitutiones congregationis clericorum regularium* (Rome, 1604).

The sack of Rome in 1527 forced the Theatine community to flee to Venice. In 1533 they spread to Naples; in 1557 they returned to Rome after failing to set up communities in Salò and Verona. The Theatines were always an elite organization. By 1550 they numbered only twenty-seven. Between 1565 and 1570 they added houses in Padua, Cremona, Piacenza and Milan. After 1600 they spread outside Italy and even did missionary work in the Middle East. By 1600 they counted 400 members, and 1400 by 1700. Thereafter decline set in.

Their impact came mainly from an setting example of parish ministry for Italian priests. Many reforming bishops came from their ranks. They developed no distinctive school of theology but did produce one spiritual classic, the *Spiritual Combat* (1589) of ·Lorenzo Scupoli (1530-1610).[3]

The Clerks Regular of St. Paul (CRSP, CBarb) are better known as the Barnabites from their mother church and community in Milan. They began with several priests who gathered around Saint Antonio Maria Zaccaria (1502-39) to form a community in Milan in 1530. After studying medicine and law at Padua, Zaccaria returned to his native Cremona in 1524 and began to do charitable work. He was ordained in 1528 and shifted his labors to Milan where he gathered eight other gentlemen to help his work and live in community, as yet without vows. His cluster of friends, under the spiritual guidance of Battista Carioni de Crema O.P. (c. 1460-1533), gradually developed into three distinct groups: the Barnabites, the Angelic Sisters of St. Paul (approved in 1535), and a lay sodality, the Married Couples of St. Paul. They soon ran into opposition. Carioni was suspected of heresy, and self-flagellation and other penances in public by priests and nuns shocked many people. After an inquiry, Paul III vindicated them, but hostile rumors continued, and the nascent Barnabites grew only slowly. Their first community outside Milan was at Pavia in 1557. When their new Constitutions were approved in 1576 they had only seven communities (six in the Po Valley, plus Rome) with forty-five priests, fifteen clerics, and twenty-one lay brothers. Real growth came after St. Carlo Borromeo gave them strong support and charged them with conducting a minor seminary. By 1607 there were 322 Barnabites, and 726 by 1700. Their small numbers encouraged talk of merging with the Jesuits or the Oratorians. They spread to France in 1610 and to Austria in 1626, where they often staffed residential colleges. In 1615 they discussed merging with the French Fathers of Christian Doctrine; in 1623 they did absorb the Fathers of Our Lady of the Assumption founded by Antonio Pagni at Pescia. The main work of the Barnabites was preaching and hearing confession; they encouraged frequent communion and the Forty Hours devotion to the Eucharist. In theology they followed Aquinas; their preaching stressed the Pauline epistles but they did not develop a distinctive spirituality. They wore a distinctive brown habit.[4]

The Somaschi (Clerks Regular of Somascha, CRS, CRSom) were founded at Venice in 1534 by St. Girolamo Emiliani (1481-1537). In

1540 Paul III approved the order, which included both priests and brothers who took the traditional solemn vows. Emiliani, a tough soldier who had undergone a conversion experience, was struck by the number of poor orphans left by war and plague; he gathered several priests and laymen to provide for them. Later the Somaschi branched into parish work and teaching, mainly at seminaries, and established a parallel order for women. They were largely restricted to Italy, and their numbers remained small: 438 members by 1600, only 450 by 1700. After discussing merging with the Jesuits or Capuchins, the Somaschi entered four short-lived mergers: most notably with the Theatines (1546-55) and with French Doctrinaires (1616-47).[5]

The Clerks Regular of the Mother of God (Matrititani, OMD, CRMD) were founded at Lucca in 1574 by St. Giovanni Leonardi (1541-1609) and received papal approbation in 1595; they were raised to a religious order in 1621. They made the traditional three vows, but like the Jesuits they stressed obedience. Members devoted themselves to parish work but lived in community. As a sign of their special devotion to Mary they dedicated all their churches to her and celebrated her feasts with special observances. When Leonardi died, they had only two communities, at Lucca and Rome, and did not spread outside Italy until after 1800.[6]

The Clerks Regular Minor (Carracciolini, CRM) were founded at Naples in 1588 by St. Francesco Caracciolo (1563-1608) and Giovanni Agostino Adorno. Their priests and brothers added a vow not to seek ecclesiastical dignities to the usual ones. Communities elected their local superior for a three year term, but a general helped by four assistants supervised the whole order from Rome. While the main strength of the order remained and still remains in Italy, houses were opened early in the seventeenth century at Madrid, Valladolid, and Alcalá. By 1700 the order had some 500 members. Their ministry has stressed devotion to the Eucharist, parishes, work among university students, and help for the sick, the dying and prisoners.[7]

More important were the Piarists (Poor Clerks Regular of the Mother of God of the Pious Schools, popularly known as the Scolopi, SchP), who were founded at Rome in 1597 by the Spaniard St. José de Calasanz (Calasanzio, 1557-1648). The son of a blacksmith, he studied both law and theology in Spain before coming to Rome in 1591 as an ambitious priest looking for advancement in the Curia. At Rome he joined two confraternities which helped the poor and taught some reading and catechism. The wealthy could pay for their sons' basic education before enrolling them in the ubiquitous Jesuit colleges, but the poor had fewer opportunities. Calasanz, a zealous and autocratic man of action, saw the need, gathered companions, and opened schools that charged no tuition and taught poor lads the three Rs, plus catechism and some Latin. That would qualify them to enter the Jesuit colleges or at least provide skills to escape destitution. At Rome the first Piarist school, financed by wealthy churchmen and by door-to-door begging, had 700 students by 1610. By then Calasanz had a community of some twenty teachers, priests and laymen, living together and teaching. He talked Paul V into uniting his followers with the Clerks Regular of the Mother of God, but the union soon foundered on differences over ministry and poverty, and the two groups went their own ways. Paul V granted autonomy to the Piarists in 1617.

Calasanz insisted on teaching to the virtual exclusion of other ministry, and members took a special fourth vow to teach. Between 1617 and 1634 the Piarists opened thirteen new schools in Italy. In 1631 they opened a school in Moravia, the first outside Italy. By 1646 there were 500 Piarists living in thirty-seven communities. Troubles soon clouded this success story. The need for teachers led Calasanz to lower standards for admission and training; tensions arose between the lay brothers who tended to teach the lower grades in the vernacular and the priests who taught older boys Latin. Many aristocrats worried about the social consequences of educating the masses. Vague questions about orthodoxy also arose. A commission of cardinals investigated and relieved the aged Calasanz of office; in 1648 Innocent X reduced the order to a congregation without vows, forbade it to accept novices, and put it under episcopal jurisdiction. About 200 members joined other orders or became laymen, but after a partial vindication in 1656 Clement IX fully restored Piarists as an order with solemn vows in 1669. Today they are the second largest order of Clerks Regular, after the Jesuits.[8]

The Camillians (Order of St. Camillus, Fathers of the Good Death, OSCam) were founded by a crippled former soldier, St. Camillus de Lellis (1550-1614), around 1582 and received papal approval in 1591. Their ministry focused sharply on hospital work, and members took a fourth vow to serve the plague stricken. When Camillus died in 1614 the order had communities in fifteen Italian cities and counted 330 members.[9]

The Brothers Hospitallers, who were neither clerks regular nor Italian, were founded by José Cuidad (St. John of God, 1495-1550), a Por-

tuguese soldier who had fought the French and the Turks. He opened
a religious bookstore in Granada, then turned his house into a hospital
for the poor. When others joined his efforts, they formed a community
of lay brothers in 1537. The bishop prescribed a habit for them, and
rules were drawn up after José's death. Pius V approved the
Hospitallers as a congregation in 1572. To the three traditional vows
they added a vow to work for the sick. The congregation spread rapidly, especially in Latin America; their membership rose from 626 in
1600 to 2,046 in 1700.

3. THE JESUITS

The Jesuits or Society of Jesus (S.J.) were the most influential and most
numerous (after the Capuchins) of the new orders. They engaged in a
wide range of different ministries; their geographical spread both in
Europe and in missionary lands was unrivalled; their ministries put
them in contact with the middle and upper ranges of society; and their
training tended to be long and rigorous.

The seed bed of the future Society of Jesus was a group of seven students at the University of Paris who in 1534 took a vow to go to Palestine and work for souls upon completing their studies. All seven were
well educated by the standards of the times; their leader, St. Ignatius of
Loyola (1491-1556), was probably the least gifted as a scholar. The
group was international from the start: two Basques, two Castilians,
an Aragonese, a Portuguese and a Savoyard. Of the seven only the Portuguese, Simao Rodrigues, was destined to work mainly in his homeland.[10] The seven, plus some new French adherents, gathered at Venice
in 1537 to sail for Palestine, but a war between the Venetians and the
Turks prevented their departure. Their Paris vow had an escape
clause: if they could not go to the Holy Land, they would put themselves at the disposal of the Pope. Paul III gave them permission to be
ordained and began to employ them as teachers and preachers, and
they also worked in the hospitals for incurables. Gradually they felt a
need to structure their work and decided to form a new religious order.

They elected Loyola as their superior; a preliminary draft of their future Constitutions was approved by Paul III in 1540. Loyola, much
aided by his gifted secretary Juan Polanco (1516-76), spent the rest of
his life drawing up the Constitutions, which were approved in 1558
and printed in 1559. The Constitutions, much longer and detailed

than earlier rules, built upon the on-going practice of the earliest Jesuits and contained many innovations. To save time for active ministries, the Jesuits prayed the divine office in private, not together in choir. They took no new names upon becoming religious. Jesuits, including the lay brothers who performed manual and clerical work, wore the black cassock of diocesan priests, not a distinctive habit. The order had eight grades of membership from novice to professed father, and only a small minority of Jesuits in the sixteenth century professed solemn vows. The professed usually added a fourth vow to go on mission if requested by the pope, but this was not a general vow of obedience to the pope, and the popes rarely invoked it. The vow was only a minor factor in the traditional Jesuit loyalty to the papacy. The Jesuit superior general, who resided in Rome, was elected for life and appointed subordinate superiors; hence authority was far more centralized than in the other orders. Jesuit generals were answerable to General Congregations, but these usually met only to elect a new general. This centralization of authority together with Loyola's stress on obedience allowed Jesuit generals to reform local communities and deal with difficult individuals much more decisively than was allowed by the friars' capitular government. The Jesuits stressed ministry to others more than personal prayer, or rather they insisted that Jesuits should be contemplatives in action so that their prayer drew strength from their ministry and vice versa.

The Jesuit innovations alarmed many friars. Three popes who had been members of religious orders, Paul IV (1555-59), Pius V (1566-72), and Sixtus V (1581-90), questioned and curtailed various innovations. When these popes died, the Jesuits returned to their old practices, arguing that their Constitutions had solemn papal approval, whereas the private directives of the three popes lapsed with their deaths.

Ignatius of Loyola provided the early Jesuits not only with Constitutions, he also published the *Spiritual Exercises* (1548), the fundamental source for Jesuit spirituality. This little book, which has appeared in more than 5,000 editions, codified methods of meditation and outlined a way of giving retreats. In 1522, shortly after his conversion, Loyola began the notes that evolved into the Exercises. He gave the Exercises to his early followers at Paris, then later to leading churchmen such as Cardinal Gasparo Contarini. Giving the Exercises, often in formats drastically reduced from the original month-long retreat, became a major Jesuit ministry down until the present. The Exercises strongly influenced both Jesuit preaching and hundreds of Jesuit meditation manuals.

The original goal of Loyola and his first companions had been Palestine. Foreign missions remained a primary Jesuit ministry. Here the pioneer was Loyola's Paris roommate, St. Francis Xavier (1506-52), who sailed for India as papal nuncio and Jesuit superior in 1541. He worked in India, Malaysia, Indonesia and Japan, setting up networks of Jesuit missionaries. During Loyola's lifetime other Jesuit missions were established in Ethiopia and Brazil, plus abortive efforts in Morocco and the Congo. In Asia the Jesuits gradually became the most important missionary order. In China Matteo Ricci (1552-1610) established a foothold at Peking by winning the Emperor's favor. It was the Jesuits who introduced the Chinese to western philosophy and science. In Japan the Jesuit mission flourished until a wave of persecutions beginning in 1597 drove them out. In the Americas the Jesuits usually built on the pioneer work of the friars; they set up colleges in major cities that copied Jesuit colleges in Europe. In the jungles in Paraguay and Brazil they set up Jesuit-run settlements called reductions in which the Indians were evangelized and protected from enslavement.

Initially Loyola had not regarded education as a major Jesuit ministry, but the success of a Jesuit college for lay students, begun at Messina in 1548, led to mounting requests. There were 144 Jesuit colleges by 1579 and 372 by 1615, and their numbers continued to grow until the suppression of the Jesuits in 1773. Requests for colleges outstripped the Jesuits' ability to staff them. Claudio Aquaviva (Jesuit general from 1581 to 1615) claimed that he turned down 150 requests during his first eight years in office. After producing several preliminary drafts, the Jesuits published in 1599 their definitive *Ratio Studiorum*, which governed their schools for three centuries. Most Jesuit colleges offered only a humanistic secondary education, but some Jesuit schools were full-fledged universities. The colleges charged no tuition (local authorities and notables were expected to provide an endowment) and were open to the poor, but since they presupposed some Latin, they attracted mainly the sons of the town elite. After 1590 the Jesuits increasingly opened boarding schools for nobles. Some 2,500 Sodalities of the Blessed Virgin Mary, a sort of confraternity to spread Jesuit spirituality among students and former students, were founded by 1773.[11] Education gradually became the most important Jesuit ministry.

Jesuit churches, rarely official parishes, were often adjacent to the

Jesuit colleges and employed the new Baroque style. They provided Masses, the Eucharist, confessions and preaching for the faithful; frequent communion and confession were encouraged. Parish priests often resented competition from the Jesuits, even when it stimulated their own ministry. Increasingly Jesuits, (for example, St. Jean François Regis, 1597-1640) preached revivalistic rural parish missions. In this work they were joined by the Capuchins, Oratorians, Eudists, and Lazarists. Working with local bishops Jesuits often supervised the reform of relaxed convents; Loyola's most tempestuous early companion, Nicolás Bobadilla (1509-90) reformed many convents in small Italian towns. Like many other Jesuits, he also served as an army chaplain. More importantly, Jesuits served as court confessors to many noblemen and monarchs, notably to several Kings of France and Holy Roman Emperors, and influenced government religious policy indirectly. In contrast, they rarely held positions in the Inquisition, which were staffed by the Dominicans and other friars.

The Jesuits were prolific in publishing works of piety, catechisms, and school books, but equally important were letters and accounts from missionaries. Intended to enlist support for the missions, these accounts taught Europeans about Asia, Africa, and the Americas. Several early Jesuits were pioneers in science, especially astronomy, but after the Galileo affair their scientific role declined. Among Jesuit theologians the three most important figures were the Dutchman St. Peter Canisius (1521-97), famous for his catechisms; the Italian St. Robert Bellarmine (1542-1621), known for his catechisms, controversial works against Protestants, and short devotional books; and the Spaniard Francisco Suárez (1548-1617), important for his metaphysics, systematic theology, and theory of law. Spain in the late sixteenth century was the center of the Second Scholasticism, a revival of scholastic methods in philosophy and theology, but also open to humanist influences. The Dominicans played the main role here, but Jesuits such as Suárez, Luis de Molina (1535-1600) and Gabriel Vázquez (1551-1604) made major contributions.

As Jesuit numbers grew, their influence spread. The thousand Jesuits when Loyola died in 1556 tripled in the next decade. There were 8,519 by 1600 and 19,998 by 1700. During the seventeenth century the Jesuits often had to turn away candidates because they lacked funds to train and support them.

The Jesuits have often been viewed as the shock troops of the Counterreformation in the struggle against Protestantism. Jesuits did indeed oppose Protestantism, mainly by their preaching and books. Protestant students were welcomed by Jesuit schools, and many became converts. But all this was secondary to reviving Catholicism. Most Jesuits were teachers or served as missionaries in Asia, the Americas or backward areas of Catholic Europe. As has been seen, only an accident prevented the first Jesuits from working in Palestine, and during Loyola's lifetime the Jesuits had their greatest impact in Portugal and Sicily, where the enemy was Istanbul and Mecca, not Wittenberg and Geneva. Before 1580 native Jesuits were thin in France, Germany and Poland, which were the critical areas of the struggle against Protestantism, and Jesuits were imported from Italy and Spain.[12]

4. CAPUCHINS AND DISCALCED CARMELITES

After the Jesuits the two most important new orders were the Capuchins and Discalced Carmelites. Since both grew out of efforts to restore a more austere and simple observance of an old rule, they can be interpreted either as new orders or as reformed branches of medieval orders.

Compared to the founding of the various orders of clerks regular, the origins of the Capuchins are convoluted and disputed. The Rule of St. Francis regarding poverty (the issue most likely to split religious orders) set an extremely difficult standard, so that efforts to mitigate or to uphold it led to endless controversies and repeated splits among the medieval Franciscans. In 1517 Leo X consolidated the Franciscans into two orders, the Conventuals and the stricter Observants, but many among the Observant friars wanted still greater austerity. Three wings partially broke off from the Observants during the sixteenth century: the Reformed (1532, mainly in Italy); the Discalced (1563, mainly in Spain, inspired by St. Peter of Alcántara, 1499-1562), and the Recollects (1579, largely in France). By 1700 there were 34,900 Observants, 12,900 Reformed, 6,200 Discalced, and 9,400 Recollects.

The Capuchins (OFM Cap) broke with the Observants even more radically; their independence was recognized by Clement VIII in 1528; the last legal subordination to the older Franciscan families was dropped in 1619. No one saintly founder stands out—the Capuchins have always looked to St. Francis himself as their ideal. Historians must choose among three flawed candidates. Matteo da Bascio[13] (d. 1552) gathered the first nucleus and introduced wearing beards and the distinctive pointed hood (*capucchio*) from which the order received its name. He served very briefly as the first vicar-general but resigned and returned to the Observants. His successor, Ludovico da Fossombrone (c. 1498-c. 1560), drew up the first constitutions (the Statutes of Albacina, 1529) but proved an arbitrary superior who quickly alienated his subjects and was eventually expelled. Bernardino d'Asti (1484-1554), the next vicar-general, governed well, played the main role in writing the definitive constitutions (1535), and secured solemn papal approval in 1536 despite objections by the Observants, who were losing many fervent friars to the Capuchins. Bernardino's work was almost undone when a new general, the celebrated preacher Bernardino Ochino (1487-1564), fled to Geneva in 1542 and became a Protestant. Paul III considered abolishing the Capuchins as infected by heresy, but an investigation vindicated their orthodoxy. Two noble-women, Caterina Cibo and Vittoria Colonna, did much to encourage the new order and protect it from papal wrath. During the next three decades the Capuchins grew very rapidly, but the Observants secured a papal order that restricted them to Italy, except for chaplains serving Italian soldiers in campaigns against Protestants and Turks. The restriction was lifted in 1574.[14]

The Capuchins, emulating the simplicity of St. Francis, generally lived in small hermitages near the towns where they begged their daily bread. They preached on street corners and in churches, but did not open schools and heard confessions rarely in their early decades, thereby avoiding friction with parish priests over jurisdiction. The Capuchins urged frequent communion and the Forty Hours devotion to the eucharist during carnival. More than any other group they devoted themselves to caring for plague victims, heedless of danger.

After 1574 their growth was rapid—nineteen provinces outside Italy by 1625, notably in France, Spain, Flanders, Austria and Germany. The Capuchins worked to convert the semi-Protestant villages of Piedmont, France and Switzerland.[15] Like the Jesuits, they were sometimes assigned to reform lax convents.[16] Often their work among the lower classes and country folk complemented that of the Jesuits who dealt mainly with urban elites. Some Catholic bishops and lay leaders preferred the Capuchins to the Jesuits since they seemed less haughty, less likely to stir Protestant antagonisms, and closer to the people and popular religion.[17]

The Capuchins came late to foreign missions compared with the Dominicans, Jesuits, and other Franciscans; they tended to work more

closely with the new Roman Congregation of the Propagation of the
Faith than the other orders, which began their missions before the
Congregation's establishment in 1622. The main focus of Capuchin
missionary effort was the Middle East, but they also worked in the
Americas and the Congo. Still more important was their preaching of
parish missions in the villages of Catholic Europe, the domestic
Indies.[18]

Unlike the Jesuits and French Oratorians who ran colleges and seminaries, the early Capuchins had little impact on Counter Reformation
theology and scholarship relative to their numbers. In theology they
tended to follow St. Bonaventure rather than the later and more subtle
Franciscan giants Duns Scotus and William of Ockham. The
Capuchins did produce many devotional works. Their greatest writer
was St. Lawrence of Brindisi (1559-1619), who worked as preacher
and diplomat from Hungary to Portugal and also served as vicar-general; for the Capuchins he was a second St. Bonaventure. Given their
identification with the poor, a surprising number of Capuchins played
important roles at royal courts as advisors, most notably the "gray
Cardinal," Père Joseph du Tremblay (1577-1638), Cardinal Richelieu's close collaborator.

The Capuchins numbered 8,803 in 1600, but doubled by 1625
when they had 42 provinces, 1260 houses, and 16,967 members. By
1700 there were 27,336 members.

The Capuchinesses, or Capuchin nuns, were an autonomous branch
of the Poor Clares who were under the direction of the Capuchin friars.
When the Capuchins arrived in Naples in 1530, they offered their services at a hospital for the incurables established by a noble Catalan
widow, Maria Laurentia Longo (1463-1542). In 1538 Paul III made
her abbess for life of a nearby convent of third order Franciscans, then
three years later elevated it to the second order, or Poor Clares, and put
the convent under Capuchin spiritual direction. Between 1553 and
1587 thirteen more Italian convents of Capuchinesses were established. Later they spread to Spain and France, but their greatest
strength remained in Italy where they numbered 2,000 by 1700. Since
they were strictly cloistered and followed an austere observance of an
old rule, they did not face the opposition encountered by active orders
for women.

The Discalced Carmelites began in Spain rather than in Italy. In the
past history of religious orders, as in society at large, males tended to
take the lead, but most male orders soon had female counterparts. The

Middle Ages produced a number of double monasteries, where the women's community was the larger, and the male community existed to serve the sacramental needs of women religious. The story of the two branches of the Discalced Carmelites (OCD) partly parallels medieval double monasteries. The lead in Carmelite reform was taken by St. Teresa of Avila (1515-82), the most remarkable woman of her century. The male branch drew inspiration from her writings and reforms and grew out of the nuns' need for sympathetic confessors.

When Teresa Sánchez de Ahumada y Cepeda entered the large convent of the Incarnation at Avila in 1536 both male and female branches of the Carmelites needed reform badly. Sins and shortcoming against all three religious vows were common in the male branch; the nuns failed in lesser ways. A nun's family rank followed her into the convent, sometimes together with several servants to wait on her. Cloister went unheeded—nuns returned home to tend to family needs. They cultivated wealthy women to encourage gifts which the convents often needed desperately. After twenty years Teresa underwent spiritual experiences which convinced her of the need for austerity and reform. As a sign of reform and humility she advocated sandals in place of shoes (hence "discalced"). She rejected fixed incomes from investments in land; rather the nuns should depend on alms and their own labor. Social differences and titles were to disappear. Dowries were not required of poor novices. All nuns, regardless of social rank, were to do manual work. Cloister was strictly enforced, but the convent walls were not to imprison the nuns so much as to free them from social obligations and liberate them for their main task, prayer. Teresa's own voluminous writings on prayer, which are a literary treasure and the summit of Spanish mysticism, were quickly published and encouraged thousands of young women to follow her in the ascent of Mount Carmel. She cut back on the singing of the Divine Office so that the nuns might have more time for contemplation.

The first Discalced Carmelite convent was opened at Avila in 1562. In 1567, encouraged by the Carmelite General Giovanni-Battista Rossi (1507-78), Teresa started a second convent, the first of new fourteen convents in Spain during the next fifteen years—her *Book of Foundations* vividly describes these labors and the opposition she had to overcome. After 1600 her reform movement spread rapidly to France.

Teresa also encouraged the beginnings of the male Discalced Carmelites since she wanted confessors imbued with the new spirit. She first broached this project to Rossi in 1567 when he was making a

visitation of the Spanish friars and insisting on his own stringent reform measures. He was generally sympathetic, but the new observance
only complicated his task of reforming the male order.[19]

The first convent of Discalced Friars opened at Avila in 1568 with
St. John of the Cross (1542-91) and two others. The Discalced Friars
embraced the austere rule approved by Innocent IV in 1247, rejecting
the mitigations of Eugenius IV (1435) and later popes. The new observance stressed continual union with God in prayer and mortification. Meat was forbidden, and the friars fasted from September 14 to
Easter. Opposition from the older Calced (or "shoed") Carmelites was
immediate since the reform movement embarrassed lax members and
drew off fervent ones. The Prior General restricted Discalced friaries
to Castile, but they soon spread to the rest of Spain. Gradually the gap
between Calced and Discalced widened until there were two distinct
orders. Partly these developments grew out of the muddled jurisdiction that Philip II and the pope granted to a series of visitators who
were assigned to inspect and reform lax communities. The Discalced
Friar Jerome Gracián acquired the power of visitator and used it to set
up Discalced communities. The old wing fought back and even imprisoned John of the Cross for eight months at Toledo. After his release he
wrote systematic expositions of Carmelite mysticism.[20] Finally Philip
II intervened: the Discalced acquired a separate province in 1581 and
were recognized as an independent religious order by Clement VIII in
1593. Subsequent legislation split the Discalced into two virtually independent orders, the original wing in Spain, Portugal and their colonies, and the Italian wing.

The Italian wing enjoyed great success and spread to France, Belgium, Germany and Poland. The 1,000 Discalced Carmelites of 1600
grew to 5,000 in 1700. By contrast, the older Calced Carmelites
counted 12,000 in 1500, 12,000 in 1600, and 14,000 in 1700. Of all
the new male orders reviewed here, the Spanish Discalced Carmelites
were the least active in ministering to the laity and the most dedicated
to prayer and mystical union with God as described in the writings of
Saints Teresa and John of the Cross. The Italian friars gave a higher
priority to active ministry.[21]

5. Congregations of Priests, Chiefly in France

The distinction between the laity and members of religious orders and congregations has been less clear cut in practice than in canon law. In the late Middle Ages the Brethren of the Common Life as well as the beguines lived together as religious communities without taking vow of poverty, chastity, and obedience. But the fact of living in a religious community has always had more practical importance than the taking of formal vows. Still less important is the distinction between solemn vows (taken in religious orders) and simple vows (taken in religious congregations such as the Vincentians). During the sixteenth and seventeenth centuries groups of priests and women set up religious communities with only simple vows or no vows at all.

The pioneers of these developments were the priests and laymen who gathered around St. Filippo Neri (1515-95) at the Roman church of San Giovanni dei Fiorentini by 1567 and lived as a community but without vows or a formal superior. In 1575 Gregory XIII recognized these *Filippini* or Oratorians (Congregation of the Oratory, CO) as a congregation of priests and authorized them to write Constitutions. The Constitutions went through several drafts before receiving final papal approval in 1612. The Italian Oratorians heard confessions, encouraged frequent communion, presented spiritual conferences, and cultivated sacred music (the oratorio as a musical form grew out of their work in Rome). Neri wanted no formal vows, largely because his followers were to be role models for the diocesan clergy. Oratorians were to retain their patrimony and contribute to community expenses. Superiors were to rule by example more than by precept.

The Oratorians began to spread to other Italian cities after 1575. Especially important was the fast growing community set up at Naples in 1586, which attracted younger, poorer and less educated men than at Rome. The leaders at Naples wanted more structure, and while they did not introduce vows, they opened a novitiate and began other practices that brought them closer to formal religious orders. It was the Neapolitan pattern that prevailed after Neri's death in the sixty-one Italian communities, each virtually independent, set up between 1591 and 1700. The Oratorians also spread to Spain, Portugal, and their American and Asian colonies during the seventeenth century. Growth in northern Europe, except for France, was much slower.

In France the great spiritual writer Pierre de Bérulle (1575-1629) took the lead in encouraging Oratorian communities. The French communities, going beyond the Naples model, were linked by a general superior and triennial General Assemblies. The main ministry of the French Oratorians was staffing seminaries and colleges, which rivalled those of the Jesuits and had a more modern curriculum. The French Oratorians produced more distinguished scholars relative to their numbers than either the Jesuits or the Dominicans. Many Oratorians inclined toward Gallicanism and Jansenism, which sharpened Jesuit antagonism against them. By 1700 the French Oratorians staffed twenty-two colleges and nineteen seminaries. Their novices came mainly from the urban elite.[22]

Similar to the French Oratorians were the Doctrinaires (Pères de la Doctrine chrétienne) founded at Avignon in 1592 by César de Bus (1544-1607) and Jean Baptiste Romillon (1543-1622) to teach the poor. They received papal approval in 1597. They lived in community but initially did not take vows. De Bus argued for a vow of obedience, which Romillon opposed, and the nascent community split in 1602. The Oratorian bishop of Avignon, Francesco Tarugi (1525-1608), gave Romillon the statutes of the Roman Oratory; he and eleven communities of his supporters joined the French Oratorians in 1619. De Bus' followers sought papal approval as an order of regulars in 1615; instead they were merged with the Somaschi until 1647. After breaking away, they obtained in 1659 the power of taking simple vows of poverty, chastity, and obedience. In this they paralleled the contemporary the Vincentians, but on a smaller scale. Their main ministry continued to be education.[23]

The Vincentians (Congregation of the Mission, Lazarists, VSC), the most important of the new French congregations, were founded by St. Vincent de Paul (c. 1581-1660). Their primary ministry was preaching rural parish missions but they also staffed parishes and seminaries. De Paul and three other priests received episcopal and royal permission to live as a community in 1626; papal approval followed in 1632. The former Priory of St. Lazar (whence Lazarists) at Paris became the headquarters of their generals (elected for life), from which the Vincentians fanned out to revivify Catholic country parishes. By St. Vincent's death there were 500 Vincentians in twenty-three communities. They also staffed fifteen French seminaries and ministered to the 10,000 galley slaves of the French fleet. Between 1642 and 1668 they established four communities in Italy plus one in Warsaw. A mission in Madagascar followed. By 1789 they were directing sixty seminaries in France and thirty elsewhere. In 1668 a general assembly drew up Constitutions; priests and lay brothers were to take simple vows of poverty, chastity, and obedience; they wore the cassock of diocesan priests and did not make a novitiate.[24]

The Eudists (Congregation of Jesus and Mary, CJM) were founded in 1643 by St. John Eudes (1601-80). He entered the French Oratorians in 1620 and worked as a preacher and parish missionary, especially in Normandy and Brittany. When the general opposed his proposed seminary at Caen, Eudes left the Oratorians and established the Eudists as priests living in community without vows who specialized in preaching parish missions and staffing seminaries. By 1670 they were operating six French seminaries. Their numbers remained small, about one hundred by 1789. The Sulpicians, founded by Jean Jacques Olier (1608-57), paralleled the Eudists. Olier, a influential writer, drew much of his spirituality from the Oratorians. In 1642 he took control of the parish of St. Sulpice at Paris and established a community of priests. Eleven years later they were staffing four French seminaries.[25]

6. THE QUEST FOR ACTIVE WOMEN'S ORDERS

The women's orders discussed so far, principally Capuchinesses and Discalced Carmelites, were all cloistered contemplatives and hence did not challenge the conviction of both ecclesiastical and civil elites that women needed the protection of either a husband or a cloister wall: *aut maritus aut murus*. Badly in need of reform, Renaissance convent life reached its nadir in the convent brothels of Venice. The bishops gathered at the Council of Trent were convinced that the solution lay in stricter cloister and a clearer distinction between nuns and lay women.[26] Yet the same religious and social needs perceived by Ignatius of Loyola and Vincent de Paul were equally obvious to devout women. Repeatedly they tried to establish active or semi-active congregations for women. Repeatedly their communities were shunted back to a semi-cloister life or suppressed. Only after a century of effort did the Daughters of Charity breach cloister walls and open the way for the active congregations which proliferated into the hundreds during the nineteenth century.

The Company of St. Ursula (later the Order of St. Ursula, OSU) began at Brescia in 1535 when twenty-eight young woman led by an older mentor, St. Angela Merici (c. 1474-1540), committed themselves to a life of virginity in serving Christ. They took no formal vows and continued to live in their family homes, but they embraced a Rule (formulated by Merici) that included poverty, chastity, and obedience, and they devoted themselves to visiting the sick, burying the dead, and especially teaching Christian doctrine to girls. After Paul III approved the primitive rule in 1544, the Ursulines spread rapidly through Italy. Even greater was their later growth in France, where they may have had as many as 12,000 members by 1700. But the French Ursulines were transformed into an order of cloistered choir nuns with formal solemn vows who followed the rule of St. Augustine and whose active work was restricted to teaching girls in their convents. At Milan in 1584 St. Charles Borromeo (1538-84) set up three Ursuline communities living in convents under episcopal control and wearing a distinctive habit, but in most Italian cities the Ursulines continued to live in their family homes. It was convent life style that spread from Milan to Avignon in 1597 and hence to the rest of France and northern Europe. Initially the Ursulines taught catechism to men and women of all ages but they gradually restricted in their ministry to teaching boarding students, usually daughters of the wealthy, plus a larger number of poor girls who came to their convents. They continued to teach catechism to older women on Sundays. Much of the pressure in France toward solemn vows and cloister (first introduced at Paris in 1612) came from wealthy fathers who feared disputes over inheritance should a daughter leave the convent.[27]

The only order, aside from the short-lived English Ladies, which was established as a direct response to Protestantism was the Filles de Notre-Dame, who built forty-five convents in southern France between 1607 and 1650. In 1606 the Baroness Jeanne de Lestonnac, encouraged by her Jesuit spiritual director, began an active congregation of sisters modelled on the Jesuits; their goal was to win women and girls from Calvinism. The sisters curtailed their devotions so they could devote time to teaching. De Lestonnac wanted a centralized order on the Jesuit model, but the archbishop of Bordeaux ensured that each convent would be under the local bishop.[28]

The Visitandines or Visitation nuns (VHM) were founded at Annecy in Savoy by St. Jane Frances de Chantal (1572-1641) working closely with St. Francis de Sales (1567-1622), who was her spiritual director and the local bishop. Their spirituality owed much to the gentle spirit of his *Introduction to the Devout Life*. Their original intent was a simple lifestyle, mitigated cloister, and visiting the sick and the poor in

their homes. They invited lay women to make retreats in their convents. Their rule sought to accommodate widows and women of frail
health; hence mortifications were to be interior, without fasting or
physical penances. When they tried to open a second convent at Lyons, the Archbishop there demanded that they accept solemn vows,
strict cloister, and the Rule of St. Augustine. It was the Lyons model
that spread rapidly through France, where there were 6,500 nuns by
1700, as well as a few scattered convents in Italy, Switzerland, Belgium, Germany, and Poland. Papal approval as a full religious order
was granted in 1618.[29]

More radical and much less successful were the English Ladies or Institute of Mary founded by Mary Ward (1586-1646). An English
Catholic linked to the Jesuits, Ward wanted to set up a congregation
modelled on the Jesuits. With six companions she opened a small
school for English girls at St. Omer in 1609. Three years later their
community numbered forty. Their goal was to return to England and
work as missionaries, where special habits and cloister were impossible. Their memorial seeking approval from Rome noted the desperate
needs of Catholics in England and argued that women could make a
special contribution to helping them.[30] Like the Jesuits, they sought to
have their superior general subject to no bishops, but directly to the
pope. They were to be excused from reciting the Office and have
grades of membership after the Jesuit pattern. They began underground work in London in 1614, copying clandestine Jesuit missionaries. On the Continent they ran schools for girls where they had ten
communities with some 200 or 300 sisters in Italy and Bavaria. But
their close association with the Jesuits won them as many enemies as
friends, both in England and on the Continent. Despite initial papal
approval in 1616, opposition mounted. Ward might have salvaged
much of her work, but she refused compromise solutions: "There is no
such difference between men and women that women may not do great
things."[31] A papal bull suppressed the English Ladies in 1631.[32]

The Ursulines and Visitandines compromised, adapted their original
structures, and flourished. The English Ladies held their ground and
were suppressed. Ultimately the Daughters of Charity (FdC, DC),
founded by Sts. Vincent de Paul (1581-1660) and Louise de Marillac
(1591-1660), were successful by evading rather than confronting the
Decrees of Trent and the prejudices against active religious orders for
women. By 1950 the Daughters of Charity were the largest religious
order, male or female. In 1633 Marillac, a wealthy widow, began

training several peasant girls to help the poor. De Paul exhorted them to have the local parish for their chapel and the city streets for their cloister. Their garb was that of French peasants, and they took only private simple vows, indeed initially some took no vows. De Paul was careful not to refer to them as nuns or an order, but only as a community or confraternity. Their work parallelled that of the rural lay Confraternity of Charity founded by de Paul. Only after they had been working for thirteen years among the poor did he ask the Archbishop of Paris to approve them as a confraternity. Papal approval came in 1668. Their lifestyle resembled that of devout members of innumerable confraternities, and because they were drawn mainly from the poor, worries about dowries and muddled claims to inheritances did not threaten wealthy families. The Daughters of Charity spread from assisting the poor in their homes to working in hospitals, from teaching catechism to running orphanages. By 1660 they had forty communities in France plus one in Warsaw.[33]

7. TASKS OF FUTURE RESEARCH

Historians have long studied male religious orders, and the bibliography is staggering. László Polgár lists 45,472 items on the Jesuits alone published between 1901 and 1980.[34] Many larger male orders have historical institutes in Rome that publish specialized journals, series of documents, and monographs.[35] The declining numbers in all the traditional orders have put these institutes and publications in jeopardy. Future research will lie much more with lay historians than heretofore. They will bring detachment and better professional training and have new questions to ask, but they will need to strive for empathy, not unlike ethnologists. The history of the women's orders has been much less cultivated. Most nuns during the Reformation era were cloistered, but contemplatives leave a thinner paper trail through history so that studying their story is more challenging. The women's orders do not have counterparts to the Roman research institutes of the Jesuits and Capuchins. Most of the history written by members of religious orders is restricted to a given writer's own order. Comparative studies are rare. Lay historians should bring a wider focus.

All the men's orders had three basic grades: priests, those in training, and lay brothers, who were largely drawn from the uneducated. Most women's orders were divided between choir nuns, who paid dowries, and lay sisters who came from poor families. The life and work of lay brothers and sister were a subculture within a subculture, one that has seldom been examined. In some orders the brothers had full voting rights, in others they did not. Did this affect morale? Did it affect the sort of applicants an order attracted? What training were lay brothers given?

The questions of the new social history are only beginning to be addressed to religious orders. What was the age profile of entrants? What was their social and educational background? How did this vary from country to country, from period to period, from order to order? What was their life expectancy, longer or shorter than lay people in the same region? Why? The reasons men and women enter the religious life need systematic research as does the perseverance rate from order to order. All the orders had to deal with recalcitrant members; the methods varied from order to order (from exhortation, to the whip, to expulsion) but have rarely been studied. What happened to those who left or were expelled? Papal indults given to individual friars often weakened discipline during the Renaissance. Did this problem touch the new orders?

Research is needed on what sorts of men and women tended to become superiors and on how family background might enhance one's role within the order. Many elite families pressured daughters into convents where dowries were modest. What steps were taken against these forced entrances that undermined religious life? There were similar though more subtle pressures on young men. It would be interesting to know the comparative likelihood of religious vocations among only sons, older sons, and younger sons. Membership in the new orders and also in most of the old orders grew throughout the seventeenth century despite a slowdown of economic and demographic growth. Did the slowdown foster or hinder the orders?

Either excessive wealth or dire penury tended to break down religious discipline. The source and level of income within the new orders needs more investigation. The per capita expenses for the new orders seems to have been considerably less than in the older orders, especially the monastic orders.[36] It would be interesting to know how much was spent on support of the community, how much on ministries such as schools and hospitals and how much financial autonomy individual communities had. Did they share with other communities of their order? The friction between the different religious orders and with the parish clergy and the bishops needs study. So does the rivalry between the new Jesuit colleges and older educational institutions.

The various orders used different strategies of conversion in Asia and the Americas. How effective were they? How well did the orders cooperate with the Congregation of Propaganda in the foreign missions? The Spanish and Portuguese kings enjoyed royal patronage over the church in their colonial empires. How did kings intervene in the life and work of the orders? How did incipient nationalism affect the orders? Jesuit Gallicanism, which might seem a contradiction in terms, was in fact widespread and awaits study. Did national rivalries affect the central direction at Rome of international orders such as the Jesuits and Capuchins? How did rivalry and war between Catholic powers affect the work of the orders?

A comparative study of preaching styles used by the main orders would have value for students of literature and of popular religion. Much research in spirituality has focused on a single order, but how much did the spirituality of Loyola and Francis de Sales really differ? How did the active orders deal with individual members, especially in Spain, who inclined to a more contemplative lifestyle? Did the active orders foster or fear mysticism? Inventories might tell us more about the sorts of books were being read in convents. How much choice of confessors and spiritual directors did nuns have? The example of the new more active orders helped to reshape the work and spirituality of the friars, but this has not been systematically examined.[37]

The new male orders narrowed the psychological, pastoral, and devotional distance between diocesan priests and the religious orders. The training, ministry and life style of members of the new orders had many similarities with parish priests. The distance that separated Benedictine monks from the medieval parish priests was enormous; that between the products of the new Tridentine seminaries and the Oratorians or even the Jesuits was less obvious—often only clear to the practiced eye. The priesthood that they shared was often a more important bond than membership in a religious order. How the diocesan clergy viewed the new orders, whether as rivals or auxiliaries, and how the laity distinguished or blended together the two groups of priests need more research.

At the same time that the gap between diocesan and regular clergy was narrowing, the church hierarchy was trying to heighten cloister walls and separate nuns from pious laywomen. Many churchmen were suspicious of the Rhenish and Flemish beguines precisely because they blurred the distinction between religious and lay women. There was a sharp decline of the beguines in the sixteenth century, but there were still 2,487 of them in Belgium in 1631. A comparative study of their life-style with the new Daughters of Charity, similar in many respects, should contrast in microcosm the religious values of the waning Middle Ages with those of the Counterreformation.

NOTES

1. I wish to thank Professors Robert Bireley and Michael Zeps for suggestions which much improved this essay.
2. Raymond Hostie, *Vie et mort des ordres religieux* (Paris, 1972), 348-57, provides useful statistical tables on membership which this essay has frequently drawn upon.
3. The most fundamental source of information on religious orders is the multi-volume *Dizionario degli istituti di perfezione* (Rome, 1974-), henceforward *DIP*. For the Theatines, see F. Andreu's article, vol. 2:978-99. Also see the essay on the Theatines by Kenneth J. Jorgensen in DeMolen (1994), 1-29. DeMolen graciously loaned me the manuscript of his work, in which all chapters give extensive bibliography.
4. Recent sources for the Barnabites are A. M. Erba's article in *DIP*, vol. 2:945-74, and the essay by DeMolen in DeMolen (1994), 59-96, which also discusses the Angelic Sisters of St. Paul. More detailed is Antonio M. Gentili, *I Barnabiti: manuale di storia e spiritualità* (Rome, 1967).
5. P. Bianchini, *Origine e sviluppo della Compagnia dei Servi dei Poveri* (Milan, 1941) gives detailed coverage. See also his article in *DIP*, vol. 2:975-78.
6. V. Pascucci, in *DIP*, vol. 2:909-12.
7. See G. La Rosa's article in *DIP*, vol. 2:925-27.
8. See G. Ausenda's article in *DIP*, vol. 2:927-45; Paul Grendler's chapter on the Piarists in DeMolen (1994), 253-78.
9. P. Sannazzaro, in *DIP*, vol. 2:912-24.
10. Generally Jesuit communities were least cosmopolitan in Spain and most mixed in eastern Europe. An extreme example was the college at Cluj in Transylvania in 1584 which had seven Poles, four Prussians, four Germans, three Italians, three Transylvanians, two Hungarians, one Lithuanian, one Silesian, one Swede, and one simply designated as a Slav.
11. Bangert (1986), 105-7. The best study of the sodalities is Châtellier (1989).
12. For an overview of the early Jesuits, see John W. O'Malley's essay on the Jesuits in DeMolen (1994), 139-63; and O'Malley (1993).
13. Capuchins, like members of many other orders, are designated by their first name in religion plus their town of origin. They are usually so listed in encyclopedias and indices.
14. For Capuchin origins with detailed bibliography, see Elisabeth Gleason's essay in DeMolen (1994), 31-57. Also useful is Melchor de Pobladura, in *DIP*, vol. 2:203-51; earlier he published a three volume history of the Capuchins in Latin.
15. Cuthbert of Brighton (1929), vol. 1:214-18; vol. 2:263-64, 280-84.

16. Ibid., vol. 2:266-70. One of the Capuchins engaged in convent reform was the noted spiritual writer Benôit de Canfield (1563-1610).

17. Forster (1992), 216-25.

18. Cuthbert of Brighton (1929), vol. 2:370-96.

19. Joachim Smet, *The Carmelites: a History of the Brothers of Our Lady of Mount Carmel* (Darien, Ill., 1976), vol. 2:1-68.

20. Ibid., 69-130.

21. For an overview of the Discalced Carmelites, see V. Macca, in *DIP*, vol. 2:523-601; Jodi Bilinkoff, in DeMolen (1994), 165-86.

22. John P. Donnelly's essay on the Oratorians in DeMolen (1994), 189-215, provides an overview and bibliography. See also Lemoine, (1956), 88-116. The Oblati dei Santi Ambrogio e Carlo, a small congregation similar to the Oratorians, was founded by Carlo Borromeo at Milan in 1578. On it see P. Calliari, in *DIP*, vol. 6:647-52.

23. See J. de Viguerie, in *DIP*, vol. 3:975-77; Lemoine (1956), 68-72.

24. Ibid., 117-30.

25. Ibid., 130-46.

26. The Council of Trent voted its decrees on the reform of religious orders on December 3 and 4, 1563: they are printed in H.J. Schroeder, ed./trans., *The Canons and Decrees of the Council of Trent* (Rockford, Ill., 1978), 217-32; on enclosure for nuns, Ibid., 220-21.

27. Recent treatments include the essay by Charmarie J. Blaisdell in DeMolen (1994), 99-136, on the first years, and Rapley (1990), 48-61; Lemoine (1956), 167-82. The Congrégation de Notre Dame, similar to the Ursulines, was founded in 1597 at Mattaincourt, Lorraine, by St. Pierre Fourier (1565-1640) and Alix Le Clerc (1576-1622); the Congregation, devoted to teaching girls, spread to France, Germany, Savoy and Belgium by 1643, on which see Rapley (1990), 61-73. Even earlier was the Congregation of Oblates of the Immaculate Conception founded by the mystic Orsola Benincasa (1550-1618), who took up a religious life-style with some companions on the outskirts of Naples in 1581. Initially she drew her inspiration from the Oratorians, but in 1618 she put her Congregation, limited to a maximum of sixty-five members, under the directions of the Theatines. Francesco Andreu, in *DIP*, vol. 1:1375-77.

28. Rapley (1990), 43-48. Somewhat parallel to the Daughters of Our Lady were the Sisters of the Blessed Virgin of Cremona, founded in 1610 by Lucia Perotti (1568-1641), who took vows and were approved as a pious association by the Bishop of Cremona. They taught young girls there under episcopal control and did not received papal approval until 1933. Paolo Calliari, in *DIP*, vol. 1:1149-51.

29. Rapley (1990), 34-41; Lemoine (1956), 183-200; Wendy Wright, in DeMolen (1994), 217-50.

30. Quoted by Rapley (1990), 29.

31. Ibid., 33.

32. Ibid., 28-34. Sometimes wrongly considered a branch of the English Ladies were the Daughters of St. Agnes founded at Douai in 1600, teaching sisters who spread to three other Belgian towns. The protection of the Archbishop of Cambrai prevented their suppression following that of the English Ladies. See Elisabeth Wetter, in *DIP*, vol. 3:1720-21.

33. G. Rocca, L. Nuovo, in *DIP*, vol. 3:1539-49, 764-69; Lemoine (1956), 201-11.

34. *Bibliographie sur l'histoire de la Compagnie de Jésus. 1901-1980*, 6 vols. (Rome, 1981-90).
35. Some of the journals are *Archivum Historicum Societatis Iesu, Archivum Scholarum Piarum, Barnabiti studi, Carmelus, Collectanea Franciscana, Regnum Dei: Collectanea Theatina*.
36. Boaga (1971), 56-57.
37. For an overview of current research and new directions, the best starting point is O'Malley (1988), especially the chapters on religious orders of men, women religious and lay, European missionary expansion, spirituality, theology, preaching and schools.

BIBLIOGRAPHY

Alden, Dauril. *The Making of an Enterprise: the Society of Jesus in Portugal, her Empire, and Beyond, 1540-1750.* Stanford, 1993.

Andrés Martín, Meliquiades. *La teología española en el siglo XVI.* 2 vols. Madrid, 1976-77.

Andreu, Francisco. *Le Lettere di s. Gaetano Thiene.* Rome, 1954.

Annaert, Philippe. *Les collèges au féminin. Les Ursulines: enseignement et vie consacrée aux XVII et XVIII siècles.* Collection Vie consacrée, vol. 3. Namur, 1992.

Astráin, Antonio, S.J. *Historia de la Compañía de Jesús en la Asistencia de España.* 7 vols. Madrid, 1902-25.

Bangert, William, S.J. *A History of the Society of Jesus.* Rev. ed. St. Louis, 1986.

Bangert, William, S.J., and Thomas McCoog. *Jerome Nadal, S.J., 1507-1580: Tracking the First Generation of Jesuits.* Chicago, 1992.

Berthelot de Chesnay, C. *Les missions de saint Jean Eudes.* Paris, 1968.

Bilinkoff, Jodi. *The Avila of Saint Theresa: Religious Reform in a Sixteenth-Century City.* Ithaca, 1989.

Bireley, Robert. *Religion and Politics in the Age of the Counterreformation: Emperor Ferdinand II, William Lamormaini, S.J., and the Formation of Imperial Policy.* Chapel Hill, 1981.

Boaga, Emanuele. "Aspetti e Problemi degli Ordini e Congregazioni religiose nei secoli XVII e XVIII." In *Problemi di Storia della Chiesa nei secoli XVII-XVIII,* 91-135. Naples, 1982.

Boaga, Emanuele. *La soppressione innocenziana dei piccoli conventi in Italia.* Rome, 1971.

Boureau, R. *L'Oratoire en France.* Paris, 1991.

Boxer, Charles R. *The Christian Century in Japan.* Berkeley and Los Angeles, 1951.

Brémond, Henri. *Histoire littéraire de sentiment religieux en France depuis la fin des guerres de religion jusqu'à nos jours.* 12 vols. Paris, 1916-33.

Brenan, Gerald. *St. John of the Cross: His Life and Poetry.* Cambridge, 1973.

Brizzi, Gian Paolo. *La formazione della classe dirigente nel sei-settecento.* Bologna, 1976.

Brodrick, James. *The Progress of the Jesuits.* London, 1940.

Caballero, Valentin. *Orientaciones pedagogicas de San José de Calasanz, el gran padagogo y su obra cooperadores de la verdad.* 2d ed. Madrid, 1945.

Caragnoni, Constanzo, ed. *I frati cappuccini. Documenti e testimonianze del primo secolo.* 3 vols in 4. Perugia, 1988-91.

Caraman, Philip. *The Lost Paradise: the Jesuit Republic in South America.* New York, 1976.

Caraman, Philip. *St. Angela: the Life of Angela Merici, Foundress of the Ursulines, 1474-1540.* New York, 1964.

Châtellier, Louis. *Europe of the Devout: the Catholic Reformation and the Formation of a New Society.* Trans. Jean Birrell. Cambridge, 1989.

Cistellini, A. *San Filippo Neri: L'oratorio e la congregazione oratoriana, storia e spiritualità.* 3 vols. Brescia, 1989.

Contrisciani, Romano. *Perfil Historico de los Barnabitas.* Palencia, 1968.

Conrad, Anne. *Zwischen Kloster und Welt: Ursulinnen und Jesuitinnen in der katholischen Reformationbewegung des 16/17 Jahrhunderts.* Mainz, 1991.

Convegno di studi storici. *450 dell'Ordine Cappuccino. Le origini della riforma cappuccina. Atti del Convegno di studi storici. Camerino, 18-21 Settembre 1978.* Ancona, 1979.

Costa, Horacio de la. *The Jesuits in the Philippines, 1581-1768.* Cambridge, Mass., 1961.

Coste, Pierre. *The Life and Work of St. Vincent de Paul.* 3 vols. Trans. J. Leonard. Westminster, Md., 1952.

Coste, Pierre, et al. *Les Filles de la Charité.* Paris, 1933.

Criscuolo, V. *I cappuccini e la congregazione dei Vescovi e regolari.* Vol. 1, *1573-1595.* Vol. 2, *1596-1605.* Vol. 3, *1606-1612.* Rome, 1989-91.

Cushner, Nicholas. *Farms and Factory: the Jesuits and the Development of Agrarian Capitalism in Colonial Quito, 1600-1767.* Albany, 1982.

Cuthbert of Brighton. *The Capuchins: a Contribution to the History of the Counter-Reformation.* 2 vols. London, 1929.

Dagens, Jean. *Bérulle et les origines de la restauration catholique (1575-1611).* Bruges, 1952.

Dainville, François de. *Les Jésuites et l'education de la société française. La naissance de l'humanisme moderne.* Paris, 1940.

DeMolen, Richard L., ed. *Religious Orders of the Catholic Reformation in Honor of John C. Olin on his Seventy-fifth Birthday.* New York, 1994.

Devos, Roger. *L'origine sociale des Visitandines d'Annecy aux XVIIe et XVIIIe siècles: Vie religieuse feminine et société.* Annecy, 1973.

Dhôtel, Jean-Claude. *Les origines du catéchisme moderne, d'après les premiers manuels imprimés en France.* Paris, 1967.

Dolan, Claire. *Entre tours et clochers: les gens d'église à Aix-en-Provence au XVIe siècle.* Sherbrooke, Quebec, 1981.

Duhr, Bernhard. *Geschichte der Jesuiten in den Ländern Deutscher Zunge.* 4 vols. in 6. Munich and Regensburg, 1907-28.

Evennett, H. Outram. "The New Orders." In *The New Cambridge Modern History,* vol. 2:275-330. Cambridge, 1965.

Evennett, H. Outram. *The Spirit of the Counter-Reformation.* Ed. John Bossy. Cambridge, 1968.

Falkner, A., and P. Imhoff, eds. *Ignatius von Loyola und die Gesellschaft Jesu, 1491-1556.* Würzburg, 1990.

Forster, Marc R. *The Counterreformation in the Villages: Religion and Reform in the Bishopric of Speyer, 1560-1720.* Ithaca, 1992.

Fouqueray, Henri. *Histoire de la Compagnie de Jésus des origines à la suppression (1528-1762).* 5 vols. Paris, 1910-25.

Frank, Karl Suso, *A Short History of Christian Monasticism and Religious Orders.* Trans. Joseph Lienhard. Kalamazoo, Mich., 1993.

Fumaroli, Marc. *L'âge de l'eloquence: Rhétorique et "res literaria" de la Renaissance au seuil de l'époque classique.* Geneva, 1980.

Ganss, George E. *Saint Ignatius' Idea of a Jesuit University: a Study in the History of Catholic Education.* 2d ed. rev. Milwaukee, 1956.

Garrido, Pablo. *La "Reforma" teresiana y la orden de Carmen. ¿Ruptura o complementa?* Rome, 1991.

Garstein, Oskar. *Rome and the Counter-Reformation in Scandinavia.* 4 vols. Oslo and Leiden, 1963-90.

Gentili, Antonio M. *The Barnabites: a Historical Profile.* Trans. S. Zanchetta and A. Bianco. Youngstown, N.Y., 1980.

Gernet, Jacques. *China and the Christian Impact: a Conflict of Cultures.* Cambridge, 1985.

Giordano, Francesco. *Il Calasanzio e l'origine della scuola popolare.* Genoa, 1960.

Grendler, Paul F. *Schooling in Italy: Literacy and Learning, 1300-1600.* Baltimore, 1989.

Gueudré, Marie de Chantal. *Histoire de l'Ordre des Ursulines en France.* 3 vols. Paris, 1957-60.

Guibert, Joseph de. *The Jesuits: Their Spiritual Doctrine and Practice.* Trans. William J. Young. Chicago, 1964.

Heimbucher, Michael. *Die Orden und Kongregationen der katholischen Kirche.* 3d ed. 2 vols. Paderborn, 1933-34.

Hengst, Karl. *Jesuiten an Universitäten und Jesuitenuniversitäten.* Paderborn, 1981.

Herrera, J. *Historia de la congregación de la Misión.* Madrid, 1949.

Ignatius of Loyola. *The Constitutions of the Society of Jesus.* Trans. George E. Ganss. St. Louis, 1970.

Jégou, Marie-Andrée. *Les Ursulines du Faubourg Saint Jacques à Paris, 1607-1662: Origine d'un monastère apostolique.* Bibliothèque de l'Ecole des Hautes Études, Section des Sciences Religieuses, vol. 82. Paris, 1981.

Jesús, Crisógono de. *Vida de San Juan de la Cruz.* 11th ed. Madrid, 1982.

Knowles, Dom David. *From Pachomius to Ignatius: a Study in the Constitutional History of the Religious Orders.* Oxford, 1966.

Konrad, Herman. *A Jesuit Hacienda in Colonial Mexico: Santa Lucia 1576-1767.* Stanford, 1980.

Lamalle, Edmond. "L'archivo di un grande Ordine religioso. L'archivo Generale della Compagnia de Gesù." *Archiva Ecclesiae* 24-25 (1981-82): 89-120.

Le Bras, Gabriel, dir. *Les ordres religieux.* 2 vols. Paris, 1980.

Ledochowska, Teresa. *Angela Merici and the Company of St.Ursula according to Historical Documents.* Milan, 1968.

Lemoine, Dom Robert. *Le droit de religieux du concile de Trente aux instituts séculiers.* Paris, 1956.

Lemoine, Dom Robert. *Le monde de religieux: l'époque moderne 1563-1789.* Vol. 15 of *Histoire du Droit et des Institutions de l'Église en Occident.* Edited by Gabriel Le Bras and Jean Gaudemet. Paris, 1976.

Lesegretain, Claire. *Les grands ordres religieux.* Paris, 1990.

Liebowitz, Ruth. "Virgins in the Service of Christ: the Dispute over an Active Apostolate for Women during the Counter Reformation." In *Women of Spirit: Female Leadership in the Jewish and Christian Traditions,* ed. Rosemary Ruether and Eleanor McLaughlin. New York, 1979.

Llompart, G. *Gaetano da Thiene. Estudios sobre un reformador religioso.* Wiesbaden, 1969.

Lukács, Ladislaus, ed. *Monumenta Paedagogica Societatis Iesu.* 3 vols. Monumenta Historica Societatis Iesu, vols. 92, 107-8. Rome, 1965-74.

McCabe, William. *An Introduction to Jesuit Theater: a Posthumous Work.* Ed. Louis J. Oldani. St. Louis, 1984.

McCormick, Ignatius, ed. *The Capuchin Reform: Essays in Commemoration of its 450th Anniversary 1528-1978.* From *Analecta Ordinis Minorum Capuccinorum* 94 (1978). Pittsburgh, 1983.

Mariani, Lucana, Elisa Tarolli, and Maria Seynaeve. *Angela Merici: contributo per una biografia.* Milan, 1986.

Martin, A. Lynn. *The Jesuit Mind: the Mentality of an Elite in Early Modern France.* Ithaca, 1988.

Martín, Luis. *The Intellectual Conquest of Peru: the Jesuit College of San Pablo, 1568-1768.* New York, 1968.

Martin, Mère Marie de Saint Jean. *Ursuline Method of Education.* Rahway, N.J., 1946.

Mauzaize, Raoul. *Histoire des Frères Mineurs Capuchins de la province de Paris (1601-1660).* Blois, 1967.

Meissner, William W. *Ignatius of Loyola: the Psychology of a Saint.* New Haven, 1992.

Melchor de Pobladura, ed. *"La Bella e Santa Riforma dei Frati Minori Cappuccini".* 2d ed. Rome, 1963.

Melchor de Pobladura, ed. *Historia generalis Ordinis Fratrum Minorum Capuchinorum.* 4 vols. Rome, 1947-51.

Michelini, Vittorio M. *Barnabiti: Chierici Regolari di S. Paolo alle radice della congregatione, 1533-1983.* Milan, 1983.

Mir, Gabriel Codina. *Aux sources de la pédagogie des jésuites: Le "modus parisiensis".* Bibliotheca Instituti Historici S.I., vol. 28. Rome, 1968.

Molette, Charles. *Guide des sources de l'histoire des congrégations féminines françaises de vie active.* Paris, 1974.

Nimmo, Duncan. *Reform and Division in the Medieval Franciscan Order from Saint Francis to the Foundation of the Capuchins.* Rome, 1987.

Oliver, Mary. *Mary Ward, 1585-1645.* New York, 1959.

O'Malley, John, ed. *Catholicism in Early Modern History: a Guide to Research.* Reformation Guides to Research, vol. 2. St. Louis, 1988.

O'Malley, John. *The First Jesuits.* Cambridge, Mass., 1993.

Le origini dei Cappuccini veneti. Studi per il 450e di fondazione (1535-1985). Venice, 1988.

Le origini della riforma cappuccina. Atti del convegno di studi storici, Camerino, 18-21 settembre 1978. Ancona, 1979.

Paschini, Pio. *S. Gaetano Thiene, Gian Pietro Carafa, e le origini dei chierici regolari teatini.* Rome, 1926.

Pastor, Ludwig von. *The History of the Popes from the Close of the Middle Ages.* Trans. Ralph E. Kerr and E. F. Peeler. 40 vols. St. Louis, 1891-1953.

Peters, Henriette. *Mary Ward. Ihre Persönlichkeit und ihr Institut.* Innsbruck, 1991.

Picard, Emile. "Les Théatins de Sainte-Anne-La-Royale (1644-1790)." *Regnum Dei: Collectanea Theatina* 36 (1980): 99-374.

Polgar, László, S. J. *Bibliographie sur l'histoire de la Compagnie de Jésus, 1901-1980.* 6 vols. Rome, 1981-90.

Ponnelle, Louis, and Louis Bordet. *St. Philip Neri and the Roman Society of His Times, 1515-1595.* Trans. Ralph Francis Kerr. London, 1932. Reprint, 1979.

Prévost, A. *Saint Vincent de Paul et ses institutions en Champagne méridionale.* Bar-sur-Seine, 1928.

Rapley, Elizabeth. *The Dévotes: Women and Church in Seventeenth Century France.* Montreal, 1990.

Ravier, André. *Ignatius of Loyola and the Founding of the Society of Jesus.* Trans. Maura Daly, et al. San Francisco, 1987.

Rigault, G. *Histoire générale de l'Institut des Frères des Écoles Chrétiennes.* 9 vols. Paris, 1937-53.

Rodrigues, Francisco, S. J. *História da Companhia de Jesus na Assistência de Portugal.* 4 vols. Porto, 1931-50.

Rollet, Henri. *La condition de la femme dans l'Eglise.* Paris, 1975.

Ruis Jurado, Manuel. *Origenes del noviciado en la Compañía de Jesús.* Bibliotheca Instituti Historici S.I., vol. 42. Rome, 1980.

Santa Teresa, Silvero de. *Historia del Carmen Descalzo en España, Portugal y América.* 15 vols. Burgos, 1935-49.

Sántha, Georgius, and Claudius Vilá Palá, eds. *Epistolarium Coaetanorum S. Josephi Calasanctii 1600-1648.* 6 vols. Rome, 1977-81.

Sántha, György, César Ahuilera, and Julián Centelles. *San José de Calasanz. Su Obra. Escritos.* Madrid, 1956.

Scaduto, Mario. *Storia della Compagnia di Gesù in Italia. L'epoca di Giacomo Lainez, 1556-1565.* Vol. 3, *Il Governo.* Vol. 4, *L'Azione.* Vol. 5, *L'opera di Francesco Borgia, 1562-1572.* Rome, 1964-92.

Schurhammer, Georg. *Francis Xavier: His Life, His Times.* 4 vols. Trans. M. Joseph Costelloe. Rome, 1973-82.

Schütte, Josef Franz. *Valignano's Mission Principles for Japan.* 2 vols. Trans. John J. Coyne. St. Louis, 1980-85.

Shiels, W. E. *King and Church: the Rise and Fall of the Patronado Real.* Chicago, 1961.

Spence, Jonathan. *The Memory Palace of Matteo Ricci.* New York, 1984.

Steggink, Otger. *La reforma del Carmelo español: la visita canónica del general Rubeo y su encountro con Santa Teresa, 1566-1567.* Textus et Studia Carmelitana, vol. 7. Rome, 1965.

Stopp, Elisabeth. *Madame de Chantal: Portrait of a Saint.* Westminster, Md., 1963.

Trevor, Meriol. *Apostle of Rome: a Life of Philip Neri, 1515-1591.* London, 1966.

Urbanelli, Callisto. *Storia dei Cappuccini delle Marche.* 3 vols. in 4. Ancona, 1978-84.

Valentin, Jean-Marie. *Le théâtre des jésuites dans les pays de langue allemande (1554-1680).* 3 vols. Bern, 1978.

Vigotti, Gualaberto. *Carlo Borromeo e la Compagnia di s. Orsola.* Milan, 1972.

Vincent de Paul: Actes du colloque international d'études vincentiennes, Paris, 25-26 septembre 1981. Rome, 1983.

Wallace, William. *Galileo and his Sources: the Heritage of the Collegio Romano in Galileo's Science.* Princeton, N. J., 1984.

Williams, Charles E. *The French Oratorians and Absolutism, 1611-1641.* New York, 1989.

Wittkower, Rudolf, and Irma Jaffe, eds. *Baroque Art: the Jesuit Contribution.* New York, 1972.

Wright, Wendy M. *Bond of Perfection: Jeanne de Chantal and François de Sales.* New York, 1985.

CATHOLIC REFORMATION, COUNTERREFORMATION AND PAPAL REFORM IN THE SIXTEENTH CENTURY

Elisabeth G. Gleason
(University of San Francisco)

The interrelation of the three terms in the title of this essay has a lengthy history in historiographical debates from the latter part of the nineteenth century to our own day. German Protestant historians were the first to label the measures adopted by Catholic princes against Protestantism and the aggressive recatholicization of much of central Europe as Counterreformation. The term was rejected by Catholic scholars because it implied that change in the Catholic church came about only in response to the Protestant Reformation, and because it took no account of reform movements within Catholicism before Luther.

Scholarship since World War II was fundamentally influenced by Hubert Jedin's *Katholische Reformation oder Gegenreformation?*, published in 1946, which proposed that both terms be retained but given more specific meaning. Jedin defined Catholic Reformation as the sum of movements and efforts, rooted in the late medieval church and continuing into the sixteenth century, to realize reform, change and purification of ecclesiastical institutions, beliefs and teaching. Counterreformation, he argued, should be used to mean quite literally the counterattack of the strengthened post-Tridentine Catholic church against Protantism. Inextricably linked with this counterattack were measures designed to spread Catholic doctrine and institute discipline among the people. Therefore, the Counterreformation involved both defense and attacks. The latter frequently built upon older ideas which predated the Reformation, and in that way were connected with currents of Catholic reform thought.

Even though Jedin's definitions have been generally accepted, some scholars have continued to question or deny the existence of a Catholic Reformation as an identifiable and significant movement apart from the reaction of the church to Protestantism which culminated in inquisition and repression.[1] On one of Jedin's key ideas, however, there is no disagreement: that the papacy played a crucial role in the process of change in the early modern Catholic church. The existence of local and even national reform, most notably in Spain, does not alter the fact that the church as a whole, in Europe and overseas, was ultimately changed as a result of decisions made by popes. This essay has as its focus the nature of reform under papal leadership in the Catholic church of the middle and later sixteenth century. Recent and lively scholarship has made this topic an important part of a new frontier in early modern studies: the examination of the Catholic Reformation and Counterreformation as historical and social phenomena rather than as a mere series of religious events touching primarily the internal history of the Catholic church, with incidental political ramifications.

1. The Past as Model: Reform Ideas and Efforts
Before the Council of Trent

The continuity of concepts of reform in the Catholic church has frequently been magnified by Catholic scholars who sought to contrast it favorably with the discontinuities for which they thought Protestants responsible.[2] But dispassionate study of Catholic reform before the Protestant Reformation, far from showing a clear line of development, turns up a bewildering mass of data but no real pattern. In older works, the discussion of reform ideas and efforts together with their schematic organization was usually along geographical lines. Thus, for example, instances of monastic or disciplinary reform in various countries were gathered, or lists compiled of writings by proponents of reform and critics of abuses in the church of a given region.

This essay proposes a different principle for understanding the character of Catholic reform in the sixteenth century by dividing its history into three stages. The first lasted from the late 1400s to the early 1540s, while the second encompassed the two middle decades of the sixteenth century. The final session of the Council of Trent from 1561 to 1563 marked the beginning of the third stage which extended well into the seventeenth century. The real issue, however, is not so much to establish precise lines of demarcation between these three stages as to understand their guiding ideas, or, to use H. O. Evennett's expression, to grasp their "spirit,"[3] and highlight the role of the papacy in each.

During the first or pre-Tridentine phase, most efforts at Catholic reform originated on the local or diocesan level rather than emanating from the popes. The common denominator of all such efforts was the dream of a return to standards of excellence that supposedly existed in the idealized church of the past. Proponents of reform during this first stage, with very few exceptions, were conservative and backward-looking, and sought restoration of what had been rather than striking out in new directions. Only by keeping this in mind is it possible to understand the character of such generally adduced examples of Catholic reform as new confraternities, above all the Oratories of Divine Love founded at the very end of the fifteenth century, which played an important role in the Italian urban milieu during the subsequent decades.[4] While testifying to the personal religious fervor and desire of their members to live a Christian life of closeness to God and service to neighbors, especially the sick, the spirituality and basic conceptual framework of the oratories were related to those of similar groups in the later Middle Ages. Their practices included such traditional forms of penance as self-flagellation.[5] Their statutes testify to a noble ideal of Christian life, but contain no innovative religious ideas. Even their biblical meditation remained within the parameters of medieval piety. Thus, using the example of confraternities as evidence of renewal in the Catholic church begs more questions than it answers. One can interpret their flowering with equal justice as evidence of continuity and tenacity of rooted concepts of Christian piety and charity, or of the importance of ritual brotherhood in Italian urban society.[6]

On a much wider scale, the same is true of the new religious orders, treated more fully in another chapter of this volume.[7] In this context it is sufficient to underline that merely listing their founders and initial dates, as is done in many general works, does not explain the reasons for the remarkable cluster of new foundations during fewer than twenty years, from 1524 to 1540. The papacy had no part in their origin. We have to look more broadly to the religious history of Italy, where almost all the new orders arose, with the famous exception of the Jesuits. That history has not yet received the kind of detailed and sophisticated analysis of the connections between religion and society, above all urban society, as can be found in the work of recent German Reformation historians, for example. It is abundantly clear that Italy formed no exception to manifestations of religious fervor so evident throughout western Europe on the eve of the Reformation. That fervor, however, found outlets through existing channels within the Catholic church. The expressed purposes of the new orders offer striking proof of their continuity with traditional concepts of Christian perfection. None of their founders initially made specific reference to the great religious debates of their own day, to the Reformation or Luther. From the documents connected with their foundation not even the suspicion emerges that there actually existed different conceptions of what constituted Christian life, as well as irreconcilable views about the relation of faith and good works, the meritorious nature of which was vigorously attacked by Protestant theologians. But then, not one of the new orders was founded for the purpose of counteracting Protestantism. On the contrary, the origins of all were curiously independent of the Reformation. Their aims were traditional: sanctification of their members and service to God, neighbor, and the church.

Thus, the Camaldolese, reformed by Paolo Giustiniani, the Theatine order instituted in 1524, the first Capuchins in the late 1520s, the orders of the following decade like the Barnabites, Somaschi, and Ursulines, or even the first Jesuits, founded in 1540, all testify to the strength of traditional devotional ideals and practices.[8] The piety of their founders was nourished by traditional sources, from which the rationale for their active apostolate was drawn. The history of the first Capuchins, for example, serves as proof that their most important inspiration was the vision of a "golden" past. Their purpose was to return to the pure spirit of St. Francis and the strict observance of the original Franciscan rule which included uncompromising poverty. Like the Jesuits, the Capuchins were transformed only later into an order in the service of a militant Counterreformation by the opening of new horizons for their activities that were unforeseen at the time of their foundation. Historical circumstances rather than design changed the nature of their apostolate and their role in European society and eventually in the non-European world as well.[9]

If the new orders were responses of their founders to what they saw as widespread needs among the people, rather than results of actions by the popes, the calling of the last pre-Reformation church council, the Fifth Lateran (1513-17), was a clear example of papal initiative. However, the intention of Julius II, who convened it, was not primarily that the council should reform the church, but that it should meet and forestall attempts to attack him through the so-called Council of Pisa, dominated by the French and by latter-day conciliarists. The decrees of the Fifth Lateran testify to the conservative and traditional orientation of their framers. That these decrees remained ineffective should not obscure their significance as indicators of ways of thinking that characterized the clerical elite.[10] The more spiritual members of this elite wished for a restoration of what supposedly had been good order in the church, observance of its laws, eradication of abuses but were not willing to confront what actually was, or to carefully examine the reasons for the dangerous and rising tide of anticlericalism and criticism of the church all over western Europe.[11]

The notable exception to this mentality at the Fifth Lateran Council (1512) was, at least to a certain extent, the *Libellus ad Leonem X*, an intriguing series of proposals for reform by the Venetian Camaldolese monks Paolo Giustiniani and Pietro Querini.[12] In the absence of supporting documentation about their origin, it is difficult to place these proposals into a satisfactory framework.

Although Giustiniani has been considered the more important author, recent studies have cast doubt on the existence of a supposed reform circle under his leadership to which the ideas of the *Libellus* might be traced.[13] The two monks appealed to the pope to reform the church, beginning with himself as its head, and to institute new measures designed to strengthen Christianity. Along with conventional views, the *Libellus* also contains innovative ideas, most conspicuously the authors' plan to effectively promote the evangelization of non-European peoples with whom Europeans had come into contact as a result of the discoveries. Giustiniani and Querini, both highly educated men, realized what an immense horizon had opened to the activities of the Christian church, and urged the pope to unequivocally assert his leadership in a global missionary thrust. But Pope Leo X lacked imagination or interest to follow their vision, and their ideas about the necessity of reconceptualizing evangelization fell on deaf ears. Giustiniani and Querini pointed to the future and had as their ideal a dynamic church, which, guided by the pope, would be willing to confront a new world.

That neither Leo X nor Clement VII were supporters of church reform is a fact that requires no emphasis. The insensitivity of the first and the indecisiveness of the second are well known to students of papal history. For both popes the fortunes of their house, the Medici, and of their city, Florence, were of primary concern. Clement VII was particularly unfortunate, or rather, inept in his political moves and provoked the disastrous sack of Rome in 1527. This terrible event and the loss of papal territory in its aftermath form the background to a singular document that allows us to glimpse reform ideas of yet another kind.

In a long dispatch to the Senate of 4 January 1529, the Venetian ambassador Gasparo Contarini reported verbatim an exchange with

Clement VII.[14] The subject was the pope's demand that Venice restore two cities of the papal state, Ravenna and Cervia, which the Republic had occupied during the troubles of the preceding two years. To Clement's complaint that the Venetians had acted illegally, Contarini replied by pointing out that in actuality Venice was doing the Holy See a favor by taking Ravenna and Cervia into protective custody in order to guard them from further evils. Contarini next developed an impassioned argument that the two cities should not matter anyway because the power of the pope was properly confined to the spiritual realm, and that a papal state was in no way necessary for the exercise of that power. On the contrary, it actually clouded the true nature of papal authority, which was that of a father over his children, not that of a prince over his subjects.

It would be easy to dismiss Contarini's ideas as Venetian excuses for illegal actions, as Clement VII did. But in actuality, they represent unsystematically formulated yet characteristic ideas of certain sixteenth-century Italian *spirituali*, or men and women who desired a serious reform of the church, and who responded to the Gospel message in a deeply personal way by embracing Pauline spirituality with its emphasis on metanoia, the reform and transformation of oneself into a follower of Christ. Contarini, who later became a conspicuous spokesman for the *spirituali*, raised the question whether the concept of a spiritual papacy was not more in conformity with the ideals of the early church, and of Christianity rightly understood, than was the papacy of his day. Clement did not want to hear what amounted to a major criticism of the status quo and of the interpretation of papal *plenitudo potestatis*, or fullness of power, with which he was familiar. He most decidedly did not consider the possibility of a papacy without a state. Even less did he consider himself as a candidate for the role of *papa angelicus*, the spiritual angelic pope of the dreamers and wandering prophets who criss-crossed Italy with their visions of church reform and the beginning of a new and better age for mankind. Therefore it was easy for him to dismiss Contarini as "more Venetian than Christian," and to ignore the idea that radical reform should begin with the pope's divesting himself of the papal state.

The most famous reform proposal of this first period, generally referred to as the *Consilium de emendanda ecclesia* of 1537, was emblematic of both the strengths and weaknesses of pre-Tridentine Catholic reform thought.[15] It was commissioned by the pope. That alone puts it into a different category from the lists of abuses and calls for change that abounded at the time, like the tract written in 1532 by Gianpietro Carafa, the future Pope Paul IV, and addressed to Pope Clement VII.[16] The *Consilium* was different from its predecessors in not just criticizing abuses, although it lists an impressive number, but in striking at the heart of the matter. The committee of cardinals and prelates who drew it up flatly stated that the source of all ills besetting the church was the exaggerated claims made for papal power, and the wrong use made of it. Reform could not begin, they wrote, let alone have much meaning, until the pope realized that he had been led astray by curial lawyers and evil counsellors who argued that his will was law. The *Consilium*, in effect, criticized the whole system of papal government because it enabled abuses to exist, and called for conceiving papal power in spiritual rather than political or economic terms. Had it led to a reexamination of the power and role of the pope in the church, this proposal would have been a major document of Catholic reform. But it clearly was nothing of the kind, notwithstanding claims for its importance made by some historians. Looked at more closely, it reveals an uneasy and ambiguous coexistence of ideas, not a consistent concept of reform.

It is true that the introductory section of the *Consilium* is radical and minces no words. But when the proposal gets down to concrete issues, like how to stem the many abuses at all levels of the church from the top down to the parish, or how to tighten discipline among the regular and secular clergy, the absence of new ideas is striking. It does not go beyond calling for traditional remedies, and breaks no new ground. Backward-looking, at times downright timid, the document shows that its nine signatories were bold in isolating the theoretical root of abuses, yet unimaginative in suggesting practical remedies. These features made it easy for Pope Paul III to shelve it, especially since there was no strong pressure group at the curia or in the college of cardinals to urge its implementation.

It did not help matters that the *Consilium* was leaked to a printer in Rome, and that it speedily reached Germany. Luther annotated it with biting reflections on the unwillingness of its authors to tackle what he considered to be the central issues, namely the theological bases on which the practices of the Roman church rested. Paul III was not another Adrian VI, whose public admission that the Catholic church was co-responsible for the crisis of the Reformation backfired tragically. From the beginning of his pontificate Paul III had announced his commitment to calling a council which would deal with the issues raised by the Reformers. The *Consilium* did not change his idea that a general council rather than piecemeal reform was necessary for the church at that junction in its history.

Although it had no practical effect, this document raises some important issues. The first concerns the intentions of Paul III, a pope who has baffled more than one historian. Side-stepping the hard question of how to interpret his words and deeds, historians have generally put him in a kind of no-man's land by calling him at once the last Renaissance pope and the first pope of the Counterreformation. Hubert Jedin, who knew the pontificate of Paul III better than any modern historian, judged that this pope cannot yet be considered the first pontiff of Catholic reform, but that he did pave its way.[17] In the absence of a modern work on the enigmatic Farnese pope himself, it is tempting to continue interpreting him as a Janus-faced figure. But such an image only masks the difficulty of uncovering the principles which guided his decisions.

Paul III was too shrewd to simply improvise, and unlike his predecessor Clement VII, he could make decisions. He understood the threat to the Catholic church posed by Protestantism, and to Italy by the devastating Habsburg-Valois wars. He was also perfectly aware that the policies of Emperor Charles V weighed particularly heavily on all Italian states after 1530. Reform for him was as much a political as a religious issue; it was essential if the Catholic church was not to lose its position in a Europe increasingly divided along religious lines. Promoting reform and calling for a council was a form of damage control. At this crucial moment in its history the church faced the aggressive Protestant Reformation in Germany, the rumblings of dissent in Italy, schism in England, and an upredictable French king. When he summoned a council, the pope was not merely cynically playing along with German or imperial demands for its convocation, but acting out of conviction that it must meet. He knew that it must deal with burning issues, and he was determined that it would not be an ineffective assembly like the Fifth Lateran. In that sense it is justified to consider Paul III more than the pope who paved the way for Catholic reform. He initiated it, and was not deflected from his purpose despite the immense political complications which stood in the way of the council, as the first volume of Jedin's magisterial *History of the Council of Trent* clearly shows.

In preparation for the council, Paul III at least considered the thorny problem of how to reform the curia, and gave the go-ahead to attempts to reform the papal *dataria*, through which venal offices were sold, and the *penitenziaria*, the office dealing primarily with dispensations. These attempts came to nothing, owing to resistance by entrenched interest groups before whose opposition the pope retreated in a series of politic moves.[18] The same was true for his abortive attempt in December, 1540, to send absentee bishops residing in Rome back to their dioceses. His bull of 1542 addressing this matter was not enforced. Taking on these interest groups would not only have amounted to reform, but to a thoroughgoing change of an entire economic system, arguably even an entire society. Paul III worked within a system, and was neither able nor willing to step outside it or to examine it dispassionately.

Paul III's commitment to reform had very definite limits. The first was his inability to conceive of the church otherwise than as it presently was, a system that included all the features the *Consilium* had singled out for particular censure: the entrenched concept of the church as property, meaning the matter-of-course acceptance of the traffic in benefices, offices, compositions, and the like. Neither Pope Paul III nor the majority of cardinals contemplated giving up lucrative financial arrangements which benefited them and their families and dependents. It has rightly been pointed out that Catholic reform proposals hit the proverbial brick wall the moment they touched upon property.[19] This was a consistent pattern throughout the tenth century and beyond. Paul III did not challenge this, let alone initiate reform in this area. That would have meant a revolution which it was hardly in his power to effect. In actuality, it was not the pope but the bankers and creditors who controlled much of church property.

The second limit to the pope's ideas of reform was his nepotism.[20] This cultivation of one's own family's interests was in reality a structural element of Italian society and an integral, even admired part of social norms in sixteenth-century Italy. Indeed, it has been shown nepotism had a sort of moral value, contributing as it did to the central and immensely important value of *pietas*, the ideal of proper behavior toward one's family and dependents in a society which placed the collectivity above the individual.[21] *Pietas* was not an excuse for nepotism, but its legitimation. Financial support of family and *familia*, or the household including retainers, had come to be considered an obligation rather than an abusive diversion of church funds.

Seen in this light, the principles according to which Paul III acted become comprehensible to our age, with its different social norms. The issue for the pope was not whether to champion ideas of reform that might threaten to deprive his family, including his grandson Cardinal Alessandro Farnese, of a huge income derived from benefices. That would have clashed with his sense of priorities and with that of his contemporaries who held comparable social rank. Rather, in his view concern for the welfare of the church was compatible with his desire to elevate the Farnese to the highest possible social position, even if that meant alienating church lands for the purpose of creating a new principality for his descendants, or of destroying the independence of abbeys so that they could become benefices in the hands of his family. Paul III, perhaps more than any other sixteenth-century pope, truly was a papal prince. All his efforts at reform therefore proceeded within parameters that were defined by this reality, and they excluded change in property arrangements or in what he considered family affairs. Reform in these areas could come only later, in consequence of the economic crises of the seventeenth century, of changing views about the nature of papal power, and last but not least, of more modern ideas about family bonds, the limits of the obligations family members had toward one other, and the relation of the family to the state.

2. THE DECADES OF SURVIVAL AND DEFENSE, 1540-1560

During the 1530s, German Protestants were no longer merely criticizing the one Christian church of which they considered themselves members, but had broken with Catholicism and were building and solidifying what in fact became a new branch of Christianity. In Protestant territories the pope had lost all power. The specter of a German national council which might codify the schism threatened as well. In this situation the pope bowed to the demand of Emperor Charles V that a legate be sent to a colloquy between German Catholic and Protestant theologians. This colloquy finally was held in conjunction with the Diet of Regensburg in the Spring of 1541. Contrary to oft-repeated statements, it was not the last opportunity to reconcile the two sides. Despite efforts by the irenic papal legate Cardinal Gasparo Contarini, nothing concrete was achieved except that the Catholics finally realized how great a gulf separated them from the Protestants, and how profound the theological differences between them were on such issues as justification, the nature of the sacraments, or papal authority.

Meanwhile, from the perspective of Rome the question of how to defend the papal state and Italy from the incursions of Protestant ideas became critical. From the time of Pope Leo X on, papal nuncios were transmitting alarming information to Rome about the growth of Protestantism all over Europe. Paul III, acting on the advice of cardinals, most notably Gianpietro Carafa, decided to reorganize and strengthen the Roman inquisition, and to establish it in its new form in July, 1542. While in Spain the inquisition was an office of the state, its Roman counterpart was under the control of a committee of cardinals responsible to the pope. The extent and nature of the control which the inquisition came to exert on Italian society are still debated,[22] but there is little doubt that the Holy Office was responsible for creating a climate of caution, if not of outright fear among both intellectuals and common people. Criticism of the church, at least in public, became dangerous. Another sort of effort to stop the spread of heterodox ideas was the index of prohibited books. The first was drawn up by the papal nuncio to Venice, Giovanni della Casa, in 1549, and the official Roman *Index librorum prohibitorum* eventually followed. Like the impact of the inquisition, the effects of ecclesiastical censorship of books on Italian culture is a topic on which scholars differ.[23] There is no disagreement, however, that whole categories of books, especially works dealing with theology and philosophy, were affected by the new mechanisms of control, even though the latter rarely functioned with complete efficiency.

Given these innovations, the question concerning the two decades of the 1540s and 1550s is whether or to what extent they marked the beginning of profound change in the Catholic church. Although the ending of the Council of Trent in 1563 is generally considered the great divide between epochs, scholars in the last ten or fifteen years have pointed to the new realities in Rome after 1541 as indicative of the end of the Renaissance church with its latitudinarian and relatively tolerant atmosphere, and the beginning of the Counterreformation church.[24] Humanistically educated and tolerant prelates, so the argument goes, were replaced by career bureaucrats convinced that it was necessary to control the expression of religious ideas and repress heterodoxy on all fronts.

While the effectiveness of the mechanisms of control should not be exaggerated, it is true that their very existence inaugurated a different concept of the Catholic community. Defense against heretics, who appear in sermons as ravenous wolves looking for victims, or as the proverbial roaring lions stalking the church on many fronts, became a priority for many Catholic prelates. A significant part of that defense became the surveillance over what was said, read, and published. Despite his age and his past as one of the famous "Renaissance cardinals," Pope Paul III was in tune with the new thinking, and espoused the view of the church as a fortress to be guarded, defended, and kept on the alert, ready for battle. Under his leadership the years following 1540 mark the beginning of the Counterreformation church. This period was still a time of transition, of piecemeal rather than sweeping structural change, and of unsystematic attempts to deal with the myriad problems facing the church and the papacy. But despite the absence of a comprehensive ideology of reform, Paul III was willing to tackle many of these problems, albeit with varying degrees of conviction and success. He was a pragmatist. In the end, it was not so much his often half-hearted actions as the signals about the necessity of reform which he sent clearly and repeatedly that separate him most sharply from his predecessors.

Although papal prince and nepotist on a grand scale, he also was the first pope of the Counterreformation. Under him the church began to change course. For example, rather than packing the College of Cardinals with his own creatures, as some of his predecessors like Sixtus IV had done, Paul III on his own initiative and without outside pressure appointed to it a significant number of proponents of church reform, like Gasparo Contarini, Jacopo Sadoleto, Reginald Pole, Gianpietro Carafa, John Fisher, Marcello Cervini, Gregorio Cortese, Giovanni Morone, Tommaso Badia, and Federico Fregoso. In addition, several curialists among his cardinals, like Bartolomeo Guidiccioni or Girolamo Ghinucci, were in their way also open to reform, as was the Spanish cardinal Juan Alvarez de Toledo. Although these men formed no homogeneous group, they were a significant and vocal minority among the cardinals. It was due to the pope, and only to him, that the composition of the Sacred College was markedly altered at a time when that college still had an important role in governing the church.

Another indication of change in his pontificate was the crackdown on suspected heretics. Most famous is the case of Bernardino Ochino, renowned preacher and Capuchin general, who was summoned before the Roman inquisition. That Ochino fled to Geneva made his case particularly clamorous, but the matter was emblematic of the new wind blowing in Rome, where defense, not accommodation became important. Others, too, were suspected, summoned, or imprisoned. In Modena, for example, the whole so-called Academy, a group of intellectuals, came under suspicion of heterodoxy, and its members thoroughly frustrated Bishop Giovanni Morone, who tried to keep the inquisition out of the affair.[25] In Italy surveillance of what people believed began in earnest. Ironically, Morone himself was imprisoned on suspicion of heresy less than ten years after the death of Paul III.

On another front, Paul III's approval of the Jesuit order proved very important to the Counterreformation. When he gave the go-ahead to Ignatius Loyola in September, 1540, he had of course no way of knowing what a signal role this order would play in the history of the church. But in accepting and approving Ignatius' concept of an unusually structured community, Paul III showed himself open to innovative ideas despite his general reluctance to multiply religious orders. He supported the Jesuits, and his grandson, Cardinal Alessandro Farnese, became one of their great patrons.

The most important contribution of Pope Paul III to the history of Catholic reform is the meeting of the long-awaited general council. That its first session finally opened in Trent in December, 1545 was the result of papal initiative and diplomacy (responding, to be sure, to the demands of Emperor Charles V), rather than of a groundswell among the Catholic lay and clerical elite like that which preceded the calling of the Council of Constance, for example. The pope was a consummate politician, but even he did not manage to resolve the conflict between the emperor and the king of France, and had to postpone the council time and again. The enormously complex history of the Council of Trent has been given its modern shape by Hubert Jedin in a multi-volume work which is the point of departure for all further studies. From it emerges the conclusion that the pope himself did not have a comprehensive reform program to propose to the council. Because he primarily reacted to perceived dangers, his priorities were the condemnation of heresy and the formulation of rebuttals to Protestant attacks on Catholic beliefs, along with such traditional objectives as peace among Christian princes and a crusade against the Turks. The emperor, on the other hand, was mainly interested in swift and effective disciplinary reform which would answer German Protestant criticism of the church as institution. Other vocal groups in the Catholic church had their own agenda, from conservative prelates who wanted merely a strengthening of existing norms to men like Cardinals Morone or Contarini who hoped for a thorough and fair discussion of doctrinal issues. It is not surprising that the small number of council fathers who gathered in Trent, predominantly Italian, did not have an independent idea of how to proceed. Against this background their deliberations began.

The council met in three sessions, from 1545-47, 1551-52, and 1561-63. It is hardly possible to speak of "The Council of Trent" in a summary fashion, since the third session was quite different from the first two. The most important task of the initial sessions was to address the main issues raised by the Protestants. In that sense these two sessions, for all their achievements, still belong to the defensive and backward-looking phase of Catholic efforts at reform. With the exception of the decree on justification, completed in 1547, little of what they produced can be called new.

One important issue from the moment the council was called concerned its relation to the pope. Was it going to be subservient to him, or could it set its own agenda? Although no pope was present at any of the meetings of the council, the papal legates who presided over it acted as links between Rome and Trent. Cardinals Cervini, Pole, and Del Monte were appointed to the first session to establish procedures and guide deliberations. These functions were continued by their counterparts at later sessions. In that sense, Trent was a council in which the popes played a dominant role, in contrast to fifteenth-century councils like Constance or Basel, or even the Fifth Lateran.

The second problem for the participants was how to address the concerns of pope and emperor, and in which order to deal with questions of doctrine and discipline. The decision in January, 1546 was to deal with both simultaneously rather than to separate them. The character of the final decrees is comprehensible only if one keeps in mind that the council fathers did not compartmentalize matters of belief and practice, but tried to consider them together.

The most notable achievement of the council's first period was the decree on justification. A perfect example of a document produced by a committee, it is also a statement of the Catholic position in answer to what had become the key doctrine of the Protestant Reformation, justification by faith alone. In Italy, too, this doctrine appealed to members of all social groups from the aristocracy down to artisans, as the council fathers were aware. The final decree was meant to counteract Luther's teaching, especially his anthropology, and hinged on a conception of the human being which had its roots in Italian humanist thought. Men and women were not conceived of as without free will and utterly dependent on the grace of God, but as a creatures capable of cooperating with divine grace despite their flaws and sins. The often sharp debates show that there was no unanimity among the council fathers, and the final decree did not include the complex views of a number of important theologians like the Augustinian Girolamo Seripando or bishop Tommaso Sanfelice. Still, the groundwork for the construction of a Catholic orthodoxy expressed in a new key had been laid. This became obvious when the council tackled such basic matters as the nature of the sacraments or the more controversial issue of the obligation of bishops to reside in their dioceses. This groundwork remained in place even when discussions temporarily ground to a halt, and as the efforts of the first session at disciplinary reform remained ineffective.

Despite the transfer of the council to Bologna in 1547 for political reasons, and its suspension in 1549, the year of Pope Paul III's death, his successor Julius III revived it. As Cardinal Del Monte he had been papal legate when the council opened in 1545, and he called it back into session in Trent in 1551. This was the only time when a small number of German Protestants attended, but no meaningful dialogue between them and the Catholics took place. The separation of the two branches of Christianity was an accomplished fact by now. More critical for the council was its inability to get down to its proper business on account of political factors, above all the hostilities between the French king and the emperor. One of the results of their long-standing enmity was to drive a wedge between the German and French bishops, and to preclude the possibility of their cooperation. When the second session was suspended in March, 1552 because of renewed war in Germany, the achievements of the council remained fragmentary.

That the initiative of the popes was crucial to the very existence of the council and to its progress is beyond dispute. Paul III brought about its opening, and Julius III insisted that its decrees were not valid without papal approval. One can only speculate what form the relation of council and pope might have taken had Cardinal Pole been elected in 1549 in a conclave where he missed becoming pope by one vote, or had Pope Marcellus II, the former Cardinal Cervini, lived longer than three weeks after his election in 1555. Both men were experienced diplomats and known proponents of church reform. But it is an exaggeration to call Marcellus II "the first pope of the Catholic Reform"[26] on the strength of his declared decision to act in order to bring about reform. His pontificate was much too brief for any concrete action by which to judge it, and all that remains are inferences concerning his intentions.

The name of his successor Paul IV Carafa has long been associated with the "typical" aspects of the Counterreformation. If that term is taken to mean suspicion, repression, inquisition, index, and fanaticism, then the association is valid. But if one takes a broader, more historical and more current view of the Counterreformation, then Paul IV is neither an archetypal nor even an adequate representative of the counterreformation papacy. In fact, he still belongs to the backward-looking proponents of reform whose program was restoration rather than innovation. Profoundly conservative, Paul IV did not contribute any new elements to Catholic reform. He mistrusted the council, and did not even consider reconvening it. His great interest in the workings of the inquisition gave that office disproportionate prominence during his reign. The imprisonment of a man like Cardinal Morone on suspicion of heresy and the pope's mistrust of all Italian *spirituali*, living or dead, remains a sure indicator of his narrow intellectual focus. He thought that Protestantism could be stopped by severity, persecution, and execution. He authorized the *Index of Forbidden Books* of 1559 which was not only sweeping in its condemnations, but which even prohibited the reading of any vernacular bibles. This prohibition had particularly dire consequences in Italy, and affected biblical culture among the Catholic laity in general.

By the time he was elected pope, Paul IV was an intolerant and fanatical man who lacked creative impulse in dealing with the great religious crisis of his time. The most constructive action of his pontificate might have been the overdue reform of curial offices like the *dataria*, had the pope not been deflected by his nepotism which transcended all limits acceptable even to his age, and by his singularly ill-considered war against the Spanish king Philip II. The end of this scandalous war in 1557 not only exposed the military weakness of the papal state, but also showed the bankruptcy of the papacy of Paul IV as a supranational force for peace, concord and reformation in Catholic Europe. What his immediate predecessors had built, the Carafa pope destroyed. A massive popular riot in Rome upon the news of his death in August, 1559 was emblematic of the resentment and hatred his papacy had inspired. Change in the church for him was admissible only as part of a strategy of defense and survival for an institution threatened on all sides by disaffection and heresy. At the time of his death it was abundantly clear that a different tack was urgently needed should the church not founder and the papacy not lose any possibility of claiming religious and moral leadership.

3. A New Era: Tridentine Reformation

The American historian Eric Cochrane urged that the term "Tridentine Reformation" replace "Counterreformation" which, in his view, had acquired too many negative connotations, above all in Italian historiography. He argued that "Tridentine Reformation" was a neutral term which would do away with fruitless or anachronistic ideological debates and allow historians to look afresh at Italian and European Catholicism, as well as at the whole spectrum of connections between culture and religion in Catholic Europe of the later sixteenth century.[27] In what follows, the term "Tridentine Reformation" will be used but given a more restricted sense than Cochrane's, to designate reform in the Catholic church after the closing of the Council of Trent in 1563, as inspired by and resulting from the council. Despite disagreements among its participants and the unfinished business it left for later generations of churchmen, Trent was the great catalyst. It has been correctly remarked that Catholic reform after this council was not only *post hoc*, but precisely *propter hoc*.[28]

During the decades following the final session of the council, Catholic reform under papal leadership was very different both in substance and spirit from what it had been during the first part of the century. It was no longer primarily directed against doctrines of the Protestants or launched in response to their criticism of Catholic belief and practice. Rather, reform under papal leadership went beyond a "Counter" Reformation to positive and constructive efforts at building a more tightly organized, better instructed, and effectively controlled church than the old institution before 1563 had been. Most striking about the Tridentine Reformation is its forward-looking character. It focused on the future rather than the past of the church. To its proponents, innovation was not a threat but a necessity, even an opportunity. The whole psychology of reform gradually changed, and the mental horizon of its most important and imaginative advocates widened to include quite literally the whole world, with a vast increase of missionary activity. A massive Catholic offensive on many fronts, in Europe and overseas, was envisioned not only by dreamers or utopians, but at the papal court as well. This positive program distinguished the later sixteenth century most clearly from the period that preceded it.

At the same time, the persistence of old patterns makes it impossible to see the decades after 1563 as a clean break with the past. The church was still regarded as property by its higher officials, and ben-

efices were not abolished nor was traffic in them curtailed. European
rulers, especially the kings of France and Spain, exercised a great degree of control over the church in their respective states, had control
over the appointment of its personnel, and frequently proved unrecep-
tive to reform ideas championed by the papacy or highly contentious in
jurisdictional matters. Far from forming one united army in the service
of papal reform, religious orders squabbled with one another over
theological issues and interfered with the work of the secular clergy.
Abuses continued. But the spirit in Rome had changed; popes sent un-
mistakable signals that at the highest levels of the church, reform was
strongly, at critical times unequivocally, supported. Despite the extremely complicated politics of this period which continued to affect all
efforts at church reform and at times to determine their limits, a new
era had opened.

The series of Tridentine Reform popes began with Pius IV, elected in
1559. Although this papal diplomat and administrator had not been
among the proponents of reform, he decided to reconvoke the Council
of Trent when an all-French synod to deal with Calvinism threatened
to institute an era of national councils, something the pope wanted to
avoid at all costs. The Council of Trent reassembled in January, 1562
for its third and by far most important session. It is ironic that an initially lackluster pope became its champion, and that his nephew Carlo
Borromeo, who was made cardinal at twenty-one for the usual family
reasons, eventually turned into the great model of a reforming bishop
for the entire Catholic church.

The decrees of the last session, at which the council arrived after political maneuvering that boggles the mind even of specialist scholars,
were crucial for the history of Catholicism for the next three hundred
years. In contrast to the teaching of all Protestant churches, the council
affirmed the character of the mass as Christ's unbloody sacrifice, the
fruits of which can be applied to the living and the dead. Private
masses were allowed, and the cup reserved to priests alone. This and
other measures underscoring the difference between the clergy and the
laity dismissed the Protestant conception of the priesthood of all believers. An *Index of Forbidden Books*, drawn up by the council, reiterated that Catholics were not free to read books by heretics.

During this session the council also faced its gravest crisis when it
reached a stalemate over the issue of episcopal residence. Spanish,
French, and some Italian bishops wanted to define the obligation of
bishops to reside in their dioceses as a matter of divine law, meaning

that the pope had no power to grant dispensations in this area. Curial cardinals and their supporters insisted that the duty of residence was based on human, not divine law, and therefore under the jurisdiction of the pope. The issue turned into a power struggle between pope and bishops, and paralyzed the council. Only the skillful mediation and diplomacy of Cardinal Morone, whom Pius IV had fully exonerated and appointed legate, brought about a compromise. Episcopal residence was defined as a divine precept (thus the pope could dispense from it) rather than a divine law, but the extent of papal power was not spelled out so as to paper over the differences among the council fathers.

The best-known decrees of the third session concerning church reform dealt with specifics. The increasingly obvious necessity of systematically educating and forming the clergy resulted in the decree that every diocese had to have a seminary. The sacraments of holy orders and matrimony were affirmed, as were the reality of Purgatory, the usefulness to the faithful of invoking the saints, and the value of indulgences. What was probably the most important decree ordered regular visitations of each diocese by its bishop and annual synods on the diocesan level. The bishop was envisioned as the hinge of the entire enterprise of reform, and the transmitter of Tridentine norms to his flock, that is to the parish priests and through them to the people, as well as the executor of Tridentine legislation. He was to be a shepherd in a literal way, keeping an eye on and being responsible for all aspects of diocesan life. Diocese and parish, bishop and priest were indissolubly linked in the work of reform. Finally, by affirming all decrees of previous sessions, the council fathers gave conciliar legislation the semblance of greater unity than it in fact possessed.

The critical question concerned the mechanism of transmitting the decrees of the council to the whole Catholic church. Pope Pius IV made the decisive move by giving all the decrees his approbation, but forbidding their interpretation without papal approval. He created a commission of cardinals, the future Congregation on the Council, on which he conferred the sole authority to interpret the conciliar decrees. No bishop could independently establish their meaning. Furthermore, no bishop had access to the voluminous acts of the council, the publication of which was begun only in the later nineteenth century. In a very real sense, after 1563 the pope determined the meaning of Tridentine reform.

Opinions about the significance of the Council of Trent for the history of the Catholic church have been sharply divided. Already in the early seventeenth century the Venetian Servite friar Paolo Sarpi, the great critic of the council, accused it of radically deforming rather than reforming the Catholic church, and of instituting innovations which were contrary to the spirit and practice of the original Christian church. His Catholic opponents, beginning with the Jesuit Pallavicino, stressed the continuity of Trent with the history and tradition of the church, and interpreted the conciliar decrees as the culmination of the long history of Catholic reform. Catholic apologists, in fact, sought to turn the tables on critics of Trent by pointing to the Protestants as the real innovators who went far beyond the doctrines of primitive Christianity.

The assessment of the council's achievement by Hubert Jedin and his successors is much more helpful to the modern student than are the polemics of the past. Jedin pointed to the achievements of Trent without ignoring what was left unclear or undone. First, the council was responsible for formulating Catholic doctrine on many contested questions, like the nature of the sacraments, and for defining Catholic teaching much more sharply than it had been defined before. In effect, it established the lines of demarcation between Catholicism and Protestantism. Second, the council initiated and shaped what was to become Tridentine Reform, which removed the most obvious abuses and brought order to a church that was undergoing remarkable expansion through missionary activities in the non-European world. But many loose ends remained, foremost among them the failure to define the central matter of papal power and discuss Catholic ecclesiology. Reform of the curia was not even touched upon. The thorny issue of relations between church and state was ignored, as was the role of rulers in the process of Catholic reform. Ultimately the success of the council's work depended not so much on the existence of its decrees as on their implementation throughout the Catholic world.

The bishop who best exemplified how the decrees of Trent were to be implemented on the diocesan level was Carlo Borromeo, archbishop of Milan from 1565 to 1584. When the layers of hagiography are removed from his conventional image, we find a man of great personal faith and sanctity, to be sure, but also an imaginative administrator of a new type, and above all a shepherd of his flock.[29] This more complex historical image has emerged clearly in recent studies.[30] Borromeo put into practice Tridentine norms; he tirelessly undertook visitations of his diocese, called and presided over diocesan synods, legislated for his church, and turned his attention to details of administration. The *Acta*

Ecclesiae Mediolanensis, documenting his activities, were published in 1582, and became the prime example and model of how a reforming bishop went about his mission of christianizing his flock. His pastoral role as bishop came to overshadow his position as cardinal, something which was not lost on the Roman curia and the successors of Pius IV. Borromeo's independent mind involved him in conflicts with the Spanish authorities in Milan. His personal asceticism was judged excessive even by some of his reform-minded fellow bishops like Gabriele Paleotti of Bologna or Domenico Bollani of Brescia. Nevertheless, his impact on the Catholic church was great precisely because of his vital fusion of pastoral, administrative, and personal activities.

It is not sufficient, of course, to look only at one bishop, even as important a figure as Borromeo, in order to examine the application of the decrees of Trent. In numerous recent studies historians have turned their attention to what happened as individual bishops applied decrees to their dioceses, and have demonstrated that many local variants existed, determined to a large extent by political factors. On the national level, too, there were great differences in the reception of the conciliar decrees. In France, for example, where the wars between Catholics and Huguenots began during the council's final session, the decrees were not published at all, and therefore had no legal standing. Despite continued efforts by papal nuncios, the French king never made the decisions of Trent the law for the church in his realm. Instead, individual bishops applied the decrees in their dioceses as they saw fit. In Spain the decrees were published with the approval of Philip II (although he had some reservations). No single generalization can cover the situation in the Catholic lands of the Holy Roman Empire. Each of the many German Catholic states has its own history of Tridentine Reform, and of accepting the council's decrees, ignoring them, or temporizing. Ironically, the most fervent champions of Tridentine Reform were not the German prince-bishops, but secular rulers like the dukes of Bavaria and Austrian Habsburgs like Ferdinand II.

In the end, the most important question was what attitude the popes would adopt. Pius IV (1559-65) and even more explicitly, his three successors Pius V (1566-72), Gregory XIII (1572-85), and Sixtus V (1585-90) proved to be decisive supporters of Tridentine Reform. During their pontificates the work of the Council of Trent was elaborated and reform was given shape. That process began with the establishment of congregations or standing committees of cardinals, each responsible for a particular aspect of church government and the work of reform. The first was the Congregation of the Inquisition, established, as we have seen, in 1542, with competence in questions concerning doctrine. It was followed, as we have also seen, by the Congregation of the Council with exclusive authority to interpret conciliar decrees (1564), and the Congregation of the Index, charged with oversight of printed works, especially those dealing with theology (1571).

Finally, Pope Sixtus V on 22 January 1588 undertook the long over-due task of reforming the Roman curia. He created fifteen congrega-tions which together formed the system of government for the papal state and the church as a whole. Before this, permanent nunciatures had been established in addition to those that already existed at the courts of the various European rules. The new ones became instru-ments of Tridentine Reform in especially critical areas like northwest Germany, Poland, and Austria. Resident papal nuncios fostered re-form and transmitted directives from Rome to local churches and rul-ers.

This whole administrative streamlining of the Catholic church has been interpreted in recent scholarship as analogous to the process of state-building by European absolute rulers. Congregations functioned like ministries, receiving power by delegation from the absolute papal monarch, and responsible to him alone. The rationalization of papal government has been seen as chronologically antecedent to the efforts at centralization of secular rulers, and even as their model.[31] Disagree-ment about this thesis has stimulated fruitful further work on the ad-ministrative history of papal government. One of its results has been a better understanding of how the College of Cardinals lost most of its traditional governing function,[32] to be replaced by the Congregations.

The restructuring of the church's administration was only one achievement of the later sixteenth-century popes. More significant for the church on the local level was a series of catechetical, liturgical, and disciplinary innovations, all emanating from Rome, which would de-termine the character of Catholic culture for centuries to come. A statement of basic Catholic beliefs, the *Professio fidei tridentina*, was completed in 1564. In 1566 the *Roman Catechism* was issued, which became the principal tool of Christian instruction for pastors and teachers of religion. Two years later the revised *Roman Breviary* ap-peared, with mandatory daily readings for the clergy. In 1570 the *Missale Romanum* codified a uniform liturgy of the mass for the entire liturgical year, for use by every church throughout the Catholic world, and in 1593 the revised Bible (the so-called *Vulgata Clementina*) was completed. That almost all these works contained the word "Roman" in their titles underlined that Rome was the nerve center of the Catholic church. From Rome the norms for the local clergy emanated, and there, too, many members of the new clerical elite were formed in institutions for the education of the clergy which were founded or strengthened, like the national colleges or the *Collegium Romanum*, the later Gregorian University. The entire elaborate structure of ecclesiastical organization culminated in the papacy not only in theory, but now also in fact. In a much stronger sense than before the Reformation, the Catholic church became Roman Catholic, which until very recently remained its apt designation.

Leading students of the Council of Trent have repeatedly called the attention of historians not only to the progress of Tridentine Reform, but also to the obstacles in its way, and cautioned against too favorable an assessment of its success. Special interest groups as well as individuals in state and church opposed reform, and overt or passive resistance to it must be built into any historical picture of post-Tridentine Catholicism.[33] Only with such a caveat in mind can one arrive at a balanced conclusion about the council's effects. Despite the many problems in its application, the letter and pervasive spirit of conciliar decrees were crucial in shaping early modern Catholicism at all levels, from academic theology to popular devotions, and in a wide range of areas from artistic decoration of churches to music. Most importantly, Tridentine Reform entailed a new kind of discipline for Catholics.

4. DIRECTIONS FOR RESEARCH

Especially important to future research will be to analyze the nature and effects of this new discipline, and establish to what extent the Council of Trent helped create a new Catholic culture in the early modern world. These broad issues are at the interface of political, social, and religious history, and offer promising topics to scholars. A number of studies already have as their focus the problem of post-Tridentine social discipline and its relation to the shape of modern Catholicism. For example, the aim to turn "collective Christians into individual ones" has been attributed to Trent.[34] An important argument has been made for the Counterreformation as a key factor in the process of modernization, itself a central feature of early modern European history.[35] The extent of papal initiative in this process should be further explored, as should the relations of later sixteenth-century popes and the theologians who emphasized the non-elitist and all-embracing nature of post-Tridentine Catholic doctrine.

What is still needed before the role of the Counterreformation papacy in shaping reform can be understood more fully are modern studies of the administrative and fiscal history of papal government, papal diplomacy, and papal relations with the episcopate. Papal pronouncements and decisions which influenced one-half of all the Catholics, namely women, need to be examined carefully, as do attitudes by popes and curial officials toward lay women and nuns.[36] Above all, new and methodologically sophisticated biographies of sixteenth-century popes are needed, especially of key figures like Paul III. The still standard *History of the Popes* by Ludwig von Pastor, immensely useful though it remains, shows signs of its age in its value judgments and apologetic approach, and clearly belongs to another era. It is doubtful, however, that crucial pontificates like that of Paul III can any longer be treated in detail by individual scholars, given the mass of available primary and secondary material. More likely, *travaux d'équipe* will eventually deal with the history of sixteenth-century popes and their pontificates.

Beyond that lie topics like the role of the papacy in the expansion of missionary activity to the non-European world and its theoretical bases, or the parameters within which the Roman curia understood and interpreted the many forms of contacts between European missionaries and other cultures in the sixteenth and seventeenth centuries. Papal pronouncements concerning non-European peoples have recently begun to be collected.[37] There is much room for historical studies which would integrate insights of modern psychology or anthropology with the vast topic of Tridentine and papal reform as Italian, European, and extra-European historical phenomena.

NOTES

1. For example, Gottfried Maron, "Das Schicksal der katholischen Reform im 16. Jahrhundert," *ZKiG* 88 (1977): 218-29; Paolo Simoncelli, "Inquisizione romana e riforma in Italia," *RSI* 100 (1988): 5-125, esp. 92-106; Firpo (1992), passim, but especially "Introduzione," 7-28.
2. Maron, "Schicksal," 209-10.
3. Evennett (1968).
4. See the survey by Daniela Solfaroli Camillocci, "Le confraternite del Divino Amore. Interpretazioni storiografiche e proposte attuali di ricerca," *Rivista di Storia e Letteratura Religiosa* 27 (1991): 315-32.
5. Giuseppe Alberigo, "Contributo alla storia dei Disciplinati e della spiritualità laicale nei secc. XV e XVI," in *Il movimento dei disciplinati nel settimo centenario del suo inizio* (Perugia, 1962), 156-252.
6. Roberto Rusconi, "Confraternite, compagnie, devozioni," in *SIA* 9 (Turin, 1986), 459-506; Christopher F. Black, *Italian Confaternities in the Sixteenth Century* (Cambridge, 1989).
7. See John Patrick Donnelly, "Catholic Reformation: the New Orders," in this *Handbook*, vol. 2: 283-315.
8. On individual orders, see *Religious Orders of the Catholic Reformation: Essays in Honor of John C. Olin on his Seventy-fifth Birthday*, ed. Richard L. DeMolen (Bronx, N.Y., 1994).
9. The recently completed collection of documents from the first century of the Capuchin order is a major source for sixteenth-century religious history: *I frati cappuccini. Documenti e testimonianze del primo secolo*, ed. Costanzo Cargnoni, 5 volumes in 6 (Rome, 1988-93).
10. See essays I-IV in Nelson H. Minnich, *The Catholic Reformation: Council, Churchmen, Controversies* (Aldershot, Hampshire, and Brookfield, Vt., 1993).
11. *Anticlericalism in Late Medieval and Early Modern Europe*, ed. Peter A. Dykema and Heiko A. Oberman, SMRT, vol. 51 (Leiden, 1993).
12. There is no modern edition of this text, printed in *Annales Camaldulenses Ordinis Sancti Benedicti*, ed. Johannes Benedictus Mittarelli and Anselmus Costadoni, vol.9 (Venice, 1773): 612-719.
13. Eugenio Massa, "Gasparo Contarini e gli amici fra Venezia e Camaldoli," in *Atti Convegno di Studio Gaspare Contarini e il suo tempo* (Venice, 1988), 39-91, and his wide-ranging *L'eremo, la Bibbia e il Medioevo in Umanisti veneti del primo Cinquecento* (Naples, 1992).
14. *Regesten und Briefe des Cardinals Gasparo Contarini*, ed. Franz Dittrich (Braunsberg, 1881), 41-46 (no.126).
15. "Consilium delectorum cardinalium et aliorum praelatorum de emendanda ecclesia S.D.N. Paulo III iubente conscriptum et exhibitum," in *Concilium Tridentinum*. (1901-), vol. 12:131-45. English translation

in *Reform Thought in Sixteenth-Century Italy*, ed. and trans. Elisabeth G. Gleason (Chico, Cal., 1981), 81-100.

16. "De Lutheranorum haeresi reprimenda et ecclesia reformanda ad Clementem VII [4. octobris 1532]," in *Concilium Tridentinum* (1901-), vol. 12:67-77.

17. *Handbuch der Kirchengeschichte*, ed. Erwin Iserloh, Josef Glazik, and Hubert Jedin, vol. 4 (Freiburg, Basel and Vienna, 1967): 477.

18. Gleason (1993), 157-76.

19. Hallman (1985).

20. Reinhard (1975).

21. Reinhard (1972).

22. Simoncelli (1988), esp. 65-66.

23. Agostino Borromeo, "The Inquisition and Inquisitorial Censorship," in O'Malley (1988), 253-72.

24. Fragnito (1988), essays 1-3.

25. Massimo Firpo, "Gli 'spirituali,' l'Accademia di Modena, e il Formulario di Fede del 1542: Controllo del dissenso religioso e nicodemismo," *Rivista di Storia e Letteratura Religiosa* 30 (1984), 40-111. Also in Firpo (1992), 29-118.

26. As Jedin does in *Handbuch der Kirchengeschichte*, vol. 4:505 (see above note 17).

27. "Counter-Reformation or Tridentine Reformation? Italy in the Age of Carlo Borromeo," in Headley and Tomaro (1988), 31-46.

28. Willaert (1960), 24.

29. Giuseppe Alberigo, "Carlo Borromeo come modello di vescovo nella chiesa post-tridentina," *RSI* 79 (1967): 1031-52.

30. Especially useful is Headley and Tomaro (1988).

31. Prodi (1987).

32. Klaus Ganzer, "Der ekklesiologische Standort des Kardinalskollegiums in seinem Wandel — Aufstieg und Niedergang einer kirchlichen Institution," *Römische Quartalschrift für christliche Altertumskunde und Kirchengeschichte* 88 (1993): 114-33.

33. Alberigo (1985a).

34. Bossy (1970), 62.

35. Especially useful are Wolfgang Reinhard, "Reformation, Counter-Reformation and the Early Modern State: a Reassessment," *CHR* 75 (1989): 383-404, and Reinhard (1977), with extensive bibliography.

36. The emblematic example of the suspicion which Mary Ward met at the highest levels of the church bears pondering, as do the reasons for the pope's rejection of her plan for a female order devoted to education of girls and modelled on the Jesuits. See Josef Grisar, "Jesuitinnen. Ein Beitrag zur Geschichte des weiblichen Ordenswesens von 1550 bis 1650," in *Reformata Reformanda. Festschrift für Hubert Jedin*, vol. 2 (Münster, 1965), 70-113, and Henriette Peters, *Mary Ward. Ihre Persönlichkeit und ihr Institut* (Innsbruck and Vienna, 1991).

37. *America pontificia primi saeculi evangelisationis (1493-1592). Documenta pontificia ex registris et minutis praesertim in Archivio Secreto Vaticano existentibus*, ed. Josef Metzler, 2 vols. (Vatican City, 1991).

BIBLIOGRAPHY

General Works

Bossy, John. *Christianity and the West, 1400-1700.* Oxford, 1985.
Camaiani, Pier Giorgio. "Interpretazioni della Riforma cattolica e della Controriforma." In *Grande Antologia Filosofica*, vol. 4:329-490. Milan, 1964.
Châtellier, Louis. *The Europe of the Devout: the Catholic Reformation and the Formation of a New Society.* Cambridge, 1989.
Delumeau, Jean. *Catholicism Between Luther and Voltaire: a New View of the Counter-Reformation.* London, 1977 [1971].
Evennett, H. Outram. *The Spirit of the Counter-Reformation.* Cambridge, 1968.
Jedin, Hubert. *Katholische Reformation oder Gegenreformation? Ein Versuch zur Klärung der Begriffe.* Lucerne, 1946.
Jedin, Hubert, and John Dolan, eds. *History of the Church.* Vol. 5, *Reformation and Counter Reformation.* New York, 1980.
O'Malley, John W., S.J. *Catholicism in Early Modern History: a Guide to Research.* St. Louis, 1988.
Prodi, Paolo. "Il binomio jediniano riforma cattolica e controriforma e la storiografia italiana." *Annali dell'Istituto storica italo germanico in Trento* 6 (1980): 85-98.
Prodi, Paolo. "Riforma cattolica e Controriforma." In *Nuove questioni di storia moderna*, 357-418. Milan, 1968.

Surveys of the Counterreformation

Alberigo, Giuseppe, and Pier Giorgio Camaiani. "Riforma Cattolica e Controriforma." *Sacramentum mundi* 7 (1977): 38-69.
Cochrane, Eric. "New Light on Post-Tridentine Italy: a Note on Recent Counter-Reformation Scholarship." *CHR* 56 (1970-71): 291-319.
Davidson, N. S. *The Counter-Reformation.* Oxford, 1987.
Dickens, A. G. *The Counter-Reformation.* London, 1968.
Lutz, Heinrich. *Reformation und Gegenreformation.* Munich and Vienna, 1982.
Mullett, Michael A. *The Counter-Reformation and the Catholic Reformation in Early Modern Europe.* London and New York, 1984.
O'Connell, Marvin. *The Counter Reformation, 1560-1610.* New York, 1974.
Schmidt, Kurt Dietrich. *Die katholische Reform und die Gegenreformation.* Göttingen, 1975.
Searle, G. W. *The Counter Reformation.* Totowa, N.J., 1974.
Willaert, Leopold, S.J. *Après le concile de Trente. La restauration catholique, 1563-1648.* Paris, 1960.
Zeeden, Ernst Walter, ed. *Gegenreformation.* Darmstadt, 1973.
Zoli, Sergio. *La Controriforma.* Florence, 1979.

The Papacy

Archivum Historiae Pontificiae. Rome, 1963- .

Aubert, Alberto. *Paolo IV Carafa nel giudizio della età della Controriforma*. Città di Castello, 1990.

Cantimori, Delio. "Italy and the Papacy." In *The New Cambridge Modern History*, vol. 2: *The Reformation, 1520-1559*: 288-312. Cambridge, 1990.

Capasso, Carlo. *Paolo III*. 2 vols. Messina, 1923-24.

Caravale, Mario, and Alberto Caracciolo. *Lo Stato pontificio da Martino V a Pio IX*. Turin, 1991 [1978].

Gleason, Elisabeth G. *Gasparo Contarini: Venice, Rome and Reform*. Berkeley and Los Angeles, 1993.

Lutz, Heinrich. "Leopold von Ranke e il papato." *RSCI* 16 (1962): 439-50.

Pastor, Ludwig von. *History of the Popes*. 40 vols. St. Louis, 1902-53.

Prodi, Paolo. *The Papal Prince. One Body and Two Souls: The Papal Monarchy in Early Modern Europe*. Trans. Susan Haskins. Cambridge, 1987.

Ranke, Leopold von. *History of the Popes*. 3 vols. New York, 1966 [1901].

Reinhard, Wolfgang. "Herkunft und Karriere der Päpste 1417-1963. Beiträge zu einer historischen Soziologie der römischen Kurie." *Mededelingen van het Nederlands Instituut te Rome* 38 (1976): 87-108.

Reinhard, Wolfgang. "Nepotismus. Der Funktionswandel einer papstgeschichtlichen Konstanten." *ZKiG* 86 (1975): 145-85.

Reinhard, Wolfgang. "Papa Pius. Prolegomena zu einer Sozialgeschichte des Papsttums." In *Von Konstanz nach Trient. Beiträge zur Geschichte der Kirche von den Reformkonzilien bis zum Tridentinum. Festgabe für August Franzen*, ed. Remigius Bäumer, 261-99. Paderborn, 1972.

Reinhard, Wolfgang. "Reformpapsttum zwischen Renaissance und Barock." In *Reformatio Ecclesiae. Beiträge zu kirchlichen Reformbemühungen von der Alten Kirche bis zur Neuzeit. Festgabe für Erwin Iserloh*, ed. Remigius Bäumer, 779-96. Paderborn, 1980.

Sparacio, Domenico. *Papa Sisto V. Profilo storico*. Perugia, 1923.

The Council of Trent and Reform (only the most important works are listed)

Alberigo, Giuseppe, et al., eds. *Conciliorum oecumenicorum decreta*. 3d ed. Bologna, 1973.

Alberigo, Giuseppe. "Du Concile de Trente au tridentinisme." *Irénikon* 54 (1981): 192-210.

Alberigo, Giuseppe. "Dinamiche religiose del Cinquecento italiano tra Riforma, Riforma cattolica, Controriforma." In *Cristianesimo nella storia* 6 (1985b): 543-60.

Alberigo, Giuseppe. "L'ecclesiologia del Concilio di Trento." *RSCI* 18 (1964): 227-42.

Alberigo, Giuseppe. "La reception du Concile de Trente par l'Eglise catholique romaine." *Irénikon* 58 (1985a): 300-20.

Alberigo, Giuseppe. "Studi e problemi relativi all'applicazione del Concilio di Trento in Italia, 1945-1958." *RSI* 70 (1958): 239-98.

Bäumer, Remigius, ed. *Concilium Tridentinum*. Darmstadt, 1979.

Il Concilio di Trento e la riforma tridentina. Atti del convegno storico internazionale, Trento 1963. 2 vols. Rome and Freiburg im Breisgau, 1965.

Concilium Tridentinum. Diariorum, Actorum, Epistolarum, Tractatuum nova collectio. Edited by the Görres-Gesellschaft. Freiburg im Breisgau, 1901- .

Jedin, Hubert. *La figura ideale del vescovo secondo la Riforma cattolica*. 2d ed. Brescia, 1985.

Jedin, Hubert. *Geschichte des Konzils von Trient*. 4 vols. in 5. Freiburg im Breisgau, 1949-75. Vols. 1-2 are in English: *A History of the Council of Trent*, trans. by Ernest Graf (London, 1957-61).

Jedin, Hubert. *Kirche des Glaubens, Kirche der Geschichte. Ausgewählte Aufsätze und Vorträge.* 2 vols. Freiburg im Breisgau, 1966.
Jedin, Hubert. *Das Konzil von Trient. Ein Überblick über die Erforschung seiner Geschichte.* Rome, 1948.
O'Donohue, J. A. *Tridentine Seminary Legislation: Its Sources and Its Formation.* Louvain, 1957.
Rückert, Hanns. *Die Rechtfertigungslehre auf dem Tridentinischen Konzil.* Bonn, 1925.
Schreiber, Georg, ed. *Das Weltkonzil von Trient.* 2 vols. Freiburg im Breisgau, 1951.
Zeeden, Ernst Walter, and Hansgeorg Molitor, eds. *Die Visitation im Dienste der kirchlichen Reformation.* Münster, 1967.

The Counterreformation and post-Tridentine European Culture

Biondi, Albano. "Aspetti della cultura cattolica post-tridentina. Religione e controllo sociale." In *SIA* 4 (Turin, 1981): 253-302.
Bossy, John, "The Counter-Reformation and the People of Catholic Europe." *PaP*, no. 47 (1970): 51-70.
Burke, Peter. "How to become a Counter-Reformation Saint." In Peter Burke, *The Historical Anthropology of Early Modern Italy: Essays on Perception and Communication.* Cambridge, 1987.
De Maio, Romeo. *Michelangelo e la Controriforma.* Rome and Bari, 1978.
De Maio, Romeo. *Riforme e miti nella Chiesa del Cinquecento.* Naples, 1973.
Firpo, Massimo. *Inquisizione romana e Controriforma. Studi sul Cardinal Giovanni Morone e il suo processo d'eresia.* Bologna, 1992.
Firpo, Massimo, and Dario Marcatto, eds. *Il processo inquisitoriale del Cardinal Giovanni Morone.* 5 vols. in 6. Rome, 1981-89.
Fragnito, Gigliola. *In museo e in villa. Saggi sul Rinascimento perduto.* Venice, 1988.
Fragnito, Gigliola. "L'edizione parigina delle opere: una impresa al servizio della Controriforma." In *Gasparo Contarini: un magistrato veneziano al servizio della cristianità,* 307-68. Florence, 1988.
Fragnito, Gigliola. *Memoria individuale e costruzione biografica.* Urbino, 1978.
Grendler, Paul. *The Roman Inquisition and the Venetian Press 1540-1605.* Princeton, 1977.
Hallman, Barbara McClung. *Italian Cardinals, Reform, and the Church as Property.* Berkeley and Los Angeles, 1985.
Headley, John M., and John B. Tomaro, eds. *San Carlo Borromeo: Catholic Reform and Ecclesiastical Politics in the Second Half of the Sixteenth Century.* Washington, D.C., 1988.
O'Malley, John W., S.J. *The First Jesuits.* Cambridge, Mass., 1993.
Prodi, Paolo. *Ricerche sulla teorica delle arti figurative nella Riforma cattolica.* Rome, 1962.
Reinhard, Wolfgang, " Gegenreformation als Modernisierung? Prolegomena zu einer Theorie des konfessionellen Zeitalters." *ARG* 68 (1977): 226-52.
Rotondò, Antonio. "La censura ecclesiastica e la cultura." In *Storia d'Italia,* vol. 5:1397-1492. Turin, 1973.
Seidel Menchi, Silvana. "Inquisizione come repressione o inquisizione come mediazione? Una proposta di periodizzazione." *Annuario dell'Istituto Storico Italiano per l'età Moderna e Contemporanea* 35-36 (1983-84): 51-77.
Simoncelli, Paolo. "Documenti interni alla Congregazione dell'Indice 1571-1590: logica e ideologia dell'intervento censorio." *Annuario dell'Istituto Storico Italiano per l'età Moderna e Contemporanea* 35-36 (1983-84): 187-215.
Simoncelli, Paolo. "Inquisizione romana e Riforma in Italia." *RSI* 100 (1988): 5-125.
Tedeschi, John A. *The Prosecution of Heresy. Collected Studies on the Inquisition in Early Modern Italy.* Binghamton, N.Y., 1991.
Witek, John W., S.J. "From India to Japan. European Missionary Expansion, 1500-1650." In O'Malley (1988), 193-210.

Part 3.
Outcomes

SETTLEMENTS: THE HOLY ROMAN EMPIRE

Thomas A. Brady, Jr.
(University of California, Berkeley)

Begun in strife, concluded in slaughter—such was for long the image of German history between the Religious Peace of Augsburg in 1555 and the Peace of Westphalia in 1648. For Leopold von Ranke and his disciples, who framed it, the era's great mystery was that the awakening between 1495 and 1520 should have yielded not a national state and a national church but 300 years of religious divisions and political weakness.[1] Nowadays, when Rankean presuppositions have sloughed away, a very different picture has emerged of the Reformation's settlements in the Holy Roman Empire.

1. Preliminary Settlements

Some settlements fell in the reformation movement's first two decades. The Peasants' War, which engulfed the southern and central sectors in 1524-26, was settled by the princes, and with it the possibility of a general reformation from below.[2] Its Anabaptist successor movement was settled when the city of Münster fell to Imperial troops in 1535.[3] The Swiss reformation's settlement came in 1531 with Zurich's defeat and Zwingli's death at Kappel.[4] These settlements left Lutheranism after the mid-1530s as the Empire's sole form of Protestant reformation.

The Lutheran reformation's survival depended on an adequate political representation of its interests at the Imperial level. At the end of the 1520s, its leaders gathered behind the Elector of Saxony, ably seconded by Landgrave Philip of Hesse (1504-64). They gained a collective voice through their protest (whence "Protestants") against the Imperial Diet of Speyer in 1529, their statement of faith (Confession of Augsburg) submitted at Augsburg in 1530, and through the military alliance, called the "Smalkaldic League," which they founded in 1531. Between then and the Smalkaldic War of 1546-47, Lutheran reformations gained time and space to spread, to grow strong, and to assume their characteristic geographical contours and institutional shapes, though not yet their doctrinal consolidation.[5]

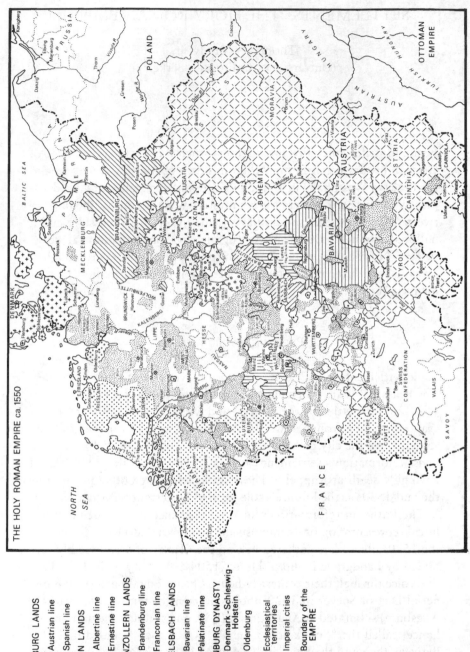

THE HOLY ROMAN EMPIRE ca. 1550

HABSBURG LANDS
Austrian line
Spanish line
WETTIN LANDS
Albertine line
Ernestine line
HOHENZOLLERN LANDS
Brandenburg line
Franconian line
WITTELSBACH LANDS
Bavarian line
Palatinate line
OLDENBURG DYNASTY
Denmark-Schleswig-
Holstein
Oldenburg
Ecclesiastical
territories
Imperial cities
Boundary of the
EMPIRE

Geographically, Lutheran gains were remarkable: three of the four lay electorates; all of the lay principalities in the northern Empire except for Cleves-Jülich; most of the lay principalities in the southern parts of the Empire, except Bavaria, Austria, and part of Baden; and all but a handful of the 65 or so free cities, though many retained important Catholic minorities. By mid-century, all of these territories and cities were "Protestant" in the sense that their rulers, princes or magistrates, professed to be "Evangelical" and not "papist." In addition, nearly a dozen bishoprics, concentrated in the Empire's northeastern quadrant, were taken or threatened, along with countless monasteries and innumerable other church properties.[6] By the 1550s the Lutheran reformation had assumed most of the geographical configuration it would maintain into the modern era.[7]

Institutionally, the Lutheran advance was equally impressive. Rulers, magistrates, and clergy had acted with impressive speed to adopt and adapt Luther's dualistic ideal—the ruler to keep law and order, the clergy to proclaim God's Word and administer the sacraments.[8] In theory, the clergy's authority was grounded in the Word alone; in practice, the Lutheran ministers could not—and many would not, or not until too late—guard religious life from intervention at will by princes and magistrates. Consequently, in the Empire with few exceptions the Protestant reconstruction of church life was undertaken by clergymen under the authority, with the permission, and as employees of princes and magistrates. It was against this type of fusion of church and state that John Calvin struggled at Geneva with some success and with important consequences for the history of Calvinism.

The fusion was hardly without precedent. Since the fifteenth century the obligation to care for the churches and monasteries had come to be regarded as a normal part of princes' and magistrates' duties.[9] In 1526 a formal magisterial right to reform (*ius reformandi*) was enshrined in Imperial law by the Imperial Diet, which declared that until a general council overcame the schism, each ruler and urban regime would act "in such a way as he will be responsible for to God and the emperor."[10] This act conferred formal religious legitimacy on the Empire's late medieval structure of dispersed governance. It also scuttled forever the fifteenth-century program of a comprehensive reform of Empire and church.

It is difficult, because of the strife and stalemate that soon followed, to recapture the ebullient mood of those halcyon days of the German Reformation, when many Protestants believed they might live to see true religion capture the entire Empire. Their hearts stirred in the early 1540s at the declaration by Elector Herman of Cologne that he would convert to the new faith if he could retain his prince-archbishopric. "In time," exulted Chancellor Gregor Brück (1482-1557) of Saxony, "our party could set up its own King of the Romans, to whom the whole Empire could be made subject and obedient, . . . and there should be no more priests."[11] It was not to be. The Cologne project faltered. Aided by Duke Moritz of Saxony—the "Judas of Meissen," his fellow Protestants named him—in 1546-47 the Emperor Charles V crushed the Smalkaldic League, and in the following year he compelled the Protestants to accept a provisional religious settlement, called the "Interim".[12] At this point, when the schism seemed almost ended, Moritz of Saxony undertook a remarkable reversal of fortunes. Backed by the French king, he rose in revolt, drove the emperor from the German lands, and signed with King Ferdinand, Charles' brother, the Treaty of Passau. This document contained the substance of the Religious Peace of Augsburg of 1555: each of the emperor's immediate subjects, the "Imperial estates," would have the right to decide which religion his subjects would practice.[13]

2. The Religious Peace of Augsburg (1555) and Its Legacy

At the Diet of Augsburg in 1555, Ferdinand I (r. 1556-62) made good on his promise to sponsor a purely political—though provisional—settlement to the Empire's religious schism.[14] The Religious Peace incorporated the religious status quo (as of 1552) into the Empire's public peace (*Landfriede*): "In order to prevent the permanent division and the ruin of the German nation, our beloved fatherland, we have agreed... [that] His Imperial Majesty and we, the Imperial estates, . . . shall maintain the following religious peace [*Religionsfriede*), together with all provisions of the . . . the established public peace."[15] The Peace guaranteed that princes, prelates, and magistrates of the Catholic faith should peacefully co-exist with those of the Confession of Augsburg, and the parties would treat "the disputed religion in no other way than by Christian, friendly, peaceful means and paths to a unanimous, Christian understanding and conciliation."[16]

The Religious Peace made rulers responsible for the religious welfare, and ultimately the consciences, of their subjects. Some years later, a Greifswald law professor, Joachim Stephan, coined for this rule the historic tag: "whose the rule, his the religion [*cuius regio, eius religio*]."[17] The Peace made two exceptions to this rule. First, in free cities where both religions were practiced, they would share the magistracies and the churches. Second and far more important, a codicil called the "Ecclesiastical Reservation," which Ferdinand promulgated without Protestant consent, protected the ecclesiastical states by forbidding secularization if a prince-bishop should turn Protestant. In return, though secretly, Ferdinand guaranteed limited religious toleration to Lutheran subjects of Catholic prince-prelates (*Declaratio Ferdinandei*).

This settlement froze the Empire's late medieval constitution as an aristocratic association and blocked the Empire's way toward centralized rule in a western European sense. The Peace also contained several inherent flaws. One was the possible unenforceability of the Ecclesiastical Reservation. Another was the Diet's lack of a way to suspend, in matters touching religion, the principle of majority rule it had adopted in 1512. A hundred years and a long war later, these problems, too, were settled in 1648.[18]

The Decades of Coexistence, 1555-1585

The skilled pragmatism of Emperor Ferdinand I, Emperor Maximilian II (r. 1564-76), and Elector August I of Saxony guarded the Empire's peace for nearly a generation. In South Germany's bi-confessional free cities, Lutherans and Catholics enjoyed the same religious and political rights, shared the magistracies and use of the churches, schools, and welfare institutions, and with some frequency married across religious boundaries. Similar conditions obtained in a few territorial states, notably in the prince-bishopric of Münster in Westphalia, where the official liturgy was a Mass with German hymns and the communion in both kinds.[19] Religious co-existence was long the norm in the Lower Rhenish duchies of Cleves-Jülich, where for years Duke William V (r. 1539-92) looked the other way while Calvinist and Lutheran congregations formed within his lands alongside Catholic parishes in which communion was received in both kinds.

It is nevertheless easy to exaggerate the Empire's possibilities for religious, as distinct from political, coexistence, for the schism had already cut deeply into everyday life. In 1549, for example, young Duke Erich II (1528-84) of Brunswick-Calenberg had written that unless his wife, Duchess Sidonia (1518-75) of Saxony, returned to "the old, true Christian faith" and abandoned her Lutheran heresy, he could not con-

tinue to live with her as man with wife.[20] It was a time drawing
boundaries, for which purpose lay to hand a rich vocabulary of division, created by the pamphlet wars of the 1520s and 1540s, which portrayed the world as a battleground between the servants of Christ and
those of Antichrist.[21] A Lutheran "Song for Children to Sing," published in 1569, begged:

> Lord, preserve us in Your Word
> And send death to Pope and Turk,
> Who hate Jesus Christ, Your only Son,
> And aim to throw Him off His throne.[22]

Meanwhile, events abroad were also working against the Empire's
peace. After the Peace of Cateau-Cambrésis (3 April 1559) proclaimed
an end to sixty-five years of Habsburg-Valois wars, during the following decade lengthy civil wars, fortified by religious conflict, erupted in
the kingdom of France and in the Habsburg Netherlands.[23] In these
lands Calvinism, a younger, more aggressive, and more internationally
minded faith than German Lutheranism, squared off to fight a reviving
Catholic Church.[24] Because of the international character of the confessions, every escalation of confessionalization consolidation and religious strife abroad tended to narrow the political space for the spirit of
accommodation on which the Religious Peace depended.

Confessional Strife Escalates

A new, harder, and more aggressive tone took definite shape during the
1580s. Confessional strife erupted over the Pope Gregory XI's new
calendar (24 February 1582), according to which the day after 4 October would be the 15th. Its adoption by Emperor Rudolph II without
consultation touched off a new pamphlet war.[25] Unlike the 1520s,
however, when Luther and his supporters had out-produced, out-writ-
ten, and out-argued their disunited Catholic opponents, by the 1580s
the Catholics were able to give as good as they got, using the printing
press both to attack the Protestants and to defend their own devotions,
both old and new.[26] In some places, notably at Augsburg, the calendar
dispute sparked disturbances of a kind unknown since the days of the
Peasants' War, as Protestants fought against being yoked by the new
papal calendar:

> The pope is brother to the Turk;
> May Jesus Christ strike them both
> Down into Hell with their calendar,
> For the Devil is their bosom pal.[27]

These strong words express the spirit of *confession*, that is, "intellectual and organizational hardening" of the religious communities into "more or less stable church structures with their own doctrines, constitutions, and religious and moral styles."[28] The currently debated "confessionalization hypothesis" holds that the three confessions—Lutheran, Reformed, and Catholic—were moving on three parallel but separate tracks, though at different speeds, toward the same goal: the regulation of religion and society in a Christian sense.[29] In many respects, such as the stricter supervision of marriage,[30] this is true, but the hypothesis cannot do justice to the radical sense of binary struggle that was growing stronger and stronger since the 1580s. The Empire had entered the confessional age.

3. THE REFORMED ADVANCE

The Coming of Calvinism
The Calvinist or "Reformed" faith formally entered the Empire around 1560 with the conversion from Lutheranism of the Palatine Elector Frederick III (1515-76).[31] As the French and Netherlandish struggles deepened, Reformed congregations were forming at Aachen, Metz, Trier, in the united duchies of Cleves-Jülich, and on the North Sea coast at Emden and Bremen. Gradually, whole Lutheran principalities were converted to Calvinism, beginning with the Palatinate around 1560, and by 1620 two of the lay electors—Brandenburg and the Palatinate—were Calvinists, along with five Silesian dukes, the prince of Anhalt, the landgrave of Hesse-Cassel, seventeen Imperial counts, and the city of Bremen.[32] Although not impressive in total land mass or aggregate population, the Reformed advance also threatened Electoral Saxony—which twice (1571-74 and 1586-91) came under the influence of "crypto-Calvinist" elites—Brandenburg, where in 1613 Elector John Sigismund (1572-1619) announced his conversion to Calvinism, Baden-Durlach, and Schleswig-Holstein. Each of these threats foundered on resistance by Lutheran elites.[33]

By the early 1590s the advance of this third, illegal Imperial confession seemed irresistible. Thirty years later, Abraham Scultetus (1566-1624), a former court preacher at Heidelberg, described the Calvinist mood at this time:

I cannot fail to recall the optimistic mood which I and many others
felt when we considered the condition of the Reformed churches in
1591. In France there ruled the valiant King Henry IV, in England
the mighty Queen Elizabeth, in Scotland the learned King James, in
the Palatinate the bold hero John Casimir, in Saxony the courageous
and powerful Elector Christian I, in Hesse the clever and prudent
Landgrave William, who were all inclined to the Reformed religion.
In the Netherlands everything went as Prince Maurice of Orange
wished, when he took Breda, Zutphen, Hulst, and Nijmegen. . . .
We imagined that an *aureum saeculum*, a golden age, had dawned.[34]
Then, however, "within twelve months the elector of Saxony, the
count palatine, and the landgrave all died, King Henry deserted the
true faith, and all our golden hopes went up in smoke."

Reformed Structures

The German-speaking Reformed reformation developed differently
from its French and Dutch counterparts in that, with few exceptions, it
was a reformation from above, initiated by rulers who exploited their
ius reformandi—guaranteed by a Religious Peace that did not recognize their faith.[35] Free presbyteries and classes in the Franco-Dutch
style did flourish in the duchies of Cleves-Jülich and in East Frisia, especially at Emden, where the constituting synod of the Dutch Reformed Church met in 1571.[36] The typical Reformed church in the
Empire nonetheless developed as a territorial church of a classic
caesaropapist kind.

The center of the Reformed faith lay from the first at Heidelberg, to
which refugees flowed from France, the Netherlands, and the German
Protestant states—e.g., Strasbourg—that had opted for orthodox Lutheranism.[37] Heidelberg's university became the center of a Reformed
network that included the universities of Marburg and Frankfurt an
der Oder, the academies of Herborn and Bremen, and a score of secondary schools of the first rank.[38] The Heidelberg Catechism, published in 1563, became the normative Reformed statement of faith (in
129 questions and answers) until far beyond the confessional era. And
the court at Heidelberg—the German Geneva—served as Reformed
Germany's political headquarters, especially under the regent John
Casimir (1543-92), who campaigned alongside the French Protestants
and maintained diplomatic ties to all of Calvinist Europe. Despite two
brief Lutheran restorations in 1576-83 and 1583-1610, the Rhine Palatinate continued to form a second hub—alongside the Dutch Repub-

lic—of Calvinism in Central Europe. From Heidelberg the faith spread
into other principalities, such as the group of Imperial counties in the
Wetterau, along the Middle Rhine's right bank, where, under the leadership of Count Johann VI of Nassau-Katzenelnbogen, there developed highly modernized and centralized institutions of ecclesiastical
and civil governance.[39]

In Europe the Reformed faith fed from the intensifying sense of confrontation with Rome; in the Empire it grew as a "Second Reformation" almost exclusively at Lutheran expense.[40] The "Second Reformation," as defined in 1596 by Wilhelm Zepper (1550-1607),
professor of theology at Herborn and Inspector in the (Reformed)
church of Nassau-Dillenburg meant that a reformation of life had to
follow the earlier reformation of doctrine. The first generation of reformers, he explained, had had "so much to do" to reform "doctrine as
the principal matter against the violent intrigues, rage, and insane
behavior of the pope and his crew," that they had no time to reform
the manner of living. At that time, indeed "the work of Christian discipline was not yet rightly understood" and was decried as a new form of
papal servitude. Now, however, it was time "to take in hand a proper
reformation in the other chief matter, the Christian way of life."[41]

Reformed Politics

To the strict Lutherans, this Reformed agenda seemed proof that the
Calvinists, having perverted true doctrine, aimed to subvert true religion as well. Seemingly untouched by the old yearning for unity and
emboldened by the fierce, bloody struggles against Catholicism in
France, England, and the Netherlands, the Calvinists also threatened
the Religious Peace. Their weakness in the Empire nevertheless forced
their leaders to seek toleration under the Peace by touting their faith as
consistent with the Confession of Augsburg. This assertion came to a
test at the Diet of Augsburg in 1566, when Duke Christoph of
Württemberg (1515-68), the foremost Lutheran prince in South Germany, complained about the "heretical catechism" (of Heidelberg). In
reply the Elector Palatine Frederick III, Christoph's cousin and exact
contemporary, stated the Reformed case for continuity with the original Protestant Reformation. The Lutheran princes, though they believed not a word, sheepishly shared Duke Christoph's admission that
if Frederick were condemned, "the persecutions in France, Spain, the
Netherlands and other similar places would grow at once by heaps,

and by that condemnation we should be guilty of shedding their blood."[42] August of Saxony's pragmatism prevailed once more, and for the next half century, the Reformed faith lived in the Empire as a legally "Lutheran" shadow confession.[43]

Even though the Lutheran powers dared not absolutely deny the Reformed claim to be Protestants, their fury against Calvinism could rage very hotly. When the second pro-Calvinist attempt on Electoral Saxony collapsed in 1601, and the chancellor who favored it was going to the block, the executioner's sword bore the inscription, "Calvinist, beware!"[44] In the same spirit, Matthias Hoe von Hoenegg (1580-1645), a Saxon court preacher, posed his question, "whether, how, and why one should have more to do with and trust more the Papists than the Calvinists."[45] The Calvinists replied in kind, meting out to Lutherans treatment fully as brutal as what the Lutherans complained of in the Catholic territories. In 1604 the "Second Reformation's" full weight fell on the University of Marburg, a famous nursery of Lutheran pastors, now to be converted to the Reformed faith by Landgrave Moritz (1572-1627) of Hesse-Cassel. When some students and faculty resisted, Moritz's troops drove them into Lutheran Hesse-Darmstadt, where from Giessen (raised to a university in 1607) they launched a mighty stream of polemic against their Reformed expropriators.[46]

The anomalous position of the Reformed as the smallest but most aggressive of the three Imperial confessions around 1600 helps to explain the political weakness of German Protestantism. It was a matter of perspective. Whereas the view from Heidelberg and Amsterdam saw the main body of German Protestants as backward but promising brethren in the great struggle against the papal Antichrist and his Habsburg lieutenants, the view from Dresden and Stuttgart looked on Calvinists as dangerous fools, ready to imitate Huldrych Zwingli, Jan van Leiden, and Thomas Müntzer in grasping the sword in the gospel's name.

4. THE LUTHERAN RALLY

Precisely when Calvinism began to penetrate the Empire during the 1560s, Lutheranism lay locked in the midst of a thirty-year doctrinal struggle over the legacy of Martin Luther.[47]

The Way to Concord

The doctrinal quarrels began in the aftermath of the Smalkaldic War between Philip Melanchthon's "Philippist" party and the Gnesio-Lutheran (Grk.: *gnesios*=legitimate) party headed the Dalmatian theologian Matthias Flacius (1520-75). The issues were fundamental: 1) whether salvation rested exclusively on God's grace (a continuation of the debate with the Catholics); 2) the manner of Christ's presence in the Eucharist (a continuation of the debate with the Zwinglians); and 3) proper relationship between the church and temporal authority (an issue critical to all confessions). The Flacians' insistence on the sovereignty of the gospel resembled militant Protestantism of the west European Calvinist-Puritan type, all the more so in that it created Protestant resistance theory to justify the right of "inferior magistrates" to resist monarchs. "When the superior authority undertakes to persecute its subjects with violence and injustice," the preachers in besieged Magdeburg proclaimed in 1550, "and to subvert divine or natural law, true doctrine, and divine services, . . . the inferior authority is obliged by divine command to maintain itself and the subjects against his superior."[48]

Ten years later, Melanchthon's death opened yet wider the floodgates of theological discord. The struggle fed from the rivalry between the two Saxonys, the dominant Albertine state being a Philippist bastion and the remnant Ernestine state the fortress of Gnesio-Lutheranism.[49] The unifying efforts, by contrast, came from the west, Brunswick and Württemberg, where the Calvinist challenge seemed more palpable, and it was Jacob Andreä (1529-90), professor of theology and chancellor of the University of Tübingen, and the Lower Saxons Martin Chemnitz (1522-86) and Nikolaus Selnecker (1530-92) who pushed hardest for doctrinal agreement. Meanwhile, in Electoral Saxony during the first half of the 1570s, the Philippists at Wittenberg—Luther's old university—were working secretly for an understanding with the Calvinists. When Elector August I purged these "crypto-Calvinists" in 1574, a corner was turned toward Lutheran doctrinal unification on an anti-Calvinist basis.

The main phase of reunification began in March 1577, when theologians assembled in the old Benedictine abbey of Bergen, an Ottonian foundation outside the walls of Magdeburg. Their twelve articles codified Lutheran doctrine against the "sects and conventicles" and against the Reformed and Catholic challenges. They agreed "to commit ourselves exclusively and only, in accordance with the pure, infallible, and unalterable Word of God, to that Augsburg Confession which was submitted to Emperor Charles V at the great imperial assembly in Augsburg in the year 1530."[50] The *Book of Concord*, which also contained several other doctrinal statements (called "symbols"), was published in 1580, the fiftieth anniversary of the Confession of Augsburg. It appeared over the signatures of fifty princes, 38 free cities, and no fewer than 8,000 clergymen.[51] This successful rallying of Lutheranism came just in the nick of time, before the Reformed challenge reached its peak, and before the Catholic revival was fairly underway.

Success and Failure in the Lutheran Reform

Although Lutheran churches existed in Scandinavia and scattered through the German diaspora in eastern Europe, they exerted little influence on Lutheranism in the Empire, which remained the most purely German in personnel and temperament of the three Imperial confessions. In many ways, too, it remained the confession least changeable and most bound to the past, a pastors' church in which most pastors came from pastoral families.[52] Some indeed have argued that Lutheranism represented a failed reformation. Gerald Strauss has argued that Lutheran clergy of the first and second generations certainly developed an aggressive program of religious and moral pedagogy, based on principles which have come to be recognized as the common pedagogy of the confessional era: self-discipline, obedience, self-control, and the acceptance of paternal, pastoral, and princely authority. This program, however, foundered on popular resistance to the new discipline.[53]

Strauss' argument about the Reformation's failure has been much debated. With dubious yield, for the debates have mixed indiscriminately urban successes with rural failures. Most of the Empire's people, after all, lived in villages, where old ways, including religious ones, stubbornly resisted all reformers. The Jesuits, for all of their successes, met their match in the villages of the prince-bishopric of Speyer, where the Capuchins, a reformed branch of the Franciscans, had later to do the whole job again.[54] Very rarely did the rural folk have the luxury of choosing their religion, and when they did, as in parts of the Swiss Confederacy and the associated states of Valais and Graubünden, they defended their own ways with great tenacity, the Reformed communities of the Toggenburg against the Catholic abbot of St. Gallen not less stoutly than the Valtellina's Catholic Italian-speakers against their Reformed occupiers from the Graubünden.[55]

The debate about the Reformation's success or failure rarely considers what barriers to religious change from above were posed by the Empire's deeply fragmented governance and considerable local autonomies. Consider how the Lutheran faith came to Ödenwaldstetten, a very poor village lying east of the Neckar Valley in the Swabian Jura.[56] The village's lord was the Catholic abbot of Zwiefalten, whose lay protector (*Vogt*) was the Lutheran duke of Württemberg. Nothing much happened at Ödenwaldstetten until the parish priest died in 1558. When the abbot asked Duke Christoph's permission to install another "Mass priest [*Messpfaffe*]," Württemberg's ruler decided that it was time to bring the gospel to the village. Two likely candidates declined the post after inspecting the situation, because "they could not detect that the mayor, officers, and jurors have any special love for the holy gospel. Also, they found a very small, cramped, crumbling . . . rectory, in which no clergyman could possible live with wife and children. And in the little church they found all sorts of papist trash, which the people continue to honor."[57] The village court consulted the Lutheran superintendent at Urach, Johann Otmar Mayländer, who organized occasional preaching at Ödenwaldstetten by a nearby pastor. When, however, he visited the village at Pentecost 1559, Mayländer was astounded to see the villagers in solemn procession, led by a volunteer Catholic priest from a nearby village, and he admonished the villagers to leave off their papistical ways. In the end, when the abbot would not pay to renovate the ruined rectory, the villagers accepted a Lutheran pastor, who served a heavily Catholic flock under their Catholic lord, the abbot. Not until around 1610 did villagers cease to demand a Catholic priest, and far into modern times, it was told, Ödenwaldstetters nodded to the spot on the church's wall where the image of the Virgin had once stood. Finally, when the village passed from Zwiefalten to Württemberg in 1750—200 years after Luther's death—the Lutheran reformation was complete at Ödenwaldstetten. This story suggests the immense difficulties under which the Lutheran reformation—and all other reformations—labored in the countryside.[58] Against Catholicism, Lutheranism had the added burden of a preaching message which condemned the past to a society based on the continuities of household, farmstead, and cultivation, and which deprecated "works," that is, human deeds and labor, to people whose lives were composed of works alone.

All three confessions were essentially town-bred, and the formation of clear confessional identities came more easily in the cities.[59] Naming was a particularly visible sign of identity, in the Empire as elsewhere in

transalpine Europe. In bi-confessional Augsburg, by the early seventeenth century Lutherans were displacing the name "Maria" for their
daughters by the confessionally neutral "Regina," while for boys,
though "Hans" and "Johann" held pride of place in both confessions,
the Lutherans turned toward Old Testament names—"Abraham,"
"Elias," and "Daniel"—and the Catholics to "Michael"—a great
Counterreformation favorite—and "Ignaz."[60] Gradually, too, confessionally mixed marriages, which had been common before the 1580s,
became less so, as the confessional lines hardened. Being on one side or
the other, or moving from one side to the other, could mean the difference between survival and ruin, since in mixed communities, such as
Augsburg, nearly all social welfare institutions were administered on a
confessional basis.[61]

Lutheran Politics

Although Lutheranism changed slowly, its achievements were not un-
impressive. By the 1580s the confession possessed a clear standard of
identity in the *Book of Concord* and a durable, bedrock policy of loyalty to the Imperial constitution in general and the Religious Peace of
1555 in particular. Indeed, it was the Lutheran jurists, not the Catholics, who developed the strongest tradition of pro-monarchical legal
thought.[62] The concentration of Lutheran powers—Saxony,
Brandenburg, and their dependents—in the east, where the Ottomans
seemed at least as threatening as the Catholics, helped the confession's
political leaders to resist being pulled by the Calvinist politicians into
the maelstrom of the western European religious wars. The most
purely Imperial of the three Imperial confessions, the Lutherans had
most to lose if the Religious Peace were disrupted. Count Henry of
Isenburg (1565-1601), a Lutheran progenitor of Calvinist heirs, stated
their position best: "Peace is better than war, for it is uncertain who
will win."[63]

5. THE CATHOLIC REVIVAL

"My church and I are destroyed," wrote Hildesheim's prince-bishop to
Rome in 1545.[64] At that time and for long after, the emperor's policy
of conciliating the Protestants dampened the freedom and will of many
of the Empire's Catholic prelates to undertake a vigorous defense of
their faith. During these decades odd conditions obtained, mixed or-

ders of worship were common, the state of ecclesiastical property was chaotic, and in some places the same man might serve as a Catholic priest and a Protestant pastor.[65] By the mid-1560s, however, change was in the wind. In 1566, three years after the Council of Trent rose for the last time, the Roman Curia, now convinced of the hopelessness of dealing with the emperor and the Imperial Diet, began to negotiate with individual bishops about introducing the Tridentine reforms.[66] The Catholic revival began with individual bishops' acceptance of the Tridentine profession of faith and promises to obey the council's canons and decrees, which were gradually incorporated via diocesan synods into the local laws.[67]

Foundations of Catholic Revival

Rome's most important contribution was to train a cadre of modern clergy at the German College (*Collegium Germanicum*), which was founded at Rome in 1552 and reorganized by Jesuits in 1573. Its graduates—in the early days mostly Netherlanders and Lower Rhinelanders—comprised an ever increasing proportion of the Catholic bishops and cathedral canons in the Empire. During the early 1580s the papacy also established permanent nuntiatures at Graz (1580) and Cologne (1584), which became important switching points for the process of Catholic reform in the Empire.[68]

Further help came from the Society of Jesus's efforts to begin the modern training of priests in the Empire.[69] Their schools, many of them founded in episcopal residential cities, became the nurseries of the Catholic reform, as the free cities had been those of the Protestant one.[70] Such schools appeared at Dillingen (for Augsburg) in the 1550s, at Mainz in 1561, at Würzburg also in the 1560s, at Eichstätt in 1584, and at Bamberg in 1586.[71] The Society, first established in the Empire at Cologne in 1544, grew even more rapidly, rising from 273 members organized into two provinces in the mid-1560s to nearly 2,500 in three provinces (Rhenish, South German, and Austrian) by the 1620s.[72] Such were its successes, so quickly did the Jesuits provide the Empire's intact Catholic communities with religious leadership and able defenders through pulpit and pamphlet, that both friend and foe tended to overestimate their powers. The Society flourished in the cities, but not in the countryside, and in Bavaria, where the Jesuits worked to great effect from pulpits, in schools, in the theater, and in the University of Ingolstadt, they took little or no part in the revitalization of the religious culture of shrines and pilgrimage that so effectively armored Bavarian Catholicism against Lutheran influence.[73] In the prince-bishopric of Speyer on the Upper Rhine, the Jesuits' efforts in the villages failed altogether, and reform had to be reestablished by the Capuchins, a far more demotic order.[74] Gradually, too, the older religious orders drew themselves together and were mobilized for the Catholic reform.[75]

The Ecclesiastical States

The key to reform was the clergy, especially the hierarchy—prince-bishops, abbots, abbesses, and cathedral canons—who, though remaining as aristocratic as ever, gradually began to change their ways of life.[76] Archbishop Wolf Dietrich von Raitenau (1559-1612) of Salzburg, a nobleman from south of Lake Constance, illustrates the transition from old to new.[77] Wolf Dietrich studied for five years at the German College in Rome before succeeding in Salzburg at the age of eighteen. There he blended the old ways with the new. He accumulated benefices with the zeal of a pre-Reformation prelate, and he even sought Rome's permission to marry Salome Alt, the lovely daughter of a Salzburg magistrate, by whom he fathered ten children. Wolf Dietrich's policies, however, fully justified Pope Sixtus V's admonition "to break the blows of the heretics and turn their deadly shots back on themselves." He introduced the Tridentine pastoral agenda at Salzburg, began to reform clerical life, harnessed the younger religious orders to the task of reform, and began—in precise imitation of Sixtus V at Rome—the Baroque transformation of Salzburg. Wolf Dietrich also had the bad judgment to clash with Duke Maximilian I (r. 1598-1651) of Bavaria, which led to his deposition and incarceration.

Archbishop Wolf Dietrich represented a Catholic version of the typically Imperial fusion between centralized authority and religious reform.[78] He and the other prince-bishops—twelve of the sees had been lost to the Lutherans—were crucial to the success of Catholic reform, because, outside of Bavaria and Austria, most of the Empire's intact Catholic communities lived under ecclesiastical lords.

Bavaria

The Bavarian dukes early assumed the leadership of the Catholic revival, because the emperors from Ferdinand I through Rudolph II were tied to the need to conciliate both the Imperial estates and the estates of the Habsburg lands.[79] In Bavaria, by contrast, already in the early 1560s Duke Albert V's (r. 1550-79) defeat of his heavily Lutheran territorial nobility enabled the duchy to become the linchpin of the Empire's Catholic reform in a Tridentine sense. Albert called the Jesuits to Munich and to his university at Ingolstadt, and he made the Landsberg League (1556-98) a military instrument for the protection of Catholic interests.

Duke Albert also began to push Catholic Wittelsbachs into endangered episcopal sees, a policy which yielded its first major fruit in the early 1580s at Cologne. Cologne's archbishop, Gebhard Truchsess von Waldburg (r. 1577-83), converted to Protestantism and tried to retain his see. This act challenged the Ecclesiastical Reservation and touched off the "Cologne War" (1583-85), which nearly became a major war. While Emperor Rudolph stood by helplessly, Duke William V (r. 1579-93, d. 1626) secured the claim of his younger brother, Ernest, to the see and began thereby the 180-year history of the great Rhenish see as a Bavarian secundogeniture. The securing of Catholicism at Cologne, in collaboration with the Spanish regime at Brussels, made possible the stabilization of the Catholic position in the Empire's entire northwestern sector, and it did so at a time when the emperor was caught between the Ottoman threat and the need to conciliate the Protestants.

The Austrian Lands

Protestantism's initial penetration of the Austrian lands met little resistance from a deeply enervated church.[80] As in Bohemia, Bavaria, and elsewhere, the new faith quickly allied with the landed nobility's struggle to preserve its liberties against princely centralism. By the early 1580s, it has been argued, most nobles and many burghers in the Austrian lands had turned to the new faith.

The Austrian Counterreformation, it has also been argued, represented the triumph of "a universal (imperial) ideology and a revived cosmopolitan (Catholic) Church" over "the vestiges of Renaissance and the ruins of Protestantism." [81] If true, this helps to explain the revival of a church once so deeply enervated that a survey of Lower Austrian monasteries in 1563 counted 122 houses containing 463 monks, 160 nuns, 199 concubines, 55 wives, and 443 children.[82] The rulers did supply some essential impulses to reform, notably Maximilian II's creation in 1567-68 of a Monastic Council (*Klosterrat*) for Upper and Lower Austria.[83] Such measures alone nevertheless cannot account for the rapid decline of the Lutheran cause after 1580. Unfavorable economic conditions helped to account for the decline of the nobles, and

the Habsburg rulers accelerated the change through the creation of
new Catholic nobles, but so did Catholic successes in the struggle for
reform at the level of the local seigniory and the rural monastery.[84]
Among rural folk, surely, the Protestant advantage was not so great as
has sometimes been asserted, for the Protestant nobles never possessed
more than about half of the pastorates in the Austrian lands, and the
majority of those were castle chaplaincies.[85]

Much depended, too, on Ferdinand I's division of the Austrian lands
in 1564 among his three sons, whose capitals lay at Vienna, Graz, and
Innsbruck.[86] While Lutheranism strongly penetrated the "lower
lands" of Upper and Lower Austria, it was weaker in Inner Austria
(Styria, Carinthia, and Carniola), and much weaker yet in the western
lands of Tyrol and Vorarlberg. At Graz and at Innsbruck the Catholic
reform received decisive dynastic support long before it did in the
"lower lands." There, except for Vienna with its durable Catholic majority, the Catholic reform began to succeed only after the great rural
insurrection of 1594/97, which the Protestant-led estates crushed.
Thereafter, the Protestant clergy were driven out of the cities and into
the castles for refuge.[87]

Vienna, demoted to a provincial capital by Rudolph II in favor of
Prague, posed a special case. In the 1580s a strong champion of
Catholic reform emerged there in the person of Melchior Khlesl (1552-
1630), son of a Protestant baker in Vienna, a graduate of Jesuits
schooling, and delegate of the bishop of Passau in the Aulic Council at
Vienna. He became the heart and soul of the struggle to beat back the
Protestant challenge in Lower Austria, though the effort faltered after
1600, when "the brothers' quarrel [Bruderzwist]" between Rudolph
and Matthias brought Catholic reform to a standstill. For a time, it
even seemed as if there would be an Austrian version of Rudolph II's
"Letter of Majesty" (1609), which confirmed the religious liberties of
the Bohemian estates. In fact, the moment for action by the Protestant
Austrian nobles was already past, and when the estates turned to arms
against Archduke Ferdinand of Inner Austria, who came to the Bohemian throne in 1617 and to the Imperial throne as Emperor Ferdinand
II in 1619, it was already too late. Catholicism, in the 1550s to 1570s
an apparently doomed religion in both the Empire and the Austrian
lands, had become by century's end the strongest of the three confessions.[88]

6. THE FAILURE OF IMPERIAL POLITICS

"There is no more friendship on this earth," the poet Theodore Höck groaned in 1601, "and each has become Devil to the other."[89] It was, indeed, a hard age, this late sixteenth century, and over its reputation stands the somber image of the reclusive Emperor Rudolph II, hiding himself away in the great Hradcany Castle at Prague, "for long stretches mentally ill, so disordered and irrationally frightened that he let imperial business slide for months and years, so depressed that he thought himself bewitched and even attempted suicide."[90] Meanwhile, all around him the leaderless Empire disintegrated into mistrust, resignation, and mutually hostile armed parties.[91]

One may not blame the listless emperor for the times, which were indeed hard. There is mounting evidence that during the 1590s Europe fell into a general crisis which adversely affected all of its lands and all aspects of its peoples' lives.[92] Not only was religious strife becoming more intense, but there were new waves of revolts in the cities and on the land.[93] By far the most ominous and most revealing sign of the crisis, however, was the onset of the great witch panic.

The Witch Panic

Between 1580 and 1660 Europe shuddered to the great witch panic, to which the Empire contributed about half of the 40-50,000 persons executed for the crime of witchcraft.[94] Its main phase began in the 1580s with an unprecedented wave of denunciations, prosecutions, and executions. In the southeast, the best studied region, about 75% of the executions for witchcraft occurred between 1586 and 1630, whereas in two core regions of witch hunting, Franconia and southwestern Germany, the peaks came later and resulted in many more executions (ca. 8,000 vs. ca. 1,800 in Bavaria and Austria).[95] The prosecutions of witches found broad approval among the common people, though not necessarily for the same reasons as it did among the elites. The latter were split, the strongest proponents of religious renewal—Catholic and Protestant—tending to be more in favor of prosecutions, but in general the skeptics gradually gained the upper hand and dampened or stopped the prosecutions earliest in the most strongly governed states.[96]

The Search for Order

Against the chaos that threatened the Empire and the world stood
forces which were, given the age's reputation, deceptively powerful. At
the center formed by the Rudolfine court worked a heterogeneous aristocracy which represented "the belief in a single universal authority
and the total, all-embracing conception of society."[97] In origin Renaissance rather than medieval, their ideal centered not on a Church Universal but a universal monarchy, the tasks of which were "to preserve
the mental and political unity of Christendom, to avoid religious
schism, uphold peace at home, and deliver Europe from the Ottoman
menace."[98]

The Rudolfine ideology of universal monarchy tried to promote Imperial stability by two means: protection of the Religious Peace and
struggle against the Ottomans. The former aim was served by a remarkably successful record of political adaptation and innovation.
Since Charles V's day much of the Imperial Diet's work, such as judicial review and financial administration, had come into the hands of
the Circles (*Reichskreise*) and a new institution, the *Reichsdeputationstag*, a kind of executive committee of the Diet.[99] In the 1590s the latter
body assumed the task of regular review of the Imperial Chamber
Court, which continued to expand its work despite competition from
another new institution, the purely royal Imperial Aulic Court
(*Reichshofrat*, est. 1559).

The Ottoman struggle tested the effectiveness of all Imperial institutions. When war came again in 1593, the Habsburg propagandists set
out to deploy anti-Ottoman sentiment against the confessional divisions. Their warnings resonated with the sentiments of many others,
among them Peter Waldner of Augsburg:

Because the Empire's princes are so contentious
The Turk has become so powerful.
There is no peace in Christendom,
So that he grazes where he will.
He knows well how things stand,
That there is no peace in Christendom.[100]

Such sentiments long mortgaged the tactic of tax refusal, which the
Protestant princes had employed so effectively against Charles V.
From 1576 to 1603, indeed, the Imperial estates voted generous taxes
against the Ottomans and, more astonishingly, paid them—rather,
they persuaded their own subjects and estates to pay them. The new
Imperial tax administrator (*Reichspfennigmeister*, est. 1566), col-

lected more than 80% of the Imperial taxes levied between 1576 and 1606—a miraculous level, considering the Empire's history. Between Charles V's abdication in 1556 and the end of the Ottoman War in 1606, the Empire paid more than 30,000,000 fl. for war against the Ottomans. [101] "While it lasted," Winfried Schulze has written, "the Ottoman threat posed an important, consolidating force in the Empire and preserved its political structure from collapsing earlier than it did." [102] Indeed, by the early years of the seventeenth century, it seemed as if the Imperial system had weathered the storms of the Reformation era and was moving down the same path on which the kingdoms of Europe's western tier were treading, toward greater centralization, cohesion, and internal uniformity.

Imperial Breakdown

The Imperial politics based on the Religious Peace of 1555 withstood internal shocks which might have broken a more fragile state. The first major test of confessional co-existence came in the early 1580s, when Spanish and Bavarian forces faced off against German Calvinist and Dutch troops in the "Cologne War." The crisis passed, and the Catholics kept the see. A similar case opened in 1592 at Strasbourg, where a double episcopal election produced Catholic and Protestant claimants to the see. Again there was threat of major war, again it was averted, and again the Catholics held the contested see. A third case involved the long confessional strife in the free city of Aachen, where the Protestant congregations had organized too late, after 1555, to be protected by the Peace. There was much internal strife and threats of external intervention, but the Catholics held the day, and in 1614/16 the Protestants were expelled from the city. In all three cases, the Catholics won out because the Catholic forces—the emperor, Bavaria, and the Spanish regime at Brussels—worked together more easily than did the western Calvinist and eastern Lutheran princes.

The Catholics possessed a tremendous advantage in a Catholic emperor, even though Rudolph's religious mentality favored the mystical, the miraculous, and the dynastic, and he abhorred confessionalism and Rome.[103] When he could make up his mind, however, he generally favored the Catholic side, as he did in a fourth case, called the "Four Monasteries Case." This was a group of suits brought by Catholic monasteries against Protestant princes, all of which the Imperial Chamber court decided in a Catholic sense—though in fact the judges probably never intended to address in principle the issue of ecclesiastical property and the *ius reformandi*.[104] No matter, for when the case came before the *Reichsdeputationstag*'s visitation of the court in 1600/1, the Protestant members demanded its referral to the Diet, the Catholics refused, and both sides left the meeting in a huff. This destroyed the effectiveness of both the *Reichsdeputationstag* and the Chamber Court and left only the Imperial Diet to oppose the creeping paralysis of Imperial governance. Then, in 1606 the Truce of Zsitva Torok with the Ottoman Sultan, who was pressed in the east by a Persian attack, removed the last major external restraint on confessional aggressiveness.[105]

This was the situation in 1608, when a dispute erupted over Catholic religious rights in the Protestant-dominated free city of Donauwörth. When the magistrates refused to protect Catholic religious processions, the *Reichshofrat* decided against them, and the emperor appointed the Duke Maximilian of Bavaria—not the commander of the Swabian Circle, the (Protestant) duke of Württemberg—to execute the sentence. Bavarian troops occupied the town, long an object of Bavarian policy, and Catholicism was restored. This action had ominous consequences, because the ensuing quarrel disrupted the Imperial Diet of Regensburg in 1608, which dissolved in acrimony without framing a recess. "This Diet had such an unfortunate end and consequence," wrote a Mainz secretary at the end of his minutes, "that it dissolved with nothing accomplished."[106] As the fear of war swept over the Empire, Rudolph II, paralyzed by his bitter quarrel with his brother, Archduke Matthias, failed to act.

With the Diet disrupted and the emperor quiescent, the confessional parties hardened into confessional alliances. At Auingen near Nördlingen on 14 May 1608 came into being the Protestant Union, in which normally traditionally loyal Lutheran cities—Nuremberg, Strasbourg, and Ulm—joined, though Elector Christian II of Saxony stayed aloof. In response, the Catholic League came into being at Munich on 10 July 1609. At first it comprised chiefly South German prelates, and its finances were closely tied to the Bavarian treasury, but in 1610 it admitted the electors of Mainz, Cologne, and Trier and two Austrian archdukes. Not only had the League greater extent than the Union, but its common confession, which the emperor officially shared, gave it greater cohesion.

Now, the old system shattered, the Empire seemed to plunge toward confessional war—and then stopped once more. The last great prewar crisis developed over the succession to the Lower Rhenish conglomerate state of Cleves-Jülich. At the death of the childless and hopelessly insane Duke John William in 1609—the year of the Twelve Years' Truce between Spain and the Dutch—the chief claimants were his brothers-in-law, Philip Louis, Count Palatine of Neuburg and a Lutheran, and Elector John Sigismund of Brandenburg, a Calvinist. At first they collaborated against a Catholic regency council headed by the dowager duchess. Meanwhile, the Protestant Union, torn between two Protestant claimants, stood pat, the emperor sat silent at Prague, and northwestern Europe mobilized for the general war the Empire most feared. At this moment (14 May 1610) came the assassination King Henry IV of France, just as the royal army was about to move, and all powers stood down. Even when Philip Louis converted to Catholicism, the confessional alliances still did not move, and by 1614 the dispute was settled by partitioning the duchies between Philip Louis and John Sigismund of Brandenburg.

The final blow to the Imperial peace came in 1618 in Bohemia. Rudolph's brother and heir, Emperor Matthias, was succeeded in Bohemia in 1618 (and in the Empire in 1619) by Archduke Ferdinand of Inner Austria (Emperor Ferdinand II). Born in 1578, Ferdinand was the first Holy Roman emperor who was wholly a child of the confessional era. His succession came at a difficult time, for Europe's rulers and politicians were waiting for the Twelve Years' Truce between Spain and the Dutch Republic to expire (in 1621), expecting it would be followed by another general European war. At Prague the Protestant nobles who led the Bohemian estates decided to forestall the uncertainty of that event by revoking their election of Ferdinand and putting a Protestant in his place. As Polyxena Lobkovic, wife of the Bohemian chancellor, remarked, "things were now swiftly coming to the pass where either the Papists would settle their score with the Protestants, or the Protestants with the Papists."[107] Bolstered by promises from Christian of Anhalt (1586-1630), the mind behind the Protestant Union, plus the Upper and Lower Austrian estates and the Prince of Transylvania, the Bohemian leaders chose themselves an alternative king. Their foolhardy choice fell on the young Elector Palatine, Frederick V (1596-1632), "a man who had never seen either a battle or a corpse, . . . a prince who knew more about gardening than fighting."[108]

7. War and Settlement

The long, terrible war of 1618-48 deserves study in its own right, for the guise in which it appears here, as the culmination of the Empire's Reformation settlement,[109] pushes to the margin some of the most interesting questions, such as the war's economic and social effects,[110] in favor of its political dimensions. Two questions need to be raised: Why did the war go on so long? Why did the war end in a restoration of the Religious Peace of 1555?

The Long War

The war lasted for thirty years because of the overwhelming quality of Emperor Ferdinand II's victories in the war's first ("Bohemian") phase in 1618-23 and second ("Danish") phase in 1624-29. His success tempted Ferdinand to declare measures that frightened his opponents, both in the Empire and abroad. His Bohemian settlement, though radical, lay within the bounds of the Imperial constitution—assuming that Bohemia lay in the Empire—and within the rights stipulated to rulers by the Religious Peace. *Cuius regio, eius religio.* The Austrian Protestants fell under the same rule, and they fell alone. The transfer of the Upper Palatinate to Bavaria also lay within royal prerogative, and one could argue that awarding the Palatine electorate to Bavaria kept it with the same dynasty and did not, therefore, violate the Golden Bull of 1356. It was difficult, however, to justify constitutionally the Edict of Restitution of 1629, which ordered restoration of all church lands and bishoprics secularized since the Treaty of Passau in 1552, not because of its strict interpretation of the Religious Peace, but because it was unilaterally issued by the emperor. Still, at this time, around 1630, " the political leaders of Germany were free to determine their own destiny," for although the war between Spain and the Dutch Republic had resumed, and although both branches of the House of Austria had become embroiled once again in a major war with France in Italy, "as long as the German princes remained neutral and unattached, there was still a chance for peace."[111] Then, in late June 1630, King Gustavus Adolphus of Sweden landed in the Empire, beginning the war's third, "Swedish" phase of 1630-34. He came, as he said, to restore the status quo of 1618, for "while an elector can sit safe as elector in his land, and a duke is duke and has his liberties, then we are safe."[112] After he fell (Lützen, 1632), and after his army was defeated (Nördlingen, 1534), France intervened to begin the war's final "French" phase (1635-48).

Settlement and Restoration

The Thirty Years' War ended in an Imperial restoration, because leading Imperial princes of both major confessions were moved by the desire to restore the Imperial constitution, so that the Empire would escape both foreign domination and a "Latin servitude" to the House of Austria. This program underlay both the Catholic League's pressure for the dismissal of Albrecht of Wallenstein (1583-1634), Ferdinand's most successful general, and the Saxon elector's perennial refusal to throw his resources whole-heartedly against the emperor. The moment for restoration seemed to strike after the Swedish defeat at Nördlingen in September 1634, when the impending French intervention pressed Emperor Ferdinand to make peace with the leading Protestant princes, Saxony and Brandenburg. The Peace of Prague (30 May 1635) ended the Imperial civil war, made the Swedish army's position in Germany hopeless, combined the hitherto hostile forces into an Imperial army, and restored the voice of pragmatism and compromise to Imperial counsels. Had it not been for the French "war of diversion," which aimed to fight Spanish power in Germany rather than "in the bowels of France," the end of the Empire's war would have ended the war in the Empire as well.[113] As it was, since the mid-1630s the old Imperial political order had begun to reconstitute itself beneath the surface of ceaseless struggle. The electors were meeting periodically, and in September 1640 the Imperial Diet convened at Regensburg for the first time since 1613. The greatest internal barrier to restoration was removed in 1641, when, over the papal nuncio's protest, Emperor Ferdinand III withdrew the Edict of Restitution. During the next six years, each French victory stiffened his resolve, and that of the leading Catholic and Lutheran princes, to make peace.

The Peace of Westphalia of 1648 completed this restoration.[114] The treaties in the main confirmed the Religious Peace of 1555, with three important changes: the Calvinist faith was recognized; the fixing of 1624 as the status quo settled the dispute about the Ecclesiastical Reservation; and the formation of two religious caucuses, the *corpus evangelicorum* and *corpus catholicorum*, which cut across the Diet's historic structure, enabled this parliament to incorporate the Empire's confessional division into its structure of governance. In addition, the Empire lost important groups of lands, the Swiss Confederacy and the Dutch Republic, from its southwestern and northwestern corners respectively.

With the Peace of Westphalia the Imperial constitution triumphed over the religious forces unleashed by the Protestant and Catholic reformations. The long war spelled defeat for two alternative visions. One was the renewed Reformed vision fashioned at Heidelberg, which held that German-speaking Protestantism's rulers should fuse their policies and resources with those of foreign Protestant rulers into a gigantic, Europe-wide league against the Habsburgs and Rome. The second was Ferdinand II's Catholic dream of extending to the Empire his style of rule, which, though it has been called "confessional absolutism," substituted religious orthodoxy for structural centralization.[115] Each of these visions looked beyond the traditional politics of compromise and accommodation to a new kind of universalism, which was neither medieval nor did it lie on the "modern path" toward absolutist centralism and the national state. The twin Imperial settlements of 1555 and 1648 defeated these projects for renewal in favor of the Imperial structure that had emerged from the fifteenth century: a monarchy caged by constituted aristocratic liberties. It would endure for another 150 years.

NOTES

1. W. Schulze (1987), 46-49. See, in general, Dickens and Tonkin (1986).
2. Peter Blickle, in this *Handbook*, vol. 2:161-92.
3. James Stayer, in this *Handbook*, vol. 2:249-82.
4. Muralt (1980); J. Wayne Baker and Miriam U. Chrisman, in Maltby (1992), 47-74, 105-28.
5. Schilling (1988a), 227-39; Rabe (1991), 317-461; Brady (1995), 206-352.
6. Cohn (1987); Schindling (1980).
7. Greyerz (1980).
8. Martin Brecht, in this *Handbook*, vol. 2:129-59.
9. M. Schulze (1991); Moeller (1987); and Berndt Hamm, in this *Handbook*, vol. 2:193-227.
10. Quoted by Brady (1995), 55.
11. Quoted by ibid., 258.
12. Rabe (1971).
13. Lutz (1964); the texts of 1552 and 1555 may be conveniently consulted in Kastner (1994), 520-31, nos. 159-60.
14. Heckel (1959).
15. Quoted by Schilling (1988a), 241.
16. Ibid., 242.
17. Heckel (1968), 80.
18. See Duchhardt (1991), 147-53, on the entire development.
19. Hsia (1984), 199.
20. *Politische Korrespondez des Herzogs und Kurfürsten Moritz von Sachsen*, vol. 4, ed. Johannes Hermann and Günther Wartenberg, Abhandlungen der Sächsischen Akademie der Wissenschaften zu Leipzig, Philologisch-historische Klasse, 72 (Berlin, Akademie Verlag, 1992), 510, no. 438.
21. Scribner (1981).
22. Ernst Walter Zeeden, in Zeeden (1985), 333-36.
23. See Wirsching (1986).
24. Oberman (1992).
25. Traitler (1989), 141-52.
26. Chrisman (1982), 81; Chaix (1981); Soergel (1993), 5-6.
27. Quoted by Vocelka (1981), 268. For Augsburg, see Roeck (1991), 84-88; Warmbrunn (1983), 360-64.
28. Zeeden (1958), 251, and (1965), 9.
29. The clearest formulation is by Schilling (1992), 205-46, and in this *Handbook*, vol. 2:641-82. On confessionalization, see Reinhard (1983); Schilling (1988b), and in English in (1992); Hsia (1989), 1-9. On the individual confessions, see Schilling (1986), Rublack (1992), and Reinhard

and Schilling (1994); and for a geographical treatment, Schindling and Ziegler (1989-93).

30. Safley (1984). Even so, Zschunke (1984) finds divergent patterns of fertility among the confessions.
31. Press (1970); Cohn (1985), 148-50. There is an important overview by J. F. G. Goeters, in Schilling (1986), 44-59; and in English see Knox (1977).
32. See Cohn (1985), 135-40, with map.
33. Klein (1962); Nischan (1994).
34. Quoted by Cohn (1985), 135; and there, too, the remaining quotes in this paragraph.
35. Schilling (1988a) and (1986); Münch (1978), who exaggerated the role of nobles in the consistories.
36. See Robert M. Kingdon, in this *Handbook*, vol. 2:229-47.
37. Press (1970); Abray (1985), 142-62.
38. See Cohn (1985), 137-38.
39. Glawischnig (1973); Georg Schmidt, in Schilling (1986), 184-213.
40. The concept is debated by William Heinrich Neuser and Heinz Schilling, in Schilling (1986), 379-86, 387-437.
41. Quoted by Paul Münch, in Schilling (1986), 296-97.
42. Hollweg (1964), 387.
43. Martin Heckel, in Schilling (1986), 11-43, here at 31.
44. Lutz (1983), 349.
45. Neveux (1967), 11.
46. Gross (1975), 105ff.
47. See Martin Brecht, in this *Handbook*, vol. 2:148-52. There is a good overview by Rabe (1991), 507-14.
48. Quoted by Schilling (1988a), 292.
49. See Ernst Koch, in Schilling (1986), 60-78.
50. Theodore G. Tappert, ed., *The Book of Concord. The Confessions of the Evangelical Lutheran Church* (Philadelphia, 1959), 8-9. See Brecht and Schwarz (1980).
51. Lohse (1980).
52. The evidence is summarized by Hsia (1989), 14-16. For the background, see Scribner (1987), 123-44.
53. Strauss (1978).
54. Forster (1992).
55. Stadler (1980), 624; Head (1994).
56. Fritz (1989).
57. Ibid., 40.
58. See, e.g., Robisheaux (1989).
59. See Abray (1985), Warmbrunn (1983), and Roeck (1991) for examples.
60. Roeck (1991), 295.
61. Ibid., 296-97.
62. Gross (1975).
63. Quoted by Schilling (1988a), 291.
64. Quoted by Bauerreiss (1965), 280.
65. Zeeden (1965), 74, 77; Evans (1979), 15.
66. Bireley (1988), 13.
67. See Molitor (1967) for a model study.
68. P. Schmidt (1984); Reinhard (1971).

69. O'Malley (1993).
70. Rublack (1978).
71. May (1983), 254-55, 242-45, 366-67, 277, 574.
72. Based on figures summarized by Hsia (1989), 48.
73. Soergel (1993), 89-90, 34-36, 152-54.
74. Forster (1992).
75. Seibrich (1991).
76. For orientation, see Wolfgang Reinhard, in Jeserich, Pohl, and Unruh (1983), 143-76; Schindling (1987); for details see Schindling and Ziegler (1989-93); and for the later history see Peter Hersche, in G. Schmidt (1989), 133-51.
77. Ortner (1981); Schindling and Ziegler (1989-93), vol. 1:72-85. The story of Wolf Dietrich is recounted by Schilling (1988a), 284-88.
78. Reinhard (1989); and see Bireley (1990), for Counterreformation statecraft.
79. Albrecht (1977a) and (1977b); Lutz (1977); Schindling and Ziegler (1989 93), vol. 1:56-71.
80. Schindling and Ziegler (1989-93), vol. 1:86-101, 102-17, 188-33, 134 52; Reingrabner (1976).
81. Evans (1979), xxiii.
82. Ibid., 4.
83. Jeserich, Pohl, and Unruh (1983), here at 512-13; Patrouch (1994).
84. MacHardy (1982), 82-83, based on Lower Austrian data.
85. Patrouch (1994), 75-76.
86. The division is explained in Jeserich, Pohl, and Unruh (1983), 472; and by Evans (1979), 158-62.
87. Schindling and Ziegler (1989-93), vol. 1:126-29.
88. Parker (1987), 19, marks the turning point in the Empire at the Cologne War (1583-88).
89. Evans (1973), 278.
90. Midelfort (1994), 128.
91. The following is based on Evans (1973) and (1979).
92. Clark (1985).
93. Schilling (1985); Roeck (1991), 62-66; Schilling (1988a), 380-81.
94. See Brian P. Levack, in this *Handbook*, vol. 2:607-40; Midelfort (1972).
95. Behringer (1988), 414-15.
96. Ibid., 417 and n. 39.
97. Evans (1973), 284.
98. Ibid., 2-3.
99. Dotzauer (1989), 27.
100. Quoted by Schulze (1978), 61 n. 99. See Vocelka (1981), 246-78.
101. Schulze (1978), 369.
102. Ibid., 366.
103. See Evans (1973), 84-115.
104. Rabe (1976).
105. See Press (1991), 161-94, for an overview.
106. Quoted by Vocelka (1981), 154.
107. Quoted by Parker (1987), 44.
108. Quoted in ibid., from a Czech source.
109. Ibid.; Schormann (1985); a good, brief overview by Bonney (1991), 188-203.

110. The long debate is summarized by Christopher R. Friedrichs in Parker (1987), 208-15; and by Schormann (1985), 112-20.
111. Parker (1987), 111.
112. Quoted by Michael Roberts, "The Swedish Dilemma, 1633-41," in Parker (1987), 157; and there, too, the following quote.
113. The quoted passages come from Parker (1987), 144.
114. Dickmann (1959).
115. R. J. W. Evans, "The Imperial Vision," in Parker (1987), 83-88.

BIBLIOGRAPHY

Abray, Lorna Jane. *The People's Reformation: Magistrates, Clergy, and Commons in Strasbourg, 1520-1599.* New Haven, 1985.

Albrecht, Dieter. "Die kirchlich-religiöse Entwicklung. Zweiter Teil: 1500-1745." In *Handbuch der bayerischen Geschichte*, ed. Max Spindler, vol. 2: 626-56. 2d ed. Munich, 1977a [1966].

Albrecht, Dieter. "Das konfessionelle Zeitalter. Zweiter Teil: Die Herzöge Wilhelm V. und Maximilian I." *In Handbuch der bayerischen Geschichte*, ed. Max Spindler, vol. 2:351-410. 2d ed. Munich, 1977b [1966].

Bauerreiss, Romuald, O.S.B. *Kirchengeschichte Bayerns.* Vol. 6, *Das sechzehnte Jahrhundert.* Munich, 1965.

Behringer, Wolfgang. *Hexenverfolgung in Bayern. Volksmagie, Glaubenseifer und Staatsräson in der Frühen Neuzeit.* Munich, 1988.

Bireley, Robert. *The Counter-Reformation Prince: Anti-Machiavellianism or Catholic Statecraft in Early Modern Europe.* Chapel Hill, 1990.

Bireley, Robert, S.J. "Early Modern Germany." In *Catholicism in Early Modern History. A Guide to Research*, ed. John W. O'Malley, S.J., 11-30. St. Louis, 1988.

Blaschke, Karlheinz. *Sachsen im Zeitalter der Reformation.* SVRG, vol. 185. Gütersloh, 1970.

Bonney, Richard. *The European Dynastic States, 1494-1660.* Oxford, 1991.

Brady, Thomas A., Jr. *Protestant Politics: Jacob Sturm of Strasbourg and the German Reformation.* Studies in German Histories. Atlantic Highlands, N.J., 1995.

Brecht, Martin, and Reinhard Schwarz, eds. *Bekenntnis und Einheit der Kirche. Studien zum Konkordienbuch.* Stuttgart, 1980.

Chaix, Gérard. *Réforme et Contre-Réforme catholiques. Recherches sur la Chartreuse de Cologne au 16e siècle.* 3 vols. Analecta Cartusiana, vol. 80. Salzburg, 1981.

Chrisman, Miriam U. *Lay Culture, Learned Culture: Books and Social Change in Strasbourg, 1480-1599.* New Haven, 1982.

Clark, Peter, ed. *The European Crisis of the 1590s.* London, 1985.

Cohn, Henry J. "Church Property in the German Protestant Principalities." In *Politics and Society in Reformation Europe: Essays for Sir Geoffrey Elton on his Sixty-Fifth Birthday*, ed. E. I. Kouri and Tom Scott, 158-87. London: Macmillan Press, 1987.

Cohn, Henry J. "The Territorial Princes in Germany's Second Reformation." In *International Calvinism, 1541-1715*, ed. Minna Prestwich, 139-65. Oxford, 1985.

Dickens, Arthur Geoffrey, and John Tonkin. *The Reformation in Historical Thought.* Cambridge, Mass., 1986.

Dickmann, Fritz. *Der Westfälische Frieden.* Münster, 1959.

Dotzauer, Winfried. *Die deutschen Reichskreise in der Verfassung des alten Reiches und ihr Eigenleben (1500-1806).* Darmstadt, 1989.

Duchhardt, Heinz. *Deutsche Verfassungsgeschichte 1495-1806.* Urban-Taschenbücher, vol. 417. Stuttgart, 1991.

Duchhardt, Heinz. *Protestantisches Kaisertum und altes Reich. Die Diskussion über die Konfession des Kaisers in Politik, Publizistik und Staatsrecht.* Wiesbaden, 1977.

Evans, R. J. W. *The Making of the Habsburg Monarchy, 1550-1700. An Interpretation.* Oxford, 1979.

Evans, R. J. W. *Rudolph II and His World.* Oxford, 1973.

Forster, Marc R. *The Counter-Reformation in the Villages: Religion and Reform in the Bishopric of Speyer, 1560-1720.* Ithaca, 1992.

Fritz, Eberhard. *dieweil sie so arme Leuth: Fünf Albdörfer zwischen Religion und Politik 1530-1750. Studien zur Kirchengeschichte der Dörfer Bernloch, Eglingen, Meidelstetten, Oberstetten und Ödenwaldstetten.* Quellen und Forschungen zur Württembergischen Geschichte, vol. 9. Stuttgart, 1989.

Glawischnig, Rolf. *Niederlande, Kalvinismus und Reichsgrafenstand (1559-1584). Nassau-Dillenburg unter Graf Johann VI.* Schriften des hessischen Landesamtes für geschichtliche Landeskunde, vol. 36. Marburg, 1973.

Greyerz, Kaspar von. *The Late City Reformation in German: the Case of Colmar, 1522-1618.* VIEG, vol. 98. Wiesbaden, 1980.

Gross, Hanns. *Empire and Sovereignty: A History of the Public Law Literature in the Holy Roman Empire, 1599-1804.* 2d ed. Chicago, 1975.

Head, Randolph C. *Early Modern Democracy in the Grisons: Society and Politics in a Swiss Mountain Canton.* Cambridge, 1994.

Heckel, Martin. "*Autonomia* und *Pacis Compositio.* Der Augsburger Religionsfriede in der Deutung der Gegenreformation." *ZSR, KA* 45 (1959): 141-248.

Heckel, Martin. *Deutschland im konfessionellen Zeitalter.* Deutsche Geschichte, vol. 5. Göttingen, 1983.

Heckel, Martin. *Staat und Kirche.* Munich, 1968.

Hollweg, W. *Der Augsburger Reichstag von 1566 und seine Bedeutung für die Entstehung der Reformierten Kirche und ihres Bekenntnisses.* Neukirchen, 1964.

Hsia, R. Po-chia. *Social Discipline in the Reformation: Central Europe, 1550-1750.* London and New York, 1989.

Hsia, R. Po-chia. *Society and Religion in Münster, 1535-1618.* New Haven, 1984.

Jeserich, Kurt G. A., Hans Pohl, and Georg-Christoph von Unruh, eds. *Deutsche Verwaltungsgeschichte.* Vol. 1, *Vom Spätmittelalter bis zum Ende des Reiches.* Stuttgart, 1983.

Kastner, Ruth, ed. *Quellen zur Reformation 1517-1555.* Darmstadt, 1994.

Klein, Thomas. *Der Kampf um die zweite Reformation in Kursachsen 1586-1591.* Mitteldeutsche Forschungen, vol. 27. Cologne and Graz, 1962.

Klueting, Harm. *Das konfessionelle Zeitalter 1525-1648.* Stuttgart, 1989.

Knox, R. Buick. "The Making of a Reforming Prince: Frederick III Elector Palatine." In *Reformation, Conformity and Dissent. Essays in Honour of Dr Geoffrey Nuttall,* ed. R. Buick Knox, 44-69. London, 1977.

Lohse, Bernhard. "Das Konkordienwerk von 1580." In *Kirche und Bekenntnis,* ed. Peter Meinhold, 94-122. Wiesbaden, 1980.

Lutz, Heinrich. *Christianitas afflicta: Europa, das Reich und die päpstliche Politik im Niedergang der Hegemonie Kaiser Karls V. (1552-1556).* Göttingen, 1964.

Lutz, Heinrich. "Das konfessionelle Zeitalter. Erster Teil: Die Herzöge Wilhelm IV. und Albrecht V." In *Handbuch der bayerischen Geschichte,* ed. Max Spindler, vol. 2: 297-350. 2d ed. Munich, 1977 [1966].

Lutz, Heinrich. *Das Ringen um deutsche Einheit und kirchliche Erneuerung. Von Maximilian I. bis zum Westfälischen Frieden 1490 bis 1648.* Propyläen Geschichte Deutschlands, vol. 4. Berlin, 1983.

MacHardy, Karin J. "Der Einfluß von Status, Konfession und Besitz auf das politische Verhalten des niederösterreichischen Ritterstandes 1580-1620." In *Spezialforschung und "Gesamtgeschichte,"* ed. Grete Klingenstein und Heinrich Lutz, 56-83. Wiener Beiträge zur Geschichte der Neuzeit, vol. 8. Munich, 1982.

Maltby, William S., ed. *Reformation Europe: A Guide to Research, II.* St. Louis, 1992.

May, Georg. *Die deutschen Bischöfe angesichts der Glaubensspaltung im 16. Jahrhundert.* Vienna, 1983.

Midelfort, H. C. Erik. *Mad Princes of Renaissance Germany.* Charlottesville, 1994.

Midelfort, H. C. Erik. *Witch Hunting in Southwestern Germany, 1562-1648: the Social and Intellectual Foundations.* Stanford, 1972.

Moeller, Bernd. *Reichsstadt und Reformation.* 2d ed. Berlin, 1987 [1962].

Molitor, Hansgeorg. *Kirchliche Reformversuche der Kurfürsten und Erzbischöfe von Trier im Zeitalter der Gegenreformation.* VIEG, vol. 43. Wiesbaden, 1967.

Münch, Paul. *Zucht und Ordnung. Reformierte Kirchenverfassungen im 16. und 17. Jahrhundert (Nassau-Dillenburg, Kurpfalz, Hessen-Kassel).* SFN, vol. 3. Stuttgart, 1978.

Muralt, Leonhard von. "Renaissance und Reformation." In *Handbuch der Schweizer Geschichte,* vol. 1:389-570. 2d ed. Zurich, 1980 [1970].

Neveux, J. B. *Vie spirituelle et vie sociale entre Rhin et Baltique au XVIIe siècle de J. Arndt à P. J. Spener.* Publications de la Faculté des Lettres et Sciences Humaines de Paris-Nanterre. Paris, 1967.

Nischan, Bodo. *Prince, People, and Confession: The Second Reformation in Brandenburg.* Philadelphia, 1994.

Oberman, Heiko A. "*Europa afflicta.* The Reformation of the Refugees." *ARG* 83 (1992): 91-111.

O'Malley, John W., S.J. *The Early Jesuits.* Cambridge, Mass., 1993.

Ortner, Franz. *Reformation, katholische Reform und Gegenreformation im Erzstift Salzburg.* Salzburg, 1981.

Parker, Geoffrey. *The Thirty Years' War.* London, 1987 [1984].

Patrouch, Joseph F. "The Investiture Controversy Revisited: Religious Reform, Emperor Maximilian II, and the Klosterrat." *Austrian History Yearbook* 25 (1994): 59-78.

Press, Volker. *Calvinismus und Territorialstaat. Regierung und Zentralbehörden der Kurpfalz 1559-1619.* Kieler Historische Studien, vol. 7. Stuttgart, 1970.

Press, Volker. *Kriege und Krisen. Deutschland 1600-1715.* Die Neue Deutsche Geschichte, vol. 5. Munich, 1991.

Rabe, Horst. "Der Augsburger Religionsfriede und das Reichskammergericht 1555-1600." In *Festschrift für Ernst Walter Zeeden,* ed. Hansgeorg Molitor, Horst Rabe, and Hans-Christoph Rublack, 260-80. Reformationsgeschichte Studien und Texte, suppl. vol. 2. Münster in Westfalen, 1976.

Rabe, Horst. *Deutsche Geschichte 1500-1600. Das Jahrhundert der Glaubensspaltung.* Munich, 1991.

Rabe, Horst. *Reichsbund und Interim: Die Verfassungs- und Religionspolitik Karls V. und der Reichstag von Augsburg 1547/48.* Cologne and Vienna, 1971.

Reingrabner, Gustav. *Adel und Reformation. Beiträge zur Geschichte des protestantischen Adels im Lande unter der Enns während des 16. und 17. Jahrhunderts.* Forschungen zur Landeskunde von Niederösterreich, vol. 21. Vienna, 1976.

Reinhard, Wolfgang. "Katholische Reform und Gegenreformation in der Kölner Nuntiatur 1584-1641." *Römische Quartalschrift* 66 (1971): 8-65.

Reinhard, Wolfgang. "Reformation, Counter-Reformation and the Early Modern State: A Reassessment." *CHR* 75 (1989): 383-404.

Reinhard, Wolfgang. "Zwang zur Konfessionalisierung? Prolegomena zu either Theorie des konfessionellen Zeitalters." *ZHF* 10 (1983): 257-77.

Reinhard, Wolfgang and Heinz Schilling, eds. *Die katholische Konfessionalisierung. Akten eines vom Corpus Catholicorum und Verein für Reformationsgeschichte veranstalteten Symposions, Augsburg, 1993.* Gütersloh, 1994.

Robisheaux, Thomas. *Rural Society and the Search for Order in Early Modern Germany.* Cambridge, 1989.

Roeck, Bernd. *Als wollt die Welt schier brechen. Eine Stadt im Zeitalter des Dreißigjährigen Krieges.* Munich, 1991.

Roper, Lyndal. *The Holy Household: Women and Morals in Reformation Augsburg.* Oxford, 1989.

Rublack, Hans-Christoph, ed. *Die lutherische Konfessionalisierung in Deutschland. Wissenschaftliches Symposium des Vereins für Reformationsgeschichte.* SVRG, no. 197. Gütersloh, 1992.

Rublack, Hans-Christoph. *Gescheiterte Reformation. Frühreformatorische und protestantische Bewegungen in süd- und westdeutschen geistlichen Residenzen.* Spätmittelalter und Frühe Neuzeit. Tübinger Beiträge zur Geschichtsforschung, vol. 4. Stuttgart, 1978.

Safley, Thomas Max. *Let No Man Put Asunder: the Control of Marriage in the German Southwest. A Comparative Study, 1550-1600.* Kirksville, Mo., 1984.

Schilling, Heinz. *Aufbruch und Krise. Deutschland 1517-1648.* Berlin, 1988a.

Schilling, Heinz. "The European Crisis of the 1590s: the Situation in German Towns." In *The European Crisis of the 1590s,* ed. Peter Clark, 135-56. London, 1985.

Schilling, Heinz. "Die Konfessionalisierung im Reich. Religiöser und gesellschaftlicher Wandel in Deutschland zwischen 1555 und 1620." *HZ* 146 (1988b): 1-45.

Schilling, Heinz, ed. *Die reformierte Konfessionalisierung in Deutschland—Das Problem der "Zweiten Reformation." Wissenschaftliches Symposion des Vereins für Reformationsgeschichte 1985.* SVRG, vol. 195. Gütersloh, 1986.

Schilling, Heinz. *Religion, Political Culture and the Emergence of Early Modern Society. Essays in German and Dutch History.* SMRT, vol. 50. Leiden, 1992.

Schindling, Anton. "Die Reformation in den Reichsstädten und die Kirchengüter. Straßburg, Nürnberg und Frankfurt im Vergleich." In *Bürgerschaft und Kirche,* ed. Jürgen Sydow, 67-88. Stadt in der Geschichte, vol. 7. Sigmaringen, 1980.

Schindling, Anton. "Reichskirche und Reformation. Zu Glaubensspaltung und Konfessionalisierung in den geistlichen Fürstentümern des Reiches." In *Neue Studien zur frühneuzeitlichen Reichsgeschichte,* ed. Johannes Kunisch, 81-112. Zeitschrift für Historische Forschungen, suppl. vol. 3. Berlin, 1987.

Schindling, Anton, and Walter Ziegler, eds. *Die Territorien des Reichs im Zeitalter der Reformation und Konfessionalisierung. Land und Konfession 1500-1650.* 4 vols. Katholisches Leben und Kirchenreform im Zeitalter der Glaubensspaltung, vols. 49-52. Münster I. W., 1989-93.

Schmidt, Georg, ed. *Stände und Gesellschaft im Alten Reich.* VIEG, Abteilung Universalgeschichte, Beiheft 29. Stuttgart, 1989.

Schmidt, Peter. *Das Collegium Germanicum in Rom und die Germaniker.* Tübingen, 1984.

Schormann, Gerhard. *Der Dreißigjährige Krieg.* Göttingen, 1985.

Schulze, Manfred. *Fürsten und Reformation. Geistliche Reformpolitik weltlicher Fürsten vor der Reformation.* Spätmittelalter und Reformation, n. s., vol. 2. Tübingen, 1991.

Schulze, Winfried. "Concordia, Discordia, Tolerantia. Deutsche Politik im konfessionellen Zeitalter." In *Neue Studien zur frühneuzeitlichen Reichsgeschichte,* ed. Johannes Kunisch, 43-79. Zeitschrift für Historische Forschungen, suppl. vol. 3. Berlin, 1987.

Schulze, Winfried. *Reich und Türkengefahr im späten 16. Jahrhundert. Studien zu den politischen und gesellschaftlichen Auswirkungen einer äußeren Bedrohung.* Munich, 1978.

Scribner, Robert W. *For the Sake of Simple Folk: Popular Propaganda for the German Reformation.* Cambridge, 1981.

Scribner, Robert W. *Popular Culture and Popular Movements in Reformation Germany.* London, 1987.

Seibrich, Wolfgang. *Gegenreformation als Restauration. Die restaurativen Bemühungen der alten Orden im Deutschen Reich von 1580 bis 1648.* Münster, 1991.

Soergel, Philip M. *Wondrous in His Saints: Counter-Reformation Propagana in Bavaria.* Berkeley and Los Angeles, 1993.

Stadler, Peter. "Das Zeitalter der Gegenreformation." In *Handbuch der Schweizer Geschichte,* 2d ed., vol. 1:571-672. Zurich, 1980.

Strauss, Gerald. *Luther's House of Learning: Indoctrination of the Young in the German Reformation.* Baltimore, 1978.

Theibault, John. "The Rhetoric of Death and Destruction in the Thirty Years War." *Journal of Social History* 27 (1994): 271-90.

Traitler, Hildegard. *Konfession und Politik. Interkonfessionalle Flugschriftenpolemik aus Süddeutschland und Österreich (1564-1612).* European University Studies, series 3, vol. 400. Frankfurt am Main, Bern, New York, and Paris, 1989.

Vocelka, Karl. *Die politische Propaganda Kaiser Rudolfs II. (1576-1612).* Veröffentlichungen der Kommission für die Geschichte Österreichs, 9. Vienna, 1981.

Warmbrunn, Paul. *Zwei Konfessionen in einer Stadt. Das Zusammenleben von Katholicken und Protestanten in den partitätischen Reichsstädten Augsburg, Biberach, Ravensburg und Dinkelsbühl 1548-1648.* Wiesbaden, 1983.

Wirsching, Andreas. "Konfessionalisierung und Außenpolitik. Die Kurpfalz und der Beginn der französischen Religionskriege (1559-1562)." *HJ* 106 (1986): 333-60.

Zeeden, Ernst Walter. *Die Entstehung der Konfessionen. Grundlagen und Formen der Konfessionsbildung im Zeitalter der Glaubenskämpfe.* Munich, 1965.

Zeeden, Ernst Walter. "Grundlagen und Wege der Konfessionsbildung in Deutschland im Zeitalter der Glaubenskämpfe." *HZ* 185 (1958): 249-99.

Zeeden, Ernst Walter. *Konfessionsbildung. Studien zur Reformation, Ggenreformation und katholischen Reform.* Stuttgart, 1985.

Zschunke, Paul. *Konfession und Alltag im Oppenheim. Beiträge zur Geschichte von Bevölkerung und Gesellschaft einer gemischtkonfessionellen Kleinstadt in der frühen Neuzeit.* Wiesbaden, 1984.

SETTLEMENTS: THE NETHERLANDS

J.J. Woltjer and M.E.H.N. Mout
(Rijksuniversiteit Leiden)

1. On the Eve of the Reformation

In the early sixteenth century the Church in the Netherlands presented roughly the same picture as in the greater part of Europe. Dioceses covered vast territories, and the bishops of Liège and (until 1528) of Utrecht reigned as princes over substantial parts of their bishoprics, which made them more like secular rulers than spiritual leaders. They were recruited from among the high nobility or even princely dynasties, for whom these episcopal sees played an important role in their struggle for power. Other bishops and many canons also belonged to the high aristocracy. Episcopal power was, however, severely limited by the privileges of archdeacons, chapters and the like. The appointment of parish priests was more often than not in the hands of the prince or the local lord. He could use his right of collation to appoint good priests, but often he used rich benefices to reward favourites or their relatives.[1] Sometimes town councils tried to take over the collations because they were dissatisfied with the priests appointed by the church authorities and might even be willing to pay extra for a good cleric.[2] It is nearly impossible to get a clear picture of the beliefs of the common man and to find out what compulsory weekly attendance at mass or annual confession and communion meant to him.

Evidence of dissident opinions and beliefs is rare. Judicial records occasionally mention blasphemy, defamation of the sacrament or of the Virgin, without, however, providing the context. One Master Herman of Rijswijk even said he was not a Christian and praised Averroes. After an earlier recantation, he was burnt as a relapsed heretic in The Hague in 1512, together with his books.[3] On the other hand, many clerics excommunicated members of their flock with the greatest ease for very minor offences or debts, thus making it clear that they themselves did not take excommunication wholly seriously.[4]

It is equally difficult to discern the seeds of change in religious life. It seems probable that the Church itself did not provide much inspira-

THE LOW COUNTRIES IN 1555

———————— Dutch provinces
– – – – – – Walloon provinces
· · · · · · · · · Linguistic boundary

tion for reform. The historiography of the early Reformation in the Netherlands used to stress the importance of the fifteenth-century spiritual lay movement of the Modern Devotion and, in its wake, of Christian humanism. Today, scholars doubt whether such a straight and simple pedigree can be constructed. The spirituality of the Modern Devotion aimed at meditation on the Passion of Christ and the imitation of His example. The Bible was read in the vernacular, but such reading was mainly restricted to the gospels because many other parts were deemed too difficult for the unlearned. Many of the houses, originally communities of lay brothers and sisters, gradually came to adopt a monastic rule of life and thus conformed to the tradition of the Church instead of seeking new paths. The Modern Devotion had a continued effect on the Jesuits rather than on the Reformation. The fact that in the seventeenth century many a Dutch Protestant wrote reverently of Thomas à Kempis' *Imitation of Christ* does not mean that there was a direct influence.[5]

Christian humanism provides a more likely foundation for early evangelical dissent and desire for reform. Humanism came relatively late to the Netherlands but it found a good school system with schoolmasters who enthusiastically attacked poor grammar and barbarous letters. The insistence of the Christian humanists on the importance of study of the Bible in the original and of the works of the Church Fathers worried many churchmen, especially after Erasmus in 1516 published his translation of the New Testament, which differed from the Vulgate. At Louvain, the Collegium Trilingue was founded (1518), where the sacred languages Hebrew, Greek and Latin were taught. But Jacobus Latomus, a leading Louvain theologian, knew that scholarship at the Collegium was not always bound by orthodox beliefs or piety. Among the first Dutch dissenters were humanists who saw a link between humanist studies and the interest in Bible reading and stressed the importance of the early Church as an example for reform plans.[6]

The initiative to reorganize the Church was, in the end, not taken by the ecclesiastical, but by the secular authorities. Their aim was to strengthen the administration in the hope that this would improve the life of the church as well. The new scheme was the fruit of an agreement between the Pope and king Philip II in 1559 after years of delay and negotiations. It was decided to create three archbishoprics and fifteen bishoprics, the boundaries of which would follow the political frontiers. Thus, no foreign prince of the Church would henceforward have authority in the Netherlands. Following the example of the

French, the king would officially only nominate, but in practice appoint the bishops.

The new scheme met with opposition of very different kinds. Six of the new bishops could only be installed in 1568-70 under the protection of the new Governor, the Duke of Alba. There was resentment in conservative church circles, among aggrieved foreign bishops and others who would loose authority and income under the new scheme. The new bishops were expected to have a degree in theology, and this automatically excluded the high nobility. There were political objections as well, because the new bishops would be creatures of the king and take their seat in the Estates, where they would boost royal influence. And, last but not least, there were secret fears that in a streamlined Church organization the new bishops would be able and willing to attack heterodoxy more effectively.[7] This posed a serious problem, for by the time the new bishoprics' scheme was implemented many people held unorthodox views in all sorts of gradations.

2. First Protestant Influences

In the Netherlands both opponents and supporters regarded Erasmus and Luther as allies in the struggle for Church reform and religious renewal. Several tracts by Luther were printed in translation in Antwerp and Leiden as early as 1520 and some Dutch writers such as the author of the *Summa der Godliker Scrifturen* (Summary of Holy Writ) expressed similar ideas. The influence of Luther's early publications was significant, but his later polemics with Erasmus about free will and his combative arguments about Holy Communion found much less response.[8]

Some believers turned away from traditional piety and ecclesiastical teachings in ways of which Luther explicitly disapproved. Thus in about 1521 Cornelis Hoen, a lawyer in The Hague, wrote a treatise in which he denied the Real Presence in the eucharist: 'this is My Body' really meant 'this signifies My Body'. The rector of the Utrecht house of the Modern Devotion, Hinne Rode, probably took the treatise to Luther—who disagreed with it—and later to Bucer and Zwingli, who gave their support.[9] There must have been many others who on the strength of their own ideas and older heterodox traditions came to similar or even more radical conclusions. In 1521 the papal nuncio Girolamo Aleander drew attention to heretics in Artois who long before had regarded the eucharist as a symbol.[10] A great diversity of opinions must have been typical of these early Protestant influences.

The Emperor Charles V and the theological faculty of Louvain made concerted efforts to stamp out dissident opinions. The faculty condemned Luther's teachings as early as November 1519, months before the Pope did, and in September 1520 the Emperor ordered the destruction of Luther's books in the Netherlands. The suppression of heresy was traditionally in the hands of the episcopal and papal inquisition, while the secular authorities executed the sentences, including capital punishment. But in 1522 Charles V appointed a layman as general inquisitor, who was, however, not a success. Heresy and heretical clerics remained a matter for the Church to judge but lay heretics were punished by secular courts because they contravened the edicts of Charles V.

Between 1518 and 1528 roughly four hundred persons were sentenced because of dissident opinions or the possession of forbidden books and twelve of them were condemned to death. The persecutions continued after 1528 and were even intensified: from 1529 every heretic, including those who repented, had to be sentenced to death. Many inquisitors thought this was wrong, because it made reconciliation of repentant heretics impossible. Dissidents had every interest in lying low, and it is therefore difficult to estimate their numbers, let alone their importance. They figure in official documents only when caught, and these sources stress only what interested the authorities. The persecution of dissidents was, however, a very unpopular cause. The higher secular authorities certainly took the lead, but local powers were often not very eager to follow and made use of all possible legal objections in order to tone down the persecutive zeal of others. Often fellow townsmen could be protected by municipal privileges, but this did not work for foreigners who were convicted with greater frequency.[11] This general unwillingness to persecute has often been linked with Erasmus. Erasmianism, a term implying aversion to religious persecution and fundamental tolerance of dissidents as long as they do not disturb the peace, is sometimes seen as a general undercurrent of Dutch history. Erasmus was, undoubtedly, by far the most famous and most influential Dutch humanist, but he did not invent 'Erasmianism', as the tradition is in all probability much older and more complex.

Luther's fellow-Augustinians in Antwerp and elsewhere were among the first to preach the new ideas. Their prior, Jacobus Praepositus, recanted in 1522, but relapsed soon afterwards. He and his successor, Hendrik of Zutphen, were fortunate enough to be able to flee. Hendrik Vos (Voes) and Jan of Essen stuck to their views and were the first to be burnt (1523). Other clerics and humanists, like the Antwerp town secretary Cornelius Grapheus and several rectors of Latin schools, were persecuted. Soon many artisans were attracted by heretical ideas. The Bible and heretical tracts were read and discussed in secret in private homes. Sometimes the documents name a priest as the centre of such a circle.[12]

In the thirties one of the sources of inspiration for dissidents became the strong eschatological tradition of the Middle Ages. Eschatological expectations assumed a central importance in the teachings of a wandering German lay preacher, Melchior Hoffman (c. 1500-43). He was convinced that only a divinely inspired prophet would be able to discover the true meaning of biblical texts. Needless to say, this conviction gave him great freedom of interpretation. In his commentary on Daniel of 1526, he predicted terrible sufferings for true Christians until the Second Coming and the Last Judgement in the year 1533. Later he began to advocate the extirpation of papists and godless people. While in Strasbourg he sided with the Anabaptists, but it is not known whether he himself was rebaptized. In 1530 Hoffman went to East Frisia where he rebaptized many local and Dutch believers, as a sign that as an adult they had joined the true church of their own free will. During the next few years the number of Melchiorites in the Netherlands grew steadily, especially in Frisia, Holland and Zeeland. Hoffman himself was said to have rebaptized about fifty people in Amsterdam during the summer of 1531. But after the execution of one of his collaborators, he ordered a staying of baptisms.[13]

In the meantime Bernhard Rothmann had turned his church in the Westphalian town of Munster into a Protestant one. As a result of the rapid spread of Protestantism the town, which harboured many fugitives from the neighbouring Netherlands, was at loggerheads with the bishop of Munster. One of Hoffman's followers in Amsterdam, Jan Matthijs of Haarlem, had received new revelations and started to rebaptize on All Souls' Day 1533. Rebaptism now acquired a special apocalyptic significance and would protect the true believers at the Last Judgement. Matthijs sent 'apostolic messengers' to Munster, who introduced rebaptism there. In due course the Anabaptists took over and drove away those inhabitants who refused to join the movement. Matthijs became the leader of this 'New Jerusalem' and after his death he was succeeded by Jan Beukelsz of Leiden. An economic crisis heightened the response to this kingdom of God and thousands wanted to obey the summons to Munster, especially in Holland and Frisia, but they were stopped by the authorities. Plans for coups in Amsterdam and Leiden were also thwarted, but in the spring of 1535 Anabaptists held a Frisian monastery for a week against government troops, and a coup in Amsterdam was defeated with much bloodshed.[14] Six weeks later Munster fell.

The destruction of Munster did not lead to the end of Anabaptism in the Netherlands. 'Batenburgers'—named after their leader Jan van Batenburg—continued the revengeful fight against the godless pillaging farms and monasteries much like ordinary robber gangs. After some time David Joris (c. 1501-56) emerged as the most important Anabaptist leader who considered it his task to reunite the Melchiorites after the disaster of Munster. He was an inspired preacher but an obscure writer who paid special attention to the Holy Cross and the sufferings of Christ, and considered the sacraments of secondary importance. He discouraged martyrdom and allowed his followers to receive the sacraments in whatever church happened to be in ascendance. His teachings became more and more spiritualist, condemning the idea of the visible church and stressing the personal responsibility of the faithful for the purity of their religious life in view of the approaching Day of Judgement. In 1544 he emigrated to Basel together with his most important followers. After his death the Jorist movement gradually disappeared, but his numerous writings continued to be read until well into the eighteenth century.[15]

The main rival of David Joris and, in the end, the most influential leader of a reorganized and spiritually revived Baptist movement was Menno Simons (1496-1561), a former priest who joined the Anabaptist movement only after the fall of Munster. His book *Dat Fundament des Christelycken Leers* (The Foundation of Christian Doctrine, first edition 1540, revised edition 1558) became very influential in the new Mennonite movement. The Mennonites were better organized than the Jorists and formed a 'brotherhood' where they practised rebaptism after the candidate had professed his faith. They shunned the evil world and the no less evil established churches. Because of their defence of free will, rebaptism and the purely symbolic significance of the sacraments they differed considerably from both Lutheranism and Calvinism. Most Mennonites refused to bear arms or to hold public offices. Their following increased considerably during the second half of the sixteenth century, but so did discord within their ranks and they became notorious for their numerous quarrels and schisms. Especially during and after the Munster troubles Anabaptists were heavily persecuted because of their often violent actions. It took a long time before the authorities realized that Mennonites were peaceful people and had lost the revolutionary drive of the Melchiorites or Batenburgers. The majority of martyrs in the Netherlands had a Baptist background.[16]

No less endangered were the members of the spiritualist sect the Family of Love, founded around 1540 by the Amsterdam merchant Hendrik Niclaes (1502-80), whose teachings were close to Anabaptism and Jorism. He repudiated the visible church as mediator between man and God and emphasized the belief that man was capable of attaining a stage of sinless perfection during his earthly life. He expected the end of the world, disliked martyrdom and permitted his followers to join any church. In view of these teachings, which were propagated in numerous writings, it is not surprising that members of the sect —and the later breakaway group the 'Liefhebbers der Waarheid' (Lovers of Truth) led by Niclaes' former disciple Hendrik Jansen van Barrevelt alias Hiël—were treated as heretics by the established churches. The sect attracted artists and intellectuals in and outside the Netherlands who subscribed to Familism during certain periods of their lives, the most famous being the Antwerp printer Christophe Plantin, the Spanish theologian Benito Arias Montano and the Dutch humanist Justus Lipsius. They combined their Familist eschatological beliefs with Christian neo-stoicism, pursuing virtue with a cheerful mind, knowing that the world was to be held in contempt because the end was near. Like the Jorists, the Familist circle dwindled after the death of their leaders.[17]

3. THE COMING OF THE CALVINISTS

In the forties Protestants of varied persuasions were to be found all over Europe. They agreed about what to reject in the old Church: mass, monastic life, indulgences, celibacy and papal power. This 'negative reformation' had sweeping consequences for the life of the old Church, but the ideas about a 'positive reformation', about what might replace what had been rejected were diverse. Luther and Melanchthon, Zwingli, Bullinger, Bucer and Calvin held very divergent opinions while spiritualists like Sebastian Franck and Caspar Schwenckfeld considered all forms of ecclesiastical organization unnecessary. They all found a response in the Netherlands through translations or summaries of their writings, and native theologians also aired their opinions. Around 1550 the Mennonites were still the only ones who had radically broken with the Church and built a new religious organization instead. The Jorists and Familists were expecting the end of the world too eagerly to care for any form of religious organization or ceremonies and simply joined the local church. Others, like Schwenckfeld, censured this behaviour but did not found their own religious groups. Most of the other dissenters did not leave the Church immediately, and not only because of the persecutions. They continued to hope for its renewal or for a compromise between old and new. They wanted to reform the Church from within and rejected a schism in the local church, which would have had much graver immediate consequences than a breach between the local church and Rome. Therefore they stayed on as 'protestantizing' Catholics rather than as Protestants in the narrow sense of the word. These protestantizing Catholics did not form a coherent group but acted as individuals, adopting Protestant beliefs in a totally eclectic way. This attitude was encouraged by the fact that neither dogmatic differences nor the limit between an internal reformation and a Protestant one were yet clearly defined. In later years, some joined a Protestant church while others reverted to orthodox Catholicism.

In 1539 a chamber of rhetoric in Ghent organized a drama festival contest. The set subject for the morality plays was: what is the best way to console the dying? Some plays were steeped in Lutheran ideas and made trust in the grace of Christ a central point. Yet the members of these chambers regarded themselves as Catholics and the authorities did not punish them.[18] Small groups consisting of clerics and laymen secretly met in order to read the Bible or theological tracts, or to pray and to sing hymns. Some were discovered and persecuted by the authorities, but others probably slipped through the net. As Luther opposed the founding of schismatic and secret churches those who accepted his sacramental doctrines stayed in the old Church. Those professing the more radical ideas of Hoen or Zwingli were in a more difficult position because they refused to kneel before the host. Some priests made changes in the mass according to their new convictions. But in the end many people, both clerics and laymen, must have conformed outwardly under the threat of persecution. Calvin, however, rejected this so-called nicodemist behaviour on the grounds that no true Christian could take part in any 'popish superstitions' and should rather leave the country. An early attempt to found clandestine Protestant congregations in a number of Walloon towns failed in 1544. Believers had asked Bucer and Calvin for a minister in order to spread the true faith but also to fight Anabaptists and spiritualists. Pierre Brully, Calvin's successor as pastor to the refugee church in Strasbourg, was sent to the Netherlands, but after only a few months he was arrested and eventually burned at the stake. Some of the members of his congregation were also executed, others recanted, some had already fled the country.[19]

This and other cases of persecution were the beginning of a wave of emigration in the mid-forties. The emigrants founded refugee churches: in Wesel (1545), in London (1550) and Frankfurt (1554), and continued to do so wherever possible. These churches often had to face dangerous situations and, moreover, became seedbeds of internal conflicts. During Mary Tudor's reign Protestant refugees were forced to emigrate from England, and in Germany they were opposed by orthodox Lutherans or by artisans who feared competition. Some inhabitants of the Netherlands emigrated for economic reasons and became Protestants only later, by joining the refugee churches of their countrymen. Refugees from the Walloon provinces often went to France, where they joined the local churches. Many others fled to Emden in East Frisia, where there were no language problems for the Dutch in the local Protestant congregations and the francophones could have their own small refugee church.[20]

In spite of persecutions and public burnings groups of dissidents continued to exist or were formed anew in the Netherlands and sometimes they were visited by an itinerant pastor. Encouraged by the refugee churches a number of these secret groups in the Southern Netherlands developed into congregations, the 'churches under the Cross', complete with administration of the sacraments, ecclesiastical discipline and pastors trained in Emden or London. The contacts between the refugee churches and the 'churches under the Cross' were quite intensive and covered organizational as well as doctrinal matters. It often happened that a pastor had to move because there was a danger that the authorities might recognize him for what he really was and another pastor, either from a secret or a refugee congregation, would come to replace him. The safest place was Antwerp, the big merchant city where foreigners were not conspicuous and two thriving secret congregations, one Flemish and one Walloon, could exist. The town became the centre of the churches under the Cross and the place where synods were secretly held from 1562 onwards.

Many were strongly influenced by Calvin's teachings, not only as far as the rejection of any compromise with the old Church was concerned, but also in their general theological beliefs. Like Calvin, many believers drew a sharp dividing line between themselves and the old Church, demanding the renunciation of the 'papist' faith. It is no coincidence that Calvin's writings against nicodemists were the first of his works to be translated into Dutch.[21] It was, however, very difficult for members of these congregations to shun the old Church completely, not only because of the obligation to attend Sunday mass, but also because the authorities would not recognize a marriage contracted outside the Church, while any secret burial without the offices of a priest would be suspect.

At first the refugee churches and the churches under the Cross harboured a variety of opinions. But the militant Calvinists knew exactly what they wanted, or rather, what God wanted of them. Their clearcut doctrines and effective organization gave them a lead over other Protestant variants and protestantizing Catholics. Against the opposition of more moderate believers these Calvinists managed during the sixties to dominate the churches under the Cross and the refugee churches and to expel those who were not in agreement with their opinions.[22] Guido de Brès, a minister who was active in Tournai and neigbouring towns such as Mons, Valenciennes and Lille, drew up a confession of faith, the 'Confessio Belgica' (published 1561 in Rouen). It was not a slavish copy of the French Calvinist 'Confessio Gallicana', but it was written in a kindred spirit.[23] Their rugged Calvinism, however, prevented these churches from becoming the centre of all criticism of the old Church. Many moderates were repelled by the prevailing atmosphere of severity and exclusivity and preferred to stay in the Catholic Church, however flawed it was, because they were certain that they would never feel at home among the militant Calvinists.

The persecutions were as unpopular as ever with most citizens and many magistrates taking a lenient point of view. The rejection of severe punishments for heretics was usually not inspired by much sympathy with their ideas, but by political and humanitarian considerations: persecutions caused social and political unrest, and as long as heretics did not stir up trouble they ought not to be punished for what were only spiritual errors. Others, however, supported the official policy of repression. Often one court case led to a number of others if the authorities managed to extort information from suspects about their co-believers. Therefore, the persecutions tended to come in waves, but even in quiet times one could never be certain how and when the severe heresy laws would be enforced. This uncertainty sometimes led to reckless behaviour by the Calvinists. Inspired by French examples Calvinists in Valenciennes and Tournai took the risk of a procession through the town singing psalms, although their pastor had opposed it. The local magistrates punished these 'chanteries' leniently, but the government in Brussels sent special emissaries to deal with it.[24]

Although the laws, and sometimes also the authorities, were merciless, persecutions came to a standstill in large parts of the Netherlands at the end of the fifties and the beginning of the sixties. After 1553 there were no more executions in Amsterdam, although the town harboured many Mennonites. In Frisia the last death sentences were pronounced under heavy pressure from Brussels in 1559. Almost everywhere the local authorities had serious doubts about the usefulness and the appropriateness of severe punishments meted out to otherwise quiet and law-abiding heretics. Sometimes there was popular protest, as in Rotterdam in 1558, where the executioner and the mayors of the town had to flee when a mob freed four Baptists who had been sentenced to death. In other places prisoners were freed from their dungeons or even on their way to the stake. In 1564 the burning of a well-known Calvinist preacher, Christophorus Fabricius, led to unrest in Antwerp. But opposition and sabotage did not stop the inquisitor Pieter Titelmans in Flanders and Tournai, and the year 1562 even became a high point with forty executions.[25]

Wherever local authorities considered themselves beyond the reach of the central government the latitude of religious beliefs which the old Church tolerated could be remarkable. A priest in Leeuwarden (Frisia) did not know whether the eucharist was the Lord's Body or not and was therefore given dispensation from celebrating mass. After he got a doctorate at the Protestant University of Heidelberg the town of Groningen did not mind employing him as a parish priest. After the death of a protestantizing priest in Deventer a successor was appointed who had studied in Calvinist Geneva. The central government forced him to step down, but the next incumbent was not orthodox either.[26]

Because of the toleration of these protestantizing attitudes within the old Church and of the successes of the Mennonites, there was not much room in the northeastern part of the Netherlands for the Calvinist churches under the Cross. Before 1566, there are no traces of Calvinist consistories north of Breda and Middelburg. An attempt made in 1557 to found a Protestant church in Groningen soon failed. Some towns, for instance Amsterdam, asked the Emden church to send pastors, but this did not lead to the formation of congregations—only to the increase of itinerant preachers.[27] Except in Mennonite congregations no Protestant, let alone Calvinist, ecclesiastical organization existed in the province of Holland before 1566, the year of the image breaking.

4. The Crisis of 1566

The continued persecutions in Flanders and neighbouring provinces led to ever growing tensions between the inhabitants of the Netherlands and their overlord king Philip II, who permanently resided in Spain and was in favour of severe repression as was the case in that country. He was out of touch with public opinion in the Netherlands, where opposition to death sentences for heretics was buttressed by the fact that in the neighbouring countries Germany and France heterodoxy was no longer punishable by death. On New Year's Eve 1564 prince William of Orange declared without qualifications in the Council of State that the heresy laws could not be enforced and that, anyway, princes did not have the right to control the conscience of their subjects. But attempts to influence Philip II in favour of a more moderate stance had no effect and in the famous 'Letters from the Segovia Forest' he ordered to continue the repression and enforce the heresy laws with full rigour. A confrontation between the severe and the lenient standpoints became inevitable. The royal letters arrived in Brussels in November 1565, whereupon a number of nobles formed an association, the so-called Compromise. In April 1566, this Compromise submitted a petition to the Governess of the Netherlands, Margaret of Parma, entreating her to suspend the heresy laws and to work out a new legal settlement of the religious problems in consultation with the States General. The Governess, well aware of the tense situation, did not dare refuse this request out of hand and tried to appease the petitioners by making loose promises about moderating the heresy laws. On the basis of her rather vague reply to the Compromise, many thought religious freedom was in sight. Exiles, among them ministers, returned from England to Flanders. Secret meetings of Protestants turned into public conventicles in the open air with a growing number of participants. When these field conventicles were banned, the participants began to carry arms.[28]

Protestants became not only more confident, some even turned to aggression. On Saturday 10 August 1566 Sebastiaan Matte, one of the ministers who had come back from England, preached near Steenvoorde, a small town in West Flanders, a region noted for its textile industry. After the sermon the believers were led to a monastery outside the town by Jacob de Buyzere, another pastor who had just returned from exile, and destroyed the images. During the next two days the same fate befell a few other monasteries. On Thursday 15 August, the day of the Assumption of the Virgin Mary, and the next two days itinerant iconoclasts destroyed the images in nearly every church, abbey and monastery in the important town of Ieperen (Ypres), in more than a hundred villages in West Flanders and in the vicinity of Lille and Tournai. Matte and De Buyzere often were in charge, and the iconoclasts were sometimes assisted by the local inhabitants. After this first round of image breaking nothing happened for two days but in the evening of 20 August and the following night a few prominent citizens of Antwerp had the churches 'purged' of images. This event in the powerful city triggered similar movements in many big towns and smaller places.

Image breaking was not the spontaneous action of mobs, but the deliberate work of relatively small, well organized groups, sometimes controlled by pastors. Other ministers, however, disapproved of unauthorized actions of private persons and preferred to see it organized by the municipality. In some cases prominent citizens or even priests took the initiative. The groups of iconoclasts, which were often small, met with surprisingly little opposition: in Antwerp crowds saw about a hundred men break the images without interfering. Only in a few places was there successful resistance. An itinerant group tried to enter the town of St Omer, but found the gates closed against them and in a neighbouring village they were chased away by the inhabitants, while elsewhere the magistrates were able to prevent image breaking. Towns where no iconoclastic movements took place include Lille, Brussels, Arras, Louvain and Bruges in the south, Dordrecht, Haarlem, Gouda and Rotterdam in the north.[29]

Amidst all these troubles the central government did not act for more than a week because it was paralysed by discord. Margaret of Parma saw the iconoclastic movements as proof of her opinion that concessions to the Protestants would only lead to disaster and, as a result, she wanted to take vigorous action. High nobles in the Council of State, among them the prince of Orange and the counts of Egmont and Horne, refused, however, to take up arms and restore order as long as it would be the old order in which Protestant sermons and field conventicles were prohibited. Only if the Governess would allow public Protestant preaching and would promise to settle the religious problem in consultation with the States General would they be willing to put an end to all violence. In the end Margaret of Parma gave in because the wave of image breaking was still spreading. She authorized the prince of Orange and his associates to negotiate, on terms which included a certain measure of religious freedom, an agreement with the nobles of the Compromise. On August 25, while the iconoclasts were still active, this agreement was arrived at and the restoration of peace could begin. The prince of Orange went to Antwerp, where he noticed that no Catholic priest dared appear in public. He had those iconoclasts who had been found guilty of looting executed and imprisoned, and restored Catholic worship as well as he could. But he assigned plots in the city to the Calvinists and Lutherans to build churches, and in doing so went beyond the agreed terms, in which preaching was allowed only outside the towns. The counts of Egmont and Horne took similar measures in Flanders and other regions, and in the autumn the prince of Orange restored order in Holland and Utrecht.[30]

Protestants optimistically interpreted these actions as a move towards freedom of worship and in Holland and Zeeland a number of protestantizing priests left the old Church and openly declared their beliefs. As soon as it seemed as if the agreement of August 25 would give the new religion an officially recognized position in the Netherlands, the Protestants in the northeastern provinces also stirred. In Leeuwarden two Protestant pastors from Emden, who had been Catholic priests in Frisia, began to preach in a private house and later in parish churches. Under the influence of these events three parish priests and one vicar left the old Church, and soon many clerics followed their example everywhere in the province. In other provinces many priests stopped celebrating mass and sometimes joined the Protestant ministers; churches were assigned to Protestant worship.

In the southern provinces of Brabant and Flanders Protestant preaching in 1566 was, as a matter of course, dominated by the fierce and strict Calvinists of the churches under the Cross and the refugee congregations who rejected all religious compromises. In Holland and

the northeastern provinces, where Protestantism acquired its organizational form only in 1566, the core was formed by individual lay
preachers and protestantizing priests who had stayed in the old Church
until the image breaking began. There, Protestantism was less well defined, more varied and often more moderate than in the south of the
Netherlands. This difference between north and south was not the result of the character of the population nor of economic conditions, but
of the fact that in Flanders and Brabant the Protestants had to operate
under close scrutiny of the central government at Brussels and the inquisitor Titelmans. There, it was much more difficult to be a protestantizing Catholic let alone a protestantizing priest. On the contrary—
the dividing line between true believers and equally firm heretics had
become quite clear in a situation in which persecution had polarized religious life. These relentless persecutions had promoted the founding
of churches under the Cross in which Calvinists had assumed control.
In Flanders and Brabant the militant refugee churches in England had
set the tone, in Holland the Protestants were more attracted to the
moderate atmosphere of the Emden church.

As early as 1566 the difference between the mentality of the 'old'
Protestants in Flanders and Brabant and the 'new' ones in Holland led
to difficulties. When Lutheran German merchants in Amsterdam
spread 'malicious rumours' about the Protestants in that town and in
particular about their doctrine of Holy Communion, the minister Jan
Arentsz read the articles of the Augsburg Confession from the pulpit
and stated that he and his flock believed nothing which was contrary to
it. This did not mean that he was a Lutheran but only that he had no
objection to collaborating with Lutherans and hoped that they would
join his church instead of founding their own congregation. Arentsz'
declaration was, however, not to the taste of the Antwerp Calvinists.
Their minister and two elders visited Amsterdam in order to lodge a
protest, but the Protestants of that town did not give in.

Until the middle of August 1566 the Protestants all over the Netherlands had profited from the sympathy the population felt for them because they were seen as underdogs suffering persecution. These feelings changed as soon as they became aggressive and attacked churches
and monasteries. Many people became convinced that it was perhaps
wiser to keep the Protestants in their place. In this way the iconoclastic
movements had the unintended effect of strengthening the government's position and playing into the hands of those who favoured rigorous measures. In the early spring of 1567 the Governess had been

able to restore her authority and, as a result, many Protestants went into exile. The stream of exiles increased after the arrival of the new Governor, the Duke of Alba, in August 1567. Nevertheless the churches under the Cross survived in many places, especially in Antwerp.

Because of the events of the 'Miraculous Year'—as the Protestants called 1566—the dividing lines between the old Church and the supporters of renewal had become much clearer. Protestantizing priests and believers had publicly left the Catholic Church and the Protestants had lost much sympathy because of image breaking. This did not mean, however, that everybody had made a conscious and open choice between the old and the new religion. A number of people were already involved with baptist or spiritualist beliefs in some form and many must have steered clear of any commitment, either from religious indifference or fear, or a combination of both.

5. The Establishment of a Protestant Church

The period of relative freedom during the 'Miraculous Year' 1566 had been too short to unify the Protestant church. Many who did not fit into the Calvinist pattern advocated the idea of a moderate church in which there would be latitude in religious belief. They feared that the Calvinists would establish an intolerant 'new popery'. Others were willing to accept Protestant ecclesiastical discipline but wanted to enforce it only in moderation. Such different opinions became the source of minor and occasionally major conflicts in the congregations themselves or even between congregations. Moreover, the international contacts of the Calvinists often brought about the involvement of foreign churches, especially Geneva.[31] Adrien Gorin, minister of the Walloon congregation in Emden, was not as orthodox as some of his elders thought necessary. They were supported by the Genevan Calvinist church, but the Emden church council judged that the elders had caused 'useless disputes'.[32]

Just as they had done before 1566 the Calvinists in the refugee churches and the churches under the Cross actively tried to ensure that Dutch Protestantism would come up to their standards. Already in November 1568 a few ministers and laymen laid down a programme for the establishment of the Dutch Protestant church. They strove for unity in doctrine and liturgy and for enforcement of ecclesiastical discipline—for the time being only in the refugee churches and the churches

under the Cross, but in future for the whole of the country, 'when the
Lord will have opened a door for the preaching of the Gospel in the
Netherlands'. No minister who did not maintain discipline would be
allowed to serve. This 'Convent of Wesel' did not have the status of an
official synod but functioned rather like a pressure group.[33] Eighteen
months later a new attempt was launched to realize this program for
the Dutch church. Prompted by Geneva, Philip Marnix of St.
Aldegonde, one of the leaders of the Dutch Revolt, and the distinguished minister Caspar van der Heijden in March 1570 addressed all
refugee churches. They proposed to collaborate in training ministers
and to keep in touch by regular correspondence as long as it was not
yet possible to convene a proper synod. This appeal, however, did not
have any effect.

A year later support for these endeavours came from unexpected
quarters: the prince of Orange desired a close-knit organization of the
exiles, hoping for collaboration between political leaders and ministers, as was the case among the Huguenots, who had held a 'synod of
princes' in La Rochelle. With his support a synod was organized in
Emden in October 1571 where many, if not all Dutch churches were
represented. The synod proved its independence from secular leaders
by ignoring every proposal the prince put forward. The Calvinists
managed to get a presbyterian-synodal order of the church adopted, as
an effective tool in the hands of whoever supported strict doctrinal and
moral control over ministers and believers. It was an important, but
not a definitive victory, because the problem of doctrinal discipline
was, in effect, a question of degree and practical considerations: nobody thought one ought to agree about the exegesis of every scriptural
passage, but, on the other hand, not every deviation could be tolerated
either. The synod decided that ministers ought to sign a confession of
faith, the 'Confessio Belgica'.[34]

In 1572 the rule of Philip II and his Governor Alba led to a revolt, in
the course of which many exiles returned. Only in large parts of Holland and Zeeland were the rebels able to hold their ground against the
Spanish armies. After four war years the States General in the royalist
provinces and the rebels in Holland and Zeeland concluded a provisional peace, the Pacification of Gent (1576), hoping that the King
would also accept it. However, he did not, and at the end of 1577
nearly all the seventeen provinces in the Netherlands were up in arms
against him, or rather against his new Governor, Don Juan of Austria.
In both cases, in 1572 in Holland and Zeeland and in 1577 in the other

provinces, the rebellion had initially been supported by large groups, among them moderate Catholics who hoped for peaceful collaboration with the Protestants. In July 1572 the States of Holland accepted a proposal of the prince of Orange for freedom of worship for both Protestants and Catholics. By the Pacification of Gent the heresy laws had been suspended, but the definitive settlement still had to be discussed by the States General and until then the status quo would be kept. Outside Holland and Zeeland, therefore, the Catholic religion would be upheld. But in 1572 (in Holland and Zeeland) as well as in 1577 (in Flanders and Brabant), the Protestants soon assumed power. The position of the Catholics was weakened because they were suspected of supporting Philip II. Catholics were distrusted even more after the massacre of St Bartholomew in France (1572), and in the following year public Catholic worship was prohibited in Holland and Zeeland. In other provinces the Protestant position was strengthened from 1578 onwards: in Ghent the Calvinists took complete control and also banned Catholic worship. The more aggressive the Protestants became, the more Catholics wondered whether, after all, Philip's rule would not be the lesser evil. In March 1580 the Catholic stadtholder of the northern provinces, Rennenberg, who had until then supported the Revolt, went over to Philip II. Thereafter, the position of Catholics siding with the rebels became completely untenable and soon Catholic worship was prohibited in every rebellious province. In this way, Catholics were driven into the arms of the new Governor, the Duke of Parma, who was able to make use of the situation and reconquer the southern half of the Netherlands.

After the rebellious provinces had concluded the Union of Utrecht (1579), in which freedom of conscience was guaranteed, they aimed at the formation of a Protestant state, but it was not at all self-evident that this would be a Calvinist state, all the more so because there were great regional differences in religious developments. Holland, where Protestants had been in control since 1572, witnessed the first vehement troubles between strict Calvinists and more moderate Protestants. Many had abhorred the persecutions and had no qualms about the dissolution of monasteries or the simplification of religious worship. But they had imagined that the renewed church would have more latitude and less narrowly defined limits and would be less polemical and less aggressive against divergent opinions. Many magistrates shared these feelings and expected that they would appoint the ministers and other functionaries much in the same way as in the old days, when they had the right of collation in the Catholic Church. Moreover, they argued that all over Europe where the church had been reformed the secular authorities had a strong hold on the appointment of pastors. According to them the task of the church was to preach, to console and to exhort—not to discipline or punish, which was the prerogative of the secular authorities. The Protestant church ought not to have any power over ministers and believers, because that would be the first step on the way to domination which was so abominable in the Church of Rome. The examination of ministers on their orthodoxy was called the 'Genevan inquisition' by magistrates who declared they would oppose it as strongly as they had opposed the Catholic inquisition. If they distanced themselves from the Calvinists, this did not mean a rapprochement to Rome.[35]

In Holland magistracy and church never reached an agreement. In Zeeland the church had more confidence in the magistrates' orthodoxy and accepted an order of the church which incorporated governmental influence. In Holland a balance was not reached by legislation but by a series of conflicts about the appointment or dismissal of individual ministers. In many cases the Calvinists were able to impose their will, sometimes with the help of orthodox regents. In practice both government and church had the right of veto: no ministers were appointed who had not been deemed orthodox by the *classis*—a meeting of ministers and elders whose task it was to oversee the Protestant church in a particular district. The Calvinists had been able to gain this important victory because the government did not want to antagonize them too much while the country was still at war with Spain and, in the end, the Calvinists got the upper hand also thanks to their clear ideas and good organization.

In Flanders and Brabant the Calvinists dominated the church before 1566. After the war broke out again in 1577 the church grew fast, but the Calvinists were able to keep their leading position, until Parma reconquered town after town and restored Catholicism everywhere. About a hundred thousand Protestants emigrated to the north. In the northeastern provinces the Protestants had not been able to maintain their position after 1566 and, therefore, a church organization was refounded in 1578 by returning Calvinist exiles with the support of the church in Holland. Protected by the magistrate, Hubert Duifhuis led an open Protestant congregation in Utrecht where discipline was not imposed. Next to it a Calvinist church existed until they were united by force during Leicester's short rule in the Netherlands (1585-87).[36]

In the nineties the Calvinists had consolidated their position in the Protestant church. But from 1604 theological tensions between two professors at Leiden university, Jacobus Arminius and Franciscus Gomarus, erupted into dissensions between moderate and strict Calvinists about the doctrine of predestination. Gomarus taught a very strict variety of this doctrine, stating that even Adam's Fall had to be attributed to God's predestinating will. Arminius and his followers held the opinion that this very severe doctrine of condemnation through predestination detracted from the glory of God and from human responsibility alike. According to them, Gomarus' teachings made any appeal to convert to the true faith sound meaningless. The followers of Gomarus, on the other hand, thought Arminius's ideas were attacking the heart of Reformed theology: the doctrine of omnipotent grace. The Arminians were supported by whoever disliked the strict Calvinists and so the dissensions grew into a severe political problem. A coup by prince Maurice of Orange which lead to a growing political influence of strict Calvinists prepared the way for the synod of Dordrecht (1618-19). The synod was attended by delegates from England, the Palatinate, Geneva, Emden and other German and Swiss Calvinist churches. The opinions of the Arminians were condemned, but the synod carefully avoided the formulations of Gomarus on predestination before the Fall. More than two hundred ministers were dismissed and forced to leave the country unless they stated that they would never preach again. However, the strictly Calvinist order of the church which was formulated at Dordrecht was nowhere accepted without some limitations.[37]

6. The Final Settlement

The Revolt of the Netherlands and the rise of the Dutch Republic did not produce a state church. On the contrary, the position of the Reformed church was characterized by great tensions: it was privileged and protected by the authorities as the established church, but it had to operate in a pluriform society. On the one hand, it wanted to do justice to its position as established church by putting its stamp on public life and taking society under its wings; on the other hand, it desired that its members accepted a severe doctrinal and moral discipline. In austere churches services were held whose most important ingredients were preaching and singing, but for fear that music would drown the

words of the psalms organs were not used until well into the seventeenth century. Because of the demands made on its members the
church remained for a long time relatively small, especially in the countryside: around 1600 it probably comprised only ten to at most twenty
percent of the population. In addition to full members there were the
so-called 'lovers of truth' who only came to services and thus were not
subject to church discipline. Baptism, however, was administered to
every child whose parents requested it, regardless of adherence to Calvinism, and thus many who were baptized never became practising
church members.

The Mennonites were especially numerous in Frisia and Holland
where they fiercely competed with the Reformed church. From time to
time Calvinist ministers asked for a banning order, but the authorities
were never willing to comply and protected the Mennonites. A Lutheran church flourished in Antwerp because of the many German
merchants there, and after Parma had conquered the city in 1585 many
Lutherans emigrated to the north where they founded congregations in
Amsterdam and a few smaller towns. In the Dutch Republic
Mennonites and Lutherans acquired the status of tolerated non-Cal-
vinist churches. Several decades after the synod of Dordrecht this status was also extended to the Arminians of the Remonstrant church.[38]
Spiritualist groups did not have separate organizations but sympathizers were probably to be found in every Protestant church and spiritualist writings were still read in the seventeenth and eighteenth century.

Catholic worship was prohibited everywhere in the Dutch Republic
and churches had either been taken over by Protestants or closed. The
property of the Church had been put to different uses and a number of
Catholics had emigrated to Cologne or other places. There was, however, a marked difference between theory and practice, because many
magistrates were unwilling to enforce the anti-Catholic laws, especially
if they were paid handsomely for their leniency. During the war with
Spain priests who were suspected of helping the enemy were harshly
dealt with, but frequently toleration was extended to the Catholics, although they could never be certain of its limits. The appointment of a
new sheriff or the pressure of the Reformed church could always lead
to strong measures against them. There were also significant regional
and local differences and in Holland the position of the Catholic
Church was easier than in some other provinces. As long as things
were done quietly much was possible. In Leiden a former canon kept a
boarding house for students with whom he discussed the Catholic

faith. The authorities prohibited these discussions but did not close down the boarding house. In Haarlem a part of the cathedral chapter was not abolished and was able to become a regional centre of Catholic activities.[39] Elsewhere priests dispensed spiritual care in secret, but for many believers it was impossible to hear mass every Sunday if only because there were not enough priests available. But in due time new Dutch priests appeared who were trained in the spirit of the Counter-Reformation first in Cologne and from 1616 onwards in Louvain. In 1592 Sasbout Vosmeer, a patrician from Delft, was appointed apostolic vicar in order to lead the so-called 'Holland mission', which counted 220 priests in 1616.[40]

In this pluriform society education became more or less tinged with Calvinism. Children's reading lessons comprised the Heidelberg catechism, but no profession of the Reformed faith was necessary in order to attend a school or even a university. The secular authorities, not the Reformed church, superintended the universities as well as the elementary and Latin schools which were to be found everywhere in the country. In many places the Catholics were even able to set up their own schools. Poor relief was not exclusively the task of the church either, but was shared between its deacons, who usually took care of the church members, and the magistrate who provided for the others. In Holland, those who did not want to marry in the Reformed church could from 1580 marry before the magistrates. In theory, holders of public offices should have been members of the Reformed church, but in practice members of the tolerated churches and sometimes even Catholics were allowed to hold such positions.

Whereas the Catholics in the Dutch Republic were officially banned and in a precarious position, they had exclusive rights in the southern or Spanish Netherlands which were reconquered for the King. Protestantism was prohibited and freedom of conscience had officially no place there. Nevertheless the re-establishment of the Catholic Church proved to be a ponderous process which took several decades. Initially there was an acute shortage of priests while the many canons of the well-endowed chapters in the towns did nothing to alleviate the plight of the poor country parish priests. It took a long time until the spirit of the Counter-Reformation had established itself in the Spanish Netherlands. In the early seventeenth century newly established seminaries began to train good priests and the university of Louvain had become a veritable bulwark of Tridentine ideas. Furthermore, the spread of the Counter Reformation was greatly helped by the efforts of the regular clergy: Franciscans, Augustinians, Jesuits and Capucins became prominent in education, spiritual care, poor relief and health care. The last heretic to be burnt (1597) was a Mennonite.[41]

During the first half of the seventeenth century a renewed and vigorous Catholicism was established in the Spanish Netherlands, as the outcome of the deep crisis of the sixteenth century. However, the result of the Reformation in the northern part of the country which became the Dutch Republic was unique. There, an established Reformed church maintained strict orthodoxy for its own members and enjoyed the protection of the magistrates; and yet this church comprised only a minority of the population. During the first half of the seventeenth century, it had to tolerate the fact that the majority stayed outside its grasp. Evidently, the strict Calvinists were fated to remain a minority, albeit a substantial one, in this complex society. During the Revolt of the Netherlands they had been able to assume control, not only thanks to their own great efforts but also to the fact that Philip II had driven many moderates into Calvinist arms by clinging to his rigid standpoint. In the Dutch Republic the secular authorities did not make use of Reformed church discipline in order to control the population. On the contrary, on the strength of the freedom of conscience guaranteed in the Union of Utrecht (1579) they protected non-Calvinists against the efforts of the Reformed church to impose its doctrines and discipline. Freedom of conscience for all had not been won during the Revolt in order to be lost to an all-embracing new church, albeit a Reformed and not a Catholic one. Dutch society was pluriform in religious matters by 1600 and it has remained so ever since.

NOTES

1. Post (1954), 87-88.
2. Boom (1987), 49-60.
3. *Nieuw Nederlands Biografisch Woordenboek* (1911-37), vol. 5:648.
4. Post (1954), 32.
5. Weiler (1984); Bange (1988).
6. Duke (1990), 1-28.
7. Dierickx (1950).
8. Visser (1969), 31-38, 152-56; Duke (1990), 11-19; Trapman (1978).
9. B. J. Spruyt, in Boom (1992), 21-42.
10. Duke (1990), 23-28, 65-70; Decavele (1975), vol. 1:591-99.
11. Duke (1990), 152-74.
12. Duke (1990), 29-59; G. Moreau (1962), 67-80.
13. Deppermann (1987), 312-48.
14. Deppermann (1987), 333-39; Mellink (1978), 39-45; James M. Stayer, "Oldeklooster en Menno," *DB* 5 (1979): 56-76.
15. Jansma (1977); S. Zijlstra, "De bestrijding van de davidjoristen aan het einde van de zestiende eeuw," *DB* 18 (1992): 11-37; Waite (1990); Valkema Blouw (1991). See James M. Stayer, in this *Handbook*, vol. 2:249-82.
16. Meihuizen (1961); Groenveld, Jacobszoon, and Verheus (1980), 62-83; Mellink (1981).
17. Hamilton (1981); Mout (1981).
18. J. B. Drewes, "Interpretatie van de Gentse spelen van 1539," *Tijdschrift voor Nederlandse Taal- en Letterkunde* 100 (1984): 241-73: Decavele (1975), 196-220.
19. G. Moreau (1962), 90-113.
20. Schilling (1972); Denis (1984); Pettegree (1986) and (1992). See Robert M. Kingdon, in this *Handbook*, vol. 2:229-47.
21. Pettegree (1992), 253. The translations were printed in Emden in 1554.
22. Patrick Collinson, *Archbishop Grindall 1519-1583: the Struggle for a Reformed Church* (Berkeley and Los Angeles, 1979), 125-52.
23. E. M. Braekman, "Les sources de la Confessio Belgica," *Bulletin de la Commission de l'Histoire des Églises Wallonnes*, 5th ser., 7 (1961): 3-24.
24. G. Moreau (1962), 168-91.
25. Woltjer (1962), 132-33, and (1971); Decavele (1975), vol. 2:57-58; *Documenta Anabaptistica Neerlandica*, vol. 2, *Amsterdam (1536-1578)*, ed. A. F. Mellink (Leiden, 1980), no. 255.
26. Woltjer (1962), 92-93; Pont (1911) 172-76.
27. Schilling (1990-92).
28. S. Groenveld et al., *De kogel door de kerk? De Opstand in de Nederlanden 1559-1609*, 3d ed. (Zutphen, 1991), 86-92.

29. Scheerder (1978).
30. Felix Rachfahl, *Wilhelm von Oranien und der Niederländische Aufstand*, vol. 2 (Halle, 1908), 738-68.
31. Vries van Heekelingen (1918-24).
32. Pettegree (1992), 205-207; J.N. Bakhuizen van den Brink, *Juan de Valdés, réformateur en Espagne et en Italie* (Geneva, 1969), 113-18.
33. Goeters (1968).
34. Nauta, van Dooren, and de Jong (1971).
35. Woltjer, in Petri (1980), 155-67; Duke (1990), 269-93; Fatio (1971).
36. Duke (1990), 269-93; Benjamin Kaplan, "Hubert Duifhuis and the Nature of Dutch Libertinism," *Tijdschrift voor Geschiedenis* 105 (1992): 1-29.
37. Woltjer, in Petri (1980), 165; Kaajan (1918); Deursen (1974), 227-371.
38. Deursen (1991).
39. P. A. M. Geurts, "Mr Willem van Assendelft, kannunik-schoolmeester te Leiden (1579-1591) en het privilegium fori der universiteit," *AGKN* 6 (1964): 1-107; Spaans (1989), 91-97.
40. Rogier (1964).
41. Pasture (1925).

BIBLIOGRAPHY

Printed Primary Sources

Bakhuizen van den Brink, J. N., ed. *De Nederlandse belijdenisgeschriften.* 2d ed. Amsterdam, 1976.

Bouterse, J., ed. *Classicale acta 1573-1620 3 Particuliere synode Zuid-Holland. Classis Rotterdam en Schieland 1580-1620.* RGPKS, vol. 69. The Hague, 1991.

Brom, G., and A. H. L. Hensen, eds. *Romeinsche bronnen voor den kerkelijkstaatkundigen toestand der Nederlanden in de 16e eeuw.* RGPGS, vol. 52. The Hague, 1922.

Coussemaker, E. de. *Troubles religieux du XVIe siècle dans la Flandre maritime 1560-1570.* 4 vols. Bruges, 1876.

Cramer, S., and J. Pijper, eds. *Bibliotheca reformatoria neerlandica.* 10 vols. The Hague, 1903-14.

Documenta Anabaptistica Neerlandica. Leiden, 1975- .

Dooren, J. P. van, ed. *Classicale Acta 1573-1620. Particuliere synode Zuid-Holland.* Vol. 1, *Classis Dordrecht 1573-1600.* RGPKS, vol. 49. The Hague, 1980.

Eeghen, I. H. van, ed. *Dagboek van Broeder Wouter Jacobsz.* 2 vols. Groningen, 1959-60.

Fredericq, P., ed. *Corpus documentorum inquisitionis haereticae pravitatis neerlandicae. Verzameling van stukken betreffende de pauselijke en bisschoppelijke inquisitie in de Nederlanden.* 5 vols. Ghent and The Hague, 1889-1902.

Goeters, J. F., ed. *Die Beschlüsse des Weseler Konvents von 1568.* Düsseldorf, 1968.

Hessels, J. H., ed. *Ecclesiae Londino-Batavae Archivum.* 3 vols. Cambridge, 1889-97.

Hooijer, C., ed. *Oude kerkordeningen der Nederlandsche Hervormde Gemeenten, 1563-1638.* Zaltbommel, 1865.

Janssen, H. Q., ed. *Bescheiden aangaande de kerkhervorming in Vlaanderen* Werken Marnix-Vereeniging, 3d ser., vol. 3. Utrecht, 1877.

Janssen, H. Q., and J. J. van Toorenenbergen. *Brieven uit onderscheidene kerkelijke archieven.* 2 vols. Werken Marnix-Vereeniging, 3d ser., vols. 2, 5. Utrecht, 1878-85.

Jelsma, A. J., and O. Boersma, eds. *Acta van het consistorie van de Nederlandse gemeente te Londen 1569-1585.* The Hague, 1993.

Knuttel, W. P. C., ed. *Acta der particuliere synoden van Zuid-Holland, 1621-1700.* 6 vols. RGPKS, vols. 3, 5, 8, 11, 15, 16. The Hague, 1908-16.

Laurent, C., et al., eds. *Recueil des ordonnances des Pays-Bas sous le règne de Charles-Quint.* 6 vols. Brussels, 1893-1922.

Livre synodal contenant les articles résolus dans les synodes des églises Wallonnes des Pays-Bas. Vol. 1, *1563-1685.* The Hague, 1896.

Marnix van St. Aldegonde, Philips van. *Godsdienstige en kerkelijke geschriften.* Ed. J. J. van Toorenenbergen. 3 vols. The Hague, 1871-91.

Meinert, H. and W. Dahmer. *Protokollbuch der niederländischen reformierten Gemeinde zu Frankfurt am Main, 1570-1581.* Frankfurt am Main, 1977.

Reitsma, J., and S. D. van Veen, eds. *Acta der provinciale en particuliere synoden gehouden in de noordelijke Nederlanden gedurende de jaren 1572-1620.* 8 vols. Groningen, 1892-99.

Roelevink, J., ed. *Classicale acta 1573-1620.* Vol. 2, *Particuliere synode Zuid-Holland. Classis Dordrecht 1601-1620. Classis Breda 1616-1620.* RGPKS, vol. 68. The Hague, 1991.

Rutgers, F. L., ed. *Acta van de Nederlandsche synoden der zestiende eeuw.* The Hague, 1899.

Schilling, Heinz, ed. *Die Kirchenratsprotokolle der reformierten Gemeinde Emden, 1557-1620.* 2 vols. Cologne, 1990-92.

Simons, Menno. *Complete Writings.* Scottdale, Pa., 1956.

Wiltens, N., ed. *Kerkelyk Plakaat-boek.* Vol. 1. The Hague, 1722.

Secondary Literature
Algemene Geschiedenis der Nederlanden. Vol. 6. Bussum, 1979.

Augustijn, Cornelis. *Erasmus. His Life, Works, and Influence.* Toronto, 1991.

Axters, S. *Geschiedenis van de vroomheid in de Nederlanden.* 4 vols. Antwerp, 1950-60.

Bange, P., et al., eds. *De doorwerking van de Moderne Devotie. Windesheim 1387-1987.* Hilversum, 1988.

Bangs, C. *Arminius: a Study in the Dutch Reformation.* 2d ed. Asbury, 1985.

Bauwhede, D. van der, and M. Goetinck, eds. *Brugge in de Geuzentijd. Bijdragen tot de geschiedenis der Hervorming te Brugge en in het Brugse Vrije tijdens de 16de eeuw.* Bruges, 1982.

Bax, W. *Het protestantisme in het bisdom Luik en vooral te Maastricht 1505-1612.* 2 vols. The Hague, 1937-41.

Bergsma, W. *Aggaeus van Albada (c. 1525-1587), schwenckfeldiaan, staatsman en strijder voor verdraagzaamheid.* Groningen, 1983.

Biografisch lexicon voor de geschiedenis van het Nederlandse protestantisme. Ed. D. Nauta, et al. Kampen, 1978- .

Biographisch woordenboek van Protestantsche godgeleerden in Nederland. Ed. J. P. de Bie and J. Loosjes. 5 vols. The Hague, 1919-49.

Bonger, H., et al., eds. *Dirck Volckertszoon Coornhert. Dwars maar recht.* Zutphen, 1989.

Boom, H. ten. *De Reformatie in Rotterdam 1530-1585.* Hollandse Historische Reeks, vol. 7. Amsterdam and The Hague, 1987.

Boom, H. ten, et al., eds. *Utrechters entre-deux. Stad en Sticht in de eeuw van de Reformatie 1520-1620.* Vierde Verzameling Bijdragen van de Vereniging voor Nederlandse Kerkgeschiedenis. Delft, 1992.

Brandt, Geeraert. *Historie der reformatie en andre kerkelyke geschiedenissen in en ontrent de Nederlanden.* 4 vols. Amsterdam, 1671-1704.

Bruin, C. C. de. *De statenbijbel en haar voorgangers. Nederlandse bijbelvertalingen vanaf de reformatie tot 1637.* Ed. F. G. M. Broeyer. 2d ed. Haarlem and Brussels, 1993.

Christophe, G. *Histoire de la Réforme protestante et de la Réforme catholique au duché de Luxembourg.* Luxemburg, 1975.

Crew, Phyllis Mack. *Calvinist Preaching and Iconoclasm in the Netherlands, 1544-1569.* Cambridge Studies in Early Modern History. Cambridge, 1978.

Decavele, J. *De dageraad van de Reformatie in Vlaanderen (1520-1565).* 2 vols. Ghent, 1975.

Decavele, J., ed. *Het einde van een rebelse droom. Opstellen over het calvinistisch bewind te Gent en de terugkeer van de stad onder de gehoorzaamheid van de koning van Spanje.* Ghent, 1985.

Denis, Philippe. *Les églises d'étrangers en Pays Rhénans (1538-1564).* BFPLL, vol. 242. Paris, 1984.

Deppermann, Klaus. *Melchior Hoffman. Social Unrest and Apocalyptic Visions in the Age of the Reformation.* Edinburgh, 1987.

Deursen, A. Th. van. *Bavianen en Slijkgeuzen. Kerk en kerkvolk ten tijde van Maurits en Oldenbarnevelt.* Assen, 1974.

Deursen, A. Th. van. *Plain Lives in a Golden Age: Popular Culture, Religion, and Society in Seventeenth Century Holland.* Cambridge and New York, 1991.

Dierickx, M. *De oprichting der nieuwe bisdommen in de Nederlanden onder Filips II (1559-1570)*. Antwerp and Utrecht, 1950.

Dis, L. M. van. *Reformatorische Rederijkersspelen uit de eerste helft van de zestiende eeuw*. Haarlem, 1937.

Dooren, J. P. van, ed. *De Nationale Synode van Middelburg in 1581. Calvinisme in opbouw in de Noordelijke en Zuidelijke Nederlanden*. Werken uitgegeven door het Koninklijk Zeeuwsch Genootschap der Wetenschappen, vol. 1. Middelburg, 1981.

Duke, Alastair C. *Reformation and Revolt in the Low Countries*. London and Ronceverte, 1990.

Estié, P. *Het vluchtige bestaan van de eerste Nederlandse lutherse gemeenten: Antwerpen 1566-1567*. Amsterdam, 1987.

Evenhuis, R. B. *Ook dat was Amsterdam*. 5 vols. Amsterdam and Baarn, 1965-78.

Fatio, Olivier. *Nihil pulchrius ordine. Contribution à l'étude de l'établissement de la discipline ecclésiastique aux Pays-Bas*. Kerkhistorische Bijdragen, vol. 2. Leiden, 1971.

Frederichs, J. *De secte der Loïsten of Antwerpsche libertijnen, 1525-1545. Eligius Pruystinck (Loy de Schaliedecker) en zijne aanhangers*. Ghent and The Hague, 1891.

Freedberg, D. *Iconoclasm and Painting in the Revolt of the Netherlands, 1566-1609*. New York, 1988.

Gelder, H. A. E. van. *De levensbeschouwing van Cornelis Pieterszoon Hooft, burgemeester van Amsterdam, 1547-1626*. 2d ed. Utrecht, 1982.

Gelder, H. A. E. van. *Revolutionnaire Reformatie. De vestiging van de Gereformeerde Kerk in de Nederlandsche gewesten, gedurende de eerste jaren van de Opstand tegen Filips II, 1575-1585*. Amsterdam, 1943.

Ginkel, A. van. *De ouderling. Oorsprong en ontwikkeling van het ambt van ouderling en de functie daarvan in de Gereformeerde Kerk der Nederlanden in de 16e en 17e eeuw*. Amsterdam, 1975.

Grell, O. *Dutch Calvinists in Early Stuart London: the Dutch Church in Austin Friars, 1603-1642*. Publications of the Sir Thomas Browne Institute, new ser., vol. 11. Leiden, 1989.

Groenhuis, G. *De predikanten. De sociale positie van gereformeerde predikanten in de Republiek der Verenigde Nederlanden vóór 1700*. Groningen, 1977.

Groenveld, S., J. P. Jacobszoon, and S. L. Verheus, eds. *Wederdopers, Menisten, Doopsgezinden in Nederland 1530-1980*. Zutphen, 1980.

Güldner, G. *Das Toleranzproblem in den Niederlanden im Ausgang des 16. Jahrhunderts*. Lübeck and Hamburg, 1968.

Hamilton, A. *The Family of Love*. Cambridge, 1981.

Hibben, C. *Gouda in the Revolt, 1572-1584*. Utrecht, 1983.

Hooft, A. J. van 't. *De theologie van Heinrich Bullinger in betrekking tot de Nederlandsche Reformatie*. Amsterdam, 1888.

Horst, B., ed. *The Dutch Dissenters. A Critical Companion to their History and Ideas*. Kerkhistorische Bijdragen, vol. 13. Leiden, 1986.

Jansma, L. G. *Melchiorieten, Munstersen en Batenburgers*. Buitenpost, 1977.

Jelsma, A. J. *Adriaan van Haemstede en zijn martelaarsboek*. The Hague, 1970.

Jong, O. J. de. *De Reformatie in Culemborg*. Assen, 1957.

Kaajan, H. *De groote synode van Dordrecht van 1618-1619*. Amsterdam, 1918.

Ketters en papen onder Filips II. Het godsdienstig leven in de tweede helft van de 16de eeuw. Utrecht, 1986.

Knappert, L. *Het ontstaan en de vestiging van het protestantisme in de Nederlanden*. Utrecht, 1924.

Kok, J. A. de. *Nederland op de breuklijn Rome-Reformatie. Numerieke aspecten van protestantisering en katholieke herleving in de Noordelijke Nederlanden 1580-1880*. Assen, 1964.

Kölker, A. J. *Alardus Amstelredamus en Cornelius Crocus. Twee Amsterdamse priester-humanisten*. Nijmegen and Utrecht, 1963.

Krahn, C. *Dutch Anabaptism. Origin, Spread, Life, and Thought (1400-1600)*. The Hague, 1968.

Kramer, C. *Emmery de Lyere et Marnix de St. Aldegonde. Un admirateur de Sebastien Franck et de Montaigne aux prises avec le champion des calvinistes néerlandais*. Archives internationales d'histoire des idées, vol. 42. The Hague, 1971.

Kronenberg, M. E. *Verboden boeken en opstandige drukkers in de hervormingstijd*. Amsterdam, 1948.

Kühler, W. J. *Geschiedenis van de doopsgezinden in Nederland*. 2 vols. Haarlem, 1932-50.

Lenselink, S. J. *De Nederlandse psalmberijmingen in de 16de eeuw van de souterliedekens tot Datheen met hun voorgangers in Duitsland en Frankrijk*. 2d ed. Dordrecht, 1983.

Loosjes, J. *Geschiedenis der Lutherse Kerk in de Nederlanden*. The Hague, 1921.

Marnef, G. *Het calvinistisch bewind te Mechelen, 1580-1585*. Standen en landen, vol. 87. Kortrijk and Heule, 1987.

Meihuizen, H. W. *Menno Simons, ijveraar voor het herstel van de nieuwtestamentische gemeente 1496-1561*. Haarlem, 1961.

Mellink, A. F. *Amsterdam en de Wederdopers in de zestiende eeuw*. Nijmegen, 1978.

Mellink, A. F. *De Wederdopers in de noordelijke Nederlanden 1531-1544*. 2d ed. Leeuwarden, 1981.

Moreau, G. *Histoire du protestantisme à Tournai jusqu'à la veille de la révolution des Pays-Bas*. BFPLL, vol. 167. Paris, 1962.

Moreau, E. de. *Histoire de l'église en Belgique*. Vol. 5, *L'église des Pays-Bas 1559-1633*. Brussels, 1952.

Mout, M. E. H. N. "The Family of Love (Huis der Liefde) and the Dutch Revolt." In *Britain and the Netherlands*, vol. 7, *Church and State since the Reformation*, ed. A. C. Duke and C. A. Tamse, 76-93. The Hague, 1981.

Mout, M. E. H. N. "Staat und Calvinismus in der Republik der Vereinigten Niederlande." In *Territorialstaat und Calvinismus*, ed. Meinrad Schaab, 87-96. VKLBW, ser. B, vol. 127. Stuttgart, 1993.

Naber, J. C. *Calvinist of libertijnsch? (1572-1631)*. Utrecht, 1884.

Nauta, D. and J. P. van Dooren, eds. *De Nationale Synode van Dordrecht 1578. Gereformeerden uit de Noordelijke en Zuidelijke Nederlanden bijeen*. Amsterdam, 1978.

Nauta, D., J. P. van Dooren, and O. J. de Jong, eds. *De synode van Emden oktober 1571*. Kampen, 1971.

Nijenhuis, W. *Adrianus Saravia (ca. 1532-1613)*. SHCT, vol. 21. Leiden, 1980.

Nijhoff, W., and M. E. Kronenberg. *Nederlandsche bibliographie van 1500 tot 1540*. 3 vols. The Hague, 1923-71.

Pasture, A. *La restauration religieuse aux Pays-Bas Catholiques sous les archiducs Albert et Isabelle (1596-1633)*. Louvain, 1925.

Petri, Franz, ed. *Kirche und gesellschaftlicher Wandel in deutschen und niederländischen Städten der werdenden Neuzeit*. Cologne and Vienna, 1980.

Pettegree, A. *Emden and the Dutch Revolt. Exile and the Development of Reformed Protestantism*. Oxford, 1992.

Pettegree, A. *Foreign Protestant Communities in Sixteenth-Century London*. Oxford, 1986.

Pollet, J. V. *Martin Bucer. Études sur les relations de Bucer avec les Pays-Bas, l'Electorat de Cologne et l'Allemagne du Nord*. 2 vols. Leiden, 1985.

Pont, J. W. *Geschiedenis van het Lutheranisme in de Nederlanden tot 1618*. Haarlem, 1911.

Post, R. R. *Kerkelijke verhoudingen in Nederland vóór de Reformatie*. Utrecht and Antwerp, 1954.

Post, R. R. *The Modern Devotion: Confrontation with Reformation and Humanism*. SMRT, vol. 3. Leiden, 1968.

Posthumus Meyjes, G. H. M. *Geschiedenis van het Waals College te Leiden 1606-1699*. Leiden, 1975.

Reitsma, J., and J. Lindeboom. *Geschiedenis van de Hervorming en de Hervormde Kerk der Nederlanden.* 5th ed. The Hague, 1949.

Rekers, B. *Benito Arias Montano, 1527-1598.* London and Leiden, 1972.

Rogier, L. J. *Geschiedenis van het katholicisme in Noord-Nederland in de zestiende en zeventiende eeuw.* 3d ed. Amsterdam and Brussels, 1964.

Roodenburg, H. *Onder censuur. De kerkelijke tucht in de gereformeerde gemeente van Amsterdam 1578-1700.* Hilversum, 1990.

Scheerder, J. *De Beeldenstorm.* 2d ed. Haarlem, 1978.

Scheerder, J. *De inquisitie in de Nederlanden in de XVIe eeuw.* Antwerp, 1944.

Schilling, Heinz. *Civic Calvinism in Northwestern Germany and the Netherlands: Sixteenth to Nineteenth Centuries.* SCES, vol. 17. Kirksville, Mo., 1991.

Schilling, Heinz. *Niederländische Exulanten im 16. Jahrhundert.* Gütersloh, 1972.

Schilling, Heinz. *Religion, Political Culture and the Emergence of Early Modern Society. Essays in German and Dutch History.* SMRT, vol. 50. Leiden, 1992.

Spaans, J. *Haarlem na de Reformatie. Stedelijke cultuur en kerkelijk leven, 1577-1620.* Hollandse Historische Reeks, vol. 11. The Hague, 1989.

Spiertz, M. G., and J. A. M. M. Jansen. *Kerkelijke archieven. Gidsen voor kerkhistorisch onderzoek.* Vol. 1-. The Hague, 1982- .

Swichum, C. A. van. *Een huis voor het Woord: het protestantse kerkinterieur in Nederland tot 1900.* The Hague, 1984.

Thijs, A. *Van Geuzenstad tot katholiek bolwerk: maatschappelijke betekenis van de Kerk in contrareformatorisch Antwerpen.* Turnhout, 1990.

Toussaert, J. *Le sentiment religieux en Flandre à la fin du Moyen-Age.* Paris, 1963.

Tracy, James D. "Heresy, Law, and Centralization under Mary of Hungary: Conflicts between the Council of Holland and the Central Government over Enforcements of Charles V's Placards." *ARG* 73 (1982): 284-308.

Tracy, James D. "With and Without the Counter-Reformation: the Catholic Church in the Spanish Netherlands and the Dutch Republic, 1570-1650." *CHR* 70 (1985): 247-75.

Trapman, J. "Le rôle des 'sacramentaires' des origines de la Réforme jusqu'en 1530 aux Pays-Bas." *Nederlands Archief voor Kerkgeschiedenis* 63 (1983): 1-24.

Trapman, J. *De Summa der Godliker Scrifturen (1523).* Leiden, 1978.

Valkema Blouw, P. "Printers to the 'Archheretic' David Joris: Prolegomena to a Bibliography of His Works." *Quaerendo* 21 (1991): 163-209.

Verboom, W. *De catechese van de Reformatie en de Nadere Reformatie.* Amsterdam, 1986.

Visser, C. Ch. G. *Luthers geschriften in de Nederlanden tot 1546.* Assen, 1969.

Vries van Heekelingen, H. de. *Genève, pépinière du Calvinisme hollandais.* 2 vols. Fribourg and The Hague, 1918-24.

Waite, Gary K. *David Joris and Dutch Anabaptism 1524-1543.* Waterloo, Ont., 1990.

Weiler, A. G. "Recent Historiography on the Modern Devotion: Some Debated Questions." *AGKN* 26 (1984): 161-79.

Wieder, F. C. *De Schriftuurlijke Liederkens. De liederen der Nederlandsche Hervormden tot op het jaar 1566.* The Hague, 1900.

Woltjer, J. J. "Het conflict tussen Willem Bardes en Hendrick Dirckzoon." *Bijdragen en Mededelingen betreffende de Geschiedenis der Nederlanden* 86 (1971): 178-99.

Woltjer, J. J. *Friesland in Hervormingstijd.* Leidse Historische Reeks, vol. 7. Leiden, 1962.

Woltjer, J. J. "Van katholiek tot protestant." In *Historie van Groningen, stad en land,* ed. W. J. Formsma, et al., 207-32. Groningen, 1981.

Woltjer, J. J. "Willem van Oranje en de godsdienstige pluriformiteit." In J. J. Woltjer, *Apologie van Willem van Oranje, 1580-1980,* 21-37. Tielt and Amsterdam, 1980.

Zijlstra, S. *Nicolaas Meyndertsz. van Blesdijk. Een bijdrage tot de geschiedenis van het Davidjorisme.* Assen, 1983.

SETTLEMENTS: FRANCE

Philip Benedict
(Brown University)

While the evangelical movement swept like wildfire across the German-speaking world, its transmission across Europe's most important linguistic frontiers involved a marked slowing of the pace of change. In France, the gradual dissemination of foreign Protestant ideas joined existing native currents of religious renewal to stimulate growing longing for a dramatic reshaping of religious life. At first, most proponents of change hoped that this might come about without breaking with the established church. With time, faced with the conservatism of the chief arbiters of doctrinal orthodoxy and intensifying persecution of those who dissented, more saw the need for a rupture. The pace of change accelerated in the mid-1550s when partisans of renewal began to organize churches of their own modelled largely on Geneva's, the city which had become the chief place of refuge for French evangelicals. These churches multiplied with extraordinary rapidity between 1555 and 1562, but they never attracted more than a fraction of the kingdom's population or gained royal sanction for a restructuring of the entire Gallican church in accordance with their practices. They also quickly encountered violent hostility from another fraction of the population still committed to Roman traditions. Nearly four decades of religious violence and civil war ensued. Amid this violence, the fondest hopes of the partisans of the "new religion" were never realized. Instead, massacre and defection thinned their ranks. Still, they succeeded in defending the legal recognition of the right to assemble for worship that they had first gained in 1562. The story of religious change in sixteenth-century France is thus, most dramatically, the story of the successful establishment of a minority church that would endure with remarkable tenacity down to the present day. It is also the story of the halting transformations that occurred over this period within the Catholic church, which emerged from the Wars of Religion with momentum gathering for its own program of internal reform.

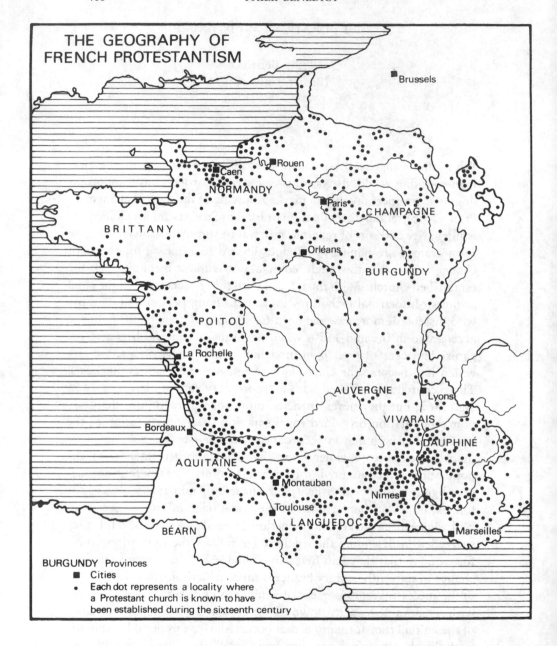

THE GEOGRAPHY OF
FRENCH PROTESTANTISM

Brussels

Rouen

Caen

NORMANDY

Paris

CHAMPAGNE

BRITTANY

Orléans

BURGUNDY

POITOU

La Rochelle

AUVERGNE

Lyons

Bordeaux

VIVARAIS

DAUPHINÉ

AQUITAINE

Montauban

Nîmes

Toulouse

LANGUEDOC

Marseilles

BÉARN

BURGUNDY Provinces
■ Cities
• Each dot represents a locality where
a Protestant church is known to have
been established during the sixteenth century

1. THE EVE OF THE REFORMATION

The most recent survey of France's religious history aptly describes the waning Middle Ages as the era of "flamboyant" Christianity. Just as decorative elements proliferated on the Gothic churches, so individual and group devotional activities multiplied within lay religious life. This was the golden age of civic mystery plays and Corpus Christi processions. Confraternities multiplied, both devotional associations dedicated to such practices as the recital of the rosary or the glorification of the Blessed Sacrament, and guild and parish brotherhoods that combined common banqueting and attendance at church services with obligations of mutual assistance to fellow members in life and death. The economic recovery that followed the end of the Hundred Years' War reinforced widely shared concern with the soul's fate in purgatory to bring the number of anniversary masses commissioned by believers to unprecedented levels. The resulting support of mass priests and chaplains in turn thickened the ranks of the secular clergy. Around the middle of the sixteenth century, nearly a quarter of the parishes in the diocese of Nantes housed upwards of ten priests. At the same time, the invention and spread of printing enriched the inner lives of prayer and meditation of that growing fraction of the population that could read. Short expositions of church doctrine, saints' lives, and above all books of hours—found by the tens of thousands in the stocks of important Paris booksellers—sold particularly well.

In the eyes of the devout, of course, "abuses" continued to riddle the church. Pluralism was widespread, most spectacularly among the bishops, where it was not uncommon for great noble prelates to accumulate several sees, which they rarely visited since their chief activities were those of courtier or royal minister, but also, increasingly, among the parish clergy as well. Although the creation of new theology faculties—at Toulouse in 1360, Avignon in 1413, and Montpellier in 1421—increased opportunities for theological education, in the regions that have been studied from 70 to 90 per cent of parish priests or their vicars still lacked university training, and few dared to preach. Enforcement of the rule had become notoriously lax in many religious houses.

Yet throughout the Middle Ages the observation of shortcomings had always been accompanied by the call for reform. The various currents of religious reform visible within the late medieval church were prominent elements of the French religious landscape as the fifteenth century gave way to the sixteenth. Observant monastic reform, which urged stricter adherence to the rules of the different religious orders, advanced on many fronts, capturing the majority of Franciscan houses and, in 1510, the celebrated Benedictine Abbey of Saint Germain-des-Prés. The pastoral reform program expressed most eloquently in the writings of Jean Gerson stimulated reforming bishops, such as François d'Estaing in Rodez or Georges d'Amboise of Rouen, to draft synodal statutes that called upon the priests of the diocese to reside in their parishes, to set forth each Sunday the articles of the faith and the works of charity, to visit the sick and dying and administer the sacraments faithfully, and to look after the proper care of the altar and church vestments. Meanwhile, the pastoral limitations of many secular priests were palliated by the efforts of the mendicant orders, whose ranks increased steadily over the last centuries of the Middle Ages and whose members offered regular preaching on the major church holidays. Several excellent recent studies have examined the content of the instruction thus dispensed. In the memorable conclusion of Hervé Martin, it conveyed:

> A Bible in crumbs, reduced to stock fragments; a Bible pressed into the service of the most disparate and at times capricious arguments; an allegorized Bible, applied metaphorically to everyday events; a reinterpreted Bible, the Old Testament understood in light of the New and of church tradition; a glossed, condensed Bible, translated with great liberty; a Bible subjected to scholastic systematization; in short, a Bible whose simple, direct meaning (the *sensus rudis* of Wyclif) was the last thing in the world to be examined, except when a religious reformer seized hold of it. And yet, constantly present in the mind of both the preachers and their audience, this Bible remained the staff of faith and the nourishment of thought and imagination.[1]

The fieriest mendicants preached in a revivalistic style that sought to move listeners to personal moral reform and could touch off great displays of collective enthusiasm. When Thomas Illyricus toured southern France in 1518-19, cities competed to attract him, thousands thronged to hear him, and his preaching was said to have had such effect that many of Toulouse's manufacturers of playing cards burned the presses that they used to make these instruments of sin and vowed henceforward to produce pious images.[2]

Institutionally, the French church had obtained considerable independence from Rome, only to fall increasingly under the control of a revived monarchy. In the midst of the Conciliar crisis, French theologians took the lead in asserting the self-governing character of the church and its independence from Papal control. Appeals of ecclesiastical court decisions to Rome were curtailed, while by the Pragmatic Sanction of Bourges of 1438 the crown embraced and codified into law the principle that cathedral chapters and religious houses were to elect their bishops or superiors independent of papal interference. This action, however, was just one step in a complicated series of maneuvers and negotiations between the crown, the papacy, and the institutions of the French church that left the manner of filling leading ecclesiastical offices a matter of contention until in 1516, when the Concordat of Bologna fixed the appointment of all bishoprics in the hands of the crown. The subservience of the church to the king should nonetheless not be overestimated. Even though the royal courts steadily eroded the jurisdiction of their ecclesiastical competitors, church courts continued to judge many issues from minor contractual disputes to marital litigation and certain cases of assault, sexual misconduct, and heresy. The leading churchmen and monastic houses remained powerful lords with extensive seigniorial rights of jurisdiction and control of key positions within the provincial Estates, while the preaching friars and university doctors of theology each considered themselves to be the moral conscience of society. As such, they felt authorized to criticize royal policies that they judged improper or tyrannical, and often did so.

2. THE NEW GOSPEL

An informed observer of the French church asked in 1500 to predict the major conflict of the next century would probably have guessed that it would be the continuation of the struggle between those who espoused internal disciplinary and pastoral reform and those who viewed their church positions as personal or family property that ought not to be encumbered with too many bothersome obligations. If the actual course of events turned out to be far more dramatic and troubled, of course, it was because there soon appeared on the scene Biblical exegetes who focused on the Bible's *sensus rudis* and expounded it in a novel manner that aroused both enthusiasm and antipathy.

The first of these were those native scholars and religious writers attracted by the promise of a humanist Christian Renaissance. The seminal figure was Jacques Lefèvre d'Etaples (c. 1458-1534), a much admired professor of philosophy at the Parisian Collège du Cardinal Lemoine. After devoting the first half of his long life to applying humanistic methods of textual scholarship to philosophy, editing and commenting upon Aristotle, the Hermetic corpus, Dionysius the Areopagite, and Ramon Lull, he turned in 1509 to the Bible. His edition of the Psalms of that year proposed several changes in the Latin text. His Biblical commentaries were sober. Like Erasmus, he was dedicated to seeing the Bible attain the widest possible circulation among "les simples vulgaires." Unlike Erasmus, he emphasized the Pauline theme of free grace in Christ. Just where such an itinerary could lead theologically was demonstrated by his observations of 1512 that questioned the scriptural basis for extreme unction and clerical confession, and by his abandonment in 1519 of a new compilation of lives of the saints because of growing doubts about their cult.

Beginning in 1521, Lefèvre had an unusual opportunity to see what fruit an intensive campaign of evangelization might bear, when he and some of his closest former students were called to the bishopric of Meaux by one of his patrons, Guillaume Briçonnet. Briçonnet had taken up residence in his bishopric and launched a program of pastoral reform. Now he offered Lefèvre a sinecure that enabled him to continue his Biblical scholarship while placing associates such as Gerard Roussel, Michel d'Arande, Martial Masurier, and Guillaume Farel in positions that allowed them to preach throughout the diocese. By 1524 the reading of Biblical passages had been incorporated into weekly services throughout the diocese, and Roussel gave a daily exposition of Paul's epistles. But by this time too, Luther had emerged as a forthright critic of the Roman church in Germany, and his ideas had been condemned as heretical by the Paris Faculty of Theology. It was becoming impossible to immunize the changes occurring in Meaux from suspicions of "Lutheranism."

Luther's writings were on sale in Paris as early as 1519. "No books are purchased with greater avidity," Glareanus soon reported to Zwingli.[3] The Sorbonne's condemnation of Luther in 1521 was quickly followed by measures making possession of his works a crime, but his ideas and those of the other reformers who emerged in his wake continued to spread through the hand-to-hand circulation of their books and the preaching of clerics attracted to their ideas. In 1522 the Franciscan François Lambert read Luther in his convent in Avignon and fled to Wittenberg to study with him. In 1523-24 Pierre Sébiville preached in Grenoble in favor of communion in both kinds and against clerical celibacy. Heresy trials or reports of attacks on Catholic holy objects indicate that by 1525 "Lutheranism"—as all dissent tended to be labelled in this period—had also reached Lyon, Orléans, Bourges, Tours, and Alençon. Reports that it was pullulating in Meaux were particularly insistent.

Just what the relationship was between the *bibliens* of Meaux and those German and Swiss theologians who were beginning to reorganize worship in their lands along lines that subsequently would be labelled "Protestant" is a complicated problem. Briçonnet condemned Luther's ideas and seems to have succeeded in blocking their spread in his diocese, but certain of his proteges corresponded before 1525 with Zwingli and Oecolampadius, both of whom would have appeared in this period to be kindred spirits in the struggle for a Christian Renaissance; Oecolampadius, in fact, first suggested the program of daily scripture lessons adopted in the diocese. In later years, one *biblien*, Farel, became a Reformer in French-speaking Switzerland; two others, Roussel and d'Arande, became Catholic bishops within France; and Lefèvre withdrew to a life of study under the protection of Marguerite d'Alençon, the king's sister, who became an important devotional writer in her own right in the 1530s. Efforts to get the aged Lefèvre to pronounce on whether the emerging Protestant or Catholic theologies were truer to the Bible reportedly received only a weary shrug of the shoulders. Aspirations for evangelical reform could lead to efforts to achieve this from within the Gallican church, to emigration and outspoken attack on the established church order, or to internal exile and the studied avoidance of taking sides on the emerging points of contention.

Several generations of sophisticated bibliographic research have revealed the history of evangelical propaganda in French over the course of the subsequent decades. Three phases can be discerned. The first, lasting into the early 1530s, was dominated by vernacular editions, excerpts, and summaries of the Bible, and by books that combined short expositions of gospel passages with prayers, such as the extremely successful *Livre de vraye et parfaicte oraison*, which went through at least 14 editions between 1528 and 1550. Luther was by far the most widely translated foreign theologian in this period, with his works of edification and piety making their way into French far more often than his overtly controversial theological writings. Frequently, his works were published without attribution in composite devotional tracts that also included pages from Erasmus or Farel. Scholarship to date has identified 22 different editions of Luther's writings published in French during his lifetime, a figure that only takes on full meaning when compared with the numbers for other languages in this same period: 2,946 editions in High German, 58 in Dutch, 28 in Danish, 14 in English, and 8 in Italian. Simon du Bois, first of Paris and then of Alençon, was the most important printer of early evangelical works in France, but many such books were imported from Antwerp or Strasbourg.

The second phase began in 1533, when Reformed Protestantism became established in Neuchâtel and then Geneva, and French language printers set up presses there. These produced the first polemical works of a more outspoken character. The first work published by Pierre de Vingle in Neuchâtel was Antoine Marcourt's immensely successful catalogue of the defective goods sold by the church of Rome, the *Livre des marchans* (1533). This was soon followed by the notorious placards posted simultaneously in several cities in 1534 denouncing the "insufferable abuses of the papal mass," then, from Geneva, the French editions of Calvin's *Institutes* and attacks on the Roman church of a more popular or satirical character by Calvin and Pierre Viret.

The third phase of reform propagandizing, after 1550, was marked by the multiplication of Genevan presses and the organization of large-scale clandestine networks for the distribution of their products within France, reinforced by the publication of Protestant writings within the country in Lyon and, after 1561, in Rouen, Caen, Orléans, and La Rochelle as well. In the early 1560s, Geneva housed at least 34 printing presses, capable of producing 27,400 copies of Beza and Marot's translation of the Psalms in a few months. Between 1536 and 1569, at least 187 editions of works by Calvin appeared in French, with 145 appearing after 1550.[4]

Faced with the rising tide of heretical books, the civil and ecclesiastical authorities adopted increasingly harsh measures against heresy, but the repression of this crime was always compromised by differences of opinion about just what constituted it and how severely it should be punished. The majority of the Paris doctors of theology had no doubt that both humanist evangelicalism and the Wittenberg theology were contrary to the teachings and traditions of the church, and they pressed for strong action against both. When the individual condemnations of heretical writings that they issued from 1520 onward were brought together into the first catalogue of prohibited books in 1544, works by Erasmus, Lefèvre, and Rabelais were listed alongside the publications of Luther and Calvin. Francis I, on the other hand, showed himself willing to defend evangelicals such as Lefèvre, Etienne Dolet, and Robert Estienne against those who would persecute them, even while he was genuinely shocked by acts of iconoclastic vandalism or "sacramentarian" attacks on the mass. Important waves of repression occurred during the king's captivity in 1525-26 and after the 1534 Affair of the Placards, which alarmed Francis both because of the placards' aggressive rejection of the real presence and because their posting in several towns at once suggested a degree of coordination not found in other manifestations of dissent. Still, royal policy in the 1520s and 1530s disappointed the most eager heresy hunters.

As Francis aged and the volume of propaganda entering France from Geneva mounted, stronger measures were decreed. In 1543, the king mandated the Sorbonne to draw up a set of articles of the faith. The document, which asserted such contested points as the sacrificial nature of the mass, the value of pilgrimages and of prayers to the Virgin and saints, and the obligatory character of monastic vows, was then ordered to be distributed to every parish in the country, with instructions to the parish priests to watch for those who did not accept its twenty-five points. Following the accession of the still stricter Henry II, a special chamber charged exclusively with the repression of heresy was created in 1547 within the Parlement of Paris, soon dubbed the "Burning Chamber" (*chambre ardente*). But the judges of the royal law courts, even those of the *chambre ardente*, were deeply divided over just how harshly the laws against heresy should be enforced. Only seven per cent of those denounced to the *chambre ardente* for heresy were condemned to death, and the percentage is lower still for the two other Parlements for which we have statistical evidence. From chronicles or other reports on the advance of Protestant opinion in specific localities, it appears that wherever groups of people won over to the new opinions began to meet regularly for discussion, gave expression to their views with acts of iconoclasm or open statements of opposition to Catholic worship, or—as a group in Meaux sought to do in 1546—organized church services of their own, such actions quickly attracted the attention of the authorities and were strongly repressed. But the repression was not intense enough to prevent the continuing circulation of heretical ideas or to lead all who fell afoul of the law to cease holding deep reservations about elements of Catholic practice. The number of heresy cases before the Parlement of Toulouse shows both the intensification of repression and the advance of heresy from 1520 to 1560. Where eight people stood trial for this crime between

1521 and 1530, 121 did so between 1531 and 1540, 257 between
1541 and 1550, and 684 between 1551 and 1560. Where evidence of
heresy was confined to a handful of cities in 1525, by 1540 the "conta-
gion" touched virtually every region of the country except Brittany and
Auvergne, where it never would have much success. After 1540, a
growing number of Frenchmen took refuge in Geneva. The city's *Livre
des Habitants*, established in 1549 to keep track of the newcomers,
lists 122 arrivals from the kingdom in 1550 and 1,204 in 1559, and it
is known that this document underestimates the numbers of those who
actually took up residence there by at least a third.[5]

Geneva's growing importance as a center for the dissemination of
reformation propaganda and as a haven for French refugees bespeaks
the exceptional role that its theologians came to play in giving shape to
stirrings for ecclesiastical change in France. To say this, however, is
not to suggest that popular heresy can be equated with Calvinist doctrine. The fullest and most vivid accounts of the underground growth
of Protestant opinion in France are provided by the correspondence of
the Genevan reformers, by Jean Crespin's *Histoire des martyrs mis à
mort pour la vérité de l'Evangile depuis le temps des apôtres jusqu'à
présent*, and the ecclesiastical history of the Reformed churches compiled under the direction of Theodore Beza. While all of these abound
with details available nowhere else, all—since the latter two were published in Geneva—view the events in France from a distinctly Genevan
perspective. Only recently have historians become fully cognizant of
the distortions that these sources might impose on our view of the early
growth of the movement and begun to read the evidence with a concern to capture the full range of ideas current among the "mal-sentans
pour la foy." Insofar as we can judge from surviving records of heresy
trials and from the character of the most widely circulated evangelical
propaganda (both of which deserve far more systematic analysis than
they have received to date), those accused of heresy were most frequently guilty of attacking mariolatry, the veneration of the saints, and
the doctrine of purgatory. The claim that the clergy had kept the Bible
from laymen so that it could invent useless rituals and peddle these for
money runs through the propaganda; this gave a new charge to old
feelings of anti-clericalism. Accusations of sacramentarianism become
more numerous in the archives of repression after 1538, but explicit
denials of the doctrine of the real presence are hard to find in the surviving interrogations of laymen, as are detailed expositions of the doctrine of justification by faith alone. Occasionally, the documents refer

to "anabaptists" or "libertines" gaining a following in one region or another. On closer inspection, it appears that the former were generally charismatic preachers drawn to antinomian or apocalyptic ideas, the latter individuals inclined toward a quietist spiritualism or, after 1555, evangelicals who spoke against the imposition of consistorial discipline within the newly established Reformed churches. The main currents of Anabaptism identified by the historians of that movement in Switzerland, the Holy Roman Empire, and the Netherlands largely bypassed France.

3. THE REFORMED CHURCHES

France's religious history entered a new phase in 1555 when groups of those disaffected from Rome began to organize a counter-church. The first two churches were established in Poitiers and Paris. Others followed, soon hundreds. Initially they met in secret. As they grew, they often dared to gather in public or even seize church buildings or public markets to hold their services. Their proliferation was nothing short of remarkable. "This entire country is so full of heretics that if our Lord does not have mercy and does not intervene this year then everything is finished," the alarmed Jesuit Jean Pelletier reported from Toulouse in 1561. "In every city ministers from Geneva preach; they have won the principal people and almost all the magistrates, who do not punish any heretics. . . . I believe that the Lord has abandoned [this country]."[6] The most careful recent estimate suggests that approximately 1,240 congregations were organized within the sixteenth-century boundaries of the kingdom between 1555 and 1570, the great majority of which took shape prior to 1562.[7] They were most numerous in Normandy, the Loire valley, and a crescent of provinces stretching from Poitou into Aquitaine and across Languedoc to the Vivarais and Dauphiné. By 1562, their membership comprised between a fifth and a third of the population of such large provincial cities as Rouen, Orléans, Caen, and Lyon, and a majority of the population of Nîmes, Montauban, and La Rochelle. Stronger in the cities and market towns than in the countryside, they nonetheless could also be found in rural villages in certain regions from the Pays de Caux to the Cévennes. Any attempt to estimate their total membership is fraught with speculation, but a reasonable guess is between 1.5 and 2 million, roughly ten per cent of the kingdom's total population.

Much of the impetus for the foundation of these new churches emanated from Calvin and Geneva. Calvin's writings vibrated with a profound abhorrence of participating in the polluting rituals of Rome, and both he and Viret had directed treatises to the faithful in France since the early 1540s urging those who had seen the light to abstain from participating in the mass. Furthermore, unlike Luther, Calvin was willing to countenance groups of laymen establishing churches of their own where the secular authorities failed to institute pure worship. Two letters addressed in 1554 to the French faithful spelled out procedures to be followed. When those who took this advice appealed to Geneva for ministers to serve their new churches, the Genevan company of pastors responded with pastors by the score—perhaps as many as 220 between 1555 and 1562.[8] The Genevan church provided the basic model for the liturgy and many of the institutions of these new churches. The confession of faith adopted in 1559 derived from a document drafted there.

But the proliferation of churches throughout France was not entirely controlled from Geneva. The dramatic speed with which new churches were established testifies to a pent-up demand for an alternative form of worship that exceeded what Geneva could supply. Many churches were led by men from within France; the Paris church played a special leadership role. From a variety of sources, we know that certain members of these new churches held views on specific issues of doctrine at variance with Calvin's. Reconstructing the full range of such viewpoints remains one of the great challenges for scholarship on this period. Furthermore, a group of churches springing up in defiance of the established authorities in towns and villages across a vast kingdom faced problems of organization for which a church reformed by government fiat in a single city and its surrounding *contado* could not always provide a model. It appears to have been the quickly perceived need to create a forum for the discussion of common concerns and the means for ensuring unity of doctrine and practice that led a group of churches within the kingdom to summon, independently of Calvin, the first national synod in Paris in 1559. The institutions established included a hierarchy of regularly assembling regional and national synods binding the different local churches together into an intercommunicating whole in a manner that had no exact counterpart in Swiss church practice. The presbyterial-synodal system thus created would be the model for a similar form of church polity in other Reformed churches. It would also prove to be an excellent means for the new churches scattered across France to coordinate resistance against political threats to their continued existence.

4. THE OUTBREAK OF VIOLENCE

Such coordination soon proved necessary, for as Reformed churches proliferated across the kingdom, events quickly spun out of control. Many of those who joined the newly emerging Protestant churches were so outraged at what they now perceived as the abuses of papal religion that they took direct action against them, ignoring pleas from leading ministers to go slow. Iconoclastic attacks proliferated. Preachers found themselves interrupted and contradicted by members of their audience. Processions were disrupted. This in turn provoked a violent response among those still attached to traditional forms of worship. Angry crowds set upon those who disrupted Catholic preaching and processions. In Paris, groups gathered to light candles and sing canticles before streetcorner images of the Virgin; passersby who refused to offer donations faced the threat of beatings. Across much of France, both faiths were mobilizing armed men by 1560-61.

The story of internal change within the Catholic church in the sixteenth century is less studied than the story of the spread of dissent and its repression, but it is scarcely less important for France's subsequent history. Diocesan synods met with some regularlity between 1516 and 1559, but only a minority of bishops were strongly committed to pastoral reform. As for the Council of Trent, Francis I and Henry II felt little enthusiasm for a conclave encouraged by their Habsburg rivals, and Gallican conciliarists questioned the validity of an assembly so strictly controlled from Rome. In 1551 Henry II and his churchmen developed plans for a national council, independent of Rome, but abandoned the project, perhaps fearful of opening the door to the ultimate triumph of Protestantism, as in England. The church's hold on the affections of Frenchmen was weakening—local studies have found fewer candidates for the priesthood, smaller offerings in church basins—yet it remained able to rally those committed to its teachings, as indicated by large new confraternities of the Holy Sacrament that reaffirmed eucharistic devotion in the face of Protestant attacks. Catholic polemicists such as Artus Désiré and Claude de Saintes responded vigorously to the swelling tide of Genevan propaganda, while mendicant preachers urged the crown to exercise its obligation to expunge heresy from the realm and warned that rulers who refused to do so merited excommunication. If such preachers could no longer draw audiences as large as they once had, comparative study would probably show that attachment to traditional Catholic practices remained stronger in France than in the Low Countries, where virtually nobody was willing to come to the defense of "the pope and his monks" when widespread iconoclasm broke out in 1566. It is of the utmost importance for France's religious history that the Catholic church still commanded a reservoir of loyalty that could be mobilized into militant outrage when objects sacred to the faith came under direct physical attack.

Much of the best recent work on this period has explored the questions of what provoked the religious violence that proliferated after 1560 and whether the converts to Protestantism might have been recruited from distinctive groups whose socio-economic interests were opposed to those who remained loyal to the Catholic church.

The intensive examination of the sociology of early Protestantism was largely inspired by Natalie Zemon Davis' 1965 article "Strikes and Salvation in Lyon."[9] This claimed that detailed examination of the local records revealed that Lyon's important Protestant church recruited its members from all of the city's major socio-economic groups in numbers roughly proportional to their place within the total urban population; that no tendency could be observed for journeymen in specific trades to line up on one side of the religious issue and masters on the other; but that the "new religion" did seem to draw more adherents from certain trades than others, notably those trades characterized by high literacy, high skills, and a high percentage of immigrants from other areas. Furthermore, Davis pointed out, the heavily Protestant printing trade experienced a series of strikes and labor disputes in precisely these same years, pitting masters and journeymen of similar religious outlook against one another. The implications of the article were broad. In opposition to assumptions that have often informed twentieth-century social historical scholarship about religious movements, it suggested that people in the past were quite capable of distinguishing between economic and religious grievances, and that religious conflicts should not be assumed to be displaced social protests on the part of people who had not yet succeeded in emancipating themselves from religious ideology. At the same time, it did not deny all connection between social realities and the spread of new religious beliefs. On the contrary, it suggested that Protestantism was likely to appeal to certain kinds of people because of social attributes that made them particularly receptive to an ideology that called upon them to reject religious traditions without Biblical foundation and the tutelage of a clergy that profited from these traditions. Literate, self-confident artisans were those most likely to believe that they could understand the Bible without clerical intermediation. Immigrants were less likely to be attached to local traditions and devotions.

Many other studies of individual urban communities soon followed. It now seems clear that the Reformed churches did not everywhere tap into the same strata of the population. In Amiens, the movement appears to have been dominated by workers from that city's large textile industry who were not notably more literate than their Catholic counterparts, but who may have been attracted to the cause—at least so one scholar has argued—because their experience with the tight regulation of the trade by Amiens' civic authorities made them suspicious of all authorities who claimed to act in their best interest.[10] In Alençon, where reform activity began in the milieu of the educated professional and legal officials closely tied to the ducal court, Protestantism was disproportionately a movement of the urban elites. Still, in most cases where the early members of the Reformed church have been identified from reliable sources that do not come primarily from the archives of repression (lists of those suspected or arrested for Protestant opinion tend to include false accusations and to be skewed toward the higher levels of society), the findings of this research have corroborated the picture first outlined by Davis. The Protestants and Catholics do not generally seem to have been divided by clear economic antagonisms. The Protestant movement cut across lines of wealth and status but tended to attract more artisans from those trades characterized by higher literacy or greater craft skill and independence. Within the urban elites, it may have had a greater appeal to legal and professional people than to merchants. Those who worked the land, however, showed little affinity for the movement. Many French cities included a sizeable component of vine-dressers or agricultural laborers, but very few of the Protestants came from these strata of society, who formed the shock troops of Catholic militancy in Dijon in the 1560s. Those rural areas where the faith struck deep roots were regions of rural industry.

A striking feature of French Protestantism was the number of noblemen attracted to the cause. At court, Louis, Prince of Condé; Gaspard de Coligny, Admiral of France; and Jeanne d'Albret, Francis I's niece and the heiress to the throne of Navarre, all embraced the faith. Regional studies have shown that, in the Beauce, the *élection* of Bayeux, and Quercy, between 26 and 40 per cent of the *noblesse campagnarde* did so as well, although percentages elsewhere may have been lower since these three were areas of strong noble Protestantism. Conversions among the Second Estate followed networks of kinship, education, and common service in certain great aristocratic households, with women playing an important role in promoting the faith. Little evidence exists, however, to suggest as was once thought that Protestantism's appeal to the nobility can be explained by its attractiveness to discontented military men who had been thrown out of work by the end of the Habsburg-Valois wars and returned home to find their revenues eaten away by inflation. There also appears to be little correlation between the location of the seigniories of those nobles who embraced the faith and the villages from which refugees left for Geneva. Where nobles converted, they rarely were able to sway or coerce many of their tenants or villagers to follow them.

One dimension missing from the recent work on the sociology of early Protestantism has been sustained attention to the geographical pattern of the faith's implantation. The outstanding French tradition of research on Catholicism's modern religious geography has revealed sharp and deeply rooted contrasts between the religious "temperament" of different regions, and a recent study has shown that such contrasts reach back to the early sixteenth century in Rouergue, where both the density of the secular clergy and the number of new confraternal foundations were significantly higher in the northern half of the diocese of Rodez than in the south. By contrast, Protestantism implanted itself far more successfully in the southern half of the diocese. What the geography of pre-Reformation religious practice might have looked like in other regions of the country, and whether or not the very strong regional differences in the degree of success obtained by the early Reformed churches can be explained by pre-existing differences in the character and intensity of Catholic devotional life in the regions in question are problems that deserve further study.

Whatever the outcome of such studies, the research to date on the sociology of early French Protestantism provides little support for the view that the subsequent conflicts of the Wars of Religion arose from pre-existing socio-economic antagonisms, although a recent book by Henry Heller has tried to reassert such a view.[11] But if the religious violence of the era did not stem from such antagonisms, what fuelled it? Here again the work of Natalie Davis has offered compelling answers. In her no less important article, "The Rites of Violence: Religious Riot in Sixteenth-Century France,"[12] she observed that recurring patterns characterized the crowd actions of the Wars of Religion. In general, Protestants were interested in mocking and physically attacking sacred objects of Catholic worship with the pedagogical intent of demonstrating their thoroughly ordinary character. Catholic violence was more often directed against the Protestants themselves with the goal of ridding the community of their presence. Ideas of pollution and the need to eliminate polluting objects or people loomed large for both. In brief, religious rioting arose from conflict between two radically different systems of the sacred and of their proper location within society.

Davis' article has now inspired a massive thesis on religious violence across the period of the religious wars by Denis Crouzet that embraces an unabashedly idealist approach to the subject and situates the violence within a grand cultural dialectic that the author claims to have discerned on the basis of extensive reading in the sermons, pamphlets, chronicles, and other published documents of the period.[13] Crouzet's vast panorama of sacred violence defies easy summary. Reduced to its essentials, it argues that the major development destabilizing religious life in the early sixteenth century was the growth of eschatological fear fueled by millenarian preaching and a striking expansion of astrological prediction epitomized by the writings of Nostradamus. This was the context for the spread of Calvin's ideas, which derived their particular potency from the reassurance that predestination offered those frightened by the imminent end of the world. But the rise of the Reformed religion only heightened anxiety further among those who remained loyal to Catholicism. The response was anti-Huguenot violence fueled by mystical aspirations to be the conduit of God's wrath and by a sense for the immanence of the divine in the Last Days. This violence would peak in the savage frenzy of the Saint Bartholomew's Massacres, an event of such violence that it subsequently provoked profound guilt on the part of those who had participated in it and a displacement of religious longings into inward penitence and exercises of self-purification. It remains to be seen whether or not further, more systematic research into the printed sermons, propaganda, and almanacs of the period will confirm that the elements that Crouzet identifies as central to this dialectic were indeed the dominant motifs within the messy amalgam of themes, topoi, and intellectual traditions that comprised French culture at this time. Predestination was certainly not central to the Protestant propaganda. Addressing the intellectual challenge raised by Crouzet's arguments nonetheless deserves to be another priority for future research.

However well Crouzet's theses hold up in the light of additional work, no account will make sense of France's religious history in this period that does not also pay close attention to the political context within which the religious changes of the era unfolded and to the variety of local and regional situations. The breakdown of order after 1560 cannot be divorced from the imbrication of the religious divisions within the rivalries of the great nobility and the context of sudden political flux that followed upon the death of Henry II—a context that also contributed a great deal to the atmosphere that allowed the Reformed churches to grow so rapidly in these years. Henry II had brought the Habsburg-Valois wars to an end with the Peace of Cateau Cambrésis largely to devote more of his resources to combatting the alarming spread of Protestantism. No sooner had he done so than he was mortally wounded, and the crown devolved upon a sickly fifteen-year-old, Francis II. Francis was under the sway of his wife's strongly Catholic uncle, the Duke of Guise, but just when he was about to bring the Prince of Condé to trial for conspiring to remove the Guises from power, he in turn died on 2 December 1560. The crown passed next to the ten-year-old Charles IX, for whom a regency government had to be set up under the direction of the Queen Mother, Catherine de Medici. Catherine had to try to maintain the loyalty of all of the influential families of the kingdom, and was attracted to the program advanced actively in these years by a number of churchmen and intellectuals whom contemporaries dubbed "moyenneurs." This group, which included several bishops, the chancellor Michel de L'Hôpital, and Etienne de la Boëtie, proposed healing the emerging religious divisions through a moderate reform of the established church that, it was hoped, might lure the Protestants back into the fold.

In pursuit of this policy, Catherine and her son wrote several bishops to urge them to seek an accommodation with the ministers of the new religion in their area, then won the assent of the Gallican church to a colloquy at Poissy in September 1561 with a delegation of the Reformed. But the colloquy only revealed the extent of the gulf between the Calvinists' interpretation of what constituted the pure worship of God and the views of the majority of French bishops. Having failed to achieve concord, Catherine legislated toleration, a makeshift in the opinion of virtually everybody at the time. The Edict of Saint-Germain of 17 January 1562, commonly known as the Edict of January, granted the Protestants permission to hold organized worship outside the walls of walled towns and forbade the clergy of each faith to insult the other. Within seven years of their foundation, France's Reformed churches had obtained legal recognition of their right to exist.

But legislating religious toleration was one thing. Creating a stable, bi-confessional *modus vivendi* was quite another. For the Protestants, in the heady spring of 1562, obtaining a measure of religious toleration seemed but a step toward their ultimate goal, the regeneration of both church and society. For the Catholic preachers who thundered against the edict at Lent, to order them to refrain from insulting members of the opposite religion was to overlook their divinely ordained obligation to call a heresy a heresy. When, on 1 March 1562, efforts by the duke of Guise to disperse a group of Protestant worshippers assembled inside the walls of the small town of Vassy led to a clash in which the duke's men slew many of those gathered, a sequence of events was set in motion that showed the instability of the political situation. Called to court to account for his actions, Guise proceeded instead to Paris, where he received a hero's welcome and the promise of troops and money from the head of the city government. Catherine turned to the prince of Condé and urged him to take the young king, then at Fontainebleau, under his protection. Condé, apparently mistrusting the Queen Mother, declined. Instead, the duke of Guise and several fellow Catholic grandees went to Fontainebleau with a large body of retainers and pressured Charles and Catherine to return to Paris with them. These "Triumvirs" declared that they would not stand for the toleration of two religions within the kingdom. Condé declared that the king had been illegally kidnapped and called for troops to assemble to defend him. In early April, the Protestants seized control of over twenty cities. The First Civil War had begun. The force of arms would now determine France's religious fate.

5. FROM CIVIL WAR TO CO-EXISTENCE

The outbreak of nationwide civil war in April 1562 initiated a cycle of violence that would repeat itself eight times until 1598. While each conflict had its own causes and characteristics, recurring patterns can be discerned. In the organized fighting of each civil war, the royal and Catholic forces nearly always had a numerical advantage over the troops that the Huguenots were able to assemble from the ranks of

Table 1. Civil Wars and Edicts of Pacification in France, 1562-1598

Conflicts and Approximate Dates	Precipitants	Edict of Pacification and Chief Provisions
First Civil War (April 1562-March 1563	Protestant mobilization and seizure of several dozen cities to preserve rights of worship thought to be in jeopardy and to remove king Charles IX from control of the Catholic Triumvirate	Edict of Amboise (7 articles) – Protestant worship allowed on lands of all noblemen possessing rights of high justice; in all cities where in existence on 7 March 1563; and in suburbs of one city per *bailliage*
Second Civil War (September 1567-March 1568)	Protestant seizure of several cities and attempt to take custody of king prompted by fears that Spanish troop movements along border betokened military action against faith	Peace of Longjumeau (14 articles) – terms of Edict of Amboise reiterated – no Protestant worship within *prévôté* and *vicomté* of Paris
Third Civil War (October 1568-August 1570)	Generalized failure of Peace of Longjumeau to restore order, military offensive of Condé and Coligny in region around La Rochelle	Peace of Saint-Germain (45 articles) – Catholic worship restored where had ceased – Protestant services allowed in localities where meeting on 1 August 1570 and in a number of specified localities in each *gouvernement*, none within 10 leagues of Paris – Protestants given four *places de sûreté*
Fourth Civil War (September 1572-July 1573)	Protestants of several regions of South and West defy royal order in wake of Saint Bartholomew's massacres to cease assemblies, expel or refuse entry to royal garrisons	Edict of Boulogne (25 articles) – Catholic worship restored where had ceased – full Protestant worship allowed in only La Rochelle, Montauban, and Nîmes – Protestant nobles possessing rights of high justice allowed to celebrate baptisms and marriages in small assemblies in their houses, except within 10 leagues of Paris – La Rochelle, Montauban, and Nîmes exempted from housing royal troops

Conflicts and Approximate Dates	Precipitants	Edict of Pacification and Chief Provisions
Fifth Civil War (September 1574-May 1576)	Failure of Edict of Boulogne to restore order as Protestant armies in Huguenot-controlled areas reject its terms; conspiracies of uncertain character involving Protestants, moderate Catholics known as "malcontents", and the king's brother, the Duke of Alençon	Edict of Beaulieu or Peace of Monsieur (63 articles) – Catholic worship restored where had ceased – Protestant worship permitted throughout realm except within 2 leagues of Paris or the court – special *chambres mi-parties* divided equally between Protestant and Catholic judges established in every Parlement to judge cases involving Protestants – Protestants granted 8 *places de sûreté*
Sixth Civil War (April 1577-September 1577)	Catholic nobles distressed by concessions of Edict of Beaulieu pressure Henry III to reopen question of peace terms and undertake new campaign against Protestants	Peace of Bergerac (64 general and 48 secret articles) – Catholic worship restored where had ceased – Protestant worship allowed on lands of all noblemen possessing rights of high justice, in all cities where in existence on 17 September 1577, and in suburbs of one city per *bailliage*, except within 2 leagues of court and 10 leagues of Paris – special chambers established in very Parlement to judge cases involving Protestants, with those of Toulouse, Bordeaux, Aix, and Grenoble to be composed of judges of both faiths – Protestants granted 8 *places de sûreté* and royal subvention to help pay for garrisons – secret articles specify concessions to Henry of Navarre and Condé
Seventh Civil War (April 1580-November 1580)	Attempts by adventuristic Huguenot commanders to seize new strongholds; fighting only limited	Peace of Fleix – reiterates terms of Peace of Bergerac with additional clarifications

Conflict and Approximate Dates	Precipitants	Edict of Pacification and Chief Provisions
Wars of the League (August 1585-March 1598)	Catholic League to forestall possibility of a Protestant succession convinces Henry III to prohibit Protestant worship through-out kingdom and to begin campaigns against regions which defy this ban. Catholic fears that campaigns not being pursued aggressively enough and provocations of Duke of Guise subsequently lead to Day of Barricades in Paris (12 May 1588). Henry III orders murder of Guise, Catholic cities across kingdom rise in revolt, and Henry III assassinated (1 August 1589). War becomes a succession struggle between Henry of Navarre and several Catholic claimants	Edict of Nantes (92 general and 56 secret articles, 2 brevets) – Catholic worship restored where had ceased –Protestant worship allowed on lands of noblemen possessing rights of high justice, in cities where in existence in 1596 or 1597, in all places where permitted under Peace of Bergerac, and in suburbs of one additional city per *bailliage*, except within 5 leagues of Paris or where other agreements were made as part of the bargains by which individual localities recognized Henry of Navarre as king – special chambers composed of judges of both faiths maintained or established in Parlements of Paris, Tou-louse, Bordeaux, and Grenoble to judge cases involving Protestants – Protestants granted 84 *places de sûreté* and royal subvention to help pay for garrisons and ministers

their faithful, with reinforcement from foreign co-religionists during certain of the wars. But mobilizing the standing army units that were dispersed across the country in peacetime and supplementing these with the mercenaries that were necessary to bring the royal army to fighting strength was always a slow and costly process, during which the Protestants typically seized the military initiative and took control of some well fortified towns. Furthermore, the crown lacked the re-sources to keep its army in the field for long, especially as the Hugue-nots siphoned off tax revenues to pay for their troops. Generally, only a few Protestant-controlled towns could be retaken before the crown chose to negotiate a new peace, granting anew rights of Reformed wor-ship on specified terms that varied in their generosity according to the course of the previous conflict.

Table 1 sets forth the chronology of the wars and the basic principles of each edict of pacification. As Bernard Chevalier accurately observes in this *Handbook*, volume 1:390, confessional violence was by no means confined to the times of formal civil war during this period; in parts of the country, religious rioting and guerrilla warfare dotted the periods of putative peace as well. Table 1 is nonetheless valuable as a guide to the crown's groping efforts to define the terms of a durable religious settlement. As can be seen, all but one of the edicts of pacification from 1563 onward parted company with the Edict of January by restricting the exercise of the "so-called Reformed religion" to specified localities. This limited the Protestants' capacity to evangelize after 1563 and probably should be considered, along with the reaction that set in against the faith on the part of many people who now perceived it as a cause of sedition and discord, as one of the fundamental reasons why it did not continue the dramatic expansion of the period 1555-62. As can also be seen, each edict of pacification tended to be longer than the preceding one, for each civil war added new layers of grievances and new problems to be resolved. Indicative of the sorts of issues that had to be addressed as the period advanced are clauses in the edicts of 1576 and 1577 annulling all cases where children were disinherited for their religion, forbidding processions to celebrate the death of the Prince of Condé or the Saint Bartholomew's massacre, and allowing people who had abjured either faith under the pressure of events to return to the religion of their choice without penalty. Over the course of the wars one can gradually see emerging the central elements that would characterize the Edict of Nantes: Protestant worship allowed in localities determined by a combination of historical precedent and regular geographic dispersion across the kingdom; special appeals courts composed of both Protestant and Catholic judges in those jurisdictions within which the Huguenots were most numerous to judge cases pitting members of the two faiths against one another or arising out of the interpretation of the edicts of pacification; and strategic strongholds placed under Protestant control to guarantee their security in case of further troubles.

In the localities, however, the terms of these edicts were often honored as much in the breach as in the observance, especially when open warfare broke out. Protestant freedom of worship was only revoked by royal decree at the outbreak of the Third and Fourth Civil Wars and under pressure from the Catholic League in 1585. This decree, however, did not stop the authorities of those towns that had remained steadfastly loyal to the crown from outlawing Protestant religious assemblies during other civil wars as well. In such times and places, close surveillance, special taxation, and other vexations were also imposed on the Huguenots. Many left such towns fearing for their safety. For their part, the new Huguenot authorities of many towns secured by the Protestants in 1562 seem to have sought at first to allow Catholic worship to continue unmolested, but this moderation was quickly swept aside as fighting intensified suspicion of those of the Catholics. Altars and church furnishings were destroyed in waves of iconoclasm; the celebration of the Mass ceased; and inhabitants were obliged to attend the Protestant *prêches*. During each subsequent civil war, the authorities of such Huguenot bastions as La Rochelle outlawed Catholic worship as a matter of course while defying the royal edicts of 1568, 1572, and 1585 forbidding Protestant services. Violent attacks on members of the Roman clergy became common. With the end of each civil war, adherents of the minority faith in any given region typically sought to reassert their rights of worship, but bitter hostility from the majority often kept them from doing so—or even, if they had fled the city, from returning to their houses—until royal commissioners intervened to enforce the peace. Such periods of attempted pacification were often punctuated by the bloodiest incidents of anti-Huguenot violence, especially during the first decade after 1562 in those areas where the Protestants remained a threatening minority presence.

Obtaining a stable religious settlement required first and foremost that an equilibrium be reached on the local level between the two parties. So many communities remained divided between important groups of partisans of each confession in the early years of the Wars of Religion that this was initially hard to do. There were localities, such as Toulouse, where the Protestant movement crested in 1561-62 and was of little significance thereafter. In that city, a Huguenot attempt to seize the town in 1562 was beaten back in five days of bloody street fighting, followed by an equally bloody wave of repression. The city's Reformed church had employed five pastors in the spring of 1562 and had constructed a temple said to hold 8,000 people, but after the events of that year it struggled to assemble regularly for worship.

In most cities which had seen the growth of an important Protestant community prior to 1562, however, the Huguenots were able to reconstruct their congregation under the terms of the Peace of Amboise and remain an important local presence. Orléans offers the example of a particularly bitterly contested city of this sort, for it was the base from which the Prince of Condé rallied his men in 1562 and 1567 but was secured by an important royal garrison in 1568. We also possess an exceptionally evocative overview of the fate of its Reformed church in the prefaces to two devotional writings written later in the century by its minister from 1562 to 1572, Daniel Toussaint. In the first years of the Reformation, Toussaint recalled, God had seemed to bless his faithful in the city. During the First Civil War, just as Orléans was besieged by the Catholics and threatened with capture and sack, peace was negotiated. In those same early years of the church:

> It was truly a triumph. . . . Although there were some hypocrites in
> the flock, there was an infinite number of good souls . . . desirous of
> enlightenment and reformation, such as shone through in several
> who changed their blaspheming into prayer and the singing of
> Psalms, their fornication and dissolution into chaste marriages, their
> excesses in dress and feasting into a withdrawn and well ordered life
> and alms to the poor. Then one could recognize a member of the
> Reformed Religion at twenty paces by his countenance, his words
> and his deeds.

But tribulations rained down after the royal troops came in 1568. Acts of violence against the Protestants multiplied. It took a year for them to reestablish their church following the Peace of Saint-Germain, during which time they "were daily threatened, beaten, robbed and . . . let and hindered . . . to enjoy the greatest part of their goods." The local reenactment of the Saint Bartholomew's massacre of 1572 was the final blow. The "greatest part" of the church was slaughtered and many others fell away from the faith, so "that it seemeth, there is no trace or path of a Church left, or that ever there had been anie reformation."[14]

The fate of Orléans' church exemplifies in particularly dramatic form that of many of the Reformed congregations in those cities of the northern half of the kingdom and in certain regions of the Midi where the Protestants had been an important minority but could not permanently secure political and military control. In these cities, the balance of power tipped towards the Catholics, the situation of the Huguenots grew more precarious, and after the outbreak of the Third Civil War and the atrocities of the Saint Bartholomew's massacre, many lost faith in the rightness of the cause or heart for the sacrifices that commitment to it entailed. In Rouen, where the church numbered roughly 16,500 members in 1564-65, less than 3,000 faithful remained by the late 1570s. In Caen, where there was less anti-Huguenot violence and no local Saint Bartholomew's massacre, abjuration and emigration

thinned the ranks of the church from about 10,750 members in 1564-
68 to 3,750 in 1578-84. With Protestant numbers dramatically reduced in this manner in many towns where they were once most threatening, and with hundreds of Huguenots having submitted voluntarily
to humiliating abjuration ceremonies that demonstrated the faith's political emasculation, local religious violence grew rare. Small Protestant minorities survived and were able to worship in times of peace,
but they no longer seemed a threat to the political order.

That they were able to worship at all is testimony to the political and
military concessions gained by their co-religionists in the "Huguenot
crescent," where perhaps half of the major towns were dominated numerically and politically by the Protestants. As the cause lost ground
elsewhere and violence continued to threaten the Reformed, their leaders in the regions stretching from Poitou to Dauphiné realized that
their continued survival depended upon maintaining military control
of their strongholds and taking organizational steps to enable them to
put an army in the field when necessary. Following the close of the
Second Civil War, the Huguenots of La Rochelle, Montauban, Castres
and a number of smaller towns refused to submit to the military authority of their royal governors; this is the origin of the system of *places
de sûreté* recognized by the edicts of pacification from 1570 onward.
Amid the fighting that followed the Saint Bartholomew's massacre,
delegates from several Protestant-controlled regions of Languedoc met
together to establish a common system for raising taxes and administering seized church properties in these areas. These assemblies soon
grew into a regular system of regional councils and national political
assemblies. They coordinated Protestant military efforts, provided a
forum for expressing shared political concerns, and nominated delegates to represent the cause in parleys with the crown.

These measures of self-defense and organization enabled the Huguenots to stave off military offensives against the towns in which they
were strongest and even to negotiate in 1576 the very favorable terms
of the Edict of Beaulieu, the one edict of pacification of the wars that
did not limit the number of localities in which the Reformed could
gather for worship. Although this in turn provoked the mobilization
of the first Catholic League and a new conflict, followed by a peace
treaty that once again restricted Protestant worship to a fixed number
of localities, the terms of this Peace of Bergerac were still more generous than those of earlier edicts of pacification. They appear to have
been implemented with a fair degree of success in most parts of the

country. It is possible to argue that the Peace of Bergerac could have become remembered in the manner that the Edict of Nantes now is, as the edict of pacification that finally brought a lasting peace, if only Henry III, a more effective ruler than posterity has conventionally judged, had been able to beget an heir.

But this is precisely what the king and his queen Louise de Vaudémont could not do, and the vicissitudes of dynastic succession consequently called the country's religious fate into question once again when the last of Henry's brothers, Francis, Duke of Alençon, died in 1584. Now the Protestant Henry of Navarre possessed the strongest claim to the succession. The scale of the Catholic mobilization that followed revealed the depth of antipathy that existed by this time to the idea of a Protestant king—even if noble ambition and rivalries, resentment at rising taxation and the spread of venal office, and Spanish aid and encouragement also fuelled the reconstruction of the Catholic League. That antipathy forced Henry III to revoke the toleration of Protestantism and to dispatch troops to fight those who defied this edict. When the fitful nature of the royal campaigning convinced militant Catholic opinion that the king's heart was not in this crusade, the Parisians took to the streets in the "Day of the Barricades" (12 May 1588). Seven months later, Henry's attempt to free himself from League tutelage by killing the duke and cardinal of Guise prompted the Sorbonne and the inhabitants of many cities in the realm to renounce their obedience to him. On 1 August 1589 the "wicked Herod" was killed by a young Dominican, said by subsequent League pamphlets to have been divinely inspired while in prayer to carry out the act.

Following Henry III's assassination, Henry of Navarre quickly proclaimed his intention to respect the established position of the Roman church, to reassure the Catholic majority that his accession would not produce a Protestant state church. At the same time, he resurrected the call for a "free" council (i.e. one not under Papal control), that, it could be hoped, might restore religious concord to the realm, and from which he promised to take instruction. A number of clerics in Navarre's service, notably Jean Hotman de Villiers and Jean de Serres, advanced schemes for the reunion of the churches. The turmoil and exaltation of the bitter succession struggle that followed Henry III's death hardly conduced to the considered examination of such schemes, however, and the promised council never assembled. Henry IV only won the allegiance of the country gradually over nine years of fighting, thanks to his own military and political genius, the internal divisions of

the Catholic League, and his decision in 1593 to convert to the Roman
church. This critical final step guaranteed that the Bourbon dynasty
that would rule France until 1789 would be a Catholic dynasty, and it
can be taken as Henry's tacit acceptance of the principle defended by
the League that the ruler of the most Christian kingdom had to be
Catholic. But Henry did not abandon the interests of his former co-
religionists. As he brought more and more towns under his control, he
allowed Protestant worship to be reestablished in many of them. The
wars of the League lasted far longer than any of the previous civil wars,
involved fighting of far broader territorial extent, and consequently
wrought far greater devastation. The Huguenots' ability to survive all
military efforts against them and to emerge with their bargaining
power enhanced drove home to the majority of Catholics that attempting to eradicate Protestantism brought consequences that were even
less agreeable than tolerating it. Some Parlements initially balked at
registering the Edict of Nantes, and its implementation required firm-
ness and patience in many regions, but the majority of a war-weary nation was now ready to submit to an edict of pacification that would finally demonstrate some durability.

Once the commissioners sent out to enforce the Edict of Nantes had
done their work, just upwards of 700 Protestant churches assembled
with some permanence within the old boundaries of the Valois kingdom. A higher percentage of these churches than in 1562 were now
clustered in the Huguenot crescent, as those located elsewhere had
proven particularly vulnerable to the events of the preceding thirty-six
years. The fuller records extant for this period enable us to estimate
the membership of these churches with reasonable accuracy at between
860,000 and one million people. Also now joined to the crown due to
the accession of the Bourbon dynasty were the slightly more than
100,000 inhabitants of the principality of Béarn, where Protestantism
had been imposed as the religion of state between 1561 and 1570.[15]

6. The Catholic Church from 1560 to 1600

The first half of the seventeenth century—the era of François de Sales,
Vincent de Paul, and many other saints and *dévots*—has always represented the heroic age of the Catholic Reformation in France. Recent
research has emphasized the transformations discernable within the
church in the later part of the sixteenth century and the important con-

tinuities between these and the subsequent flowering of the French Counterreformation. Even while the established church was buffeted by the attacks of Huguenot iconoclasts and the material destruction of the civil wars, the introduction of new religious orders, the promulgation at the diocesan level of many of the decrees of the Council of Trent, and a dramatic devotional élan that gathered strength over the 1580s and 1590s altered the character of French Catholicism and prepared the way for the still greater changes to follow.

The first new orders of the Counterreformation spread into France just as the Wars of Religion broke out. Jesuit novices had been sent to Paris for their education as early as 1540, and a bishop well disposed to the young order had placed it in charge of the faltering college in the small town of Billom in Auvergne in 1556, but opposition from the Faculty of Theology and the Parlements impeded the Society's efforts to gain formal permission to establish itself until 1562. During the 1560s and 1570s, itinerant Jesuit preachers such as Antonio Possevino and Emond Auger visited many cities, stiffening the resolve of Catholics in strongly Protestant areas, encouraging charitable initiatives and eucharistic devotion, and organizing innovative catechetical instruction. Permanent houses were soon established in a growing number of cities—11 by 1575, 20 by 1594, and 37 by 1615. The secondary schools whose operation became the chief activity of the order quickly gained such prestige that Reformed consistories had to admonish church members not to send their children to them. They incorporated elements of humanist instruction into the curriculum, but formed pupils with a depth of commitment to orthodox doctrine that distinguished them from those educated in the municipally-controlled colleges of the first two thirds of the century. Their proliferation was critical in shaping the outlook of the social elites of the *grand siècle*.

The Capuchins soon followed. This austere offshoot of the Franciscan order established its first French house in 1575. By 1596, 35 houses lodged 456 brothers. The Capuchins directed their ministry toward the broad mass of the population. They were soon known for their devoted service to the victims of plague epidemics, their missions, and their encouragement of dramatic ceremonies of reverence for the contested mysteries of the Catholic faith. Particularly important was the Forty Hours devotion, where rotating groups of the faithful prayed continuously before an elaborately decorated altar on which the consecrated host was exposed, a ceremony that began to spread through France in the late 1580s.

It was not simply the new religious orders that promoted change in the mood and style of Catholic piety in this period. Non-residence remained the norm and dedicated pastoral reformers a distinct minority among France's bishops. Furthermore, published synodal statutes survive from only 32 bishoprics for the period 1559-98 as opposed to 61 for the years 1516-59, suggesting slackening episcopal oversight. Still, a majority of the country's archbishops took at least the first step toward implementing the decrees of the Council of Trent, convening provincial councils to promote their adoption.

The Tridentine decisions were highly controversial in France, for while a contingent of French bishops had been dispatched to Trent after the failure of the colloquy of Poissy, they arrived too late to have much influence on the outcome of its work, while certain decrees were seen as challenges to regalian power or the ancient liberties of the Gallican church. Support for the decrees nonetheless gathered within the First Estate, and the 1579 clerical Assembly of Melun unanimously urged their incorporation into French law. The tenacious opposition of the law courts thwarted this, just as it would later defeat similar demands from the Catholic League, and later yet would block Henry IV from delivering on his promise to Pope Clement VIII, made in exchange for the Pope's recognition of his conversion, that he would see to it that the decrees became law. But only the canons on ecclesiastical justice and pontifical authority offended. After the request of the Assembly of Melun was rejected, eight of the kingdom's fourteen archbishoprics made an end run around the legists and, between 1581 and 1590, convened provincial ecclesiastical councils to consider the remainder of the Tridentine program. Most of these adopted the overwhelming majority of Trent's liturgical, theological and disciplinary regulations. If never formally enacted into law, the guidelines for church reform laid down at Trent thus came to be known and accepted throughout much of France by 1590.

Perhaps the greatest force for change in Catholic religious life was simply the impact of the events of the era on the sensibilities of those faithful to the church. Outrage at the Huguenot attacks on sacred doctrines and objects, dismay at the devastation wrought by the civil wars, and the widespread tendency to attribute these hardships to the avenging hand of a wrathful God all combined to spur a revival of communitarian Catholic rituals and an upsurge of penitential piety that gathered strength as the Wars of Religion advanced. In 1567-68, hundreds of inhabitants of towns across Burgundy gathered in their ruined churches to revive the confraternities of the Holy Ghost that had been numerous in the region in the late Middle Ages but had ceased to function by the middle of the sixteenth century. Among the obligations that members assumed were to exchange gifts and contribute grain at Pentecost for the baking of communal loaves of bread, a symbolic expression of their longing to repair a sense of community that had been violated by the events of the recent past; to keep arms ready for use whenever their superiors required; and communicate with each other about the movements of the Huguenots in the region. Companies of Penitents spread out of their original toehold in the region between Marseille and Avignon across much of southern France and even, temporarily, into parts of the north during the League. In 1583-84, the inhabitants first of Champagne and then of a large portion of the region around Paris organized vast regional processions in which, barefoot and dressed in white, they begged God's mercy for their sins. Such processions were repeated in Paris and other towns in the early years of the League. Other signs of a broad rallying to the gestures and traditions of the church may be found in the revival of pilgrimages to certain formerly abandoned shrines and an upturn in the level of pious giving to ecclesiastical collection basins, while the publication of many books by Spanish devotional writers in the 1580s and 1590s introduced new currents of Catholic religiosity destined to have great influence.

Any general picture of Catholic religious life during this period must also take into account the interruption of worship and devastation of church property in many regions by marauding Protestant troops, the forced alienation of about five per cent of the church's property in subventions demanded by the crown to help fight the religious wars, and a drop in the number of clergymen resulting from rising requirements for ordination as well as the insecurities of a clerical career in this era. In the particularly troubled diocese of Toulouse, the number of priests fell by nearly fifty per cent between 1538 and 1596. Still, the archbishop of that city could report to Rome in 1594, "There remains the very great consolation that piety and devotion have grown because of the troubles, so that as much as the material goods [of the church] have been damaged, by just as much has zeal and ardor for piety and religion increased among all the people of Toulouse."[16] As the seventeenth century dawned, the renewal of Catholic religious life was gathering force, even while France's Reformed minority had obtained a more secure position of legal toleration than ever before.

✖ ✖ ✖

No dictum has been more emphasized by French historiography over the past two generations than the importance of envisaging problems over the *longue durée*. If this chapter closes its account of religious change in France in 1600, the long view reminds us that the legal framework of the religious settlement obtained by that date would not endure for the rest of the Ancien Régime. The toleration of two faiths in one kingdom was still not accepted by the great majority of the political nation as anything other than a necessary evil. Many Huguenots continued to believe that only constant vigilance could preserve their privileges from erosion by a hostile majority, and this would combine once again with the confused ambitions of their leading noble chieftains to produce risings in the 1620s that ended with the loss of their *places de sûreté*. The steady advance of the Counterreformation would meanwhile stiffen Catholic conviction, and as the military might of the crown grew, the argument that Protestantism had to be tolerated to maintain civil peace lost its force. In 1685, the Edict of Nantes would be revoked, and French Protestantism would enter a second period during which those of its adherents who remained in the country had to gather for worship in defiance of the law. This time the churches under the cross would wander in the desert for more than a century before they were granted freedom of worship again in 1787.

But on a deeper level, the basic confessional patterns that would characterize the country for centuries to come had taken shape by the end of the sixteenth century. The longings for evangelical reform that had developed among a fraction of the population in the first six decades of the century had been funnelled into an organized church of Calvinist theology that, despite comprising only a small minority of the population, had already demonstrated its extraordinary capacity to survive. The militance of much of the Catholic population had ensured that the Bourbon dynasty that would last to the Revolution would be Catholic. In large measure because of the challenge posed by the growth of Protestantism, the forces of reform were also gaining the upper hand in their long struggle with the forces of inertia within French Catholicism, and these forces would keep on gathering strength over the next generations. As for the dream of the "moyenneurs" of defining a distinctive Gallican *via media* to reunite the country in a single church, this would live on in the schemes advanced for the reunion of the churches by a variety of eirenicists throughout the seventeenth century. As during the sixteenth century, however, this dream would be no match for the institutional and ideological dynamic pushing all of Europe toward confessional polarization.

NOTES

1. Martin (1988), 268.
2. Marie-France Godfroy, "Le prédicateur franciscain Thomas Illyricus à Toulouse (novembre 1518-mai 1519)," *AM* 97 (1985): 101-14.
3. Imbart de la Tour (1905-35), vol. 3:170. This work remains the fullest and most authoritative account of the early Reformation in France.
4. *Index Aureliensis: Catalogus Librorum Sedecimo Saeculo Impressorum* (Baden-Baden, 1962-), part 1, vol. 6.
5. Amédée Roget, *Histoire du peuple de Genève*, (Geneva, 1870-1883), vol. 3, 134; Paul-F. Geisendorf ed., *Livre des habitants de Genève*, vol. 1: *1549-1560* (Geneva, 1957), 4-10, 146-218; E. William Monter, *Calvin's Geneva* (New York, 1967), 166.
6. A. Lynn Martin, *The Jesuit Mind: The Mentality of an Elite in Early Modern France* (Ithaca, 1988), 90.
7. Garrisson-Estèbe (1980), 83.
8. Kingdon (1956), 79; Peter Wilcox, "L'envoi de pasteurs aux Eglises de France: Trois listes établies par Colladon (1561-1562)" *Bulletin de la Société de l'Histoire du Protestantisme Français* 139 [1993], 347-74.
9. *ARG* 56 (1965): 48-64; reprinted in Davis (1975).
10. Rosenberg (1978).
11. Heller (1986).
12. *PaP* 59 (1973), 51-91; reprinted in Davis (1975).
13. Crouzet (1990).
14. Daniel Toussaint, *The Exercise of the faithfull soule* (London, 1583), dedication; "L'Arche de Noé, Traité nécessaire en ce temps, pour consoler les pauvres Fideles, de longtemps agités de diverses tempêtes, que pour se résoudre des marques de la vraie Eglise, addressé et dedié aux Eglises Réformées de la France" (1596) in *Mémoires de la Ligue* (Amsterdam, 1758), vol. 6:378.
15. Philip Benedict, *The Huguenot Population of France, 1600-1685: the Demographic Fate and Customs of a Religious Minority*, TAPS, vol. 81 (Philadelphia, 1991), 75-76.
16. Le Goff and Rémond (1988), 306.

BIBLIOGRAPHY

Anquez, Léonce. *Histoire des assemblées politiques des réformés de France (1573-1622).* Paris, 1859.

Aspects de la propagande religieuse. THR, vol. 28. Geneva, 1957.

Audisio, Gabriel. *Les vaudois du Luberon. Une minorité en Provence (1460-1560).* N.p., 1984.

Baccrabère, G. "La pratique religieuse dans le diocèse de Toulouse aux XVIe et XVIIe siècles." *AM* 74 (1962): 287-314.

Baumgartner, Frederic J. *Change and Continuity in the French Episcopate: the Bishops and the Wars of Religion 1547-1610.* Duke Monographs in Medieval and Renaissance Studies, vol. 7. Durham, N.C., 1986.

Bedouelle, Guy. *Lefèvre d'Etaples et l'Intelligence des Ecritures.* THR, vol. 152. Geneva, 1976.

Belle, Edmond. "La Réforme à Dijon des origines à la fin de la lieutenance générale de Gaspard de Saulx-Tavanes (1530-1570)." *Revue Bourguignonne* 21 (1911): 1-245.

Benedict, Philip. "The Catholic Response to Protestantism: Church Activity and Popular Piety in Rouen, 1560-1600." In *Religion and the People 800-1700*, ed James Obelkevich. Chapel Hill, 1979.

Benedict, Philip. *Rouen during the Wars of Religion.* Cambridge, 1981.

Bergin, Joseph. "Henry IV and the Problem of the French Episcopate," in *From Valois to Bourbon: Dynasty, State and Society in Early Modern France*, ed. Keith Cameron. Exeter, 1989.

Berthoud, Gabrielle. *Antoine Marcourt, Réformateur et Pamphlétaire du "Livre des Marchans" aux Placards de 1534.* THR, vol. 129. Geneva, 1973.

Broutin, Paul. *L'évêque dans la tradition pastorale du XVIe siècle.* Bruges, 1953.

Cameron, Euan. *The Reformation of the Heretics.* Oxford, 1984.

Cassan, Michel. "Laïcs, Ligue, et réforme catholique à Limoges." *Histoire, économie et société* 10 (1991): 159-75.

Cassan, Michel. "Les multiples visages des confréries de dévotion: l'exemple de Limoges au XVIe siècle." *AM* 99 (1987): 35-52.

Chevalier, Bernard, and Robert Sauzet eds. *Les Réformes. Enracinement socio-culturel.* Paris, 1985.

Constant, Jean-Marie. *Nobles et paysans en Beauce aux XVIe et XVIIe siècles.* Lille, 1981.

Crouzet, Denis. *Les guerriers de Dieu. La violence au temps des troubles de religion (vers 1525-vers 1610).* Seyssel, 1990.

Davis, Natalie Zemon. "The Sacred and the Body Social in Sixteenth-Century Lyon." *PaP* 90 (1981): 40-70.

Davis, Natalie Zemon. *Society and Culture in Early Modern France: Eight Essays.* Stanford, 1975.

Davies, Joan. "Persecution and Protestantism: Toulouse, 1562-1575." *HistJ* 22 (1979): 31-51.

Delumeau, Jean. *Catholicism between Luther and Voltaire: a New View of the Counter-Reformation.* London, 1977 [1971].

Denis, Philippe. "Viret et Morély: Les raisons d'un silence." *BHR* 54 (1992), 395-409.

Diefendorf, Barbara B. *Beneath the Cross: Catholics and Huguenots in Sixteenth-Century Paris.* Oxford, 1991.

Dompnier, Bernard. "Un aspect de la dévotion eucharistique dans la France du XVIIe siècle. Les Prières des Quarante Heures." *RHEF* 67 (1981): 5-31.

Eire, Carlos M. N. *War Against the Idols: the Reformation of Worship from Erasmus to Calvin.* Cambridge, 1986.

Estèbe, Janine. *Tocsin pour un massacre ou la saison des Saint-Barthélémy.* Paris, 1968.

Evennett, H. Outram. *The Cardinal of Lorraine and the Council of Trent: a Study in the Counter-Reformation.* Cambridge, 1930.

Farge, James K. *Orthodoxy and Reform in Early Reformation France: the Faculty of Theology of Paris, 1500-1543.* SMRT, vol. 32. Leiden, 1985.

Farr, James R. "Popular Religious Solidarity in Sixteenth-Century Dijon." *French Historical Studies* 14 (1985): 192-214.

Febvre, Lucien. *Amour sacré, amour profane. Autour de l'Heptaméron.* Paris, 1944.

Febvre, Lucien. *Au coeur religieux du XVIe siècle. La réligion de Rabelais.* Paris, 1957.

Fouqueray, Henri. *Histoire de la Compagnie de Jésus en France des origines à la suppression (1528-1762).* Paris, 1910.

Galpern, A. N. *The Religions of the People in Sixteenth-Century Champagne.* Cambridge, Mass., 1976.

Garrisson-Estèbe, Janine. *Protestants du Midi, 1559-1598.* Toulouse, 1980.

Garrisson-Estèbe, Janine. *Les protestants au XVIe siècle.* Paris, 1988.

Gascon, Richard. *Grand commerce et vie urbaine au XVIe siècle. Lyon et ses marchands.* Civilisations et Sociétés, vol. 22. Paris, 1971.

Greengrass, Mark. "The Anatomy of a Religious Riot in Toulouse in May 1562." *JEccH* 34 (1983): 367-91.

Greengrass, Mark. *France in the Age of Henri IV: the Struggle for Stability.* Studies in Modern History. London, 1984.

Greengrass, Mark. *The French Reformation.* Historical Association Studies. Oxford, 1987.

Guggenheim, Ann H. "The Calvinist Notables of Nimes during the Era of the Religious Wars." *SCJ* 3 (1972): 80-96.

Guiraud, Louise. *Etudes sur la Réforme à Montpellier.* Montpellier, 1918.

Harding, Robert R. "The Mobilization of Confraternities against the Reformation in France." *SCJ* 11 (1980): 85-107.

Hauser, Henri. *Études sur la Réforme française.* Paris, 1909.

Heller, Henry. *The Conquest of Poverty: the Calvinist Revolt in Sixteenth-Century France.* SMRT, vol. 35. Leiden, 1986.

Higman, Francis M. *Censorship and the Sorbonne: a Bibliographical Study of Books in French Censured by the Faculty of Theology of the University of Paris, 1520-1551.* THR, vol. 172. Geneva, 1979.

Higman, Francis M. "Le domaine français 1520-1562." In *La Réforme et le livre. L'Europe de l'imprimé (1517-v. 1570),* ed. Jean-François Gilmont. Paris, 1990.

Higman, Francis M. "Les traductions françaises de Luther, 1524-1550." In *Palaestra Typographica. Aspects de la production du livre humaniste et religieux au XVIe siècle,* ed. Jean-François Gilmont. Aubel, Belgium, 1984.

Holt, Mack P. "Wine, Community and Reformation in Sixteenth-Century Burgundy." *PaP,* no. 138 (1993): 58-93.

Imbart de la Tour, Pierre. *Les origines de la Réforme.* Paris, 1905-35.

Kaiser, Wolfgang. *Marseille im Bürgerkrieg. Sozialgefüge, Religionskonflikt und Faktionskämpfe von 1559-1596.* Göttingen, 1991.

Kelley, Donald R. *The Beginning of Ideology: Consciousness and Society in the French Reformation.* Cambridge, 1981.

Kingdon, Robert M. *Geneva and the Coming of the Wars of Religion in France, 1555-1563.* THR, vol. 22. Geneva, 1956.

Kingdon, Robert M. *Geneva and the Consolidation of the French Protestant Movement, 1564-1572.* Madison, 1967.

Knecht, R. J. "Francis I, 'Defender of the Faith'?" In *Wealth and Power in Tudor England: Essays Presented to S. T. Bindoff*, ed. E. W. Ives, R. J. Knecht, and J. J. Scarisbrick. London, 1978.

de Lacombe, Bernard. *Les débuts des guerres de religion (Orléans, 1559-1564). Cathérine de Médicis entre Guise et Condé.* Paris, 1899.

Lamet, Maryélise Suffern. "French Protestants in a Position of Strength: the Early Years of the Reformation in Caen, 1558-1568." *SCJ* 9 (1978): 35-56.

Lefebvre-Teillard, Anne. *Les officialités à la veille du Concile de Trente.* Paris, 1973.

Le Goff, Jacques, and René Rémond, eds. *Histoire de la France religieuse.* Vol. 2, *Du christianisme flamboyant à l'aube des Lumières (XIVe-XVIIIe siècle).* Paris, 1988.

Lemaitre, Nicole. *Le Rouergue flamboyant: le clergé et les fidèles du diocèse de Rodez, 1417-1563.* Paris, 1988.

Le Roy Ladurie, Emmanuel. *Paysans du Languedoc.* Paris, 1966.

Martin, Henri-Jean, and Roger Chartier, eds. *Histoire de l'édition française.* Vol. 1, *Le livre conquérant.* Paris, 1982.

Martin, Hervé. *Le métier de prédicateur en France septentrionale à la fin du Moyen Age (1350-1520).* Paris, 1988.

Martin, Victor. *Le Gallicanisme et la Réforme catholique. Essai historique sur l'introduction en France des décrets du concile de Trente (1563-1615).* Paris, 1919.

Mentzer, Raymond A., Jr. *Heresy Proceedings in Languedoc, 1500-1560.* TAPS, vol. 74. Philadelphia, 1984.

Moeller, Bernd. "Luther in Europe: His Works in Translation 1517-46." In *Politics and Society in Reformation Europe: Essays for Sir Geoffrey Elton on Sixty-Fifth Birthday*, ed. E. I. Kouri and Tom Scott. New York, 1987.

Molinier, Alain. "Aux origines de la Réformation cévenole." *AÉSC* 39 (1984): 240-64.

Moore, W. G. *La Réforme allemande et la littérature française.* Strasbourg, 1930.

Nicholls, David J. "Inertia and Reform in the Pre-Tridentine French Church: the Response to Protestantism in the Diocese of Rouen, 1520-1562." *JEccH* 32 (1981): 185-97.

Nicholls, David J. "Looking for the Origins of the French Reformation." In *Power, Culture, and Religion in France, c. 1350-c. 1550*, ed. C. Allmand. Woodbridge, Suffolk, 1989.

Nicholls, David J. "The Nature of Popular Heresy in France, 1520-1542." *HistJ* 26 (1983): 261-75.

Nicholls, David J. "Sectarianism and the French Reformation." *Bulletin of the John Rylands University Library* 70 (1988): 35-44.

Nicholls, David J. "Social Change and Early Protestantism in France: Normandy, 1520-62." *European Studies Review* 10 (1980), 279-308.

Nicholls, David J. "The Social History of the French Reformation: Ideology, Confession, and Culture." *SH* 9 (1984): 25-43.

Pannier, Jacques. *Les origines de la Confession de foi et la Discipline des Eglises réformées de France: Etude historique.* Paris, 1936.

Poujol, Jacques. "De la Confession de Foi de 1559 à la Conjuration d'Amboise." *BSHPF* 119 (1973): 158-77.

Rabut, Elisabeth. *Le roi, l'église et le temple. L'Exécution de l'Edit de Nantes en Dauphiné.* N.p., 1987.

Renaudet, Augustin. *Préréforme et humanisme à Paris pendant les premières guerres d'Italie.* Paris, 1916.

Richet, Denis. *De la Réforme à la Révolution. Études sur la France moderne.* Paris, 1991.

Roelker, Nancy Lyman. "The Appeal of Calvinism to French Noblewomen in the Sixteenth Century." *Journal of Interdisciplinary History* 2 (1972): 391-418.

Romier, Lucien. *Catholiques et huguenots à la cour de Charles IX.* Paris, 1924.

Romier, Lucien. *La conjuration d'Amboise. L'aurore sanglante de la liberté de conscience. Le règne et la mort de François II.* Paris, 1923.

Romier, Lucien. *Les origines politiques de guerres de religion.* Paris, 1913-14.

Romier, Lucien. *Le Royaume de Cathérine de Médicis. La France à la veille des guerres de religion.* Paris, 1925.

Rosenberg, David L. Social Experience and Religious Choice: a Case Study, the Protestant Weavers and Woolcombers of Amiens in the Sixteenth Century. Unpublished Ph.D. dissertation, Yale University, 1978.

Salmon, J. H. M. *Society in Crisis: France in the Sixteenth Century.* New York, 1975.

Sauzet, Robert. "Le milieu dévot tourangeau et les débuts de la réforme catholique." *RHEF* 75 (1989), 159-66.

Smith, Malcolm C. *Montaigne and Religious Freedom: The Dawn of Pluralism.* Geneva, 1991.

Sunshine, Glenn S. From French Protestantism to the French Reformed Churches: The Development of Huguenot Ecclesiastical Institutions, 1559-1598. Unpublished Ph.D. dissertation, University of Wisconsin, Madison, 1992.

Sutherland, Nicola M. *The Huguenot Struggle for Recognition.* New Haven, 1972.

Taylor, Larissa J. *Soldiers of Christ: Preaching in Late Medieval and Reformation France.* Oxford, 1992.

Turchetti, Mario. *Concordia o Tolleranza? François Bauduin (1520-1573) e i "Moyenneurs".* THR, vol. 200. Geneva, 1984.

Veissière, Michel. *L'éveque Guillaume Briçonnet (1470-1534). Contribution à la connaissance de la Réforme catholique à la veille du Concile de Trente.* Provins, 1986.

Venard, Marc. *L'Eglise d'Avignon au XVIème siècle.* Lille, 1980.

Venard, Marc. "France. III: Le XVIe siècle." *Dictionnaire d'histoire et de géographie ecclésiastiques,* vol. 18:51-78. Paris, 1980.

Venard, Marc. "Une réforme gallicane? Le projet de concile national de 1551." *RHEF* 67 (1981): 201-25.

Venard, Marc. *Réforme protestante, Réforme catholique dans la province d'Avignon—XVIe siècle.* Paris, 1993.

Vivanti, Corrado. *Lotta politica e pace religiosa in Francia fra Cinque e Seicento.* Turin, 1963.

Wood, James B. *The Nobility of the Election of Bayeux, 1463-1666: Continuity through Change.* Princeton, 1980.

Wood, James B. "The Royal Army During the Early Wars of Religion, 1559-1576." In *Society and Institutions in Early Modern France,* ed. Mack P. Holt. Athens, Ga., 1991.

SETTLEMENTS: THE BRITISH ISLES

W. Ian P. Hazlett
(University of Glasgow)

There was no such thing as a 'British Reformation'. The concept of 'Britain' at the time belonged mainly to humanist antiquarianism and bardic fantasy, though it came to be employed to enhance unionist notions. Since the geographic British Isles reflected a typically European political, ethnic, cultural, and linguistic heterogeneity, the Reformation in the four nations is four tales. The Tudor regimes did sponsor an English-style Reformation in Wales and Ireland, but with disparate results. In Scotland, the Reformation established itself contrary to the will of her monarch and most of the Church hierarchy – uniquely in Europe – and so eminently contrary to the religion-of-the-ruler principle. Accordingly, Reformation historiography of the British Isles is fourfold, usually practised separately. If the predominance of the English Reformation in Wales and Ireland is recognised, the English and Scottish Reformations are conventionally, though not always helpfully, treated apart. Traditional Scottish affinity with the Continent, along with an English isolationist ethos helps account for this.

In the wider field, the reformations in the British Isles continue to be relegated as peripheral and derivative.[1] This is enhanced by axiomatic value judgements of the English Reformation in particular as a (mere) political 'act of state' or an abortive 'half Reformation'. The disparagement is compounded by the universal tendency to stress its unique features due to inadequate distinction between primary and secondary elements. However, concentration on perceived Continental 'centres' and 'norms' will never reveal the whole truth about the entire European Reformation. Two postulates are of relevance: firstly, that 'accompanying the pan-European echo of the Reformers' message was an equally universal No'.[2] Secondly, that the Reformation needs to be seen as 'not only Protestant and northern but also as Christian and European. Neither confessional nor racial-cultural explanations of the place of the Reformation in European history have survived the fire of historical criticism'.[3] The assumption governing this chapter is that the reformations in the British Isles were typically European and Christian

REFORMATION IN THE BRITISH ISLES

ORKNEY
ISLANDS

HEBRIDES
ISLANDS

NORTH SEA

Dornach
Rosemarkie
Elgin

Moray Firth

Aberdeen

Dunkeld
Brechin
Dundee
Perth
St.Andrews

Lismore
Iona

F. of Lorne

Dunblaine

Firth of Forth

Liniithgow   Pinkie
Edinburgh Leith
Glasgow   Langside
Melrose   Kelso
Jedburgh   Flodder Field
           Teviotdate

ATLANTIC
OCEAN

Firth of Clyde

Lochmaben
Dumfries

Solway
Moss
Carlisle

Newcastle

Durham

Derry
Raphoe
Ardstraw

Connor

Whithorn

Solway Firth

Kendal

Clogher
Armagh

Killala
Achonry

Downpatrick
Dromore

ISLE OF
MAN

Lancaster

York
Marston Moor

Mayo
Elphin
Ardagh
Tuam Roscommon
Clonmacnoise
Clonfert
Kilmacduagh
Kilfenora
Killaloe
Limerick
Emly
Ardfert
Lismore
Aghadoe
Cork
Ross

Kilmore

Enaghdune

Trim

Kildare

Dublin

IRISH SEA

Bangor

St.Asaph

Manchester

Doncaster

Lincoln

Chester

Nottingham

The Wash

Lichfield

Mousehold Heath
Peterborough
Norwich

Leighlin
Ferns
Cashel Kilkenny

Waterford

CARDIGAN
BAY

Coventry
Naseby

Ely

Cambridge

Worcester
Hereford
Gloucester

St.Davids

Llandaff

Cloyne

Oxford
Westminster
Windsor Greenwich
London
Rochester

Bristol

Bath Salisbury

Canterbury
Dover
Calais

Bristol Channel

Wells

Winchester
Southampton
Portsmouth

Chichester

Exeter
Warham

ISLE OF
WIGHT

Plymouth

ARMADA 1588

‡ Archbishoprics
† Bishoprics
x Battles
• Major Monasteries
   dissolved, 1539
▨ The Pale around 1550
⣿ Plantations under the
   Tudors and James I

ambivalent responses to the breakdown of the religious and theological consensus. Acknowledged as pertinent are variable combinations of socio-economic shifts and circumstances or 'conjunctures', which help make up the still unassembled 'whole orchestra',[4] regional or Continental.

Another presupposition is a threefold distinction between Reformation 'movement', 'legislation', and 'process' of inculcation. This is designed in part to avoid the mildly metaphysical debate about the characteristics of the 'Second Reformation'. Applied to the British Isles the notion implodes, at least in relation to physiognomy and periodisation. The time-span considered is the period 1525-c. 1635. Not however till 1690 was any Reformation in the British Isles settled.

1. ENGLAND

Historiography

The English Reformation is often handled in a polemical and emotional manner.[5] Far from abating, controversy has currently intensified with the formation of new battle lines. This helps explain the recent 'Niagara'[6] of publications. In the past (but not only), studies were confessionally conditioned – Protestant, Catholic, Anglican. They were then joined by the influential 'Whig' (liberal, secularised Protestant) school. This understood the Reformation as the midwife delivering England from the Dark Ages to the threshold of modernity, and so a turning-point of progress. A subsequent neo-Marxist interpretation reducing it to an epiphenomenal manifestation of economic decline has never commanded wide acceptance. It has however encouraged research into groups like landed gentry (old and new), merchants, and lawyers, which made capital gains.

Modern work reveals four identifiable schools, symbolised by the names of Geoffrey Elton, Geoffrey Dickens, Christopher Haigh, and Patrick Collinson. Elton concentrates on the dirigiste 'top' of the early modern Church-State or State-Church, its mechanics of policy-making and organs of implementation and enforcement.[7] For him, the real manufacturer of the new order was not Henry VIII (1491-1547), but the Principal Secretary of State, Thomas Cromwell (c. 1485-1540). An undercurrent of the Weber-Tawney paradigms in Elton's approach has not been noticeably developed at large. While the religious reorientation is evaluated positively, inherent and, alas, influentially limiting in

Elton's posture is a dismissive attitude to the prophetic spirit and the theology of keen conviction. These are regarded as meddlesome 'intrusions' from 'fanatics' and 'bigots'.[8]

In contrast, Dickens considers more the religious and subjective side of the Reformation movement and its spread.[9] His perception is dual: of course the Reformation was imposed from the top (like everywhere else in Europe), but accompanying this were perceptible pressures or aspirations from below. However, while ordinary people should not be neglected due to high profiles accorded to monarchs, prelates, monasteries, liturgies, etc., an exclusively socio-biographical heuristic method will not open all windows either. Apart from uncertainty about where the 'below' begins, Dickens has been criticised for underestimating the strength of residual and revived Catholicism. None-the-less, his book does retain the status of being standard, especially in view of its uncommon cognisance of the European context and of its religious *nous*. With the studies of David Loades, this position is also marked with perspectives on the teleological significance of the Reformation for Anglo-British development.

A third school, making the subject combustible, is characterised as 'revisionist'. Alongside Haigh, some other names are Scarisbrick, Rex, Duffy, and, with qualifications, Collinson. For them, the 'coercion/acceptance' and 'response-to-public-opinion' models are defective. Rather they propose 'coercion/compliance or coercion/occasional-prudential-conformity', so that sulky obedience rather than conversion is what the State Reformation induced. Haigh disavows the negationist extremes of Scarisbrick virtually writing Protestants out of the script. But a hint of populism mixed with a reductionist tradition compels him to deny any autonomous existence to 'the Reformation in England': the English State Reformation, an essentially political story, just 'coincided' with the European Reformation 'accidentally' and was not to the people's taste.[10] 'The English Reformation' is reduced as it were to a nominalist icon or a semantic conceit. Apart from a series of statutory 'Reformations by instalment', there was albeit a genuine evangelical movement among (chiefly) a well-educated minority of Christians; its growth was, however, constantly retarded and adventitious until the Elizabethan period.

Characteristic of revisionism is micro-study involving flight from keystone 'elitist' sources to local parish, diocesan, guild, borough, legal records, and ostensibly telltale wills. There is a zeal to establish 'how things really were' – but often with judgmental overtones. The absence of a real comparative sense with the rest of the British Isles and the Continent is also patent. Further, the lines between natural feet-dragging, uninformed apathy or antipathy, and educated active resistance are very blurred indeed. Accordingly, evaluation of such pessimistic historiographical recasting is in abeyance.

Lastly, Collinson and others are identified with the overdue correction of astigmatic perceptions of Elizabethan Protestantism and 'Puritanism'.[11] This has remedied a certain conceptual and terminological aporia in regard to theological landscape at that time. The damagingly fashionable 'history from hindsight' approach held that the problems were caused by (alien, unenglish) 'Calvinist Puritan' impatience with the quintessential 'Anglican via media' of the English Reformation. It is now better understood that while all Church Puritans were Calvinist, not all Church Calvinists were Puritans or 'precisionists'. This insight is common among historians today as it was in earlier 'ecclesiastical' historians, like Basil Hall and Buick Knox. Only later in England – as elsewhere – did the broad Reformed consensus in soteriology crack with relapses into semi-Pelagian and proto-Arminian ideas. Until then, Church of England theology was radically Augustinian and firmly Reformed, tempered by an adiaphorist attitude to externals. It is conceded, therefore, that the developed theological profile of the English Church – be it described as Calvinist (or Reformed) consensus, or 'indigenous latitudinarianism'[12] – did not reflect any via media between Catholic and Reformation theology, rather one between various hues of Protestant doctrine. Such a phenomenon was far from unique to England. This is not to detract from a groping in the 1530s for a chimerical mean between Romanism and Lutheranism, not unique to England either. Like everywhere else after 1541, it was superseded.

Generally, recent focus has shifted from a long preoccupation with the Henrician 1530s. Revisionist concerns, less hagiographic interest in Catholicism, serious study of genuine radicals, and more objective study of Reformation and Puritan theology, have all contributed to this realignment of the field. Work long overdue on Catholic bishops in Henry's reign like John Fisher (1469-1535) and Stephen Gardiner (c. 1497-1555) has also been provided. Thereby a myopic and romantic fixation with Thomas More (1478-1535) has been broken. Finally, Collinson has blown the whistle on a brand of studies on early modern English towns of a socio-economic reductionist character. Demoting reformation in urban contexts to a tangential ephemeron, such an approach contrasts with the conventional study of civic reformations on the Continent, although similar studies have also been done on some English cities.[13]

Genesis of the Launching-pad

The quickest route to the core of the English Church Reformation is to visit the Swiss National Museum in Zurich. Its silver collection includes four inscribed items from the sixteenth century. All were gifts to either the Zurich city council or the city's church and the reformer, Henry Bullinger (1504-75). Some of the pieces were tokens of gratitude from three members of the community of English Protestants who took refuge in Zurich during the Catholic restoration in England (1553-58). These men, including John Jewel (1522-71), subsequently became Elizabethan bishops. The fourth item is from Queen Elizabeth (1533-1603) to Bullinger, acknowledging services rendered. These symbols were more than just tokens of thanks. They represented general sympathy with the Zurich Reformation and solidarity with the exemplary 'magisterial' nature of the Zurich church. In other words, there were parallels between the religious authority assumed by the Zurich city government and that expressed in England by the Royal Supremacy exercised in part through Parliament and statute. This revolution had been legitimated in England by the Act of Supremacy (1534) in the course of the 'Reformation Parliament' (1529-36).

While Zurich was hardly a conscious model for England, there were many ideological and theological similarities. For example: a qualified caesaropapism; an arrogation by the secular authority of the right to be the guardian and arbiter of doctrine and practice; a blurring of the traditional jurisdiction between church and state in the interests of uniting the Christian Commonwealth along more organically unitary lines; the notion of a reformation of the church and of society; the domestication of clergy by abolishing clerical immunity; a laicisation of social services; an appeal to Constantinian or Theodosian Church-State paradigms in the Early Church; the citation of the Israelite monarchy and the kingly reformers of religion; and the claim that new legislation was declaratory, not innovative – hence the assault in England on the clericalist cult of Thomas à Becket. In relation to post-Hildebrandine Western tradition the new situations were of course innovative, but not when compared to Eastern or Byzantine tradition.

There is a striking contrast with the Swiss example: while it was initially twinned with Reformation theology, the English Church revolution was not. Granted that Catholics like Bishop Fisher and Thomas

More repudiated the Royal Supremacy, granted that Cromwell had un-ambiguous Protestant leanings, it may be seen that apart from the *defensor fidei* (Henry VIII) himself, there were Catholic bishops like Stephen Gardiner, Catholic jurists like Christopher St. German (c. 1460-1540)[14], and political theorists like the Catholic humanist, Thomas Starkey (c. 1499-1538) among the chief apologists of the new order. Apropos Zurich, particularly Starkey provides a clue. Italian-educated at Padua, his reasoning derived from his study of Aristotle and Plato, Paul, Marsiglio (c. 1280-1342) and the Early Church[15] – as was the thinking of Huldrych Zwingli (1484-1531). Hence the Swiss magisterial and the English royal-parliamentary reformations were not intrinsically an effluence of Reformation theology. Rather they were recycled semblable responses to prior concepts mediated by Human-ism. Later the concept became indissolubly wedded to Reformed the-ology in England, just as earlier, Cromwell, Archbishop Thomas Cranmer (1489-1556), and Bishop Edward Foxe (c. 1496-1538) had accommodated it to Lutheran theology. In sum: the ideological es-sence of the Royal Supremacy was procreated by neither the Tudor monarchy nor the English Church.

Reform under Henry, 1531-1547

In the first of three legislative phases constituting the English Reforma-tion, papal jurisdiction was abolished following a *coup d'église* ema-nating from Henry's divorce from Catherine of Aragon (1485-1536); the monarch was proclaimed the 'supreme head on earth' of the Eng-lish Church and in whom resided by virtue of 'imperial' sovereignty an inalienable responsibility for religion; monasteries were dissolved, their property leased or sold by the Crown; a limited iconoclasm was sanc-tioned; holy-days were restricted and pilgrimages effectively prohib-ited; indulgences for souls in purgatory were condemned; an English Bible was ordered to be placed in every church, and a formulary of faith – the *Ten Articles* (1536) – was issued to restrict 'diversity in opinions' (showing that even if there was still no 'Reformation' in the way that revisionists would gainsay by a reconstructed exit-poll proce-dure, the Catholic theological consensus had fragmented). The Latin Mass was left untouched, though an English litany was permitted in 1544. The measures were laced with social, economic, and educa-tional exhortations about the individual and common good, to which proper religion should be harnessed.

Much ink has flowed estimating how far to ascribe this to Renais-

sance and Christian humanism, Catholic reformism, enlightened Tudor despotism, discreet Lutheranism, economic exigency, political ex-
pediency, or a combination of all of them. Even contemporary ana-
lysts must have found it difficult to read the signs of the times. Under
More's chancellorship (1529-32), England's first six Protestant martyrs were burned[16] – largely of the Lutheran persuasion. And in 1535,
twenty-five Anabaptists were executed, as were Fisher, and More himself, plus six principled Carthusian priors. The King thereby demonstrated that the Royal Supremacy was lord of the individual conscience. Even if the English 'schism' cannot be decribed as an adoption
of *the* Reformation – doctrinally it was well to the right of the
Augsburg Confession – it represented more than a commodious semantic shift. The crushed northern Catholic crusade, the Pilgrimage of
Grace (1536-37), seems to corroborate this.

The next decade is often interpreted as a 'conservative' or (non-
papalist) Catholic 'reaction'. In reality it was more of a political attempt to steer the Church along pre-Tridentine Catholic Reform lines
within a caesaropapist framework. This necessitated doctrinal intervention by the King, the ungrateful disposal of Cromwell, the respectful containment of Cranmer, the resignation of evangelical bishops like
Hugh Latimer (c. 1485-1555), and the execution of the leading Lutheran, Robert Barnes (1495-1540). The entente between the French
and the Hapsburgs at this time left England, as a lesser power, vulnerable because of a suspect religious image. English exports were largely
locked into the Antwerp market. Accommodation with the big powers, especially England's traditional ally, Spain, was more relevant than
the speculative alliance with the remoter Smalkaldic League in Germany. France's ally, firmly Catholic Scotland, completed the encircle-
ment. So the diplomatically stranded Henry placated Catholic Europe
– especially after his excommunication in 1538. The enhanced Catholic flavour of the *Six Articles* (1539) and the *King's Book* (1543), as
well as discreet Protestant emigration or prudential conformism, is to
be seen in this light, and not just in that of indigenous Catholic pressure or loyalism.

Reformation under Edward, 1547-1553

The second phase of official Reformation occurred during Edward VI's
reign. The King being a minor, authority was exercised first by the
Lord Protector, the Duke of Somerset, Edward Seymour (c. 1500-52),
and then later by the Lord President of the regency council, the Duke of

Northumberland (later Earl of Warwick), John Dudley (c. 1504-53). All three figures represent a victory for the Protestant element in the political nation. Under this regime, the royal right of Reformation was exercised in such a way that official religion experienced a quantum leap. To rephrase Jerome's words following the imagined Arian take-over of the Early Church in 360: 'The whole of England groaned and was astonished to find itself Protestant'.[17]

Encouraged by Protestants like John Knox (c. 1512-72), whom the government recalled from France, the Zwinglian Bishop John Hooper (d. 1555), the Strangers' Churches Superintendent, Jan Laski (1499-1560), committed Protestant bishops like Nicholas Ridley (c. 1500-55) and Cranmer, plus the import of influential theologians like Martin Bucer (1491-1551), Peter Vermigli Martyr (1500-62) and Bernard Ochino (1487-1564), not to overlook the memoranda of Calvin (1509-64) and Bullinger, the English Church underwent a Protestant lurch. In an Erastian manner, bishops were to be government appointed; chantries were dissolved (not just to fund a Scottish war); the Latin Mass was abolished, and by Acts of Uniformity, parish worship was restructured through English-language editions of the *Book of Common Prayer* in 1549 and 1552 (the first still just a modification of the Roman Canon, the second decidedly Reformed); a *Book of Homilies* (1547) was issued; clerical marriage was legalised; and the forms of ministry were reduced to the three of the settled Early Church, viz., bishop, presbyter, and deacon. Finally, *Forty-Two Articles* (1553) of doctrine – distanced firmly from both Catholic and Anabaptist theology – were promulgated. These developments – along with a conservative Social Gospel rhetoric[18] – embody, it has been claimed, a theology constructed 'with bricks manufactured in upper Germany'.[19] Simultaneously, however, the kingdom was convulsed by two serious regional revolts which were in part religious, two foreign wars against the French and the Scots, bad harvests and disease. These elements contributed to the 'mid-Tudor crisis', which with the monarch's premature death meant that the Edwardian Reformation was stillborn.

Morphology of the Reformation till 1553

Opinions vary regarding a Protestant movement and process until Edward's demise. The significance of Lollardy (the pre-Reformation tradition of dissent derived from Wycliffe), of anticlericalism (if any), of Erasmian humanism, of the efficacy of Lutheran ideas, of broadening literacy, and of popular moods, is still unclear. The paradox remains that the English Reformation is a 'hugely documented, but in some respects still obscure story'.[20] A rough consensus suggests that 'popular' support for the Reformation was insubstantial outside London and some counties in the far south-east until well into the reign of Elizabeth; that innovative religious ideas and books were in circulation, and not just in the universities, London law schools, or Hanseatic business centres, nor just in Latin; and that in the Edwardian era, a definite if temporary boost was given to the Protestant cause.

Some hold that the Reformation movement was either inexplicable or illusory. This is justified by referring to the sound state of the pre-Reformation English Church (unlike most other places, its higher clergy were not scions of the aristocracy)[21], or to the apparent preference of the population for traditional religion (by which is really meant traditional culture).[22] Yet hinting at the old "deformation" concept, as do some modern writers, is hardly helpful. It is not possible to ignore both the ultimate revolution of dogma and new spirituality of the Reformation which entailed preaching, edification, catechising, and discipline aimed at conversion and effective sanctification. This met with as much natural popular resistance in England as in Germany and elsewhere.[23] It would be naive to imagine that fundamental Reformation doctrines could hardly appeal to ordinary people. This was not true of concepts such as that of unmerited, classless, and even-handed grace, or that of the democratically equal share in the undiminishable reality of sin, irrespective of financial, ecclesiastical or 'spiritual' status. John Fines' compilation dispels the myth that the Reformation was 'a sordid monument of middle-class self-interest'.[24]

Inevitably, the role of non-religious factors is elusive. For example: the bearing of agrarian and social discontent, price rises, inflation, striking urban imbalance, population growth, vagrancy, unemployment, superstition, land enclosures, coin debasements, rebellious youth, disease, colportage, secularisation, and literacy. One thing does seem certain: the Reformation attracted primarily the more physically and mentally mobile, progressive classes of lay people, like merchants of the London-Antwerp nexus, mariners, entrepreneurial craftsmen, teachers, students, lawyers, and teenagers. It was from among such people that the English Bible translations of the martyred William Tyndale (c. 1494-1536) were paid. Top merchants like Richard Hilles, also acted as go-betweens with the Strasbourg and Zurich Churches. These were the people in the Reformation movement most concerned about socio-economic renewal and development. Apart though from

Bucer's *On the Kingdom of Christ*, theologians in England were unable to devise a global programme, rarely advancing beyond appeals to moral rectitude.

The Roman Restoration under Mary, 1553-1568

After Edward's demise came the chastening – or liberating – Catholic restoration by Queen Mary I (1516-58), daughter of Henry VIII and Catherine of Aragon, and wife-to-be of King Philip of Spain (1527-98). One must say that if positive Reformation developments in England are to be ascribed largely to 'foreign' influences, then recatholicisation under Mary was even more obviously dependent on other foreign and political influences. This was consequent on England's clientage now to Spain, the chief sponsor of the Counter Reformation. Guided by the papal legate, Cardinal Reginald Pole (1500-58), all previous religious legislation was repealed with two important exceptions: firstly, Parliament insisted that Mary retain the Royal Supremacy, and secondly, there was no question of restoring expropriated assets to the Church.

The ca. 300 executions for heresy in the Marian era included a showpiece incineration of the elderly bishops Cranmer, Ridley, and Latimer. Other notable Protestant figures died similarly, like Bishop Hooper, the biblical translator John Rogers (c. 1499-1555) and the northern evangelist John Bradford (c. 1510-55). In addition, Martin Bucer's bones were disinterred and ritually burned at Cambridge. Retrospectively, this blood of the martyrs was to be seed indeed, along with that of 800 Protestant activists allowed to emigrate.

Historians differ about the efficacy of the Catholic restoration.[25] Some see it as successful and popular, frustrated only by Mary's premature death, and ironically corroborated by Jewel's comment in 1559 that the nation had relapsed into a 'wilderness of superstition'.[26] Others see it as botched affair and a gift to the Reformation movement, fortifying it with a typological arsenal, such as divine punishment for previous religious compromises and toleration of idolatry, persecution, exile, eschatological expectation, and deliverance. Moreover, the religious reinstatement can be seen as handicapped by the stern Anglo-Aragonese Catholicism of the Queen, the hispanicisation of Court circles, and the pathological antipathy of Pope Paul IV (1476-1559) to the Spanish interest as well as his inveterate hostility to the theologically suspect Pole. If at the popular level the much lamented old 'merry England' and epicurean Catholic culture went hand in hand, evidence for this in the sombre Catholic puritanism of the royal entourage was not abundant.

The Reformation under Elizabeth, 1558-1603

The third and last phase of the legislative Reformation was the 'Elizabethan Settlement', though its chief consequence was lack of settlement. Usually dated as 1559-62, a better finish date is 1571, when the provisional quality of earlier arrangements had disappeared. If Henry VIII was 'next to God', and Edward VI a young 'Josiah', Protestant opinion superimposed on Elizabeth the attributes of the 'new Deborah'. Her reign did facilitate the general protestantization of England in earnest. As Claire Cross aptly states, the Settlement was 'not the climax of the English Reformation, but only the end of the beginning'.[27]

If the constructor of the Henrician edifice was Cromwell, that of the Elizabethan strategy was the Queen's durable Principal Secretary, William Cecil, later Lord Burghley (1520-98). His role illustrated how the actual 'face' of the English Reformation was the work of committed lay officials with minds of their own. Cecil favoured a general rather than a 'precisionist' Reformation, believing that the 'religion of Christ'[28] was too important to be left to the Church. Implementing of the Reformation meant practising the art of the possible on a large national and territorial scale of an extent paralleled nowhere else.

The legislation of the Settlement was enshrined in the Act of Supremacy and Uniformity (1559), the third *Book of Common Prayer* (1559) and the *Thirty-nine Articles* passed by the Church in 1563, but not sanctioned by Parliament in their English form till 1571. The enactments assuaged the Edwardian programme of 1552, and included a redefinition of the royal headship as 'Supreme Governor'. This last is often perceived as a concession to classical Calvinist aversion.

A conventional view was that the 1559 enactments derived from a difficult struggle between a conservative Queen and a fervidly Protestant Commons.[29] Now it is argued that they issued from a contest between on the one hand a mildly Protestant Queen and a broadly Protestant majority in the Commons, and a still Catholic episcopate and conservative House of Lords on the other.[30] Consequently, the liturgy and confession of the substitute Protestant episcopate aimed at adopting Reformed theology without utterly alienating the Catholic party. Far from being derived from an English spirit of compromise, they are rooted in the irenic tradition of Bucer and Melanchthon as mediated by Cranmer and the new archbishop, Matthew Parker (1504-75). In view of the context, the Church of England's creed was just as political as, but no more so than, the Confession of Augsburg. The *Articles* do not

constitute a substantive via media in reality. They were however sufficiently irenic and moderate to frustrate increasingly Protestant opinion
as time went on, particularly in the areas of the extent of the atone-
ment, grace, Church polity, and pastoral discipline. Initially though,
the more forward Protestants were content to acquiesce in monarchical
episcopacy on provisional *bene esse* principles. The Church also issued
a *Catechism* (1570), drawn up by Alexander Nowell (c. 1507-1602).
Strongly Erastian, its fundamental theology is unmistakably derived
from the *Genevan Catechism* and *Heidelberg Catechism*.

In addition to these foundational documents, the English Reformation Church was furnished in time with a corroborative literary package. Firstly, John Jewel's *Apology of the Church of England* (1562),
was an exposition of the principle of 'Catholic and Reformed' which
was warmly applauded in Zurich.[31] Secondly, the *Laws of Ecclesiastical Polity* (1591-1600) was published by Richard Hooker (1544-
1600). This work defended episcopacy against presbyterian theory articulated by Beza (1519-1605), and in England by Walter Travers (c.
1548-1635), Thomas Cartwright (1535-1603), and John Field (1545-
88). Hooker like Jewel – but unlike Adrian Saravia (c. 1532-1613) –
was no advocate of divine-right episcopacy. Thirdly, more directly
formative of Protestant public opinion than anything else was the *Acts
and Monuments*, or *Book of Martyrs* (1563ff.) by the ex-Marian exile,
John Foxe (1516-1587). This *tour de force* helped form the Protestant
nation, if not quite a nation of Protestants. It was placed in all parish
churches. Foxe directed a belated wave of English Luther-translations,
though with no obvious impact on the 'Helvetic' Church of England.[32]
Lastly, the sophisticated English *Geneva Bible* (1560) was to be the
preferred text for biblical study by the public and the clergy – despite
Establishment anxiety that its annotations were too provocatively Reformed at places. Its popularity endured beyond the *King James Version* of 1611.

A Failed Reformation or a Failed Reformed Church?

The Rubicon-crossing of the Reformation movement was occasioned
by the papal bull excommunicating Elizabeth in 1570 – *Regnans in
excelsis* – and a promulgation releasing Catholics from loyalty to her.
Not surprisingly, the English hierarchy appealed to Zurich for support
and a vindication of the English Reformation. Bullinger obliged with
his *Confutation of the Pope's Bull*, published in Latin, English, and
German.[33] The bull certainly expedited the sea change which synthe-

sised Protestantism, dynastic and national security, cultural identity, independence, and chauvinism into an indivisible reality. Papal demonisation of the English Church, the bogle of the Catholic Mary Stewart's claim to the English throne until her execution in 1587, occasional English Catholic plots at home and abroad against Elizabeth, the spectre of the Spanish 'Enterprise of England', and an associated perceived threat from Ireland, – all gave *gestalt* to the Protestant nation and ideology, making England part of the so-called 'Calvinist International'. Hence English support for foreign reformations in Scotland, France, Geneva, the Rhine Palatinate, and the Netherlands, as well as the effort, if bungled, to protestantise Ireland. All this culminated in the design of James VI & I (1566-1625) to form a pan-European Protestant coalition headed by himself. In this overall sense then, the Reformation hardly failed in England.

But as for the Church herself and the process of popular religious re-education, judgement is much more controverted. Never comprehensive in reality, the State Church failed to absorb survivalist Catholics of the periphery, or a remnant of elite Catholics reinvigorated by Jesuit and other missionaries operating from English Catholic centres at Louvain, Rheims or Douai. During the era, over a hundred priests or missioners were executed for treason. The statutory Church was never comfortable with the energy of Puritan godliness or the broadening of theological access, as the sequestration of Archbishop Edmund Grindal (c. 1519-83) for defending prophecyings against the Queen's wishes shows. The Establishment also developed a paranoia about gathered separatists as seen in the example of the participative Strangers' Churches.[34] A kind of sterile bureaucratic legalism held sway. There was no coherent strategy for evangelisation due to problems of finance and ministerial training, to a juridical-canonical rather than a pastoral approach to discipline, and to restrictive parochial laicisation, – granted that the common man was a 'recalcitrant subject for Gospel tutelage'.[35] Yet committed Church-Protestant piety is often ignored and most people are placed in special categories: recusants (non-complying Catholics), Puritan conformists, non-conforming Puritans within the Church, parish Anglicans, Church Presbyterians, statute Protestants, Church papists, Prayer-Book Protestants, separatists, instinctive Pelagians, Church secularists, *politiques*, Familists, nullifidians, 'neuters', or 'lukewarm Laodiceans'.[36]

It may well be apt to apply Aristotle's appraisal of the middle way to the English Reformation Church, that 'some people fail to realise that a nose which deviates from perfection by being either hooked or snub is still an excellent nose.'[37] But so long as people were captive to the concept of mandatory uniformity, an internal time-bomb would tick. One ingredient was disagreement over polity and discipline. Another was the corrosion of the English Reformed consensus on justification, predestination, and grace.[38] This emanated locally from Pierre Baro (1534-99) and Launcelot Andrewes (1555-1626) at Cambridge, and Antonio del Corro (1527-91) at Oxford.[39] The Church's *Lambeth Articles* (1595), the Calvinist orthodoxy of James VI & I, the replication (1618) of the strongly Augustinian *On God's Case against Pelagius* by Thomas Bradwardine (d. 1349), and English participation at the Synod of Dordrecht (1618-19) failed to check this contraflow. All this contributed to the mayhem engulfing English Christianity and society in the subsequent Civil War and Revolution.

2. WALES

Current Historiography

The four dioceses of Wales were long part of the province of Canterbury, so that all changes in the English area of the province applied automatically to the Welsh Church. In most historiography, the ultimately successful Reformation in Wales has usually been relegated to a passing reference or footnote. Yet it is of compelling interest in its own right. Though subject to the English Crown, Wales had very few of those preconditions attending the Reformation elsewhere in Europe. A remote poor upland country, she had no capital city, no government centre, no university, an impoverished Church, an absentee English higher clergy, a semi-feudal particularism, a limited urban and middle class, no printing press, an ancient European language and bardic culture, a mixture of folk-Catholicism and paganism, no obvious anticlericalism or dissent, no excess of law and order, and an avaricious nobility and landed class. Yet such a place has confounded all the theories and paradigms of historians by metamorphosing within a century into a Protestant nation. The story has been rescued from oblivion almost solo by Glanmor Williams, one of the most astute observers of the Reformation anywhere in the British Isles.[40] Williams' approach cannot be called 'revisionist', since there was little to revise and he offers a sober realism devoid of historiographic triumphalism.

Renaissance, Reformation, and the 'Welsh' Monarchy

We have been changed by the faith of the Saxons [=the English],
    Our hearts are not sympathetic towards it.
Thus wrote the poet, Thomas ab Ieuan ap Rhys,[41] articulating majority
opinion for a long time to come, though Protestant doctrine did have
some early bardic utterance in Gruffudd ab Ieuan Lylwelyn Fychan.
How then did the Welsh dragon come to change its religious colour?

To dismiss the Reformation in Wales as the consequence of an English government fiat would be too simplistic. The Welsh Reformation
was dependent rather on a political realignment and a rewriting of history and myth to make both political and religious changes palatable.[42]
The chief political change, namely the Union with England 1536-43
according full political rights and parliamentary representation to
Wales, was made acceptable by appealing to the Welsh origins of the
quasi-messianic Tudors. They were perceived by the Welsh as the
bearers of the pre-Anglo-Saxon authentic 'British' kingship of
Arthurian legend that had survived the Roman conquest. The religious
change was coated with two layers. First, Welsh Protestant humanists
argued that while previous papist captivity and bondage to the English
had gone hand in hand, the Reformation in the context of equal rights
meant the restoration of the original, allegedly Rome-free Celtic Christianity of antiquity. Second, humanists convinced Parliament that the
Reformation in Wales could not be initiated through the medium of a
foreign language, English. In consequence, key texts were translated to
the effect that 'more than anything else, the Reformation kept Wales
Welsh'.[43]

Thus the package for a new Wales was composed of various elements: union with England and loyalty to the Tudor dynasty, political
and legal equality in the new entity of 'England and Wales', a Reformed Church, scriptures, liturgy and preaching all in Cymric
(Welsh), appeal to Celtic Christian antiquity, a college for Welsh students de facto at Oxford (Jesus), and a landed class (profiteers from
Tudor stripping of Church assets) guaranteeing the changes in the localities. The mutation involved viewing Catholicism, sedition, obscu-
rantism, political subservience and foreign threats as the same things.

The chief contributors to the religious reorientation were the following: the ex-Augustinian Henrician bishop, William Barlow – the near-
est Wales almost had to a John Knox, except that he was English and
something of a maverick which meant that he had little impact.[44] But

among English-speakers in towns he disseminated Reformation doctrines. More appreciable was the work of a Protestant humanist elite. In 1546, the first Welsh printed book, *Yny Lhyvyr Hwnn* [*In This Book*] – an anticlerical primer – was published by the influential Erasmian gentleman-scholar, Sir John Price. In 1551, Welsh portions of the New Testament were published by the native dux of the New Learning, William Salesbury (c. 1501-84)[45] who with the Puritan Bishop Richard Davies (c. 1501-81)[46] published in 1567 the first complete Welsh New Testament, along with the *Book of Common Prayer*. Lastly, Bishop William Morgan (c. 1547-1604) published a whole Welsh Bible in 1588, which met with crucial bardic acclamation.[47] The arduous task of instructing the people remained and perhaps made less urgent by the Counter Reformation's complacency about Welsh Catholic loyalty. This misjudgement impaired the internal resistance campaign which was unable to stem the sluggish, popular Church Protestant drift.[48]

3. IRELAND

The limited impact of the Reformation in mainland Ireland means that the expression 'Irish Reformation' is for many a solecism beyond the pale. An English dominion since the twelfth century, Ireland's status was in Henry VIII's reign upgraded to a kingdom (1541) to enhance royal authority and 'civility' in the entire country. This was consonant with the general Tudor policy of both centralising authority and rationalising government in the peripheral and outlying parts of the Crown dominions.[49] Unlike Wales, however, 'Ireland' was a semi-autonomous old Anglo-Norman colony with a Parliament in Dublin, politically and culturally other than the large but balkanised Gaelic world to the west and north – dominated by military, bardic, and in part hereditary clerical castes. Following Irish old-colonial obstructionism, Tudor forward policy culminated in flooding Irish government with New English officials, in fresh colonisation (initiated by the Catholic Mary I) and military conquest. This last was completed in 1603 with the hugely expensive campaign against The O'Neill of Ulster[50] – the starting point of modern Irish history. Accompanying the process was a naive Anglo-ethnocentrism typical of European mental inadequacies at the time. An inextricable part of these policies (except in Mary's reign), the Reformation seemed therefore bound to enhance colonial hegemony. In Crown eyes, it was also related to the need to fortify the English Reformation on the international plane. Accordingly, Tudor religious legislation was replicated in the Irish Parliament. Yet if subjugation succeeded, why was the practical Reformation only partial?

Current Historiography

This is largely a meditation on failure. Securing only small indigenous allegiance the Reformation became largely confined ultimately to the 'Protestant Ascendancy'.[51] The paradox was unequalled in Europe: a practising Catholic majority in a Protestant state, and for centuries to come. The modern epistemology of failure has advanced from hoary explanations such as: the divinely ordained Catholicism of the Irish (Gaelic?) people; Protestantism meant (only) English rule and New Scottish infiltration; Catholicism (must have) meant 'Irish' or 'national' political resistance; the eventual strict Reformed, episcopalian Church of Ireland had little mission incentive since the Catholic 'wild' Irish were regarded as eschatologically reprobate – a controversial diagnosis recently recalled.[52]

Current thinking has revamped the terms of the discussion. The basic hermeneutical circle is nevertheless hard to evade, namely whether 'Protestantism failed because Catholicism succeeded, or Catholicism succeeded because Protestantism failed'.[53] Was Catholic success due to the indefectibility of the old Irish faith or to the vigour of revival Catholicism? It is nonetheless clear that the old 'two-way sorting'[54] is anachronistic, that Protestant failure was not predetermined, that native and old colonial rejection was neither universal nor automatic, that extraordinary circumstances were not a sufficient excuse, that government incoherence, lack of resources, long-established laicisation of the Gaelic Church, Continental seminarian mission, Old Iro-English civic conservatism,[55] and practical incompetence were major factors. Identified as apparently disjointed has been reforming strategy, now persuasive (Bishops William Casey, Edward Staples, Nicholas Walsh, and Hugh Brady[56]), now coercive, now dismissive (Archbishop James Ussher (1581-1656). Bradshaw has mooted that the coercion policy of archbishops like George Brown (d. 1556, former provincial of the English Augustinians), Adam Loftus (c. 1552-1605), and civil officials like Edmund Spenser (c. 1552-99), was elementally Reformed due to the doctrine of unattenuated original sin.[57] The implication of this has been rejected by Canny by appealing to transconfessional historical analogies; to this one can add that the sources of state-sponsored religious coercion are Augustine's 'compel them to come in' and the Theodosian Code, adopted, hallowed and bequeathed by Catholic tradition. Canny also exonerates reformers in Ireland from the despondent attitude of 'letting [Catholics] go to hell their own way',[58] and rebuts the suggestion that a supremacist 'apartheid' ideology (Bradshaw) was conceptually devised. Rather, it was hoped that the reformed Church would magnetically attract Gaelic Catholics 'to heaven the state's way',[59] – a trickle-down Reformation.

Achievements

The Reformation in Ireland was not an unmitigated failure. Some achievements are noteworthy, even if their importance is disputed. In 1571 Seaan O Kearnaigh published an evangelical *Gaelic Catechism*, the first Gaelic publication in Ireland. In 1603, an epic Gaelic New Testament translation based on Erasmus' Greek text, originated by the Queen, was completed by Uilliam O Domhnaill (d. 1628), later the fervidly Reformed Archbishop of Tuam in Connacht. A consultant was the Munster bard, Maoilin Og Mac Bruaideadha. O Domhnaill also published in 1608 a Gaelic version of the *Book of Common Prayer*.[60] All three publications came too late, it is conventionally believed, either to advance the Reformation or help secure the future of Irish Gaelic. In 1611 and 1618, some Catholic works of piety appeared in Gaelic for the first time, by Bonaventura O hEodhasa and the influential Aodh MacAingil – but the Gaelic medium was never to be crucial to the survival or revival of Catholicism in Ireland. Then in 1592, Trinity College was founded in Dublin as Ireland's first university, and training ground in the humanist and reformation world view. Lastly, following the stiffening of reformation resolve in the 1590s, the Puritan Church of Ireland adopted an explicitly predestinarian alignment with its 104 *Irish Articles* 1615,[61] though superseded in 1635. This meant that in terms of official dogmatic self-definition, the Irish State Church was for a generation the most categorically 'Calvinist' in the British Isles.

4. SCOTLAND

The Scottish Reformation has been peculiarly myth-ridden, though it is debatable whether modern reappraisal clarifies or obscures the view. The primacy accorded to John Knox (c. 1514-72), who was never

Moderator, is no longer widely accepted, although the reasons are variable. In much of the Knox literature, polemical axes – overt or covert – are often wielded. Few would deny that his prophetic, evangelistic and inspirational intervention at key moments was crucial. Catholic contemporaries however tended to regard the now hardly known John Willock (d. 1585), future Reformed Superintendent of Glasgow and five-times Moderator, as the 'primate' of the Reformation church. Knox neither created the Scottish Reformation nor determined its subsequent development. His historic function was that of a catalyst. If the traditional exaggeration of his role is explicable by the part he allocated himself in his *History*, the cutting-down effect of more sober (or hostile) evaluations can however generate other distortions. For Knox bequeathed to the Reformed Kirk its most distinctive trait: namely the priority of faith and Christian conscience over religious 'policy' and accommodation. This spirit was created originally with the sudden but limited public opposition to the perceived idolatry and blasphemy of the Mass, leading to a (bloodless) religio-political revolution; it was a precedent which would pay dividends in the Kirk's epic struggles with Erastianism and English-style notions of royal authority and supremacy in the Church, polity, and liturgy. Such notions appealed understandably to Scottish rulers, notwithstanding their firm 'Calvinism'.

Another myth is that the 'Scottish Reformation' was a short, sharp affair out of the blue in 1558-60, and a uniquely clean-cut, comprehensive Calvinist conquest. This emanates from the glamour and fixation with those few fateful years. It is like confining the German Reformation to 1517-20. It also follows from the well-nigh universal habit, friendly or inimical, of attributing super-Calvinist proportions to the Scottish Reformation. For example, in assaulting the idea of the 'Second Reformation' as determined by exclusively Calvinist impetus, Heinz Schilling regularly cites 'Scotland, *from the outset* Calvinist' as the chief exception.[62] Yet a broader view of the Reformation encompassing prior 'movements' in anything but cushioned circumstances shows that Scotland (like England, France, and the Netherlands) also manifested prior Lutheran and Zwinglian streams. The martyrdoms of the Lutheran Patrick Hamilton (c. 1504-28), and the broadly Zwinglian George Wishart (c. 1513-46) testify to that. Moreover, the familiar perception of the 1560 Reformation as the culmination of a crusade of card-carrying Calvinists resulting in the establishment of a uniquely autonomous Church is faulty too. Knox himself stated that at the hour of triumph in the Scottish Parliament, 'divers men were of divers judgements'.[63] In fact the Scottish Reformation was beyond cavil a 'long Reformation', extending from c. 1525-1690, when the presbyterian polity, but still not yet full Church automomy, was finally legalised.

Current historiography

Dating back to 1960, the revisionist process in Scotland precedes by far that for most other Reformations. Three main reassessments have transpired. First, that the pre-Reformation Church was a victim of circumstances and propaganda rather than inherently corrupt. Second, that the idea of an inevitable Calvinist-presbyterian Reformation is a view from hindsight. Third, that popular support for the Reformation was limited and that subsequently, the process of protestantisation was erratic.

The first view was advanced in a work of largely Catholic writers edited by David McRoberts.[64] The secularised system whereby the Crown and the nobility held de facto the Church and much of its wealth in thraldom was highlighted. It was stressed that the Reformation ideology along with a form of nationalism legitimated the substitution of Protestant English for the traditional Catholic French alliance or clientage. And impious Catholics like James V (1512-42), Cardinal David Beaton (c. 1494-1546) – despite their anti-heretical zeal – and the temporising Regent, Mary of Guise (1516-60) were criticised. The Scottish Catholic Reform movement was stymied by aristocratic vested interest in the status quo. When it redefined its interest, the nobility's most effective propaganda weapon was acquired by hijacking the 'neurotic' Knox[65] into the service of political revolution. The Catholic bishops' 'kerygmatic failure', or lack of pastoral leadership, however was not identified.[66]

The second development has involved an amicable feud between Gordon Donaldson and James Kirk. The former's basic premiss was that while all presbyterians were Calvinist, not all Calvinists were presbyterian. Also, Scottish Reformation theology was no more Calvinist than that in the English Church.[67] Accordingly, seeing more continuity than discontinuity, Donaldson revived the episcopalian interpretation of the early Reformed Kirk, seen as reflexing in the direction of true evangelical episcopacy. Not till the late 1570s, under the influence of the Protestant humanist, Andrew Melville (1545-1622), Beza, and English presbyterian theorists, did a doctrinaire presbyterian party

emerge. The implication of these views has been stoutly negated by
Kirk. He insists that at least the notions of ministerial parity and presbyterial discipline were central to the 1560 Reformers' thinking, and
that, committed to a 'radical root and branch Reformation' and not
disposed to 'tarry for the magistrate',[68] they were champing at the bit
from the start, set on here-and-now implementation.

Donaldson and Kirk coalesce to rebut the naively reductionist view
that the Scottish Reformation was just 'political' and imposed from the
top. They have been given limited discreet support from the more radically revisionist Michael Lynch. He concedes that the religious impulse
was primary, but argues that it was astutely politicised to gain broader
immediate support, compensating for the lack of wide sympathy.[69]
Further, contrary to received tradition, both Kirk and Donaldson have
good things to say about the appropriateness of the religious policy of
the Queen, Mary Stewart (1542-87), until her enforced abdication
(1567) brought about by an apocalyptic imperative. The young widow
of Francis II (1544-60) perhaps influenced by the conciliatory policy of
Catherine de Medici (1519-60) in France, accommodated herself in the
period 1560-67 to a remarkable compromise in Scotland unparalleled
in Europe – a Catholic monarch at the head of Protestant state, and
who put Crown funds at the disposal of the new Church.

The third main feature of modern study is associated with the names
of Ian Cowan and Michael Lynch. The illusion that the religious Reformation was a democratic aspiration is targeted. Accordingly, evidence for the tardy, muddling and often unwelcome progress of the
Reformation among the people is keenly sought. Cowan shows this in
the regions, Lynch and others in the some towns and cities – apart from
a more activist Protestantism in Dundee, St. Andrews, Stirling, and
Ayr. Both writers acknowledge that the process was handicapped by
the Kirk's underendowment due to the nobility's impropriation of two-
thirds of the ecclesiastical patrimony at the outset – for which addic-
tion to Mammon they were excoriated by the Reformers. But it is
Keith Brown who makes the timely point that more urgent than the regeneration of the commonalty was the moral acculturation and
christianisation of the nobility with its feuding elements, not without
success.[70] All writers stress the participative laicisation of the new
Church, Donaldson and Kirk in relation to religious principles, Lynch
and Brown more in terms of class interest and the politics of kinship.

Two other upshots are worth mentioning. One is the rediscovery of
Scotland's Lutheran heritage and the second is a helpful refinement on

Calvinism and capitalism in Scotland.[71] It has been long known that an obvious Achilles' heel in Max Weber's thesis about Protestantism and capitalism was Scotland: if Scotland was the super-Calvinist nation it was supposed to have been, then it ought to have pioneered the way to capitalism. In reality, it remained one of Europe's more under-developed countries until the eighteenth century. Earlier, James McEwen demonstrated that the Weber-Calvinist 'prudential view of Providence' was at variance with the views of Calvin and Knox.[72] Rather they had maintained that calamity and deprivation were truer signs of God's benevolence. Gordon Marshall agrees: the ethic of the this-worldly ascetic vocation was religious and inimical to self-interest, and the Kirk's economic utterances were conservative and restrictivist. By the next century the mutation of 'blessings' into material well-being was widespread, enunciated by ministers like Robert Bruce (c. 1534-1631), yet still no economic growth ensued.

From Church of the Cross to Hidden Church to Church Militant
After 1560 in Scotland, moderate Calvinist or Reformed theology was essentially uncontested. The Scots Confession of the 1560 Parliament, the *Second Helvetic Confession*, and the *Heidelberg Catechism* along with Calvin's *Institutes* embodied the favoured parameters. Notwithstanding this consensus, the lack of unanimity on church order and relations with the equally 'Calvinist' but sometimes ungodly Magistrate seriously vexed the Scots for a long time. Like the Elizabethan Settlement in England, the 1560 Scottish settlement begat generations of energy-sapping unsettlement.

Nearly forty years earlier, Lutheran theology had penetrated Scotland, securing a toe-hold in 'stations of high tension' like St. Andrews University, the sea ports, some Augustinian and Dominican houses, and in the households of a small number of gentry and burghers. Persecution, especially the burning of Marburg's first graduate, the well-connected Patrick Hamilton, was sufficiently deterring to create a Scottish Protestant diaspora or an underground Church of the Cross at home. Reformation Scotland however was to experience little of the mutual religious killings that defaced contemporary England. Notable exports were explicit Lutherans like John Gau (d. 1563) and the ex-Dominican John MacAlpine or Macchabeus (d. 1557), both of whom worked with the Reformation in Denmark. Also, the ex-Augustinian Alexander Alane or Alesius (1500-65), Cromwell's expert on Luther in England settled in Germany. Of apparently Zwinglian predisposition was the Glasgow ex-Dominican, John Macdowell (d. 1555), who found refuge in the English Church. Troubled relations with England ironically emboldened Protestantism in Scotland. The return and preaching of the exile, George Wishart, English translator of the *First Helvetic Confession* resulted however in his burning (1546), fresh repression of his work and an exodus of the priveleged.

Among the new exilic generation were 1560 Reformers like Knox and the ex-Dominican, John Willock, – the former in England, Germany, France and Geneva, the latter in England and East Frisia. Knox's story was a remarkable odyssey from French galley-slave to Minister of Edinburgh. Popular Lutheran theology was disseminated through the vernacular *Gude and Godlie Ballatis* influenced by Wittenberg Scots. While there was obviously no mass Protestant movement before 1560, there was a closet Church, usually sheltered in noble, gentry and patrician households. This Church was occasionally externalised in most towns, but rarely in Edinburgh. Nor was this 'privy Kirk' induced into conformity by the Scottish Catholic Reform Councils (1549-59), led by Archbishop John Hamilton (c. 1511-71). It was this shadow Church-in-waiting which was represented by the small first General Assembly in 1560.

Propitious international and domestic situations enabled the pro-Reformation minority to 'come out', and led by some key nobles encouraged by Knox, effect two seigneurial revolutions in 1560 and 1567. The religious commitment of the (still inadequately researched) five original bonded 'Lords of the Congregation' is not questioned. One, John Erskine of Dun (1509-90), the first Moderator, had a long Reformation pedigree, and became a Superintendent as well as grey eminence in the Kirk. The first revolution was the overthrow of Roman Catholicism at the 1560 Parliament without royal consent (given 1567), but with decisive English support. Last-ditch Catholic defence was offered in vain by reformists like Ninian Winzet (c. 1518-92) and the Cluniac abbot, Quintin Kennedy (1520-64). The second was the coup d'état of 1567 by which Mary abdicated and her infant son, James VI, was declared King. Thereafter, despite a lengthy transconfessional war over the rightful monarch issue, the way was cleared for moderate Protestant 'policy' to prevail, driven originally by Erastian *politiques* like William Maitland of Lethington (c. 1528-73), irrespective of pressures from what Lynch calls (Calvinist) 'hawks'.[73] Not till 1573 was an Act of Uniformity passed. James was to be tutored, and trained in Reformed theology by the humanist, British unionist and theorist of tyrannicide, George Buchanan (1506-82) – later a General Assembly Moderator.

Subsequent development was vitiated by a see-saw struggle between autonomous presbyterian aspirations and Erastian-episcopalian policies of the government. The conflict was epitomised by James' maxim: 'no bishops, no king', and – as a function of his Two Kingdoms theory – by Andrew Melville's proposition that in the Church, 'God's silly vassal [the King] is neither lord, nor head, but a member'.[74] The imbroglio of de facto presbytery co-existing with an official episcopacy was resolving in favour of the latter, especially after the new triple monarchy (1603) whereby the orthodox Calvinist James became Supreme Governor of the English and Irish Churches. From 1610 the General Assembly was banned. But in 1638, the revolutionary National Covenant movement forced Charles I (1600-49) to allow the Assembly to convene at Glasgow. This abolished prelacy, and alien Anglican practices advanced by the monarch, as 'popish'.

Momentously significant in that gesture was aristocratic commitment to allegedly bourgeois presbyterianism, a turning-point in a national resistance campaign. Opposition to Anglican innovations was inseparable from that to alien centralising and interventionist notions of monarchical authority in church and nation, perceived as 'tyranny'. Only from this point on do 'Calvinism' and 'presbyterianism' become interchangeable in Scotland. The Covenant was the third seigneurial ace played since 1560, this time repelling the limits of secular sovereign assertion, and initiating the imminent wider struggle against absolutism and ideas of Divine Right. Scotland's older traditions had been corporatist. Though expressed in the form of a 'highly devolved feudal monarchy', the monarch was more the chief of the nobles than 'sovereign'. So the politics of therapeutic liberation do not explain what happened. The anti-encroachment politics were interwoven with theology. Old social, kinship, locality, communalist, cultural and class divisions were now transcended by the 'celestial glue' of the Covenant of Grace provided by federal theology. However, the basic oppositional Word of God theology had been bequeathed by Knox and Melville. Added to this were ideas of popular sovereignty, and of the already exercised rights of resistance and deposition, imparted by the Conciliarist, John Mair[75] (c. 1467-1550), and Buchanan, the one Catholic, the other Reformed. Even so, presbyterian Church settlement (1690) as such was not to be realised until the era of William of Orange (1650-1702), in a national, but not a 'state' Church.

The foundational documents of the *ecclesia scoticana* in this era include the following works: the *Scots Confession* of 1560, which was composed by a panel of six Reformers.[76] It was broadly 'Catholic and Reformed' in theology with a Calvinist but not explicitly predestinarian flavour. The Confession's equivocation on obedience to secular authority has often been controversial.[77] The *Book of Common Order* or 'John Knox's Liturgy' (1564) laid down guidelines for worship, practice and procedure in the Kirk. Derived from Calvin's *Forme des prières*, it was rendered into Classical Common Gaelic by the bardically trained Eóin Carsuel (d. 1572), Superintendent of Argyll and Bishop of the Isles. His landmark text – *Foirm na n-Urrnuidheadh* [*Form of Prayer*] (1567)[78] – was the first Gaelic book ever published. No extraordinary reconversion strategy for the large sub-Catholic and feudal areas in Gaelic Scotland was planned, but there is no evidence of wanting to abandon them to a predestined cold *ifrinn* [hell] either. Work by Jane Dawson will reveal an intelligent and successful accommodation of Calvinism to a boisterous, pastoral Gaeldom of clans, oral tradition, fairy Celtic other-worlds, and ancestor veneration. This should help familiar paradigms of the social anthropology of Calvinism to be revised. National reconstruction programs were embodied in the *First Book of Discipline* (1560)[79] and the proto-presbyterian *Second Book of Discipline* (1578),[80] neither of which were fully sanctioned in law. They embodied the Kirk's aspirations rather than achieved reality. Yet their educational, social welfare, and disciplinary policies appealed to ordinary people – even if such ideas were what revisionist ardour calls 'the more respectable face of Protestantism'.[81] Certainly relevant were the pleas for the 'poor labourers of the ground' and the redemption of the historic financial deficit in the parishes – but the nobility refused to release appropriate church endowments, and burghers declined to pay taxes to such ends. Freewill church offerings became the mechanism. Finally, while the *Genevan Catechism* and the *Heidelberg Catechism* were used, the chief indigenous primer sanctioned was *A Shorte Summe of the Whole Catechisme* (1581)[82] composed by John Craig (c. 1512-1600), an ex-Dominican converted to the Reformation while at Bologna in Italy. He was also author of the binding *King's Confession* (or *Negative Confession*) of 1581, designed to flush out crypto-Catholics at a time of heightened dread of international Catholicism.

❈ ❈ ❈

Conclusion and Prospect

A satellite picture of the British Isles in the Reformation era incontestably reveals religious atmospheric developments similar to those on the Continent. That the understanding, reception, and implementation of Reformation ideas was diverse is no surprise either. There are two obvious reasons for this. First, while previously part of a wider religious whole, the British Isles did not constitute a geographical, political, or cultural unity. Second, this was true of the Continent also. Accordingly, just as the Reformation on the Continent was variable, partial and asymmetrical, so also was it in Britain and Ireland. In regard then to the global picture, the evolution and sequel in the British Isles was characteristically European.

The contrasts within the British Isles are conspicuous, perhaps more so in retrospect than at the time, when there was more consciousness of vulnerability as well as potential for a monochromatic clean sweep. The Anglo-Welsh Protestant episcopalian State Church had to cope with presbyterian and other challenges. The Kirk had to balance *fait accompli* presbytery with official State sponsored episcopacy, and its principle of autonomy with government Erastian pretensions. In both Churches, much hung in the balance for several generations. And the Church of Ireland became confined essentially to elements in the old, and to the new Anglo-Scottish, colonial minority, though significant presbyterian secession diminished crucial Irish Protestant solidarity. The puzzle of outlawed continuing mass Catholicism in Ireland is unique in Europe, where normally Catholic integrity depended on secular real power. All the Reformation Churches lived in a state of permanent anxiety about the Counter Reformation and political Catholicism, from within and without. Accordingly, the Reformations in Wales, Ireland, and Scotland depended for long on English political preponderance and support. Seventeenth century revolution, rebellion, civil wars and militarisation of the British Isles were due partly to the unresolved clash between episcopalian, Erastian, presbyterian, separatist, and Catholic ideologies, and partly to disputed theologies of political sovereignty.

However, following the increasingly explicit Catholic inclinations of the monarchy under James II, the religious struggle for the British Isles was settled on the battle field. This necessitated wider European aid to impose the arrangements which became statutory and definitive, namely a Protestant episcopalian England and Wales, a presbyterian Scotland, and a British state-sponsored, but two-tier minority Protestant presence in Ireland. This resulted from the intervention of a Dutch-led Continental Protestant army in 1688-90. Such a compromise was based on the recognition that no religious and ecclesiastical unity or uniformity was feasible, despite the Three Kingdoms sharing one monarch (but different governments) since 1603. Thereafter, the chief real guarantees of the settlements were collective exhaustion, the depoliticisation of confessional Protestantism and Irish Catholicism, grudging toleration of dissent and nonconformity, and the popular entrenchment and interiorisation of heterogeneous pieties. The Three Kingdoms were to remain fundamentally disunited, in religion as in politics.

NOTES

1. For example, see *History of the Church*, ed. Hubert Jedin, et al., (London 1981); Euan Cameron, *The European Reformation* (Oxford, 1991).
2. Pierre Fraenkel, "Johann Eck und Sir Thomas More 1525 bis 1526," in *Von Konstanz nach Trient*, ed. Remigius Bäumer (Munich, 1972), 486-87.
3. Thomas A. Brady, Jr., "Social History," in *Reformation Europe: A Guide to Research*, ed. Steven Ozment (St. Louis, 1982), 176.
4. Fernand Braudel, *On History* (London, 1980), 30.
5. O'Day (1986) and Loades (1992), 1-5.
6. Compare Dickens (1989), 9.
7. Elton (1977) and id., *Policy and Police: The Enforcement of the Reformation in the Age of Thomas Cromwell* (Cambridge, 1972).
8. Elton (1977), 354-82.
9. See also Claire Cross, *Church and People 1450-1660: The Triumph of the Laity in the English Church* (London, 1976).
10. Haigh (1993), 13.
11. MacCulloch (1990), and id., "The Myth of the English Reformation," *JBS* 30 (1991): 1-19.
12. White (1992).
13. Collinson (1988), 28-93, Compare Brigden (1989) and Skeeters (1993).
14. Rex (1993), 14-16, and William J. Sheils, *The English Reformation 1530-1570* (London, 1989), 18.
15. Mayer (1989), 216-27. See Helmut Kressner, *Schweizer Ursprünge des anglikanischen Staatskirchentums* (Gütersloh, 1953).
16. William A. Clebsch, *England's Earliest Protestants 1520-1535* (New Haven, 1964), 277ff.
17. *Altercatio luciferani et orthodoxi*, 19, in *Patrologiae cursus completus, sive bibliotheca universalis, series latina*, ed. Jacques-Paul Migne (Paris, 1844-1902), vol. 23:155ff.
18. Geoffrey Elton, "Reform and the 'Commonwealth Men' of Edward VI's Reign," in *The English Commonwealth 1547-1640*, ed. Peter Clark et al., (Leicester, 1979), 23-38.
19. Geoffrey Elton, "England und die oberdeutsche reform," *ZKiG* 89 (1978): 3-11.
20. Dickens (1989), 12.
21. Thomson (1993). See Elton (1977), 10.
22. Duffy (1992), 3-6, and Skeeters (1993).
23. Gerald Strauss, *Luther's House of Learning* (Baltimore & London, 1978).
24. Dickens (1989), 332, and id., "The Early Expansion of Protestantism in England," *ARG* 78 (1987): 187-222. See also Brigden (1989), 411.
25. See David M. Loades, *The Reign of Mary Tudor*, 2d ed. (London & New York, 1991).

26. *The Zurich Letters, Comprising the Correspondence of Several English Bishops and Others,* Publications of the Parker Society, vol. 50 (Cambridge, 1842), 44-45.
27. *The Elizabethan Religious Settlement* (Bangor, Gwynedd, 1992), 20.
28. Quoted in Stanley T. Bindoff, *Tudor England* (Harmondsworth, 1950), 203. See Hudson (1980), 100.
29. See John Neale, *Elizabeth I and Her Parliaments* (London, 1953).
30. See Hudson (1980) and Jones (1982).
31. W. M. Southgate, *John Jewel and the Problem of Doctrinal Authority* (Cambridge, Mass., 1962), 62.
32. Geoffrey Elton, "Luther in England", in *Luther in der Neuzeit,* ed. Bernd Moeller (Gütersloh, 1983), 121-34.
33. David J. Keep, "Bullinger's Defence of Queen Elizabeth," in *Zürcher Beiträge zur Kirchengeschichte,* vol. 8, 2 (Zurich, 1975), 231-42 and Robert C. Walton in ibid., 243-56.
34. Andrew Pettegree, *Foreign Protestant Communities in Sixteenth Century London* (Oxford, 1986).
35. Wallace (1982), 75.
36. Walsham (1993), 107.
37. *Politics* V, 9.
38. See Tyacke (1987) and Wallace (1982), 29-78.
39. Dent (1983), 110-25.
40. Williams provides a handy summary in *The Reformation in Wales* (Bangor, Gwynedd, 1991).
41. Quoted in Herbert and Jones (1988), 111.
42. Roberts (1972).
43. Williams (1987), x.
44. Williams (1967), 111-24, and E. Gordon Rupp, *Studies in the English Protestant Tradition* (Cambridge, 1949), 62-72.
45. Williams (1967), 191-205. Also his "Religion and Welsh Literature in the Age of Reformation," *Proceedings of the British Academy* 69 (1983): 371-408. See Gruffydd (1990).
46. Williams (1967), 154-90.
47. Thomas (1988).
48. Williams (1987), 315-31 and Roberts in Fritze et al. (1991), 530.
49. Ellis (1985).
50. Hiram Morgan, *Tyrone's Rebellion: The Outbreak of the Nine Years' War in Tudor Ireland* (Woodbridge and Rochester N.Y., 1993).
51. See Canny (1986) and Clarke, "Bibliographical Supplement 1534-1691," in Moody (1991), 696-702.
52. Ford (1987), 225-28.
53. Clarke (1989), 105.
54. Clarke in Moody (1991), 699.
55. Lennon (1989).
56. Walshe (1989).
57. See Bradshaw (1978) and id., "The Elizabethans and the Irish: a Muddled Model," *Studies* 70 (1981): 233-44.
58. Ford (1987), 228.
59. Canny (1986), 110.
60. See Ford (1987), 123-37 and Mac Craith (1990).
61. See Ford (1987), 194-201.

62. Heinz Schilling, *Die Reformierte Konfessionalisierung in Deutschland: Das Problem der "Zweiten Reformation"* (Gütersloh, 1986), 389 and note 5, 400.
63. *John Knox's History of the Reformation in Scotland*, ed. William C. Dickinson (Edinburgh, 1949), vol. 1:342.
64. David McRoberts, ed., *Essays on the Scottish Reformation, 1513-1625* (Glasgow, 1962).
65. Ibid., 345.
66. Mullan (1986), 12.
67. Gordon Donaldson, *The Scottish Reformation* (Cambridge, 1960).
68. James Kirk, "Reformation and Revolution, Kirk and Crown 1560-1690," in Wormald (1991), 90.
69. Michael Lynch, "Calvinism in Scotland 1559-1638," in *International Calvinism 1541-1715*, ed. Menna Prestwich (Oxford, 1985), 225-55.
70. See also Keith Brown, "The Nobility of Jacobean Scotland," in Wormald (1991), 61-71.
71. See McGoldrick (1989) which leans heavily on the pioneering work by James Cameron and John Durkan. See Marshall (1980).
72. *The Faith of John Knox* (London, 1961), 88-95.
73. See note 69 above, especially page 248.
74. Ed. James Kirk (Edinburgh, 1980), 128.
75. Sometimes called John Major.
76. Best edition by Theodor Hesse in *Bekenntnisschriften und Kirchenordnungen*, ed. Wilhelm Niesel (Zollikon-Zurich, 1938).
77. Hazlett (1987), 315-19.
78. *Scottish Gaelic Texts*, 11, ed. Robert Thomson (Edinburgh, 1970).
79. Ed. James K. Cameron (Edinburgh, 1972).
80. See note 74.
81. Lynch (1981), 103.
82. See *The School of Faith*, ed. Thomas F. Torrance (London, 1959).

BIBLIOGRAPHY

Entries for England are limited to monographs published since 1980, excluding biographies of monarchs and leading statesmen and works in the bibliography by David M. Loades in this *Handbook*, vol. 1:429-35. The material for Wales, Ireland, and Scotland is less constrained.

England
Bedouelle, Guy, and Patrick Le Gal, eds. *Le "Divorce" du Roi Henry VIII: Etudes et Documents*. THR, vol. 221. Geneva, 1987.
Birch, D. *Early Reformation English Polemics*. Salzburg Studies in English Literature: Elizabethan and Renaissance Studies, vol. 92, pt. 7. Salzburg, 1983.
Bossy, John. *The English Catholic Community, 1570-1850*. London, 1983.
Brachelow, Stephen. *The Communion of Saints: Radical Puritan Thought and Separatist Ecclesiology, 1570-1625*. Oxford, 1988.
Brigden, Susan. *London and the Reformation*. Oxford, 1989.
Bryant, James C. *Tudor Drama and Religious Controversy*. Macon, Georgia, 1984.
Collinson, Patrick. *The Birthpangs of Protestant England: Religious and Cultural Changes in the Sixteenth and Seventeenth Centuries*. Basingstoke, 1988.
Collinson, Patrick. *The Religion of the Protestants: The Church in English Society 1559-1625*. Oxford, 1982.
Davis, John F. *Heresy and Reformation in the South-East of England 1520-1559*. Royal Historical Society in History, vol. 34. London, 1983.
Dent, Christopher M. *Protestant Reformers in Elizabethan Oxford*. Oxford, 1983.
Dickens, A. Geoffrey. *The English Reformation*. 2d ed. London, 1989.
Duffy, Eamon. *Stripping the Altars: Traditional Religion in England, c.1400-c.1580*. New Haven, 1992.
Dures, Alan. *English Catholicism 1558-1642: Continuity and Change*. Harlow, 1983.
Elton, Geoffrey. *Reform and Reformation 1509-1558*. London, 1977.
Fines, John. *A Biographical Register of Early English Protestants and Others Opposed to the Roman Catholic Church 1525-1558*. Courtenay Studies in Reformation Theology, vol. 3. Abingdon, 1981.
Fritze, Ronald H. et al., eds. *Historical Dictionary of Tudor England, 1485-1603*. New York, 1991.
Gilman, Ernest B. *Iconoclasm and Poetry in the English Reformation: Down went Dagon*. Chicago, 1986.
Greaves, Richard L. *Society and Religion in Elizabethan England*. Minneapolis, 1981.
Haigh, Christopher. *English Reformations: Religion, Politics and Society under the Tudors*. Oxford, 1993.
Hannay, Margaret P., ed. *Silent but for the Word: Tudor Women as Patrons, Translators, and Writers of Religious Works*. Kent, Ohio, 1985.
Helmholz, Richard H. *Roman Canon Law in Reformation England*. Cambridge, 1990.
Houlbrooke, Ralph A. *The English Family, 1450-1700*. New York, 1984.
Hudson, Winthrop S. *The Cambridge Connection and the Elizabethan Settlement of 1559*. Durham, N.C., 1980.

Ingram, Martin. *Church Courts, Sex and Marriage in England, 1570-1640.* Cambridge, 1987.

Jones, Norman L. *Faith by Statute: Parliament and the Settlement of Religion 1559.* London, 1982.

Lake, Peter. *Anglicans and Puritans: Presbyterianism and English Conformist Thought from Whitgift to Hooker.* London, 1988.

Loades, David M. *Revolution in Religion: The English Reformation 1530-1570.* Cardiff, 1992.

MacCulloch, Diarmaid. *The Later Reformation in England 1547-1603.* Basingstoke, 1990.

McKim, Donald K. *Ramism in William Perkins' Theology.* American University Studies, series VII, vol. 15. New York, 1987.

Marshall, Peter. *The Catholic Priesthood and the English Reformation.* Oxford, 1994.

Mayer, Thomas F. *Thomas Starkey and the Commonweal: Humanist Politics and Religion in the Age of Henry VIII.* Cambridge, 1989.

Moreau, Jean-Pierre. *Rome ou L'Angleterre? Les Réactions Politiques des Catholiques Anglais au Moment du Schisme (1529-1553).* Paris, 1984.

Morgan, John P. *Godly Learning: Puritan Attitudes to Reason, Learning and Education.* Cambridge, 1986.

Nijenhuis, Willem. *Adrianus Saravia (c.1532-1613).* SHCT, vol. 21. Leiden, 1980.

O'Day, Rosemary. *The Debate on the English Reformation.* London, 1986.

Reventlow, Henning G. *The Authority of the Bible and the Rise of the Modern World,* 73-146. London, 1984.

Rex, Richard. *Henry VIII and the English Reformation.* Basingstoke, 1993.

Rex, Richard. *The Theology of John Fisher.* Cambridge, 1991.

Skeeters, Martha C. *Community and Clergy: Bristol and the Reformation, c. 1520-1570.* Oxford, 1993.

Smeeton, Donald D. *Lollard Themes in the Reformation Theology of William Tyndale.* SCES, vol. 6. Kirksville, Mo., 1986.

Solt, Leo F. *Church and State in Early Modern England, 1509-1640.* Oxford, 1990.

Thomson, John A. F. *The Early Tudor Church and Society, 1485-1529.* London and New York, 1993.

Tyacke, Nicholas. *Anti-Calvinists: The Rise of English Arminianism, c.1590-1640.* Oxford, 1987.

Wallace, Dewey, D. *Puritans and Predestination: Grace in English Protestant Theology, 1525-1695.* Chapel Hill, N.C., 1982.

Walsham, Alexandra. *Church Papists: Catholicism, Conformity and Confessional Polemic in Early Modern England.* Royal Historical Publications, vol. 68. Woodbridge, Suffolk, 1993.

Warnicke, Retha. *Women of the English Renaissance and Reformation.* Westport, Conn., 1983.

Watt, Tessa. *Cheap Print and Popular Piety, 1550-1640.* Cambridge, 1991.

White, Peter O. G. *Predestination, Policy and Polemic: Conflict and Consensus in the English Church from the Reformation to the Civil War.* Cambridge, 1992.

Zaret, David. *The Heavenly Contract: Ideology and Organization in Pre-Revolutionary Puritanism.* Chicago, 1985.

Wales

Gruffydd, R. Geraint. "The Renaissance and Welsh Literature." In *The Celts and the Renaissance: Tradition and Innovation,* ed. Glanmor Williams and Robert O. Jones, 41-56. Cardiff, 1990.

Herbert, Trevor, and Gareth E. Jones, eds. *Tudor Wales.* Cardiff, 1988.

Jones, J. Gwynfor. *Early Modern Wales, c.1525-1640.* Basingstoke, 1994.

Jones, J. Gwynfor. *Wales and the Tudor State: Government, Religious Change and the Social Order, 1534-1603.* Cardiff, 1989.

Jones, J. Gwynfor, ed. *Class, Community and Culture in Tudor Wales.* Cardiff, 1989.

Roberts, Peter R. "The Union with England and the Identity of 'Anglican' Wales." *TRS* 22 (1972): 49-70.

Thomas, Isaac. *William Morgan a'i Feibl: William Morgan and his Bible.* Cardiff, 1988.

Williams, Glanmor. "Medieval Wales and the Reformation." In *An Introduction to Celtic Christianity,* ed. James P. Mackey, 206-37. Edinburgh, 1989.

Williams, Glanmor. *Recovery, Reorientation and Reformation: Wales c. 1415-1642.* Oxford, 1987.

Williams, Glanmor. *The Welsh and their Religion: Historical Essays.* Cardiff, 1993.

Williams, Glanmor. *The Welsh Church from Conquest to Reformation.* Rev. ed. Cardiff, 1976.

Williams, Glanmor. *Welsh Reformation Essays.* Cardiff, 1967.

Ireland

Bottigheimer, Karl S. "The Failure of the Reformation in Ireland: Une Question Bien Posée." *JEccH* 36 (1985): 196-207.

Bottigheimer, Karl S. "The Reformation in Ireland." *JBS* 15 (1976): 140-49.

Bradshaw, Brendan. *The Dissolution of the Religious Orders in Ireland under Henry VIII.* London, 1974.

Bradshaw, Brendan. "The Edwardian Reformation in Ireland." *Archivum Hibernicum* 34 (1977): 83-99.

Bradshaw, Brendan. "The Reformation in the Cities: Cork, Limerick, and Galway, 1534-1603." In *Settlement and Society in Medieval Ireland,* ed. John Bradley, 445-76. Kilkenny, 1988.

Bradshaw, Brendan. "Sword, Word and Strategy in the Reformation in Ireland." *HistJ* 21 (1978): 475-502.

Brady, Ciáran et al., eds. *Politics, Religion and Society in Ireland, 1515-1641.* Dublin, 1992.

Canny, Nicholas P. *The Elizabethan Conquest of Ireland: A Pattern Established, 1565-1576.* Hassocks, 1976.

Canny, Nicholas P. *From Reformation to Restoration: Ireland 1534-1660.* Dublin 1987.

Canny, Nicholas P. "Protestants, Planters and Apartheid in Early Modern Ireland." *Irish Historical Studies* 25 (1986): 105-15.

Canny, Nicholas P. "Why the Reformation Failed in Ireland: Une Question Mal Posée." *JEccH* 39 (1979): 432-50.

Clarke, Aidan. "Varieties of Uniformity: The First Century of the Church of Ireland." In *Churches, Ireland and the Irish,* ed. William J. Sheils and Diana Wood, 105-22. Studies in Church History, vol. 25. Oxford, 1989.

Dawson, Jane. "Two Kingdoms or Three? Ireland in Anglo-Scottish Relations in the Middle of the Sixteenth Century." In *Scotland and England, 1286-1815,* ed. Roger A. Mason, 113-38. Edinburgh, 1987.

Edwards, R. Dudley. *Ireland in the Age of the Tudors: The Destruction of Hiberno-Norman Civilization.* London, 1977.

Ellis, Steven G. "Economic Problems of the Church: Why the Reformation Failed in Ireland." *JEccH* 41 (1990): 139-65.

Ellis, Steven G. *Tudor Ireland: Crown, Community and the Conflict of Cultures, 1470-1603.* London, 1985.

Ford, G. Alan. *The Protestant Reformation in Ireland, 1590-1641.* Studien zur Interkulturellen Geschichte des Christentums, vol. 34. Frankfurt a. M., 1987.

Lennon, Colm. *The Lords of Dublin in the Age of Reformation.* Blackrock, 1989.

Mac Craith, Míchéal. "Gaelic Ireland and the Renaissance." In *The Celts and the Renaissance: Tradition and Innovation,* ed. Glanmor Williams and Robert O. Jones, 57-89. Cardiff, 1990.

Moody, Theodore W. et al. *A New History of Ireland.* Vol. 3, Early Modern Ireland, 1534-1691. Rev. ed. Oxford, 1991.

Trevor-Roper, Hugh. "James Ussher, Archbishop of Armagh." In *Catholics, Anglicans and Puritans,* ed. id., 120-65. London, 1989.

Walshe, Helen C. "Enforcing the Elizabethan Settlement: The Vicissitudes of Hugh Brady, Bishop of Meath, 1563-84." *Irish Historical Studies* 26 (1989): 353-76.

Scotland

Bardgett, Frank D. *Scotland Reformed: The Reformation in Angus and the Mearns.* Edinburgh, 1992.

Blake, William. *William Maitland of Lethington 1528-1573: A Study of the Policy of Moderation in the Scottish Reformation.* Studies in British History, vol. 17. Lewiston, 1990.

Brown, Keith M. *Bloodfeud in Scotland 1573-1625: Violence, Justice and Politics in an Early Modern Society.* Edinburgh, 1986.

Brown, Keith M. "In Search of the Godly Magistrate in Reformation Scotland." *JEccH* 40 (1989): 553-81.

Cameron, James K. "The Cologne Reformation and the Church of Scotland." *JEccH* 30 (1979): 39-64.

Cameron, Nigel de S. et al., eds. *Dictionary of Scottish Church History and Theology.* Edinburgh, 1993.

Cowan, Ian B. *The Scottish Reformation: Church and Society in Sixteenth Century Scotland.* London, 1982.

Cowan, Ian B., and Duncan Shaw, eds. *The Renaissance and Reformation in Scotland.* Edinburgh, 1983.

Dawson, Jane E. A. "The Two John Knoxes: England, Scotland and the 1558 Tracts." *JEccH* 42 (1991): 555-76.

Dilworth, Mark. "The Counter-Reformation in Scotland: A Select Critical Bibliography." *RSCHS* 12 (1984): 85-100.

Donaldson, Gordon. *All the Queen's Men: Power and Politics in Mary Stewart's Scotland.* London, 1983.

Donaldson, Gordon. "Reformation to Covenant." In *Studies in the History of Worship in Scotland,* ed. Duncan Forrester and Douglas Murray, 33-51. Edinburgh, 1984.

Donaldson, Gordon. *Scottish Church History.* Edinburgh, 1985.

Durkan, John. "Scottish 'Evangelicals' in the Patronage of Thomas Cromwell." *RSCHS* 21 (1982): 127-56.

Durkan, John. "Heresy in Scotland: The Second Phase, 1546-58." *RSCHS* 24 (1992): 320-65.

Graham, Michael F. "Equality before the Kirk: Church Discipline and the Elite in Reformation-Era Scotland." *ARG* 84 (1993): 289-310.

Graham, W. Fred. "The Reformation in Scotland." In *Reformation Europe: A Guide to Research,* ed. William S. Maltby, 235-51. St. Louis, 1992.

Greaves, Richard L. *Theology and Revolution in the Scottish Reformation: Studies in the Thought of John Knox.* Grand Rapids, 1980.

Hazlett, W. Ian P. "'Jihad' against Female Infidels and Satan. John Knox's First Blast of the Trumpet." In *Calvin: Erbe und Auftrag,* ed. Willem van 't Spijker, 279-90. Kampen, 1991.

Hazlett, W. Ian P. "The Scots Confession 1560: Context, Complexion and Critique." *ARG* 78 (1987): 287-320.

Hewitt, George D. *Scotland under Morton 1572-80.* Edinburgh, 1982.

Janton, Pierre. *Concept et sentiment de l'Église chez John Knox, le réformateur écossais.* Paris, 1972.

Jordan, Constance. "Women's Rule in Sixteenth Century Political Thought." *RenQ* 40 (1987): 421-51.

Kirk, James. "Early Scottish Protestants." In *Humanism and Reform: the Church in Europe, England and Scotland 1400-1643,* ed. James Kirk, 361-411. Studies in Church History, Subsidia, vol. 8. Oxford, 1991.

Kirk, James. *Patterns of Reform: Continuity and Change in the Reformation Kirk.* Edinburgh, 1989.

Kirk, James. "The Scottish Reformation and the Reign of James VI: A Select Critical Bibliography." *RSCHS* 23 (1987): 113-55.

Kyle, Richard G. *The Mind of John Knox.* Lawrence, Kansas, 1984.

Lynch, Michael. *Edinburgh and the Reformation.* Edinburgh, 1981.

Lynch, Michael. *Scotland: A New History, 171-244.* London, 1992.

Lynch, Michael, ed. *The Early Modern Town in Scotland.* London, 1987.

Macdougall, Norman, ed. *Church, Politics and Society: Scotland, 1408-1929.* Edinburgh, 1983.

McFarlane, Ian D. *Buchanan.* London, 1991.

McGoldrick, James E. *Luther's Scottish Connection.* Rutherford, N.J., 1989.

Marshall, Gordon. *Presbyteries and Profits: Calvinism and the Development of Capitalism, 1560-1707.* Oxford, 1980.

Mason, Roger A., ed. *John Knox: On Rebellion.* Cambridge, 1994.

Müller, Gerhard. "Protestant Theology in Scotland and Germany in the Early Days of the Reformation." *RSCHS* 22 (1985): 103-117.

Mullan, David G. *Episcopacy in Scotland: The History of an Idea, 1560-1638.* Edinburgh, 1986.

Sanderson, Margaret H. B. *Cardinal of Scotland: David Beaton, c. 1494-1546.* Edinburgh, 1986.

Sanderson, Margaret H. B. *Scottish Rural Society in the Sixteenth Century.* Edinburgh, 1982.

Shaw, Duncan. "Zwinglian Influences on the Scottish Reformation." *RSCHS* 22 (1985): 119-39.

Vershuur, Mary B. "Perth Craftsmen's Book: The Interpretation and Utilization of Protestant Thought by Sixteenth-Century Scottish Townsmen." *RSCHS* 23 (1988): 157-74.

Wiedermann, Gotthelf. "Some Ideas Concerning the Debate on Lutheran Theology at the University of St. Andrews 1525-1530." *RSCHS* 22 (1984): 13-34.

Wormald, Jenny. *Court, Kirk, and Community: Scotland 1470-1625.* London, 1981.

Wormald, Jenny, ed. *Scotland Revisted.* London, 1991.

SETTLEMENTS: SPAIN'S NATIONAL CATHOLICISM

Christian Hermann
(University of Nantes)

At the dawn of the fifteenth century Spain lay at the edge of Christian Europe.[1] It contained kingdoms lacking prestige and kings lacking the sacral authority possessed by the Holy Roman emperor and the king of France. Spain was also the meeting-place of Christianity, Islam, and Judaism, whence flowed into Europe the ancient philosophy and science recovered and reinterpreted by Islamic and Jewish thinkers.

At the end of the sixteenth century, by contrast, Europe was living in an age of Spanish hegemony. King Philip II's empire dominated Catholic Europe, and his Spain, the only realm truly safe from Protestantism, presented the last hope of the papacy and of the obdurate French, German, English, and Irish Catholics. Spain's theologians spoke loud and clearly at the Council of Trent; its mystics inspired a new Catholic spirituality; and the Jesuits, of Spanish origin, had become the vanguard of Roman Catholicism. The English and the Dutch characterized the phenomenon in two highly emotionally and imaginatively charged words: "Spanish papacy." Today, we prefer to speak of Spain's "national Catholicism."

Spain's history between 1400 and 1600 poses many unanswered questions. Why did Spain enclose itself within an exclusive religious identity? What share did Spain have in the religious Reformation, and why did it exercise, until well into the seventeenth century, such a powerful influence on the Catholic world? What were the origins and true nature of Spanish relations with the papacy? To raise these questions, and answer them, is to weigh the reality and the emotive force contained in the traditional polemical term "papalism." In this chapter we will examine Spanish national Catholicism as seen by those who shaped it—monarchs, mystics, and theologians. There is another story, waiting to be uncovered, about the local religious life of the Hispanic peoples, but it cannot yet be told.[2]

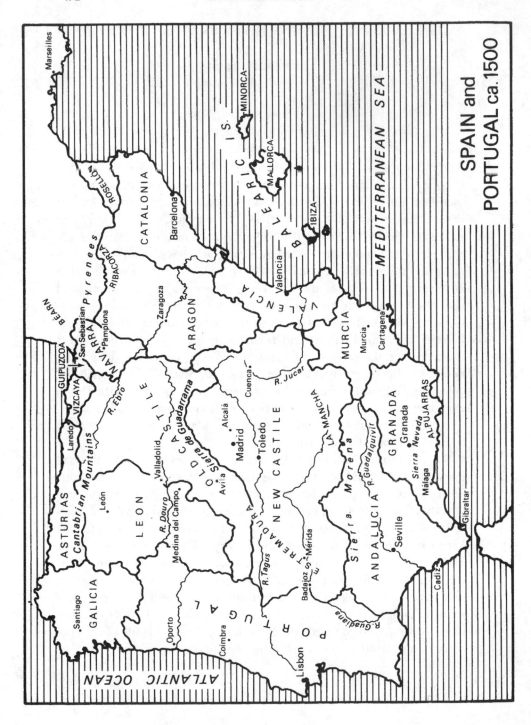

SPAIN and PORTUGAL ca. 1500

1. FROM RELIGIOUS PLURALITY TO INQUISITIONAL CATHOLICISM

The End of Coexistence

Around 1400 the medieval coexistence (*convivencia*) of the three Iberian religions came to an end. The first large-scale pogroms exploded in 1391; in 1413 at Tortosa, the Christian theologians confronted the Jewish rabbis and called upon them to convert; in 1412/14 the kings of Castile and of Aragon promulgated the first discriminatory measures against Jews. This trend, which culminated in the mass expulsion of 1492,[3] promoted from the beginning a massive conversion of Jews to Christianity, in which it is impossible to determine the relative importance of intimidation, and of the natural ascendancy of a dynamic religion of the majority. This movement created a socio-cultural group of "New Christians [*cristianos nuevos*]," who were despised by the Jews as renegades and by the "Old Christians [*cristianos viejos*]" as insincere converts.

As in medieval Europe generally, fifteenth-century antisemitism in Spain fed from an envy of evident privilege, a hatred of royal fiscalism—of which the New Christians were regarded as agents—and the lower classes' identification with an exclusive concept of Christianity, tainted with millenarianism. Spain had long been the country of the "three religions of the Book," as the *Koran* called them. Whatever their inferior legal status, Moors and Jews were protected by Christian kings, just as Jews and Christians were and sometimes still are in the modern Islamic lands. In the fifteenth century, however, a new desire to be part of Christian Europe, based on an exclusive, united faith, required a repudiation of this traditional religious plurality. Royal policy eventually complied, so that, two centuries after England and a century after France, Spain expelled its Jews in 1492.

Before and after the expulsion, the target of anti-Jewish sentiments in Spain was the powerful community of Jewish renegades, the New Christians, many of whom rose to high positions in the Spanish church. The splendid development of a central role in intellectual and religious life that made Spain the beacon of the Tridentine reform and of Catholic Europe cannot be understood without their contribution. Their success evoked envy from the less well educated nobility, whom they crowded out of the best ecclesiastical offices, and hatred from the popular classes, who saw their Christianity being "judaized." Hence, Spanish antisemitism targeted the converted Jews as much as, or more then, the practicing ones. Indeed, the Holy Office of the Inquisition was institutionalized mainly to curb the alleged crypto-Judaism of New Christians, for by 1500 few openly practicing Jews were left in Spain. It was the New Christians who stayed, around whom Spanish antisemitism crystalized during the following two centuries.

The chief weapon against New Christians, rules requiring "purity of blood [*limpieza de sangre*]," restricted their access to religious orders, cathedral and other chapters, military religious orders, town councils, guilds, and universities, which demanded proof of Old Christian ancestry and held even a distant Jewish or Moorish ancestor to be a mark of infamy. Although such laws eventually became a Spanish national obsession, they were resisted from the first by the New Christians in the higher clergy and by others, such as the three leading theologians who opposed the first such laws at Toledo in 1449 and argued for the equality of all Christians, regardless of the date of their conversion. During the fifteenth century, the Crown, too, tried to hinder the advance of such discrimination, though without ever confronting it directly. The decisive turning point was probably the imposition of a "purity of blood" rule on the cathedral chapter of Toledo by Archbishop Siliceo in 1547. The Society of Jesus, in the first fifty years the most fervent adversary of these rules, itself adopted them for its Spanish provinces in 1593.

The Fate of the Moriscos

Although the fall of Granada, Iberia's last Islamic state, was not connected to the expulsion of the Jews except by simultaneity, the two events had roots in the same late fifteenth-century situation: the prosperity of Castile and of Aragon and their movement into the rank of major European powers. Initially, there was no sign that this meant an end to the centuries-long tradition of religious plurality associated with the "reconquest [*reconquista*]," when Christian rulers had guaranteed the legal status and the religious freedom of their new Islamic subjects. After Granada's fall, a royal decree or "capitulation" repeated this guarantee, and the first archbishop of Granada, Hernando de Talavera, sought to convert the Muslims by purely peaceful means. The times, however, were against him, for the Castilian desire to join Christian Europe and the new Ottoman challenge both promoted unity of faith as a guarantee of national identity. In 1499, a more severe policy toward the Granadan Muslims, promoted by the primate of Spain, Francisco Jimenez de Cisneros (1437-1517), provoked the first revolt of the Granadan Moriscos. Three years later, the Muslims had to choose between conversion and exile, though, unlike the Jews, the majority decided to stay. Although Islamic law legitimized simulated conversion under pressure if necessary to preserve the real faith, conversion proved a dangerous, if convenient, solution, because it placed the Moriscos under the Inquisition, whose goal was to seek out equivocation and eliminate it.

The Muslims of Aragon and of Valencia did not face the test until the revolts of 1521-22, when the popular associations (*germanías*) in the Valencian towns rose against the aristocracy and then turned against the Muslims, many of whom were forcibly baptized. In 1525 King Charles I (the Emperor Charles V) legalized these measures and imposed the Granadan doom—conversion or exile—on all Muslims in the kingdoms of Aragon and Valencia. Thereafter the lot of the Moriscos, the Muslims who stayed, progressively worsened, not least because the Ottoman challenge constantly cast them as an enemy within the gates. King Philip II had the Valencian and Aragonese Moriscos disarmed in 1563, well before the great revolt in the mountainous district of Las Alpujarras in Granada (1568-70). The policy of the Catholic missionaries and the Inquisition toward the Moriscos vacillated between optimistic zeal and disillusioned resignation, while the Valencian and Aragonese nobles, whose wealth depended upon a Moorish laboring class, long remained the Moriscos' only defenders. Finally, in 1609 King Philip III ordered their general expulsion, and by 1614 a relieved Spain was inhabited only by Christians of long standing.

Spain and the Protestant Reformation in Europe[4]

In Spain "Christian" was at this time a synonym for "Roman Catholic." Although the condition of the church and the kingdoms' political and commercial integration into Europe favored a reception of Protestant ideas, in fact Protestantism made far less impact on Spanish Christianity than Judaism did, thanks to the long *convivencia* and to the fifteenth-century Jewish conversions. The New Christians suffused Spanish religious culture with a rich spiritual, philosophical, and exegetical tradition, and the Protestant goal of restoring early Christianity meant also a recovery of the Jewish heritage. But Protestantism came to Spain only in the second half of the 16th century, and must not be confused with the home-grown reform of the first half of the century. This perspective is crucial to understanding the impact of Protestantism on Spain, which was confined to a few urban conventicles of theologians, influential clergymen, and patricians. The chief ones, at Seville and Valladolid, were eradicated in the 1550s, though it proved more difficult to prevent the diffusion of Bibles translated by eminent Spaniards.

The phenomenon of Erasmianism illustrates the equivocal nature of pre-Tridentine Spanish reform. Erasmus' audience was for a long time as large in Spain as elsewhere, and it included two Inquisitor-Generals, one of whom, Cisneros, in 1516 requested Erasmus' collaboration on the polyglot Bible of Alacalá.[5] Mistrust set in, however, with the second edition of Erasmus' Latin New Testament (1519), and by 1527, when a meeting of theologians was convened in Valladolid, there was an increasingly general hostility to Erasmus' works. Although the protection of Pope Clement VII and of the Inquisitor-General, A. Manrique, saved Erasmus from a condemnation, by 1530 his disciples started to be cited before the Inquisition, and little-by-little his influence waned.

A more important and uniquely Spanish expression of dissent was the mystical movement called the "illumined ones [alumbrados]," small groups who searched for a more authentic spiritual life beyond official ecclesiastical structures. Though without any direct ties to Protestants, the alumbrados shared some of their concerns, for they emphasized faith, the abandonment of self to divine love, interior peace and illumination, personal piety, and reading the Bible, while they de-emphasized rituals, the sacraments, the cult of the saints, purgatory, and the contribution of good works and free will to salvation. They more or less rejected clerical, papal, and royal claims to religious authority. The alumbrados were prosecuted by the Inquisition between 1520 and 1540, and then again during the 1570s.

2. The Catholic Reformation in Spain

Concern for reform of the clergy was voiced, earlier in Castile than in Aragon, by clergymen, by the kings, and by the parliament (cortés). They all wanted an educated clergy who led irreproachable lives, but they also wanted to enhance, not obliterate, the sacerdotal character of the clergy and its distinction from the laity. This meant removing clerical status from those who were tonsured but not ordained and who expected to live on the church without serving it; in the religious orders it meant a restoration of rigorous vows, strict community life, and stricter observance of claustration; and for all the clergy it meant stricter separation between clerical and lay jurisdictions and properties. In practice, the reform of the Spanish clergy during the fifteenth and sixteenth centuries affected only the religious orders. Among the secular clergy the only sixteenth-century significant reform was the Crown's recruitment of bishops who displayed education, competence, and generally exemplary morals.

The Advance of the Monastic Observance

Since around 1400, the monastic reform movement called the "Observance" flourished in Castile under royal protection and with papal encouragement. It began with King John II's (r. 1406-54) support for the chief organizers of the Observance among the Franciscans, Dominicans, Cistercians, and Hieronymites. After mid-century Popes Calixtus III and Sixtus IV broke this royal-papal alliance to support the opponents, called "Conventuals," but monastic reform again became royal policy under the Catholic Kings, Isabella of Castile and Ferdinand of Aragon. The ambitious program adopted by a national council meeting at Seville in 1478 reflected the monarchs' particular concern for the regular orders, and eleven years later, after a long period of papal caution, even hostility, to royal policy, Pope Innocent VIII restored the old policy of collaboration and ordered the reform of the Spanish Benedictines, Cistercians, and Augustinians. By then, however, the monarchs wanted much more: papal authorization to impose the Observance on the convents and to interdict appeals to Rome. They got what they wanted. Pope Alexander VI granted the right to appoint commissioners empowered to introduce the Observance and deny appeals to Rome. To this task the Catholic Kings appointed the Franciscan Jimenez de Cisneros and the Dominican Diego Deza, whose powers the papacy progressively widened between 1494 and 1499 to include all Conventuals. By the death of Cisneros in 1517, the Observants' triumph over the Conventuals was so complete in Castile that Pope Leo X had only to approve, which he did in the same year.

The conflicts between Charles V and the papacy interrupted the alliance for about a dozen years, but it resumed under Pope Clement VII in 1530-31. The chief remaining tasks were to reduce resistance to monastic reform in Galicia and in the Asturias and to introduce it into the kingdoms of Aragon and Navarre. The Crown's use of Castilian clergy stirred up patriotic reactions against the threat of Castilianization in those kingdoms. The Holy See, now anxious to avoid regalism, withdrew its support for the royal commissioners, and in 1548 it vigorously opposed a plan to break the obstinacy of the Catalan nuns by entrusting their reform to the Inquisition: the defense of a moderate standard of discipline was not tantamount to heresy!

Philip II, who wished to bring the stalled reform to a conclusion, failed to learn from his father's failures. The program he issued between 1561 and 1563 sought to impose, without concessions, the Castilian Observance by Castilian commissioners on the monasteries of Aragon, an enterprise which met with growing skepticism and resistance at Rome. Against this royal program, the Holy See regarded the decrees of the Council of Trent, which rose for the last time in 1563, as the sole, universal norm for the Catholic world, to which the practices of national churches ought to yield. On the discipline of regular clergy, the Tridentine decrees were less rigorous than the Observance evolved in Spain during the fifteenth century and imposed by the monarchy since the Catholic Kings. In 1566-67, however, Pope Pius V, an advocate of the strictest monastic ideals, abandoned his predecessors' opposition and yielded to all of the Spanish Crown's demands, and by 1570 a papal-royal modus vivendi on monastic reform had been achieved. This allowed the reform commission, which Philip II had installed a few years earlier, and to which he named the General Inquisitors Fernando de Valdés and Diego de Espinosa, and by the Franciscan Royal Confessors, Bernardo de Fresneda and Francisco Pacheco, to work in concert with the papal nuncio at Madrid. Thenceforth, the Observance moved ahead more slowly but, especially in the kingdom of Aragon, more surely.

Spanish Mysticism in the Golden Age

The reigns of Charles V and Philip II were the harvest time of religious reform in Spain. The dazzling development of Spanish mysticism, focused on the goal of personal perfection, exceeded all expectations of its fifteenth-century predecessors. It blossomed in the convents and the monasteries, because the ideal of a rigorous religious life had been restored. Nor did the reform remain within the monastery walls, for treatises on spiritual direction, on moral edification, and pastoral works by monastic authors guided the religious life of the lay elites, if not of the faithful masses. The reform's influence is suggested by frequent new editions of such works during the sixteenth and seventeenth centuries and by many translations into all the languages of Catholic Europe. The French "century of the saints" (the first half of the seventeenth century) possessed deep roots in this Spanish spirituality.

The central doctrine of this spiritual movement was the soul's mystical journey in three stages: purgation, illumination, and union. In the first stage, purgation, body and spirit are purified through mortification, asceticism, meditation, study, and training of the conscience, which together detach the individual from secular interests and dispose one to internalize the spiritual life. Detachment does not mean flight from professional, social, or familial responsibilities. Faith, the Spanish mystics believed, is expressed by action: good works, religious rites, and above all charity. Teresa of Avila's (1515-82) biographies show that she knew the trivial difficulties of everyday life; she gave the communities she had founded practical household advice.[6] And Ignatius of Loyola (1491-1556) passed on to the Society of Jesus his taste for the active life and his organizational genius.

During the second stage, illumination, the soul, now disposed to perfection and divine grace, progresses from permanent prayer into dialogue. The typical method of prayer is presented in numerous works, such as the Alonso de Madrid's *Art of Serving God* (*Arte para servir a Dios* [1521]), and Ignatius' *Spiritual Exercises* (1521). Francisco de Osuna (d. ca. 1540) distinguishes three kinds of prayer—vocal, intellective, and mental or meditative—which correspond to the stages of the soul's progress from the purgative to the unitive state.[7] During the progress toward illumination, one descends into the self, re-centers it on the soul, and detaches it from the sensual faculties in order to seek God, in Whose image humanity was created. Such contemplation makes possible a purely spiritual form of prayer and opens the way to union with God.

The third stage, union, is the soul's ascent to God. It is a journey, the mystics' ultimate goal, attested by the titles of such mystical works as Bernardino of Laredo's (1482-1545?) *Ascent of Mount Zion* and John of the Cross' (1542-91) *Ascent of Mount Carmel*.[8] In this stage the natural faculties are passive, as only the will, seized by divine grace, continues to act, while the intellect and the senses enter a supernatural state in which they perceive the world only in the light of the love of God. One's entire life now becomes an act of prayer in this loving communion, as it is called in the John of the Cross' *Spiritual Song*. The blessings of divine love are now understandable, but only with the help of Christ, for the entire scheme is profoundly christological. As early as the journey's first stage, meditation on the blessings of Christ becomes part of methodical mental prayer and leads to the stage of illumination. The self's identification with His humanity thus prepares the approach to the mystery of His divinity. The Christocentric perspective adopted by Spanish mysticism, clearly revealed in Teresa's *Libro de las moradas o Castillo interior* (1588), also inspired Luis Ponce de Léon (1527-91) to write the *Nombres de Cristo* (1585).

Like peoples in other parts of Europe, Spaniards experienced the same dissatisfaction with the ritualism and legalism of the official church, the same aspiration to follow the Bible and to commit oneself to the imitation of Christ. To this challenge the Spanish mystics supplied a Roman Catholic response. Looking at the methods of spiritual asceticism alone, it is very difficult to distinguish orthodox mysticism from heterodox Illuminism (*alumbradismo*), except in the mystics' relationship to the official church. The movement's monastic leadership safeguarded the church's magisterial authority and its sacramental life, which the mystics, unlike the Illuminists, did not deprecate. The mystics did not claim to offer a superior authenticity but urged only that questing souls not be content with what they are, but always to reach further. This touchstone allowed the Inquisition to separate the grain from the chaff.

In its own way, Spanish mysticism also responded to a second challenge from Protestant Europe, the call for the priesthood of all believers. Asceticism, meditation, the study of the sacred texts, the ideal of Christian perfection, until this time the province of the regular clergy, were now offered to all laymen, according to their capacities. Over several generations the most accessible spiritual practices were widely diffused through Spanish society, leading some theologians and other clergy to worry that the vulgarization of Christian perfection would pose a danger to the beliefs of the faithful and the clergy's authority. Then, too, women who departed from traditional paths of piety posed a threat to a male clergy, and it is intriguing to note that the mystics were as generally feminist in attitude as their opponents were antifeminist. This is one reason why the relationships among the mystics, the theologians, and the Inquisition were often stormy and marked by defiance and suspicion. True enough, few mystics were condemned by the Inquisition—the placement of two of Luis de Granada's works on the Index in 1559 is the most famous case—but almost all had encounters with the Inquisition at some point in their lives. Two prestigious Jesuit saints, Francisco de Borja (1510-72) and Ignatius himself, are cases in point.

Theology and Humanism

The rise of mysticism in sixteenth-century Spain coincided with the rebirth of Spanish theology. Here, too, the regulars led the way. Spanish scholastic theology had developed at the University of Salamanca from 1396, followed by Valladolid (1418) and Lerida (1430). The world of the high clergy became international, and the late medieval councils brought it into contact with Italian humanism. Although Spanish theologians of the conciliar era kept active, the fifteenth-century ossification of the scholastic method did not spare Spain. Then came renewal, and by 1600 Spain contained more than thirty schools of theology, half of which had been founded between 1500 and 1550. A parallel expansion of the preparatory schools and houses of studies of the religious orders raised the intellectual formation of the regulars and the elite of the secular clergy.

The renaissance of theology was sponsored by Francisco Jiménez de Cisneros (1437-1517), the major promoter of the monastic Observance under Isabella the Catholic. He shared the humanists' belief in the primacy of observation and experience over logical virtuosity and in human capacity for moral and intellectual progress. He also shared their confidence in critical method, philology, and the study of ancient tongues and sources. In order to counter the sectarianism of the scholastic schools, at the new University of Alcalá of Henares he ordered the simultaneous teaching of all three current schools of thought—nominalism, Scotism, and Thomism. Thereafter, little by little innovation gained a footing in the country's universities.

The next step was the edition by a scholarly team at Alcalá of a great multilingual Bible, called the *Complutensian Polyglot*, which appeared in six volumes in 1522.[9] This monument of European humanism was the first critical edition of the Latin Vulgate, the first edition of the Septuagint, and the first edition of the Hebrew Old Testament by Latin Christians. The impulse Cisneros gave to biblical studies did not weaken during the sixteenth century, and even before the Council of Trent prescribed in 1546 the establishment of a Biblical chair in each faculty of theology, Spain had one in each of its three principal universities: Salamanca (1416), Alacalá de Henares (1532), and Valladolid (1542). The effort culminated in two works. The *Poliglota Regia* (1569-72), which completed what the *Complutensian Polyglot* had begun, appeared under royal patronage and with papal endorsement. Edited by Benito Arias Montano (1527-98), a lay biblical scholar and theologian, it was printed in eight volumes by Plantin at Antwerp.[10]

The second key work was Martin Martinez Cantalapiedra's extensive exegetical treatise, *Libri decem hypotyposeon . . . ad intelligendum Scripturas divinas* (1583).

This return to the Bible did not have all the repercussions that one might expect. It was accessible only to those familiar with ancient tongues, and in practice it passed to the laity through the filter of the clergy, for the possession of a vernacular Bible, already prohibited by the Catholic Kings, became in the sixteenth century grounds for suspicion of heresy. The division of Europe into religious parties tainted Bible study with a suspicion of Protestantism, and in the Spanish stereotype a Protestant soon became a layman who read the Bible.

At the end of the 1530s, a generation of Dominicans consolidated the theological renaissance. The new, humanist-influenced method that emerged in Melchior Cano's (1509-60) *De locis theologicis* of 1563 no longer applies logical rules to a question but rather investigates sources of positive knowledge to which reason can respond. The hierarchy of sources thus established reaffirms the primacy of divine mystery, of revelation, and of tradition, over natural reason, positive science, and individual speculation: Holy Scripture and Apostolic tradition stood first; natural reason, philosophy, history, and other sciences were subsidiary; and the acts of the councils, the church's traditions, and the works of the Fathers formed an intermediate tier. Cano's positive theology was thus clearly Catholic in that its hierarchy of sources blocked any development toward religious scientism or relativism.

The renewal of moral theology, which establishes the principles of social organization and personal behavior in conformance with providential design, was undertaken by Francisco de Vitoria (1486-1546), whose *Relecciones de Indis* appeared in 1557, and Domingo de Soto (1495-1560), author of *De Iusticia et Iure* (1554). Deeply engaged in the political, economic, and social debates of the age, they developed less a humanist theology than a theocentric humanism. All rights and authority come from God, but man, created in God's image (as human institutions are not) is the source and measure of the law. The hierarchy of divine, natural, and positive law is not invalidated by sin or infidelity, so that positive laws established by rulers and communities are subordinate to natural human rights.

For half-a-century, this theocentric humanism born at Salamanca in the mid-sixteenth century flourished in the Society of Jesus, reaching its apogee in Juan de Mariana (1536-1624)[11] and Francisco Suarez (1548-

1617),[12] and in 1588 exploding into dogmatic theology with the publication of Luis Molina's (1535-1600) major work.[13] Their accent on natural human freedom led these Spanish theologians to emphasize the coordination of conscience and actions and their connection with the assurance of salvation through faith and through a gracious God's mercy. Molina provided the most radical formulation of this perspective. The Creator's omnipotence cannot compel to goodness or faith an individual who wishes to turn away from Him, and divine grace becomes effective for salvation only through the concurrence of human free will. The storm Molina aroused in Catholic Europe led to the seventeenth-century struggle between Jansenists and Jesuits, just as the analogous Dutch controversy between Arminians and orthodox Calvinists rocked the theologians of Protestant Europe. At the center of each controversy lay the issue of the nature of divine power and its relation to human fate.

During the first half of the sixteenth century, the Spanish theologians also formulated a political doctrine, the roots of which lay in the religious unification, the Catholic reform, and the monarchy's imperial expansion. They were theorizing a Castilian historical experience and legitimizing its outcome, but they had the courage to risk opposing in certain ways narrow Spanish interests. The keystone in the arch of this doctrine is the juncture of fideism and political providentialism, otherwise known as the "divine reason," which opposes, or may oppose, reason of the state. Its most complete expression came from the Jesuit Pedro Rivadeneira (1527-1611), whose title is a manifesto: *Treatise on the Religion and the Virtues a Christian Prince Must Have in Order to Govern and Conserve His States. Against the Doctrines Taught by Nicholas Machiavelli and the Politiques of Our Time* (1595). Refusing to desacralize politics, Rivadeneira underlined the superior moral authority of religion, because of the ends it pursues. God's providential plan for humanity points to a temporal destiny, which cannot be adequately accounted for by reason, the law of nations, and positive law alone. Because the human being is but a creature in God's image, and human reason contains but a parcel of divine intelligence, the political community can find its temporal and spiritual fulfillment only through submission to revelation's superior authority. This idea, clearly inspired by the Old Testament covenant between the Hebrew people and Yahweh, left no room for religious or confessional plurality, for it rested the state's authority on the political body's religious unity: one faith, one king, one law.

This doctrine, which revitalized the Thomist thesis of the church's indirect sovereignty in temporal matters, was deepened and sharpened by Francisco Vitoria (1483/86-1546)[14] and acquired its definitive formulation from Robert Bellarmine (1542-1621)[15] and Francisco Suarez (1548-1617).[16] It then became an official teaching of the Roman Catholic Church. It is important to recall that these Jesuit doctors were refuting the absolutist theses advanced by an eminent Protestant theologian, King James I of England and VI of Scotland. Suarez, who explicitly attacked James' assertion of the ruler's responsibility to God alone,[17] held that if the pope and the emperor were supreme in their respective spheres as spiritual and temporal heads of Christendom, the superiority of spiritual to temporal ends meant that the pope held indirect authority over any temporal government of Christians. What was true of the papacy vis-à-vis the emperor, held for every national church vis-à-vis its prince. The church thus became a kind of constitutional court that guaranteed principles of governance without being able to administer them or to make laws. It could not only censure a temporal ruler's acts, it could compel him to repeal them, if their religious or moral consequences affected the higher, spiritual ends. The analogous, indirect spiritual authority of the rulers, on the other hand, was limited to the defense of religion.

How could the Holy Roman emperor be regarded as the defender of the faith in a Europe divided among rival national monarchies? Both Rivadeneira and Suarez answered that the pope could charge any temporal ruler with this mission.[18] Historical circumstances, not divine right, made Spain the temporal army of the Roman Church. Just like the Hebrew people under the old law, Spain was called to assume the defense of the faith, which the Holy Roman emperors had formerly supplied.

Vitoria and, following him, Suarez extended this argument to the relationships between rulers and ruled in general and argued that only the church's authority came directly from divine law, while all temporal authority proceeded from that law only mediately: "No temporal rule comes immediately from God [*Nullus principatus est immediate a Deo*]." The mediator, however, is not the church but the people constituted as a political community: "All power comes from God through the people [*Omnis potestas a Deo per populum*]." Sovereignty is delegated to kings by the people, and the delegation is conditional, resting on the original pact that formed the political community. The community, in turn, establishes the monarchy and the state, which continue to depend on the contract of delegation. The ruler's abuse of legitimate authority violates the pact and the constitution, offends natural law and Christian faith, and makes the ruler into a tyrant who can therefore be opposed, removed, or, if need be, killed. To be sure, the legitimization of regicide by Suarez, and later by Juan de Mariana (1536-1633/34), was so hedged with prudent restrictions as to be little more than an intellectual exercise. Yet, in the political context of early seventeenth-century Europe it is easy to understand why their works were solemnly condemned and burned in England and in France. One can also understand why they later became the bêtes noires of absolutist monarchies.

Rather traditional with respect to European affairs, Spanish political theology acquired a prophetic quality in Vitoria's *Relecciones de Indis* (1557), which deals with the relationship between Europeans and the peoples of the New World. Since the 1510's, when the Dominicans on San Domingo and Bartolomé de las Casas (1474-1566) had mounted their protests, the Spanish colonists' operations and the Indians' lot had become a major topic of debate in high-ranking circles of the Spanish state, but also among the educated public at large. Vitoria, writing a few years before the New Laws of 1542, proceeded in the spirit of theocentric humanism to develop all the consequences of natural law with respect to the issue. By what right did the Spaniards take possession of the New World and subject its inhabitants to their authority? Vitoria discarded all arguments of a traditional kind, arguing that no such right arose from a special gift of God, from the authority of pope or emperor, or from the Indians' alleged sins against nature (cannibalism, sodomy). Nor could it arise from the right of discovery, because of the Indians' natural right to form their own political communities, nor again from abdications by native princes in the Spanish king's favor. The sole bases of legitimate authority over such peoples, Vitoria asserted, were the need to assure free communication and the solidarity of members of the human species (whence the right to evangelize), the free choice of the subject peoples, and perhaps the need of barbarous peoples for tutelage from more civilized ones. All in all, Vitoria, along with Las Casas and Suarez, belong with the great mystics among the most eminent the Spanish contributions to the Catholic Reformation.

3. The Conciliar Movement and the Hispano-Roman Alliance

The role of Spain and its national Catholicism in the European Counterreformation depended fundamentally on Spanish relations with the papacy and on what may be called the "Hispano-Roman alliance." Its foundations were laid during the age of conciliarism, that is, the first half of the fifteenth century. In 1400 the Spanish monarchies were still a cluster of second-rate powers with divided interests: Aragon defended its claims to Sicily against France; Castile held loyally to France against Portugal and its English ally; and Navarre's king drew more from his fiefs in the Paris basin than from his poor Pyreneean kingdom. The three dynasties agreed only in their common support for the Avignonese claimant to a divided papacy, the Iberian Benedict XIII. Their loyalty was tested when the Council of Pisa's (1409) pitiful failure brought the great powers behind the Council of Constance (1414-18) and its successful effort to reunite the papacy. The Iberian monarchs now withdrew from Benedict's obedience, though their clergies stayed loyal to him.

The settlement of the Great Western Schism at Constance threatened to allow conciliar principles to triumph in the church and bring the national churches under royal domination.[19] Castile and Aragon help to save the Holy See from this fate by supporting deferral of reform until after the election of a single new pope, Martin V, thus sealing the first Hispano-Roman alliance. King John II of Castile opposed conciliarism for the sensible reason that if the General Council came to govern the church, the Castilian parliament (cortés) might be tempted to imitate the solution in Castile. King Alphonse V of Aragon, who already had to share governance with his parliament (corts), was in fact better disposed toward the conciliar movement and was long the ally of Emperor Sigmund, a chief sponsor of conciliarism. His main goal, however, Catalan-Aragonese domination of the western Mediterranean, required support from the pope, who was the legal suzerain of Naples, Sicily, and Sardinia. Alphonse therefore joined the Castilian position, adding to the new Iberian weight in European international relations during the first half of the fifteenth century.

In fact, both kings' support for Rome was provisional. Alphonse of Aragon's aimed to secure papal investiture with the kingdom of Naples at the death of Queen Joanna, whereas the Holy See wanted to maintain a division of southern Italy between an Angevin Naples and an Aragonese Sicily. To pressure the pope, the king restored the Avignonese obedience in 1423 and fanned the flames of radical conciliarism, regalism, and anti-clerical nationalism, a program for which his arch-bishop of Palermo, Nicholas Tudeschi, spoke brilliantly at the Council of Basel.[20] Alphonse's cynical manipulation of the conciliar crisis gained the desired effect, as the pope gave in and endorsed the unifica-tion of Sicily and Naples under Aragonese hegemony.

In Castile, meanwhile, John II's papal sympathies placed him in a delicate position with respect to his French ally, his parliament's anti-clerical sentiments, his divided clergy, and they made him prudent, hesitant and inclined to compromise. At the Council of Basel, the first generation of Salamanca theologians, making their remarkable debut in European intellectual life, mirrored the king's indecision: Juan de Segovia emerged as an eloquent conciliarist, while Juan de Torquemada defended the papal position, for which Pope Eugenius IV created him cardinal.

At this point, in 1438, the twisting policies of Castile and Aragon suddenly converged to save the papacy once again. Both kings op-posed the Council of Basel's deposition of Pope Eugenius, and sup-ported translation of the Council to Ferrara, as Eugenius wished, in 1437. It had become clear to them that the subordination of the Holy See to the Council meant in practice domination of the Church Univer-sal by the emperor or by the king of France. None of the Iberian mon-archs wanted this, least of all the king of Aragon, who stood to forfeit Naples, the apple of his eye, to France. When Pope Eugenius IV in-vested him with Naples by the Treaty of Terracina in 1443, Alphonse might have remarked that Italy was worth the price of conciliarist dreams. Spain had saved the papacy for a second time.

During the later fifteenth century the Hispanic kingdoms, united by the marriage of Isabella and Ferdinand in 1469, rose to the rank of a great power. Castile adopted the cause of Spanish hegemony in Italy, and Aragon repudiated conciliarism and adopted the Castilian view of coordination between papacy and monarchy. The alliance benefited Rome, because, though defeated, conciliarism lived on wherever mon-archs and nobilities longed to curb the judicial meddling and cut back the foreign incomes of Rome. As the Ottoman power rose to menace Italy and the entire western Mediterranean, the papacy had no choice: Spain was its only reliable ally.

The Hispano-Roman alliance worked splendidly, especially during its honeymoon under Isabella and Ferdinand and its maturity under Philip II, despite the latter's political and military failures that tinged it with a certain bitterness. The alliance's earlier successes, however, were unalloyed, from the conquest of Granada to the American enterprise to the successful defense of Naples against French claims since 1494. By 1514 Ferdinand's hold on Naples was secure, and the traditional Franco-Castilian amity was dead. When King Louis XII of France tried to resurrect conciliarism by staging the Council of Pisa (1509) to threaten Pope Julius II, he failed miserably. Cardinal Bernardino de Carvajal spoke in a mighty conciliarist voice at Pisa, but he stood alone, now an instrument of French policy. Meanwhile, home in Iberia, conciliarism continued its long, unbroken decline.

Spanish participation in the Fifth Lateran Council (1512) occasioned the formulation by the royal council—Isabella had died in 1504—of the basic Spanish understanding of the alliance's basis. The king recognized the pope's supremacy over the General Council, holding that while the Council had periodically to define doctrine and laws, the pope had to govern the church. The papacy, on the other hand, had to respect canon law and conciliar decrees, which it could not vacate or ignore at will. Further, in the matters of papal reservations of benefices and the position of the clergy in society, Spain continued to share the anticlerical and patriotic prejudices of other countries. The royal councils asserted that the reserved benefices should be abolished or at least reduced, episcopal authority should be restored, benefices should be reserved to natives, and church courts and properties should be brought under the law of the land and regulated by the Crown. This statement, an artful recognition both of papal supremacy over the Church Universal and of royal domination of the kingdoms' churches, fixed Spanish policy toward Rome.

Hispano-Roman relations nonetheless foundered once more, temporarily, under Charles V (r. 1516-56). The issue was the Italian question, the "liberty of Italy," for the sake of which the papacy wished to restore French rivalry to Spain and thereby to prevent Italy's domination by either. Charles V made war on the papacy, which remained allied to France through much of his reign. This situation long crippled their collaboration against the German Protestants, though not that against the Ottomans.

Charles' position, which his theologians pressed during the first two sessions of the Council of Trent (1546-49, 1551-52), rested on a distinction between the welfare of the church and Rome's authority and fiscal system. The Council should give priority to reform of the Church "in its head and in members," using the conventional phrase, which decoded meant to abolish the papal reservation of benefices and the prerogatives of the Roman Curia. The pope, by contrast, insisted that doctrine, not discipline, take priority, which turned the conciliar front against the German Protestants rather than against Rome. Understandably, this made trouble for Charles V, of course, who was obliged as emperor to treat with his German Protestant subjects and as Spanish king to defend Catholic orthodoxy and papal primacy in the church. Faced with a choice between a mutinous Empire and a loyal Spain and pressed by papal intransigence, Charles ended, as he usually did, by taking the Spanish side. Once again, Spain saved the Holy See.

Philip II's reign witnessed the apogee of the Hispano-Roman alliance. It began with the settlement of the Italian question. The military defeat in 1557 of France, backed by Pope Paul IV, sealed Spanish domination of Italy for the next 150 years. Defeated on the Italian question, the papacy could console itself with the victory of its position at Trent, while Philip, an ardent supporter of reform, resigned himself to the Council's adjournment without a reform of the situation at Rome. Yet, Philip's position had improved, for by now the papacy had become utterly dependent on Spain, because the emperor at Vienna had to tolerate Lutheranism in the Empire and even in his own Austrian lands, and France's religious fate lay in the balance during the era of its civil wars. As champion of the Holy See and crusader against the Ottomans, Spain was now a great, even the principal, power and the unrivaled leader of Catholic Europe. A truce with the Ottomans after the Battle of Lepanto (1571) allowed a reorientation of the Hispano-Roman alliance against the rebellious Dutch heretics, as pope and king collaborated closely in a *reconquista* of Protestant Europe. While Philip II was sincere in proclaiming his desire to support the Irish, English, and French Catholics against their sovereigns, he was too clever to ignore the benefits that Spanish imperialism drew from the Hispano-Roman alliance.

4. BETWEEN THEOCRACY AND CESAROPAPISM

The Spanish Crown both recognized the church and governed it. On the one hand, its adherence to the idea of a divine providential order as the sole source of legitimacy forced it to recognize the church's indirect sovereignty over temporal matters—the common opinion of contemporary Catholic theologians. On the other hand, the Crown, supported by Roman law, affirmed regalian prerogatives and required the submission of church and clergy—except in purely spiritual matters—to the kingdoms' laws. The king's commissioner always presided over the church's councils and synods, the statutes of which were published only after royal approval. The Crown also regarded the church's wealth as an adjunct to its own resources, a position shared by the parliaments (*cortés*), which also argued for royal control over church properties held in mortmain (rarely enforced) and church tribunals, as well as for secularization of all temporal rights held by prelates. Finally, the Crown exercised royal authority over the church via the *recurso de Fuerza*, which transferred to royal courts the business of ecclesiastical courts that had abused their jurisdictions, and by referring all papal bulls to the king's council before publication in Spain.

The Hispanic churches were thus thoroughly integrated into their respective kingdoms. Their offices and incomes were reserved for natives alone, a measure for which the *cortés* had begged throughout the fifteenth century, and which the Crown rigorously enforced during the sixteenth—though it also generously naturalized foreigners it wished to patronize. The boundaries nevertheless remained, both between Spain and foreign countries and among the Hispanic kingdoms.

Regalism and Hispano-Papal Relations

Iberia possessed a long tradition of ecclesiastical "nationalism" under royal leadership. It underlay Philip II's efforts to separate his kingdoms from France, now threatened by Calvinism. He obtained papal permission to shift his Navarrese regions from the diocese of Bayonne to that of Pamplona, and though he did not try to alter the provincial boundaries of the religious orders, the Crown did promote the autonomy of their Spanish branches from foreign superiors: the Castilian Cistercians in 1561, the Aragonese Benedictines in 1592, and, in the following reign, the Cistercians of Aragon and of Navarre in 1616. The Habsburg monarchs, who were grand-masters of the military-religious orders, opposed the authority of the Cistercian abbots of Morimond over the orders of Alcantara and Calatrava, and although Philip II obtained papal permission to end this situation as early as 1560, French opposition delayed the change for nearly a century.

A vigorous tradition of Crown and parliaments thus promoted the church's integration into the political community and into the nation, aiming to regulate its relations with the other bodies of society, and to delimit its autonomy in the name of public rights. This tradition has been called "regalist," and it is true that eighteenth-century regalist theorists justified their proposed legislation by appeal to the authority of earlier kings. In fact, early modern Spanish church-state relationships, which had emerged between 1480 and 1520, produced a papal-royal co-government of the Hispanic churches. The division of authority, though differing among the realms, always respected the Roman primacy. What emerged was less a secularization of the church's law than a papal-royal co-government of the Hispanic churches.

What co-government meant in practice may be illustrated in fiscal terms. In Aragon the clergy bore the same tax obligations as the laity, while in Castile the clergy were immune from direct taxes, though with notable exceptions. Despite openings presented by the kingdom's laws, the monarchs hesitated to tax the church by royal authority, while a major portion of the church's payments to the Crown derived not from royal prerogative but from papal concessions. Such grants were intended to support the Crown's efforts against the infidel, from the medieval reconquest to the seventeenth-century fight against the Barbary pirates. The three most ancient such taxes were the *tercias reales*, the *decimes*, and the *cruzada*. All three dated from the thirteenth-century campaigns against the Moorish kingdoms, though they continued to be collected during the subsequent pause in the reconquest. Martin V, the pope elected at Constance in 1417, granted John II of Castile and Alphonse V of Aragon *decimes* of 80,000 and 60,000 florins respectively, while Eugenius IV added 100,000 florins and 200,000 florins respectively, aiming to detach these kings from the causes of conciliarism and ecclesiastical nationalism *à la française*. The *tercias reales* represented two-ninths—a third of two-thirds—of the yield of the ecclesiastical tithe, and by the end of the fifteenth century it was combined with the *alcabalá*. The *decimes*, also called *subsidios*, were assessed on the clergy according to their incomes. Charles V restored this tax in Castile in 1519; it was extended to Aragon by 1534, when he was mobilizing the campaign against Tunis; and it was fixed just before the Battle of Lepanto at a level deemed enough to arm sixty galleys. The *cruzada* was raised through the proclamation of papal-approved indulgences, and from all subjects, not just the clergy. Charles V obtained the right to make the tax permanent in Castile and extend it to Aragon, including Sardinia and Sicily, and in 1574 it was extended to the Indies as well.

The growth of the "royal patronage [*padronado real*]" over the church, with papal approval, further swelled the church's contribution to the Crown. The Catholic Kings' assumption of the grand-masterships of the military-religious orders enriched the Crown from these offices' incomes and properties. Then, in 1523, the monarch received the general right to nominate bishops, together with the right, long reserved to the Roman Curia, to collect incomes from vacant sees. In 1567 Pope Pius V conceded a second royal claim on the tithes, the *excusado*, to help finance the war in the Low Countries, and in 1591 the pope authorized a new tax on the clergy, called the *millones*.

The Crown also tapped ecclesiastical wealth through the expansion of public credit in the form of the royal treasury's sale of annuities (*juros*).[21] The Crown's appropriation of some kinds of ecclesiastical property has been referred to as the "secularization" of the sixteenth century, though unlike what happened in the nineteenth century, its object was not to despoil the church by selling its wealth to reduce the public debt. True, ecclesiastic jurisdictions and seigniories were sold, but their former possessors were indemnified in *juros*, the interest from which was supposed to cover the lost incomes. This operation was quite advantageous to the Crown: it reduced the seigniorial power of the large ecclesiastical bodies; it transformed ownership of land into fixed capital, to the profit of public finances; and it tied the economic interests of the clergy to those of the state.

One can not precisely measure the church's contribution to Spanish royal finance, though some figures are available. The church's contribution as a whole, including both taxes paid by the clergy and the *cruzada*, which everyone paid, yielded an average of 740,000 ducats during the 1530s, 3,500,000 in the 1590s, and 4,500,000 in the 1630s. It thus made up about a third of what came into the treasury (the *real hacienda*), far more than the famed royal fifth of American bullion.[22] If we consider only what the clergy paid, it still matched the royal fifth. No other contemporary monarchy in Europe obtained anything like as much from its clergy, an advantage to maintain which the Spanish monarchs could well afford to respect papal primacy over the church in theory and law.

The Royal Patronage

Public laws and the royal duty to protect them nourished the Spanish monarch's rule over their realms' churches, which since around 1500 took the formal name of "the royal patronage (*padronado real*)." Like their European brothers, the Castilian and Aragonese kings enjoyed patronage—the right to appoint to ecclesiastical offices—over royal chapels, monasteries and convents, collegiate churches, hospitals, and parishes within the royal domain. Though lucrative, this limited patronage was not sufficient to permit control of the church as a whole, the real key to which was the right to nominate bishops. The Crown needed to protect the episcopacy from the aristocracy, for not only did many bishops come from aristocratic families, but some also were grand seigniors by virtue of their episcopal offices.

Around 1400 the papacy, having reduced to formalities the cathedral chapters' primordial right to elect and the Crown's to confirm bishops, had become the de facto nominator of Hispanic bishops. The kings of Castile and Aragon began to reverse this situation by virtue of their actions during the schism and the conciliar crisis. Martin V made concessions with the object of detaching the monarchs from the cause of his rival, Benedict XIII. No other major changes occurred between 1420 and 1520, though the Catholic Kings did obtain the permanent, general right to nominate bishops to Granadan and American sees. Then, in 1523 Pope Adrian VI granted to Charles V and his successors the perpetual right of presentation to all the bishoprics, abbeys, and consistorial benefices in Spain. No doubt the Concordat of Bologna between France and the Holy See in 1516 stood behind this grant, since the pope could not long withhold from His Catholic Majesty of Spain what had been granted to His Christian Majesty of France. Seventy years later, in 1586, Pope Sixtus V extended the royal patronage to Sicily and Sardinia, and this right was made perpetual in 1621.

The Royal Patronage Extended

Medieval Christian Spain was a frontier land in the Christian *reconquista* from the Muslims, in which the military-religious orders took a prominent part. Their many seigniories, which followed the Tagus River from Extremadura to the southern Iberian coast, embraced one-tenth of Spain's inhabitants as their vassals or tenants. The orders' lands cut Spain nearly in two, and their autonomy threatened in principle the Castilian monarchy's cohesion. Understandably, therefore, the Castilian monarchs long strove to acquire the offices of grandmasters of the military-religious orders, and in 1492 Pope Alexander VI conferred them for life on the Catholic Kings. The grant was renewed to Charles V, who was granted perpetual possession of the grand-masterships of the three Castilian military orders: Alacantara, Calatrava, and Santiago. In 1587 Pope Sixtus V granted Philip II similar rights over the Aragonese Order of Montesa.

Although the Crown had by 1523 secured the church's political loyalty, the papacy's favors did not provide a basis for royal intervention in its governance, except in Granada and Spanish America. The royal patronage of Granada, defined by papal bulls between 1486 and 1504, covered not the much reduced Muslim kingdom conquered in 1492 but the largest historic extent of that realm, plus the Canary Islands. It also covered the personnel and resources of most religious institutions, except for the monasteries; and the royal obligation to protect the churches evolved into a royal right of presentation to all secular, but not monastic, benefices.

The royal patronage of the Indies, granted by Pope Alexander VI in 1501 and 1508, replicated all the characteristics of the Granadan patronage.[23] Before that, two bulls of 1493 had in effect created a royal vicariate over the church: the first bull legalized the American enterprise by conceding to the Castilian kings and their successors sovereignty over and the duty to evangelize the lands west of the ocean; the second forbade anyone to enter these lands without the king's permission. The royal jurists tendentiously interpreted the pope's recognition of a royal evangelizing mission as constituting a royal vicariate, that is, that all papal authority over the church in America was mediated by the king as papal vicar and perpetual legate. In principle, therefore, during the sixteenth century direct communication between the Holy See and the churchmen of the New World was forbidden, though Rome never recognized this theory of a royal vicariate. Papal bulls and briefs were scrutinized by royal councilors (*regium exequatur*), and no papal nuncios or collectors of revenue were allowed to set foot in Spanish America. In 1573 Philip II obtained a privilege whereby the archiepiscopal courts would serve as final instance of appeals in ecclesiastical suits in Spanish America, and appeals to Rome would no longer be recognized. The same was true in Sicily, where a royal tribunal established in 1578 revived the privilege of 1098 that granted immunity to appeals. In the seventeenth century, when the Roman Congregation for the Propagation of the Faith was serving as a central agency for missionary activities, the Crown opposed the extension of its activities to the Indies. Once again, the Crown called upon its theory of a royal vicariate over the secular clergy, an authority unparalleled in Catholic Europe. It founded convents and monasteries without the consent of the bishops or the Holy See; it nominated the inspectors sent by the generals of the regular orders; and it forbade any clergyman to sail for the Indies or return to Europe without royal permission.

The central piece in this royal edifice was the Holy Office of the Inquisition. Authorized by Pope Sixtus IV in 1478, the court administered canon law, its members were clergymen, and its secular auxiliaries depended on ecclesiastical powers, but the Crown, who nominated its personnel, was its only real master. The Inquisition's jurisdiction expanded to cover Aragon (1486), Sicily (1487), Sardinia (1492), and Spanish America (1569). The royal Council of the Inquisition, founded in 1483, supervised the tribunals, which grew by 1600 to number nineteen, fourteen of which operated in Spain. The Inquisition's officials were assisted in preliminary investigations by auxiliaries, called "qualifiers," and they directed a network of laymen, called "familiars," who worked among the people—more than 6,000 of them working for a few hundred clergymen at the Inquisition's peak in the sixteenth century.

Following a few fruitless attempts to forestall the unforeseen consequences of its authorization, the Holy See in 1487 reserved for itself only suits concerning bishops and other higher clergy. This reservation permitted Archbishop Hernando de Talavera of Granada to escape from Inquisitorial jurisdiction to Rome, where he was acquitted on the day before his death in 1507. After one last attempt to regain control, in 1520 Pope Leo X dismissed his appointees, except for the Inquisitor-General, Cardinal Adrian of Utrecht, who succeeded him as pope in 1522. This was the end of papal authority over the Spanish Inquisition. Under Philip II the Inquisition issued its own Index of Prohibited Books, which the Council of Trent decided not to challenge, and it prosecuted Bartolomé Carranza, himself an eminent member of the Inquisition and intimate of Philip II. Although Carranza was hardly suspected of Protestant sympathies, the Inquisition investigated the catechism he had written in defense of the Catholic faith.[24] This time numerous Tridentine fathers rose to the accused's defense, and a scandalized papacy translated the case to the Roman Inquisition, only to yield subsequently to royal pressure and declare him, two weeks before Carranza died in 1576, suspect of heresy.

It is an error to examine royal authority over the Spanish church without considering the authority of Rome as well. The latter expressed itself especially in the papal reservations, powers which the Holy See had reserved for itself: reserved presentations to specific benefices; reserved jurisdiction or appeals jurisdiction in certain cases; and powers to dispense from certain prescriptions of canon law. The fees connected with these transactions constituted an important source of papal revenue, for beneficiaries paid half the benefice's revenue (called a "half-annate") for the first year, and the Apostolic treasury also claimed the personal properties of deceased bishops and the revenues of vacant bishoprics. In accepting, alone of all Catholic powers, the papal reservations in their greatest extent, the Crown showed itself far more friendly to Rome than even the best-intentioned Italian states.

Since 1529 the nuncio represented the Roman tribunals in Spain, a situation found in no other Catholic country, and the nuncios routinely possessed legatine full powers and functioned as collector-general for the papal treasury. In a word, the nuncio *was* the Holy See in Spain. The Crown's recognition of these powers was the price it paid for the far-reaching royal authority over the Hispanic churches and those of Naples, Sicily, and Milan—not to speak of Spanish America and the royal vicariate.

❈ ❈ ❈

Spain fully participated in the European movements of religious reform and humanism between 1400 and 1600. It did not choose the Roman Catholic route. Rather, the chronology of Spain's ecclesiastical, theological, and spiritual reforms shows that Roman Catholicism chose the Spanish route. The Council of Trent, for example, was as much Spanish as universal. The universities of Salamanca and of Alcalá were the church's intellectual arsenals, and Spanish representation during its three phases was second only to the Italian presence. Then, too, half of Italy lived under the direct influence of the Crown of Spain.

Two movements shaped the country's religious evolution: one animated by the demands of Christian perfection, the assimilation of modernity, and intellectual and moral courage; the other marked by fanaticism, exclusivist rejection, and repressive dogmatism. If antithetical, the two movements were not contradictory. Let us remember that Francisco Jimenez de Cisneros, who led the Observant reform, supervised the editing of the polyglot Bible of Alacalá, and sponsored the theological renaissance, was also the organizing Inquisitor-General of the Holy Office. We must rather see them as the two faces of an indomitable energy. Tolerance and pluralism, after all, were as rare in other countries as in Spain, and in sixteenth-century Europe a plurality of religions was a misfortune to be avoided or endured, but not condoned. It was the unquestionable, if by most estimates the only, benefit of the Inquisition to have guarded Spain from wars of religion. At a very high price. The New Christians, true, were not the only architects of Spain's mystical and theological renaissance, but the Catholic reform doubtless owed its vigor and originality largely to them. Perhaps the Spanish Church, which surely possessed sufficient resources to meet the Protestant challenge without, believed it had too few to prevent a Judaic reform within. Suarez, Mariana, John of the Cross, and Teresa of Avila were the last great voices of Spanish theology and spirituality. After them came conformity and self-censorship.

The Hispano-Roman political alliance was distinct from the religious alliance, each possessing its own logic and perspectives. They are nevertheless mutually dependent. Rome did not make Spain a great hegemonic power, yet it is doubtful that without Rome, Spain would have become a great power so soon. Spain had no interest in attacking Rome. To attack or destroy the papacy's centralizing absolutism would have undermined the legitimacy of Spain's direct government of one half of Italy and domination of the other. It would have reduced Spain's prestige as leader of the anti-Ottoman crusade. It would have diminished the Spanish king's legitimacy as guardian of the Catholic side in the northern religious wars. Finally, it would have removed the mantle of religious legitimacy from the Spanish colonial empire. The popes and the Curia recognized this situation, which explains Roman intransigence about the reform of the papal government: at Rome they knew that in the end, Spain would bend.

Internal needs also tied together the interests of kings and popes. In Spain the monarchy had no sacral tradition or tradition of national identity, which might have enabled it to subject the clergy to the law and the fiscal needs of the state, on the pretext of liberating from Roman despotism. Even the French monarchy, which had these means, forced the clergy to pay taxes only under the threat of Calvinism's advance. Instead, the Spanish kings renewed the medieval cooperation between conquering rulers and papal legates and thereby found an original path in between the Gallican model, which left Rome only a purely spiritual primacy, and an all-powerful Holy See which ruled over a clergy entrenched with its immunities. Sharing the authority and the benefits with Rome, the Spanish monarchs established an ecclesiastical regalism, founded not on regalian prerogatives and national sovereignty, but on a delegation of powers that made the king the pope's vicar.

This arrangement helped the Spanish empire to remain a constellation of kingdoms and principalities united in a simple dynastic union, but otherwise independent and sovereign, conserving their political institutions, their fiscal organization, their money, their military and naval forces. The unified command of foreign policy and war was thus the only attribute of central power, except for the Holy Office of the Inquisition. This reveals the importance of the rigorous unity of faith in assuring the submission of the people to the Spanish state, for it served to awake and sustain a common political identity. For better or for worse, the Catholic faith was the cement of a Hispanic multi-national state. Spanish papalism was truly a reality; it was the reality of a national Catholicism.

Translated by Laura Glass-Gerard

NOTES

1. For the secular history of Iberia and for further bibliography, see Henry Kamen, in this *Handbook*, vol. 1:467-98.
2. Christian (1981a) and (1981b).
3. See Robert Bonfil, in this *Handbook*, vol. 1:263-302.
4. See Kamen (1994).
5. On Cisneros, see Erika Rummel, in this *Handbook*, vol. 2:261-91.
6. Libro de su vida (1588); Libro de las fundaciones (1610).
7. *Abecedarios espirituales* (1527-30).
8. Respectively, *Subida de monte Sion* (1538) and *Subida del monte Carmelo* (1618).
9. See Ronald G. Witt and Erika Rummel, in this *Handbook*, vol. 2:93-125, 261-91.
10. It was for this reason also called the "Plantin Bible" or "Antwerp Bible."
11. *De Rege et Regis Institutione* (1599).
12. *De legibus ac Deo legislatore* (1612).
13. *Concordia liberi arbitrii cum gratiae donis* (1588).
14. *Releccio de potestate civilis* (1528).
15. *Tractacus de potestate Romani Pontificis in rebus temporalibus* (1610).
16. *De legibus ac Deo legislatore* (1612).
17. *Defensio fidei contra Iacobum regem Angliae* (1613).
18. In *Historia eclesiastica del cisma de Inglaterra* (1588) and *De legibus ac Deo legislatore* (1612) respectively.
19. On the late medieval councils and conciliarism, see John van Engen in this *Handbook,* vol. 1:305-28; here at 317f.
20. Called "Panormitanus," his important works on canon law became current once again in the eighteenth century, when the Jansenists exploited them.
21. See James D. Tracy, in this *Handbook*, vol. 1:563-88.
22. Christian Hermann, "La fiscalité monarchique sur l'Eglise d'Espagne," in *Les Eglises et l'argent* (Paris and the Sorbonne, 1989), 9-19.
23. See Wolfgang Reinhard, in this *Handbook*, vol. 1:637-64.
24. *Catecismo Cristiano* (Antwerp, 1558), published in the year of his promotion to archbishop of Toledo.

BIBLIOGRAPHY

General Works

Diccionario de Historia Eclesiastica de Espana. 5 vols. Consejo Superior de Investigaciones Cientificas. Madrid, 1972-87.

Garcia Villoslada, Ricardo, ed. *Historia de la Iglesia en Espana.* Vol. 3, *La Iglesia en la Espana de los siglos XV y XVI.* 2 parts. Biblioteca de Autores Cristianos. Madrid, 1980.

Hermann, Christian, ed. *Le premier âge de l'Etat en Espagne, 1450-1700.* Paris, 1989.

Historia de Espana. Vol. 17, *La Espana de los Reyes Catolicos,* by L. Suarez Fernandez (2 parts., 1969). Vol. 20, *La Espana del emperador Carlos V,* by M. Fernandez Alvarez (1979). Vol. 22, *Espana en tiempo de Felipe II,* by F. Luis Fernandez and F. de Retana (2 parts., 1977). Madrid.

From Religious Plurality to Inquisitional Catholicism

Bataillon, Marcel. *Erasme et l'Espagne.* Geneva, 1990.

Bennassar, Bartolomé, ed. *L'Inquisition espagnole (XVe-XIXe siècle).* Paris, 1979.

Bujanda, Jesus Maria de. *Index de l'Inquisition espagnole, 1551, 1554, 1559.* Index des livres interdits, vol. 5. Sherbrooke and Geneva, 1984.

Cardaillac, L. *Morisques et chrétiens. Un affrontement polémique (1492-1640).* Paris, 1977.

Domínguez Ortíz, A. *Los judeoconversos en Espana y América.* Madrid, 1971.

Domínguez Ortíz, A., and B. Vincent. *Historia de los moriscos. Vida y tragedia de una minoria.* Madrid, 1978.

Hamilton, Alastair. *Heresy and Mysticism in Sixteenth-Century Spain: the Alumbrados.* Toronto, 1992.

Huerga, A. *Historia de los alumbrados (1570-1630).* 2 vols. Madrid, 1978.

Huerga, A. *Predicadores, alumbrados e Inquisicion en el siglo XVI.* Madrid, 1973.

Kamen, Henry. *Inquisition and Society in Spain in the Sixteenth and Seventeenth Centuries.* Bloomington, 1985.

Kamen, Henry. "Spain." In *The Reformation in National Context,* ed. Bob Scribner, Roy Porter, and Mikulas Teich, 202-14. Cambridge, 1994.

Kamen, Henry. "Toleration and Dissent in Sixteenth-Century Spain: the Alternative Tradition." *SCJ* 19 (1988): 3-23.

Kinder, Gordon. *Spanish Protestants and Reformers in the Sixteenth Century.* London, 1983.

Marquez, A. *Los alumbrados. Origenes y filosofia (1525-1559).* Madrid, 1972.

Menéndez y Pelayo, Marcelino. *Historia de los heterodoxos espanoles.* Madrid, 1965.

Montalvo Anton, J. M. *Teoria y evolucion de un conflicto social. El antisemitismo en la Corona de Castilla en la Baja Edad Media.* Madrid, 1985.

Novalin, G. *El inquisidor general Fernando de Valdès.* 2 vols. Oviedo, 1968.

Pérez Villanueva, J., and B. Escandell Bonet, ed. *Historia de la Inquisicion en Espana y América.* Vol. 1, *El conocimiento cientifico y el proceso historico de la institucion.* Madrid, 1984.

Sicroff, A. *Les controverses des statuts de pureté de sang en Espagne du XVe au XVIIe siècle*. Paris, 1960.
Tellechea Idigoras, J. I. *Tiempos recios. Inquisicion y heterodoxias*. Salamanca, 1977.

The Catholic Reformation in Spain

Andrés Martin, M. *Los recogidos. Nueva vision de la mistica espanola (1500-1700)*. Madrid, 1976.
Andrés Martin, M. *Reforma espanola y reforma luterana*. Madrid, 1975.
Andrés Martin, M. *La teologia espanola en el siglo XVI*. 2 vols. Madrid, 1976-77.
Azcona, Tarsicio de. *La eleccion y reforma del episcopado espanol en tiempo de los Reyes Catolicos*. Madrid, 1960.
Bada, Joan. *Situació religiosa de Barcelona en el segle XVI*. Barcelona, 1970.
Bakhuizen van den Brink, J. N. *Juan de Valdès, réformateur en Espagne et en Italie, 1529-1541. Deux études*. Geneva, 1969.
Bilinkoff, Jodi. *The Avila of Saint Teresa: Religious Reform in a Sixteenth-Century City*. Ithaca, 1989.
Camillo, O. di. *El Humanismo castellano del siglo XV*. Valencia, 1976.
Christian, William. *Apparitions in Late Medieval and Renaissance Spain*. Princeton, 1981a.
Christian, William. *Local Religion in Sixteenth-Century Spain*. Princeton, 1981b.
Cruz, Anne J., and Mary Elizabeth Perry, eds. *Culture and Control in Counter-Reformation Spain*. Minneapolis, 1992.
Dombrowski, Daniel A. *St. John of the Cross: an Appreciation*. Albany, 1992.
García Oro, José. *Cisneros y la reforma del clero español en tiempo de los Reyes Catolicos*. Biblioteca "Reyes Catolicos." Estudios, no. 13. Madrid, 1971.
Kamen, Henry. *The Phoenix and the Flame: Catalonia and the Counter Reformation*. New Haven, 1993.
Nalle, Sara Tilghman. *God in La Mancha: Religious Reform and the People of Cuenca, 1500-1650*. Baltimore, 1992.
Nieto Sanjuan, J. C. *Juan de Valdès, 1509-1541. Background, Origins and Development of his Theological Thought*. Ann Arbor, 1968.
Redondo, A. *Antonio de Guevara (1480-1545) et l'Espagne de son temps*. Geneva, 1976.
Ricard, R. *Estudios de literatura religiosa espanola*. Madrid, 1964.
Sainz Rodríguez, Pedro. *Introduccion a la historia de la literatura mistica en España*. Madrid, 1984.
Santos Diez, J. L. *Introduccion a los origenes de la Observancia en Espana. Las reformas de los siglos XIV y XV*. Madrid, 1957.
Santos Diez, J. L. *Politica conciliar postridentina en Espana*. Rome, 1969.
Steggink, O. *La reforma del Carmelo espanol*. Rome, 1965.
Tellechea Idigoras, J. I. *El arzobispo Carranza y su tiempo*. 2 vols. Madrid, 1968.
Tellechea Idigoras, J. I. *El obispo ideal en el siglo de la reforma*. Rome, 1963.

The Conciliar Movement and the Hispano-Roman Alliance

Ametller y Vinyas, J. *Alfonso V de Aragon en Italia y la crisis religiosa del siglo XV*. 3 vols. Gerona, 1903-28.
Arranz Guzman, A. "La imagen del pontificado en Castilla a través de los Cuadernos de Cortes." *Hispania Sacra* 42 (1990):721-60.
Beltran de Heredia, V. "Noticias y documentos para la biografia del cardenal Juan de Torquemada." *Archivum Fratrum Praedicatorum* 30 (1960):53-148.
Binder, K. *Konzilsgedanken bei Kardinal J. de Torquemada, O.P.* Vienna, 1976.
Brandmüller, W. *Das Konzil von Pavis-Siena*. 2 vols. Münster, 1968-74.

Doussinague, J. M. *Fernando el Catolico y el cisma de Pisa.* Madrid, 1946.
Fromberg, U. *Johannes von Segovia als Geschichtsschreiber des Konzils von Basel.* Basel, 1960.
Fromme, B. *Die spanische Nation und das Konstanzer Konzil.* Münster, 1896.
Goni Gaztambide, J. *Los espanoles en el concilio de Constanza. Notas biograficas.* Madrid, 1966.
Gutiérrez, C. *Espanoles en Trento.* Valladolid, 1951.
Hinojosa, R. de, ed. *Despachos de la diplomacia pontificia en Espana.* Madrid, 1896.
Massi, P. *Magistero infallibile del papa nella teologia di Giovani da Torquemada.* Turin, 1957.
Norr, K. N. *Kirche und Konzil bei N. de Tudeschis, Panormitanus.* Cologne and Graz, 1964.
Prelsswerk, E. *Der Einfluss Aragons auf den Prozess des Basler Konzils gegen Papst Eugen IV.* Basel, 1902.
Renaudet, Augustin. *Le concile gallican de Pise-Milan. Documents florentins.* Paris, 1922.
Serrano, L., ed. *Correspondencia diplomatica entre Espana y la Santa Sede durante el pontificado de Pio V.* 4 vols. Madrid, 1914.
Vera Fajardo, G. *La eclesiologia de Juan de Segovia en la crisis conciliar (1435-1447).* Vitoria, 1968.

Between Theocracy and Cesaropapism

Arranz Guzman, A. Cortes medievales castellano-leonesas: participacion eclesiastica y mentalidades religiosas. Unpublished dissertation, University of Alcalá de Henares, 1988.
Arranz Guzman, A. "Los enfrentamientos entre concejos y poderes eclesiasticos en las Cortes castellanas: sincronizacion de los conflictos?" *Hispania* 171 (1989): 5-68.
Arranz Guzman, A. "El tercer estado castellano ante las relaciones realengo-abadengo. Siglos XIII-XV." *Hispania* 172 (1989):443-76.
Catalano, G. *Controversie giurisdizionali tra Chiesa e Stato nell' eta di Gregorio XIII e Filippo II.* Palermo, 1955.
Egana, A. de. *La teoria del Regio Vicariato espanol en Indias.* Analecta Gregoriana, vol. 95. Rome, 1958.
Estal, J. M. del. "Felipe II y su perfil religioso en la historiografia de los siglos XVI y XVII." *Ciudad de Dios* 187 (1974): 549-81.
Estal, J. M. del. "Felipe II y su perfil religioso en la historiografia de los siglos XVIII y XIX." *Ciudad de Dios* 189 (1976): 84-117.
Fernández Santamaría, J. A. *The State, War and Peace: Spanish Political Thought in the Renaissance, 1516-1559.* Cambridge, 1977.
Gutiérrez Martin, L. *El privilegio de nombramiento de obispos en Espana.* Rome, 1967.
Hermann, Christian. "L'Eglise selon les Cortes de Castille, 1476-1598." *Hispania Sacra* 27 (1976): 201-35.
Hermann, Christian. *L'Eglise d'Espagne sous le Patronage Royal (1476-1834).* Bibliothèque de la Casa de Velazquez, no. 3. Madrid, 1988.
Leturia, P. *Relaciones entre la Santa Sede e Hispanoamérica. 1493-1835.* Analecta Gregoriana, 101-103. Rome, 1959-60.
Nieto Soria, J. M. "La configuracion eclesiastica de la realeza trastamara en Castilla, 1369-1474." *La Espana Medieval* 13 (1990):133-62.
Nieto Soria, J. M. *Fundamentos ideologicos del poder real en Castilla, siglos XII-XVI.* Publicaciones del gobierno de Castilla y Leon. Madrid, 1988.
Rouco Varela, A. M. *Staat und Kirche im Spanien des XVI. Jahrhunderts.* Munich, 1965.

SCANDINAVIA, 1397-1560

Michael F. Metcalf
(University of Minnesota)

The long century and a half between the founding of the Kalmar Union
in 1397 and the deaths of Christian III of Denmark in 1559 and Gustav
Vasa of Sweden in 1560 encompassed the passing of the Middle Ages
in Scandinavia and the rise of two competing early modern state systems that would dominate the region throughout the seventeenth and
eighteenth centuries and into the Napoleonic period. Central to this
process was the rising importance of Baltic trade in the economy of the
maritime powers during the sixteenth century. The nuances and tex-
tures of this issue and other aspects of the transition from the medieval
to the early modern era in Scandinavia offer rich materials for comparison both within the region and with other areas of western Europe,
but only the broadest picture can be presented in this essay.

1. SCANDINAVIA IN THE LATE MIDDLE AGES

Dominating the high latitudes of Europe then as now, late medieval
Scandinavia accounted for an enormous share of Europe's geographical area, but for only a very small portion of its population. At the
time of the Black Death, the region remained divided into the three
monarchies of Denmark, Norway, and Sweden that, by the mid-
twelfth century, had consolidated their political positions in the Roman Catholic ecumene.[1] Nonetheless, the extensive privileges and the
indebtedness of the Danish crown to North German princes meant that
German merchants drew much of the advantage of Scandinavian trade
and that numerous Danish castles lay under the administration of the
crown's foreign creditors in the 1340s. The North Atlantic islands of
Iceland, Greenland, the Faeroes, Orkney, and Shetland all owed allegiance to the Norwegian crown, as did the Hebrides and the Isle of
Man in the Irish Sea. The Swedish realm, which throughout this period included all of Finland, was the most compact of the three, sharing
borders with Norway and Denmark in the west, Denmark in the south,

SIXTEENTH-CENTURY SCANDINAVIA

ICELAND

† Holar

NORTH SEA

RUSSIA

KINGDOM OF DENMARK-NORWAY

KINGDOM OF SWEDEN

Trondheim

Bergen

Stavanger

† Hamar

† Oslo

† Abo

Helsingfors

Västerås †

‡ Uppsala

Strängnäs †

† Stockholm

Narva

Reval

Linköping †

BALTIC SEA

Viborg

† Växjö ‡

Kalmar

‡ Riga

Aarhus

Ribe

Copenhagen

† Lund

Malmö

† Schleswig

Lübeck   Danzig

‡ Archbishopric
† Bishopric

F.D. '95

and the lands of Muscovy in the east, while Denmark's territory remained largely what it had been since the Viking Age, encompassing the Baltic Sea island of Bornholm, Schleswig, and Jutland on the European mainland, the three most southerly regions of the Scandinavian peninsula (Blekinge, Halland, and Skåne), and the numerous and prosperous islands that lay between Jutland and the southern Scandinavian peninsula, including, most prominently, Sjælland and Funen.

The peoples of Scandinavia were few in number, with the two most populous kingdoms, Sweden and Denmark, claiming but nine and eight hundred thousand subjects respectively as late at the 1630s and 1640s, for which period the first reliable estimates are available (Norway's population is estimated to have been around 200,000 in the 1520s and 450,000 by 1645).[2] In the Late Middle Ages, economic life in the North was dominated by agriculture, although fishing was a very important aspect of the Norwegian economy and mining had already gained considerable importance in Sweden. Both climate and soil conditions favored agriculture in the Danish realm over that in other parts of Scandinavia and meant that the Danish lands were by far the most densely populated in the region. The agricultural productivity of the Danish realm, the density of its population, and its favorable geographical location between the Baltic and the North Seas all contributed to the foundation and survival of many more towns than could be sustained in either Sweden or Norway.[3] Urban population, too, accounted for a greater percentage of the Danish population despite the fact that noble families tenaciously held onto their right to conduct foreign trade in order to meet the needs of their own estates.

By the end of the Middle Ages, the Church had acquired considerable amounts of arable land throughout Scandinavia, controlling approximately 40 percent of the arable in Norway proper, a third in Denmark, and 21 percent in the Swedish realm. At the same time, the arable controlled by the nobility and the crown was approximately 15 to 20 percent and 7 percent, respectively, in Norway and 22 percent and 5.5 percent, respectively, in Sweden.[4] We are much less well informed about land distribution between the crown and the nobility in Denmark prior to the Reformation, but between 1560 and 1650 the nobility controlled about 44 percent of the arable. Quite remarkable is the fact that peasants owned some 51 percent of the arable in the Swedish realm and that peasants and burghers owned between 35 percent and 37 percent of the arable in Norway proper, while the comparable figure for Denmark, while not known for the Late Middle Ages, may be hinted at by the fact that the percentage of arable owned by peasants between 1560 and 1650 remained stable at about 6 percent.[5] The emphasis in Danish and Swedish agricultural production in the fifteenth century began to turn away from grains and toward livestock, for while the growth of population in North German and Dutch towns began to provide better export opportunities for grains, Baltic ports such as Danzig and Riga were able to export them more inexpensively than were ports in Scandinavia. The importance of fish in the European diet, and the fact that dried and salted fish served as protein-rich foodstuffs that could be preserved for relatively long periods of time, kept exports of both stockfish from the west coast of Norway and herring from the important Skåne market in the Danish realm booming, but this trade was controlled by the Hanseatic towns, thus reducing its overall importance to the Danish and Norwegian economies. Iron exports from Sweden, in the meanwhile, were growing in importance, but they too were dependent on Hanseatic capital to meet production costs, as well as on German merchants and their commercial networks to sell the iron overseas.

The social organization of the Scandinavian realms was clearly being defined in terms of estates by the Late Middle Ages, with the clergy and nobility enjoying their particular privileges vis-à-vis the crown, the burghers in their towns constituting a population treated separately from the unprivileged rural population in terms both of legal codes and taxes, and those peasants who owned their own land paying taxes to the crown. Over and above these populations were the poor, the infirm, and people who labored in the towns and in the countryside. The social construct of a society of estates was emerging quite clearly, although the estates were not to acquire clear political representation until the early modern period, and then only imperfectly in Denmark and hardly at all in Norway. In the interim, only the two privileged estates—and especially the bishops and the wealthiest noblemen—enjoyed a political voice through the respective royal councils and the broader assemblages of great men that were held periodically.[6] Indeed, the councils had come to exercise considerable influence and power over the course of the fourteenth century, and the fact that intermarriage across the three kingdoms (especially between the Danish and Swedish nobilities) was frequent and profitable opened perspectives toward international political cooperation. During the fifteenth century, these councils would elaborate constitutional positions for themselves that laid claim to their special guardianship of the sovereignty of their respective realms. Thus emerged the notion of the council of the realm and practices of governance that would have far-reaching consequences for the nature of the monarchy and, later, the nature of the early modern state in Scandinavia.[7]

Finally, it is important to mention the challenges to Hanseatic domination of Scandinavian and Baltic trade that would arise in the fifteenth century and that would ultimately have considerable influence on the course of Scandinavian history in the late medieval and early modern periods. The first of these challenges would come from within Scandinavia, when in 1422 King Erik of Pomerania, who was anxious for English and Dutch merchants to gain access to the Baltic trade as a counterweight to Lübeck and its allies, temporarily denied passage through the Sound to all Hanseatic ships. It was during this conflict that Erik introduced the Sound dues on all ships passing through the narrow waters between Helsingør and Helsingborg, although in later negotiations Lübeck and the other Wendish towns were granted freedom from these fees. Erik's challenge of the Hanseatic cities thus failed, but over the course of the century English and especially Dutch ships would sail in and out of the Baltic through the Sound in increasing numbers, thus posing an increasing threat to the Hansa's domination of Baltic trade that Scandinavian monarchs were able to utilize politically in their dealings with Lübeck. By 1500, Dutch ships came to dominate the trade between the Baltic and western Europe, and their payment of the Sound dues went a long way to improving the personal finances of the kings of Denmark, thus strengthening their hands in domestic terms, as well as in terms of commercial policy. Equally important was the fact that the Dutch markets came to dominate the demand for Scandinavian and Baltic agricultural produce and naval stores in the sixteenth century, thus further involving the Netherlands in the commercial and power politics of the region, and further jeopardizing the traditional influence of Lübeck and the other Hanseatic towns.

2. ARISTOCRATIC CONSTITUTIONALISM VS. ROYAL AMBITION

By 1396 the accidents of dynastic alliances in Denmark and Norway, the determination by Sweden's aristocracy to limit royal power and protect the privileges of native-born men, and intermarriage among Scandinavian aristocrats had produced a situation in which Margaret of Denmark had been hailed as regent in each of the three realms and her grand nephew Erik of Pomerania had been recognized as heir to the throne of Norway (1388), hailed as king of Denmark (1396), and elected king of Sweden (1396).[8] The daughter of the king of Denmark, the widow of one king of Norway, and the surviving mother of a second, Margaret had been hailed as regent by the Swedish council in 1388 with the express purpose of driving Albrecht of Mecklenburg from the Swedish throne. Once that was accomplished and Erik assured the crowns of Denmark and Sweden, a new initiative was undertaken in 1397 at a meeting of the regent, the king, and representatives of the councils of Denmark, Norway, and Sweden held at the town of Kalmar on the southeast coast of Sweden. Erik was crowned and hailed as king in all three realms, thus giving rise to the Kalmar Union, which would be both a unifying factor and a point of contention until its ultimate demise in 1523.

Following the death of the still-reigning and much-respected Margaret in 1412, Erik enjoyed a decade of peaceful rule before launching an increasingly vigorous foreign policy that challenged Lübeck and its Hanseatic allies in an attempt to reduce German commercial dominance in his realms and to promote his own interests in northern Germany. His policies eventually provoked the first real crisis in the Union's short history, namely, a serious revolt that broke out in 1434 among certain sectors of Swedish society which objected to the king's policies because they jeopardized the smooth operation of the Bergslagen mining industry that depended on Lübeck's ability to finance its operations and to market its products abroad.[9] This revolt was so effective and the economic burden of the king's wars so burdensome that the councils of all three realms ultimately renounced their allegiance to King Erik by 1441. The Danish and Swedish councils took the lead in this development, opening a new chapter in the history of the Union when they met at Kalmar in 1438 to discuss the problems the king was creating for them and to formulate a new contract concerning the Union. The two councils made clear their desire and intent that the Union should remain in place, preferably under King Erik, but even if the two realms were in the future to have different kings.[10] Thus, the two councils effectively claimed and assumed responsibility for guarding the fundamental interests of their respective realms; the next year both the Danish and Swedish councils renounced their allegiance to the king, while the Norwegian council followed suit two years later. All three councils thereby confirmed in action their assumption of the roles of councils of the realm with shared—or even ultimate—responsibility for the sovereignty of their respective kingdoms.

All three councils elected Christopher of Bavaria as the Union's new king, but his death without issue in 1448 led to the situation that the Danish and Swedish councils had discussed a decade earlier. While an assembly of Swedish nobles joined with the council of the realm in the spring of 1448 to elect the prominent Swedish nobleman Karl Knutsson as Sweden's new king, their Danish counterparts hailed Christian of Oldenburg as king in September, and the Norwegian council followed suit in the spring of 1449. With these actions, then, the precedent was set for hailing separate monarchs within the Kalmar Union; the way was thus paved for a seventy-five year struggle to determine whether the Union would survive or whether Sweden would seek an independent future under a Swedish dynasty. Tensions rose between the Danes and the Swedes because of Karl Knutsson's claim to Norway, but these were diffused at a meeting of the two councils (the Norwegians did not attend) in the spring of 1450 at which Karl Knutsson recognized Christian's right to the Norwegian crown. The two councils had never decided what procedure to follow when a Union monarch died, but at this meeting they agreed that, upon the death of either Christian or Karl Knutsson, twelve members of each of the two councils would meet to discuss whether the royal vacancy would be filled by the recognition of the surviving monarch by the council whose king had died. Were this solution to be rejected, then a regent would be selected to serve in the vacated realm until the death of the other monarch, whereupon twelve members of each council would once again meet to negotiate the election of a single Union monarch.[11]

Clearly, the aristocratic Danish and Swedish councils of the realm continued to find the concept of the Union to be in their best interests and in the best interests of their kingdoms in 1450. Not only did the persistence of the Union offer the best prospects for peace within Scandinavia—and thus for the continued ability of aristocratic families to pursue interests across the borders of the Scandinavian realms—but it also offered the best prospects for the councils to maintain their political influence at home and to maximize the aristocracy's ability to protect its interests against possible royal encroachment. Indeed, the election of different kings in Denmark and Sweden led to an extended period of warfare between the two monarchs, and, when faced with military defeat at the hands of Christian I, the Swedish council ultimately utilized the possibilities that the continued Union offered by renouncing its allegiance to Karl Knutsson in 1457 and hailing Christian as king of Sweden. At the same time, however, three developments over the course of the late fifteenth century contributed to the strained relations between the Danish kings and their Swedish rivals, all of whom, with the exception of Karl Knutsson, carried the title of regent. First of all, Christian I, who had come to the Danish throne with the strong backing of his powerful relative, Duke Adolf of Holstein, was elected duke of Schleswig and Holstein following Adolf's death in 1459. Because of the economic vitality of the duchies, and because Holstein was an imperial fief, Christian and his Oldenburg successors to the Danish throne would be drawn into North German politics in ways that would complicate their relationship with Sweden. Second, Sweden's geopolitical situation exposed it to an expanding Muscovy during the late fifteenth and early sixteenth centuries, which situation created the need for effective military leadership within Sweden to deal with the eastern borderlands and the defense of Finland. This military threat could not be met collectively by a body like the council of the realm, which therefore had to rely on a regent or captain of the realm to do the job; the council thus had to tolerate strong military leaders who inevitably asked for more and more resources and authority. Related to both of these circumstances over the course of the late fifteenth and early sixteenth century, finally, was the expanding transformation of military technology toward the use of cannon and firearms and the concomitant need to build more solid and powerful defense works and to enlist specialists in the use of these advanced technologies. In both Denmark and Sweden, as elsewhere in Europe, these changes in military technology drove up the cost of warfare and defense and thus presented monarchs with the challenge of finding ways to pay for them. Because the problem was the same, this affected both the kings of Denmark and the high Swedish officers charged with defending the realm. The pressures toward increasing princely authority and control of resources inevitably drove both Danish kings and Swedish regents to seek the same sorts of enhanced prerogatives and revenue streams, and their interests inevitably clashed with those of the aristocratic councilors who stood to lose some of their political influence and some of the revenues they and their relatives derived from administrative fiefs.

The late medieval struggle between aristocracy and monarchy in Scandinavia was carried out under circumstances that gave the Danish and Swedish councils of the realm considerable influence and left them considerable room to maneuver. This was not, however, the case in

Norway, whose clergy and nobility—the latter already relatively small in number—had suffered much more heavily from the plagues of the fourteenth century than had their Scandinavian counterparts. In Denmark, Christian I was succeeded by his son Hans in 1481 and his grandson Christian II in 1513, but although the Oldenburgs were well ensconced in Denmark and Norway, they did need the support of the Danish council if they were to succeed in preserving and solidifying the Kalmar Union under their scepters. The Swedish council shifted its loyalty to Karl Knutsson once again in 1464, recognizing him as king for a brief two-year period before retracting that recognition and restoring it once again between 1467 and Karl's death in 1470. The reign of Christian I was thus plagued by his recurring attempts to secure recognition in Sweden, and while these efforts required support from the Danish council for fiscal, diplomatic, and military measures, the king did not hesitate to seek that support elsewhere, as well. Thus, in 1468, Christian I summoned what was Denmark's first meeting of estates to encompass the council, the nobility, and representatives of the burghers and the peasants. It was a gambit on the king's part to secure from a broader representative body a number of things which the council of the realm had not granted him, and, because it was successful, it left the king more powerful and led the council to be more forthcoming vis-à-vis his requests and needs. Christian I claimed that his recognition as king of Sweden in 1457 was irreversible, and he appeared to be in a strong position to enforce his claim by military force following Karl Knutsson's death in 1470. But those Swedish aristocrats who opposed the king's claims triumphed on the battlefield at Brunkeberg just outside of Stockholm in 1471 and drove Christian from Sweden.[12] The man who led this effort was Sweden's new regent, Sten Sture the Elder, who would serve in that capacity for the next sixteen years and develop monarchical tendencies of his own when it came to his dealings with the Swedish council.

Renewed discussions between the Danish and Swedish councils in 1476 failed not least because the Swedish council insisted that Christian I recognize the right of rebellion against tyranny, but the king's death in 1481 opened a new possibility that all three councils might join in recognizing his son Hans as Union monarch. While his succession was not disputed in Denmark, Hans' recognition as king of Denmark was delayed for two years as the members of the Danish council of the realm worked to secure the support of their Norwegian and Swedish counterparts. Several meetings were held and appear to have

shaped the accession charter Hans accepted in 1483 upon his election
as king by the Danish and Norwegian councils in such a fashion as to
make it possible for the Swedish council to follow suit. This charter
recognized the right of rebellion and placed more limits on the prerogatives of the Union monarch than had any previous document. The king
was to rule each of the three realms according to its own laws, was to
rotate his residence one year at a time among the three kingdoms, was
to appoint four members of the councils in each of the two other
realms to conduct business for him in his absence, and was to meet
with three councilors from each of the three realms in late July of each
year to discuss Union matters.[13]

Despite the fact that many of the points in King Hans' accession
charter were designed to placate Swedish concerns and demands, the
Swedish council failed to join the Danes and Norwegians in electing
him king. Instead, they kept the negotiations open through two more
meetings into 1484, asking for additional clauses and attempting to
reach internal consensus about a Swedish acceptance of the Union
monarch. The stumbling block was and remained the elected regent,
Sten Sture, who was opposed to the arrangement not least because it
would, in effect, leave the governance of Sweden in the hands of the
council.[14] He and those who supported his opposition succeeded in
blocking a Swedish election of Hans in the 1480s, but the constitutional principles that had been negotiated between the Danish and
Swedish councils continued to exercise an influence on Swedish domestic politics for decades to come. Similarly, Sten Sture's opposition led
King Hans, in his attempt to secure Swedish recognition as Union monarch, to work against the regent's interests both at the Holy See and in
Moscow. But it was not until 1497 that he would succeed in winning
election in Sweden after invading that kingdom from the west when it
was at war with Muscovy in the east. Even then, King Hans' rule in
Sweden would last a mere four years before Sten Sture and others re-
belled in 1501 on the grounds that the king had not kept his promises
and had put Swedish castles in the hands of Danish nobles. The clash
of wills and the clash of interests between Danish monarchs and Swedish regents would persist for another two decades, culminating in
Christian II's military imposition of his rule in 1520 and his politically
disastrous execution of scores of leading members of the Swedish opposition immediately after his coronation. It was these actions in 1520
and the visceral Swedish reaction to them that led to Sweden's complete rejection of the Union in 1523.

In the meanwhile, the Kalmar Union had served to educate the aristocratic councils of the three realms in constitutional arguments and in
how to put them into practice in a way that solidified their self-con-
scious concept of themselves as the guardians of the sovereignty of
each of their realms. That this position was self-interested is, of course,
beyond dispute, but this simply cemented their determination all the
more. Out of the Union came a tradition that would continue to have
salience in these circles in Denmark and in Sweden into the early seventeenth century, long after the Norwegian aristocracy had ceased to
have the demographic or political wherewithal to prevent its political
demise by the mid-sixteenth century. In addition, the kings and would-
be kings of Denmark and Sweden had also undergone political schooling on the job, learning not least the efficacy of reaching beyond the
councils of the realm to broader meetings that included members of
many or all of the estates. By the reign of Christian II (1513-23), the
transition from medieval to early modern forms of thought and governance was in full swing, although the struggles between councils of
the realm and monarchs would not be settled until later.

3. THE NEW MONARCHY IN THE EARLY SIXTEENTH CENTURY

Strongly implicated in the strength and success of the councils of the
realms were the archbishops and bishops in each of the three
Scandinavian kingdoms. Representing the Church, its collective property, and their own particular interests as bishops, these episcopal
members of the councils had also, during most of the Middle Ages, monopolized the office of chancellor thanks to their ready access to clerical help and archival facilities. All of this had changed by the late fifteenth and early sixteenth century in Denmark and Sweden, for the
level of education of council members, the number of literate lay
clerks, and the availability of secure archival space in secular structures
had all conspired to level the playing field or even to shift it in favor of
the lay lords of the realm. Yet the episcopal voices remained very important within the councils (this was especially true in Norway), and
the imposition of excommunication as a political tool remained in use
on extraordinary occasions of high politics.

In the Scandinavian realms, the consolidation of royal power in the
sixteenth century and the rise of the new monarchies was to be influenced profoundly by the Reformation, but the roots of that consolida-

tion lay in the demands on material and human resources posed by warfare and defense. Indeed, the efforts of King Hans and of Sten Sture the Elder pointed in the direction of consolidating royal power, as did, even more clearly, those of Christian II and Sten Sture the Younger, Sweden's regent from 1512 to 1520. In both Denmark and Sweden, these rulers ran into considerable resistance to their policies, with Danish noblemen not only complaining that King Hans violated their right to serve the crown and to receive administrative fiefs, but also that he broke the terms of his accession charter by entrusting fiefs and judgeships to burghers and by allowing them to purchase lands that could rightfully be owned only by the nobility. These complaints, of course, demonstrated that the nobility and the council of the realm had not succeeded in enjoying the fruits of what they had been promised upon Hans's election to the throne in 1483, and that was but a sign of the growing ability of the monarch to find alternative solutions to those offered by traditions received from the past.

Neither the council nor the nobility had lost its ability to exercise influence over the king, but the conflicts between monarch and council were becoming increasingly evident as the former found it necessary and desirable to exercise more power than the constitutional formula of 1484 could accommodate. In Sweden, too, Sten Sture the Elder was told by the archbishop that the constraints placed by that constitutional scheme on King Hans also applied to him as regent. When Hans died in 1513 and negotiations were held with his son Christian II concerning the terms of his accession charter, the Danish council tried to bring political theory and political reality back into balance concerning the prerogatives of the king, but they were to be disappointed once again. Christian II accepted essentially the same limitations on royal power that King Hans had accepted in 1483, including a recognition of the right to rebellion against a tyrannical monarch. Indeed, he went even further in recognizing the rights of the secular and ecclesiastical lords over their property. Yet, the new king's readiness to accept these conditions appears to have been informed largely by his realization that the extent to which his father had really had to observe the charter he had accepted had boiled down to a simple matter of whether he or the council was able to muster more brute force. There was very little that Christian II held to for long, but his recognition of the right to rebellion was one clause in his accession charter that would come back to haunt him a decade later.

It was during the years of Christian II's rule in Denmark and Sten

Sture the Younger's regency in Sweden that the striving toward royal prerogatives and the challenges to the now-traditional powers of the councils of the realm became a real threat to the constitutional arrangements that had been hammered out over the history of the Union. Christian II had been raised among the burghers of Copenhagen, to whom his father had turned more and more, and his reign would be marked by attempts to promote the interests of burghers and peasants alike, as well as by a policy of promoting the commercial interests of Copenhagen and Malmö in direct contravention of the interests of the Hanseatic towns. This latter policy was not least grounded in King Hans' promotion of the Dutch as a counterweight to Hanseatic dominance of Scandinavian trade, but Christian's Dutch connections went much farther. Already during his father's life time, he had taken a young Dutch commoner named Dyveke as his mistress and had found her mother Sigbrit Villoms' advice on financial matters useful and instructive. Perhaps nothing captures the flavor of the aristocratic aversion to Christian II's decade of rule better than his snubbing of the council and the conventions of the day by giving the Dutch commoner, Sigbrit Villoms, considerable practical influence in the Danish chancery and placing her in charge of administering the Sound dues. To add insult to injury, Christian refused to abandon Dyveke following his marriage in 1515 to the then fifteen-year old Isabella of Burgundy, one of the sisters of the future Emperor Charles V.

Whereas Christian II flaunted his promotion of bourgeois and peasant interests vis-à-vis the council of the realm and the aristocracy in general by issuing decrees that—had they been allowed to stand— would have seriously altered the social and economic legal frameworks of Danish society, Sten Sture the Younger—regent rather than monarch—challenged the power and prestige of the aristocratic council in other ways. Following in the footsteps of his predecessors, Sture utilized a close alliance with the commoners of the mining regions and with the merchants of Stockholm in his competition for power and resources with the council, which was divided between those who supported his policies and those who, led by the archbishop of Uppsala, were very critical of them. Like the Danish kings, Sten Sture the Younger had been forced to accept something akin to an accession charter prior to being elected regent by the council.[15] Because he was the leader of the country's military forces, however, he was able at critical junctures to treat the fetters of that document as cynically as Christian II treated those imposed on him by his accession charter.

The resulting political situation, in which the regent sought and found ways to balance the support of the council when he was in agreement with it and the support of other social and economic circles when he was not, created tensions that would ultimately have dire consequences. Nonetheless, by mobilizing the vocal support of assemblies he convened around the realm, the regent was able to hold the council to a policy of rejecting Christian II's demands that Sweden either recognize him as king or pay an annual tribute to the Danish crown, alternatives to which the Danish and Swedish councils had agreed in 1512.

The fates of Christian II and Sten Sture the Younger became intertwined with the outbreak of war in 1517, when the Danish king turned to armed force in an attempt to assert his claims on Sweden. Although Christian had largely succeeded in cowing the Danish council into cooperation in this venture, Sten Sture was faced with a power struggle at home that pitted his authority and policies against those of the new archbishop of Uppsala, Gustav Trolle, who had been carefully selected in 1514 precisely because of his potential ability to rally the council opposition in its struggle for power with the regent.[16] Figuratively speaking, Stockholm faced Uppsala in a struggle for political control that Sten Sture characterized as the Church's attempt to usurp the fiefs and rights of the crown, and that the archbishop portrayed as defending the Church's liberty. The new archbishop secured the Pope's blessing to maintain an armed retinue of four hundred men to defend and retake properties belonging to the Church, as well as papal confirmation of the archiepiscopal claim to a key fief and castle called Stäket and his permission to bar from the sacraments anyone who opposed these moves. Because Sten Sture insisted that Stäket was crown property, the lines of a battle royal had been drawn; by the fall of 1516, the regent, who openly accused the archbishop of plotting with Christian II against Sweden, lay siege to Stäket Castle.

Christian II's initial naval attack on Sweden in 1517 was repulsed, but it brought the regent's feud with the archbishop to a head and prompted the Swedish council to agree to subjecting the archbishop to a tribunal. But whereas the council expected to sit in judgment in this case, Sten Sture demanded that the archbishop be tried by a meeting of the realm that brought into play his supporters among the miners, burghers, and peasants, as well as providing him a stage on which to unleash his considerable rhetorical powers. Needless to say, the meeting found Gustav Trolle guilty and formed a confederation with the regent for mutual support in the event that the archbishop succeeded in having them denied the sacraments of the Church. Following this decision, Stäket Castle was destroyed, and the archbishop was imprisoned and forced to resign his seat. Just as Christian II had relied successfully on nontraditional segments of society to support him in his dealings with the Danish council, Sten Sture had outmaneuvered the Swedish council by appealing to broader circles in Swedish society and mobilizing their vocal and public support for his positions.[17] One might almost say that the new monarchy had arrived in both Scandinavian realms despite the fact that Sten Sture was never elevated to royal status.

By January 1520, Christian II had assembled the full force of his armed might and deployed it against the recalcitrant Sten Sture in a decisive battle for supremacy. Prior to the invasion, however, the Danish archbishop executed the pope's threat of denying the sacraments to Sten Sture and his supporters, and Christian made it clear that he was serving as the armed fist in the service of the Church in his campaign against the Swedish regent and his men. In a major battle in mid-January, the Swedish regent was mortally wounded; the Danish king continued his march toward Stockholm, agreeing in March with those Swedish councilors who had opposed Sten Sture that Sture's supporters would be offered amnesty for all of their misdeeds, except for those against the Church. His offer to Stockholm's defenders in September, however, extended the amnesty even to those matters, and Christian was subsequently hailed and crowned as king of Sweden in November 1520. For a very short moment, then, it appeared that the Danish king had achieved all that he could have desired in his long struggle to make the Kalmar Union a tangible reality under his sole scepter. With new sources of revenue from the Swedish realm, he might have returned to Denmark in an even better position to pursue his several goals in the areas of commercial policy and legal reform. Instead, Christian II joined with the now-restored Archbishop Gustav Trolle in an act of duplicity and brutality that would brand him a tyrant and lose him Sweden, Denmark, and Norway by 1523. Reneging on the amnesty he had declared, Christian II passively supported the summary trial and execution of more than four score of Sten Sture's supporters in Stockholm's great square.[18]

The reaction in Sweden to the events of November 1520 was swift and predictable. A new leader, who was closely related to the Stures and a number of whose relatives had been executed at Stockholm, immediately emerged to rally the same circles that had supported Sten

Sture's party and opposed Christian II's promotion of Copenhagen's and Malmö's commercial interests. Deploying the rhetorical strategies of the late regent, Gustav Eriksson Vasa quickly succeeded in raising formidable peasant armies in opposition to the new regime. Christian II had left what remained of the Swedish council in charge as he returned to Denmark, but the moral credentials of that rump body had been destroyed by its cooperation with the tyrant, and Gustav Vasa was able to become master of Sweden by August of 1521, when he was elected regent by a meeting of the realm. In all of this, Vasa was supported by Lübeck, whose major position in the Baltic trade was being challenged both by Christian II's policies and by the commercial rise of Danzig.

In Denmark, Christian II returned to face a council of the realm that now, in addition to its opposition to his legislation on behalf of the unprivileged estates and its unhappiness at the burden of taxes occasioned by his wars with Sweden, was alienated by the king's bloody actions in Stockholm.[19] His prestige and personal authority badly weakened by the events of 1520, Christian II was faced in late 1522 with a conspiracy of aristocrats who renounced their allegiance to him and hailed his uncle, Duke Frederick of Holstein, as Denmark's new king. Although he never abdicated the throne, Christian II recognized that he was powerless to remain in Denmark, and in April 1523 he sailed from Copenhagen, only to return as a prisoner a decade later. Frederick was now elected king of Denmark, while Gustav Vasa was elected king of Sweden in the same year. The project of the Kalmar Union was now rejected by the Swedes and abandoned by the Danes, although it would resurface decades later on a number of occasions. An epoch had come to an end, but the consequences for the two kingdoms were very different indeed. Whereas Gustav Vasa had come to the throne through military rebellion against Christian II and under circumstances in which a large part of the council aristocracy had died, gone into exile, or been discredited during the events of 1520, King Frederick had been borne to his new position by a proud and determined Danish aristocracy which together with the council of the realm was acting in defiance of Christian II and of the very idea of a powerful monarch.

The settlement of 1523 removed from Scandinavian politics the bone of contention and the dilemma that had been common to monarchs, regents, and councils of the realm alike since at least the middle of the fifteenth century, namely, how to manage the Union. In Sweden,

Gustav Vasa and his supporters now set about creating a regime in their own image that would emphasize royal power and prerogative, while, in Denmark, where King Frederick continued to reside at his family castle in Schleswig, the Danish council and aristocracy attempted to create a regime in *their* own image that would keep royal power in check. In this situation, even the Norwegian council was able to extract recognition of its powers and prerogatives from the new Danish monarch, although this would never be repeated. For the moment, the Danish council was able to bask in the light of its success in exercising its claim as the repository of sovereignty, since it had rejected Christian II, rejected much of his legislation, and elected Frederick in his stead. Yet, the logic of monarchy remained the same, and thus Frederick followed in much the same direction as had Christian II when it came to the exercise of royal power. One factor and one factor alone seems to have led the council and the king to minimize their differences over matters of policy and power, and that was the fact that the deposed Christian II continued to present a potential political and military threat for the entire decade of Frederick's rule.

4. The Reformation in Scandinavia

In both Danish and Swedish historiography, 1523 has come to mark a symbolic transition from the medieval to the early modern era, partly because of the Union's end, but not least because it was during the reigns of Frederick I and of Gustav Vasa that the Reformation reached Scandinavia from Northern Germany and began to shake the traditional political and economic power of the Church.[20] That process was more gradual and more rooted in questions of faith in Denmark than it was in Sweden or in Norway, but the swiftest transition took place in those parts of Schleswig-Holstein which Frederick I placed under the administration of his son Christian in 1525. A dedicated Lutheran, Duke Christian quickly seized the opportunity to reform the church in the lands under his control, completing the process by 1528. His father was much more cautious. Because Frederick owed his crown to the Danish council's ecclesiastical as well as secular lords, any attempt to carry out a princely reform of the church would jeopardize his relations with that body. And since the still-Catholic and still-exiled Christian II, occasionally backed by his imperial brother-in-law Charles V, continued to pose a potential threat, this was a risk that Frederick did not find worth contemplating.[21] Although evangelical thought made considerable headway in the Danish towns during the decade between 1523 and 1533, and although the king demonstrated considerable sympathy for Lutheranism in both his official toleration of evangelical preaching and his personal behavior, Frederick died without confronting the Catholic Church and proclaiming the Reformation in Denmark. That act would not take place until 1536, after the election of Frederick's son to succeed him as King Christian III of Denmark.

Unlike Frederick and Christian, Gustav Vasa showed no personal interest in the new religious teachings emanating from Wittenberg.[22] Yet, it was he who promoted policies that eventually led to the break with the Catholic Church. Of decisive importance to the king of Sweden was the fact that the Church controlled some 21 percent of Sweden's arable land and that Martin Luther's political teachings clearly opened the door to rethinking the rightful disposition of that property. Moreover, the actions of Rome and of Archbishop Gustav Trolle between 1514 and 1520 provided the king with considerable propaganda against the Church and cost the bishops on the council of the realm most of their political influence. It was thus relatively easy for Gustav Vasa to launch an all-out economic and political attack against the Church, demanding that more and more of the tithe be paid to the crown rather than to the Church and, at the meeting of the estates held at Västerås in 1527, securing the decision of that meeting to place all lay properties of the Church under royal administration and to deprive the bishops of all their castles and fortifications (never again would bishops sit on the council of the realm). In these latter acts, the king had the support of the estates thanks both to his argument that taxes on the peasantry and contributions from the towns would otherwise have to be raised and to his proposal that the nobility be given the right to reclaim any lands donated to the Church since 1454. These were, of course, bold and audacious moves–indeed, they were preceded by a threat of abdication should the estates not support him. But the king was concerned about content rather than form, and while a break with Rome was never formally proclaimed, the cumulative effect of developments in Sweden after 1527 led to a de facto split by 1531. Clearly, reasons of state rather than reasons of faith dictated Gustav Vasa's actions; the financial gains for the crown were so substantial that the king persisted in his policy despite armed rebellions among his unreconstructed subjects. Between 1521 and the end of Gustav Vasa's reign in 1560, it is estimated that the crown's share of arable lands in

Sweden proper grew from 5.5 percent to over 28 percent, with almost all of that gain coming from the former Church lands.[23]

The Reformation was proclaimed in Denmark only after the interregnum between Frederick I's death in 1533 and Christian III's election in 1536, during which period the council of the realm once again asserted its role as the repository of sovereignty. Because the council was dominated by the bishops and their aristocratic relatives, it was not surprising that it did not move immediately to support the Lutheran Duke Christian as his father's rightful successor to the Danish throne. Moreover, Denmark's relationship with Norway was complicated by the fact that the deposed Christian II had landed in Norway with a military force in 1531, had been welcomed by the Norwegian archbishop and others who were unhappy with Frederick I's reign, and was now, following negotiations that led to a broken promise of safe passage, a prisoner in the Danish castle of Sønderborg. Instead of electing a new king in 1533, then, the Danish council and an assembly of noblemen postponed the election until the next year. On the eve of the assembly to be held in the summer of 1534, however, Denmark was plunged into a civil war that was closely connected with the foreign policy of Lübeck's revolutionary new leader, Jürgen Wullenwever. With Duke Christian's recognition as regent in Schleswig and Holstein in 1533, and with the duchies' close alliance with the Netherlands, Lübeck was determined to prevent his accession to the Danish throne and instead threw its support behind the imprisoned Christian II, finding support for this policy among the burghers of Malmö. The extent of Wullenwever's plan is clear from the contract Lübeck entered into with Count Christopher of Oldenburg, who agreed to lead its military effort. As spoils of war, Lübeck was to be given the castles of Helsingør and Helsingborg at the mouth of the Sound, as well as the right to collect the Sound dues.[24]

The invasion of Denmark in 1534 by Lübeck's forces under the leadership of Christopher of Oldenburg not only delayed the election of a new king, but split the council and the nobles between those from Sjælland and Skåne, who chose to accept Christopher's occupation of Sjælland and Copenhagen as a fait accompli, and those from Jutland and Funen, who offered the crown to Duke Christian and hailed him as King Christian III. As the war for control of the realm progressed, advances by Count Christopher and his forces were accompanied by uprisings against the nobility by burghers and peasants, and with time the common threat to the nobility from the unprivileged orders transformed the character of the civil war. Following Jürgen Wullenwever's fall from power in the late summer of 1535, Lübeck's new leadership moved swiftly to negotiate a peace with Christian III in early 1536, and by July the king was in full control of his realm. Like Gustav Vasa in 1523, Christian had come to power through military action rather than through an election sanctioned by the council of the realm. He was the first of the Oldenburgs to have come to the throne without first accepting an accession charter, and he was quick to rearrange the political landscape. Two weeks after the capitulation of Copenhagen, Christian III imprisoned all the Danish bishops, demanding and obtaining a letter from the secular councilors of the realm condoning his action and recognizing that only his descendants could succeed him as king. Summoning the estates (including the burghers and peasants, but excluding the clergy) to a meeting in Copenhagen, the king secured their approval of a series of moves that replaced the bishops with Lutheran superintendents and assigned to the crown all lands formerly belonging to the bishops and the cathedrals. Thus, the Lutheran Reformation was officially introduced to Denmark, and, as in Sweden, the council of the realm was never again to count bishops and archbishops among its members. Here, as in Sweden, the monarchy had dealt the aristocracy a severe political blow, but in contrast to Gustav Vasa in Sweden, Christian III supported a continued central role for the council of the realm. Although the Danish council sustained a severe blow when the king's accession charter, negotiated in 1536, stated explicitly that, upon his death, the royal castles were to be held in the name of his successor and not in the name of the council of the realm, the king and the council issued a document to the assembled estates that laid out constitutional arrangements in a way that enhanced the council's status. This document continued to recognize Denmark as an electoral monarchy, while explicitly acknowledging the council of the realm as representing the entire society and stating that the chancellor must be selected from amongst the council families.[25] In effect, the document was a joint statement by king and council that recognized their joint responsibility for governing the realm. Finally, as punishment for its welcome of Christian II in 1531 and as a measure of its marginal status, Norway was proclaimed to be a part of Denmark, rather than an independent kingdom. Disbanding the Norwegian council of the realm altogether, Christian III went on to impose the Lutheran Reformation on Norway in the face of considerable elite and popular opposition.

5. THE CONSOLIDATION OF ROYAL POWER AND
THE EARLY MODERN STATE

The reigns of Gustav Vasa in Sweden (1523-60) and Christian III in
Denmark (1536-59) witnessed the consolidation of royal power and a
restructuring of government that clearly marked the arrival of the early
modern state in both realms. In Sweden, the fact that only nine of the
39 members of the council of the realm who had been in office in 1520
remained alive and in the country in 1522 meant that Gustav Vasa was
able to secure direct control of many more of the castles and administrative districts than had any of the Swedish regents during the Kalmar
Union.[26] This forced the king to introduce reforms to make the administration of these districts and the royal estates more rational so that
surplus tax revenues paid in kind (including butter, hides, and grain)
could be successfully marketed for sale at home or abroad. These revenues and those from the church lands confiscated in 1527 were further enhanced in the years after 1540 by the rising prices on the European market, but the king also had important incomes from both the
export of iron and copper and from the proceeds of a rich new silver
mine developed in the 1530s. Not only did the royal treasury thrive
under these circumstances, but the king was simultaneously able to
build up a permanent navy numbering nearly fifty ships of various sizes
by 1560, to develop a standing army of professional troops, and to
strengthen existing and build new royal strongholds. In addition to
these measures, Gustav Vasa introduced many economic measures and
regulations which were designed to maximize his regime's ability to
meet foreign and domestic crises by capitalizing on and increasing domestic production so that Sweden could withstand crop failures and
blockades, as well as purchase necessary goods from abroad. By the
late 1530s, the political circumstances under which the king operated
and the practical reforms that he had introduced had brought about a
remarkable concentration of power. Gustav Vasa used this situation in
1540 to secure the acceptance by a meeting of the nobility and some of
the bishops of what for Sweden was an entirely new concept, that is,
hereditary monarchy. This concept, later accepted at a meeting of the
estates in 1544, was accompanied by a transformation of the council of
the realm into a royal council as well as by the approval by the estates
of another concept that was entirely foreign to Swedish tradition,
namely, the granting by the monarch of hereditary duchies to his sons.

In similar fashion, Christian III's reign witnessed a dramatic

strengthening of the Danish monarchy and of the Danish state, although here the emphasis was on administrative, legal, and economic
reforms. Naval power was maintained and expanded, but unlike
Gustav Vasa, King Christian continued to rely on peasant and bourgeois levies, rather than on a standing professional army, to supplement the knight service still owed by the nobility (Denmark was, of
course, much closer to the steady supply of willing mercenaries in Germany and Scotland than was Sweden). As in Sweden, the confiscation
of church properties in 1536 enhanced the crown's revenues enormously, just as the confiscation of the bishops' well-defended castles
increased the king's ability to project power domestically. Moreover,
the monarch's incomes from land taxes increased dramatically as the
terms under which the realm's numerous administrative districts were
governed were altered significantly in the king's favor during the
course of his reign. Smaller districts were consolidated or joined with
larger ones, and the practice of strictly defining the limits of what a fief
holder could retain from the revenues of his district, a practice already
introduced on a small scale by Christian II and Frederick I, was now elevated to a universal maxim on the appointment of new fief holders.
To deal more effectively with the enhanced revenues, the Danish
crown, like the Swedish crown before it, developed a central treasury
that was capable of auditing the accounts of the fief holders. For the
first time, extensive land registers were developed in both Denmark
and Sweden to enable the monarchs to exercise more control over the
resources of their respective realms.[27] This and other manifestations of
power on the part of Christian III and the council of the realm in Denmark differed significantly from those carried out by Gustav Vasa in
Sweden in that they were accompanied by serious reforms designed to
meet many needs of Danish society in the areas of legal reform, poor
relief, education, and the like. Whereas the Swedish monarch appears
to have been driven in his actions by the motive of consolidating the
ability of his regime to cement its integrity and cope with potential foreign threats, Christian III and the Danish council seem to have been
animated by concepts of social responsibility for the subjects of the
crown that were part and parcel of the Lutheran ideology to which
they subscribed.

6. SCANDINAVIA IN 1560: A VIEW TO THE FUTURE

The change in land holding patterns brought about in Scandinavia in conjunction with the Reformation was perhaps the most striking single economic change in sixteenth-century Scandinavia, but rather than creating new wealth it merely shifted that wealth from the Church to the crown. Far more important in altering the economic picture was the long period of rising prices on European markets in the years after 1540, for the Scandinavian kingdoms were net exporters and experienced a long period of improving economic circumstances and expanding capital resources. The growing population and commercial expansion of the Netherlands and of cities in other parts of northwestern Europe created a demand for foodstuffs, timber, masts, pitch, iron, and numerous other Scandinavian and Baltic products, a number of which the Danes, Norwegians, and Swedes were able to supply at competitive prices. In the agricultural sector, this led in Denmark and Sweden to shifts from grain to livestock production, since animal fats were in high demand and the Scandinavians were better able to compete successfully in this sphere than in grains, although the Danes did well in the latter market, as well. The most important upshot of this development in Sweden was the considerable boost in revenues received by the crown thanks to its organized export of in-kind tax payments. In Denmark, on the other hand, both merchants and the nobility experienced a windfall through the export of cattle and grain. The tangible results of this economic boom included the construction of the numerous and elaborate Renaissance manor homes that still grace the Danish landscape today, as well as the creation of a number of merchant fortunes. At the same time, the Danish and Swedish peasantries appear to have thrived in this economy, even if they were not in a position to participate directly in international trade. The fact that the crown to whom they paid taxes or the landlords to whom they paid rents were realizing growing incomes thanks to the price revolution appears at a minimum to have obviated any need for those parties to press for new tax or rent concessions. Just how profitable land was proving to be during these boom years is illustrated by the fact that the price of a productive unit of tax-free land (i.e., that reserved to the nobility) rose in Denmark by 600 percent between 1540 and 1600.[28]

While the rising importance of the Baltic in European trade brought economic boom to the Scandinavian kingdoms, it also heightened the strategic importance of the Sound in European politics and led to a struggle between Denmark and Sweden for supremacy in the Baltic Sea basin in the years following 1560.[29] Ironically, one of the effects of the Reformation in weakening and ultimately destroying the Teutonic Order that had controlled Estonia and Livonia for much of the Middle Ages was to create a power vacuum that drew the two Scandinavian kingdoms, Russia, and Poland into a race for control of the Order's former territory. The importance of these lands was directly linked to the Baltic trade with western Europe, for ports like Narva, Reval, and Riga were notable transshipment points for produce from their vast hinterlands that was highly valued in European markets. With effective administrative organs, growing navies, and sufficient revenues to mount extensive military campaigns, the early modern states that Gustav Vasa and Christian III had built were not only in a position to compete for control of the Baltic Sea and its trade, but found it in their explicit interest to do so. Under their sons and immediate successors Erik XIV and Frederick II, Sweden and Denmark fought their first and inconclusive war over this issue between 1563 and 1570. It was a contest that would lead to war between the neighboring Scandinavian kingdoms four more times between 1570 and 1660, and that would end in Sweden's ultimate triumph.[30] That long struggle would create the increasing demands on both polities to mobilize material and human resources that would drive them to refine the early modern state project even further.

NOTES

1. The best treatment of medieval Scandinavia in English is Sawyer and Sawyer (1993).
2. Hørby *et al.* (1980), 377.
3. For the most convenient treatment of issues of historical geography in late medieval and early modern Scandinavia, see Mead (1981).
4. For Norway, see Nagel (1980), 160-61; for Sweden, Rosén (1961), 359.
5. For Denmark, see Hørby *et al.* (1980), 383; for Norway and Sweden, see note 4.
6. It is important to keep in mind the absolute size of the Danish and Swedish nobility, which is estimated to have been approximately 2,000 individuals in Denmark (Hørby *et al.* [1980], 383) and about 550 adult males in Sweden (Samuelson [1993], 46-47) at any given time between 1560 and 1600.
7. See, for example, Roberts (1967).
8. The best general treatment of the creation and early decades of the Kalmar Union is Christensen (1980).
9. Readers of English have few treatments of this rebellion to turn to; the treatment by Murray (1944) is simplistic and too influenced by the contemporary propaganda promoted by the supporters of Karl Knutsson.
10. Hørby *et al.* (1980), 168.
11. Ibid., 183.
12. See Lönnroth (1938).
13. Hørby *et al.* (1980), 214-15.
14. Rosén (1961), 322-23.
15. Ibid., 333-34.
16. See Wisselgren (1949) for the fullest treatment of the struggle between the regent and the archbishop.
17. Schück (1987) discusses the importance of these broader quasi-representative meetings in the political tactics of the Swedish regents; see especially, 27-36.
18. Roberts (1968), 16-19.
19. See the works of Mikael Venge, which deal thoroughly with the crisis Christian II faced in Denmark.
20. The best overview in English is Grell (1992); Dunkley (1948) presents a more comprehensive, yet now dated treatment of the Danish Reformation, while the essays in Grane and Hørby (1990) are very useful.
21. Concerning Christian II in exile, see Beyer (1986).
22. Michael Roberts has described Gustav Vasa as looking at the Church "with the insensitive and unsentimental eye of an efficiency-expert"; Roberts (1968), 83.
23. Rosén (1961), 380.

24. Hørby et al. (1980), 306.
25. Ibid., 319-21.
26. Rosén (1961), 391.
27. For a careful inventory of Gustav Vasa's holdings and operations in Uppland, see Söderberg (1977).
28. Hørby et al. (1980), 407.
29. See Kirchner (1954) and Attman (1979).
30. Roberts (1979), 1-82.

BIBLIOGRAPHY

Åström, Sven-Erik. "Swedish Imperialism under the Microscope." *Scandinavian Economic History Review* 30 (1982): 227-33.

Attman, Artur. *The Struggle for Baltic Markets: Powers in Conflict, 1558-1618.* Gothenburg, 1979.

Bagge, Sverre. "Nordic Students at Foreign Universities until 1660." *Scandinavian Journal of History* 9 (1984): 1-29.

Benedictow, Ole Jørgen. "Fra rike til provins 1448-1536." *Norges historie*, ed. Knut Mykland, vol. 5. 15 vols. Oslo, 1976-80.

Beyer, Jens Christian. "King in Exile: Christian II and the Netherlands 1523-1531." *Scandinavian Journal of History* 11 (1986): 205-28.

Carlsson, Gottfrid. "Preussische Einfluss auf die Reformation Schwedens. Ein Beitrag zur preussisch-schwedischen Geschichte in den 20er Jahren des 16. Jahrhunderts." In *Festschrift für Otto Scheel. Beiträge zur deutschen und nordischen Geschichte*, ed. Harald Thurau, 36-48. Schleswig, 1952.

Christensen, Aksel E. *Kalmarunionen og nordisk politik 1319-1439.* Copenhagen, 1980.

Christopherson, K. E. "Lady Inger and Her Family: Norway's Exemplar of Mixed Motives in the Reformation." *CH* 55 (1986): 21-38.

Dunkley, E. H. *The Reformation in Denmark.* London, 1948.

Fladby, Rolf. "Gjenreisning." *Norges historie*, ed. Knut Mykland, vol. 6. 15 vols. Oslo, 1976-80.

Garstein, Oskar. *Rome and the Counter-Reformation in Scandinavia until the Establishment of the S. Congregatio de Propaganda Fide in 1622.* 2 vols. Oslo, 1963, 1980.

Gissel, Svend, Eino Jutikkala, Eva Österberg, Jørn Sandnes, and Björn Teitsson. *Desertion and Land Colonization in the Nordic Countries c. 1300-1600.* Stockholm, 1981.

Grane, Leif, and Kai Hørby, eds. *Die dänische Reformation vor ihrem internationalen Hintergrund.* Göttingen, 1990.

Grell, Ole Peter. "Scandinavia," in *The Early Reformation in Europe*, ed. Andrew Pettigree, 94-119. Cambridge, 1992.

Grell, Ole Peter. "The City of Malmø and the Danish Reformation." *ARG* 79 (1988): 311-39.

Häpke, Rudolf. *Die Regierung Karls V. und der europäische Norden.* Lübeck, 1914.

Hill, Charles E. *The Danish Sound Dues and the Command of the Baltic: a Study of International Relations.* Durham, N.C., 1926.

Hørby, Kai, Mikael Venge, Helge Gamrath, and E. Ladewig Petersen. "Tiden 1340-1648." *Danmarks historie*, ed. Aksel E. Christensen, H. P. Clausen, Svend Ellehøj, and Søren Mørch, vol. 2. Copenhagen, 1980.

Johannesson, Kurt. *The Renaissance of the Goths in Sixteenth-Century Sweden: Johannes and Olaus Magnus as Politicians and Historians.* Trans. James Larson. Berkeley and Los Angeles, 1991.

Kirby, David G. *Northern Europe in the Early Modern Period: the Baltic World, 1492-1772.* London, 1990.

Kirchner, Walther. *The Rise of the Baltic Question.* Newark, Del., 1954.

Lindegren, Jan. "The Swedish 'Military State,' 1560-1720." *Scandinavian Journal of History* 10 (1985): 305-66.

Lönnroth, Erik. "Slaget på Brunkeberg och dess förhistoria." *Scandia* 11 (1938): 159-213.

Lundbak, Henrik. . . . *Såfremt som vi skulle være deres lydige borgere. Rådene i København og Malmø 1516-1536 og deres politiske virksomhed i det feudale samfund.* Odense, 1985.

Mead, W. R. *An Historical Geography of Scandinavia.* London, 1981.

Murray, John J. "The Peasant Revolt of Engelbrekt Engelbrektsson and the Birth of Modern Sweden." *JMH* 19 (1947): 193-209.

Nagel, Anne-Hilde. "Oversikter, årstall, tabeller." *Norges historie,* ed. Knut Mykland, vol. 15:132-386. 15 vols. Oslo, 1976-80.

Nordstrom, Byron J., ed. *Dictionary of Scandinavian History.* Westport, CT, 1986.

Oakley, Stewart P., ed. *Scandinavian History 1520-1970: a List of Books and Articles in English.* London,1984.

Oakley, Stewart P. *War and Peace in the Baltic 1560-1790.* London & New York, 1992.

Österberg, Eva. *Mentalities and Other Realities: Essays in Medieval and Early Modern Scandinavian History.* Trans. Alan Crozier. Lund, 1991.

Österberg, Eva, and Dag Lindström. *Crime and Social Control in Medieval and Early Modern Swedish Towns.* Stockholm, 1988.

Petersen, E. Ladewig. *The Crisis of the Danish Nobility 1580-1660.* Odense, 1967.

Petersen, E. Ladewig. "Fra standssamfund til rangssamfund 1500-1700." *Dansk social historie,* vol. 3. 6 vols. Copenhagen, 1979-80.

Pulsiano, Phillip, Kirsten Wolf, Paul Acker, and Donald K. Fry, eds. *Medieval Scandinavia: an Encyclopedia.* New York, 1993.

Riis, Thomas. *Should Auld Acquaintance Be Forgot . . .: Scottish-Danish Relations, c. 1450-1707.* 2 vols. Odense, 1988.

Roberts, Michael. *The Early Vasas: a History of Sweden, 1523-1611.* Cambridge,1968.

Roberts, Michael. "On Aristocratic Constitutionalism in Swedish History, 1520-1720." In Michael Roberts, *Essays in Swedish History,* 14-55. London and Minneapolis, 1967.

Roberts, Michael. *The Swedish Imperial Experience, 1560-1718.* Cambridge, 1979.

Rosén, Jerker. "Tiden före 1718." Vol. 2 of Sten Carlsson and Jerker Rosén. *Svensk historia.* Stockholm, 1961.

Samuelson, Jan. *Aristokrat eller förädlad bonde? Det svenska frälsets ekonomi, politik och sociala förbindelser under tiden 1523-1611.* Lund, 1993.

Sawyer, Birgit, and Peter Sawyer. *Medieval Scandinavia: From Conversion to Reformation circa 800-1500.* Minneapolis, 1993.

Schousboe, Karen. "Culture and History: The Social Dynamics of Cultural Signification in Denmark 1400-1600." *Ethnologia Scandinavica* (1984): 5-24.

Schück, Herman. "Sweden's Early Parliamentary Institutions from the Thirteenth Century to 1611." In *The Riksdag: A History of the Swedish Parliament,* ed. Michael F. Metcalf, 5-60. New York, 1987.

Skarsten, Trygve R. "The Reception of the Augsburg Confession in Scandinavia." *SCJ* 11 (1980): 87-98.

Skarsten, Trygve R., ed. *The Scandinavian Reformation: A Bibliographic Guide.* St. Louis, 1985.

Söderberg, Ulf. *Gustav I:s arv och eget i Uppland—en godsmassas framväxt, organisation och förvaltning.* Stockholm, 1977.

Szelagowski, Adam. *Der Kampf um die Ostsee (1544-1621).* Munich, 1916.

Thoren, Victor E. *The Lord of Uraniborg: a Biography of Tycho Brahe.* New York, 1991.

Venge, Mikael. *Christian 2.s fald. Spillet om magten i Danmark januar-februar 1523.* Odense, 1972.

Venge, Mikael. *"Når vinden føjer sig . . ." Spillet om magten i Danmark marts-december 1523.* Odense, 1977.

Wisselgren, Greta. *Sten Sture d.y. och Gustav Trolle.* Lund, 1949.

REFORMATION AND COUNTERREFORMATION IN EAST CENTRAL EUROPE

Winfried Eberhard
(Ruhr-Universität Bochum)

The historic core of East Central Europe was formed by the crown lands of Poland, Bohemia (Bohemia, Moravia, Silesia, and Lusatia), and Hungary. In many respects the social and constitutional structures of these kingdoms were comparable, and the Reformation movement in particular found in them two basic conditions that shaped its own course and articulation. First, since the fourteenth centuries these kingdoms had developed vigorous parliamentary regimes in which the upper nobles (magnates and barons) formed a strong counterweight to the king. Second, in each kingdom the Reformation movement confronted a Catholic monarch who opposed the movement or worked actively against it. This situation had two consequences. On the one hand, the constitutional polarity of parliament and crown thus offered the Reformation a basis that was greatly enhanced by actual conflicts between the king and the parliamentary estates. On the other, the Reformation movement introduced into the structural polarity a dynamism that could radicalize the parliamentary system. Religious opposition to the kings lent a new, superior legitimacy to the estates' self-consciousness and to their political aim to consolidate their autonomy.

The parliamentary systems of Poland, Hungary, and Bohemia-Moravia rested on the large numbers of nobles who possessed their lands outright. Above the mass of petty nobles rose a truly dynamic middling nobility, whose goal was economic and political aggrandizement. The decisive element, however, both for the political success of the estates and for the advance of the Reformation was the special estate of upper nobles, who possessed vast estates and great political influence, both in their own regions and in the offices of the kingdom. Except in Bohemia, there existed alongside this estate a politically powerful and richly endowed episcopate, which formed the monarch's natural ally against the Reformation movement. In Hungary and Poland the estate of free, royal cities was utterly unimportant, though in Bohemia it was able until the mid-sixteenth century to support the Protestant party in the Bohemian diet or parliament. Cities nonethe-

EAST CENTRAL EUROPE
ca. 1570

F.D.'95

International boundaries
Boundaries of principalities
duchies and vassal states
Ottoman boundaries
Holy Roman Empire

less everywhere formed the starting points and spiritual centers of the Reformation movement. In all three kingdoms the estates had developed a consciousness of representing, along with the king, the kingdom as a whole (*monarchia mixta*). Their power rested on the right to elect or to confirm the king and on the king's need for their consent to taxes and for their cooperation in framing new laws in the parliaments of the respective kingdoms. Moreover, the upper nobles held the kingdoms' highest offices and seats in the high courts (the Senate in Poland). Their power, which rested on vast possessions, had been growing since the fifteenth century through the progressive mortgaging to them of the royal domain. In Poland and Hungary, above all, these great magnates also took over the provincial administrations (*wojewodine, komitate*). The situation helped the Reformation movement to establish itself against royal wishes, because, especially in times of weak royal power, the crown depended on the diets' consent and especially on their financial assistance.[1]

1. BOHEMIA-MORAVIA

The first reformation in Latin Christendom was the Hussite revolution during the years 1419 to 1436 in the kingdom of Bohemia-Moravia. After their victory over the radical Taborites, who wanted to abolish both crown and clergy, the moderate Hussite party, the Utraquists, gained through the treaties of 1436 their own recognition from Emperor Sigmund, the Council of Basel, and the Bohemia Catholics.[2] They nevertheless continued to form a separate church, which combined Apostolic succession, the Mass, and the other sacraments with Communion under both kinds (*sub utraque specie*, hence "Utraquists"), which was held to be necessary to salvation for the laity as well, and they rejected the papal claim to universal jurisdiction and magisterial authority. The church's spiritual center was the Charles University in Prague. The Utraquist church was governed by an administrator and a consistory elected by the estates, over whom the clerical synods and the Utraquist diets stood as higher instances. Based on the Compacts of 1436, Utraquism became the established church by means of the Religious Peace of Kuttenberg (1485) in Bohemia and the provincial law framed by the nobles (ca. 1485) in Moravia. Each new king had to swear to respect the liberties of both the Utraquist and the Catholic churches. By the late fifteenth-century, therefore, this kingdom possessed an established church under parliamentary authority.[3]

Catholicism continued to exist only on the southern, northern, and northwestern margins of Bohemia, in southern Moravia, and above all in a few royal cities. The majority of the nobility and the Bohemian towns, by contrast, became Utraquist. The archbishopric of Prague, vacant since the original Hussite revolution, was governed by an administrator supported by the cathedral chapter. While the nobles had appropriated most of the ecclesiastical properties in Bohemia, in Moravia the bishop of Olomouc/Olmütz and some of the monasteries were able to preserve both their possessions and their seats in the parliament. In Bohemia, by contrast, the ecclesiastical house of the diet was abolished, and the Utraquist church abolished clerical benefices.

The political victors in this first reformation were the lay estates of the diet. Above all the nobles increased their economic power through the expropriation of the clergy and the retention of mortgaged crown lands. Alongside the magnates (*páni, Herren*) in the parliament sat the estate of the knights and that of the royal cities, led by Prague. Only with these estates' consent could the financially weakened crown collect taxes or organize the military defense of the land. Moreover, the nobles possessed the high offices and the supreme court of the land (*zemské právo*). The strong position of the parliamentary estates in these lands was fortified under weak rulers, Vladislav and Louis, the last two kings of the Jagiellonian dynasty, and remained as a powerful base of opposition under the Habsburg kings between 1526 and 1620.

Alongside the two officially recognized confessions, there developed during the second half of the fifteenth century in both Bohemia and Moravia the communities of Bohemian Brethren (*Unitas Fratrum*), who took up the traditions of the Hussite group known as "Taborites." They rejected priesthood, the Mass, and the Catholic sacraments and interpreted the Eucharist in a purely spiritual sense. They lived as pacifists according to the Bible and maintained a stern moral discipline. Since they had rejected the Utraquist church, they enjoyed no official protection from the law and depended on the protection of sympathetic nobles. The Brethren consolidated their doctrine and organization toward the end of the fifteenth century, placing four elected Seniors and a Small Council of twelve over the congregations led by preachers, all under the supreme authority of a synod.

The Protestant Reformation in Bohemia and Moravia thus encountered a religious structure already largely reformed. It had three distinct encounters with the two Hussite confessions and with Catholicism in the Catholic regions and towns. The Utraquist church had developed two distinct parties well before Luther's time: a conservative party which moved toward Catholicism and an opposition which, influenced by the Brethren, wanted a more Biblicist practice and an elimination of Catholic elements and connections. This left wing of the Utraquists came into contact with Luther ever since he spoke positively of Hussitism during the Leipzig Debate (1519). The "New Utraquists," who comprised chiefly clergymen, nobles, and burghers of Prague, saw in Luther a confirmation of their own program. A change of regime in 1523 brought their leaders into power in the provincial offices and the city council of Prague. It also changed the ecclesiastical leadership in their favor, as Gallus Cahera (d. 1545), a disciple of Luther, became administrator of the church. In 1524 a synod formulated principles which reveal the goals of the New Utraquists: the Bible as an absolute norm; reduction of the sacraments to two, Baptism, and the Eucharist; rejection of the sacrificial theory of the Mass and of the Real Presence of Christ in the Eucharist. This quasi-Lutheran New Utraquist program soon foundered on a conservative coup in Prague's city council and on the new king's religious policy.

King Ferdinand I (r. 1526-64) of the Habsburg dynasty sought to block all innovations and favored conservative Utraquism and used it as a bridge to the confessional unification of the kingdom. He succeeded in forming a loyal royalist party by installing Catholics and conservative Utraquists in the kingdom's offices and in the Prague city council, and traditionalists also secured a majority in the Utraquist consistory. New Utraquism nonetheless continued to spread among the clergy, the parliamentary estates, and some cities, because of the stream of Bohemian students to the University of Wittenberg, the contacts of Prague faculty to Philip Melanchthon, and the support of some Prague city councilors. By 1540 this party had once more the upper hand, and in 1543 an Utraquist synod made overtures to the Bohemian Brethren and began to neutralize royal influence in their church. The king responded by banishing their principal leader, Dr. Václav Mitmánek (d. after 1553), and purging the church's leadership on behalf of the conservative party.

The Bohemian Brethren also made contact with Luther by means of the letters exchanged between him and their leading Senior Brother Lukas of Prague (1458-1528).[4] Their attempt to reach an understanding, however, foundered on the issues of Christ's Real Presence in the Eucharist and Luther's doctrine of freedom, against which the Brethren emphasized the idea of strict communal discipline in a Christian sense.

Still, Lukas' successor, Jan Augusta (1500-72), was sympathetic to Lutheranism. Under his leadership the Brethren admitted several nobles to their community (1530), thereby weakening their separation from the world, and sent several students to study at Wittenberg. A sense of impending pressure from the crown prompted the Brethren in 1535 to send King Ferdinand their "Account of the Faith [*Rechenschaft des Glaubens*]," which became their definitive statement of belief and underwent several new editions down into the seventeenth century. On the issue of justification, the "Accounting" comes close to Luther, who in 1530 wrote a preface to the Latin version of the document which he had printed at Wittenberg. This convergence of the Brethren and Lutheranism nonetheless did not lead to a rapprochement of the dominant party with the New Utraquists. On the contrary, rivalry flared up between Utraquism and the Brethren, who were spreading their communities over the land, and gave rise to heated polemics between the two confessions' clergies.

A point of entry for early Lutheran influence was the Catholic borderlands of Saxony in northern Bohemia. Here Protestantism secured an early and strong position in the western parts of the district of Elbogen/Loket. A region prospering from silver mining, here the nobles and the rapidly growing population enjoyed close contacts to Saxony. The predominant noble family were the Counts Schlick, who introduced the reformation by means of the first Evangelical church ordinance in 1523. Their new, very prosperous mining town of St. Joachimsthal/Jáchymov became Bohemian Lutheranism's most influential center, above all because of its Latin school. From 1532 its rector was Johannes Mathesius (d. 1565), Luther's table companion, who from 1545 to 1565 also worked as pastor and gifted preacher to stabilize the city's Evangelical church. Lutheran schools also sprang in other towns of northern Bohemia and gained great importance for the expansion and consolidation of Lutheranism in the region. During the 1520s and 1530s other nobles of the region opened their lands' congregations to Evangelical preaching and employed their rights of patronage to install Evangelical clergymen in them. In later decades the rise of the glass, linen, and cloth industries promoted a migration into northern Bohemia by Saxons, who brought the Reformation with them. North Bohemian Lutheranism lacked, however, a common institutional framework, for it was established only in the form of local churches sponsored by noble families, who thereby were able to intensify seigniorial control of the parishes and their properties. Some of the royal cities of northern Bohemia also introduced Lutheran clergymen and ordinance in their churches, notably Leitmeritz/Litoměřice, Kaaden/Kadaň, Saaz/Žatec, and Trautenau/Trutnov.[5] This was made possible by the catastrophic shortage of Catholic priests. So obvious was Lutheranism's spread in traditionally Catholic districts that by 1539 the Administrator of Prague complained of the loss of 250 parishes. At first the king was hardly in a position to take countermeasures, since he required the Bohemian parliament's consent for taxes to fight the Ottomans and had, therefore, to avoid awakening the estates' opposition to the crown. From about 1538, however, parliamentary opposition to royal requests based themselves increasingly on confessional grounds, a policy on which New Utraquists, Brethren, and Lutherans united under the growing predominance of Lutheranism.

The Smalkaldic War of 1546/47, in which Charles V defeated the German Protestant leaders, naturally influenced the situation in Bohemia. Without asking the parliament, in 1546 King Ferdinand ordered an army to mobilize against the kingdom's Protestant neighbors in the Empire. The parliament's majority protested these breach of the constitution and refused to obey. The protest grew into a revolt by the Lutheran and Brethren nobles and the cities, who aimed to expand the estates' constitutional rights. They aimed to deprive the king of the right to intervene in religious matters and to strengthen the power of the non-Catholic confessions by means of a united Hussite or united Evangelical parliamentary party. As, however, the majority of the nobles would support only a legal resistance to the king's violation of the constitution, not a struggle for religious goals, the revolt failed. At this time, Lutheranism had not yet gained its eventual role as leader of the non-Catholic estates. The rebels were punished with death sentences, banishment, and confiscation of property. The Bohemian Brethren, threatened by the dissolution of their communities, migrated in droves to Poland, while others fled to the protection of the Moravian nobility, who had not participated in the revolt. After a constitutional revision in a royal sense eliminated the political possibility of legal resistance to the crown, opposition assumed more and more a confessional face.

The Evangelical confessions were defeated but not broken. The Brethren's communities lived on under noble protection in Moravia and soon revived in Bohemia. Since the 1550s and 1560s Lutheranism underwent its great expansion in northern and western Bohemia, where, despite temporary banishments of Lutheran pastors by a royal edict of 1554, ever more nobles and towns installed Evangelical clergy and schoolmasters in their communities. Finally, in 1549 the New Utraquist estates refused to sign the articles of faith which the king hoped would pave the way to reunion with the Catholic church. They also protested often, though in vain, that the king since 1554 forbade the estates to appoint the Utraquist consistory and the noble "Defenders."[6] The king, for his part, aimed to prevent the Lutheranization of Utraquism and, eventually, reunion with the Catholic church, by promoting a traditionalist, pro-Roman leadership, which mean that the "Old Utraquist" consistory progressively lost authority among the estates and the congregations and encouraged their drift toward Lutheranism. This situation increasingly polarized the Utraquist church and made a minority of the Old Utraquists. King Ferdinand, however, had to forego positive measures of counterreformation, because improving his fiscal situation required the good will of the princes in the Empire and the estates in Bohemia. He had to cover not only his old debts but also the costs of the new Ottoman war which broke out in 1551. Therefore, instead of repression he undertook to support an inner reform of Catholicism by calling the Jesuits to Prague in 1556 and by persuading the pope in 1561 to restore the archbishopric of Prague and concede the chalice to the laity. After some initial difficulties, the Jesuit college at Prague began to produce both an educated priesthood and a new generation of Catholic nobles, who introduced the counterreformation in their seigniories. The college at Prague was followed by foundations at Böhmisch Krumau/Český Krumlov (1581), Komotau/Chomutov (1589), and Neuhaus/Jindřichův Hradec (1592).

Meanwhile, the non-Catholic estates increasingly accepted Lutheran leadership. Under the new king, Maximilian II (r. 1564-76), they not only refused to renew the old Compacts, which they felt to be Catholic chains, but in 1571 they demanded—to no avail—toleration of the Confession of Augsburg. By 1575 the estates, bent on achieving their religious liberty, were exploiting the needy king's struggle in Hungary, Habsburg designs on the Polish throne, and above all their right to approve and crown Rudolph (II) as king of Bohemia. Under the leadership of Baron Bohuslaus Felix Hassenstein von Lobkowitz (1517-83), the Lutherans and New Utraquists produced a common "Bohemian Confession [Confessio Bohemica]," which leaned heavily on the Confession of Augsburg. They also drafted a common church ordinance which placed the church's governance in the estates' own hands. The Brethren and the New Utraquists recognized one another's confessions as orthodox. The emperor, pressed by the archbishop and the Catholic estates, gave the confession only his oral assent, promised the nobles religious liberty comparable to his concession to the Austrian nobles in 1568, and conceded to them the right to elect noble Defenders of the church.[7] Even though these steps did not provide the Evangelicals with a common church ordinance, the Bohemian Confession represented a major step toward their solidarity, which they called either "the Evangelical estates" or the "estates under both [species, i.e., Utraquist]."

Under Emperor Rudolph II (r. 1576-1612) the Bohemian reformation developed undisturbed. While Lutheranism consolidated itself in the German-speaking regions, the clergy and nobles of the Unity of Bohemian Brethren came under Calvinist influence. Evangelical Bohemian nobles went abroad to the Protestant universities of Heidelberg, Marburg, Herborn, Leiden, Basel, and Geneva. At court, Evangelical councilors won influence alongside that of conciliatory Catholic officials. Since the transferal of the Imperial court to Prague in 1583, however, forces began gathering for a Catholic restoration. In 1584 the papal nuncio, Giovanni Bonomi, drafted a plan for a counterreformation strategy and prompted the two leading Bohemian officials, Oberstburgraf Wilhelm von Rosenberg and Obersthofmeister Georg Popel von Lobkowitz, to accept an obligation to foster the Catholic religion. From 1589 on, the Old Utraquists administrators and the consistory even promised obedience to the pope, so that the archbishop acquired great influence on the Utraquist leadership. Catholic barons and converted nobles restored Catholicism in their Bohemian and Moravian lordships, and they and the emperor transferred their rights of lay patronage to the archbishop or the bishop of Olmütz. The new archbishop, Zbyněk Berka von Dubá (1593-1606) received papal confirmation only after promising to take counsel from the nuncio and the Jesuit provincial.

In Moravia three post-Tridentine bishops of Olmütz were all educated in Rome—Wilhelm Prusinovský (1565-72), Stanislaus Pavlovský (1579-98), and Franz Cardinal von Dietrichstein (1599-1636). They undertook deliberate measures of restoration on their own estates, on those of the Catholic nobles, and in the royal cities, and they also played a stronger role at court.[8] In the Moravian parliament, unlike that of Bohemia, the ecclesiastical estates had survived the Hussite revolution, and the bishop possessed a key political position. On the other hand, since the 1520s many Catholic nobles, plus such Catholic royal cities as Olmütz/Olomouc, Iglau/Jihlava, Znaim/Znojmo, and Brünn/Brno gradually went over to Lutheranism and installed Lu-

theran preachers in their pulpits.[9] Royal and episcopal countermeasures had no effect. Protected by the old noble privilege of religious liberty, in Moravia the Utraquists, who withdrew from the jurisdiction of
the Prague consistory, the Bohemian Brethren, and the Lutherans were
joined by other groups fostered by the land's officials, most of whom
were not Catholics. These included breakaways from the Unity of
Brethren and later on Calvinists and Anti-trinitarians, but the principal
group were the Anabaptists, who began to arrive in Moravia in 1526.[10]
South German Anabaptists fled into southern Moravia, where under
Balthasar Hubmaier's leadership they formed new communities. After
his execution in 1528, the Tyrolean Jakob Hutter united the communities and gave them a new constitution. The characteristic feature of
these "Hutterites" was a way of life thought to be based on a primitive
Christian communism of production and consumption. Their consolidation suffered only temporarily from measure of persecution and
King Ferdinand's order of expulsion. The Moravian nobles defended
their religious rights, notably in 1550 in a direct confrontation with
Ferdinand in the Moravian parliament. The Moravian reformation's
strength was its individual religious liberty; its weakness was its fragmentation.   In practice there arose a right of reformation (*ius
reformandi*) of the lords, while the Moravian estates paid little attention to the problem of Protestant unity, so that they posed no united
front to the Counterreformation. On the contrary, bishop Pavlovský
was able to lay the foundations for a Catholic restoration and to publish the Tridentine decrees at a synod held in 1591. As in Bohemia, so
in Moravia the Catholic reform and counterreformation were supported by the Jesuits, who in 1566 opened a college for training priests
in Olmütz. Other orders were also important for the inner Catholic reform in Moravia and Bohemia, notably the Premonstratensians, whose
General-Visitor, the abbot of Prague-Strahov and later Archbishop
Johannes Lohelius, was working hard since 1587 for discipline and the
improvement of education in his own order. The popular new order of
the Capuchins, who arrived in Bohemia and Moravia in 1600, undertook preaching and pastoral work. The Catholic renewal, therefore,
developed from two sides: from below in the domain of clerical formation, preaching, and pastoral work by the reformed orders; from above
through the strategy of the bishops and nuncios, aided by the Catholic
nobles, to push back Protestantism.

A noticeable turn in favor of the Catholics can be detected around
1600. In 1599 Nuncio Filippo Spinelli persuaded the emperor to dis-

miss Protestant officials and to install as Grand Chancellor, a most influential office, a representative of Catholic absolutism, Zdenek Adalbert Popel von Lobkowitz (d. 1627). Supported by the regime at Prague, in Moravia, as in Bohemia, the highest offices were brought into Catholic hands, and the Protestants were expelled from the city councils. In 1602 came Imperial edicts against the communities of the Brethren in both Bohemia and Moravia, and in the next year the emperor raised the archbishop of Prague to the rank of prince in order to strengthen his political authority. Shortly thereafter, in 1605, the archbishop was able to call a diocesan synod for the first time and formally to publish the Tridentine decrees.

The political restoration of Catholicism led to increasing confessional polarization in Bohemia and Moravia, just as in contemporary Hungary. The Protestant estates, which since 1575 had repeatedly struggled for recognition of the religious liberty and for a common church, came together under the leadership of Václav Budovec von Budov (ca. 1547-1621), a noble from among the Calvinist-influenced Brethren. They were able to put considerable pressure on the emperor because of the costly war against the Ottomans and the conflict within the House of Habsburg over the Imperial succession. But they took different courses. Whereas the Moravian estates joined the Hungarian-Austrian federation and recognized Archduke Matthias,[11] the Bohemians remained loyal to Emperor Rudolph and secured in exchange the famous Letter of Majesty (1609). This edict confirmed religious liberty for the nobles and cities and guaranteed the Protestants their own ecclesiastical leadership, the administration of the University of Prague, and the right to build churches and schools. From this point on the Defenders, appointed as the churches' supervisors and censors, formed a kind of Protestant shadow government of Bohemia. The new emperor, Matthias (r. 1611-19), developed a policy of deliberate Catholic restoration, guided by Melchior Cardinal Khlesl (1553-1630) of Vienna and Archbishop Johannes Lohelius (r. 1612-22) of Prague. Against this program the Protestant estates entered protests and sought an alliance with the estates of the other Habsburg dynastic lands. The new policy of counterreformation in the cities and the forceful closure of churches heightened the confessional tensions, and an assembly of the Bohemian estates, called by the Defenders despite a royal prohibition, led to the famous defenestration of Prague in 1618. The Protestant estates now organized a new regime of 30 Directors, who began to mobilize an army, struck contacts to anti-Habsburg forces abroad, and in the following year provoked the Moravians into joining their revolt. The confederation of all the crown lands, which the Austrian states also joined, gave the Bohemian estates a new, federal constitution to protect the Protestant regime and their own prerogatives against the monarchy.   So provided, they deposed the strongly Catholic restorationist king, Ferdinand II (r. 1619-37) and elected in his place Elector Palatine Frederick V, a Calvinist. He, however, turned out to be militarily incompetent and the strong Calvinist intervention caused confessional conflicts within the regime, so that the revolt foundered on the lack of both domestic military support and foreign military aid. The rebels' defeat by the Imperial forces with Bavarian backing was sealed in 1620 by a brief battle on White Mountain near Prague.

    This revolt introduced the Thirty Years' War. Not surprisingly, for the Bohemian conflict arose from a situation common in Central Europe, the struggle between the principle of particularistic liberties of estates, stiffened by the claims of several Protestant groups, and the absolutist claims of the monarchical unitary state, allied to a universalist Catholicism. The entire situation was intensified by the position of the powerful House of Habsburg. In Bohemia and Moravia, defeat and punishment of the rebels was followed by an enforcement of the Counterreformation. Between 1621 and 1628 the non-Catholics confronted the alternatives of conformity or emigration. In 1627/28 a new, absolutist constitution abolished both the Protestant Reformation and the power of the parliamentary estates in both countries.

2. HUNGARY

The course and outcome of the Hungarian reformation depended to a large measure on the strong position of the nobility, especially the upper nobles or magnates, vis-à-vis the crown in the kingdom as a whole and in the administrative districts (comitats). In the latter the administration had long been in the hands of the magnates, whose economic, political, and military power derived from their immense estates. Here, like in Moravia, Luther's teachings began to spread already around 1520 among the German-speaking burghers of Upper Hungary (Slovakia) and Transylvania. It was above all the merchants who carried the ideas along the routes that traditionally linked these cities to the more northern lands. In Hungary, more than in Bohemia and far more than in Poland, the German-speaking burghers spearheaded the reception of the Protestant Reformation. At the court in Buda, Margrave George of Brandenburg-Ansbach, a royal councilor, and Queen Mary, a Habsburg princess, fostered a group of humanists who favored Luther's ideas, among them Simon Grynaeus, the librarian and schoolmaster, and the court preachers Konrad Cordatus and Johannes Henckel.[12] The "national" party among the Magyar nobility nonetheless looked askance on the Lutheran heresy, as they did on any foreign influence at court. Accordingly, in the wake of a decision by the Hungarian diet in 1523 and of royal mandate of 1525, which threatened to punish the Lutherans as heretics, the court preachers were dismissed.

The great turning point came with the catastrophic defeat at Ottoman hands in 1526 near Mohács. The king and most of the bishops and leading magnates had fallen, and the Ottomans now occupied south central Hungary.[13] Upon the nobles fell the task of securing law and order in the other parts of the kingdom. They occupied some of the lands of the vacant episcopal sees, while the king took the rest to help finance the struggle. In the ensuing struggles between the two rivals for the Hungarian throne, Jan Zapolya/Szapolyai (r. 1526-40) and Ferdinand of Habsburg, Ferdinand depended on the German, pro-Lutheran party, and only Zapolya, with his patriotic Magyar noble following could initially move with any success against the German heresy. More important, perhaps, was the near total dysfunction of the Catholic ecclesiastical system, since prelates were nominated to the vacant sees either by both of the rival claimants to the throne or by neither. The chief consequences of Mohács were the triple division of the realm—an Ottoman region, a Habsburg western and Upper Hungary, and an eastern Hungary and Transylvania under Zapolya—the organizational and economic problems of the church, the weakness of the monarchy, and the enhanced position of the magnates in their regions. All of these posed favorable conditions for the spread of the Protestant Reformation, which accordingly developed in plural forms with corresponding ethnic and regional concentrations. Its first agents in Hungary, as elsewhere, were itinerant preachers, its chief instruments were schools and printshops, and its principal assets were the protection of urban magistrates and noble patrons. Then, too, numerous students streamed from Hungary toward Wittenberg, more than from Bohemia and many more than from Poland.

Itinerant preachers representing unclear or eclectic theologies spread Protestantism during the 1520s and 1530s in the mining towns of Upper Hungary and the county of Zips/Spiš, such as Schemnitz/Banská

Štiavnica, Käsmark/Kesmarok, Neusohl/Banská Bystrica, Kaschau/ Košice, Kremnitz/Kremnica, Eperies/Prešov, and Leutschau/Levoča. At the same time the Anabaptist Andreas Fischer won many adherents among the urban artisans, and their numbers were swelled by Anabaptist refugees from Moravia.[14] Lutheranism, on the other hand, stabilized in this regions only during the 1540s, principally under the influence of Michael Radašin of Neusohl/Banská Bystrica, who since 1546 was the Protestant Senior of the northeastern Hungarian cities, and above all Leonhard Stöckel (1510-60), since 1539 rector of the humanist school at Bartfeld/Bardějov.[15] He made this school extremely influential, and numerous future officials of Hungary were educated there. Stöckel also drafted the first Hungarian Protestant confession of faith, the "Five-City Confession," which the five royal cities of Upper Hungary adopted in 1549. The association of pastors of the twenty-four towns of the county of Zips accepted Protestantism in 1544 and subsequently adopted this confession. In this region an influential promoter of Protestantism was the magnate Alexius Thurzó, who was also King Ferdinand's viceroy. By mid-century Lutheranism was finally well established in the Upper Hungarian towns and had spread to the Slovak population as well. Two other confessions were drafted, the "Confessio Montana" or "Seven Cities' Confession adopted by the seven mining towns in 1559 and the "Confessio Scepusiana" of the towns of Zips in 1573. These documents, all based on the Confession of Augsburg, were designed to justify Lutheranism to the king and to mark it off from Swiss-style Protestantism, which the Hungarian diet had proscribed in 1548. The king, however, had already recognized Stöckel's statement.

In Transylvania Protestantism also spread among the urban Germans (the "Saxons") and moved along trade routes with the merchants and foreign preachers. Their centers included Kronstadt/Brassó, Hermannstadt/Sibiu, and Schäßburg/Sighişoara. In this region the leading reformer was Johannes Honter (1498-1549), who, after his studies at Vienna, Cracow, and Basel, was called in 1533 to his native town of Kronstadt. Here he reformed the school, established a printshop, and in 1544 became a pastor.[16] After the death of King John Zapolya in 1540 and the Ottoman conquest of Buda and the archbishopric of Gran/Esztergom in 1541, the clergy turned Protestant, and it became possible to alter the liturgy and to accept a church ordinance composed by Honter, the "Formula reformationis Coronensis ac Barcensis totius provinciae" (1543). Other towns followed Kronstadt's example, and soon the political assembly of the German "nation" in Transylvania, called the "Universitas Saxorum," ordered a common church ordinance to be drafted on the basis of Honter's "Formula." This was called the "Reformatio ecclesiarum Saxonicarum in Transsylvania." Its articles on clerical office, communal discipline, and the necessity of good works took a Melanchthonian line. The capstone on the Transylvanian Lutheran church was the election in 1553 of Paul Wiener as the first Protestant bishop during a vacancy in the Catholic see of Weißenburg. His successor was able to defend Lutheranism against the Transylvanian Anti-trinitarians.

Protestantism was also spread among the Transylvanian Magyars by the magyarized Saxons Kaspar Heltai or Helth and Franz Dávid (Hertel). Despite opposition from the bishop of Weißenburg, some of his canons sympathized with Protestantism and later openly joined it. One of them, Martin Kálmáncsehi (d. 1557), became an important Calvinist reformer in Hungary. Heltai and Dávid also opted for Calvinism, so that, while the Saxon "nation" identified itself with Lutheranism, the Transylvanian Magyars and many of them in Hungary proper went over to Calvinism, which received especially strong support from Transylvania's anti-Habsburg nobles and since 1559 from its rival king, Jan Sigismund Zapolya. A similar pattern of ethnicity and confession is found in Poland. Only in the Székler villages of the Transylvanian mountains did Protestantism fail to make inroads, and the people remained loyally Catholic. Elsewhere, however, their Polish contacts helped the Anti-trinitarians (Unitarians) to gain considerable influence in Transylvania. They were protected by Queen Isabella and later by King Jan Sigismund Zápolya (d. 1571), who became one of them. The theologian Franz Dávid also went over to them. The Unitarians, a radical splinter of Calvinism, threatened mainly this confession, finding their adherents among the Magyar nobles and burghers.

Eventually, official religious toleration grew out of this variegated Transylvanian reformation. When the diet of Thorenburg/Thorda in 1550 decreed toleration, this represented a victory for Protestant demands. Seven years later, however, the diet decreed that each person might retain his own faith and recognized officially Catholicism, Lutheranism, and Calvinism as "approved religions." This principle of co-existence was often reaffirmed, and in 1571 the Unitarian confession was also recognized as "approved." Romanian Orthodox Christianity, which was not even mentioned, was nonetheless tacitly tolerated in Transylvania.[17]

In Hungary's Magyar regions, including those occupied by the Ottomans, Protestantism spread more slowly than elsewhere, and down to mid-century it represented a certain theological eclecticism between Wittenberg and Zurich and Geneva, though it leaned toward the Swiss tendency. Here the leading preachers and organizers were Johann Sylvester, Mathias Dévai Biró, Michael Sztárai, Gallus Huszár, Stephan Szegedi Kis, and, most important, Peter Meliusz.[18] In contrast to Upper Hungary, Zips, and Transylvania, in these regions Protestantism depended less on confessional decisions in the city than on the patronage of powerful magnate families, such as the Nádasdy, Perényi, Drágffy, Török families, plus (somewhat later) the Bocskay, Béthlen, Rákóczy, and Tököly families. The itinerant preachers, who moved and had to move frequently, had mostly studied at Wittenberg. Sylvester (d. 1552) taught since 1539 in schools on Thomas Nádasdy's estates in the comitats of Eisenburg/Vas and Ödenburg/Sopron, where in 1541 he edited the first complete translation of the New Testament into Magyar. Dévai (d. 1545) preached since 1531 at Buda and Kaschau and later on the estates of Thomas Nádasdy. In 1539 he became court preacher to Peter Perényi and later worked on those of Gáspár Drágffy. His last post was in Debrecen, a town belonging to the magnate family of Török and eventually the chief center of Hungarian Calvinism. His loyalty to Wittenberg doctrine later brought him the nickname, "the Hungarian Luther." Indeed, the first Protestant synod in Magyar-speaking Hungary, which met at Erdöd in 1545, did declare for the Revised Confession of Augsburg. Michael Sztárai (d. 1575), who preached in the western part of Ottoman Hungary, had by 1551 founded more than 120 congregations there. He, too, stood under the influence of Luther and Melanchthon, though since 1555 he found himself positioned between the Lutheran and Calvinist fronts. During the 1550s Gallus Huszár preached in northwestern Hungary, where he founded both a printing house and a school for training clergymen. Since 1560 he worked at Kaschau, though he later fled to Debrecen, where he continued to print materials for the Reformed Confession. Even though Huszár retained the Lutheran form of worship, he strongly supported the line of Bullinger and Calvin. The most important and most learned of these Magyar reformers of the first generation was Stephan Szegedi Kis (1502-72). After taking his doctorate at Wittenberg, he worked since 1548 in several regions, notably in the district of Temesvár, which was under Transylvanian administration. Here the congregations of the old diocese of Csanád, now mostly under Ottoman rule, reorganized themselves in 1549-50 into a Reformed church and elected Matthias Gönci as their bishop. When Temesvár was transferred to King Ferdinand's rule, Szegedi moved to serve Reformed communities in Ottoman Hungary, where he organized the school at Tolna to train clergymen in the Swiss brand of Protestantism and later was elected to be general superintendent. Though he, too, recognized the authority of Luther and Melanchthon, his writings, which betray more strongly an affinity to Bullinger and Calvin, were printed posthumously at Geneva, Basel, Zurich, and London.

Analogous to the mobility of its representatives, the first generation of Magyar-speaking Protestantism reveals a definite theological pluralism or eclecticism, though leaning progressively more strongly in the Swiss direction. After the defeat of the Protestant League of Smalkalden in the Empire in 1547, King Ferdinand sought to reverse Protestant progress in his own lands as well. In 1548 the Hungarian diet, meeting at Preßburg/Bratislava, issued laws against the Protestants and introduced the Inquisition, which moved mainly against the Anabaptists and "Sacramentarians," the latter in the Swiss sense. Since 1555 the Lutherans, hoping to secure toleration via the protected Confession of Augsburg, drew the boundary to Swiss Protestantism with a new sharpness, against which the Calvinists of non-Habsburg Hungary reacted by defining their position more precisely. During the 1560s the conflicts between Lutherans and Calvinists gained new heat from their counterparts in the Empire. In the synod at Debrecen, where they enjoyed the protection of the Transylvanian governor, Peter Petrovics, the Reformed theology and liturgy emerged victorious from the conflicts with the Lutherans. Reformed confessionalization was led by Martin Kálmáncsehi (d. 1557), former cathedral canon of Großwardein/Nagyvárad/Oradea Mare, who became a Reformed bishop in this region. In eastern Hungary the most important Reformed organizer was his successor, Peter Meliusz (1505-72), a Wittenberg graduate whom Szegedi Kis won over to the position of Bullinger and Calvin. From the very beginning of his episcopal service he set the goal of reaching agreement on the Lord's Supper with the Magyar-speaking congregations of the neighboring regions of Transylvania and Upper Hungary. At synod of Neumarkt/ Marosvásárhely/Tirgu Mures in 1559, Meliusz' Reformed formula was accepted, the first confessional document in Magyar. Meliusz also translated Calvin's catechism into Magyar. Between 1561 and 1571 he made Debrecen into "the Hungarian Geneva," composing numerous popular tracts and making available a vernacular Bible, church ordinance, order of worship, and hymnbook. His confessional statement, the "Confessio Catholica Debrecinensis" of 1562, fixed the Reformed loyalty of Magyar-speaking Protestantism. Religious life at Debrecen was radically tailored to Zurich's pattern, partly, perhaps, because of the rivalry posed to Calvinism in this region by the Transylvanian Anti-trinitarians. Finally, at the synod of Debrecen in 1567, the Reformed church organization beyond the River Theiß was consolidated under the aegis of Bullinger's Second Helvetic Confession (*Confessio Helvetica Posterior*), so that Anti-trinitarianism remained confined to Transylvania.

To the north, in eastern Upper Hungary, where the Protestants lay in struggle against the bishop of Erlau/Eger, they also adopted the Reformed confession. Beginning at the synod of Gönc (south of Kaschau) in 1566, a Reformed polity was constructed of the type presided over by a Senior under the leadership of Gáspár Károlyi (1530-91). The statutes of a synod held at Hercegszölös, ten years later, show that the Reformed organization was also adopted by congregations in Ottoman Hungary. The Ottomans rarely interfered with the Reformed clergy and schools and even, on occasion, supported them against the Catholics, for they found the autonomous communal structure of Protestantism more advantageous than that of Catholicism, with its ties abroad. The Reformed confession's strict discipline may also have been welcome to the Ottoman administration.

By 1560 a majority of the Hungarian nobility and their subjects had gone over to Protestantism, and by 1570 the division of Hungary into Reformed, Lutheran, and residual Catholic regions had been fixed. Because of the fluctuating triple division of the realm and of the nobles' dominant position, this situation played the decisive role in Protestantism's spread and survival. The nobles' sense of autonomy and the cities' desire for self-administration also favored the Protestant religion. The magnates' centrality to confessional geography became clear around 1590, when in western Hungary, where the Catholic church had survived, the nobles supported Lutheranism. Despite Calvinist influences, the magnate Franz Nádasdy held a religious colloquy and obliged his clergy to adopt the Confession of Augsburg. In Slovenia and Croatia, too, Lutheranism was promoted by magnate families, the Ungnad, Erdödy, and Zrinyi. The Captain-general (*Landeshaupt-*

mann) of Styria, Hans Ungnad von Sonneck, turned Lutheran and traveled to Württemberg, where he opened a printing firm in Urach. Here he printed the writings and translations of the Slovene reformer Primoz Truber and the Croat Stephan Konsul, including works by Luther and Melanchthon, bibles, catechisms, songs, and school-books.[19] Despite the countermeasures taken since 1565 by the bishop of Zagreb, Georg Draskovics, and despite the barring of Protestants from owning land or holding office in Croatia, the Zrinyis were able to protect Protestantism, of a Reformed type, on their estates.

By the end of the sixteenth century, only a minority of the Hungarian estates and a dwindling remnant of the population remained Catholic, chiefly in the northwestern region. Because of the Ottoman expansion, Tyrnau/Trnava had in 1543 become the seat of the exiled archbishop of Gran/Esztergom. Archbishop Nikolaus Oláh (r. 1554-68) did call the Jesuits and tried to found a seminary for training priests, but these plans did not bear fruit until around 1590. Meanwhile, Jesuits and other clergy were imported from Austria, and the German-Hungarian College at Rome began to train priests of a post-Tridentine type. Prince Stephan Báthory (r. 1571-86) of Transylvania promoted Catholicism, fought the Anti-trinitarians, and permitted the Jesuits to establish colleges, though the Hungarian diet suppressed the latter in 1588, fearing that they would disrupt the balance among the "four approved confession." Although most of the Hungarian sees remained vacant or only intermittently filled, and although most of the ecclesiastical properties were confiscated, the dioceses themselves continued in principle to exist. Not only did the diet's Protestant majority never attempt to abolish the sees, it repeatedly asked that they be filled. In 1556 the Hungarian diet even confirmed the church's rights and liberties, including the tithe. Its apparent object was to uphold the estates' privileges and the effectiveness of the kingdom's offices and the diet, while the victorious spread of Protestantism meant that the estates could renounce a formal change of religion in order to avoid direct conflict with the king and with the bishops in the diet's upper house. This was a miscalculation, for during the seventeenth century the bishops became the centers of Catholic renewal in Hungary.

A certain policy of Catholic restoration is detectable already under Emperor Rudolph II toward the end of the sixteenth century. Rudolph increasingly entrusted administrative offices to the bishops, who thereby dominated the royal council. This policy evoked anticlerical demands

from the nobles in 1605. And in Transylvania, which had been transferred to the emperor in 1602, there was growing dissatisfaction with
the efforts to restore Catholicism. Then, too, anti-Protestant measures
were underway on the remaining ecclesiastical estates and royal cities
in Upper Hungary. The intensification began when the bishop and cathedral chapter of Erlau, driven out by the Turks, settled in Kaschau in
1597 and in 1604 took possession of the cathedral. They were backed
by Archduke Matthias as the emperor's own representative. The coming of the Jesuits to Kaschau, the expulsion of the Protestant clergy,
and an episcopal visitation in the Protestant cities of the Zips region led
gradually to solidarity among the Protestants of the various regions
and of the nobles and cities in the Hungarian diet, in which they demanded their liberty of religion. Instead, Matthias prefaced diet's conclusions with an article that renewed the legal protection for the
Catholic religion and forbade the diet to entertain grievances concerning religion. This affront sparked a revolt which the Protestant magnates, who until now had stood on the sidelines, joined. The Protestant estates announced their rejection of Matthias' article, their
solidarity with the towns, and their customary right of armed resistance. Shortly thereafter, the Transylvanian Calvinist magnate Stephan
Bocskay, who aimed to unite politically all the Protestants, came into
military conflict with the emperor's general in Hungary. At this point
the Transylvanian and Upper Hungarian Protestants united in resistance, as Calvinists and Lutherans abandoned their rivalry in the fact of
pressure from the Catholic restoration. The Upper Hungarian towns
opened their gates to Bocskay, the Transylvanian ones elected him
their prince, and in 1605 the Hungarian diet named him king. Despite
these victories, Bocskay declared his willingness to treat with the emperor, and the Treaty of Vienna (1606) secured liberty of religion for
the nobles and towns. Not only did King Matthias confirm this grant
before his coronation in 1608, but he was forced to extend it to all subjects. Furthermore, the Upper Hungarian Protestants obtained the
right to have their own ecclesiastical organization and thus became legally independent from the bishops. In addition the kingdom's office
were opened to Protestants. This outcome of Bocskay's rebellion,
which both Lutheran and Calvinist magnates had backed, made impossible a Catholic restoration from above, such as happened in Bohemia.
Down to the beginning of the eighteenth century, the Protestant magnates of Hungary again and again defended their rights by means of
both political and military resistance, so that Hungary remained the

only land in East Central Europe in which Protestantism survived as an important social element.[20] Furthermore, at the beginning of the seventeenth century Bocskay's success and his international connections provided an important impulse for the resistance of Protestant nobles in Bohemia, Moravia, and Poland.

The foundations of Catholicism's partial restoration in Hungary were laid by Archbishop Peter Pázmány of Gran/Esztergom (r. 1616-37) with support from Emperor Ferdinand II's absolutist policies. Pázmány, son of a Reformed noble family in Großwardein/Nagyvárad/ Oradea Mare, turned Catholic in 1583 while studying in the local Jesuit school, and he later taught as a professor in Graz. His apologetical works introduced the Catholic position to Hungarian audiences. He established seminaries at Vienna and Tyrnau for the education of Catholic priests and laymen, together with the University of Tyrnau, later moved to Budapest, and its noble colleges. These institutions were operated by the Jesuits, whose educational policy aimed to win the nobles back to the Catholic church. In the event, Pázmány won back thirty magnate families. The emperor supported this strategy by appointing only Catholics to royal offices. By 1637 there were hardly any Protestant magnates left in western Hungary. The Catholic restoration never embraced the entire nobility, as it did in Poland, because the Protestant confessions had already built a strong organization and tradition, and above all because in Hungary, unlike in Poland, the king always confronted a Protestant political opposition.

3. POLAND

Protestantism established itself organizationally and politically in the Polish lands later than in the other realms of East Central Europe. As in the Magyar-speaking lands of Hungary, where the variegated reformation movement attained organizational solidity and theological clarity around mid-century, in Poland this delay meant the introduction of the more radical, modern form, Calvinism, which was better able than Lutheranism was to bolster the legitimacy and opposition of the estates. There also existed a patriotic motive for marking off the boundary to "German Lutheranism."

During the second half of the fifteenth century, much as in Hungary, a strong and similarly constituted parliamentary constitution had formed in Poland. Here, too, the power of the very numerous nobility rested on the legislative and financial powers of the diet (*sejm*) and on noble administrative control of the districts (*województwa*).[21] Just as the Hungarian comitats had their assemblies, so did their Polish counterparts (*sejmiki*), which instructed their delegates to the diet of the realm. In the diet these delegates, who mostly belonged to the middling nobility (*szlachta*), formed the second house (*izba poselska*). In the upper house, where the magnates were represented, sat the bishops, the district governors, castellans, and officials of the central government.

Just as in Hungary, in Poland the early adherents of Protestantism were German burghers in royal Prussia. In neighboring Great Poland the nobles spread Lutheran writings, the possession of which was punishable already by 1523. In Gdánsk/Danzig the civic commune seized the initiative and, following an attack on the monasteries, staged a movement against the city council that ended in the introduction of Evangelical religion.[22] King Sigismund I (r. 1506-48), bent on restoring the old order by force, threatened in his "Statuta Sigismundi" the death penalty for apostasy from the Catholic religion. Protestants could therefore not openly form congregations until mid-century. Instead, the new religion spread gradually among the nobility, many of whom attended Protestant universities abroad. Lutheranism also spread at Danzig.

One important center for the Polish reformation was Königsberg, the capital of the state of the Teutonic Knights, a Polish fief which in 1525 had become the secularized, Lutheran duchy of Prussia. Since 1530 Protestant works were being printed at Königsberg, and during the 1540s appeared the Prussian church ordinance, catechisms, and hymnbooks in Polish. A new university, founded in 1544, also helped to spread Protestantism in Poland. A third center of such activity was the capital, Kraków/Cracow, where Lutheran books early circulated in the university. Here, too, formed a circle of humanist scholars associated with the German-speaking patriciate, which since 1542 moved toward Protestantism under the leaders of Francesco Lismanini, a Franciscan who later went over to Calvinism. The Protestants of Cracow soon extended their influence to the local nobility.

In general, Polish Protestantism was led not by the towns but by the nobles. In Little Poland since the 1540s this meant above all the middling, rising nobility, who sent—as nobles from other regions did later—mostly Protestant envoys to the diet. After 1550 the magnates began installing Protestant clergymen in the churches, and in 1565 even the Wojwode of Cracow joined the Protestants. In Little Poland and elsewhere, one motive for the nobles' favoring Protestantism was animus against the large concentration of estates in ecclesiastical hands and the church's immunity to the lay courts and to taxation. In Little Poland the clergy owned 15 percent of the land, and in the district of Cracow they possessed as much as the king did.[23] The clergy nonetheless contributed to taxes and defense only voluntarily, and the ecclesiastical courts, backed by royal officials, prosecuted all who refused to pay tithes.

Protestant anticlericalism could nonetheless not develop openly until the reign of King Sigismund II (r. 1548-72). Although he corresponded with Melanchthon and Calvin and appointed the Lithuanian magnate Nikolaus Radziwiłł, a Calvinist, as grand chancellor, Sigismund remained a Catholic. He nevertheless tolerated the formation of Protestant congregations, granted religious liberty to the Prussian towns, and approved the adoption of the Confession of Augsburg by the diet of Royal Prussia in 1559. From 1550 on, the nobles' attacks on ecclesiastical courts formed a constant theme in the diet, in which the Protestants dominated the lower, noble house. From the 1560s, for a while, the upper house also possessed a Protestant majority among the lay members. Between 1552 and 1565, only Protestants were elected as presidents (marshals) of the diet, and in 1552 the diet decided to vacate the enforcement of ecclesiastical courts' sentences against tithe-resisters and "heretics." When this decision was generalized and extended in 1565, coupled with the royal policy of toleration it became tantamount to a declaration of religious freedom. The diet had already in 1555 adopted an "Interim," that is, religious toleration for the nobles until a general council should meet.

The spread of Protestantism in Poland nevertheless varied greatly by region and confession.[24] Since open confession of the new faith and the formation of congregations was possible only since 1548, Calvinism spread very rapidly among the Polish and Lithuanian nobles as an alternative to "German" Lutheranism. The most susceptible to its message were the rich, most powerful stratum of magnates and the middling nobles, also the lesser nobles, but only in Lithuania and Volhynia, not in Masovia, which remained entirely Catholic. While Lutheranism was taking root in the nobles and cities of Royal Prussia and Great Poland, the nobles of Little Poland, Ruthenia, and Lithuania tended to adopt Calvinism. Some of the Lutheran congregations of

Great Poland formed a synodical association, which since 1565 was governed by a superintendent. In Lithuania Prince Nikolaus Radziwiłł introduced Calvinist worship wherever possible and established a printshop to produce a vernacular Bible (the Brest Bible, 1563). In Little Poland the most important Calvinist figures was Jan Łaski (Johannes a Lasco, 1499-1560), who after long stays in Germany and other foreign lands returned to Cracow in 1556. Here he collaborated with Lismanini to organize Polish Protestantism into a national church along Genevan lines.[25] Lutheran opposition and Laski's early death, however, prevented this attempt to overcome Protestant fragmentation in Poland. Anti-trinitarian influence on the Calvinists of Little Poland—Lismanini even joined this movement—led to the splitting off of the Cracow Anti-trinitarians as a "Ecclesia minor." The leading theologian of this group was Fausto Sozzini (ca. 1537-1604), and its organizational and spiritual center lay in the city of Raków. Yet a fourth Protestant confession established itself in Poland, the Bohemian Brethren, whose expulsion from Bohemia brought some of them to Great Poland. They gained adherents among the nobles and in other social strata, forming centers at Poznań/Posen, Koźminek, and Leszno.

Although neither a general nor regional confessions of faith halted this confessional fragmentation of Polish Protestantism, efforts at the formation of a consensus did bear some important fruits. Allured in 1555 the Calvinists of Little Poland formed in Kozminek a union with the Great Polish Bohemian Brethren, themselves already heavily influenced by Calvinism. The next step, the *Consensus Sandomirensis* of 1570, included the Lutherans as well, though this was no doctrinal union but merely an act of mutual recognition. A common synod of these groups was provided for, but by 1595 it had met only four times. Although the Protestant nobles did not form a solid parliamentary party during this era of Protestant expansion under Sigismund II, after the king's death, when they were threatened by a Catholic royal election, they formed the Warsaw Confederacy to fight Catholicism. In 1573 this alliance forbade any punishments on account of religion, established full religious liberty for the nobles, and, by means of the electoral capitulation of the new king, Henry of Valois, lay the basis for religious toleration in Poland.[26] Neither at this time nor at any other did there emerge a common name for the Protestants, who also did not form a single party in the diet. They used for themselves the term coined by others, "religious dissidents (*dissidentes de religione*)."[27]

Polish Protestantism reached its zenith in the Warsaw Confederacy.

King Stefan Báthory (r. 1575-86), a Catholic who was also Prince of Transylvania, pursued the same policy of toleration in Poland that he had accepted in Transylvania. At the same time, Protestantism began to suffer from its own internal weaknesses: confessional fragmentation, the lack of adequate clerical leadership and schools, and above all the fact that Protestantism remained almost entirely an affair of the nobles, and never of a majority of them. A Protestant victory in Poland required collaboration between the magnates and the nobles (szlachta), but the possibility for this had been destroyed during the 1560s by the "execution movement" of the nobles against the magnates' domination and their appropriation of royal domains.[28] When a proposal for review of the royal domains in magnate hands succeeded in the diet, it split the Protestant party. Thereafter the magnates no longer supported the nobles' demands for secularization of ecclesiastical lands and suppression of the tithe, but rather defended these traditional rights. The conflict with the nobles drove the magnates into alliance with the Crown, and in Poland there had never existed such sharp conflicts between nobles and king as in Bohemia and Hungary. The magnates needed the king's favor in bestowal of estates and offices in order to hold their position. King Sigismund III's (r. 1587-1632) policy of appointing only Catholics to royal offices enhanced the wave of magnate conversions to Catholicism, which had begun in 1569. By 1582 almost all the Polish senators were Catholic, and the only Protestant senators left were Lithuanians.[29]

The return of nobles to Catholicism was made possible by the Catholic revival since the Council of Trent. Stanislaus Cardinal Hosius, since 1551 bishop of Ermland, had already been active through apologetical writings and in founding Jesuit colleges to support the Catholic restoration in Poland.[30] Following the council an active Catholic party of magnates formed in the diet in 1564, and the conflicts among the Protestants—Brethren, Lutherans, and Calvinists—at this time brought the Catholic party many supporters. The magnates' consolidation in alliance with the crown and the clergy against the nobles thus formed a political counterpart to the advance of the counterreformation, which did not occur by force. Yet, toward the end of the sixteenth century occurred growing numbers of attacks on Protestant churches in the royal towns. The Protestant noble opposition, led by two magnates, Nikolaus Zebrzydowski and Janusz Radziwiłł (1579-1620) moved again these unpunished provocations, against the king's favoring of bishops and Catholic magnates for royal offices, and against civil arm's aid for ecclesiastical courts. When the king asked the diet of 1606 for a permanent tax, a standing army, and a reform of the diet, the parliamentary opposition, which feared an absolutist coup, banded together with the Protestants. In the same year the Protestant nobles formed a league to defend themselves, but in 1607 it was crushed by the king and the magnates, who by now were almost exclusively Catholics. There the struggle ceased, for instead of punishing the rebels the king declared an amnesty. Thereafter, over the course of the seventeenth century the counterreformation achieved peacefully most of its aims. In 1607 the political influence of the Protestant nobles was broken forever.

The Polish reformation thus stands in stark contrast to those in Hungary and Bohemia. It failed because of its late development, its meager organizational abilities, its lack of a clear tradition of opposition to the king, and above all, the political conflict between the nobles and the magnates, who quickly returned to Catholicism.[31]

All three core kingdoms of East Central Europe possessed similar political conditions for the reception of Protestantism: a highly developed parliamentary constitution with a strong, numerous upper nobility, whose oligarchical tendencies posed a potential counterweight to the monarchy. All three lands experienced a delay in the Reformation's onset and development, because the Catholic monarchs opposed the movement and the non-German nobilities regarded it with coolness. The only exception was Bohemia-Moravia, where an earlier, Hussite reformation had promoted the formation of a Czech-speaking, non-Catholic parliamentary party of estates, which allied with German Lutheranism during the second half of the sixteenth century. It is also noteworthy that the reception of Protestantism, and hence the forms of confessional pluralism, varied greatly from region to region, which produced different forms of religious co-existence. In the end, the Catholic church was able to re-stabilize itself in all three lands.

Alongside these general similarities of the development of the Reformation, there were distinct differences among the three lands: the resistance to the monarch, the regional shape of confessional pluralism, and the degree of Protestant solidarity. In Bohemia there existed since the Hussite revolution a tradition of opposition of the non-Catholic confessions to the Catholic monarchy. This was the basis for the confessional solidarity that developed since about 1540, for the consensus expressed in the Confessio Bohemica of 1575, and for the mounting Protestant opposition that culminated in the estates' revolt of 1618-20. Bohemia witnessed the strongest Protestant opposition to the monarchy, which responded with especially harsh countermeasures that led to the severest type of conflict, the Protestant estates' rebellion. In Moravia, by contrast, the nobles, concerned solely for their individual religious liberty, formed no front against the king, who could in general count on their loyalty. The Hungarian estates' opposition to the Habsburg ruler developed, like the Protestant solidarity, relatively late. The kingdom's unstable triple division and the Ottoman danger meant that royal interventions against the Protestant were not effective before 1600. After the Bocskay revolt against the royal anti-Protestant policy, the dynasty's need for legitimation under Matthias led to a successful compromise, not to the annihilation of Protestantism as in Bohemia. In Poland there was no fundamental opposition to the ruler, so that the political motive for the nobles to become Protestants was correspondingly weak, arising as it did solely from hostility to the clergy. Poland thus lacked an effective basis for an enduring Protestant front or for the formation of a Protestant opposition. As in Moravia, the Protestant collaboration aimed only at individual religious liberty for the nobles and at mutual recognition among the Protestant groups. Then, too, the Polish reformation was weakened by its late development after 1548 and above all by the political differences between the nobles and the magnates. So, the only Protestant resistance to the Catholic restoration came in 1606, and it was a complete failure.

Religious pluralism in East Central Europe was most clearly defined by region in Poland and Hungary, while Bohemia-Moravia was far more mixed because of the divisions among Lutheranism, Utraquism, and the Bohemian Brethren, and also because of the linguistic distinctions among regions. During the 1520s and 1530s the Protestant initiative lay in all lands with the German-speaking cities or regions (northwestern Bohemia, Royal Prussia, Upper Hungary-Zips, Transylvania), which received Lutheranism and passed it on to neighboring regions, such as Great Poland. In this way Lutheranism became the dominant tendency in Bohemia-Moravia for the Utraquists, while Calvinism played a role through the Brethren only after 1600. In Poland and Hungary, by contrast, the social distance of the indigenous nobility to the German burghers and especially the late formation of Protestant communities promoted the more "modern" Calvinism to a dominant position. This happened initially in the regions farthest from German influences, such as central and eastern Hungary, Little Poland, and Lithuania. In Hungary, Calvinism, with its center in the eastern regions, even became for a long time the politically dominant confession.

Protestantism's strong thrust, though unable to wipe out the Catholic Church, and its plural formations forced the Protestants in all three kingdoms to practice an intra-Protestant toleration and a co-existence with the Catholics. In Bohemia this co-existence gave way to increasing polarization toward the end of the sixteenth century, but in Moravia even the bishops recognized until 1617 the nobles' traditional religious liberty. In Poland and Transylvania, in the interests of peace the plurality of confessions was even legally established and guaranteed through agreements, not as a result of revolts. Tolerant pluralism of confessions thus became a special feature of the East Central European reformation, which distinguished it from those of the German lands and western Europe. Where it succumbed to polarization, as in Bohemia-Moravia, the process of Catholic restoration was forceful and complete. In Poland, by contrast, the Catholic restoration trod the path of liberty, and in Hungary-Transylvania the confessional co-existence lasted into the age of absolutism.

Translated by Thomas A. Brady, Jr.

NOTES

1. On the constitutional background, see Rhode (1964), Schramm (1985), and Dillon (1976). Schramm (1965), 220-314, presents the East Central European type of Protestant reformation against the monarchy.
2. Malcolm D. Lambert, *Medieval Heresy: Popular Movements from the Gregorian Reform to the Reformation*, 2d ed. (Cambridge, Mass., 1992), 284-389; Howard Kaminsky, *A History of the Hussite Revolution* (Berkeley and Los Angeles, 1967); John M. Klassen, *The Nobility and the Making of the Hussite Revolution* (Boulder, Colo., 1978); Ferdinand Seibt, *Hussitica. Zur Struktur einer Revolution*, 2d ed. (Cologne and Vienna, 1990); František Šmahel, *Husitiská revoluce*, 4 vols. (Prague, 1993).
3. Eberhard (1981), 112-19, and (1986).
4. Amadeo Molnár, "Luther und die Böhmischen Brüder," *Communio Viatorum* 24 (1981): 47-67; Brock (1957); Heymann (1968).
5. Heribert Sturm, *Skizzen zur Geschichte des Obererzgebirges im 16. Jahrhundert* (Stuttgart, 1965); idem, "Johannes Mathesius," in *Lebensbilder zur Geschichte der böhmischen Länder*, ed. Karl Bosl, vol. 2 (Munich, 1976): 29-51; Rudolf Wolkan, "Studien zur Reformationsgeschichte Nordböhmens," *JGPÖ* 3 (1882): 55-65, 107-19, and 4 (1883): 67-95, 145-67; Wilhelm Wostry, "Das Deutschtum Böhmens zwischen Hussitenzeit und Dreißigjährigem Krieg," in *Das Sudetendeutschtum, sein Wesen und Werden im Wandel der Jahrhunderte* (Brünn, 1937), 295-370; Georg Loesche, *Johannes Mathesius, ein Lebens- und Sittenbild aus der Reformationszeit*, 2 vols. (Gotha, 1895).
6. Krofta (1911). On the institution of the Defenders, see Eberhard (1981), 50.
7. Hrejsa (1912); Pánek (1982), 101-19.
8. Gatz (1995).
9. Paul Dedic, "Die Geschichte des Protestantismus in Olmütz," *JPGÖ* 52 (1931): 148-74; F. Schenner, "Beiträge zur Geschichte der Reformation in Iglau," *Zeitschrift des deutschen Vereins für Geschichte Mährens und Schlesiens* 15 (1911): 222-55 and 16 (1912): 84-102, 374-406.
10. Waclaw Urban, *Der Antitrinitarismus in den Böhmischen Ländern und in der Slowakei im 16. und 17. Jahrhundert* (Baden-Baden, 1986); Jarold K. Zeman, *The Anabaptists und the Czech Brethren in Moravia: a Study of Origin and Contacts* (The Hague, 1969).
11. Bahlcke (1994), 309-42.
12. Louis Neustadt, *Markgraf Georg v. Brandenburg als Erzieher am ungarischen Hofe* (Wrocław, 1883).
13. István Nemeskürty, *Ez történt Mohács után . . . 1526-1541*, 2d ed. (Budapest, 1968).
14. Urban, *Antitrinitarismus*, 119-27.

15. Leonhard Stöckel, *Leges scolae Barthphensis (1540)*, ed. Johann Samuel Klein (Rinteln, 1770); Iserloh (1967), 337.
16. Oskar Netoliczka, *Johannes Honterus' ausgewählte Schriften* (Vienna and Hermannstadt, 1898).
17. Binder (1976), 88-123.
18. Bucsay (1977), 53-69, 91-99, 104-25.
19. Ernst Benz, "Hans Ungand und die Reformation unter den Südslawen," in Ernst Benz, *Wittenberg und Byzanz* (Marburg, 1949), 141-246; Günther Stöckl, *Die deutsch-slavische Südostgrenze des Reiches im 16. Jahrhundert. Ein Beitrag zu ihrer Geschichte, dargestellt an Hand des südslavischen Reformationsschrifttums* (Wrocław, 1940).
20. Jean Bérenger, *Les "Gravamina." Remontrances des Diètes de Hongrie de 1655 à 1681* (Paris, 1973).
21. Russocki (1980); Stanisław Russocki, "The Parliamentary System in 15th-Century Central Europe," in *Poland at the 14th International Congress of Historical Sciences in San Francisco* (Wrocław, 1975), 7-21; J. Bardach, "La formation des assemblées polonaises au XVᵉ siècle et la taxation," *Ancien Pays et Assemblées d'Etats* 70 (1977): 249-96.
22. Bogucka (1993).
23. Schramm (1965), 41, 188-89.
24. Ibid., 162-63.
25. Henryk Gmiterek, "Bucer und Polen," in *Martin Bucer and Sixteenth Century Europe. Actes du colloque de Strasbourg (23-31 août 1991)*, ed. Christian Krieger and Marc Lienhard (Leiden, 1993), 547-56.
26. Lecler (1955); Tazbir (1977); K. Jordt-Jörgensen, *Ökumenische Bestrebungen unter den polnischen Protestanten bis zum Jahre 1645* (Wrocław, 1942).
27. Eduard Opalinski, "The Local Diets and Religious Tolerance in the Polish Commonwealth (1587-1648)," *Acta Poloniae Historica* 68 (1993): 43-57.
28. Z. Wojciechowski, "Les débuts du programme de 'l'exécution des lois' en Pologne au début du XVIe siècle," *Revue Historique du Droit Français et Étranger* 29 (1951): 173-92; Schramm (1965), 42-43, 174-76.
29. Schramm (1965), 177-78.
30. Joseph Lortz, *Kardinal Stanislaus Hosius. Beiträge zur Erkenntnis der Persönlichkeit und des Werkes* (Münster, 1931).
31. Schramm (1965) 5, 20, 179-80, 188.

BIBLIOGRAPHY

General
Betts, Reginald R. "The Reformation in Difficulties. Poland, Hungary and Bohemia" and "Constitutional Development and Political Thought in Eastern Europe." In *The New Cambridge Modern History*, vol. 2: *The Reformation 1520-1559*, 2d ed. G.R. Elton, 244-67 and 526-39. Cambridge, 1990.
Daniel, David P. "Ecumenicity or Orthodoxy: The Dilemma of the Protestants in the Lands of the Austrian Habsburgs." *CH* 49 (1980): 387-400.
Evans, R. J. W., and T. V. Thomas, eds. *Crown, Church and Estates. Central European Politics in the Sixteenth and Seventeenth Centuries.* London, 1991.
Hutter, Ulrich, ed. *Martin Luther und die Reformation in Ostdeutschland und Südosteuropa.* Beihefte zum Jahrbuch für Schlesische Kirchengeschichte, vol. 8. Sigmaringen, 1991.
Iserloh, Erwin. "Die Reformation in Osteuropa." In *Handbuch der Kirchengeschichte,* ed. Hubert Jedin, vol. 4: 324-41. Freiburg im Breisgau, 1967.
Krimm, Herbert, ed. *In oriente crux. Versuch einer Geschichte der reformatorischen Kirchen im Raume zwischen der Ostsee und dem Schwarzen Meer.* Stuttgart, 1963.
Lecler, Joseph. *Histoire de la Tolérance au Siècle de la Réforme.* Paris, 1955.
Pettegree, Andrew, ed. *The Early Reformation in Europe.* Cambridge, 1992.
Rhode, Gotthold. "Die Reformation in Osteuropa. Ihre Stellung in der Weltgeschichte und ihre Darstellung in den 'Weltgeschichten'." *Zeitschrift für Ostforschung* 7 (1958): 481-500.
Rhode, Gotthold. "Stände und Königtum in Polen/Litauen und Böhmen/Mähren." *Jahrbücher für Geschichte Osteuropas* 12 (1964): 221-46.
Russocki, Stanisław. "Lokale Ständeversammlungen in Ostmitteleuropa im 15.-18. Jahrhundert als Faktor der politischen Kultur." In *La Pologne au XVe Congrès International des Sciences Historiques,* 171-89. Wrocław, 1980.
Russocki, Stanisław. "Les structures politiques de l'Europe des Jagellons." *Acta Poloniae Historica* 39 (1979).
Schramm, Gottfried. "Armed Conflict in East-Central Europe: Protestant Noble Opposition and Catholic Royalist Factions, 1604-20." In Evans and Thomas (1991), 167-95.
Schramm, Gottfried. "Polen-Böhmen-Ungarn: Übernationale Gemeinsamkeiten in der politischen Kultur des späten Mittelalters und der frühen Neuzeit." *Przegląd Historyczny* 76 (1985): 417-37.
Wild, Georg. *Der Protestantismus in Ostmitteleuropa.* Leer, 1963.

Bohemia and Moravia
Bahlcke, Joachim. *Regionalismus und Staatsintegration im Widerstreit. Die Länder der Böhmischen Krone im ersten Jahrhundert der Habsburgerherrschaft (1526-1619).* Schriftenreihe des Bundesinstituts für ostdeutsche Kultur und Geschichte, vol. 3. Munich, 1994.
Bretholz, Bertold. *Neuere Geschichte Böhmens.* Vol. 1: *Der politische Kampf zwischen Ständen und Königtum unter Ferdinand I. (1525-1564) und Maximilian II. (1564-1576).* Gotha, 1920.
Brock, Peter. *The Political and Social Doctrines of the Unity of Czech Brethren in the Fifteenth and Early Sixteenth Centuries.* The Hague, 1957.

Dillon, Kenneth J. *King and Estates in the Bohemian Lands 1526-1564*. Studies presented to the International Commission for the History of Representative and Parliamentary Institutions, vol. 57. Brussels, 1976.

Eberhard, Winfried. "Bohemia, Moravia and Austria." In Petegree (1992), 23-48.

Eberhard, Winfried. "Entstehungsbedingungen für öffentliche Toleranz am Beispiel des Kuttenberger Religionsfriedens von 1485." *Communio Viatorum* 29 (1986): 129-54.

Eberhard, Winfried. "Entwicklungsphasen und Probleme der Gegenreformation und katholischen Erneuerung in Böhmen." *RQ* 84 (1989): 235-57.

Eberhard, Winfried. *Konfessionsbildung und Stände in Böhmen 1478-1530*. Veröffentlichungen des Collegium Carolinum, vol. 38. Munich and Vienna, 1981.

Eberhard, Winfried. *Monarchie und Widerstand. Zur ständischen Oppositionsbildung im Herrschaftssystem Ferdinands I. in Böhmen*. Veröffentlichungen des Collegium Carolinum, vol. 54. Munich, 1985.

Eberhard, Winfried. "Ständepolitik und Konfession." In *Bohemia Sacra*, ed. Ferdinand Seibt, 222-35. Düsseldorf, 1974.

Evans, R. J. W. *The Making of the Habsburg Monarchy 1550-1700*. Oxford, 1979.

Evans, R. J. W. *Rudolf II and his World: a Study in Intellectual History, 1576-1612*. Oxford, 1973.

Fichtner, Paula Sutter. *Ferdinand I. of Austria: the Politics of Dynasticism in the Age of Reformation*. East European Monographs, vol. 100. New York, 1982.

Gatz, Erwin, ed. *Die Bischöfe des Heiligen Römischen Reiches 1448-1648. Ein biographisches Lexikon*. Berlin, 1995.

Gindely, Anton. *Geschichte des Dreißigjährigen Krieges*. 4 vols. Prague, 1869-80.

Gindely, Anton. *Geschichte der Gegenreformation in Böhmen*. Leipzig, 1894.

Heymann, Frederick G. "The Hussite-Utraquist Church in the Fifteenth and Sixteenth Centuries." *ARG* 52 (1961): 1-26.

Heymann, Frederick G. "The Impact of Martin Luther upon Bohemia." *CEH* 1 (1968): 107-30.

Hoensch, Jörg K. *Geschichte Böhmens*. 2d ed. Munich, 1992.

Hrejsa, Ferdinand. *Česká konfesse, její vznik, podstata a dějiny*. Prague, 1912.

Hrejsa, Ferdinand. *Dějiny křestanství v Československu*. 6 vols. Prague, 1947-50.

Janáček, Josef. *Doba předbělohorská 1526-1547. České dějiny*, vol. 1, parts 1-2. Prague, 1968-84.

Kadlec, Jaroslav. *Přehled českých církevních dějin*. 2 vols. Rome, 1987.

Kalista, Zdeněk. "Die katholische Reform von Hilarius bis zum Weißen Berg." In *Bohemia Sacra*, ed. Ferdinand Seibt, 110-44. Düsseldorf, 1974.

Kroess, Alois. *Geschichte der böhmischen Provinz der Gesellschaft Jesu*. Vol. 1. Vienna, 1910.

Krofta, Kamil. "Boj o konsistoř podobojí v letech 1562-1575 a jeho historický základ." *Český Časopis Historický* 17 (1911): 28-57, 178-99, 283-303, 383-420.

Macek, Josef. *Jagellonský věk v českých zemích (1471-1526)*. 2 vols. Prague, 1992-94.

Macek, Josef. *Jean Hus et les traditions hussites (XVᵉ-XIXᵉ siècles)*. Paris, 1973.

Machilek, Franz. "Böhmen." In *Die Territorien des Reichs im Zeitalter der Reformation und Konfessionalisierung. Land und Konfession 1500-1650*. Vol. 1: *Der Südosten*, eds. Anton Schindling and Walter Ziegler, 134-52. Münster, 1989.

Molnár, Amedeo. "Aspects de la continuité de pensée dans la Réforme tchèque." *Communio Viatorum* 15 (1972): 27-50, 111-25.

Molnár, Amedeo. "Der Hussitismus als christliche Reformbewegung." In *Bohemia Sacra*, ed. Ferdinand Seibt, 92-109. Düsseldorf, 1974.

Müller, Josef T. *Geschichte der Böhmischen Brüder*. 3 vols. Herrnhut, 1922-31.

Pánek, Jaroslav. "The Opposition of the Estates in the beginnings of the Habsburg Re-Catholicization of Bohemia." In *History and Society*, eds. Jaroslav Purš and Karel Hermann, 353-62. Prague, 1985b.

Pánek, Jaroslav. "The Religious Question and the Political System of Bohemia before and after the Battle of the White Mountain." In Evans and Thomas (1991), 129-48.

Pánek, Jaroslav. "Das Ständewesen und die Gesellschaft in den Böhmischen Ländern in der Zeit vor der Schlacht auf dem Weißen Berg (1526-1620)." *Historica* 25 (1985): 73-120. [= 1985a]

Pánek, Jaroslav. *Stavovská opozice a její zápas s Habsburký 1547-1577. K politické krizi feudální třídy v předbělohorském českém státě.* Prague, 1982.

Polišenský, Josef. *Der Krieg und die Gesellschaft in Europa 1618-1648. Documenta bohemica bellum tricennale illustrantia.* Vol. 1. Prague, 1971.

Říčan, Rudolf. *Das Reich Gottes in den böhmischen Ländern. Geschichte des tschechischen Protestantismus.* Stuttgart, 1957.

Richter, Karl. "Die böhmischen Länder von 1471-1740." In *Handbuch der Geschichte der böhmischen Länder,* ed. Karl Bosl, vol. 2:97-412. Stuttgart, 1974.

Seibt, Ferdinand, ed. *Bohemia Sacra. Das Christentum in Böhmen 973-1973.* Düsseldorf, 1974.

Válka, Josef. "Moravia and the Crisis of the Estates' System in the Lands of the Bohemian Crown." In Evans and Thomas (1991), 149-57.

Zeman, Jarold K. *The Hussite Movement and the Reformation in Bohemia, Moravia and Slovakia (1350-1650): a Bibliographical Study Guide.* Ann Arbor, 1977.

Hungary

Bak, Janos M. *Königtum und Stände in Ungarn im 14.-16. Jahrhundert.* Quellen und Studien zur Geschichte des östlichen Europa, vol. 6. Wiesbaden, 1973.

Barton, Peter F. *Die Geschichte der Evangelischen in Österreich und Südostmitteleuropa.* Vol. 1: *Im Schatten der Bauernkriege, die Frühzeit der Reformation.* Studien und Texte zur Kirchengeschichte und Geschichte, vol. 2, part 10. Vienna, 1985.

Benda, Kálmán. "Habsburg Absolutism and the Resistance of the Hungarian Estates in the Sixteenth and Seventeenth Centuries." In Evans and Thomas (1991), 123-28.

Benda, Kálmán. "La Réforme en Hongrie." *Bulletin de la Société de l'Histoire du Protestantisme Français* 122 (1976): 1-53.

Binder, Ludwig. *Grundlagen und Formen der Toleranz in Siebenbürgen bis zur Mitte des 17. Jahrhunderts.* Siebenbürgisches Archiv, series 3, vol. 11. Cologne and Vienna, 1976.

Binder, Ludwig. *Die Kirche der Siebenbürger Sachsen.* Erlangen, 1982.

Bónis, Gyula. "The Hungarian Feudal Diet (13th-18th centuries)." In *Anciens pays et assemblées d'Etats,* vol. 306 (1965): 287-307.

Borbis, Johann. *Die evangelisch-lutherische Kirche Ungarns in ihrer geschichtlichen Entwicklung.* Nördlingen, 1861.

Bucsay, Mihály. *Der Protestantismus in Ungarn 1521-1978. Ungarns Reformkirchen in Geschichte und Gegenwart,* Part 1: *Im Zeitalter der Reformation, Gegenreformation und katholischen Reform.* Studien und Texte zur Kirchengeschichte und Geschichte 1/III, vol. 1 Vienna, Cologne and Graz, 1977.

Daniel, David P. *The Historiography of the Reformation in Slovakia.* Sixteenth-Century Bibliography, vol. 10. St. Louis, 1977.

Daniel, David P. "Highlights of the Lutheran Reformation in Slovakia." *Concordia Theological Quarterly* 41 (1978): 21-34.

Daniel, David P. "Hungary." In Pettegree (1992), 49-69.

Doumergue, Emile. *La Hongrie Calviniste.* Toulouse, 1912.

Evans, R. J. W. "Calvinism in East Central Europe: Hungary and Her Neighbours." In *International Calvinism, 1541-1715,* ed. Menna Prestwich, 167-96. Oxford, 1985.

Göllnerová, A. "Počátky reformace v Banskí Bystrici." *Bratislava* 4 (1930): 580-612.

Lencz, Géza. *Der Aufstand Bocskays und der Wiener Frieden.* Debrecen, 1917.

Macartney, Carlile A. *Hungary: a Short History.* Edinburgh, 1962.

Molnár, Andrea. *Fürst Stefan Bocskay als Staatsmann und Persönlichkeit im Spiegel seiner Briefe 1589-1606.* Studia Hungarica, vol. 23. Munich 1983.

Nagy, Barnabás. "Geschichte und Bedeutung des Zweiten Helvetischen Bekenntnisses in den osteuropäischen Ländern." In *Glauben und Bekennen. Vierhundert Jahre Confessio Helvetica Posterior. Beiträge zu ihrer Geschichte und Theologie,* ed. J. Staedtke, 109-204. Zurich, 1966.

Pindor, Josef. *Die evangelische Kirche Kroatiens und Slavoniens in Vergangenheit und Gegenwart.* Essen, 1902.

Pokoly, József. *Az erdélyi református egyház története (1556-1880).* 5 vols. Budapest, 1904-5.

Ravasz, László, Révész, Imre and Kováts, János István. *Hungarian Protestantism.* Budapest, 1927.

Reinerth, Karl. *Die Reformation der siebenbürgisch-sächsischen Kirche.* Schriften des Vereins für Reformationsgeschichte, vol. 173. Gütersloh, 1956.

Révész, Imre. *History of the Hungarian Reformed Church.* Washington, D.C., 1956.

Rhode, Gotthold. "Ungarn vom Ende der Verbindung mit Polen bis zum Ende der Türkenherrschaft (1444-1699)." In *Handbuch der europäischen Geschichte,* ed. Theodor Schieder, vol. 3:1061-1117. Stuttgart, 1971.

Roth, Erich. *Die Reformation in Siebenbürgen. Ihr Verhältnis zu Wittenberg und der Schweiz.* Siebenbürgisches Archiv, 2-4. 2 vols. Cologne and Graz, 1962-64.

Sinor, Denis. *History of Hungary.* London, 1959.

Stökl, Günther. "Religiös-soziale Bewegungen in der Geschichte Ost- und Südosteuropas." *Ostdeutsche Wissenschaft* 2 (1955): 257-75.

Tóth, William. "Highlights of the Hungarian Reformation." *CH* 9 (1940): 141-56.

Tóth, William. "Luther's Frontier in Hungary." In *Reformation Studies. Essays in Honor of Roland H. Bainton,* ed. F. H. Littel, 75-91. Richmond, Va., 1962.

Tóth, William. "Stephen Kis of Szeged, Hungarian Reformer." *ARG* 44 (1953): 86-103.

Poland

Bardach, Juliusz. *Historia państwa i prawa Polski.* 2d ed. Warsaw, 1966.

Bogucka, Maria. "Die Wirkungen der Reformation in Danzig." *Zeitschrift für Ostforschung* 42 (1993): 195-206.

Fedorowicz, Jan K., ed. *A Republic of Nobles. Studies in Polish History to 1864.* Cambridge, 1982.

Gmiterek, Henryk. *Bracia Czescy a Kalwini w Rzeczypospolitej, połowa XVI - połowa XVII wieku.* Lublin, 1987.

Hoensch, Jörg K. *Geschichte Polens.* 2d ed. Stuttgart, 1990.

Maczak, Antoni. "Confessions, Freedoms and the Unity of Poland-Lithuania." In Evans and Thomas (1991), 269-86.

Olesch, Rainer and Rothe, Hans, eds. *Fragen der polnischen Kultur im 16. Jahrhundert.* Gießen, 1980.

Rhode, Gotthold. *Geschichte Polens.* 3d ed. Darmstadt, 1980.

Rhode, Gotthold. "Polen-Litauen vom Ende der Vergindung mit Ungarn bis zum Ende der Vasas (1444-1669)." In *Handbuch der europäischen Geschichte,* ed. Theodor Schieder, vol. 3:1006-60. Stuttgart, 1971.

Schramm, Gottfried. *Der polnische Adel und die Reformation 1548-1607.* VIEG, vol. 36. Wiesbaden, 1965.

Skwarczyński, Paweł. "Poland and Lithuania." In *The New Cambridge Modern History.* Vol. 3: *Counterreformation,* ed. R.B. Wernham, 377-403. Cambridge, 1960 [2nd ed. 1990].

Stasiewski, Bernhard. *Reformation und Gegenreformation in Polen: Neue Forschungsergebnisse.* Münster, 1960.

Tazbir, Janusz. *Geschichte der polnischen Toleranz.* Warsaw, 1977.

Topolski, Jerzy. *Kirchengeschichte Polens.* Warsaw, 1985.

Völker, Karl. *Kirchengeschichte Polens.* Grundriß der slawischen Philologie und Kulturgeschichte, vol. 7. Berlin and Leipzig, 1930.

Zeeden, Ernst W. "Calvins Einlenken auf die Reformation in Polen-Litauen." In *Syntagma Friburgense. Historische Studien Hermann Aubin zum 70. Geburtstag dargebracht,* 323-59. Lindau and Constance, 1957.

NEW PATTERNS OF CHRISTIAN LIFE

Hans-Christoph Rublack
(Eberhard-Karls-Universität Tübingen)

The lives of all Europeans—except for the Jewish minority and the European Muslims living under Ottoman rule—were Christian in the sense that life's meaning and stages were more or less deeply touched by Christian cosmological ideas and were judged by Christian ethical standards. There were nonetheless significant varieties of Christianity not only in thought but also in life. In the pre-Reformation era such differences existed not only among socio-political strata (estates) but also between laity and clergy, higher and lower clergy, secular as well as regular. These differences reflected varying intensities and styles of Christianized social life, all of which had formed well before 1400. The Reformation surely added new patterns, though it remains an open question whether 'new' should be understood in terms of negations or of modifications of traditional ways of life. Moreover, despite the all-embracing connotation of the term 'Christian,' ecclesiastical norms and practices and the main lines of religious life can be correlated to large social and economic factors. There nonetheless did appear some new patterns, such as the way of life the Protestant reformers called 'epicurean'[1] or 'atheist', by which term they meant a worldview which emphasized the experience of contingency and denigrated God's action in this world.[2]

1. PERCEPTIONS OF LIFE

Our life here in this time is nothing but sorrows, anxiety and dearth, one suffering follows the other. Even if we have many pleasures, we have all the more heartache. Take youth, what else is it but permanent distress and anguish. Youth is subject to toil, and a series of foolish desires. Old age is nothing but permanent illness, dislike and hatred of life, one sickness on top of another. There is much trouble. If you are rich, you cannot eat one bite in peace, if powerful and the ruler of many subjects, you have a lot to fear. The poor man knows nothing but suffering and misery.[3]

Johann Jakob Wick, a minister at Zurich, lived almost the entire sixteenth century. He was born in 1522, the year Zurich's reformation
began, and died in 1588.[4] He is known for his collection of broad-
sheets, pamphlets, and the news he recorded during the latter part of
his life. As funneled through Zurich, a major Protestant center of information, local, regional, and international news focused on miraculous and portentous celestial and climatic events, murders and fatal accidents. Some events reflected human sinfulness, some the devil's
work, and some God's intervention in this world. Many marvels,
Wick commented, displayed how God's wrath was calling men to
change their sinful lives and announcing the imminent end of this
world. This traditional outlook, which formed long before the wave of
pessimism and melancholy we associate with the seventeenth century,
perceived the world as standing between God's punishment of sin and
the Devil's wickedness, between the Fall and the Last Judgment, running right down to its end. Such pious commonplaces were encouraged by dearth and the fragility of life caused by catastrophes, be they
hunger and indebtedness or violence and death, against which humans
were helpless.

The meaning lent to everyday life by this worldview differed radically from the modern, secularised understanding of the world. Life in
this world continued after the rupture of death in a world beyond,
where there was a real second life of different quality, everlasting in
heaven, fullfilled, without any distress, full of harmony and happiness,
and culminating in the vision of God.

This did not mean that earthly life did not resonate to sacral power.
God and the Devil were held to be an omnipresent entities who granted
blessings or inflicted harm. God acted in storm, hail, and lightning,
punishing unrepentant sinners, while the Devil seduced women and
men to evil, most poignantly by transforming women to witches.
Witchcraft and harmful magic were believed to cause real damage. Because the Protestant Reformation abolished sacramentals and deprived
the clergy of their aura of sacral power, Protestant laymen seem to
have become even more inclined—though this point cannot be
proven—to resort to magic for protection against the many agents that
threatened life. Magic healing, soothsaying, prognostications were
available in or near every village.[5] In this world the religious supernatural was tangible and immanent rather than intangible and transcendent.[6] The century-long campaign by Protestant ministers—replicated with modifications by the Catholic priests—against superstitious

uses of magic had little success among the peasants. The pastors were often unaware that the peasants held these 'superstitions' to be compatible with Christian religion, or supplementary to, if not derived from, liturgical usage.

It is worthwhile to contrast this more popular Christian pattern of life with the image of life and living which the Protestant ministers tried to implant in the minds of their congregations. In general terms, preachers saw life as characterized by misery, suffering, instability, harm, change and unhappiness. Its beginning already signified its end: 'As soon as a human being begins to live, he already starts to die', said one Lutheran minister in typically late medieval fashion.[7] Life meant above all survival, beginning with birth—the first confrontation with mortality—and in the ministers' view the best one could hope for was a quiet end, that death would come as sleep. True life began thereafter with the resurrection of the body at the second coming of Christ. Over against this second life, the first appeared highly unstable. A more positive view of the matter was that life is a pilgrimage, a metaphor for moving and struggling through this vale of tears to a desired end, through death to life eternal. Labour, associated with sweat and trouble, was required in this world, but ultimate success depended on God's blessing. The farmers' need for His blessing took its rhythm from the seasons, for the harvest depended on God's help in the form of good weather. Wealth could quickly turn to poverty—more enduring than wealth—and property was fragile, a gift of God to be administered for His purposes, sustenance and charity. It was easy for ministers to back up their teaching with examples from real life: crises, endangered food production, sudden deaths, dying babies; dying children were all frequently cited, as were catastrophes caused by weather. Theologically all this misfortune was said to be caused by sin, a condition deriving both from individual misdeeds and more importantly from Original Sin. Only faith in God and Christ relieved this existential condition, true faith also demanded obedience to God's commands. So the ministers expounded God's law, as contained in the Decalogue, in their sermons and in catechism lessons. At the same time, however, they taught that only those could live up to this law who were saved by grace. Here, in the antithesis between God's wrath and God's grace, formed the gap between the faith of the Protestant elite and the common people's religion. The common man would believe, as one of them stated, that 'eternal God derives his name from goodness in that He is a good and pious God', to which another might add: 'God is a good man with whom one can live more harmoniously than with the parsons'.[8] Lutheran ministers, by contrast, would stress that God's grace was His gift only, unwarranted by human achievement or disposition. It had to be received in true faith in God's Word, granted freely by God in Christ, who had justified sinners by His crucifixion and—some true Lutherans would add—His continuous and ubiquitous presence in his humanity.[9] Under these conditions, this work of God would fullfill the law, and the fruit would be love of neighbor. Yet, even in the state of being simultaneously justified and a sinner, man would still act contrary to God's law. The only escape from the world, therefore, was to accept its order as God's order and to recognize His continual agency in it. This basically meant to accept social stability without upward mobility and without avarice and to avoid enrichment at the cost of others, the sum total of social wealth being rather inflexible. It also meant contentment with what God granted and the giving of assistance to one's neighbour. Such were the basic practical teachings of the Lutheran clergy.

Compared to the Lutherans, Calvinist reformers earned a reputation for being at once more rigid in discipline and more open to the social demands of Christian life. Though they agreed with Lutheran theologians on most doctrinal points and made common polemical front against the Roman church, the Calvinists also stressed some elements of the Protestant faith and—what seems to be more important—developed a zeal for their implementation. Their God was a Lord who had decreed that some were regenerate, others reprobate, and whom Christians were bound to honour by the conduct of their lives. Some Calvinists—though not Calvin—therefore included ecclesiastical discipline as an essential mark of the church (*nota ecclesiae*)[10] and made sanctification, as distinct from justification, an essential. To them, regenerate life made itself manifest in godliness of behaviour and self-discipline, through which not only was life controlled, but God's special providence displayed the signs of His election.[11] Although the pursuit of Protestant piety based on an internalized style of life reached a high point in seventeenth-century England, its roots lie in the preceding age. Its practitioners tended to convert an 'inscrutable, mysterious God' into a 'father figure'.[12] The obverse of this individual piety was a Reformed church discipline, institutionalized in the localized congregations under the regime of a Geneva-type consistory, a body of elected or coopted magistrates and clergy who met regularly to observe and reprimand deviant behavior. Its aim was to keep the congregation pure for the Lord's Supper. Though to be holy in the Calvinist sense never meant to be able to resist sin, some progress was possible towards this goal. Thus, the Reformed churches of the sixteenth and seventeenth centuries lived what might seem a paradox, promoting individualism within a religious culture shaped by collective moral discipline.

Christians of this era, whether Catholic or Protestant, saw in the cosmos not nature to be admired or used for human purposes, but a structured, sacred, and hence moral, order. Participation in the sacral order came either through the sacraments (Catholic) or through believing in God's Word alone (Protestant), which gave access to God's grace, without which—with or without good works—man's sinful state could not be overcome. Grace was indispensable to the possibility of a second life in heaven, but it was also indispensable to living morally in this world in obedience to God's Decaloque as interpreted by the clergy. Though recognizing that neither the power of God nor that of the Devil, His cooperative antagonist, was bound by the church's means, official religion attempted to monopolize the basic attitudes toward this world and the next.

The experiences of laymen and -women might conform to, or deviate from, these clerical teachings. The laity regarded the clergy as paid administrators of the sacred, whose intervention became necessary in cases of extreme danger, such as storms and plagues. In such instances they would pray, or even better ring the weather bell, to appeal to God for help. If they had sufficient food, they did not deem it necessary to pray, as the peasant suggested to a Protestant pastor: 'Dear children, you need not learn how to pray, as you have sufficient food without it, let those say prayers who have no bread to live on'.[13] According to the same pastor, the Tübingen preacher Jakob Heerbrand, a popular saying in this society of scarcity and survival, where 'to have God, and sufficient' was an ultimate concern, identified its basic desires as a 'quiet conscience, peace, health, food, and what we need in this temporal and the yonder eternal life'.[14]

2. FRAMEWORKS: CHANGES IN ECCLESIASTICAL INSTITUTIONS

In the towns, especially, and less so in the countryside, Protestantism radically simplified the plural ecclesiastical structures of the later Mid-

dle Ages by making the parish in its traditional form into the sole necessary unit of Christian life. This step removed the possibility for
changing one's religious life by looking beyond the local community,
and it made all Christian life the province of the local pastor. Outside
the local church there was literally no religious life: no communities or
convents, no baptism, confession, wedding, or burial. This concentration could intensify dependence on the local pastor, but it could also
mean an intensification of discipline and religious life, exemplified by
the Reformed churches. Its most general meaning, however, was a reduction of the flexibility and the variety of ways of life recognized as
Christian and of their flexibility. This intensified localization of religious life went hand-in-hand with a simplification of the ecclesiastical
hierarchy and a stabilization of pastoral clergy within the localities.
The clergy were required, and did, reside in their parishes, and neither
the cure of souls nor lay patronage was disturbed by monastic intrusions. Perhaps even more important was the clergy's apparent loss of
its sacral character, which turned them into officeholders who
preached God's Word and administered the sacraments in the vernacular language. As the medieval system of benefices was largely retained,
and the recruitment of pastors was limited to burghers who in practice
were closely related to the administrative elite, the basis of a pastor's
status shifted from sacral power to social distance within the local
communities, where the pastor was nonetheless a householder, just like
his parishioners. The derivation of clerical income from the parishes
supplied potential for a range of conflicts between pastor and parish
commune, which were overlain by admonitions to fulfill God's law.[15]
What Protestant laymen expected was a holy message of consolation
for their troubled lives and a Lord's Supper that confirmed their communal bonds and social value system. They paid the pastor for his
services and tended to reject demands that interfered with their lives.
They also expected their pastor to conduct the services accompanying
the life cycle—baptism, wedding, and burial—whereby he administered the sacred economy and brought sacral power into their world.[16]
Those ministers who deviated from lay expectations of them as holy
servants and tried to be ministers of God's law independent of lay
needs, met with resistance, indifference, or enmity. Because the villagers, the majority of common folk, held the honorable pastor to be a
godly man, their hostility was a sin that kept them from confession and
communion.[17]
    Out of this localized religious structure, which partly reduced and

partly refashioned traditional religious life, arose the characteristic patterns of religious life in Protestant churches. With the number of feast days reduced, saints' cults and relics abolished, and pilgrimages and processions abandoned, the Sunday service centred on preaching and Communion. Sunday routine was distinguished from daily work by going to church and by some form of rest, then gathering in taverns, or visiting distant relatives, maybe fairs, even dancing, gambling, and drinking. Weekday services, by contrast, were attended only by some of those too young or too old to work. The Sabbath's sacral character was reduced to attendance at the service and reduced there by the chatting and snoozing that were common behavior in all confessions. What Protestant peasants and citizens accepted was the major change, a shift of the centre of the service from the Eucharist to preaching. Pastors complained that the saying of laymen 'we have been to the sermon' was often taken literally, as laymen appeared just before the sermon and left, as if a fire had broken out, after it ended.[18] Their actions suggest an acceptance of the service's new core, and so did the children's 'playing church': 'One of them steps forward, takes a book, and preaches to the others'.[19] Protestant services always included some elements of lay participation. The congregation sang at least one hymn and, in village churches that lacked cantors, two or three, singing them, at least in the sixteenth century, by rote, since they could not read.[20] The hymns were prescribed either by the church ordinances or by the pastors.

   Protestant religion's cognitive turn becomes clearer in catechetical instruction. Down to the eighteenth century, the youths soon forgot what they had learned,[21] since they had not learned it 'by heart', and religious ignorance remained common among Protestant villagers and urban lower classes.[22] In the cities, where male literacy was becoming more common, religious books were more popular, ranging from hymnals and prayerbooks through partial or whole Bibles to devotional tracts and works.[23] Another indication of increasing religious reading are the printed funeral sermons, which spread from the upper class down into the middle class.[24] An upper-class woman might read through the Bible seven times during her lifetime, apart from praying and singing hymns, 'and this was her best treasure and comfort'.[25] If laymen for whatever reasons decided not to attend church, they might claim to have read a spiritual lesson instead, insinuating that they had done nothing much different from the pastor preparing his sermon. Protestant pastors certainly became more literate during the sixteenth century, because a university training in theology, and not just literacy, was required for acceptance into the clergy.[26] From the mid-sixteenth century on, pastors asked for studies to be installed in the parsonages, another mark which set them off from the laity.

Reform of the Catholic clergy, too, led to increased social distance from the laity, though in different ways than among the Protestants, because Catholic reforms reaffirmed the priest's sacral character. Although clerical concubinage had been sharply criticized in the fifteenth and sixteenth centuries, in practice having a wife was often thought to be indispensable to a rural clerical household. Although initially the priests and the villagers probably did not differ mentally more than burghers and villagers did, the clergy's increasingly elaborate training, their more missionary understanding of their office, and closer supervisions through visitations enhanced the aura of clerical holiness. The distance created by this aura was characteristically symbolized by the grill that separated penitent from priest during confession. Like their Protestant colleagues, priests were asked to stay out of taverns, which excluded them from much local communication. The Latin language was retained for the Mass, and hosts for the Eucharist, which laymen (with certain exceptions) continued to receive in one kind only. The rituals met the laity's chief expectation, though priests also preached and taught the catechism. As in Protestant lands, the parish was the essential forum of Catholic reform,[27] though it was but the lowest tier of an elaborate and multi-layered institutional hierarchy. At the top stood the Roman Curia and the pope, who had finally secured the leadership of ecclesiastical reform during the Council of Trent's final session in 1562-63. The next subordinate level, the episcopacy, retained its essential magisterial office, which it reinforced by means of visitations.

Unlike the Protestant churches, the Roman Catholic church did not simplify its structure. Indeed, it added new institutions, such as the Society of Jesus with its lay sodalities and female congregations such as the Ursulines.[28] And it reinvigorated old ones, such as the Franciscans, which produced a new offshoot in the Capuchins. Moreover, Catholic parish life was not closed but demonstratively mobile, moving the sacred out into public space by means of processions or moving toward sacred places on pilgrimage. Control of local religious life, often—as in Bavaria—initiated by intensifying state bureaucracy, was balanced by spontaneous devotion and by the new orders' extraordinary missionary efforts,[29] which successfully re-directed popular religion toward sacramental life in the local churches. The focal point of this new piety was Christ crucified as presented in the Eucharist sacrament, ranking higher than saints.

It seems too easy to feature the Catholic reform as a regeneration, because this requires the biased assumption that the late medieval church was dying. The Roman church's vitality lay in its mobilizing dynamics and its missionary expansion, even to the new worlds, which clashed with the Protestant reduction of the church to its local foundations. The confessions nonetheless possessed some common traits in their ritual lives, their increased distance between clergy and laity, and the weight they placed on relatively new media communication—sermons and books.

3. PRACTICES OF CHRISTIAN LIFE

The new Protestant churches' continuity with traditional Christian religion was most obvious in their rites of passage, especially baptism and burial. A newborn was to be baptised as soon as possible in order to protect it from the Devil's assaults, and its mother received a special blessing, the rite of 'churching', to guard her from similar attacks. Churching brought the new mother alone to the church forty days after the birth. Although initially, several Lutheran church ordinances forbade the practice, and the Reformed churches abolished it altogether, later it regained popularity. Lutheran ministers then offered non-theological reasons for the rite's reinstatement, noting that women in this blessed state of giving birth should give thanks to God and should be relieved both from hard work and their husbands' sexual desires. Eventually, some Lutherans came to believe that these needs did not justify the rite of churching, which they argued should be suppressed.[30].

More acceptable to Protestant lay folk was the idea of death as a period of sleep. Following Luther, they came to speak of death in these terms: he or she fell peacefully asleep. Various rites aimed to prevent the return of the deceased were traditional part of burials, which culminated in the official Lutheran prescription of a graveside sermon and the popular practice of a post-burial meal, at which the community reaffirmed its own survival. Yet, lay people in villages kept their old burial customs, such as opening a window for the soul to escape or setting down the coffin on the threshold three times. When reprimanded by the pastor for honouring such customs, they replied that this had been done by their ancestors as well. The funeral sermon was often turned into praise for the deceased's life, or at least made the best of it, making special note of the final days, hours, minutes. In this way the medieval 'art of dying' (*ars moriendi*) was adapted by Protestant laymen and ministers.

Weddings became even more open to social influence, once the Protestant theologians had abolished the sacramental character of marriage. They therefore removed legitimacy from the private act—the couple's vows to one another—which the canon law had held to constitute, when followed by consummation, a valid marriage. The Council of Trent held that a fully legal marriage required in addition publicity, a public ceremony before a priest. Moving more radically in the same direction, the Protestant clergy and authorities fought a long battle against traditional 'clandestine' marriages and required the parent's consent to their children's decision. This requirement favored secure property transfers in the interest of propertied burghers and peasants. By enforcing a public proclamation of the forthcoming marriage and the going to church, the Protestant wedding was in effect re-sacralized. Again, social and ecclesiastical influences mixed to frame an important stage in life.

The annual cycle, like the life cycle, was accentuated by religious highlights, which could very well differ from the contents of the sermons.[31] Thus, the twelve nights after Christmas were a favorite time for prognostications, while Good Friday and Easter Sunday were marked by special popular responses. Even attending communion could be part of a cycle, for it was regular connected to the beginning or end of labour in the fields.[32]

Most persistent, despite almost continuous Protestant preaching against them, were the magical practices that the clergy called 'superstitions'. One might argue that the transfer of salvation to God's grace in Christ alone, denying to human effort any potential for achieving grace, plus the suppression of sacramentals, created among lay Protestants a need for specific means to meet special needs. Pastors, indeed, reported a growth and persistence of such magical practices during the sixteenth and subsequent centuries. Most common were magic safeguards against illness of children and cattle, dangers to pregnant and birthing women, and death. Laymen assimilated Protestant means to the task of making life less exposed to danger. They used God's words, as employed in liturgy, such as 'In the name of the Father, the Son, and the Holy Ghost'. They defended this practice with the argument that 'as God's word owned wonderful power, to convert the souls, and to bend the hearts of human beings, so it may help as well in other accidents'.[33] Popular attachment to the sacramental character of holy communion is revealed in such customs as not walking barefoot for three days following the reception of communion, or, even more telling, refusing to spit on the day following—which cannot be explained except by a belief in transubstantiation. The threshold of the church building was considered sacred, so that earth removed from alongside it helped against tooth-ache, and the keys to the church were employed to heal illness of cattle. Some practices were purely local, others widespread, and all were, of course, kept secret from the pastors. They persisted through formulae, repeated literally and by heart with a power of recall that surprised pastors, who were frustrated by popular inability to remember the catechism, and through persons whose names were known to everyone except the authorities.[34]

The pattern of Christian life in a Lutheran village around 1600 cannot be considered de-sacralized. The decisive moments of changes in life were sanctified by the local pastor in rituals which took place in the selfsame church where more or less everybody gathered once a week to hear the sermon. Hearing sermons, considered a normal part of village life, was done by a congregation ranged in pews commensurate with 'honour,' that is, social standing. Communion was taken once or twice a year on dates tied to the harvest cycle. The pastor tended to be considered as agent of the sacred, not—as he understood his own office— as a teacher or as enforcer of God's law. Lay people understood the division of roles: they had to work and had no time left to pray.

Only at the end of the early modern era did there appear in the villages a form known earlier in some noble and patrician families, the household church (*Hauskirche*), in which the father, substituting for the pastor, questioned children and servants about sermons and catechism and led the hymns and prayers. This form of piety, which Luther had urged for catechetical instruction, possibly became a habit at pious courts and houses of noblemen during the following century. An incident in Ulm reveals its existence among patricians, but also its use to fend off the pastors' claim to examine every child's knowledge of catechism in public.[35] Because life was fraught with accidents unforeseeable and potentially catastrophic, at best bringing about misery, the villagers expected the pastor to comfort them with the highest authority—God's Word. To guard against more personal dangers they helped themselves by magical means. The policing of morals in the villages was controlled by the commune according to its notion of what was honourable. In the Lutheran cities, though as yet little is known about piety in detail, there would be more devotional books, and the upper middle class would make use of prayer books, especially for purposes of consolation.[36] The pastors would also be of urban origin and therefore more at home among their congregations.[37]

We know more details about Reformed villages.[38] After ca. 250 years of preaching, a Bernese village pastor could echo Calvin's mid-sixteenth century assessment, 'we see that religion is collapsing in the whole Christian world' (*videmus statum religionis in toto orbe christiano fere collapsum*).[39] The villagers, he complained, did not attend sermons, and 'even if they do occasionally turn up, they don't listen; if they listen, they don't understand it; if they understand something, they don't believe it; if they believe it, they don't respect or love it; and when they love it, they are not obedient, they do not live up to it, they do not act accordingly'.[40] The Reformed church was characterized by its discipline, and the prosecution of irreverence for God's law depended on the pastor's zeal as well as communal interest. Usually pastors became more weary of such work, the longer they stayed in office. Though their tale—at least in villages—is evidently no success story, it must be rated as a remarkable long-term effort, at least in contrast to Lutheran village life. There was some social discipline, and some successes were registered during hard times. Otherwise—as we know from Zurich's villages—the religious life of Reformed villagers 'was restricted to the pedantic and precise execution of ritual actions':[41] morning and noon prayers, in the evening occasional reading of the Bible or devotional tracts, and on Sundays regular attendance at church. If pastors and theologians considered this as below the minimum, historians are free to regard it as average. There was obviously more zeal, and more success, in Reformed urban congregations, where discipline did improve among the middle class.

It is, moreover, worth noting that Reformed moral discipline originated from an intention to achieve a purer congregation at the Lord's Supper, and that its model, the Genevan consistory, devoted itself primarily not to punishment but to reconciliation. The ideal community, whether household or congregation, was one of peace and harmony.[42] The subject of 'social discipline' has recently caught historians' attention and has become the object of major local and comparative research projects,[43] and its content has become clear. Support by local elites granted the efforts some success, as did the absolutist state's parallel prosecution of crime,[44] which was equally based on the model of classifying deviant behaviour according to the Decalogue. Yet, the long-term civilizing effects of Christian social discipline have been called into question by quantitative studies, which, in the case of the Bernese villages, indicate that the final outcome was not discipline but secularization. Even if this sincere, though not heroic, effort to repress human sins paved the way toward modernity, it certainly did not lead to individualism or to a refinement of human feelings. It therefore seems worthwhile to consider whether those who were discriminated against by orthodox Protestant ministers as subversive 'epicureans', blamed for their libertine consciousness, their insistence on happiness and their right human innerwordliness, should not equally be ranged among the forerunners of modern life styles. As an eighteenth-century Bernese village pastor confirmed, the Reformed reformation failed in its attempt to transfer religious knowledge in any more than a purely mechanical way. Christian life in these villages was not impregnated by religious literacy.

In Roman Catholic villages the reforms did not change the expectations of villagers, which were rather similar to Protestant ones, chiefly comfort and blessing. But the means employed remained sacramental, the elevation at Mass drew the crowd into church, and the people asked the priest for assurance of a holy death. Sacramentals, such as holy water, were employed to cure illness and prevent harm, processions continued to be held in villages and in the fields, and people continued to go on pilgrimage. Though rural confraternities appear first in the sixteenth century, they began to flourish only in the seventeenth. Catechetical instruction did not become popular, and the people continued to expect their priest to act for them, mediating between the supernatural world and their own.[45] The villagers resisted priests who tried to change their code of behaviour, resorting even to contesting his means of income. Based on a recent study of the diocese of Speyer, it seems that Catholic villages remained most traditional and resistent to change.[46]

Cities were far more diversified and complex than villages. Not only were there many types of cities—large and small, artisan or patrician ruled and rural towns, free, imperial, or territorial ones—but they differed in confessional status and development. At Augsburg, where Catholics had declined to a minority, they gained new strength from the Jesuit mission and the Fugger family's influence.[47] At Münster

Protestants and Catholics lived peacefully together, as in other episcopal cities, Würzburg and Bamberg, until the end of the sixteenth century, when Counterreformation measures began to drive them apart.[48]
At Lyon the Reformed Protestants ruled for one year,[49] while in Paris
the Protestant minority was slaughtered in 1572.[50] In Protestant Ulm a
Catholic minority lived relatively peacefully,[51] and so, until the end of
the sixteenth century did a Protestant minority in the now Catholic city
of Constance, which was deprived of its status as imperial city but restored as an episcopal see.[52] Catholic cities were rich in churches, convents of religious orders, and confraternities, especially where the Jesuits and Capuchins founded Marian confraternities, though the revival
of other orders came later, after 1600. The burghers had many religious opportunities outside their own parishes for hearing sermons,
participating in processions, confessing their sins, attending perform-
ances of Jesuit plays, and reading for private devotion.

The experience of conversion has been studied only for one direction, from the Protestant to the Catholic faith.[53] Conversion presup-
poses a consciousness of confessional identity, which was theologically
shaped by learned texts and socially implemented by the clear separation of groups of families. In view of the fact that conversion was not
only an individual's decision but also a collective movement,[54] the phenomenon needs to be studied in various contexts, along with the
growth of confessional social identity, which had by no means reached
its climax by 1600.[55]

By the end of the Reformation century, the patterns of Christian life
were still developing into the shapes they would retain for the next century or two. The age of confessional churches has been rightly described as one in which the Christian religion had an impact comparable to those of political and social forces. But since the results of
Protestant reformation and Catholic reform measures from above varied, they cannot easily be summed up, and moreover by 1600 they still
operated on a very local level. Local communities shaped their own
ways of life, and supervision from above by no means always produced
the desired result. Furthermore, they depended for effect very much on
the local pastor or priest or on the clergy as a body or the religious orders. The most important aspect remains the flexibility and plurality
of patterns.

NOTES

1. Oberman (1992), 103.
2. Haag (1992), 77-80; Rublack (1988), 150.
3. Sermon by Johann Jakob Wick, 11-12 February 1545, Zürich, Zentralbibliothek, Ms. D 79, 59v, quoted by Senn (1976), 259: "Unser läben hie in diesem zyt ist nüt anderist den iamer angst und not, ein lyden über das ander. Hand wir schon vil fröuden, so hand wir dester meer herzleyden. Nemglich die iuget, was ist sy anderist dan ein stäts gramen und grymen. Die Iuget ist der rûoten der arbeyten, und den torrechtigen begerden ergen. Das alter ist nüt anders dan ein stete krankheyt, übel mögende und verdruz des läbens, da kumpt ein krankheyt über die ander. Da ist vil sorgen. Der rych darff kein rüwigen mumpfel essen, wer gwaltig ist und über vil herschet der mûoß auch vil fürchten. Der arm hat nütt den lyden und iamer."
4. Senn (1975); Weber (1972)
5. See Thomas (1978), 207ff., for a classic account.
6. Scribner, "Cosmic Order," in Scribner, (1987), 1-16.
7. Rublack (1993), 365.
8. Quoted in Rublack (1992a), 146 note 22, 143 note 10.
9. Baur (1992).
10. Neuser (1980), 257.
11. Greyerz (1990).
12. Greyerz (1993), 282.
13. "Liebe Kinder / ihr doerffet nicht lernen beten / habt ohn das gnug zu essen: lasset die beten / die kein brot haben." Moses Pflacher, *Postill*, 509, quoted in Rublack (1992a), 363.
14. Jakob Heerbrand, *Herbst vnnd Ernst Predig...* Tübingen 1584, quoted in Rublack (1992a), 357.
15. Scribner (1991); Rublack (1989).
16. Scribner, "Cosmic Order," in Scribner (1987).
17. Bossy (1975).
18. Graff (1937) vol. 1:72, and 177 note 5.
19. Gregor Strigenitz, *Ieremias vocatus ...* Leipzig 1601, 11, as quoted in Rublack (1992b), 163 note 123.
20. Graff (1937), vol. 1:255f.
21. Strauss (1978); for an exceptional case of success, see Kittelson (1982) and (1985).
22. Thomas (1978), 189-97.
23. Weyrauch (1985); figures in Hartmut Lehmann (1980).
24. Moore (1991).
25. Ibid., 291, from the funeral sermon for Blandina Borg (1615-57).
26. Vogler (1981).

27. Bossy (1970).
28. Conrad (1991).
29. Chatellier (1989).
30. On churching and burial customs, see Scribner (1990).
31. Scribner, "Cosmic Order," and "Ritual," in Scribner (1987).
32. Rublack (1993).
33. Johann Ludwig Hartmann, *Greuel des Segensprechens* (Nuremberg, 1680), 247f.
34. Rublack, "Luthertum und Aberglaube," forthcoming in Bob Scribner and R. Po-chia Hsia, eds., *Problems of Historical Anthropology* (Wiesbaden 1995); Scribner (1990); Thomas (1978).
35. Hagenmaier (1989), 135 note 330. See also Veit (1992).
36. Vogler (1992a) and (1992b).
37. Lehmann (1984).
38. Schmidt (1993).
39. Oberman (1992), 102.
40. Schmidt (1993), 209.
41. Schär (1985) 163.
42. Kingdon, "Calvinist Discipline," in Guggisberg and Krodel (1993), 665-79.
43. Schilling (1983), (1989), (1994).
44. Schnabel-Schüle (1994).
45. Beck (1988); Lang (1982).
46. Forster (1992); Becker (1989).
47. Warmbrunn (1983).
48. Hsia (1984).
49. Davis (1965).
50. Diefendorf (1991).
51. Lang (1977).
52. Zimmermann (1994).
53. Luria (1993).
54. For example, the ca. 900 persons converted in Augsburg between 1559 and 1560 through Peter Canisius' preaching. Warmbrunn (1983), 240.
55. François (1991).

BIBLIOGRAPHY

Alldridge, Nick. "Loyalty and Identity in Chester Parishes 1540-1640." In *Parish, Church, and People. Local Studies in Lay Religion 1350-1750*, ed. Susan J. Wright, 85-124. London, Melbourne, Auckland, and Johannesburg, 1988.

Baur, Jörg. "Lutherische Christologie." In Rublack (1992a), 83-124.

Beck, Rainer. "Der Pfarrer und das Dorf. Konformismus und Eigensinn im katholischen Bayern des 17./18. Jahrhunderts." In *Armut, Liebe, Ehre. Studien zur historischen Kulturforschung*, ed. Richard van Dülmen, 107-34. Frankfurt am Main, 1988.

Becker, Thomas Paul. *Konfessionalisierung in Kurköln. Untersuchungen zur Durchsetzung der katholischen Reform in den Dekanaten Ahrgau und Bonn anhand von Visitationsprotokollen 1583-1761*. Veröffentlichungen des Stadtarchivs Bonn, vol. 43. Bonn, 1989.

Bossy, John. *Christianity in the West 1400-1700*. Oxford, 1987.

Bossy, John. "The Counter-Reformation and the People of Catholic Europe." *PaP* 47 (1970): 51-70.

Bossy, John. "Godparenthood: the Fortunes of a Social Institution in Early Modern Christianity." In *Religion and Society in Early Modern Europe*, ed. Kaspar von Greyerz, 194-201. London, 1984.

Bossy, John. "The Social History of Confession in the Age of the Reformation." *TRS*, 5th series, (1975): 21-38.

Brecht, Martin. "Lutherische Kirchenzucht bis in die Anfänge des 17. Jahrhunderts im Spannungsfeld von Pfarramt und Gesellschaft." In Rublack (1992a), 400-20.

Brecht, Martin. "Protestantische Kirchenzucht zwischen Kirche und Staat. Bemerkungen zur Forschungssituation." In Schilling (1994), 41-48.

Chaix, Gérald "Die schwierige Schule der Sitten - christliche Gemeinden, bürgerliche Obrigkeit und Sozialdisziplinierung im frühneuzeitlichen Koln, etwa 1450 - 1600." In Schilling (1994), 199-217.

Chatellier, Louis. *The Europe of the Devout: the Catholic Reformation and the Formation of a New Society*. Cambridge and Paris, 1989.

Conrad, Anne. *Zwischen Kloster und Welt. Ursulinen und Jesuitinnen in der katholischen Reformbewegung des 16./17. Jahrhunderts*. VIEG, vol. 142. Mainz, 1991.

Davis, Natalie Zemon. "Strikes and Salvation at Lyons." *ARG* 56 (1965): 48-64.

Diefendorf, Barbara B. *Beneath the Cross. Catholics and Huguenots in Sixteenth-Century Paris*. New York, 1991.

Diefendorf, Barbara B. "The Huguenot Psalter and the Faith of French Protestants in the Sixteenth Century." In Diefendorf and Hesse (1993), 41-63.

Diefendorf, Barbara B., and Carla Hesse, eds. *Culture and Identity in Early Modern Europe (1500-1800). Essays in Honor of Natalie Zemon Davis*. Ann Arbor, 1993.

Estèbe, Jeannine, and Bernard Vogler. "La genèse d'une société protestante: Étude comparée de quelques registres consistoriaux languedociens et palatins vers 1600." *AÉSC* 31 (1976): 362-388.

Forster, Marc R. *The Counter-Reformation in the Villages: Religion and Reform in the Bishopric of Speyer, 1560-1720*. Ithaca, 1992.

François, Etienne. *Die unsichtbare Grenze. Protestanten und Katholiken in Augsburg 1648-1806*. Abhandlungen zur Geschichte der Stadt Augsburg, vol. 33. Sigmaringen, 1991.

Friedeburg, Robert von. "Anglikanische Kirchenzucht und nachbarschaftliche Sitten-reform: Reformierte Sittenzucht zwischen Staat, Kirche und Gemeinde in England 1559-1642." In Schilling (1994), 153-82.

Gordon, Bruce. *Clerical Discipline and the Rural Reformation. The Synod in Zürich, 1532 - 1580.* Zürcher Beiträge zur Reformationsgeschichte, vol. 16. Bern, Frankfurt am Main, New York, Paris, and Vienna, 1992.

Gordon, Bruce. "Die Entwicklung der Kirchenzucht in Zürich am Beginn der Reformation." In Schilling (1994), 65-90.

Graff, Paul. *Geschichte der Auflösung der alten gottesdienstlichen Formen in der evangelischen Kirche Deutschlands.* Vol. 1, *Bis zum Eintritt der Aufklärung und des Rationalismus.* Göttingen, 1937.

Greyerz, Kaspar von. "Biographical Evidence on Predestination, Covenant, and Special Providence." In *Weber's Protestant Ethic. Origins, Evidence, Contexts,* ed. Hartmut Lehmann, 273-84. Cambridge, 1993.

Greyerz, Kaspar von, ed. *Religion and Society in Early Modern Europe.* London, 1984.

Greyerz, Kaspar von. *Vorsehungsglaube und Kosmologie. Studien zu englischen Selbstzeugnissen des 17. Jahrhunderts.* Veröffentlichungen des Deutschen Historischen Instituts London, vol. 25. Göttingen, 1990.

Guggisberg, Hans R., and Gottfried G. Krodel, eds. *The Reformation in Germany and Europe: Interpretations and Issues.* Special vol. of the Archive for Reformation History. Gütersloh, 1993.

Haag, Norbert. *Predigt und Gesellschaft. Die Lutherische Orthoxie in Ulm 1640-1740.* VIEG, Abteilung Religionsgeschichte, vol. 145. Mainz, 1992.

Hagenmaier, Monika. *Predigt und Policey. Der gesellschaftspolitische Diskurs zwischen Kirche und Obrigkeit in Ulm 1614-1639.* Nomos Universitätsschriften Geschichte, vol. 1. Baden-Baden, 1989.

Heiss, Gernot. "Konfessionsbildung, Kirchenzucht und frühmoderner Staat. Die Durchsetzung des 'rechten' Glaubens im 'Zeitalter der Glaubensspaltung' am Beispiel des Wirkens der Jesuiten in den Ländern Ferdinands I." In *Volksfrömmigkeit. Von der Antike bis zum 18. Jahrhundert,* ed. Hubert Ch. Ehalt, 191-220. Kulturstudien, vol. 10. Vienna and Cologne, 1989.

Holtz, Sabine. *Theologie und Alltag. Lehre und Leben in den Predigten der Tübinger Theologen 1550 - 1750.* Spätmittelalter und Reformation, new series, vol. 3. Tübingen, 1993.

Hsia, R. Po-chia. *Society and Religion in Münster 1535-1618.* New Haven, 1984.

Hsia, R. Po-chia. *Social Discipline in the Reformation: Central Europe 1550-1750.* London, 1989.

Julia, Dominique. "Discipline ecclesiastique et culture paysanne aux XVIIe et XVIIIe siècles." In *La religion populaire,* 199-209. Colloques Internationaux du Centre Nationale de la Recherche Scientifique, no. 576. Paris, 1979.

Kingdon, Robert M. "Calvinist Discipline in the Old World and the New." In Guggisberg and Krodel (1993), 665-79.

Kingdon, Robert M. "Social Control and Political Control in Calvin's Geneva." In Guggisberg and Krodel (1993), 521-32.

Kittelson, James M. "Successes and Failures in the German Reformation: The Report from Strasbourg." *ARG* 73 (1982): 153-75.

Kittelson, James M. "Visitations and Popular Religious Culture: Further Reports from Strasbourg." In *Pietas et societas: New Trends in Reformation Social History. Essays in Memory of Harold J. Grimm,* ed. Kyle C. Sessions, and Phillip N. Bebb, 89-101. SCES, vol. 4. Kirksville, Mo., 1985.

Lang, Peter Thaddäus. "Ein grobes, unbändiges Volk." Visitationsberichte und Volksfrömmigkeit." In *Volksfrömmigkeit in der Frühen Neuzeit,* ed. Hansgeorg Molitor, and Heribert Smolinsky, 49-63. Katholisches Leben und Kirchenreform im Zeitalter der Glaubensspaltung, vol. 54. Münster, 1994.

Lang, Peter Thaddäus. "Die tridentinische Reform im Landkapitel Mergentheim bis zum Einfall der Schweden 1631." *Rottenburger Jahrbuch für Kirchengeschichte* 1 (1982): 143-71.

Lang, Peter Thaddäus. *Die Ulmer Katholiken im Zeitalter der Glaubenskämpfe: Lebensbedingungen einer konfessionellen Minderheit.* Europäische Hochschulschriften, series 3, vol. 89. Frankfurt am Main, 1977.

Lehmann, Hartmut. "The Cultural Importance of the Pious Middle Classes in Seventeenth-Century Protestant Society." In Greyerz (1984), 33-41.

Lehmann, Hartmut. *Das Zeitalter des Absolutismus. Gottesgnadentum und Kriegsnot.* Christentum und Gesellschaft, vol. 9. Stuttgart, 1980.

Lenman, Bruce. "The Limits of Godly Discipline in the Early Modern Period with Particular Reference to England and Scotland." In Greyerz (1984), 124-45.

Luria, Keith P. "Rituals of Conversion: Catholics and Protestants in Seventeenth-Century Poitou." In Diefendorf and Hesse (1993), 65-81.

Molitor, Hansgeorg. *Kirchliche Reformversuche der Kurfürsten und Erzbischöfe von Trier im Zeitalter des Gegenreformation.* VIEG, vol. 43. Wiesbaden, 1967.

Molitor, Hansgeorg, and Heribert Smolinsky, ed. *Volksfrömmigkeit in der Frühen Neuzeit.* Katholisches Leben und Kirchenreform im Zeitalter der Glaubensspaltung, vol. 54. Münster, 1994.

Moore, Cornelia Niekus. "Erbauungsliteratur als Gebrauchsliteratur für Frauen im 17. Jahrhundert: Leichenpredigten als Quelle weiblicher Lesegewohnheiten." In *Le livre religieux et ses pratiques. Etudes sur l'histoire du livre religieux en Allemagne et en France à l'époque moderne. Der Umgang mit dem religiösen Buch. Studien zur Geschichte des religiösen Buches in Deutschland und Frankreich in der frühen Neuzeit,* ed. Hans Erich Bödeker, Gerald Chaix, and Patrice Veit, 291-315. Veröffentlichungen des Max-Planck-Instituts für Geschichte, vol. 101. Göttingen, 1991.

Münch, Paul. "Kirchenzucht und Nachbarschaft. Zur sozialen Problematik des calvinistischen Seniorats um 1600." In *Kirche und Visitation. Zur Erforschung des frühneuzeitlichen Visitationswesens,* ed. Ernst Walter Zeeden and Peter Thaddäus Lang, 216-48. SFN, vol. 14. Stuttgart, 1984.

Münch, Paul. *Lebensformen in der frühen Neuzeit.* Frankfurt am Main and Berlin, 1992.

Münch, Paul. "Volkskultur und Calvinismus. Zu Theorie und Praxis der `reformatio vitae' während der `Zweiten Reformation.'" In *Die reformierte Konfessionalisierung in Deutschland - das Problem der "Zweiten Reformation",* ed. Heinz Schilling, 291-307. SVRG, no. 195. Gütersloh, 1986.

Neuser, Wilhelm. "Dogma und Bekenntnis in der Reformation: Von Zwingli und Calvin bis zur Synode von Westminster." In *Die Lehrentwicklung im Rahmen der Konfessionalität,* ed. Carl Andresen, 167-352. Handbuch der Dogmen- und Theologiegeschichte, vol. 2. Göttingen, 1980.

Oberman, Heiko A. "Europa afflicta: the Reformation of the Refugees." *ARG* 83 (1992): 91-111.

Roodenburg, Herman. "Reformierte Kirchenzucht und Ehrenhandel. Das Amsterdamer Nachbarschaftsleben im 17. Jahrhundert." In Schilling (1994), 129-51.

Rublack, Hans-Christoph. "Augsburger Predigt im Zeitalter der lutherischen Orthodoxie." In *Die Augsburger Kirchenordnung von 1537 und ihr Umfeld,* ed. Reinhard Schwarz, 123-56. SVRG, no. 196. Gütersloh, 1988.

Rublack, Hans-Christoph. "Gesellschaft/Gesellschaft und Christentum VI: Reformationszeit." In *Theologische Realenzyklopädie* 13 (1981): 1-13.

Rublack, Hans-Christoph. "Lutherische Beichte und Sozialdisziplinierung." *ARG* 84 (1993): 127-55.

Rublack, Hans-Christoph, ed. *Die lutherische Konfessionalisierung in Deutschland.* SVRG, no. 97. Gütersloh, 1992a.

Rublack, Hans-Christoph. "Lutherische Predigt und gesellschaftliche Wirklichkeiten." In Rublack (1992a), 344-95.

Rublack, Hans-Christoph. "Reformation and Society." In *Martin Luther and the Modern Mind. Freedom, Conscience, Toleration, Rights,* ed. Manfred Hoffman, 239-78. Toronto Studies in Theology, vol. 22. New York, 1985.

Rublack, Hans-Christoph. "Success and Failure of the Reformation: Popular 'Apologies' from the Seventeenth and Eighteenth Centuries." In *Germania Illustrata. Essays on Early Modern Germany presented to Gerald Strauss,* ed. Susan Karant-Nunn and Andrew Fix, 141-65. SCES, vol. 18. Kirksville, Mo., 1992b.

Rublack, Hans-Christoph. "Der wohlgeplagte Priester". Vom Selbstverständnis lutherischer Geistlichkeit im Zeitalter der Orthodoxie." *ZHF* 16 (1989): 1-30.

Sabean, David. *Power in the Blood: Popular Culture and Village Discourse in Early Modern Germany.* Cambridge, 1984.

Schär, Markus. *Seelennöte der Untertanen. Selbstmord, Melancholie und Religion im Alten Zürich 1500-1800.* Zurich, 1985.

Schilling, Heinz. "Chiese confessionali e disciplinamento sociale. Un bilancio provvisorio della ricerca." In *Disciplina dell'animo, disciplina del corpo e disciplina della società tra medioevo ed età moderna*, ed. Paolo Prodi, 125-60. Annali dell'Istituto storico italo-germanico Quaderno, vol. 40. Bologna, 1994.

Schilling, Heinz. "Einleitung." In *Die Kirchenratsprotokolle der Reformierten Gemeinde Emden 1557 - 1620, Teil 1: 1557-1574*, ed. Heinz Schilling, and Klaus Dieter Schreiber, ix-xxviii. Stadteforschung. Veröffentlichungen des Instituts für Vergleichende Städtegeschichte in Münster, series C, vol. 3, part 1. Cologne and Vienna, 1989.

Schilling, Heinz. "Die Kirchenzucht im frühneuzeitlichen Europa in interkonfessionell vergleichender und interdisziplinärer Perspektive - eine Zwischenbilanz." In Schilling (1994), 11-40.

Schilling, Heinz, ed. *Kirchenzucht und Sozialdisziplinierung im frühneuzeitlichen Europa.* Beiheft der Zeitschrift für Historische Forschung, vol. 16. Berlin 1994.

Schilling, Heinz. "Reformierte Kirchenzucht als Sozialdisziplinierung? Die Tätigkeit des Emder Presbyteriums in den Jahren 1557-1562." In *Niederlande und Nordwestdeutschland. Studien zur Regional- und Stadtgeschichte Nordwestkontinentaleuropas im Mittelalter und in der Neuzeit*, ed. Wilfried Ehbrecht and Heinz Schilling. 261-327. Cologne and Vienna, 1983.

Schilling, Heinz. "Sündenzucht und frühneuzeitliche Sozialdisziplinierung. Die calvinistische presbyteriale Kirchenzucht in Emden vom 16. bis 19. Jahrhundert." In *Stände und Gesellschaft im Alten Reich*, ed. Georg Schmidt, 265-302. Wiesbaden, 1989.

Schmidt, Heinrich Richard. *Dorf und Religion. Reformierte Sittenzucht in Berner Landgemeinden der Frühen Neuzeit.* Unpublished Habilitationsschrift. Bern, 1993.

Schmidt, Heinrich Richard. *Konfessionalisierung im 16. Jahrhundert.* Enzyklopädie Deutscher Geschichte, vol. 12. Munich, 1992.

Schmidt, Heinrich Richard. "Pazifizierung des Dorfes - Struktur und Wandel von Nachbarschaftskonflikten vor Berner Sittengerichten 1570-1800." In Schilling (1994), 91-128.

Schnabel-Schüle, Helga. "Calvinistische Kirchenzucht in Württemberg? Zur Theorie und Praxis der württembergischen Kirchenkonvente." *Zeitschrift für württembergische Landesgeschichte* 49 (1990): 169-223.

Schnabel-Schüle, Helga. "Kirchenzucht als Verbrechensprävention." In Schilling (1994), 49-64.

Schneider, Bernhard. "Wandel und Beharrung. Bruderschaften und Frömmigkeit in Spätmittelalter und Früher Neuzeit." In *Volksfrömmigkeit in der Frühen Neuzeit*, ed. Hansgeorg Molitor and Heribert Smolinsky, 65-87. Katholisches Leben und Kirchenreform im Zeitalter der Glaubensspaltung, vol. 54. Münster, 1994.

Scribner, Robert W. "Cosmic Order and Daily Life: Sacred and Secular in the Pre-industrial German Society." In Scribner, (1987), 1-16.

Scribner, Robert W. "The Impact of the Reformation on Daily Life." In *Mensch und Objekt im Mittelalter und in der frühen Neuzeit*, 315-43. Sitzungsberichte der Österreichischen Akademie der Wissenschaften, Philosophisch-Historische Klasse, no. 568. Vienna, 1990.

Scribner, Robert W. "Pastoral Care and the Reformation in Germany." In *Humanism and Reform: The Church in Europe, England and Scotland, 1400-1643.* Essays in Honour of James K. Cameron, ed. James Kirk, 77-97. Studies in Church History. Subsidia, vol. 8. Oxford, 1991.

Scribner, Robert W. *Popular Culture and Popular Movements in Reformation Germany.* London, 1987.

Scribner, Robert W. "Ritual and Popular Belief in Catholic Germany at the Time of the Reformation." In Scribner (1987), 17-48.

Senn, Matthias. "Alltag und Lebensgefühl im Zürich des 16. Jahrhunderts." *Zwingliana* 14 (1976): 251-62.

Senn, Matthias. *Die Wickiana. Johann Jakob Wicks Nachrichtensammlung aus dem 16. Jahrhundert.* Küssnacht-Zürich, 1975.

Spufford, Margaret. "Puritanism and Social Control?" In *Order and Disorder in Early Modern England*, ed. Anthony Fletcher and John Stevenson, 41-57. Cambridge, 1985.

Strauss, Gerald. *Luther's House of Learning. Indoctrination of the Young in the German Reformation.* Baltimore, 1978.

Thomas, Keith. *Religion and the Decline of Magic.* Harmondsworth, England, 1978 [1971].

Veit, Ludwig Andreas, and Ludwig Lenhart. *Kirche und Volksfrömmigkeit im Zeitalter des Barock.* Freiburg im Breisgau, 1956.

Veit, Patrice. "Das Gesangbuch in der Praxis Pietatis der Lutheraner." In Rublack (1992a), 435-54.

Veit, Patrice. "Private Frömmigkeit, Lektüre und Gesang im protestantischen Deutschland der frühen Neuzeit: Das Modell der Leichenpredigten." In *Frühe Neuzeit - Frühe Moderne? Forschungen zur Vielschichtigkeit von Übergangsprozessen.* 271-95. Göttingen, 1992).

Venard, Marc. *Histoire du christianisme des origines à nos jours.* Vol. 8, *Le temps des confessions (1530-1620/30).* Paris, 1992.

Vogler, Bernard. "Die Entstehung der protestantischen Volksfrömmigkeit in der rheinischen Pfalz zwischen 1555 und 1619." *ARG* 72 (1981): 158-195.

Vogler, Bernard. "Die Gebetbücher in der lutherischen Orthodoxie." In Rublack (1992a), 424-34.

Vogler, Bernard. "Les livres de prières de l'orthodoxie luthérienne face aux crises (1575-1799)." In *Krisenbewußtsein und Krisenbewältigung in der Frühen Neuzeit - Crisis in Early Modern Europe. Festschrift für Hans-Christoph Rublack*, ed. Monika Hagenmaier and Sabine Holtz, 245-53. Frankfurt am Main, 1992b.

Warmbrunn, Paul. *Zwei Konfessionen in einer Stadt. Das Zusammenleben von Katholiken und Protestanten in den paritätischen Reichsstädten Augsburg, Biberach, Ravensburg und Dinkelsbühl von 1548 bis 1648.* VIEG, vol. 111. Wiesbaden, 1983.

Weber, Bruno. *Wunderzeichen und Winkeldrucker 1543-1586. Einblattdrucke aus der Sammlung Wikiana in der Zentralbibliothek Zürich.* Dietikon Zurich, 1972.

Weyrauch, Erdmann. "Die Illiteraten und ihre Literatur." In *Literatur und Volk im 17. Jahrhundert. Probleme populärer Kultur in Deutschland*, ed. Wolfgang Brückner, Peter Blickle, and Dieter Breuer, 465-74. Wiesbaden, 1985.

Wright, Susan J., ed. *Parish, Church, and People. Local Studies in Lay Religion 1350-1750.* London, Melbourne, Auckland, Johannesburg, 1988.

Zeeden, Ernst Walter. "Aspekte der katholischen Frömmigkeit in Deutschland im 16. Jahrhundert." In *Konfessionsbildung. Studien zur Reformation, Gegenreformation und katholischen Reform*, ed. Ernst Walter Zeeden, 314-31. SFN, vol. 15. Stuttgart, 1985.

Zimmermann, Wolfgang. *Rekatholisierung, Konfessionalisierung und Ratsregiment. Der Prozess des politischen und religiösen Wandels in der österreichischen Stadt Konstanz 1548-1637.* Konstanzer Geschichts- und Rechtsquellen, vol. 34. Sigmaringen, 1994.

THE GREAT WITCH-HUNT

Brian P. Levack
(University of Texas-Austin)

Between 1450 and 1750 European ecclesiastical and secular courts tried and executed tens of thousands of individuals, most of them women, for the crime of witchcraft. Because the scale and intensity of these prosecutions was so great, and the fears underlying them so deep, this judicial operation is often referred to as the "witch-craze." As a description of the entire set of early modern European witchcraft trials this term is somewhat misleading, since it implies that all those who accused and tried witches were either acting irrationally or suffering from some kind of delusion.[1] A more appropriate term is "witch-hunt," a phrase coined in the twentieth-century to describe the accusation and harassment of undesirable individuals either for beliefs they held or for crimes they did not commit.[2]

The historical investigation of the great European witch-hunt involves four separate but related enterprises. The first is the reconstruction of the beliefs of those persons who made the accusations and brought the witches to trial. These witch-beliefs, which underwent a remarkable development in the fifteenth and sixteenth centuries, formed the intellectual foundation of the hunt. The second is a study of the judicial processes that were used to prosecute witches. Since the hunt was primarily a judicial operation, conducted in ecclesiastical and secular courts, it is necessary to discover how the prosecutions were initiated and what procedures were used to secure the witches' conviction. The third is an analysis of the data regarding the social identity of the witches and the geographical distribution of the trials. This investigation helps to explain why individuals possessing certain social characteristics and living in particular countries or regions were especially vulnerable to accusation and prosecution. The fourth is an explanation why witch-trials became more numerous in the fifteenth, sixteenth and early seventeenth centuries and why they eventually declined in number in the late seventeenth and eighteenth centuries.

WITCHCRAFT TRIALS IN WESTERN EUROPE, 1580-1650

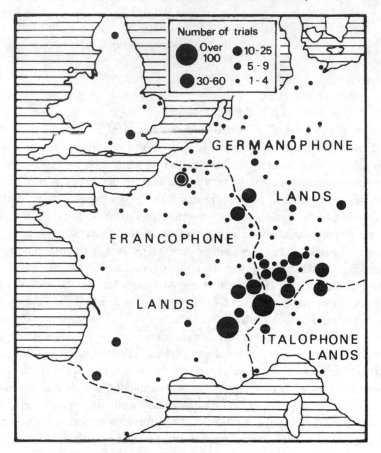

EXECUTION OF WITCHES IN RELATION TO TRIALS

a. Habsburg Netherlands

NAMUR (1509-1646)

CAMBRÉSIS (1446-1680)

LUXEMBOURG (1550-1650)

b. Franco-Swiss borderlands

FRANCHE COMTÉ (1599-1667)

PRINCE-BISHOPRIC OF BASEL (1570-1677)

NEUCHATEL (1568-1677)

FRIBOURG (1607-1683)

GENEVA (1537-1681)

0   100   200   300   400

Number of ▨ trials and ▧ executions

1. WITCH-BELIEFS

The prosecution of witches in early modern Europe was based upon, and to a great extent inspired by, a set of beliefs regarding who witches were and what types of activities they allegedly engaged in. These witch-beliefs were embodied in, and transmitted through, a large body of literature, written for the most part by inquisitors or judges who had actually tried witchcraft cases. According to these men, many of whom were clerics, witches were individuals who practiced harmful or maleficent magic (*maleficium*) and who also worshipped the Devil. There was a close connection between these two forms of activity, for ever since the early years of Christianity theologians had insisted that all magic was caused by the power of the Devil; consequently, all magicians had commerce with demons.

By the beginning of the sixteenth century the nature of this diabolical commerce had been greatly embellished. It was now believed that practitioners of *maleficium* had made face-to-face pacts with the Devil, a charge that scholastic theologians had leveled against ritual magicians in the thirteenth century and only later applied to the illiterate, predominantly female peasants who allegedly practiced maleficent magic. The idea of a pact with the Devil led to the classification of all magicians, and later all witches, as idolaters, heretics and apostates. Witches were also believed to have worshipped the Devil collectively in nocturnal assemblies or sabbaths, at which they allegedly participated in promiscuous sexual activity, naked dancing, cannibalistic infanticide, and other forms of amoral or anti-human activity. During the Middle Ages, theologians had made such charges against heretics, such as Cathars and Waldensians, as well as ritual magicians and Jews. These charges were leveled in the early fifteenth century against the new sect of witches with which authorities became increasingly concerned. A belief also arose that witches, benefiting from the power of the Devil with whom they had made a pact, flew to and from their nocturnal assemblies, often covering great distances.[3]

Taken together, these beliefs, often referred to as the composite or cumulative concept of witchcraft, explain why both secular and ecclesiastical authorities developed such great concern about the crime of witchcraft during the early modern period. Witches were not only using their magical powers to injure or kill human beings and domestic animals, but they had also sold their souls to the Devil and were engaged in a large conspiracy to undermine Christian civilization. They were guilty therefore of a spiritual as well as a temporal crime. And since they were allegedly acting in concert with hundreds, if not thousands of other witches, these heretical magicians represented a political threat as well.

It was once believed that this stereotype of the witch was fully formed in a series of trials conducted by papal inquisitors at Toulouse and Carcassonne in the early fourteenth century. It has since been discovered, however, that the records of those trials were the product of an early nineteenth-century forgery.[4] The evidence that we now have suggests that the stereotype did not begin to appear in its full form until the early fifteenth century in parts of western Switzerland, south-eastern France and northern Italy.[5] In some of the areas where it first appeared inquisitors had also been pursuing Waldensian heretics, and the two groups were naturally seen as related threats. There is no evidence, however, that the inquisitors who conducted these trials actually confused the two groups. These new witches, unlike the Waldensians, were regarded as having magical powers, and some of them also confessed to flying through the air.

The cumulative concept of witchcraft did not take root in some regions for a full century after its original formation. The belief in *maleficium* was widespread, if not universal, but the belief that witches (*maleficae*) made pacts with the Devil and worshipped him collectively gained credence slowly, and only in certain intellectual circles. Belief in the sabbath did not penetrate either Scotland or Poland until the late sixteenth century, and it was only in the seventeenth century that it made its way into England, Hungary and Finland. In some areas, such as southern Spain, the Dutch Republic, and Russia, it never found fertile ground. Even in those areas where learned witch-beliefs took shape relatively early, the literature did not always reflect the full concept of the witch until well into the seventeenth century. The widely circulated *Malleus maleficarum* which was written by two German inquisitors in 1486, had very little to say about the sabbath, while the belief in nocturnal flight received little or no attention in many sixteenth-century demonological treatises.

While the witch-beliefs of educated clergymen and judges have been the subject of historical research for more than a century, the beliefs of the accused witches and their neighbors have only begun to command serious scholarly attention within the last twenty-five years.[6] This reorientation of witchcraft studies reflects a broader historical interest in "popular culture," an enterprise which owes much of its inspiration to the work of anthropologists. Underlying this work has been a will-ingness to treat such belief systems as having more coherence than is implied in references to "peasant superstition." This scholarship has revealed the profound differences that existed between popular and learned beliefs about witchcraft. Illiterate villagers appear to have de-fined witchcraft mainly as *maleficium* and made few if any connections between that harmful magic and the power of the Devil, simply attrib-uting the witches' magic to mysterious powers possessed by certain members of the community. University educated elites, on the other hand, viewed the witch's activities in predominantly theological terms, emphasizing the witch's commerce with the Devil. In witchcraft trials, which were usually controlled by members of the ruling class and which often involved torture or other forms of judicial coercion, the learned interpretation of the crime was often superimposed on the popular. For this reason an accused witch would often be convicted not simply of harming her neighbor but of making a pact with the Devil and attending the sabbath.

The argument that the lower classes were totally ignorant of the Devil and the sabbath can no longer be maintained. Even if preaching did not produce a theologically sophisticated populace, it did instill more than a transitory view of the Devil. In England, where there was less judicial coercion than in most countries of Europe, a belief in the pact with Devil apparently penetrated the lower classes by the end of the sixteenth century.[7] Contemporary narratives of demonic posses-sion, documents that appear to have been uncontaminated by judicial authorities, suggest a significant popular knowledge of the Devil, even if the view differed in some respects from that of learned demonolo-gists.[8] Likewise the process of demonic temptation, and even the orgies that allegedly took place at the sabbath, were by no means incompat-ible with a popular mentality.

Interest in popular witch-beliefs, especially those which relate to the Devil, has also raised the question whether the origins of some features of the learned stereotype of the witch can be traced to popular sources. There is a spectrum of opinion on this issue. At one end stand those scholars who see the learned concept as essentially a clerical fantasy to which ignorant peasants were forced to confess.[9] In such circum-stances the popular contribution to learned beliefs was limited to the specific details they provided while responding to leading questions. At the other end stand those who see the lower classes providing the basic material out of which inquisitors molded their ideas. Many of the sources for the clerical idea of witches' flight, for example, appear to have come from folk beliefs regarding cannibalistic screech owls and nocturnal processions of women led by the goddess Diana.[10] Likewise the English belief that witches were assisted by demonic familiars in animal form can trace its origin to the popular belief in the magical powers of animals.[11] Carlo Ginzburg has discovered in northeastern Italy a belief that certain men could defend the community by going out at night in spirit to fight the witches.[12] It remains uncertain whether such popular ideas can be considered a major source of the inquisitorial notion of collective Devil-worship. It is true, however, that the idea of the sabbath was compatible with certain folk-beliefs, especially those of Scandinavian origin, regarding the gathering of witches at specific locations. The effect of all this work suggests that learned and popular ideas may have influenced and modified each other in more complex ways than was previously believed.

Closely related to the question of the origin of witch-beliefs is the extent to which they have a foundation in reality. Very few scholars would adopt the position that the accused witches actually engaged in all the activities of which they were accused or deny that the great majority of witches were falsely accused. The difficult question is whether the entire crime was the product of either learned or popular fantasy, a delusion to which eventual "enlightenment" was the only cure, or whether witches did actually do some of the things with which they were charged. It is almost certain that some witches practiced magic, although the number of such practitioners was probably very small, and much of the magic they practiced was probably beneficent rather than malignant.

Much more controversial is whether or not accused witches worshipped the Devil or engaged in a sort of collective activity that contemporaries could interpret as diabolism. It has often been argued, for example, that witches were actually members of an ancient fertility cult which the Church was determined to wipe out.[13] One of the problems with such theories is that the evidence upon which they are constructed—the confessions of witches themselves—is often contaminated, since the confessions were obtained as a result of torture or other forms of judicial coercion. Those trial records that are clearly uncontaminated, such as the original depositions made against witches by their neighbors, usually refer only to *maleficium*, not diabolism.[14] The only sources that might be used to support the claim that witches actually worshipped the Devil or gathered collectively for some other purpose are the free confessions of witches, and even those cannot always be relied upon as statements of fact, especially when they were the product of either youthful imagination or hallucination induced by drugs.[15] Such confessions can greatly illuminate the nature of popular witch beliefs, but they still do not tell us very much about the actual activities that witches engaged in.

The reception of learned witch-beliefs in the various countries of Europe had only a limited impact on the official definition of the crime. In most secular jurisdictions, even those where theories of Devil-worship found widespread acceptance, the statutes or edicts upon which prosecutions were based referred mainly to the performance of *maleficium* and made no explicit reference to the demonic pact or the sabbath. In some cases, as in Scotland, Finland, Hungary and Poland, the passage of witchcraft legislation preceded the introduction of learned ideas. In England, where the clerical stereotype of the witch was never fully accepted, even by the educated and ruling elites, the Elizabethan law upon which most prosecutions were based did not even mention the pact. Only in the final witchcraft statute of 1604 did it become a felony to "consult, covenant with, entertain, employ, feed, or reward any evil and wicked spirit."[16]

In a few countries the heretical aspect of witchcraft, a pact with the Devil, served as the main definition of the crime. This was true in both the Spanish kingdoms and the Italian territories, where the Inquisition maintained its jurisdiction over witchcraft, as well as in some German principalities like Saxony. In colonial Massachusetts the witchcraft law of 1648 was written exclusively in terms of diabolical compact, so much so that most cases brought by villagers exclusively on the basis of alleged *maleficium* could not be successfully prosecuted.[17]

2. THE JUDICIAL PROCESS

Extensive research on witch trials throughout Europe has shed considerable light on the different ways in which prosecutions originated. The main question has been whether the initial charges came from "above," i.e., from members of the judicial elite or the ruling classes, or "below," i.e., from the accused witches' lower-class neighbors. It was once believed that on the Continent, where an inquisitorial form of criminal procedure prevailed, most witchcraft prosecutions came from above—from local officials who secretly denounced suspected malefactors or from judges acting *ex officio* on the basis of rumor. Only in England, where officials lacked the authority to initiate prosecutions by themselves, did the charges originate in complaints brought by villagers.

This over-simplified picture is gradually being redrawn. On the one hand, it is becoming obvious that in many Continental jurisdictions there was significant pressure from local communities on judicial authorities to initiate prosecutions, so much so that in some cases villagers took up collections in order to cover the costs of prosecution. The initial charges were often brought by the people themselves.[18] Even in those places where inquisitorial procedure had been introduced, accusation by a wronged party was by no means precluded.[19] The use of inquisitorial procedure simply meant that once those accusations were lodged, the judicial process was taken over by the state and thereby "officialized."[20] On the other hand, in England, where all prosecutions apparently originated from below, the role of both clerical and lay elites in encouraging accusations and assisting in prosecutions is becoming more evident.[21]

To some extent the question regarding the high or low origin of witchcraft prosecutions is misleading, since the individuals who seem to have taken the greatest initiative in the prosecution of accused witches were the middling group of local officials who often straddled the boundaries between elite and popular culture. These men—priests, elders, parish officials, and small landowners—did not exercise great political authority, and only a small percentage of them were university educated. They were, however, usually literate, and constituted a village or parish elite. As such they were responsible for the operation of local judicial tribunals and had sufficient power at least to direct the accusations of their neighbors into the proper judicial channels. Unlike central judicial authorities, who often manifested either indifference or skepticism toward allegations of witchcraft, these men usually supported the vigorous prosecution of the crime. Their attitude can be attributed, at least in part, to their personal knowledge of the witches and their determination to rid their communities of undesirable and dangerous individuals. Witchcraft trials took place in a variety of ecclesiastical and secular courts. In some cases authorities from both spiritual and temporal jurisdictions cooperated in prosecutions. Once again the complexity of the situation has made generalizations difficult. It is evident, however, that as witch-hunting became more intense in the late sixteenth century, the secular courts assumed control over the large bulk of prosecutions. Indeed, the only ecclesiastical tribunals that tried a significant number of these cases after 1550 were the Spanish, Portuguese and Roman inquisitions, all of which should be distinguished from the older episcopal institution, usually referred to simply as the Inquisition, which had tried many of the fifteenth-century cases.

The assumption of secular control over witchcraft prosecutions in most countries was to some extent the result of the passage or promulgation of witchcraft laws, although secular authorities could also proceed against accused witches on the basis of earlier laws against either magic or heresy.[22] Increasing secular control of witchcraft prosecutions was partially responsible for the dramatic increase in the conviction- and execution-rates in the late sixteenth century. Unlike the ecclesiastical courts, the secular courts were able to harness the full power of the state against the accused, and they were also more concerned with punishment than with the correction of religious error.[23] The Spanish and Roman Inquisitions, moreover, developed a set of procedural safeguards that made convictions more difficult to obtain and which required a review of all death sentences by central inquisitorial authorities.[24] In addition, the Spanish Inquisition made efforts to regulate the jurisdiction of the municipal courts, which were generally more severe in their treatment of witches than the Inquisition itself.[25]

The practice of automatically appealing cases in which witches were condemned to death also became established in certain secular jurisdictions. Wherever such a procedure was instituted, as in Denmark in 1576 and in those parts of France subject to the jurisdiction of the Parlement of Paris in 1624, it had a negative effect on the conviction- and execution-rates. This supports the further generalization that when central or national authorities exercised some supervision over the prosecution of witches, either as members of an appeals court or as itinerant justices (as in England), the conviction-rates in those areas remained relatively low. By contrast, in small jurisdictional units which did not have a regular appeals process, as in many German states, conviction rates were exceptionally high.[26] Some of the worst areas were those German territories in which a cleric exercised unrestricted secular power, as in the Fürstpropstei of Ellwangen.

One of the procedural abuses that central judicial authorities tried to prevent was the unwarranted use of torture. There is no question that torture, and the inquisitorial procedure with which it was usually associated, were responsible for many of the confessions that witches made, especially those involving acts of diabolism. It is also true that in many witchcraft cases the restrictions that had been established to regulate the application of torture were relaxed or completely ignored on the grounds that witchcraft was a *crimen exceptum* in which the normal judicial rules did not apply. We have, for example, reports of witches being tortured repeatedly and with such brutality that the accused died in the torture room. It would be wrong, however, to assume that all persons accused of witchcraft were routinely tortured. England was not the only country that prohibited its use except in cases of treason, and many of those countries that permitted torture in certain circumstances did not use it in all witchcraft trials. In some jurisdictions torture was administered with such restraint that many witches endured it without confessing.[27]

After applying torture to obtain the confession of a single person, authorities sometimes used it again to secure the names of accomplices. When those persons were themselves tortured in order to secure confessions and the names of additional accomplices, the witch-hunt could take a heavy toll. Large chain-reaction hunts of this sort usually took place in German territories, with the most notorious examples at Trier in 1589, Würzburg in 1628-30, and Bamberg in 1630. One of the main characteristics of such hunts was that as they developed, fewer victims conformed to the traditional stereotype of the witch. It was not uncommon in the later stages of such hunts for accusations to be lodged against young attractive women, prosperous members of the community, and even children. This breakdown of the stereotype, which also can be observed in the witch-hunt at Salem, Massachusetts in 1692, often led to a loss of confidence in the operation of the judicial machinery and a sudden termination of the hunt.[28]

3. PATTERNS OF PROSECUTION

Although we will never have complete figures, owing mainly to the loss of judicial records, we now have enough evidence to make some reasonable estimates of the numbers of trials, convictions and executions in different parts of Europe. The total number of trials, although still the source of some controversy, appears to lie in the range of 100,000 to 200,000.[29] These figures are much lower than those with which many earlier scholars worked. They are based, however, on careful historical research, much of which has resulted in a correction of the high numbers claimed at the time by alarmed officials or boastful

witch-hunters. Of those accused witches who were tried, a sizable majority were convicted, although historians have discovered more ac-
quittals than expected.[30] Perhaps the most surprising result of this research has been the establishment of wide variations in the
execution-rates of those tried for witchcraft in different parts of Europe, ranging from single-digit percentages in the Spanish empire to
more than 90 percent in some German, French and Swiss areas. Overall, it appears that the execution rate was only marginally higher than
50 percent.[31]

The proliferation of national, and regional witchcraft studies has
given us a considerable amount of data regarding the geographical distribution of prosecutions throughout Europe.[32] By taking into account
differences in the size of the population of different areas, it has also
become possible to establish the relative *intensity* of prosecutions and
executions in these countries and regions.[33] It is important, for example, to note that Scotland executed about three times as many witches
as England, but that statistic becomes even more revealing when we
recognize that Scotland had only one quarter of England's population.
A comparison between the duchy of Lorraine and the county of Essex
in England, both of which had approximately the same population, reveals that their rates of prosecution were roughly the same, although
the execution-rate in Lorraine was more than three times that of Essex.[34] In similar fashion, the prosecution of hundreds of witches in
small German territories, such as the 133 witches executed on one day
in lands of the convent of Quedlinburg, take on an even more dramatic
character in light of the relatively small population of those tiny political units.

For many years the only geographical distinctions that historians of
witchcraft made were between England, where as few as 500 witches
were executed in the sixteenth and seventeenth centuries, and "the
Continent." This picture has now been radically revised. There are
numerous areas besides England where witch-hunting claimed only a
limited number of victims. Countries or provinces on the periphery of
Europe, with the exception of Poland and Scotland, experienced at
times much less intense witch-hunting with fewer witch trials and executions than those that lay near the center. The zones of lesser intensity included the northwestern provinces of France, the Spanish kingdoms, the Italian territories, the Scandinavian countries, Russia, and
Hungary. In contrast, the most intense prosecutions took place within
the southern and western areas of Germany, the western cantons of

Switzerland, the southern provinces of France, and the relatively independent duchies and principalities that lay to the east of France. Another way of describing the uneven distribution of trials is to note that as many as 75 percent of all prosecutions took place within the mid-sixteenth-century boundaries of the Holy Roman Empire, an area which embraced the German territories, the Swiss cantons, Lorraine, Franche-Comté and Savoy but which contained less than half of the entire European population.

There were three main determinants of this geographical distribution of witchcraft cases. The first was the nature of the witch-beliefs that prevailed in certain areas and the strength with which those beliefs were held. Wherever witchcraft was believed to involve the collective worship of the Devil, witch-hunting took a heavier toll than when the crime was viewed as simply that of *maleficium*. The second determinant was the nature of the judicial machinery and the degree to which it was controlled by central authorities. Those jurisdictions which employed inquisitorial procedure, allowed the regular use of torture, and permitted local tribunals to prosecute witches without adequate supervision tended to have much higher numbers of convictions and executions than those countries which did not. The use of torture to implicate accomplices was particularly important in this regard, since large chain-reaction hunts that progressed by means of such torture were largely responsible for the high number of total executions in many areas. The third determinant was the intensity of religious fervor in a particular locality. Large witch-hunts, as opposed to the occasional prosecution of individuals for sorcery, were often inspired by a determination of religious reformers, Protestant or Catholic, to achieve a godly society and to reform popular culture. Since these hunts were controlled to a great extent by ruling elites, they lasted longer and involved more suspects than those prosecutions that came from below.

The uneven regional distribution of witchcraft prosecutions has led historians to qualify many of the generalizations that they made only a generation ago. Even the generally accepted argument that witchcraft was almost exclusively a rural phenomenon cannot be accepted without qualification. It is true that a solid majority of witches came from the countryside and that within the large cities it was more common to find learned magicians or women practicing love magic than maleficent witches. It is also true that many of the prosecutions that took place in cities and towns brought the accused from surrounding geographical areas. Nevertheless, significant numbers of witches did actually reside in towns. In fact, when we take into account the relatively small percentage of the early modern European population that lived in towns, urban witches may have been overrepresented among those tried for witchcraft. One reason for this is that many of the large chain-reaction hunts, in which convicted witches named their accomplices, who in turn named others, took place in towns, especially in Germany.

Within the rural areas, where the majority of accused witches resided, we can state with relative certainty that most came from agricultural villages rather than mountain hamlets. Much has been made of the fact that some of the first individuals prosecuted for witchcraft came from mountainous regions of Switzerland and France, where it is argued the residents were more credulous regarding preternatural phenomena and more resistant to the official culture of the Church.[35] There is no question that some of the early witches, whom the inquisition considered to be heretics, came from the same mountainous regions where Waldensian heresy had been strong. The bulk of all prosecutions, however, even in the early years of the great hunt, took place within the stable, nucleated villages that characterized arable regions rather than in more sparsely populated mountainous climes.

Detailed research has given us a clearer sense where witches came from and a better account of when the largest number of prosecutions took place. We are presented with a picture of extraordinary diversity, in which prosecution began, peaked, and ended at different times in different places throughout Europe. Four distinct periods of European-wide prosecution are identifiable. The first, which lasted from the earliest trials in the fifteenth century until the 1520s, witnessed numerous prosecutions within a fairly limited geographical area, which included the Rhineland, the Swiss cantons and some of the areas in southern France and northern Italy. These trials, which were held as the cumulative concept of witchcraft was taking shape, cannot always be distinguished from prosecutions for ritual magic.

The second period—between 1520 and 1560—shows an overall decline in witchcraft prosecutions, although witch-hunts occurred from time to time in the Low Countries, the Basque-speaking region of Spain, a number of German cities like Nuremberg, and the northern Italian diocese of Como. After 1560 the total number of trials began to rise again. During 1580 and 1650 Europe entered the third and most intense phase of witch-hunting. Many of the persons prosecuted during this period were involved in mass trials, although the majority of all witches were certainly prosecuted individually or in groups of two or three. In this period, trials spread to virtually all portions of western Europe. The last period of prosecution, from 1650 to 1750 was characterized by a sharp decline and termination of trials in western European regions but an intensification in Poland, Russia, Austria, Hungary and Transylvania. The reasons for this late development of witch-hunting in eastern Europe are not clear, although the late arrival or reception of learned ideas of witchcraft, a delayed development of religious conflict (as in Poland) and an intensification of social and economic conflict all played some role in the process.

4. WHO WERE THE WITCHES?

The proliferation of local witchcraft studies in recent years has made possible not only a more precise determination of the geographical and chronological distribution of prosecutions but also a more detailed portrait of the witches' social identity. These studies have produced a substantial body of data regarding the sex, age, marital status, social standing, wealth, and occupations of those persons accused of witchcraft. The records yield more information regarding the sex of the witches than any other personal or social characteristics, and those data confirm what contemporaries and subsequent historians have always known: the overwhelming majority of witches were female. The percentage of female witches has varied from region to region, ranging from 37 percent in Russia to 92 percent in England, but the aggregate percentage is approximately 75 percent. It is clear, therefore, that early modern European witchcraft was a sex-related activity, even if a solid number of men were accused of the crime, especially during its early phases, when it was closely associated with both ritual magic and heresy. Indeed, the female sex linkage may be even closer than the figure of 75 percent would suggest, since some of the male witches were accused mainly because they were related by either blood or marriage to female witches.

A reading of many of the witchcraft treatises of the fifteenth and sixteenth centuries, beginning with the notoriously misogynistic *Malleus maleficarum*, suggests that clerical inquisitors were primarily responsible for the identification of women as witches. One theory holds that a traditional clerical fear of female sexuality, especially that of older, unmarried women, coupled with a clerical belief that women were more prone than men to demonic temptation, led monks and clerical judges to suspect women of witchcraft more readily than men. The nature of the alleged pact with the Devil, in which sexual temptation played an important role, and the sabbath, where naked dancing and promiscuous sexual activity allegedly took place, reinforced learned belief in this regard. The recognition, however, that witchcraft prosecutions came from below as well as above, from secular as well as clerical authorities, and from women as well as men has given rise to alternative explanations of the fact that most witches were women.[36] These theories can be grouped into those which emphasize the witch's social and economic standing, those which focus on the functions she performed in the community, and those which relate to her personality. In each case there is an effort to take into account the fact that accusations of witchcraft were not made against women indiscriminately; rather they were directed at women who shared some physical, social, economic, or personal characteristics.

The socio-economic answer to this question is based upon the fact that the great majority of women accused of witchcraft were old and poor, and sometimes relied on the charity of their neighbors. Their dependent status was accentuated by the fact that a disproportionately large number of them were either widowed or single. Women in such straitened economic circumstances were particularly vulnerable to witchcraft prosecutions, since the more prosperous members of the community either resented having to provide for such individuals or felt guilty for having refused to do so. In either case identification of the woman as a witch represented a response to the unease of their accusers. Once charged with witchcraft, these isolated and poverty-stricken women had few personal or financial resources on which they could draw for their defense. Some of these same women may have actually practiced magic, or threatened to practice it, as the sole means of defending themselves or retaliating against their accusers, thus confirming the original suspicion that they were witches.

A second set of explanations for the preponderance of female witches centers on the functions that women performed in village communities. Here the argument is that traditionally female activities made them vulnerable to accusations of sorcery by both their neighbors and their superiors. Female involvement in the preparation of food, for example, lies behind numerous accusations of witchcraft as well as the conventional depiction of witches brewing magical concoctions. And the almost exclusive involvement of women in childbirth apparently made midwives vulnerable to the accusations of their neighbors. In this respect learned theory confirmed popular suspicions, since clerics believed that midwives had the opportunity to provide unbaptized infants for sacrifice to the Devil. The identification of witches as midwives has recently been challenged, and it is true that there is very little direct or uncontaminated evidence showing that large numbers of accused witches served in this occupation.[37] Nevertheless, midwifery remains one of the few occupations of witches recorded in judicial proceedings. More generally, it is clear that the process of childbirth and the care of infants was the focus of many witchcraft accusations, as charges against lying-in-maids at Augsburg suggest.[38]

Far more common than midwives or lying-in-maids among the victims of witchcraft prosecutions were healers or wise-women. These women provided basic medical care, often in the form of herbal and magical remedies, to rural populations which had only infrequent contact with physicians. Since healers performed useful functions in society, they were generally tolerated by their neighbors. They were, however, particularly vulnerable to accusations of witchcraft when the condition of their patients worsened or they died. Contemporaries frequently observed that those who had the power to cure by magical means could likewise cause harm.

Healers were also identified with witches in the minds of many religious reformers, especially Protestants, who considered their practice of white magic no less heretical or diabolical than the *maleficia* of witches.[39] It remains uncertain how many of the thousands of women prosecuted for witchcraft were in fact healers. There is more evidence of their prosecution for superstitious practices in the ecclesiastical courts than for witchcraft in the secular courts, and their crime was not commonly confused with that of witchcraft. Nonetheless, many of the local and regional studies of witchcraft trials, especially those in France, Switzerland, England, Scotland, Austria, Hungary, and New England, have shown that a significant proportion of those accused were in fact wise-women.[40]

A third approach to the problem of women as witches focuses on their personal attributes. The judicial record provides abundant evidence that most witches exhibited behavior that did not conform to contemporary male standards of proper feminine conduct. Witches were often described as aggressive and quarrelsome, and many of them had violated conventional standards of sexual morality. They also displayed frequent signs of religious, social and sexual independence. Seen in this context, witchcraft accusations and prosecutions represented efforts to maintain traditional standards of feminine behavior or perhaps even establish new ones.[41] This is a plausible line of argument, but it does not explain why some quarrelsome or assertive women were accused of witchcraft, while others were not. It is more likely that those women who acted in such as way also were involved in some activity that led their neighbors to suspect them of either *maleficium* or diabolism.

Concerning the age of accused witches the trial records provide much less information than we have regarding their sex. It is apparent, however, that they were on average quite old, at least by the standards of their times. In most areas they were older than fifty, which in early modern Europe was well beyond the age of menopause, and in some countries, such as England and Geneva, the average age hovered closer to sixty.[42] The old age of witches served mainly to reinforce theories regarding their sex. Old witches were more dependent upon the community than young ones; they were more likely to be midwives and healers; and they were also more likely to be difficult to deal with personally. There were, however, some striking exceptions to the norm of the older witch. In the seventeenth century large numbers of children became involved in witch-hunts. In some cases they were named in the latter stages of large chain-reaction hunts. In others children were encouraged by either their parents or their priests to confess freely to attending the sabbath, as in Sweden in 1668-69 and the Basque country in 1609-10.[43] These same children could also be the source of witchcraft accusations, naming those who went to the sabbath with them and sometimes accusing their own parents.

5. THE RISE OF WITCH-HUNTING

The main historiographical question in the history of witchcraft is how to account for the rise of witch-hunting in the fifteenth century and its dramatic intensification in the late sixteenth and early seventeenth centuries. Since the great witch-hunt was composed of many individual hunts, each of which had its own specific causes, it is difficult to offer a single comprehensive explanation of its origins and development. Mono-causal explanations of the hunt, such as those which attribute the entire episode to changes in medical thought or the spread of syphi-

lis in Europe, have proved to be either implausible or unpersuasive.[44]
We can, however, identify five approaches to this question, each contributing to an understanding of the rise of witch-hunting.

Ideology

The formulation of the cumulative concept of witchcraft, its dissemination throughout Europe, and its reception by those men who controlled the judicial machinery of church and state has occupied a prominent place in most explanations of the great hunt.   The Spanish
inquisitor Alonso de Salazar Frías underlined the singular importance
of ideology in this process when, at the height of the great Basque
witch-hunt of 1609-14, he observed that "there were neither witches
nor bewitched until they were talked and written about."[45]   The invention of printing in the middle of the fifteenth century and its rapid
growth in the sixteenth century obviously played a crucial role in this
process, but the oral communication referred to by Salazar, both in
learned and popular contexts, was equally important.   Written instructions from judicial authorities also formed part of this discourse.   In
many German communities, local judges acquired a knowledge of the
heretical aspects of witchcraft from the members of university law faculties, who were asked for judicial guidance in the handling of witchcraft cases.[46]

We now have a fairly clear idea of how the cumulative concept of
witchcraft took shape, but there remains a great deal of work to be
done on the treatises through which it was propagated.   The *Malleus
maleficarum* has attracted the lion's share of this historical work, but
other major works, such as those of Jean Bodin, William Perkins, and
James I, have also received systematic analysis.[47]   Historians are also
exploring a much larger body of work composed by less well known
demonologists and preachers, and this is giving us a better sense of the
extent to which certain ideas spread among the educated classes.[48]
Closely related to this enterprise is the study of artistic materials, especially those engravings and woodcuts which were used to illustrate
witchcraft treatises.   These visual materials provide a vehicle for understanding the sources and content of demonological fantasy, as well as
the nature of its appeal.[49]

The literature and iconography of witchcraft provide compelling
evidence that fears of the demonic became more intense between the
early fifteenth century, when the trials began, and the late sixteenth
and early seventeenth centuries, when they reached a peak.   Not only

did the figure of the Devil become more frightening, but men's confidence in God's triumph over him was weakened. In both visual and literary sources the image of the sabbath became more horrific, the witches demonstrated greater eagerness to serve the Devil in a religious fashion, and the traditional insistence on the necessity of God's permission for all diabolical activity was weakened. Treatises such as Pierre de Lancre's *Tableau de l'inconstance de mauvais anges et démons* (1612) and Henri Boguet's *Discours des sorciers* (1602) reveal a more extreme view of diabolical power than those written in the fifteenth century, including the *Malleus maleficarum.*

The question remains why this shift in learned attitudes took place and why the men who prosecuted witches were receptive to it. Part of the answer may lie in theological developments. The revival of Augustinianism in the fifteenth century and its continued influence for more than two hundred years may have gradually led to an emphasis on the power of demonic forces in the universe, although Augustine himself had always insisted upon God's omnipotence.[50] It has also recently been argued—though against the best modern scholarship—that a separation of nature and grace by nominalist theologians allowed the Devil more freedom than he had in the earlier scholastic tradition, which emphasized the operation of natural law.[51] Another source of the new outlook may have been the replacement of the Seven Deadly Sins by the Ten Commandments as the basis of Christian ethics. This change, which had begun in the fifteenth century but was not complete until the middle of the sixteenth century, directed the moral attention of both clergy and laymen to the sin of idolatry, which was prohibited by the First Commandment, and with which diabolism was equated. The Commandments helped to turn the Devil from the fiend who was the enemy of Christ into the anti-type of God the Father, the source and object of false worship, especially by witches.[52]

One of the reasons why ruling elites were receptive to these depictions of unprecedented demonic influence in the world is that they were increasingly frightened by the prospect of rebellion and disorder within their communities. The early modern period witnessed frequent agrarian disturbances, numerous political uprisings, and some devastating civil wars. The crime of witchcraft and that of rebellion were identified in Scripture, while the ideology of witchcraft, especially in its exaggerated, late sixteenth-century form, was suffused with the imagery of rebellion. The Devil was the first rebel and his confederates, the witches, were accused of treason against God, meeting collectively

in large numbers, and challenging the established moral and social order. The imagery of the sabbath, in which everything is inverted, reflects not only an exaggerated belief in demonic power but also the fear
that witches would turn the world upside-down.[53]

The Reformation

Although the Protestant Reformation did not begin until about 100
years after the first witch trials, it has often been argued that the Protestant and Catholic reformations, taken together, constituted one of
the main causes of the intensification of witch-hunting in the late sixteenth century. The nature of that connection, however, remains very
much a point of controversy. Some of the older theories, such as those
that attributed witch-hunting to one denomination or another and
those that considered witch trials as merely veiled attempts to eliminate
religious rivals, have not survived rigorous testing. There is widespread recognition that the Reformation contributed in various ways
to the heightened fear of the demonic that lay at the foundation of all
witch-hunting. Likewise, the biblicism that characterized Protestant
preaching and writing led to a new emphasis on condemnations of
magic in the Old Testament, especially Exodus 22:18: "Thou shalt not
suffer a witch to live." At the very least this scriptural injunction
served to reinforce secular laws against contemporary witchcraft, with
which Hebraic divination and sorcery were readily but erroneously
identified. In some cases, when the biblical injunction against witchcraft became the subject of a sermon, it inspired a community to identify and prosecute witches in their midst.[54]

Somewhat more controversial is the extent to which witch-hunting
represented an effort by religious reformers to bring about a general
moral reform of society. It is true that in some reformed communities
campaigns against sins like fornication, adultery, sodomy, prostitu-
tion, and blasphemy included witchcraft among the offenses which
were to be targeted. In Scotland witch-hunting became part of a more
general campaign by ministers and laymen to establish a godly state,
and a similar impulse may have inspired some of the witch-hunts in Puritan England, as at Newcastle in 1649.[55] It remains uncertain how
many witches were tried as part of such operations, although the involvement of clerics in many witch-hunts suggests that the numbers
may be large.[56] Much work needs to be done in this area, especially on
the influence of millenarian sentiment in inspiring both the programs
for reform and the witch-hunts themselves.[57]

Closely related to those theories which link witch-hunting to programs of moral reform are those which associate it with the efforts of religious reformers to eliminate many of the superstitious and magical practices that flourished in the countryside. According to this interpretation, witch trials represented the efforts of religious reformers to destroy the "animist mentality" of a population that was only superficially christianized by the middle of the sixteenth century. One of the main premises of this argument—that the rural population before the Reformation was essentially pagan—has not gone unchallenged, especially since so much of the popular magic that reformers attacked had specifically ecclesiastical sources. Nevertheless, the conflict between priest and magician that Jean Delumeau has referred to was very real, and it formed part of a more general assault on popular culture, a campaign to "acculturate" the masses, that has become a centerpiece of recent French historiography.[58] The concept of acculturation may not be the most appropriate term to describe this development,[59] but the connection between such campaigns and witch-hunting has been established in a number of local studies.

In addition to attacking popular magic and superstition, Protestants also endeavored to eliminate the magical aspects of Roman Catholicism. These manifestations of ecclesiastical "magic" ranged from the "hocus pocus" of the Eucharist to the lay use of holy water and candles to exorcise evil spirits. The elimination of these magical practices almost certainly had an indirect effect on some witchcraft prosecutions, especially in England, since it eliminated one of the means by which individuals traditionally protected themselves against witchcraft. Without such rituals at their disposal, villagers were forced to take legal action against those persons who were allegedly causing them supernatural harm.[60] This thesis, however, has only limited applicability in Catholic circles, and it also works only in those situations in which accusations came from the witch's neighbors.

Social and economic change

The tensions generated by the rapid increase in the population of Europe, the unprecedented inflation between 1500 and 1640, the reduction of real wages, the decline in the standard of living for the lower classes, and the advent of agricultural capitalism contributed to the personal tensions that found their expression in witch-hunting. There are some clear chronological correlations, moreover, between crises of subsistence and periods of intense witch-hunting, especially in the Pays de Vaud and in many German states.[61] Such correlations are not universal and some of the conflicts which resulted in witchcraft accusations did not originate within an economic context.[62]

It is even more problematic whether the entire European witch-hunt can be attributed primarily to economic and social change. The rise of witch-hunting in the fifteenth century had little to do with such developments, especially since the most dramatic economic and social changes of the early modern period did not occur until the middle of the sixteenth century. It is more plausible to link such changes with the more intense prosecutions of the late sixteenth and early seventeenth centuries. Alan Macfarlane has interpreted the rise of witch-hunting in Essex county, England in the late sixteenth century as a reflection of a breakdown of traditional communal values and good neighborliness under the pressures of economic change.[63] In these circumstances witchcraft accusations represented efforts by hard pressed villagers to reverse the guilt they experienced for refusing to help those in need. A somewhat different dynamic operated at Salem, Massachusetts in 1692, where the victims of witchcraft included more prosperous members of the community. These accusations, however, also arose in response to the advent of a commercial society.[64] In both cases, however, witch-hunting was related to shifts in values, not simply to increased competition for economic resources.

Closely related to social and economic change were the combined effects of disease and war on the European population. We cannot establish any direct connection between outbreaks of the plague and periods of intense witch-hunting, except in those cities like Geneva and Milan where persons identified as plague spreaders were prosecuted as witches.[65] The plague did, however, have devastating long-term consequences in many European communities, and thus it contributed to the general deterioration of living conditions that encouraged accusations of witchcraft. The effects of early modern warfare on the European population for many years after the incidence of armed conflict, played an important, though indirect, role in the rise of witch-hunting. During actual periods of armed conflict, however, witchcraft accusations tended to decline, as communities found different sources for anxiety and different scapegoats for their problems.[66]

Gender

The history of witchcraft has been one of the main areas in which the relatively new fields of women's history and gender studies have found

extremely fertile ground. Scholars working in these areas have established gender as an analytical category that is relevant to virtually every
aspect of witchcraft studies. It remains uncertain, however, whether
gender is central or ancillary to an explanation of the rise of witch-
hunting. In order to establish its centrality, it is necessary to show that
a new misogynism emerged during the early modern period or that
women were perceived as constituting a new threat to a male-domi-
nated society.[67]

Those who emphasize the ideological origins of witch-hunting in
some ways have the greatest difficulty in establishing a gender-based
explanation of the witch-hunt. The problem does not lie in the nature
of the stereotype of the witch, which is essentially female, suffused with
sexual imagery and reflective of a deep hatred and fear of women. The
problem is that this stereotype has a long history, especially in clerical
circles, and represented little that was new in the early modern period.
In order to establish the existence of a new misogynism—one that
would account for the early trials of the fifteenth century or the massive prosecutions of the late sixteenth and early seventeenth century—
it is necessary to illustrate the intersection of that ideology with novel
intellectual or religious trends.

One way of demonstrating this linkage has been to stress the fusion
of the old misogynism with Catholic and Protestant programs for reform, especially those involving efforts to change popular sexual
behavior.[68] Another has been to emphasize changes that took place in
attitudes toward women during the Reformation, and to argue either
that witches suffered by comparison with a higher standard or that
they were the victims of a lower one.[69] A third has been to stress the
contemporary identification of women with disorder, a view that combined a traditional medieval view of uncontrolled female sexuality
with a distinctly early modern fear of rebellion and the destruction of
conventional gender relationships.

The possibility that women represented a new threat to male social
and economic power suggests a different way of using gender to explain the rise of witch-hunting. Interpretations of witchcraft trials as
efforts by physicians to destroy midwives or healers who threatened
their professional monopoly or by clerics who wished to eliminate the
dissemination of contraceptive techniques can be dismissed as either
anachronistic or insubstantial. Much more plausible are those theories
which stress the impact of demographic and economic change on
women, especially those who were old and unmarried. The tensions

that these changes generated often led to witchcraft accusations, as un-attached women found it more difficult to make a living and as com-munities tried to cope with the social effects of their poverty and inde-pendence. The only question in this regard is whether the growth of this impoverished and unaccommodated group of women was suffi-ciently widespread and alarming to serve as the main cause of witch-hunting throughout Europe. Even if we accept the proposition that gender is central to all social and economic relations, we still cannot es-tablish a persuasive explanation of the rise of witch-hunting that fo-cuses exclusively or even primarily on gender.

The State

A final approach to the rise of witch-hunting links it in various ways with the rise of the modern state, a development of sufficiently long du-ration to coincide with the entire period of prosecution. There is wide-spread acceptance of the fact that some aspects of state-building, espe-cially the extension of secular jurisdiction over ecclesiastical crimes and the development of inquisitorial procedure, served as necessary pre-conditions of the great witch-hunt. Proponents of the "state thesis," however, have argued for much more, depicting the great witch-hunt as one of the means by which the centralized, absolutist state curbed localism and particularism, produced a more obedient population, and legitimized new regimes. At the same time the state was able to assist the church in acculturating the peasant masses and bringing about godly reform.[70]

The state thesis has great appeal, both because it can be combined with a religious or ideological explanation of witch-hunting and be-cause the involvement of the state in the prosecutions is readily appar-ent. The problem, apart from its inapplicability in areas where pros-ecutions came mainly from below, is that it ascribes to central authorities a leading role in witch-hunting. Even if central govern-ments did pass witchcraft edicts or statutes, they rarely took the initia-tive in prosecutions, and they often did more to restrain witch-hunting than to encourage it. The concentration of trials in outlying regions of France, for example, where the state thesis is most readily applied, had much more to do with the independence of these regions from central judicial control than with the efforts of the central government to re-duce them to obedience.[71]

6. The Decline of Witch-hunting

The decline of witch-hunting, viewed as both a local and a general European development, has attracted much less scholarly attention than its rise. Much of what has been written concerns the termination of specific witch-hunts, especially those involving large numbers of victims. In many cases these large hunts ended when the local community or higher authorities came to the conclusion that innocent persons were being prosecuted. In some of the larger chain-reaction hunts, this loss of confidence in the process of witch-hunting arose when persons who did not conform to the stereotype of the witch were accused.[72] In some other mass trials the revelation that the accusations had been brought deliberately and maliciously had the same effect. In still others, the intervention of higher authorities was sufficient to bring the vicious cycle of accusations and implications to a halt.

Much more controversial than the cessation of specific witch-hunts has been the end of all trials in a particular region or country. Traditionally this has been attributed to a process of philosophical and scientific enlightenment, an approach that has paralleled the emphasis placed by historians of the liberal rationalist school on scholasticism, credulity and superstition as the causes of witch-hunting. Although historians no longer speak about the dispelling of "delusion" among the learned elite, many still emphasize the new intellectual currents of the mid and late seventeenth century as the main reason for the end of witch-hunting.[73] For these scholars the emergence of the mechanical philosophy and the growing conviction that there were natural explanations of allegedly supernatural phenomena led men in positions of authority to challenge those beliefs upon which prosecutions had been based. This ideological approach to the end of witch-hunting emphasizes the rise of Cartesian thought and its rejection of both the Aristotelian and neo-Platonic cosmologies.

The difficulty inherent in this philosophical approach to the decline of witchcraft is that many of the men who discouraged or terminated witch-hunts still believed in the reality of witchcraft and even more so in the possibility of diabolical intervention in the world. There is only limited evidence of the new mental outlook in the lawyers and magistrates who criticized the trials in France, England, Scotland, Spain and Germany in the early seventeenth century. These men, and many others who urged restraint in the prosecution of witches and imposed new rules for the conduct of the trials, based their skepticism on legal rather than philosophical grounds. They were much more concerned with confessions produced under torture and false charges made by demoniacs and frauds than with the reality of demonic power. They also developed more demanding standards for proving that an act of maleficent magic had actually taken place. Much more work needs to be done on the changes that took place in legal procedure and in the mentality of the judicial elite during the seventeenth century before we can fully understand why trials came to an end, often with great suddenness.

Changes in the religious outlook of the ruling elites may have also contributed to their reluctance to allow accusations of witchcraft to come to trial. The development of natural theology, with its central assumption that God worked through the processes of nature, tended to minimize the possibility of any supernatural intervention in the world and also helped to make the mechanical philosophy compatible with religious orthodoxy. At the same time an apparent decline in religious zeal and enthusiasm in all western European countries after 1650 deprived witch-hunting of an important source of its inspiration and energy.

Those scholars who have emphasized the socio-economic causes of the great witch-hunt have also advanced corresponding explanations for its termination. There is a general correlation between the stabilization of the European population and a leveling off of prices on the one hand and the decline of witch-hunting on the other. It remains to be shown, however, whether a general improvement in economic conditions in the late seventeenth and early eighteenth centuries actually caused the reduction in witchcraft accusations. It is equally uncertain whether the construction of a new gender ideology in which women were domesticated and subordinated to men made it less necessary for the proponents of that ideology to use witchcraft accusations to control women.[74] Further research on the decline of witch-hunting in specific localities will be needed in order to address these questions.

The persistence of popular witch beliefs long after the great witch-hunt had come to an end and the occasional illegal execution of suspected witches by their neighbors suggest that the main responsibility for bringing the witch-hunt to an end lay with the ruling classes, not the common people. Whether officials and judges abandoned witch-hunting because the absolutist state had finally triumphed and had succeeded in reforming popular culture remains at the very least unproven.[75] To be sure, central authorities in almost every European country took the lead in bringing that hunt to an end, but in so doing they were acting as they had throughout the period of witch-hunting, when they had almost always demonstrated more restraint in prosecuting witches than the men who occupied positions of power within local communities.

The decline and ultimate termination of officially sanctioned witch-hunting in the late seventeenth and eighteenth centuries emphasizes the fact that the great witch-hunt was a time-bound and a culture-bound phenomenon. Confined exclusively to European countries and their overseas possessions, it lasted only from the fifteenth to the eighteenth century. It began only after late medieval theologians and judges developed the stereotype of the witch as a Devil-worshipping magician and after ecclesiastical and secular judicial authorities acquired the judicial tools necessary to prosecute the crime. Once the trials began, they increased in intensity throughout Europe as the result of a potent combination of ideological, socio-economic, political, and religious forces. The end of witch-hunting occurred not simply when those forces lost strength but when the very intellectual and legal foundations of the phenomenon were undercut—when educated Europeans questioned the ability of the Devil to intervene in human affairs and when judges refused to convict accused witches on the basis of insufficient evidence.

NOTES

1. Another term, "witch-panic," is appropriate for some of the larger individual hunts, in which accusations and prosecutions became particularly intense.
2. Larner (1984), 88-91.
3. On the development of witch-beliefs in the Middle Ages see Cohn (1975) and Peters (1978).
4. Cohn (1975), 126-28; Kieckhefer (1976), 16-18.
5. Blauert (1989); Cohn (1975), 225-28; Monter (1976), 17-24; Kieckhefer (1976), ch. 5.
6. Thomas (1971); Ginzburg (1983).
7. Holmes (1984), 100-1.
8. Midelfort (1989), 104-5.
9. See, for example, Muchembled (1990).
10. Cohn (1975), 210-19.
11. Holmes (1984), 97.
12. Ginzburg (1983) and (1991).
13. Murray (1921). Ginzburg (1983), xiii, 20-22, claimed that there was a "kernel of truth" in Murray's thesis since the members of a fertility cult in the Friuli were prosecuted as witches, but there is no evidence that these persons ever participated physically in assemblies that could be interpreted as the witches' sabbath.
14. Kieckhefer (1976), ch. 3.
15. Henningsen (1980), 390; Harner (1973).
16. Thomas (1971), 442-43.
17. Wiseman (1984), ch. 7; Godbeer (1992), ch. 5. On the few successful prosecutions for *maleficium* see Fox (1968), 36-40.
18. Soman (1978), 42-43; Henningsen (1980), 17; Schormann (1981), 109-10.
19. Unverhau (1983), esp. 116.
20. Langbein (1974), 130-31.
21. Holmes (1984), 92-93.
22. Burghartz (1988), 62-63.
23. On the attitude of the Venetian Inquisition toward witchcraft see Martin (1989), esp. 248-49.
24. Henningsen (1980), 366-77; Tedeschi (1990).
25. Gari LaCruz (1980).
26. Levack (1987), 85-90; Soman (1989).
27. Soman (1986), 44-45; Tedeschi (1990), 97-104; Monter (1976), 96-97.
28. Midelfort (1979), 177-88.
29. Levack (1987), 19-22; Barstow (1994), 19-23.
30. Godbeer (1992), ch. 5; Heikkinen and Kervinen (1990), 324; Behringer (1987), 58; Henningsen (1980), 17.

31. Levack (1987), 1-24.
32. Macfarlane (1970); Midelfort (1972); Monter (1976); Dupont-Bouchat (1978); Schormann (1977); Muchembeld (1979); Larner (1981); Behringer (1987); Ankarloo and Henningsen (1990); Briggs (1989); Martin (1989).
33. See for example Demos (1982), 11-13.
34. Briggs (1984), 12.
35. Hansen (1900); Trevor-Roper (1969)
36. Burghartz (1988); Sharpe (1991); Holmes (1993).
37. Harley (1990).
38. Roper (1991), 30-31.
39. Clark (1990); Sawyer (1989).
40. Horsley (1979), 700-12; Larner (1981), 138-42; Sawyer (1989); Soman (1978), 43; Demos (1982), 81-84.
41. Karlsen (1987), 138.
42. Macfarlane (1970), 161; Monter (1976), 123; Bever (1982), 181.
43. Ankarloo (1990), 284-317; Henningsen (1980).
44. Estes (1984); Andreski (1982).
45. Kors and Peters (1972), 341.
46. Schormann (1977), 9-44.
47. Anglo (1977); Segl (1988); Lange (1970); Clark (1977); Larner (1984).
48. Clark (1990).
49. Zika (1989); Hults (1987); Hoak (1985).
50. Wright (1982), 1-50.
51. Cervantes (1991), 14-19.
52. Bossy (1988).
53. Clark (1977) and (1980); Levack (1987), 57-60.
54. Boyer and Nissenbaum (1974), 168-78.
55. Larner (1981), 67-68, 71-75.
56. On the different degrees of clerical involvement in witch-hunting compare Muchembled (1979), 259-60, 266-67, and Briggs (1989), 71-72.
57. Lamont (1969), 98-100.
58. Delumeau (1978); Muchembled (1979) and (1985); Klaits (1985), ch. 3.
59. Burke (1982).
60. Thomas (1971), 493-98.
61. Kamber (1982), 26-28; Behringer (1987), 98-106.
62. Blauert (1989), 20-23; Briggs (1989), 74.
63. Macfarlane (1970), 192-99.
64. Boyer and Nissenbaum (1974), 179-216.
65. Monter (1976), 44-48.
66. Monter (1976), 81; Kamber (1982), 27.
67. Hester (1992); Barstow (1994).
68. Klaits (1985), 65-85; Muchembled (1979), 266-67, 259-60.
69. Coudert (1989); Brauner (1989); Karlsen (1987).
70. Muchembled (1985), 235-78; Larner (1981), 193, 198-99.
71. Briggs (1989), 13-14.
72. Midelfort (1979).
73. Trevor-Roper (1969); Easlea (1980), 196-252.
74. For the development of this argument with respect to New England see Karlsen (1987).
75. Muchembled (1985), 235-78.

BIBLIOGRAPHY

Andreski, Stanislav. "The Syphilitic Shock." *Encounter* 58 (1982): 7-26.
Anglo, Sydney, ed. *The Damned Art: Essays in the Literature of Witchcraft*. London, 1977.
Ankarloo, Bengt, and Gustav Henningsen, eds. *Early Modern European Witchcraft: Centres and Peripheries*. Oxford, 1990.
Baranowski, Bohdan. *Procesy Czarownic w Polsce w XVII i XVIII Wieku*. Lodz, 1952. [With a French summary.]
Barstow, Anne Llewellyn. *Witchcraze: a New History of the European Witch Hunts*. San Francisco, 1994.
Behringer, Wolfgang. "'Erhob sich das ganze Land zu ihrer Ausrottung...': Hexenprozesse und Hexenverfolgungen in Europa." In *Hexenwelten: Magie und Imagination vom 16.-20. Jahrhundert*, ed. Richard van Dülmen, 131-69. Frankfurt am Main, 1987.
Behringer, Wolfgang. *Hexenverfolgung in Bayern: Volksmagie, Glaubenseifer und Staatsräson in der Frühen Neuzeit*. Munich, 1987.
Bever, Edward. "Old Age and Witchcraft in Early Modern Europe." In *Old Age in Pre-industrial Society*, ed. P. Stearns, 150-90. New York, 1982.
Blauert, Andreas. *Frühe Hexenverfolgungen: Ketzer-, Zauberei- und Hexenprozesse des 15. Jahrhunderts*. Hamburg, 1989.
Boguet, Henri. *An Examen of Witches*. Trans. E. A. Ashwin. Ed. Montague Summers. London, 1929.
Bossy, John. "Moral Arithmetic: Seven Sins into Ten Commandments." In *Conscience and Casuistry in Early Modern Europe*, ed. Edmund Leites, 214-34. Cambridge, 1988.
Boyer, Paul and Stephen Nissenbaum. *Salem Possessed: The Social Origins of Witchcraft*. Cambridge, Mass., 1974.
Brauner, Sigrid. "Martin Luther on Witchcraft: a True Reformer?" In Brink (1989), 29-42.
Briggs, Robin. *Communities of Belief: Cultural and Social Tension in Early Modern France*. Oxford, 1989.
Briggs, Robin. "Witchcraft and Popular Mentality in Lorraine, 1580-1630." In *Occult and Scientific Mentalities in the Renaissance*, ed. Brian Vickers, 337-49. Cambridge, 1984.
Brink, J. R., et al., eds. *The Politics of Gender in Early Modern Europe*. SCES, vol. 12. Kirksville, Mo., 1989.
Brucker, Gene A. "Sorcery in Early Renaissance Florence." *Studies in the Renaissance* 10 (1963): 7-24.
Burghartz, Susanna. "The Equation of Women and Witches: a Case Study of Witchcraft Trials in Lucerne and Lausanne in the Fifteenth and Sixteenth Centuries." In *The German Underworld*, ed. Richard J. Evans, 57-74. London, 1988.
Burke, Peter. "A Question of Acculturation?" In *Scienze credenze occulte livelli di cultura*, 197-204. Florence, 1982.
Byloff, Fritz. *Hexenglaube und Hexenverfolgung in den Österreichischen Alpenländern*. Berlin and Leipzig, 1934.
Caro Baroja, Julio. *The World of the Witches*. Trans. O. N. V. Glendinning. Chicago, 1965.

Cervantes, Fernando. *The Idea of the Devil and the Problem of the Indian: The Case of Mexico in the Sixteenth Century*. London, 1991.

Clark, Stuart. "Inversion, Misrule and the Meaning of Witchcraft." *PaP* 87 (1980): 98-127.

Clark, Stuart. "King James's Daemonologie: Witchcraft and Kingship. " In *Anglo* (1977), 156-81.

Clark, Stuart. "Protestant Demonology: Sin, Superstition, and Society (c. 1520-c. 1630)." In Ankarloo and Henningsen (1990), 45-81.

Cohn, Norman. *Europe's Inner Demons*. London, 1975.

Coudert, Allison P. "The Myth of the Improved Status of Protestant Women: The Case of the Witchcraze." In Brink (1989), 61-94.

Delumeau, Jean. *La Peur en occident XIVe - XVIIIe siècles*. Paris, 1978.

Demos, John P. *Entertaining Satan: Witchcraft and the Culture of Early New England*. New York, 1982.

Dupont-Bouchat, Marie-Sylvie. "La répression de la sorcellerie dans le duché de Luxembourg aux XVIe et XVIIe siècles." In M. Dupont-Bouchat, et al., *Prophètes et sorciers dans les Pays-Bas XVIe-XVIIIe siècles*, 41-154. Paris, 1978.

Easlea, Brian. *Witch-hunting, Magic and the New Philosophy: an Introduction to the Debates of the Scientific Revolution 1450-1750*. Brighton, 1980.

Estes, Leland. 'The Medical Origins of the European Witch Craze: a Hypothesis." *JSH* 17 (1984): 271-84.

Fox, Sanford J. *Science and Justice: The Massachusetts Witchcraft Trials*. Baltimore, 1968.

Gari Lacruz, Angel. "Variedad de competencias en el delito de brujería 1600-1650 en Aragùn." In *La Inquisición Española: Nueva visión, nueva horizontes*, ed. J. Perez Villanueva, 319-27. Madrid, 1980.

Gijswift-Hofstra, Marijke. "The European Witchcraft Debate and the Dutch Variant." *Social History* 15 (1990): 181-94.

Gijswijt-Hofstra, Marijke, and Willem Frijhoff, eds. *Witchcraft in the Netherlands: from the Fourteenth to the Twentieth Century*. Trans. R. M. J. van der Wilden-Fall. Rotterdam, 1991.

Ginzburg, Carlo. *Ecstasies: Deciphering the Witches' Sabbath*. New York, 1991.

Ginzburg, Carlo. *The Night Battles: Witchcraft and Agrarian Cults in the Sixteenth and Seventeenth Centuries*. Trans. John A. Tedeschi and Anne Tedeschi. Baltimore, 1983.

Godbeer, Richard. *The Devil's Dominion: Magic and Religion in Early New England*. Cambridge, 1992.

Hansen, Joseph. *Zauberwahn, Inquisition and Hexenprozess im Mittelalter, und die Entstehung der grossen Hexenverfolgung*. Munich, 1900.

Hansen, Joseph, ed. *Quellen und Untersuchungen zur Geschichte des Hexenwahns und der Hexenverfolgung im Mittelalter*. Bonn, 1901.

Harley, David. "Historians as Demonologists: the Myth of the Midwife-Witch." *Social History of Medicine* 3 (1990): 1-26.

Harner, Michael J. *Hallucinogens and Shamanism*. New York, 1973.

Heikkinen Antero and Timo Kervinen. "Finland: the Male Domination." In Ankarloo and Henningsen (1990), 319-38.

Henningsen, Gustav. *The Witches' Advocate: Basque Witchcraft and the Spanish Inquisition, 1609-1614*. Reno, Nev., 1980.

Hester, Marianne. *Lewd Women and Wicked Witches: A Study of the Dynamics of Male Domination*. London, 1992.

Hoak, Dale. "Art, Culture and Mentality in Renaissance Society: The Meaning of Hans Baldung Grien's Bewitched Groom (1544)." *RenQ* 38 (1985): 488-510.

Holmes, Clive. "Popular Culture?: Witches, Magistrates and Divines in Early Modern England." In *Understanding Popular Culture: Europe from the Middle Ages to the Nineteenth Century*, ed. S. Kaplan, 85-111. Berlin, New York and Amsterdam, 1984.

Holmes, Clive. "Women: Witnesses and Witches." *PaP* 140 (1993): 45-78.

Horsley, Richard A. "Who Were the Witches?: the Social Roles of the Accused in the European Witch Trials." *JIH* 9 (1979): 689-715.

Hults, Linda C. "Baldung and the Witches of Freiburg: the Evidence of Images." *JIH* 18 (1987): 249-76.

Kamber, Peter. "La Chasse aux sorciers et aux sorcières dans le Pays de Vaud: aspects quantitatifs (1581-1620)." *Revue Historique Vaudoise* 90 (1982): 21-33.

Karlsen, Carol. *The Devil in the Shape of a Woman: Witchcraft in Colonial New England.* New York, 1987.

Kieckhefer, Richard. *European Witch Trials: Their Foundations in Popular and Learned Culture, 1300-1500.* London, 1976.

Kivelson, Valerie A. "Through the Prism of Witchcraft: Gender and Social Change in Seventeenth-Century Muscovy." In *Russia's Women: Accommodation, Resistance, Transformation,* ed. B. E. Evans, B. A. Engel and C. D. Worobec, 74-94. Berkeley and Los Angeles, 1991.

Klaits, Joseph. *Servants of Satan: The Age of the Witch-hunts.* Bloomington, 1985.

Klaniczay, Gábor. "Decline of Witches and Rise of Vampires in 18th-Century Habsburg Monarchy." *Ethnologia Europaea* 17 (1987): 165-80.

Klaniczay, Gábor. "Hungary: the Accusations and the Universe of Popular Magic." In Ankarloo and Henningsen (1990).

Kors, Alan C., and Edward Peters, eds. *Witchcraft in Europe, 1100-1700.* Philadelphia, 1972.

Kramer, Heinrich, and James Sprenger. *The Malleus Maleficarum.* Trans. and ed., Montague Summers. New York, 1971.

Kunze, Michael. *Highroad to the Stake: A Tale of Witchcraft.* Trans. William E. Yuill. Chicago, 1987.

Lamont, William. *Godly Rule.* London, 1969.

Lange, Ursula. *Untersuchungen zu Bodins Démonomanie.* Frankfurt, 1970.

Langbein, John. *Prosecuting Crime in the Renaissance: England, Germany, France.* Cambridge, 1974.

Larner, Christina. *Enemies of God: The Witch-Hunt in Scotland.* Baltimore, 1981.

Larner, Christina. *Witchcraft and Religion: the Politics of Popular Belief.* Oxford, 1984.

Lea, Henry C. *Materials toward a History of Witchcraft.* Ed. Arthur C. Howland. 3 vols. New York, 1957.

Levack, Brian P. "The Great Scottish Witch Hunt of 1661-1662." *JBS* 20 (1980): 90-108.

Levack, Brian P. *The Witch-Hunt in Early Modern Europe.* London, 1987.

MacDonald, Michael, ed. *Witchcraft and Hysteria in Elizabethan England.* London, 1990.

Macfarlane, Alan. *Witchcraft in Tudor and Stuart England.* London, 1970.

Mandrou, Robert. *Magistrats et sorciers en France au XVIIe siècle: une analyse de psychologie historique.* Paris, 1968.

Martin, Ruth. *Witchcraft and the Inquisition in Venice, 1550-1650.* Oxford, 1989.

Midelfort, H.C. Erik. "The Devil and the German People: Reflections on the Popularity of Demon Possession in Sixteenth-Century Germany." In *Religion and Culture in the Renaissance and Reformation,* ed. Steven Ozment, 99-119. SCES, vol. 11. Kirksville, Mo., 1989.

Midelfort, H. C. Erik. "Johann Weyer and the Transformation of the Insanity Defense." In *The German People and the Reformation,* ed. R. Po-Chia Hsia, 234-61. Ithaca, 1988.

Midelfort, H. C. Erik. *Witch-hunting in Southwestern Germany, 1562-1684: the Social and Intellectual Foundations.* Stanford, 1972.

Midelfort, H. C. Erik. "Witch Hunting and the Domino Theory." In Obelkevich (1979), 277-325.

Monter, E. William. *Frontiers of Heresy: the Spanish Inquisition from the Basque Lands to Sicily.* Cambridge, 1990.

Monter, E. William. *Ritual, Myth and Magic in Early Modern Europe.* Athens, Ohio, 1983.

Monter, E. William. *Witchcraft in France and Switzerland: The Borderlands during the Reformation.* Ithaca, 1976.

Muchembled, Robert. *Popular Culture and Elite Culture in France, 1400-1750.* Trans. Lydia Cochrane. Baton Rouge, 1985.

Muchembled, Robert. "Satanic Myths and Cultural Reality." In Ankarloo and Henningsen (1990), 139-60.

Muchembled, Robert. "The Witches of the Cambrésis: the Acculturation of the Rural World in the Sixteenth and Seventeenth Centuries." In Obelkevich (1979), 220-76.

Murray, Margaret A. *The Witch-Cult in Western Europe.* Oxford, 1921.

Naess, Hans E. "Norway: the Criminological Context." In Ankarloo and Henningsen (1990), 367-82.

Obelkevich, James, ed. *Religion and the People, 800-1700.* Chapel Hill, N.C., 1979.

Oberman, Heiko A. *Masters of the Reformation.* Trans. Dennis E. Martin. Cambridge, 1981.

O'Neil, Mary. "Magical Healing, Love Magic and the Inquisition in late Sixteenth-century Modena." In *Inquisition and Society in Early Modern Europe*, ed. Stephen Haliczar, 88-114. Totowa, N.J, 1987.

Paulus, Nikolaus. *Hexenwahn und Hexenprozesse, vornehmlich im 16 Jahrhundert.* Freiburg im Breisgau, 1910.

Pearl, Jonathan L. "Witchcraft in New France in the Seventeenth Century: The Social Aspect. " *Historical Reflections* 4 (1977): 191-205.

Peters, Edward. *The Magician, The Witch and the Law.* Philadelphia, 1978.

Peters, Edward. *Torture.* Oxford, 1985.

Pollock, Adrian. "Social and Economic Characteristics of Witchcraft Accusations in Sixteenth and Seventeenth-Century Kent." *Archaeologia Cantiana* 95 (1979): 37-48.

Remy, Nicolas. *Demonolatry.* Trans. E. A. Ashwin. Ed. Montague Summers. London, 1930.

Roper, Lyndal. "Witchcraft and Fantasy in Early Modern Germany." *HWJ* 32 (1991): 19-43.

Russell, Jeffrey B. *Witchcraft in the Middle Ages.* Ithaca, 1972.

Sawyer, Ronald C. "'Strangely Handled in All Her Lyms': Witchcraft and Healing in Jacobean England." *JSH* 22 (1989): 461-85.

Schormann, Gerhard. *Hexenprozesse in Deutschland.* Göttingen, 1981.

Schormann, Gerhard. *Hexenprozesse in Nordwestdeutschland.* Hildesheim, 1977.

Scribner, Bob (R.W.). "Witchcraft and Judgement in Reformation Germany." *History Today* 40 (1990): 12-19.

Segl, Peter. *Der Hexenhammer: Entstehung und Umfeld des Malleus maleficarum von 1487.* Cologne, 1988.

Sharpe, J. A. "Witchcraft and Women in Seventeenth-Century England: Some Northern Evidence." *Continuity and Change* 6 (1991): 179-99.

Silverblatt, Irene. *Moon, Sun and Witches: Gender Ideologies and Class in Inca and Colonial Peru.* Princeton, 1987.

Soman, A. F. "Decriminalizing Witchcraft: Does the French Experience Furnish a European Model?" *Criminal Justice History* 10 (1989): 1-22.

Soman, A. F. "The Parlement of Paris and the Great Witch-hunt (1565-1640)." *SCJ* 9 (1978): 30-44.

Soman, A. F. "Trente procès de sorcellerie dans le Perche (1566-1624)." *L'Orne littéraire* 8 (1986): 42-57.

Souza, Laura de Mello e. *O diabo e a terra de Santa Cruz.* Sao Paulo, 1987.

Teall, John L. "Witchcraft and Calvinism in Elizabethan England: Divine Power and Human Agency." *Journal of the History of Ideas* 23 (1962): 22-36.

Tedeschi, John A. "Inquisitorial Law and the Witch." In Ankarloo and Henningsen (1990), 83-118.

Thomas, Keith. *Religion and the Decline of Magic.* London, 1971.

Thorndike, Lynn. *A History of Magic and Experimental Science.* 8 vols. New York, 1923-58.

Trevor-Roper, H. R. *The European Witch-Craze of the Sixteenth and Seventeenth Centuries and Other Essays.* New York, 1969.

Unverhau, Dagmar. "Akkusationsprozess-Inquisitionsprozess: Indikatoren für die Intensität der Hexenverfolgung in Schleswig-Holstein." In *Hexenprozesse: Deutsche und skandinavische Beiträge*, ed. C. Degn, H. Lehmann, and D. Unverhau, 59-142. Neumünster, 1983.

Valentinitsch, Helfried, ed. *Hexen und Zauberer: Die grosze Verfolgung—ein europäisches Phenomen in der Steiermark.* Graz, 1987.

Walker, D. P. *Unclean Spirits: Possession and Exorcism in France and England in the Late Sixteenth and Early Seventeenth Centuries.* Philadelphia, 1981.

Weyer, Johann. *Witches, Devils and Doctors in the Renaissance: Johann Weyer's De Praestigiis Daemonum.* Ed. George Mora. Medieval and Renaissance Texts and Studies, vol. 73. Binghamton, 1991.

Wiseman, Richard. *Witchcraft, Magic and Religion in Seventeeth-Century Massachusetts.* Amherst, 1984.

Wright, A. D. *The Counter-Reformation: Catholic Europe and the Non-Christian World.* New York, 1982.

Zguta, Russell. "Witchcraft Trials in Seventeenth-Century Russia." *AHR* 82 (1977): 1187-1207.

Zika, Charles. "Fears of Flying: Representations of Witchcraft and Sexuality in Early Sixteenth-Century Germany." *Australian Journal of Art* 8 (1989): 19-48.

CONFESSIONAL EUROPE
Heinz Schilling
(Humboldt-Universität zu Berlin)

Between 1560 and 1650, Europe's history was shaped by what we call "confession," the modern variant of Christianity. A confession was defined by an explicit statement of doctrine (Lat., *confessio*), of which the most significant were: for Lutheranism, the Confession of Augsburg (1530) and the Book of Concord (1580); for the Reformed (Calvinist) confession, the Helvetic Confessions (1536, 1566), the Zurich Consensus (1549), and the canons of Dordrecht (1619); for Anglicanism, the Book of Common Prayer (1549) and the Thirty-Nine Articles (1563); and for Catholicism, the Council of Trent's doctrinal canons, especially the "Tridentine Profession of Faith [*professio fidei tridentina*]" of 1564 and certain papal statements. Based on their respective confessions of faith, the three great confessions (four, including Anglicanism) developed into internally coherent and externally exclusive communities distinct in institutions, membership, and belief. Each in its own way, their churches entered into alliances with the early modern states, the coercive power of which enhanced the churches' ability to manage religion, though with results that usually lagged far behind their aims. The confessions also formed a "balance-of-confessions" connected to the European balance-of-power that was forming in these same decades.

1. THE CONCEPT OF CONFESSIONALIZATION[1]

Europe housed other, non-confessional religious communities, notably the Anabaptists and other heirs of the radical reformation, and there were always counter-trends to orthodoxies within the confessional churches. Interconfessional contacts and extraconfessional movements nevertheless tended to be limited to private circles, at least until 1640 or so, when the process of deconfessionalization began to give them greater freedom. Beyond the Christian confessions vital Jewish communities existed in many European countries, though they, too, were isolated and deprived of any chance to influence the larger European societies of this era.[2]

The term "confessional Europe" for the era following the Reformation does not represent an idealist denigration of demographic, economic, political, and social factors in favor of theological or religious ones. On the contrary, the emphasis on ecclesiastical and religious structures and tendencies arises from reflections on the sociology of religion in premodern Europe in general and on the initial phase of European modernity in particular. They help us to overcome, on the one hand, the Marxists' demotion of religion to a mask for the *real* driving forces of history and, on the other, the idealist approach that has long dominated the humanities and theological studies on both sides of the Atlantic. Instead, we seek a historically accurate conception of the social effects of religion and the churches.

In the social constellation we call "premodern Europe," religion, especially in the structured form of a "confession," was a dominant element in a complex of factors, each of which can be considered—as in a medical syndrome—both separately and in its interaction with the others. Whereas the modern understanding of religion and church holds them to be mere subordinate parts of a larger secular system, in those days they were considered central, load-bearing pillars of the entire social order. Accordingly, religious change was also social change, or, as the seventeenth-century German lawyers put it, "religion is the bond of society [*religio vinculum societatis*]."

This kind of structural-functional approach to religion and church offers us perspectives and possibilities for comparison and evaluation unmatched by either materialist or idealist approaches. It demonstrates, for example, how the history of confessional Europe meant in the long run a tremendous revolutionary shift. More importantly, it rejects the long dominant view of post-Reformation religious history as a matter of competition and mutual exclusion and emphasizes the confessions' structural and functional *similarities* rather than on the *differences* among them. The confessional hypothesis focuses both on the cultural, intellectual, social, and political functions of religion and confession within the early modern social order and on the confessions' roles as spurs and barriers to the emergence of modernity. These are two sides of the historical paradigm we call "confessionalization." It holds that the late sixteenth-century emergence of confessions was one of the key events in early modernization, because the doctrinal and organizational strengthening of the churches became a powerful prelude to political and social reorganization in the following era. The confessional churches lay at the center of this process. Although similar tendencies appeared among the sects, especially the Anabaptists, these lacked any positive connection to state-building and, hence, any larger social consequences.

The goal of our study of "confessional Europe" is thus a comprehensive analysis of society. Rather than deny the spiritual and theological differences that have for centuries occupied the historians, it asserts a new set of questions about motors of and barriers to the social changes that enabled Europe in time to exchange its "traditional" or "feudal" social system for a modern one based on citizenship and a market economy. The confessional paradigm thus pushes the discussion about transition into the early modern era, fixing on the decades around 1600 as the "warm-up time of modernity" *(Vorsattelzeit der Moderne).*[3]

This concept of the social role of religion lends historical depth to the concept of modernization, which, originally oriented to the present age alone, is now indispensable for the early modern era as well. Its deployment liberates our historical vision from the dominance of purely secular social and economic relations, however appropriate the latter may be for the recent era, and allows us to conceive of the early modern social order in terms of a sociology of religion that includes demographic, political, and economic, along with the social and social-psychological, connections. Religious change, conceived as social change, thus serves as a heuristic indicator for the secularizing forces within the entire process.

Two further characteristics of the era around 1600 suggest the special importance of "confessional Europe's" religion and churches. The first is the simultaneous secularizing and re-sacralizing tendencies produced by the Reformation itself.[4] Second, there is the simultaneity of confessionalization and the formation of the early modern state, which strove to construct a unified, disciplined society of subjects, either in an absolutist sense or in that of a society based on estates *(Ständestaat)*. The primary axis of social change thus ran right through the zone in which the concerns of church and state overlapped, where the secularizing forces, important as they were, were neither the exclusive nor even the primary driving elements.[5] The decisive force, on the contrary, was resacralization.[6] To sum up, the state became more sacral before it became more secular.

Three main categories are needed to describe "confessional Europe" from a bird's-eye view: 1) the confessional churches themselves and their forms of religious mentality and practice; 2) state and society and their culture under the influence of confessionalism; and 3) the pre- or non-confessional forces, which, though in the background, later acquired decisive influence on the emergence of modern Europe. What follows is organized in these three categories.

The context for this discussion is the crisis that gripped Europe around 1600.[7] The crisis was climatic, coinciding with the depth of the "Little Ice Age," when colder, wetter winters, drove down harvests and led to a recession of vegetation in marginal areas.[8] The crisis was also demographic, for by 1600 the sixteenth-century population growth turned to stagnation and decline: more deeply in southern and central Europe, less deeply in England and Scandinavia, and hardly at all in the Dutch Republic.[9] The economic situation was complicated and regionally diverse, though in general it can be said that the "commercial revolution" of the sixteenth century was coming to an end.[10] The shift of major trade movements from the north-south routes (between northern and central Europe and the Levant via Italy) to east-west ones (from Russia and the Baltic through the Netherlands to Spain and the Americas) was now complete, and the most active centers of trade and production had shifted from Italy, southern France, and South Germany to the Atlantic rim, the Netherlands and later England. As western Europe grew ever more dependent on Baltic grain, unemployment, falling real wages, and inadequate food supplies plunged urban industry into a decisive structural crisis around 1600. While luxury goods continued to come from highly skilled guildsmen in the old urban centers, craft production began to shift to a "proto-industrial" rural sector based in households.[11]

The coincidence of these demographic and socio-economic problems with collective and individual feelings of insecurity gave rise to the psychological anxieties that marked the end of sixteenth century.[12] These feelings found relief in expectations of the end of the world, which spread among the political and cultural elites as eschatological or chiliastic views of history, among the masses as astrology and belief in portents and prodigies. The most extreme consequences of anxiety were the persecution of witches and heretics, the waves of violence against the Jews and others, depredation by mercenary soldiers, and waves of protest, mainly in the countryside. Actions against those allegedly responsible for contemporary evils were often connected with interpretations of the age and its portents, as a veritable flood of pamphlets—equal in size to that of the 1520s—fed public discussion. Whereas formerly the discussion had centered on the right to salvation and the character of the true church, this time it focused on the consequences for the world if the victory lay with the true or the false faith, with the followers of Christ or those of Antichrist. This discourse was thoroughly international.[13]

The anxiety of the times took various forms in different areas of Europe: in Spain the *autos da fé* organized by the Inquisition; in southern Italy the anti-Spanish insurrection inspired by the Joachite millenarianism of Tommaso Campanella (1568-1639); in France the massacres of the Religious Wars; in England and in the Netherlands the Calvinist polemics against the Spanish Antichrist; in Switzerland the socio-confessional conflicts in Appenzell, the Valais, Graubünden, and the Valtellina; in Sweden the bitter struggles of the Lutheran nobles and the bishops against the Crown's Calvinizing and Catholicizing tendencies; in Bohemia the deeply anti-Catholic insurrection of the estates against the Habsburgs; and finally in revolts of German-speaking burghers in Poland against the spread of Calvinism. The international public discourse of the separate confessions placed each of these disturbances—but particularly the rise of the Jesuits since the 1540s, St. Bartholomew's Day (1577), and the defeat of the Spanish Armada (1588)—in a Europe-wide context.[14] These events tended to push anxiety to extreme heights in Central Europe, where the ideological and political fronts coincided.[15] After all the political and legal tools of compromise failed and as the wars dragged on, the physical struggle for daily life overcame anxieties about the future.

2. CONFESSIONALIZATION OF THE CHURCHES

Confessionalization modernized, above all, the churches themselves. Where the Reformation succeeded, the period after 1550 witnessed institutional reconstruction of doctrine and liturgy in a great burst of church ordinances, confessional statements, and confessional alliances. This happened above all in central Europe, where each of the dozens of Protestant territorial states and each of the free cities issued a more or less independent church ordinance, and where the boundaries between Lutheranism and Calvinism remained to be staked out.[16] In the Netherlands, France, and Scotland, by contrast, reformation and confessionalization largely coincided. The new Protestant gains, whether in western or in east central and southeastern Europe (Poland, Bohemia, Transylvania, Hungary, and Austria) mostly benefited Calvinism.

The movement did not achieve total reform of state and society, not even in the northern Netherlands, where Calvinism acquired the status of a "public church" (*publieken kerke*), to which all magistrates had to belong, although it remained a minority in a multi-confessional and relatively tolerant society.[17] In England, although Queen Elizabeth I tried to forestall confessionalization, both because it contradicted her temperament and because she wished to avoid giving greater influence to the clergy, Puritan confessionalism developed as an oppositional movement within the state church.[18] This outcome proved all the more disruptive, because it developed uninterruptedly for several generations and reached a resolution only in the 1640s—fifty-to-a-hundred years later than in Germany, France, and the Netherlands.

In the Catholic lands, confessionalization of the church involved both a reaction to the Protestant advance (the Counterreformation) and a development of pre-Reformation tendencies (the Catholic reformation). Although the former should not be underestimated, it is true that early modern bureaucratization and rationalization (which in Protestant lands ran parallel to doctrinal and ritual reforms) and the renewal of monastic and lay piety had already begun in the late medieval era.

In some respects the European Reformation can be understood as a "modernization crisis," a response to the rapid fifteenth-century transformation of the Roman Curia, which was met north of the Alps by misunderstanding and mistrust. The late medieval beginnings of modernization, however, had failed to develop within the intact church, because the interests of the clerical hierarchy had opposed them, and because the Renaissance popes had posed more pressing agendas. Luther and the Reformation thus to some degree rescued the late medieval reforms in the old church and enabled the Catholic confessionalization of the late sixteenth century to employ them.[19] The Protestants took the lead in modernizing the church and held it for three or four generations, while with the Council of Trent the Catholics began to follow, though with painful slowness.[20] The true Counterreformation, recovery of lands lost to Protestantism, was successful only in part. Certain parts of Germany were recovered, above all the ecclesiastical territories and much of the Habsburg dynastic lands. Poland, too, which had in many regions developed a multi-confessional and tolerant political order under Protestant influence, began at the end of the sixteenth century to be returned to Catholicism. And although the Jesuits also attempted the same in Sweden, there and in the other Scandinavian lands they made no headway against Lutheranism's deep rootedness in the elites and the people. Similar conditions obtained in England, Scotland, the Dutch Republic, and the Protestant parts of Germany and Switzerland. In these lands Catholicism could at best maintain Jesuit missions or underground congregations, which in the post-confessional age would provide a basis for a new Catholic ecclesiastical organization.[21]

As different as the experiences of confessionalization were, they reveal common tendencies, of which four seem especially important: 1) alliance of church and state; 2) focus on the "middle zone" between church and state; 3) means to realize Christian norms in the belief, thinking, and behavior of people; and 4) formation of a typically early modern church personnel, which included varying degrees of lay participation.

The Alliance of Church with State

The church's institutional and social reliance on the early modern state was particularly pronounced in the Protestant states of Scandinavia, England, and Switzerland (especially in Zurich), and in the territorial and urban churches in the Empire—the Calvinist no less than the Lutheran ones. In these lands the clergy acquired a quasi-official status under the ruler as "chief bishop [*summus episcopus*]" or "supreme head of the church," and the ecclesiastical bureaucracy grew as a branch of its civil counterpart. Calvinism, which, unlike the Zwinglian form of Reformed Christianity, recognized in principle the autonomy of the church vis-à-vis the state, formed in practice no exception. Indeed, the Calvinist presbyteries and consistories were normally closely coordinated to the political elite, even where they were not recruited, as they partly were in Geneva, from the magistrates themselves.[22] Calvinism achieved a de facto autonomy in ecclesiastical and congregational matters only where it was not the dominant confession, and where it had to build its church independently from, or even against, the temporal authority. This was true of the French Huguenots, of the congregations which formed underground or "under the cross" on the

Lower Rhine, and of the English Puritans. If an ecclesiastical or congregational autonomy free from state influence developed anywhere, and if there was any path from the presbyterian-synodal church of the early modern era toward modern democracy, then it was in such minority churches, whose members were excluded from all state offices. Further, if capitalism truly had socio-religious roots, they may be sought in this Calvinism of the diaspora, whose adherents were freed from the conservative and feudal restraints of government to devote themselves to religion and business. Bolstered by the triad of congregation, family, and economy, in this milieu developed a socio-religious type—in origin not only Calvinist but also sectarian—which became something like an early modern bourgeoisie.[23]

The post-Tridentine Catholic lands preserved at least in principle the church's medieval organization. The need, however, for Catholicism to enter alliances with the temporal rulers—either to retake lost areas or to guard its own lands against Protestant heresy—greatly enhanced the state's influence in ecclesiastical matters, already traceable in the late Middle Ages. Normally this influence was regulated by treaties with the Roman Curia (called "concordats") or with the diocesan bishops and metropolitans, though the instruments of lay supervision varied from place to place. In the German lands, for example, central administrations developed special organs for church affairs, comparable to the Protestant consistories. Bavaria had its Spiritual Council (*Geistlicher Rat*) of theologically educated clergymen and legally trained laymen, who were appointed by the duke to supervise the subjects' religious life, monasteries, parish clergy, and collegiate churches. In Spain a supreme council for ecclesiastical and religious affairs, namely, the Inquisition (*Consejo de la Suprema y General Inquisicion*) was part of the royal regime. And in France the important instrument of state influence was the royal right to nominate bishops, which the Concordat of Bologna had confirmed in 1516.[24]

Overlapping Authorities

The states' activities also intensified in what had lain largely in the church's hands during the Middle Ages, when the state had lacked the capacity to manage them. The most important such matters were marriage and the family, education, poor relief, and social welfare. Except for Catholic marriage, which remained a sacrament and thus did not fall under the "mixed matters," in both Protestant and Catholic lands such matters came under the jurisdiction of both authorities. And if in the long run the state's competence grew at the church's expense, the norm was their coordination, despite the frequent differences of opinion and even conflicts between them.

The individual confessions were nonetheless quite differently equipped to protect the church's interests in mixed matters. Calvinist responsibility for these matters was especially explicit and instrumentally rational in the modern sense: it lay primarily with the congregational presbytery and secondarily with the synod. Where Calvinism was the established religion, both bodies coordinated their activities with those of the civil magistrates.[25] In Lutheran lands, by contrast, the powers of the local congregation were incorporated into the territorial bureaucracy, which allowed the state possibilities for influence and even control.[26] In Catholic lands most of the medieval institutions survived, though here, too, the drive for agreement and coordination can be traced in the episcopal authority, which the Council of Trent strengthened, in the new religious orders, such as the Jesuits, and above all in the state itself.[27] Best known are the Jesuits establishment of schools and universities. In 1576 Peter Canisius (1521-97) could still complain "that the Catholics have so few universities, and such poor ones." He and others nonetheless pressed forward energetically on this front since the late sixteenth century, and gradually the gap diminished. The essential difference between Protestant and Catholic education consisted in the fact that behind the Calvinist and Lutheran efforts normally stood a territorial patron or even a national state, while in Catholic lands the main effort was borne by internationally organized religious orders, whose colleges, seminaries, and houses of study contributed to the progress of learning, including the natural sciences.[28]

Under Calvinism social welfare—care of the poor, orphans, and the sick—belonged to a special institution, the diaconate, governed by the deacons under the presbytery's supervision. The Calvinist cities developed effective systems of district or neighborhood responsibility for a deacon, or a pair of deacons, who collected alms and supported the needy. In some places this system, which always meant supervision as well as support, became models for secular welfare institutions in the nineteenth century. Lutheranism established the "common chest" at the parish level, though this seldom led to a separate local welfare system, which instead was supplied by the territorial church and the state. Catholicism retained here, too, the medieval plurality of institutions, though with attempts to rationalize them.[29] Independently from these ecclesiastical efforts, the state became active in social welfare, especially in the German territorial states, where the political traditions favored the promotion of the common good through legislation. Hundreds of regulations and poorlaws were issued, mostly based symbiotically on religious and political elements without much variation from confession-to-confession.[30]

For marriage and the family, as well as generally for relations between the sexes, confessionalization had important long-term consequences.[31] The development of modern marriage is to a large degree the history of marriage and married life as the confessional churches shaped them. Here, too, despite theological differences, the functional equivalence of the three streams of confessionalization remains valid, because the chief problem everywhere was to liberate the making of marriages from the kinfolk and bring it into the public sphere, where it could be regulated, supervised, and documented. This normally involved an obligation to announce from the pulpit intentions to marry, the introduction of church weddings—at which the consent of the bridal couple and their parents or other relations before witnesses was required—and the registration of marriages in the parish registers kept by every parish priest and pastor.

In the two Protestant churches marriage was "a worldly matter," both based on the promises of the spouses and bound by the norms of Christian fidelity, honesty, and responsibility to one's neighbor. The confirmation of Catholic marriage as a sacrament by the Council of Trent, by contrast, in principle excluded a secularization of marriage. It also affirmed the Catholic Church's primary responsibility for marriage affairs and its autonomy vis-à-vis the state, which the Protestants, having denied the sacramental character of marriage, could not claim. Still, as the Protestant confessions did not dare to draw the practical consequences from their desacralization of marriage in principle—relinquishing marriage and the family entirely to the state—in practice the role of religion remained primary in the Protestant lands as well. The only exceptions were the Dutch Republic and, for a time, England, where a free civil marriage was temporarily introduced respectively at the end of the sixteenth and in the mid-seventeenth century. On the other side, the sacramental marriage bond of Tridentine Catholicism was in reality no more stable than the secular vows taken by Protestant partners, the respecting of which was strictly policed by the Calvinist presbyteries and the Lutheran consistories. It is indeed quite possible that a quantitative comparison between the annulment decrees of episcopal tribunals and the Roman Rota, on the one hand, and the Protestant divorce decrees (with which especially the Lutherans were quite stingy), would show that the secular vow as the basis of Protestant marriage was in practice more stable than the sacramental marriage of Catholicism.[32]

Such similarities aside, the pressure to marry within one's own confession altered traditional regional or social strategies concerning marriage and replaced or supplemented them by a confessional criterion. Given the confessional and territorial fragmentation of Central Europe, here confessional boundaries determined marriage connections more strongly than did territorial boundaries. Although confessionally "mixed marriages" were concluded in all social strata, they entailed many individual and social problems, which in the confessionally mixed zones troubled European society long after the confessional era ended.[33]

Discipline and Supervision

The construction of the ability to manage and supervise in the interest of inculcating Christian norms of belief, thought and behavior was bound to the churches' engagement in education, marital affairs, and social welfare.[34] They employed quite similar instruments, notably catechisms,[35] which were by no means, as is often assumed, a purely Protestant phenomenon.[36] Catholicism's rich variety of instruments for supervising religion and morals included more or less regular visitations and synods, the ecclesiastical courts of the deaneries, dioceses, provinces, the Roman Curia, the Inquisition (in Italy and Spain), and the papal nuntiatures. The religious orders also worked to discipline both their own members and others, an enterprise in which the Jesuits, with their network that spanned Europe and its colonies, were especially active as teachers, preachers, and princely confessors.[37] In Lutheranism, except for excommunication and quasi-bureaucratic supervision by visitors, superintendents, and consistories, specialized institutions of religious discipline emerged only in a few places. Here the task of discipline fell chiefly on the sermons and pastoral care, together with the state's laws and supervision. A similar situation emerged in the Zurich model of Swiss Reformed religion, where morals courts (*Chorgerichte*) and synods (chiefly to discipline the clergy) were dominated by the civil magistrates. The Anglican Church maintained a distinct institutional continuity with the Middle Ages in that formally the bishops and archbishops were responsible for visitations and the ecclesiastical courts. Royal policy promoted the centralization, nationalization, and control

of this system, in the day-to-day management of which the elders—laymen annually elected by the parish—played an important role. The
much more strongly congregational ideal of the Puritans imitated Geneva, where Calvin's model provided the soundest theological and institutional basis for a comprehensive influencing of society in the spirit
of early modern confessionalism and its norms of thought and
behavior. The most important organ of management was the consistory (*consistoire*), whose members were coopted elders and pastors,
and which normally convened each week to review the church's administrative work and to exercise discipline. Calvin had designated discipline in his *Institutes* (based on Matt. 18:15-18) as the central pillar of
Reformed churchmanship, and some Calvinist confessions, such as the
Confessio Gallica and the *Confessio Belgica*, even declared it to be, together with preaching and administration of the sacraments, a third
"mark of the [true] church [*nota ecclesiae*]."

Driven by their concern for confessionally correct belief and
behavior, the churches' leaders effected deep changes in the churches
and in religion. Jean Delumeau has rightly portrayed the changes as an
early modern wave of "christianization," for as the reformed religiosi-
ties of the established churches spread across the territorial states, they
decisively undermined or weakened the old, preconfessional forms of
popular religiosity, especially the animistic and magical rites connected
to events of nature, to the annual cycle of sowing and reaping, to the
rites and festivals connected with individual and familial life-cycles—
birth, maturity, marriage, and death—and to the healing of humans
and animals. In cooperation with the early modern state, the confessional churches—each in its own way—set about purifying, standard-
izing, and unifying religious life. They varied nonetheless markedly in
their capacity for integrating popular religiosity. Tridentine Catholicism and often Lutheranism, too, could supply the peasants' needs for
the visual representation of the holy by means of the decoration of
churches and the maintenance of statues, altars, and church bells. Calvinism displayed this integrative power only rarely and in very limited
measure, because its drive for rationality and purity forbade any compromise with the sensual forms of popular religion.[38]

The religious shaping of the people by the church and religion was
not effected through discipline alone, but also by other means, notably
by print: hymnals, prayerbooks, and books of private devotion; homilies, lives of the saints, and edifying dramas; manuals of married life
and Christian behavior; and funeral sermons—to name only the princi-

pal genres. There were new forms of devotion, too, such as the "Spiritual Exercises" of the Jesuits, as well as the many aspects of the plastic arts, which, though most highly developed in Catholicism, were not absent from Protestantism. Finally, it must be noted that in all four of the major confessions, at the turn of the sixteenth to the seventeenth century emerged a new "simple" piety of the heart, which over the course of time would push confessionalism itself aside.[39]

Recruitment of Clergy

The Protestant clergies differed decisively in origin, self-image, and lifestyle from their medieval counterparts. This was as true in Anglicanism and the Lutheran lands, which retained a clerical hierarchy from parish pastor to superintendent to General Superintendent, president (*Präses*), or bishop, as it was in Calvinism, where in principle an equality of clergy obtained. When Protestantism abandoned the claim to sacral power, it also surrendered the clergy's special status in society, for Protestant clergymen were citizens and subjects, just like their parishioners.[40] The right of Protestant clergy to marry led to a de facto obligation to marry. Most of them did marry and often had large families, and they assumed a quite different position in civil society than the Catholic priests did. Their work had become a profession, which presupposed a formal training and a set of professional norms, the theoretical grounding of which lay in the Protestant clergy's dedication to preaching the Word. The Protestant clergyman attained his office through examinations and ordination, and in the state churches, he thereby acquired a quasi-official status that bound him to the ruler's policies and made him a representative of the state in the village or the town. This status and the required education promoted, as Rosemary O'Day has shown for the Anglican clergy, the development of an esprit de corps, which tended to create an unbridgeable distance between the clergy and their congregations, especially rural ones. Its counterpart was the social closeness to possessors of the same or similar academic training, which in the German territories meant the bourgeois lawyers and officials.

In the Protestant churches the lay officials formed another sector of what may be called the "society of churchmen" (*Kirchendiener-Gesellschaft*). This term applies strictly only to Calvinism, where, in addition to the preachers, elders, deacons, those who staffed the colleges, academies, and other schools were officials of the church.[41] Laymen nonetheless also participated in ecclesiastical affairs in the Lutheran and Anglican churches, though on a theologically and institutionally more limited basis, for here they possessed only special competences over the financial maintenance of church building and poor relief, in the case of the Lutheran *Kastenherren* or *Kirchenprovisoren*, and in addition service in the visitations and episcopal courts, in that of the Anglican elders.

In Catholicism, too, confessionalization also meant forming a new kind of clergy. Since the Council of Trent explicitly reaffirmed the traditional sacerdotal basis of ecclesiastical office, marked by the requirement of celibacy, the post-Tridentine Catholic priestly clergy appears quite different from the Protestant magisterial clergy. A social-historical perspective, however, reduces the difference greatly, providing that comparisons are correctly made: the Protestant pastors corresponded to the regular orders in pastoral work and to the secular parish priests, but not to the prelates and the bishops. The latter remained aristocrats until the end of the Old Regime, especially in the Empire. Otherwise, the differences between Protestant and Catholic clergies seem much reduced, both because the former's level of professionalization was often very low in practice, leaving the village clergy fixed in premodern social conditions, and because the Catholic clergy, both regulars and seculars, were prepared for their callings in the universities and seminaries, uniting the modern qualification of education to the traditional sacral powers. Indeed, it has been shown that even in the Roman Curia, often viewed as the guardian of a traditional, "feudal" pattern of recruitment, a type of professionalization emerged in the sixteenth century in the figure of the career prelate.[42] Just as their social and political integration into the state by no means deprived the Protestant clergy of the possibility of critical distance and even opposition,[43] so the responsibility of the Catholic priests to their bishops and the pope did not prevent them from acting in reality as agents of the temporal authority.

Even the principle of lay participation in church affairs made no practical difference, because the Calvinist presbyteries and synods generally had no lay participants. Theologians set the tone, in Geneva as in the Dutch Republic, where their domination aroused charges of "rule by the pastors (*domineesheerschappij*)" and a new sort of "papistry (*papisterij*)." In addition, although Catholic confessionalization did not prescribe a role for laymen in the church's governance, it did not exclude their participation. Already in the Middle Ages, lay participation had become usual in parish financial administration, in visi-

tations, and in the episcopal courts, and now it became especially pronounced in the Jesuits' Marian congregations, though the leadership
remained in clerical hands.[44] Concerning the level of lay participation
and its possibilities for mobilizing the laity and thereby strengthening
the confessional system, there is some evidence that the Catholic
priestly clergy had greater success than the Protestant magisterial
clergy.

Finally, it is important to emphasize another common feature of the
early modern confessional churches in personnel matters, namely, the
maintenance of the male monopoly of offices, even while women were
being more closely integrated. Such were the Calvinist experiments
with female deacons, the new social position of the Protestant pastor's
wife,[45] the emergence of leading Catholic nuns—notably Teresa of
Avila (1515-82)— who profoundly influenced Catholic spirituality, or
the direct or indirect incorporation of wives and daughters in the
Marian confraternities.[46]

3. STATE AND SOCIETY

The interpenetration of religion and society made the formation of
confessional churches a political and social fact. The coincidence of
this process with the fundamental political, legal, and administrative
transformation that produced the early modern state justifies our
speaking of confessional Europe as the "warm-up time of modernity."
In the beginning, the confessional church set the tone and used the state
for its purposes, which is why one can speak in this period of the "confessional state" or even the "sacral state." Thereafter, of course, European jurists and politicians discovered ways to harness confessionalism's autonomous power and bind it to the interests of state. This was
as true of the republican and parliamentary regimes as of the absolutist
ones. In the long run the alliance of state and church profited the
former far more than it did the latter. The modernizing resacralization,
which confessionalization promoted, produced the modernizing
secularization of the modern era. This transformation requires comments, though there is not space here to draw the connections between
confessionalization and the rise of capitalism or European culture.

Confessionalization and the Early Modern State
The general political consequences of confessionalization may be de-

scribed in terms of Norbert Elias' concept of the civilizing process as a
form of "monopolization." Elias recognizes in the state's exclusive
command of military and financial power the decisive "monopolies"
that determined the rise of the early modern state, but he overlooks the
state's monopolization of the church and religion, which both preceded the other two processes and made them easier.[47] Confessionalization influenced four main aspects of state development: 1) the theoretical and ideological foundations of the early modern state's
authority; 2) the state's human and material resources; 3) the formation of a political and cultural identity to integrate the subjects into the
state; and 4) the growth of a system of European states, including their
overseas missionary and colonizing efforts.

Political Conceptions

Political theory and culture in confessional Europe was decisively
shaped by a profound change in ideas about rulership. The change
from the medieval rule over persons to the modern of rule over things,
which underlay the ruler's emergence as the holder of a supreme, unified state authority, received important support from the sacralization
of governance that confessionalization promoted. The change's roots
lay in the Reformation era and the ensuing confessional conflicts, in
which the victory or defeat of a confession depended on the decision of
the prince who acted as "defender of the church [*defensor ecclesiae*]"
or as a reforming ruler. As constructors of Protestant churches the
princes were accorded the position of "supreme bishop," "supreme
head," or at least "principal member of the church." This entailed a
sacralization, unintended by the theologians, of state power understood in terms of the prince's person. One sign of this was the title "by
the grace of God," used by rulers of all ranks, including sometimes urban magistrates. Another was routine Sunday prayers for the ruler in
all parishes and congregations and prayers for special occasions, such
as changes of regime and conclusion of treaties, or special events in the
lives of the ruler and his family, such as travels, illnesses, pregnancies,
births, and deaths. Similar things were done in the Catholic states,
though based on different legal and political concepts. In the Spanish
monarchy, for example, the church played a central role in the ceremonies for royal births, baptisms, confirmations, anointings, coronations,
funerals, and posthumous remembrances of members of the royal family.

One result of this sacralization was the rise of a quasi-numinous separation of the prince from his subjects, which, together with other tendencies—especially the advance of Roman law and Jean Bodin's doctrine of sovereignty—led to an escalation of and a qualitatively modernizing change in the image and impact of state power. This happened not through the instrumentalization of religion but via a characteristically early modern piety toward rulers, of which neither the sincerity nor the political utility is open to doubt.[48]

The long-term political and constitutional consequences of this sacralization depended on its legal and social context. Germany and England represent the two extremes in Protestant Europe. In the German lands, sacralization and the legal principle of "whose the rule, his the religion [*cuius regio, eius religio*]" gave rise since the late 1500s to the union of throne and altar that fostered autocracy in nineteenth-century Prussia and elsewhere. In England, by contrast, where the king possessed legislative power only in cooperation with Parliament, the ruler's supremacy over the church was restricted in practice by Parliament and the common law. By the mid-seventeenth century, after all attempts to alter this situation had failed, the law of the land (*lex terrae*) triumphed over the law of the church (*lex ecclesiae*), and thereafter the king was bound by law and the constitution in church matters as much as in civil ones. Instead of converting the papal heritage to the service of an English absolutist monarchy, it was accommodated to a constitutional monarchy.[49]

In other lands, too, confessionalization long influenced political theory and the political ideas. The older literature saw here only stark contrasts: an ethos of obedience and a strengthening of the absolutist and autocratic structures in Lutheranism and Catholicism; an ethos of freedom and constitutional and democratic impulses in the Reformed religion, especially in Calvinism.[50] This simplistic dichotomy has given way to a quite different picture of the political impact of the early modern confessions: besides confessionalization's integrating, stabilizing effects, it could also unite with oppositional parliamentary forces in territorial states or the burghers in the cities. Conflicts, for example, between the state and the dominant church, on the one side, and a confessional minority, on the other, expanded and made more secure the political space for anti-government forces. This was true to the same degree of Lutheran, Calvinist, and Catholic minorities.

The same picture of interchangeability emerges concerning political theory and political culture. The alleged resistance theory of western European Calvinism grew in fact from roots in the tracts of Lutheran theologians who supported the city of Magdeburg against the Emperor Charles V. These Lutheran anti-monarchists had their exact counterparts in the Catholic monarchomachs, and the authoritarian reformation of princes, often held to be typically Lutheran, took its purest form in the so-called "Second Reformation" under the banner of Calvinism. Indeed, as the basically undemocratic structures of Calvin's own theology have become more clearly defined, so has the realization that, as Robert M. Kingdon has written, Geneva became a "political model" because of urban political traditions and a specific historical constellation of forces. The ideology of freedom and natural rights first came to the fore not in Calvin's Geneva but in the American and French revolutions, independent of all confessional associations, although "traces of ideas of natural rights" may be found in all the confessions, though not always to the same degree.[51]

Agents of the State

Confessionalization aided early modern state-building directly or indirectly through clerical administrative organization and recruitment that supplemented and strengthened the still quite incomplete civil administrations. In Protestant lands and cities one can speak of a second, ecclesiastical branch of the state's bureaucracy, while in the Catholic lands the state's institutions normally employed the church's counterparts indirectly or as supports only, when the interests of the two authorities coincided. These relationships were especially important for the state's penetration of the villages and small towns, which had hitherto largely eluded its authority.

In such settings important functions of supervision and discipline devolved upon the clergy, the quasi-official pastors of the Protestant state churches and also the Catholic priests, whose church, while formally independent and universal, had entered manifold ties and agreements with the state. The clergy's maintenance, for example, of baptismal, marriage and death registers, which began contemporaneously with confessionalization, supplied the basis of the state's policy on population, a connection particularly notable in what has been called the "peopling policy [*Peuplierungspolitik*]" of the German territorial states.

The clergy also formed a web of communication between the state's bureaucratic center and the periphery, where they announced the state's decrees to village communities and urban neighborhoods. The web functioned in both directions, for the clergy also relayed from "below" to "above" information that proved indispensable to accurate and effective management by early modern civil administrations. In a certain sense the clergy—Protestant more than Catholic—formed the first, still incomplete examples of the "commissar," the delegated officials who accomplished so much for the early modern state despite local society's capacity for absorbing them.[52]

The framing and enforcement of innumerable laws for the protection and regulation of religious and ecclesiastical life enormously expanded the hitherto weakly developed business of state. The state also acquired new jurisdictions, notably over marriage and the family, the schools and education, and poor relief and social welfare, which in pre-Reformation times had been mainly the church's concern. Once the churches had reclaimed at least partial responsibility for these areas, the symbiosis of state and church, so typical of confessional Europe, permitted the rulers to appropriate primary jurisdiction over them— with the churches' blessing. Ecclesiastical property was treated in a similar manner, and in various ways the properties were turned to the advantage of the state's finances while these were still quite weak and imperfectly developed.

Confession and Identity

Although research on confessionalization's concrete effects on the rise of national identities in Europe, the formation of the international system, and European expansion abroad lies in its infancy, the basic outlines can be described. Confessionalization not only promoted early modern state-building, it also influenced the formation of modern European nations. Religion and politics were closely intertwined and remained so until the nineteenth and even the twentieth century, most clearly, perhaps in Catholic Spain, Italy and Ireland, and Protestant England and Scandinavia.[53] More complex histories determined that multi-confessional identities should emerge in the Dutch Republic, Germany, and Switzerland, where national formation was blocked by both the existence of the Empire and its multiplicity of territorial states. These countries possessed not two confessional identities, but three, which hindered their nineteenth-century attempts to catch up in nation-building and, in Germany at least, became a mortgage of quasi-metaphysical quality on the modern political culture. The excess of confessional and ideological feeling, it has been said, has shaped German culture from the confessional era down to the present day and made Germany a "belated nation."[54] In France, too, the relationship between confessional and political identity was complicated. Although since the days of Henry IV and even more strongly those of Louis XIV, Catholicism held its power over the French identity, again and again this identification was trumped by the political rivalry with Spain and the House of Habsburg, which drove France perennially into the arms of the Protestant powers. Cardinal Richelieu, scrupulous as he was in religious matters, found this configuration a heavy political and spiritual burden, which he would have gladly abandoned—had circumstances permitted—for an international policy in tune with France's Catholic identity.[55]

Confessional Alignments in Europe

It has long been recognized that confessional antagonisms played a role in European power relations during the sixteenth, seventeenth, and even the eighteenth century.[56] No systematic study, however, has ever been made of the connections between confessionalization and the rise of an international system of sovereign states in Europe, despite the obvious coincidence of the two processes around 1600. The first tentative researches have produced the hypothesis "that the confessional forces worked in modernizing fashion in the formation of the modern type of international system, just as they did in the inner articulation of the early modern state. Further, that in this process the mutuality of religious-ecclesiastical and political forces played an important role."[57] Something very similar may be said about confessionalization and the European overseas expansion, a question which is ripe for review. In any structural-functional analysis of Christianity's role in the social changes unleashed by the discoveries and conquests, special attention should be given to the unleashing of a new phase of "christianizing," "civilizing," and "modernizing" activity. It is simply incorrect to allege that the transfer of the confessional paradigm into the history of the European expansion represents a lapse into an obsolete eurocentric historiography of developmentalism. Indeed, the use of quotation marks with "civilizing" and "modernizing" signifies the violent and destructive effects of the intrusion of European processes, including confessionalized evangelization, into alien social and cultural systems. How destructive, we can conceive only in the late twentieth century, when the dominance of the European perspective, along with the confessional phase of European history, has come to an end.[58]

Social Formation

Confessionalization helped to reshape society at its very roots, for its spiritual and moral ethos exercised an enduring power on the public and private lives of all social strata, the elites and the burghers more than the rural folk. Its effects combined with those of the state to produce a relatively unified society of subjects (*Untertanengesellschaft*) and inculcated modern, disciplined, and "civilized" (in Norbert Elias' sense) forms of behavior, thought, and mentality. Confessionalization also promoted unification by neutralizing or weakening the intermediate powers of the clergy, the nobles, and the cities. At least down to the later seventeenth century, the new clergy—such as the Jesuits—gained a considerable independence and freedom of action from this alliance with the state, though later on, when the state lost interest, it abolished clerical independence in favor of the unrestricted domination of the state, what is sometimes called "confessional absolutism." This happened in France under Louis XIV by the latest, and in Austria a bit later. The subjection of the clergy and the estates sometimes occurred under the banner of a pronounced anticonfessionalism, as in Prussia, where state-managed toleration was an important tool of absolutist politics and social policy.

The term "social discipline" as label for the early modern shaping of human behavior and thinking was introduced by Gerhard Oestreich to designate the incorporation of individuals and social groups into a homogeneous association of subjects, plus the stripping away of regional and particular interests in favor of a "common good" defined by the state. By a long process, begun in the later Middle Ages, the prince and his officials came to define the meaning of "the common good."[59] At its peak in the late sixteenth century, confessionalization decisively accelerated this process, for it possessed special importance for all questions of legitimacy. The early modern state's marked deficiency of legitimacy made the sixteenth- and seventeenth-century churches indispensable agents for obligating individuals and social groups to the new system of moral, political, and legal norms. The good Christian was taught to live with the family and neighbors in fraternal peace and to exercise seriously, knowledgeably, and conscientiously the "office" God conferred on him or her in domestic and public affairs. This meant educating and supervising children and servants and fulfilling conscientiously one's calling as civil servant, artisan, entrepreneur, or merchant. Through sermons and pastoral care, house visitations and religious societies—such as the Catholic confraternities and congregations—the confessional churches helped to routinize obedience and good behavior toward the master and mistress of the house, toward the lesser and middling magistrates and officials, and toward the ruler himself.

Whereas they collaborated with the state to impede crimes, the churches' most important discipline, religious discipline, operated through special institutions aimed to curb sin.[60] Even the policing of sin by the free or underground churches, such as the Puritans in England or the Calvinists in Catholic France and the Lower Rhineland, which had no alliance with the state, strengthened the social discipline of the state, because churches and state inculcated the same norms. The churches disciplinary work was essential to modernization, because the pre-absolutist state, lacking adequate instruments of supervision and manipulation of its own, depended on religious sanctions to internalize the new values.

Long, nearly complete series of presbyterial minutes reveal the Calvinist "police of sin" that influenced European society for a very long time. It promoted a rational, sober, disciplined type of behavior, which more or less spread over early modern Europe and became a prerequisite for the successful transformation of premodern Europe into the modern bourgeois society of the industrial age. The Calvinist congregations worked tirelessly against deviations from the fixed principles of belief and worldview; against neglect of religious duties to oppose contentiousness, force, and dishonesty; against excess, unconstrained luxury, excessive gambling, drinking, dancing, and pleasure-seeking; against sexual indiscipline, fornication, and adultery; and against drunkenness, uncleanliness, sloth, and all the other deviations, great and small, from the modernized code of Christian moral norms that characterized the sixteenth-century confessionalization. In all of this, the congregations showed that they were not only agents of a closed Calvinist system of belief and values, but also and above all promoters of emotional control, a rational and modern lifestyle, endurance and self-discipline, and a sober sense of responsibility for one's own life and that of one's neighbor within the marriage, the family, the congregation, and the society as a whole.[61]

The much less numerous studies of the "police of sin" by the Anglican, Lutheran, and Catholic churches reveal a similar, if more muted, picture. Like the Calvinist consistories and synods, the worldwide Jesuit network contributed to the formation of modern habits of thought and behavior among the princes, the nobles, and the new strata of civil servants and teachers in the towns—though hardly in the countryside. The Jesuits, indeed, introduced "enough novelties concerning the family and the social order, and about how to live one's religion, to disturb the guardians of tradition." They and their counterparts in the other confessions taught a programmatic combination of religious inwardness and a morally responsible way of life in and for the Christian community and for the family, the church, and the urban public sphere. Each of the confessional churches in its own way represented a "modern Christianity," and all three "merged, so to speak, with the origins of the bourgeois ethos in Europe."[62]

The connection between confessionalization and the bourgeois mentality was enhanced by the attacks on pre-confessional popular religion, which made headway in the cities, though not on the land. The purification of faith and piety from magic, the didactic (and thus rational) character of religion, and the anchoring of religion in inner conviction rather than in an externalized ritual came all the easier in the cities, because these very tendencies had already been promoted by the late medieval reform movements, such as the *devotio moderna*, and by the elective affinity between early Reformation piety, on the one hand, and the early modern bourgeois spirit, on the other.

Finally, confessionalization's effects on the premodern European model of gender relations can hardly be overestimated. From the new anthropology taught by both Protestantism and Catholicism, the agents of confessionalization derived new notions of gender relations, of the roles that men and women played in marriage, family, household, and the public sphere, and rooted them deeply in European societies. The new understanding of marriage and the formalization of weddings contained far-reaching consequences for gender relations. This is clearest in Protestantism, because "with the new, biblically based understanding, marriage became the central social order governing the two sexes."[63] The relations between man and wife, and between parents and children, were now framed in a system of Protestant norms different from the old esteem for chastity and celibacy as worthy ideals of human self-realization. Catholic confessionalization, however, also contained new social consequences for the family. Its model was not the pastoral family, as in Protestantism, but the Holy Family, dominated by Mary with Joseph standing in the background.[64]

While the transformation of gender relations had begun in the late Middle Ages, when powerful economic, demographic, and political forces had pushed it forward, the decisive breakthrough came during the confessional age.[65]   Its effects are best known in the Protestant lands, especially the Lutheran ones, though our picture of them is filled with contradictions. On the one hand, it is said that Protestant anthropology, particularly the appreciation of marriage, brought about a depreciation and "domestication" of women, and orthodox Lutheran sermons are said to have been characterized by "the view that uncontrolled women were dangerous to themselves and society."[66] On the other hand, it has been shown that Luther's theology enhanced the position of women, in that "also married and single women were called to the priesthood of all believers," the bearing of children was praised as "God's special miracle," and the old taboos, such as "the notion that women's bodily process (menstruation, conception, pregnancy, birthing, and lying-in) made them impure," were rejected.[67] This change was heightened by Reformed Protestantism, which realized the theory of general priesthood in the office of deaconess.[68] Case studies of practice, naturally, show a varying picture. At Augsburg, for example, although the Protestants did not "deem there to be any differences in the kind of spirituality appropriate to men and women, they evolved "a two-kingdom theory of sexual difference [based on the idea that] their offices in life on earth were different." Although this resulted in "a more exclusively male-run Church," it did not effect religiosity proper, so that "Protestant women may have been able to developed a female-centered piety."[69] Another study shows that in the German Protestant pastor's household, the pastor's wife worked alongside her husband as "companion" and "co-ruler," based on an "office of housemother" that corresponded to that of "housefather." Inequality nevertheless endured, as this female "lordship" was defined in terms of male lordship, an observation which corresponds to the Reformed model of gender relations in southern French cities.[70] Finally, there is the special case of the Protestant Imperial abbesses, who maintained an independent ecclesiastical position in Lutheranism, even though the Lutheran church was in principle a male church.[71]

Confessional religious discipline was not overtly gender-specific, that is, "confessionalizing measures were not directed specifically against or toward women."[72] A long-term study of Calvinist Emden, for example, has shown that "the double standard appeared relatively late," and that it arose from a specifically Pietist religiosity and the state's supervisory measures against unwed mothers. Church discipline at Emden did not, however, "discriminate against either males or females regarding the norms or standard of Christian sexual life."

Men and women were in equal measure obliged to live according to the norms of Christian responsibility, love, and peacefulness, a requirement which could only lead to improvement for women. This is supported by the demonstration that "during the first century of church discipline in Emden (ca. 1550-1650) males were more frequently cited before the church council."[73]

Catholic confessionalization, though on a different theological basis, also promoted a thoroughgoing change in traditional gender relations, though here, too, the findings are contradictory. On the one hand, "Catholicism nurtured a peculiarly female style of devotion" and developed a whole cosmos "of female saints," while, on the other, this "holiness could be attained only by divesting oneself of the sexual, feminine 'bodiliness.'"[74] In the area of advanced female education, Catholicism seems to have promoted, both in theory and practice, more univocally than Protestantism did, "the intellectual equality of women and their capacity for and right to learning."[75] In the Catholic regions of central Europe, confessionalization displaced the old cosmos of saints, "which had been chiefly ordered by the relationship of lord and subject and by the communal life of a largely closed rural order," in favor of a cosmos of saints "keyed to the model of man, wife, and child." The "patriarchial order of the peasant mentality" was replaced by an early modern mentality oriented to the Holy Family, in the center of which stood Mary. In the background stood Joseph, "in whom the male functions of rule over wife, child, household, and form were reduced to exclusively protective ones." This change introduced "a brief phase of matriarchally influenced norms" and a "matriarchal model of family."[76] Jesuit anthropology and pastoral principles, too, promoted changes in gender relations, namely, "a new concept of the family—marked by heightening of the sacrament of marriage, a division of responsibilities between the spouses, and a lessening of the father's despotic power—was emerging. The patriarchal family and the 'Holy Family' were not the same."[77] Here we find, therefore, a tendency to embourgeoisement and interiority, just as in confessional Protestantism.

These characteristic trends of the confessional age did not spread unchecked. After the mid-seventeenth century a change came over Catholic female education, as "the elan of the founders was shattered, and the discrepancy between male and female education began to grow again." The same thing happened to "the matriarchal model of the family" and the active participation of women in "the priesthood of all

believers."[78] These changes show that in the history of gender relations, as in other areas, the nineteenth-century "barriers" to women
were not direct products of the Reformation and confessionalization,
but rather the results of later retreats from the modernizing impulses
they unleashed.

The Confessional Cultures

The degree to which confessionalization shaped Europe's cultures can
only be suggested here. In art and literature the measured harmony of
the Renaissance gave way to the nervous dynamics of the Baroque,
which stood in the zone of tension between insecure fragmentation and
a fervent security of faith. Theodore K. Rabb has interpreted this
change as the search of a deeply unsettled age for a new security.[79]
This "struggle for stability" developed in alliance with the
confessionalizing process and manifested itself in art. The Baroque
was congenial to confessional Europe, because it resacralized art following its desacralization by the Renaissance. As in politics and society, however, this meant not a return to a predominantly ecclesiastical
art, as in the Middle Ages, but a new union of sacred and profane in art
and culture which opened the way, over the long run, to secularization.

The Baroque was an expression of confessional Europe, too, in that
it made—and makes, as any traveler to Central Europe can see—the religious schism visible. Differences between North and South aside, the
Renaissance style was unified and international, just like the humanist
republic of letters. The Baroque, by contrast, was fragmented and
torn, chiefly along confessional lines. At first glance, this difference
may seem to contradict our thesis of the functional equivalence of Protestant and Catholic confessionalization, for how could one conceive a
greater incompatibility than that between the riot of color, form, and
life of the southern, image-oriented Catholic Baroque and the cool,
northern sobriety of the rationally controlled word- and oratorio-ori-
ented Protestant Baroque?[80]

The Baroque cultures nonetheless did exhibit trans-confessional
similarities, notably in church architecture, where a common rationality and deliberate effect reigned. This is true of the precisely emotional
purpose aimed at by Jesuit architecture, the model of which was the Il
Gesu in Rome, built in the 1570s. It is also true of Salzburg Cathedral
and of the Church of the Fourteen Saints in Franconia, and of new
Protestant churches, such as Hendrik de Keyser's (1567-1621) in the
Netherlands and Christopher Wren's St. Paul's in London. The same

could be said, moreover, of the Baroque palace architecture of both the Catholic and the Protestant courts. And also of painting, where the extremes are marked by the heavenward-looking holy humans and human saints of a Guido Reni (1575-1642), on the one hand, the Biblical scenes of Rembrandt van Rijn (1606-69), on the other. The genres and manners of expression of these pictures are undeniably quite different, but their spirits reveal a common rationality and striving for effect. If one accepts the rational program of color, form, and light in Italian and Spanish Baroque painting and in the great churches of Catholic Europe, one cannot deny that this southern, image-oriented Baroque is of a no less modern character than the Protestant Baroque of northern and western Europe. The ideal-typical postulate of their opposition, which reflects the prejudices and clichés of the Enlightenment and the nineteenth century, thus needs to be relativized.

The same point is suggested by the recent rediscovery of the linguistic power of Catholic confessionalism, while, at least in its Anglican and Lutheran forms, Protestantism cannot be said to have lacked possibilities for the plastic arts.[81] Even the new, Tridentine conception of the communion of saints, which long perpetuated itself in the high and the popular cultures of Catholic Europe by means of ceiling frescoes in palaces and churches, the giving of Christian names, celebrations of patron saints' days, pilgrimages, and millions of holy pictures—even this image rested on a rational psychology and perspective. It, too, contributed importantly to the modernizing transformation of cultures and habits of thought.[82]

4. Beyond Confessionalization

One cannot speak of "confessional Europe" without devoting attention to the forces that opposed confessionalization and to the passing of confessionalism. The non- and anti-confessional forces also possessed modernizing potential, though it became visible later, during the Enlightenment.[83] Just as important were the anti-confessional tendencies within confessionalism itself, the quasi-dialectical process of which set loose forces that endured long into the post-confessional era. The state, too, continued to draw internal strength from its alliance with confessionalism long after the end of the confessional era. Eventually, when the state had become strong enough to function effectively without the aid of church or religion, it could reject the maxim that "religion is the bond of society" and embrace a plurality of churches and worldviews. By this time, too, the acceptance of a multi-confessional Europe of the great powers obtained in international relations as well.

The Limits

Despite the dynamic and pervasive character of the confessionalizing process, some important social and political sectors resisted its claims to totality. Chief among them was the law, especially Roman but partly also canon law, which the Protestants still looked to in some matters, such as consanguinity as an impediment to marriage. In Germany it was true as well of Imperial law.[84] Indeed, in a Europe divided by confession, it was the jurists, educated in a common European jurisprudence, who retained the indispensable social and political relations between the confessional blocks. The most notable such group were the politiques in France, who held that public law was neutral and superior to the confessions. There were also the teachers of the law of nature and of nations, such as Hugo Grotius, who worked to dampen the apparently irreconcilable religious struggle by keeping it within legal bonds and by setting as an ultimate goal reconciliation under a new regime of peace. Some essential sectors of daily life, such as the laws of marriage and inheritance, which generally remained valid over the confessional boundaries, also resisted confessionalization. The European noble houses also retained their ties across confessional lines, and so did the world of diplomacy.

Nor, despite the educated classes' role in confessionalization, was European culture life ever entirely fractured, as the histories of literature, art, and humanism clearly show.[85] Despite the confessionalization of schools and universities, important sectors of scientific discourse also resisted the split, especially the natural sciences and medicine, which were moving toward a modern sort of empiricism. Another such field was political thought, where Jean Bodin (1530-96) and Justus Lipsius (1547-1606) were not identified with any confession, because they marked out paths toward social and political modernization open to Catholic and Protestant states alike.

When, after the mid-seventeenth century, the dominant syndrome of confessionalization began to weaken, these and other forces of modernization came to the fore. They included secular processes, such as the rise of legal individualism or the modern category of "self-interestedness,"[86] and the religiously rooted forces of modernization arising from the radical reformation and the sects to which it gave birth. Such forces had been able to exert no general social effects during the preceding era, because they "had been willing to push social change forward beyond the point possible at the beginning of the early modern period." Only when "the structural necessity of a coalition between the early modern state and confessionalism had vanished" could the modernization potential of Protestant dissent gain general social influence.[87] This happened earliest in the Dutch Republic and in England, where the Glorious Revolution sealed the compromise between the Anglican confessional church and the Protestant dissenters. In other European lands this task remained to be accomplished by the Enlightenment, which radically secularized the spiritual and institutional foundations of European society, and the ensuing political revolutions, which swept away the pre-modern type of church-state alliance.

Fading Away

The end of confessional Europe, properly speaking, came around 1650, nearly 150 years before the French Revolution. It happened both through the internal dissolution of orthodoxy and through the state's deconfessionalization of politics and society. The inner renewal of the major European churches began already in the first third of the seventeenth century, when the spirit of an ecumenical religiosity of the heart began to resist the reigning dogmatism and to tread new paths— Pietist, Puritan, and Jansenist.[88] Simultaneously, preconfessional and trans-confessional forces, long concealed but not extirpated by the Reformation and confessionalization, emerged into view. Some were secularizing forces, such as the emancipation of the arts and sciences, plus humanist concepts and attitudes that tended to replace revealed religion with philosophy and morality.[89] Some of the forces were themselves deeply religious, notably the sects and the "libertines," whose spirituality was not, as it is often but falsely alleged, characterized by "secularization or Renaissance enlightenment" but an "innovative synthesis of spiritualism, pietism, . . . and early Protestant religious sentiments."[90] Finally, the ideal of Christian unity, which had been shattered by the failure of interconfessional conversations during the 1560s, reappeared in the form of a new irenicism.[91]

The decisive external forces for deconfessionalization arose from the bitter experience of Europe's civil and international wars: the French Civil Wars, the English Civil War, and above all the Thirty Years' War. Gradually, the idea won out among lawyers and politicians, but also in European public opinion that churchmen who thought in terms of a total confrontation of worldviews would, if not politically restrained, plunge the state into external and internal chaos. Practically contemporaneously with confessionalism, therefore, attempts began to hedge it in politically and legally and to chain its dynamism to the interests of state. Within the German Catholic and Protestant lands this happened largely in peaceful ways, since the Peace of Augsburg's principle of "whose the rule, his the religion" provided the requisite legal means. In France, it fell to royal jurists under the name "politiques" to formulate in the midst of confessional civil war in the 1570s and 1580s, the theory of the absolute primacy of the state over religious factions. Later, under Henry IV they put this theory into practice in the name of a post-confessional Catholicism. In this circle the maxim of the new, post-confessional state was framed, "state and religion have nothing in common," which swept across Europe during the seventeenth century.[92] In England more than fifty years later, a similar political constellation led to the framing of two strategies. One was that of Thomas Hobbes' (1588-1679) power state, named "Leviathan," which demoted religion to a private matter and claimed absolute authority over its public manifestations. This model was realized, however, not in England but, if at all, in some of the continental absolutist states. The other, liberal strategy won out in England with the Glorious Revolution, which left Anglicanism as the established religion but opened the way to religious pluralism in practice. In international relations, the fire storm of the Thirty Years' War sealed the deconfessionalization of Europe.

From around 1650, when politics and religion began to be uncoupled both in theory and in practice, confessionalism lost its basis, even though confessional forces continued to play a role within and between states. This change opened the way to a major transition. The confessional state of the earlier part of this era, which devoted itself to the victory of true doctrine in Europe and the salvation of its subjects' souls, gave place to the secular, tolerant administrative state of the later period, which pursued secular raison d'état externally and the "common good"—the mundane happiness of its subjects—within. This shift changed, too, the position of the confessional churches. The Enlightenment accorded them at most the legal status of associations for the pursuit of the religious and cultic interests of their members.[93] Even where the established church continued to be protected and fostered by the state, it had to surrender confessionalism's holistic claims and in the long-run to accept being one community of belief among many.

Translated by Thomas A. Brady, Jr.

NOTES

1. The theoretical basis for this is fully developed in Schilling (1981), 15-49, and (1992), xiv, 205ff., 247ff. Confessionalization has been the subject of three symposia sponsored by the Verein für Reformationsgeschichte: Schilling (1986); Rublack (1992); and Reinhard and Schilling (1995). On the international reception of the "confessionalization" paradigm, see Schmidt (1992); Hsia (1989); Prodi (1992); Cameron (1991), 361ff.; Chevalier and Sauzet (1985); and Venard (1992).
2. G. Vogler (1994); Lehmann (1980); Israel (1989). See Robert Bonfil, in this *Handbook*, vol. 1:263-302.
3. Following Reinhard Koselleck, "'Sattelzeit' der Moderne ab 1750," introduction to *Geschichtliche Grundbegriffe*, vol 1 (Stuttgart, 1972): xv. Eric W. Cochrane comes to a similar conclusion in Headley and Tomato (1988), 31-46, at 43 ("an age of consolidation").
4. Prodi (1992), esp. 228f.; Schilling (1981), 23-24, esp. 26.
5. Fundamental is Winfried Schulze, "Vom Gemeinnutz zum Eigennutz," *HZ* 243 (1986): 591-626, and (1987).
6. Baur and Sparn (1990), 954. On the oath, see Prodi (1992), 282ff.; Brecht and Schwarz (1980), 351-78.
7. Parker and Smith (1978); Rabb (1975); Zeller (1971-78), vol 2:1-13; Lehmann (1980); Clark (1985).
8. Pfister (1985).
9. See Jan de Vries, in this *Handbook*, vol. 1:1-50.
10. De Vries (1976); on trade and industry, see Bartolomé Yun and John H. Munro, in this *Handbook*, vol. 1:113-46, 147-96.
11. Van der Wee (1988), 307-81.
12. Ankerloo and Henningsen (1990); Behringer (1988); Hsia (1988b), esp. 197-230.
13. Tschopp (1991); Jean Delumeau, Jacques Solé, in Chevalier and Sauzet (1985), 7-13, 57-64.
14. Maltby (1971); Kingdon (1988).
15. Schilling (1988), 371-419.
16. Schilling (1986); Henry J. Cohn, in Prestwich (1985), 135-66; Rublack (1992); Reinhard and Schilling (1995).
17. Van Deursen (1974); Duke (1990), and in Prestwich (1985), 109-34; Tracy (1985); Schilling (1992a), 353-412; Kaplan (1989); Marnef (1987) and (1991).
18. Collinson (1982), (1983), and in Prestwich (1985), 197-224. See also O'Day (1986); Cross (1987); Tyacke (1987); Watts (1985).
19. Volker Reinhardt, in *Deutschland in Europa*, ed. Bernd Martin (Munich, 1992), 90; Gordon (1992), 23-36.
20. Even for France, the influence of Trent has recently been acknowledged. See Bergin (1987).

21. O'Malley (1988); Reinhard and Schilling (1995); Headley (1988); Garstein (1963-80, 1991); Rogier (1947); Tracy (1985); Jerzy Kloczowski, in Venard (1992).

22. Schilling (1991), 105-61.

23. Schilling (1994).

24. Roland Mousnier, *Les institutions de la France sous la Monarchie absolue, 1598-1789*, vol 1 (Paris, 1974): 222ff.; Baumgartner (1986). For Spain, see Henry Kamen, *Spain, 1469-1714* (London, 1983), 177-90; Christian Hermann, in this *Handbook*, vol. 2: 491-522.

25. Van Deursen (1974), 1ff., 227ff.; Schilling (1992), 360ff., 401ff., and (1991), 105ff. See Marnef (1987), 243ff., 300ff., and (1991); Münch (1978); Kingdon, (1967), chap. 1; Stauffenegger (1983); Garrison-Estèbe (1980), 89ff.; Michael Lynch, "Calvinism in Scotland", in Prestwich (1985), 225-55.

26. An outstanding source is Veit Ludwig von Seckendorff, *Teutscher Fürstenstaat* (Frankfurt am Main, 1656), 8, of which an expanded edition appeared at Jena in 1720 (reprinted, Aalen, 1972).

27. Venard (1992), chap. 5; Becker (1989); Lottin (1984); John W. O'Malley, *The First Jesuits* (Cambridge, Mass., 1993).

28. The quote is from Canisius' letter to Giovanni Cardinal Morone, Regensburg, summer 1576, in Otto Braunsberger, ed., *Epistulae et Actae* (Freiburg in Breisgau, 1896-1926), vol. 7:358-66. See Stichweh (1991), 38-42, 170-87, with references.

29. On Calvinist societies, see Mckee (1984); Kingdon (1985), 81-90; van Deursen (1974), 102-27. On the Catholic lands, see Châtellier, (1987); Dinges (1988); Pullan (1971), and id., "Catholics and the Poor in Early Modern Europe," *TRS*, 5th ser., 26 (1976): 15-34, at 33.

30. Friedrich Battenberg, "Obrigkeitliche Sozialpolitik und Gesetzgebung," *ZHF* 18 (1991): 33-70; Dinges (1988).

31. Safley (1984), and in Hsia (1988a), 173-90; Ingram (1987); Greaves (1981), 115-376; Addy (1984), 161-98.

32. Schilling (1993a).

33. Peter Schöller, *Die rheinisch-westfälische Grenze zwischen Ruhr und Ebbegebirge*, (Münster, 1953), 40; François (1991).

34. Robert Jütte, "Poor Relief and Social Discipline in 16th Century Europe," *European Studies Review* 11 (1981): 25-52; Martin Dinges, in *GG* 17 (1991), 5-29.

35. Colin, et al. (1989).

36. Catholicism: Reinhard and Schilling (1995); Châtellier (1987); Zeeden and Lang (1984); Seidel Menchi (1992). Calvinism and Lutheranism: Mentzer (1994); Schilling (1991), 41-68; Schilling (1993b); Kingdon (1985), part 8; Gordon (1992). Anglicanism: Ingram (1987); Addy (1984); Rosemary O'Day, in Zeeden and Lang (1984).

37. Bireley (1975) and (1981). On the Inquisition, see Monter (1990); Grendler (1977); Haliczer (1986). A case study of a nuntiature is Reinhard (1971).

38. Muchembled (1978); Greyerz (1985). Case studies: Freitag (1991); Hörger (1975).

39. Zeller (1971-78); Breuer (1984); Lehmann (1980); Rublack (1992); Bödeker, Chaix, and Veit (1991); Chevalier and Sauzet (1985).

40. J. F. G. Goeters, ed., *Akten Synode Emden*, para. 1. On the social and

cultural history of the early Protestant clergy, see B. Vogler (1976); Susan C. Karant-Nunn, in Fix and Karant-Nunn (1992), 121-40; Schorn-Schütte (1991); Groenhuis (1977); Rosemary O'Day, *The English Clergy: the Emergence and Consolidation of a Profession, 1558-1648)* (Leicester, 1979); Cameron (1991), 389ff.

41. John Calvin, *Institutio christianae religionis* (ed. of 1559), Book IV, chaps 3-4.

42. Wolfgang Reinhard, "Herkunft und Karriere der Päpste 1417-1963. Beiträge zu einer historischen Soziologie der römischen Kurie," *Mededelingen van het Nederlands Instituut te Rome* 38 (1978): 87-108. On the parish clergy, see André Schaer, *Le clergé paroissial catholique en haut Alsace sous l'ancien régime* (Paris, 1966); Marc Venard, "Pour une sociologie du clergé au 16e siècle. Recherches sur le récrutement sacerdotal dans la province d'Avignion," *AESC* 23 (1968): 987-1016; Sauzet (1979); B. Vogler (1987); Vladimir Angel, Georges Viard, in Venard (1989); Becker (1989), 77-146. Comparative interconfessional studies are rare, but see Wolfgang Reinhard, "Kirche als Mobilitätskanal frühneuzeitlicher Gesellschaft," in *Ständische Gesellschaft und soziale Mobilität*, ed. Winfried Schulze (Munich, 1988), 333-51; Schilling (1992), 179-87.

43. Sommer (1988), a profound analysis.

44. Heinz Schilling, in *Anticlericalism in the Late Middle Ages and Reformation*, ed. Peter Dykema and Heiko A. Oberman (Leiden, 1993), 655-68; Châtellier (1987).

45. Schorn-Schütte (1991), and in Wunder and Vanja (1991), 109-53.

46. Châtellier (1987), 156ff.; Efrén de la Madre de Dios and Otger Steggink, *Tiempo y vida de Santa Teresa*, 2d ed. (Madrid, 1977); Conrad (1991) and in Opitz (1993).

47. Norbert Elias, *Über den Prozeß der Zivilisation*, vol. 2, 2d ed. (Bern, 1969), 142ff. For criticism, see Schilling (1981), esp. 365ff.

48. Dieter Breuer, "Absolutistische Staatsreform und neue Frömmigkeitsformen," in *Frömmigkeit in der frühen Neuzeit*. ed. Dieter Breuer (Amsterdam, 1984), 5-25; Anna Coreth, *Pietas Austriaca* (Munich, 1959).

49. Geoffrey R. Elton, "Lex terrae victrix: Der Rechtsstreit in der englischen Frühreformation," *ZSRG, KA* 70 (1984) 217-36, at 236.

50. Hermann Vahle, "Calvinismus und Demokratie im Spiegel der Forschung," *ARG* 66 (1975): 182-221.

51. Winfried Schulze, in Blickle, et al. (1985), 199-216; Robert M. Kingdon, "John Calvin's Contribution to Representative Government," in *Politics and Culture in Early Modern Europe: Essays in Honour of H. G. Koenigsberger*, ed. Phyllis Mack (Cambridge, 1987), 183-98; Horst Dreitzel, "Grundrechtskonzeptionen in der protestantischen Rechts- und Staatslehre im Zeitalter der Glaubenskämpfe," in *Grund- und Freiheitsrechte*, ed. Günter Birtsch (Göttingen, 1987), 180-214; Bireley (1990).

52. Dietrich Gerhard, "Amtsträger zwischen Krongewalt und Ständen," in *Alteuropa und die moderne Gesellschaft. Festschrift Otto Brunner* (Göttingen, 1963), 230-47.

53. Treated in more detail by Heinz Schilling, "Nationale Identität und Konfession in der europäischen Neuzeit," in *Nationale und kulturelle Identität. Studien zur Entwicklung des kollektiven Bewußtseins in der Neuzeit*, ed. Bernhard Giessen (Frankfurt am Main, 1991), 192-252.

54. Helmuth Plessner, *Die verspätete Nation* (Frankfurt am Main, 1974 [1957]).
55. Klaus Malettke, "Richelieus Außenpolitik und sein Projekt kollektive Sicherheit," in *Kontinuität und Wandel in der Staatenordnung der Neuzeit*, ed. Peter Krüger (Marburg, 1991), 47-68, esp, 50ff.
56. Bernard Vogler, "La dimension religieuse dans les relations internationales en Europe au 17ᵉ siècle (1618-1721)," in *Histoire, économie et société* (1991): 379-98. See also Johannes Burkhardt, *Abschied vom Religionskrieg*, (Tübingen, 1985).
57. Schilling (1993c), 592, with references in notes 3-4.
58. For South America one must note not only religious syncretism but also modern "liberation theology." See Heinrich Lutz, "Dreißig Jahre nach Guardinis 'Ende der Neuzeit': Für ein Einbringen unserer kulturkritischen Tradition in heutige globale Pespektiven," in *Festschrift für Wilhelm Messerer zum 60. Geburtstag* (Cologne, 1980), 383-97; Reinhard (1989); Alain Milhou, Minako Debergh, and Claudia von Collani, in Venard (1992), part II, chaps. 7-9.
59. Winfried Schulze, "Gerhard Oestreichs Begriff 'Sozialdisziplinierung in der Frühen Neuzeit,'" *ZHF* 14 (1987): 265-302.
60. Heinz Schilling, "'History of Crime' or 'History of Sin?'" in *Politics and Society in Reformation Europe*, ed. E. J. Kouri and Tom Scott, (London, 1987), 289-310.
61. Schär (1985); Peter Hersche, "Die protestantische Laus und der katholische Floh. Konfessionspezifische Aspekte der Hygiene," *Ansichten von der rechten Ordnung*, ed. Benedikt Bietenhard (Bern, 1991), 43-60.
62. Châtellier (1987), 127, 151. "Christianisme modern" is my coinage, based on his "catholicisme moderne."
63. Wunder (1992), 67, a fundamental work; Merry E. Wiesner, "Beyond Women and the Family: Towards A Gender Analysis of the Reformation," *SCJ* 18 (1987): 311-21; Opitz (1993).
64. Châtellier (1987), 163.
65. Merry E. Wiesner, *Working Women in Renaissance Germany*, (New Brunswick, N.J., 1986), esp. 149-98; Heide Wunder, in Wunder and Vanja (1991), 12-26, and (1992); Susan C. Karant-Nunn, in Marshall (1989), 29-47, esp. 42f.
66. Dagmar Lorenz, "Vom Kloster zur Küche: Die Frau vor und nach der Reformation Dr. Martin Luthers," in *Die Frau von der Reformation zur Romantik*, ed. Barbara Becker-Cantarino (Bonn, 1985) 7-35; Susan C. Karant-Nunn, in Fix and Karant-Nunn (1992), 121-40, at 121; Mary Wiesner, in Obelkevich, et al. (1987), 295-308.
67. Gerta Scharffenorth, in Wunder and Vanja (1991), 97-108, at 106f.
68. Thus in the *Canones* (V, para. 10f.) of the Dutch and Low German Calvinists at Wesel. J. F. G. Goeters, ed., *Die Beschlüsse des Wesler Konvents* (Düsseldorf 1968), 15.
69. Roper (1989), 256, 265.
70. Luise Schorn-Schütte, in Wunder and Vanja (1991), 109-53.
71. Mary Wiesner, in Fix and Karant-Nunn (1992), 192ff.
72. Westphal (1994), 345, a rare investigation of the gender-specific consequences of confessionalization.
73. Schilling (1991), 62-63, and (1993a). See Robert M. Kingdon in this *Handbook*, vol. 2: 229-47.

74. Roper (1989), 263. See Marshall (1989).
75. Anne Conrad, in Wunder and Vanja (1991), 156.
76. Hörger (1975), 273, 297, 307f.; Hans Dünninger, *Maria siegt in Franken. Die Wallfahrt Dettelbach als Bekenntnis* (Würzburg, 1979).
77. Châtellier (1987), 163.
78. Anne Conrad, in Wunder and Vanja (1991), 178. Gertha Scharffenorth (ibid., 107) argues that Luther's favorable remarks on women were omitted from New High German editions of his tract on marriage as "obsolete." See also Hörger (1975), 307ff.
79. Rabb (1975).
80. Details by Schilling (1988), 293ff. I know of no larger, interconfessional study, though helpful are: Werner Hofmann, ed., *Luther und die Folgen für die Kunst* (Munich, 1983); Jan Knipping, *Iconography of the Counter Reformation in the Netherlands* (Nieuwkoop, 1974); Emile Male, *L'Art religieux de la fin du 16e siècle du 17e siècle. Étude sur l'iconographie après le concile de Trente*, 2d ed. (Paris, 1951); Sibylle Ebert-Schifferer, ed., *Guido Reni und Europa. Ruhm und Nachruhm. Katalog Ausstellung Schirn* (Frankfurt a.M., 1988).
81. Valentin (1980); Breuer (1979).
82. Conrad Wiedemann, in Breuer, et al. (1994); Hörger (1975).
83. A coinage analogous to Gerhard Oestreich's "das "Nichtabsolutistische am Absolutismus.""
84. Helmholz (1992). On Imperial law, fundamental is Martin Heckel, *Gesammelte Schriften*, 2 vols. (Tübingen, 1989). See also Michael Stolleis, in Breuer, et al. (1994).
85. Werner von Koppenfels, in Breuer, et al. (1994).
86. Winfried Schulze, "Vom Gemeinnutz zum Eigennutz" (note 5 above), and "Ständische Gesellschaft und Individualrechte," in *Grund- und Freiheitsrechte von der ständischen zur spätbürgerlichen Gesellschaft*, ed. Günter Birtsch (Göttingen, 1987), 161-79. The notion of "self-interest" occurs first around 1600 in those societies—Holland and later England—which had been least shaped by confessionalism. See Heinz Schilling, "Der libertär-radikale Republikanismus der holländischen Regenten," *GG* 10 (1984): 498-533, here at 528-33; Albert Hirschman, *The Passions and the Interests* (Princeton, 1977).
87. See Schilling in Fix and Karant-Nunn (1992), 119.
88. For a (rare, alas) comparative perspective, see Erich Angermann, "Religion - Politik - Gesellschaft im 17. Jahrhundert. Ein Versuch in vergleichender Sozialgeschichte," *HZ* 214 (1972): 26-29; and in general, see Lehmann (1980).
89. Fundamental are van Gelder (1961); Wollgast (1988).
90. Kaplan (1989), 30-90, with the quotes at 36, 90. See also Schilling in Fix and Karant-Nunn (1992), 99-120.
91. Gustav Adolf Benrath und Reimar Hansen, in Schilling (1986).
92. An anonymous source of 1591, cited by Diethelm Klippel, "Souveränität," in *Geschichtliche Grundbegriffe*, vol. 6 (Stuttgart, 1990), 108 note 65.
93. The Prussian General Code of 1794, one of the most progressive (in the Enlightenment's sense) in Europe, designates the churches and sects as "Kirchengesellschaften" or "geistliche Gesellschaften." *Allgemeines Landrecht*, ed. Hans Hattenhauer (Frankfurt am Main, 1970), chap. 11, 542-84.

BIBLIOGRAPHY

Addy, John. *Sin and Society in the Seventeenth Century.* London, 1984.

Ankerloo, Bengt, and Gustav Henningsen, eds. *Early Modern European Witchcraft.* Oxford, 1990.

Baumgartner, Frederic J. *Change and Continuity in the French Episcopate. The Bishops and the Wars of Religion. 1547-1610.* Durham, 1986.

Baur, Jörg, and Walter Sparn. "Orthodoxie (Lutherische Orthodoxie)." In *Evangelisches Kirchenlexikon,* fasc. 8, coll. 953-59. Göttingen, 1990.

Becker, Thomas. *Konfessionalisierung in Kurköln.* Bonn, 1989.

Behringer, Wolfgang. *Hexenverfolgung in Bayern: Volksmagie, Glaubenseifer und Staatsräson in der Frühen Neuzeit.* Munich, 1988.

Bergin, Joseph. *Cardinal de la Rochefoucauld. Leadership and Reform in the French Church.* New Haven, 1987.

Bireley, Robert. *The Counter-Reformation Prince: Anti-Machiavellianism or Catholic Statecraft in Early Modern Europe.* Chapel Hill, 1990.

Bireley, Robert. *Maximilian von Bayern, Adam Contzen, S.J., und die Gegenreformation in Deutschland, 1624-1635.* Göttingen, 1975.

Bireley, Robert. *Religion and Politics in the Age of the Counterreformation. Emperor Ferdinand II., William Lamormaini, S.J. and the Formation of Imperial Policy.* Chapel Hill, 1981.

Blickle, Peter, et al., eds. *Zwingli und Europa—Referate und Protokoll des Internationalen Kongresses aus Anlaß des 500. Geburtstages von Huldrych Zwingli vom 26. bis 30. März 1984.* Zurich, 1985.

Bödeker, Hans Erich, Gérald Chaix, and Patrice Veid, eds. *Le Livre religieux et ses pratiques. Etudes sur l'histoire du livre religieux en Allemagne et en France à l'époque moderne.* Göttingen, 1991.

Bossy, John. *Christianity in the West, 1400-1700.* Oxford, 1985.

Brecht, Martin. *Kirchenordnung und Kirchenzucht in Württemberg vom 16. bis zum 18. Jahrhundert.* Stuttgart, 1967.

Brecht, Martin, and Reinhard Schwarz, eds. *Bekenntnis und Einheit der Kirche: Studien zum Konkordienbuch.* Stuttgart, 1980.

Breuer, Dieter. *Oberdeutsche Literatur 1565-1650. Deutsche Literaturgeschichte und Territorialgeschichte in frühabsolutistischer Zeit.* Munich, 1979.

Breuer, Dieter, ed. *Frömmigkeit in der Frühen Neuzeit. Studien zur religiösen Literatur des 17. Jahrhunderts in Deutschland.* Beihefte zum *Daphnis,* vol. 2. Amsterdam, 1984.

Breuer, Dieter, Barbara Becker-Cantarino, Heinz Schilling, and Walter Sparn, eds. *Religion und Religiosität im Zeitalter des Barock. Akten des 8. Barocksymposiums an der Herzog-August-Bibliothek.* Wiesbaden, 1994.

Cameron, Euan. *The European Reformation.* Oxford, 1991.

Chaix, Gérald. *Réforme et Contre-réforme catholiques. Recherches sur la Chartreuse de Cologne aux 16e siècle.* Analecta Cartusiana, vol. 80. 3 vols. Salzburg, 1981.

Châtellier, Louis. *L'Europe des Dévots.* Paris, 1987.

Châtellier, Louis. *Tradition chrétienne et renouveau catholique dans le cadre de l'ancien diocèse de Strasbourg (1650-1770).* Paris, 1981.

Chevalier, Bernard, and Robert Sauzet, eds. *Les Réformes. Enracinement socioculturel.* Paris, 1985.

Clark, Peter, ed. *The European Crisis of the 1590s*. London, 1985.
Colin, Pierre, Elisabeth Germain, Jean Joncheray, and Marc Venard, eds. *Aux origines du catéchisme en France*. Tournai, 1989.
Collinson, Patrick. *Godly People: Essays on English Protestantism and Puritanism*. London, 1983.
Collinson, Patrick. *The Religion of Protestants: the Church in English society 1559-1625*. Oxford, 1982.
Conrad, Anne. *Zwischen Kloster und Welt. Ursulinen und Jesuitinnen in der katholischen Reformbewegung des 16./17. Jahrhunderts*. VIEG, vol. 142. Mainz, 1991.
Cross, Claire. *Church and People, 1450-1660*. Glasgow, 1987.
Delumeau, Jean. *Le catholicisme entre Luther et Voltaire*. Paris, 1971.
Delumeau, Jean. *Un chemin d'histoire. Chrétienté et christianisation*. Paris, 1981.
Deursen, Aadrian Theodor van. *Bavianen en Slijkgeuzen: Kerk en kerkvolk ten tijde van Maurits en Oldenbarnevelt*. Assen, 1974.
Dinges, Martin. *Stadtarmut in Bordeaux (1525-1675)*. Bonn, 1988.
Dülmen, Richard van. *Religion und Gesellschaft. Beiträge zu einer Religionsgeschichte der Neuzeit*. Frankfurt, 1984.
Duke, Alastaire. *Reformation and Revolt in the Low Countries*. London, 1990.
Evans, Robert John Weston. *The Making of the Habsburg Monarchy 1550-1700*. Oxford, 1979.
Fix, Andrew, and Susan Karant-Nunn, eds. *Germania Illustrata. Essays in Early Modern Germany Presented to Gerald Strauss*. Kirksville, Mo., 1992.
Ford, Alan. *The Protestant Reformation in Ireland, 1590-1641*. 2d ed. Studien zur intellektuellen Geschichte des Christentums, vol. 34. Frankfurt am Main, 1987.
François, Etienne. *Die unsichtbare Grenze. Protestanten und Katholiken in Augsburg 1648-1806*. Sigmaringen, 1991.
Freitag, Werner. *Volks- und Elitefrömmigkeit in der Frühen Neuzeit. Marienwallfahrten im Fürstbistum Münster*. Paderborn, 1991.
Garrison-Estèbe, Janine. *Protestants du midi, 1559-1598*. Toulouse, 1980.
Garstein, Oskar. *Rome and the Counter-Reformation in Scandinavia*. Vol 1, *1539-1583*. Vol 2, *1583-1622*. Vol 3, *1622-1656*. Oslo, 1963-80; Leiden, 1991.
Gelder, H. A. Enno van. *The Two Reformations in the 16th Century. A Study of the Religious Aspects and Consequences of Renaissance and Humanism*. The Hague, 1961.
Gordon, Bruce. *Clerical Discipline and the Rural Reformation: the Synod in Zürich, 1532-1580*. Bern, 1992.
Greaves, Richard L. *Society and Religion in Elizabethan England*. Minneapolis, 1981.
Grendler, Paul F. *The Roman Inquisition and the Venetian Press, 1540-1605*. Princeton, 1977.
Greyerz, Kaspar von, ed. *Religion and Society in Early Modern Europe (1500-1800)*. London, 1985.
Groenhuis, G. *De Predikanten: de sociale Positie van de gereformeerde Predikanten in de Republiek der Verenigde Nederlanden voor 1700*. Historische Studies, vols. 33. Groningen, 1977.
Haliczer, Stephen, ed. *Inquisition and Society in Early Modern Europe*. London, 1986.
Headley, John, and John Tomato, eds. *San Carlo Borromeo. Catholic Reform and Ecclesiastical Politics*. Cransbury, N. J., 1988.
Helmholz, Richard H. *Canon Law in Protestant Lands*. Berlin, 1992.
Hörger, Hermann. "Dorfreligion und bäuerliche Mentalité im Wandel ihrer ideologischen Grundlagen." *ZBLG* 38 (1975): 244-316.
Hoffmann, Philip. *Church and Community in the Diocese of Lyon, 1500-1789*. New Haven, 1984.
Hsia, R. Po-chia, ed. *The German People and the Reformation*. Ithaca, 1988a.
Hsia, R. Po-chia. *The Myth of Ritual Murder. Jews and Magic in Reformation Germany*. New Haven, 1988b.
Hsia, R. Po-chia. *Social Discipline in the Reformation. Central Europe 1550-1750*. London, 1989.

Ingram, Martin. *Church Courts, Sex and Marriage in England, 1570-1640.* Cambridge, 1987.

Israel, Jonathan Irvine. *European Jewry in the Age of Mercantilism, 1550-1750.* 2d ed. Oxford, 1989.

Jedin, Hubert. *Geschichte des Konzils von Trient.* 4 vols. Freiburg im Breisgau, 1951-75.

Kamen, Henry. *The Iron Century: Social Change in Europe, 1550-1660.* 2d ed. London, 1976.

Kaplan, Benjamin Jacob. Calvinists and Libertines: The Reformation in Utrecht, 1578-1618. Ph.D. diss., Harvard University, 1989.

"Katholische Reform. Symposion im Campo Santo Teutonico, 26. bis 29. September 1988." *RQ* 84 (1989): 1-270.

Kingdon, Robert M. *Church and Society in Reformation Europe.* London, 1985.

Kingdon, Robert M. *Geneva and the Consolidation of the French Protestant Movement, 1564-1572.* Geneva, 1967.

Kingdon, Robert M. *Myths about the St. Bartholomew's Day Massacres, 1572-1576.* Cambridge, Mass., 1988.

Kolb, Robert. *For all the Saints. Changing Perceptions of Martyrdom and Sainthood in the Lutheran Reformation.* Macon, Ga., 1987.

Lehmann, Hartmut. *Das Zeitalter des Absolutismus. Gottesgnadentum und Kriegsnot.* Christentum und Gesellschaft, vol. 9. Stuttgart, 1980.

Lottin, Alain. *Lille. Citadelle de la Contre-Réforme? (1598-1668).* Dunkirk, 1984.

Maltby, William S. *The Black Legend in England: the Development of Anti-Spanish Sentiment, 1558-1660.* Durham, 1971.

Marnef, Guido. *Antwerpen in Reformatietijd. Ondergronds Protestantisme in een internationale handelsmetropool, 1550-1577.* Manuskript Doctoraat Letteren en Wijsbegeerte, Leuven, 1991.

Marnef, Guido. *Het Calvinistisch Bewind te Mechelen 1580-1585.* Kotrijk-Heule, 1987.

Marshall, Sherrin, ed. *Women in Reformation and Counter-Reformation Europe: Public and Private Worlds.* Bloomington, 1989.

Mckee, Elsie Anne. *John Calvin on the Diaconate and Liturgical Almsgiving.* Geneva, 1984.

Mentzer, Raymond. *Sin and the Calvinists.* Kirksville, Mo., 1994.

Monter, E. William. *Frontiers of Heresy: the Spanish Inquisition from the Basque Lands to Sicily.* Cambridge, 1990.

Muchembled, Robert. *Culture populaire et culture des élites dans la France moderne.* Paris, 1978.

Münch, Paul. *Zucht und Ordnung. Reformierte Kirchenverfassungen im 16. und 17. Jahrhundert (Nassau-Dillenburg, Kurpfalz, Hessen-Kassel).* Stuttgart, 1978.

O'Day, Rosemary. *The Debate on the English Reformation.* London, 1986.

Obelkevich, Jim, Lyndal Roper, and Raphael Samuel, eds. *Disciplines of Faith: Studies in Religion, Politics and Patriarchy.* London, 1987.

Oestreich, Gerhard. *Geist und Gestalt des frühmodernen Staates. Ausgewählte Aufsätze.* Berlin, 1969.

O'Malley, John W., ed. *Catholicism in Early Modern History. A Guide to Research.* St. Louis, Mo., 1988.

Opitz, Claudia, et al., eds. *Maria in der Welt. Marienverehrung im Kontext der Sozialgeschichte 10.-18. Jahrhundert.* Zurich, 1993.

Parker, Geoffrey, and Lesley Smith, eds. *The General Crisis of the Seventeenth Century.* London, 1978.

Péronnet, Michel, ed. *Les églises et leurs institutions au XVIème siècle.* Montpellier, 1977.

Pettegree, Andrew. *Emden and the Dutch Revolt: Exile and the Development of Reformed Protestantism.* Oxford, 1992.

Pfister, Christian. *Bevölkerung, Klima und Agrarmodernisierung 1525 bis 1860.* 2d ed. Bern and Stuttgart, 1985.

Plazaola, Juan, ed. *Ignacio de Loyola y su tiempo. Congresso International de Historia (9-13 septiembre 1991).* Bilbao, 1992.

Prestwich, Menna, ed. *International Calvinism 1541-1715.* Oxford, 1985.

Prodi, Paolo. *Il sacramento del potere. Il giuramento politico nella storia costituzionale dell' Occidente.* Bologna, 1992.

Pullan, Brian. *Rich and Poor in Renaissance Venice: The Social Institutions of a Catholic State to 1620.* Oxford, 1971.

Rabb, Theodore K. *The Struggle for Stability in Early Modern Europe.* New York, 1975.

Rabut, Elisabeth. *Le roi, l'église et le temple. L'exécution de l'Edit de Nantes en Dauphiné.* Paris, 1987.

Ravitch, Norman. *The Catholic Church and the French Nation, 1589-1989.* London, 1990.

Reinhard, Wolfgang. "Christliche Mission und Dialektik des Kolonialismus." *HZ* 109 (1984): 353-70.

Reinhard, Wolfgang. "Gegenreformation als Modernisierung? Prolegomena zu einer Theorie des konfessionellen Zeitalters." *ARG* 68 (1977): 226-52.

Reinhard, Wolfgang. "Katholische Reform und Gegenreformation in der Kölner Nuntiatur 1584-1621." *RQ* 66 (1971): 8-65.

Reinhard, Wolfgang. "Reformation, Counter-Reformation and the Early Modern State: a Reassessment." *CIIR* 75 (1989): 383-404.

Reinhard, Wolfgang and Heinz Schilling, eds. *Die katholische Konfessionalisierung. Wissenschaftliches Symposion der Gesellschaft zur Herausgabe des Corpus Catholicorum und des Verein für Reformationsgeschichte.* Gütersloh and Münster, 1995.

Rogier, L. J. *Geschiedenis van het Katholicisme in Noord-Nederland in de 16e en de 17e eeuw.* 2 vols. 2d ed. Amsterdam, 1947.

Roper, Lyndale. *The Holy Household: Women and Morals in Reformation Augsburg.* Oxford, 1989.

Rublack, Hans-Christoph, ed. *Die lutherische Konfessionalisierung in Deutschland. Wissenschaftliches Symposium des Vereins für Reformationsgeschichte.* SVRG, no. 197. Gütersloh, 1992.

Safley, Thomas Max. *Let No Man Put Asunder: The Control of Marriage in the German Southwest.* Kirksville, Mo., 1984.

Sauzet, Robert. *Contre-réforme et Réforme catholique en Bas-Languedoc: le diocèse de Nîmes au 17e siècle.* Paris and Louvain, 1979.

Sauzet, Robert, ed. *Les frontières religieuses en Europe du 15e au 17e siècle.* Paris, 1992.

Schär, Markus. *Seelennöte der Untertanen. Selbstmord, Melancholie und Religion im Alten Zürich 1500-1800.* Zurich, 1985.

Schilling, Heinz. *Aufbruch und Krise. Deutschland 1517-1648.* Siedlers Deutsche Geschichte, vol. 5. Berlin, 1988.

Schilling, Heinz. *Civic Calvinism in Northwestern Germany and The Netherlands, Sixteenth to Nineteenth Centuries.* Kirksville, Mo., 1991.

Schilling, Heinz. "Confessional Migration as a Distinct Type of Old European Long Distance Migration." In *Le migrazioni in Europa (secc. 13-18). Atti della XXV Settimana di Studi.* Prato, 1994.

Schilling, Heinz. "Frühneuzeitliche Formierung und Disziplinierung von Ehe, Familie und Erziehung im Spiegel calvinistischer Kirchenratsprotokolle". In *Glaubensbekenntnisse, Treueformeln und Sozialdisziplinierung,* ed. Paolo Prodi. Munich, 1993a. English translation in Mentzer (1994).

Schilling, Heinz, ed. *Kirchenzucht und Sozialdisziplinierung in interkonfessionell vergleichender Perspektive.* Berlin, 1993b.

Schilling, Heinz. "Konfessionalisierung und Formierung eines internationalen Systems während der Frühen Neuzeit." In *The Reformation in Germany and Europe: Interpretations and Issues,* ed. Hans Guggisberg and Gottfried Krodel, 591-613. Gütersloh, 1993c.

Schilling, Heinz. "Die Konfessionalisierung von Kirche, Staat und Gesellschaft - Profil, Leistung, Defizite und Perspektiven eines geschichtswissenschaftlichen Paradigmas." In Reinhard and Schilling (1995), 1-35.

Schilling, Heinz. *Konfessionskonflikt und Staatsbildung: Eine Fallstudie über das Verhältnis von religiösem und sozialem Wandel in der Frühneuzeit am Beispiel der Grafschaft Lippe.* Gütersloh, 1981.

Schilling, Heinz. *Religion, Political Culture and the Emergence of Early Modern Society. Essays in German and Dutch History.* SMRT, vol. 50. Leiden, 1992.

Schilling, Heinz, ed. *Die reformierte Konfessionalisierung in Deutschland - Das Problem der "Zweiten Reformation". Wissenschaftliches Symposium des Vereins für Reformationsgeschichte.* SVRG, no. 195. Gütersloh, 1986.

Schindling, Anton, and Ernst Walter Zeeden, eds. *Die Territorien des Reiches im Zeitalter der Reformation und Konfessionalisierung. Land und Konfession 1500-1650.* 5 vols. KLK, vols. 49-53. Münster, 1989-93.

Schmidt, Heinrich Richard. *Konfessionalisierung im 16. Jahrhundert.* Munich, 1992.

Schorn-Schütte, Luise. Evangelische Geistlichkeit in der Frühneuzeit. Ihr Beitrag zur Entfaltung frühmoderner Staatlichkeit und Gesellschaft. Unpublished Habilitationsschrift, Giessen, 1992.

Schulze, Winfried. "Concordia, Discordia, Tolerantia. Deutsche Politik im konfessionellen Zeitalter." In *Neue Studien zur frühneuzeitlichen Reichsgeschichte,* ed. Johannes Kunisch, 43-80. ZHF, Beiheft 3. Berlin, 1987.

Seidel Menchi, Silvia. *Ketzerverfolgung im 16. und 17. Jahrhundert.* Wiesbaden, 1992.

Solé, Jaques. *Le débat entre protestants et catholiques français de 1598 à 1685.* Lille, 1986.

Sommer, Wolfgang. *Gottesfurcht und Fürstenherrschaft. Studie zum Obrigkeitsverständnis Johann Arndts und lutherischer Hofprediger zur Zeit der altprotestantischen Orthodoxie.* Göttingen, 1988.

Stauffenegger, Roger. *Église et Société. Genève au 17e siècle.* 2 vols. Geneva, 1983.

Stichweh, Rudolf. *Der frühmoderne Staat und die europäische Universität. Zur Interaktion von Politik und Erziehungssystem im Prozeß der Ausdifferenzierung (16.-18. Jahrhundert).* Frankfurt, 1991.

Strauss, Gerald. *Luther's House of Learning: Indoctrination of the Young in the German Reformation.* Baltimore, 1978.

Tazbir, Janusz. *A State without Stakes: Polish Religious Toleration in the 16th and 17th Centuries.* Wydawniczy, 1972.

Thomas, Keith. *Religion and the Decline of Magic.* Harmondsworth, 1975.

Tracy, James D. "With and Without the Counter-Reformation: the Catholic Church in the Spanish Netherlands and the Dutch Republic, 1580-1650." *CHR* 71 (1985): 547-75.

Tschopp, Silvia Serena. *Heilsgeschichtliche Deutungsmuster in der Publizistik des Dreißigjährigen Krieges.* Frankfurt am Main, 1991.

Tyacke, Nicholas. *Anti-Calvinists: the Rise of English Arminianism, c. 1590-1640.* Oxford, 1987.

Valentin, Jean-Marie, ed. *Gegenreformation und Literatur. Beiträge zur interdisziplinären Erforschung der katholischen Reformbewegung.* Beiheft zum *Daphnis,* vol. 3. Amsterdam, 1979.

Valentin, Jean-Marie. "Gegenreformation und Literatur: das Jesuitendrama im Dienste der religiösen und moralischen Erziehung." *HJ* 100 (1980): 240-256.

Valentin, Jean-Marie. *Le théâtre des Jésuites dans les pays de la langue allemande (1554-1680): salut des âmes et ordres des cités.* 3 vols. Bern and Frankfurt am Main, 1978.

Valentin, Jean-Marie, ed. *Le théâtre des Jésuites dans les pays de langue allemande. Répertoire chronologique des pièces représentatées et des documents conservés (1553-1773).* 2 vols. Stuttgart, 1983-84.

Van der Wee, Hermann, ed. *The Rise and Decline of Urban Industries in Italy and the Low Countries (Late Middle Ages-Early Modern Times).* Leuven, 1988.

Venard, Marc, ed. *Les débuts de la Réforme catholique dans les Pays de la langue Français (1560-1620)*. Themenheft der *Revue d'histoire de l'Eglise de France*, vol. 75. Paris, 1989.

Venard, Marc. "Le prêtre en France au début du XVIIe siècle." *Bulletin de Saint Sulpice* (1982): 197-213.

Venard, Marc, ed. *Le temps des confessions (1530-1620/30)*. Histoire du christianisme des origines à nos jours, vol 7. Paris, 1992.

Vogler, Bernard. *Le clergé protestant rhénan au siècle de la Réforme 1555-1619*. Paris, 1976.

Vogler, Bernard, ed. *L'institution et les pouvoirs dans les églises de l'Antiquité à nos jours. Colloque de Strasbourg 1983*. Brussels, 1987.

Vogler, Bernard. *Vie religieuse en pays rhénan dans la seconde moitié du 16e siècle (1556-1619)*. Lille, 1974.

Vogler, Günter, ed. *Alternatives Denken vom 16. bis zum 18. Jahrhundert*. Weimar, 1994.

De Vries, Jan. *The Dutch Rural Economy in the Golden Age, 1500-1700*. New Haven, 1974.

De Vries, Jan. *The Economy of Europe in an Age of Crisis (1600-1750)*. Cambridge, 1976.

Watts, Michael R. *The Dissenters: From the Reformation to the French Revolution*. Oxford, 1985.

Westphal, Siegrid. *Frau und lutherische Konfessionalisierung. Eine Untersuchung zum Fürstentum Pfalz-Neuburg, 1542-1614*. Frankfurt am Main, 1994.

Wollgast, Siegfried. *Philosophie in Deutschland zwischen Reformation und Aufklärung, 1550-1650*. Berlin, 1988.

Wunder, Heide. *"Er ist die Sonn', sie ist der Mond": Frauen in der Frühen Neuzeit*. Munich, 1992.

Wunder, Heide, and Christina Vanja, eds. *Wandel der Geschlechterbeziehungen zu Beginn der Neuzeit*. Frankfurt am Main, 1991.

Zeeden, Ernst Walter. *Die Entstehung der Konfessionen. Grundlagen und Formen der Konfessionsbildung*. Munich, 1965.

Zeeden, Ernst Walter, and Peter Thaddäus Lang, eds. *Kirche und Visitation: Beiträge zur Erforschung des frühneuzeitlichen Visitationswesens in Europa*. Stuttgart, 1984.

Zeller, Winfried. *Theologie und Frömmigkeit. Gesammelte Aufsätze*. 2 vols. Marburg, 1971-78.

APPENDIX 1: THE COINAGES
OF RENAISSANCE EUROPE,
CA. 1500

Before the more widespread diffusion of negotiable credit instruments, early-modern European economies utilized primarily commodity moneys in the form of metallic coinages: gold, silver, and copper. Both the gold and silver coinages were alloyed, in varying degrees, with some copper as a base-metal hardening agent. Alloys with proportionately more copper were also used, rather than just smaller size, to distinguish lower from higher denomination coins.[1] Thus most petty coinages were predominantly copper (hence *base* coinage), some with virtually no silver; but not until 1543 was Europe's first all-copper petty coinage issued, in the Habsburg Netherlands, to mark an important step towards fiat money, i.e. money whose exchange value is established solely by government decree.

European governments, however, also played a crucial role in determining the domestic values of their gold and silver coins, so long as they were able to enforce a monopoly on domestic minting. Through their mint indentures and monetary ordinances, they stipulated the three essential components of all coins struck: the weight or the *taille*, as the number of coins struck from the legal mint-weight; the fineness or alloy; and the exchange rate or "nominal value", expressed in the domestic money-of-account. That nominal money-of-account value had to be greater than the current market value for the coin's bullion contents (its commodity value), in order to cover the costs of minting, in the form of the mint-master's *brassage* fee and the government's *seigniorage* fee. Normally, coins did command such a premium over bullion, because the transaction costs in effecting exchanges were much lower with legal-tender coins, bearing the government's stamp to certify its value, than with raw bullion (especially when trading in bullion was prohibited by law). Most governments also permitted the circulation of certain good-quality foreign gold coins (*not* silver), though at rates that accorded a smaller premium than those enjoyed by domestic coins. If, for any reason, the public lost confidence in the domestic coinage, that coinage would lose its essential premium and the domestic mints would no longer receive any bullion. For then the market values of both bullion and foreign coins would rise proportionally above the values assigned to domestic coins, as expressed in the domestic money-of-account.

Most early-modern moneys-of-account, an accounting system for reckoning and recording coin values, prices, wages, rents, etc., were based on the current domestic silver penny: with 12 pence to the shilling and 20 shillings to the pound (£1 = 20s = 240d). Thus a sum expressed as 6s 8d was always worth 80 currently circulating pennies. When Carolingian officials established this system, c.800, the "pound" was in fact the pound weight of silver, from which 240 pence were meant to be struck; but subsequent changes in coin weights, alloys, and nominal values forever severed that original relationship. Any increase in the coin's *taille* (reducing its weight), nominal value, or its copper alloy (reducing its fineness) constituted a *debasement* that proportionally increased the total money-of-account value of coinage struck from the *pound*, *marc*, or other mint-weight of fine metal. Conversely, any reduction in the *taille* (increasing the coin's weight), its face value, or its copper alloy (increasing the fineness) constituted a *renforcement* (strengthening) that proportionally reduced the total money-of-account value of coinage struck from the *pound*, *marc*, etc. of fine metal. Those relationships, which indicate the total money-of-account or "tale" value of the coinage struck from the legal mint-weight of fine gold or silver (*pound*, *marc*), can be expressed by this formula:[2]

TALE VALUE =

TAILLE (NUMBER STRUCK PER POUND) X COIN'S FACE VALUE/PERCENTAGE FINENESS

The following tables on the leading west European coins in 1500 provide their weights and fineness in modern metric terms, and their official values in terms of three moneys-of-account: the English pound sterling, the Flemish *livre gros* (*pond groot*), and the French *livre tournois*. They also indicate the relative purchasing power of these coins in 1500, expressed in terms of: (1) major consumer goods in the Antwerp-Mechelen-Brussels region of Brabant; and (2) the summer daily wage of an Antwerp master mason. Self-evident from this table is the fact that an Antwerp mason would then have consumed far more North Sea herring than luxury woolens from Ghent, and that gold coins were usually reserved for just very high-value transactions.

1. England was an exception in doing so by weight alone, so that a farthing weighed 25% of the penny.
2. The proportional changes in these relationships involve reciprocal values that are expressed by the formula $\Delta TV = [1/(1-\chi)]-1$. TV represents the total money-of-account value of coinage struck from the mint-weight of pure metal (silver or gold): Δ represents percentage change; and χ represents the percentage reduction of silver (or gold) in the money-of-account unit. As late as 1278, only 242d were being struck to the English Tower Pound (12 oz), which weighed 349.914 grams; in 1500, however, almost double that amount, 450d (though of the same sterling fineness), was struck from the Tower Pound. The mint-weight for both France and the Netherlands was de *marc de Troyes* (8 onces), weighing 244.753 grams. The Cologne *Mark* weighed 233.856 grams; the Florentine *libbra* (12 oncie), 339.542 grams; and the Venetian *marco* (8 oncie), 238.50 grams.

Table 1. A Selection of Gold and Silver Coins Circulating in Western Europe in 1500: Weight, Percentage Fineness and Intrinsic Fine Metal Contents, and their Nominal Values in Flemish (Habsburg Netherlands'), French, and English Moneys-of-Account.

COIN	Place of Issue	Struck (in this form) during or since	Weight in Grams	Percent Fineness	Grams Fine Metal (Gold or Silver)	Value in pence gros of Flanders[a]	Value in sous tournois of France	Value in pence sterling of England
GOLD								
florin	Florence	1252	3.528	97.90[b]	3.454[b]	79	38.76	55
ducat	Venice	1284	3.560	[99.50[c]]	3.542[c]	79	38.76	55
genovino	Genoa	1252	3.560	[97.90[b]]	3.485[b]	79	38.76	55
ducat	Hungary	1308	3.536	[97.90[b]]	3.462[b]	79	38.76	55
Rhenish florin	Germany: Four Electors	1490	3.278	77.08	2.527	58	28.76	41
postulaat de Bourbon	Liège	1456-1482	2.331	62.50	1.457	32	15.28	22
cavalier (rijder)	Burgundian Netherlands	1433-1454	3.626	99.22	3.598	79	38.76	54
lion (leeuw)	Burgundian Netherlands	1454-1466	4.257	95.83	4.079	92	45.00	63
florin of St Andrew	Burgundian Netherlands	1466-1496	3.399	79.17	2.691	61	30.00	42
florin of St Philip	Habsburg Netherlands	1496-1500	3.300	66.67	2.200	50	24.50	36
toison d'or	Habsburg Netherlands	1496-1500	4.490	99.17	4.453	100	49.06	72
florin of St Philip	Habsburg Netherlands	1500	3.300	66.33	2.189	50	24.50	36
écu à la couronne	France	1474	3.399	96.35	3.275	71	35.00	50
écu au soleil	France	1475	3.496	96.35	3.368	74	36.26	51
Henricus noble	England	1412-1464	6.998	99.48	6.962	153	75.00	108
angel-noble	England	1465	5.184	99.48	5.157	116	56.88	80
ryal or rose noble	England	1465	7.776	99.48	7.736	173	85.00	120
sovereign	England	1489	15.552	99.48	15.471	346	170.00	240
cruzado	Portugal	1457	3.780	98.90	3.738	84	41.00	58
florin	Aragon	1346-1476	3.480	75.00	2.610	58	28.75	40
excelente	Spain	1497	3.780	98.90	3.738	84	41.00	58

COIN SILVER	Place of Issue	Struck (in this form) during or since	Weight in Grams	Percent Fineness	Grams Fine Metal (Gold or Silver)	Value in pence gros of Flanders[a] in d gros	Value in sous tournois of France in d tournois	Value in pence sterling of England in d sterling
toison d'argent	Habsburg Netherlands	1496-1521	3.399	87.85	2.986	6.00	34.88*	4.12*
stuiver or patard	Habsburg Netherlands	1496-1521	3.098	31.94	0.990	2.00	11.63*	1.38*
gros or groot	Habsburg Netherlands	1496-1521	1.827	25.95	0.474	1.00	5.81*	0.69*
courte or double mite	Habsburg Netherlands	1496-1521	1.078	2.66	0.029	0.083 2 mites = 1/12d	0.48*	0.06*
groat	England	1464-1526	3.110	92.50	2.877	5.82*	33.82*	4.00
penny	England	1464-1526	0.778	92.50	0.720	1.45*	8.45*	1.00
halfpenny	England	1464-1526	0.389	92.50	0.360	0.73*	4.23*	0.50
gros de roi	France	1488-1519	3.547	91.84	3.258	6.19*	36.00	4.22*
grand blanc à la couronne (douzain)	France	1488-1519	2.846	35.94	1.023	2.06*	12.00	1.41*
demi-blanc (sizain)	France	1488-1519	1.423	35.94	0.511	1.03*	6.00	0.70*
denier tournois	France	1488-1519	0.971	8.00	0.078	0.17*	1.00	0.12*
grosso or matapan (= 32 denari piccioli)	Venice	1421	1.600	95.20	1.523	3.07*	17.87	2.12*
soldino (= 8 denari piccoli)	Venice	1421	0.400	95.20	0.381	0.77*	4.47*	0.53*
grosso (of 6s 8d in denaro picciolo)	Florence	1489	2.310	95.83	2.214	4.46*	26.00*	3.08*
quattrino (4 denari piccioli)	Florence	1490	0.786	16.67	0.131	0.26*	1.54*	0.18*

* Money-of-account values of silver coins estimated on the basis of relative silver contents.

a. The *livre gros* (*pond groot*) of Flanders was the common money-of-account for the Burgundian and then Habsburg Netherlands (from 1433-34). £1 *livre gros* (= 20s = 240d = 5760 mites) = £1.50 *groot* of Brabant = £6.0 Artois = £12.0 *parisis* (of Flanders). From c.1460 the *gulden* money-of-account (or guilder, based on the 1460 value of the Rhenish florin) = 20 stuivers = 40d gros Flemish = £1.0 Artois.

b. Nominally the Florentine florin was 24 carats fine, i.e. 100% pure gold; but no gold coins were finer than 99.7%. The fineness (and also the weight) of the Florentine florin in this table is taken as the mean fineness of those coins actually struck from 1496 to 1507; and that fineness has been arbitrarily assigned to the Genoese and Hungarian gold coins.

c. The Venetian mint accepted bullion that was 23.5 carats (23 carats 2 grains) or 97.92% fine and further refined it, but probably not beyond 99.5% - 99.7% pure.

Table 2. The Puchasing Power of Selected Gold and Silver Coins and of a Master Mason's Daily Summer Wage in the Antwerp-Mechelen-Brussels Region in 1500.

Relative Quantities of Selected Goods Purchased by the following coins:

Commodity and Unit (Metric)	Price per Unit in Flemish d gros	Flemish Stuiver (2d gros)	Flemish Florin of St Philip (50d gros)	French écu à la couronne (71d gros)	Italian florin or ducat (79d gros)	English angel-noble (116d gros)	Purchasing Power of Antwerp Masons's Daily Summer Wage (8.33d gros)
Rhine Wine, red: liter	2.46d	0.81	20.29	28.80	32.05	47.06	3.38
Butter: kilogram	2.97d	0.67	16.82	23.89	26.58	39.03	2.80
Rye: liter	0.17d	11.94	298.60	424.01	471.79	692.75	49.76
Wheat: liter	0.25d	8.00	199.86	283.80	315.78	463.68	33.31
Peas: liter	0.25d	7.86	196.59	279.16	310.61	456.09	32.76
Beef, salted: kilogram	1.86d	1.07	26.81	38.08	42.37	62.21	4.47
Herrings, smoked red: number	0.19d	10.42	260.42	369.80	411.46	604.17	43.40
Eggs: by number	0.10d	20.88	521.92	741.12	824.63	1,210.86	87.00
Sugar-loaf: kilogram	8.51d	0.24	5.88	8.35	9.29	13.63	0.98
Pepper: kilogram	78.70d	0.03	0.64	0.90	1.00	1.47	0.11
Ginger: kilogram	36.16d	0.06	1.38	1.96	2.18	3.21	0.23
Candles, tallow: kilogram	4.00d	0.50	12.51	17.76	19.76	29.02	2.08
Flax, combed: kilogram	4.08d	0.49	12.26	17.42	19.67	28.45	2.04
Linen sail-cloth: 1 meter long	4.71d	0.42	10.61	15.07	16.77	24.62	1.77
Wool/worsted Cloth, coarse grey, from Weert/Maaseik: 1 meter	17.27d	0.12	2.90	4.11	4.58	6.72	0.48

Commodity and Unit (Metric)	Price per Unit in Flemish d gros	Flemish Stuiver (2d gros)	Flemish Florin of St Philip (50d gros)	French écu à la couronne (71d gros)	Italian florin or ducat (79d gros)	English angel-noble (116d gros)	Purchasing Power of Antwerp Masons's Daily Summer Wage (8.33d gros)
Woolen Cloth:* Ghent *Dickedinnen* fine black: 1 meter long by 1.75 m.	167.62d	0.01	0.30	0.42	0.47	0.69	0.05
Woolen Cloth:* Mechelen black *Rooslaken* fine: 1 meter long by 1.75 m.	110.55d	0.02	0.45	0.64	0.71	1.05	0.08

* The Ghent *dickedinnen* woolen broadcloths (made from English Staple wools), fully finished, measured 21.0 by 1.75 meters (30 by 2.5 ells) and cost £14 13 4d gros Flemish. Mechelen's black *Rooslaken* woolen broadcloths, also made from fine English wools, measured 20.67 by 1.75 meters, fully finished, and cost £9 10s 5d gros Flemish.

Sources

Bernocchi, Mario, *Le monete della repubblica fiorentina*, Vol. III: *documentazione* (Florence, 1976).

Blanchet, A., and Dieudonné, A., *Manuel de numismatique française*, 2 vols. (Paris, 1916).

Lane, Frederic, and Mueller, Reinhold, *Money and Banking in Medieval and Renaissance Venice*, Vol. I: *Coins and Moneys of Account* (Baltimore and London, 1985).

Munro, John, "Money and Coinage of the Age of Erasmus," in R.A.B. Mynors, D.F.S. Thomson, and W.K. Ferguson, eds., *The Correspondence of Erasmus*, Vol. I: *Letters 1 to 141, 1484 to 1500* (Toronto, 1974), pp. 311-47.

Spufford, Peter, "Coinage and Currency," in M.M. Postan and E.E. Rich, eds., *The Cambridge Economic History of Europe*, Vol. III (Cambridge, 1963), pp. 576-602.

Spufford, Peter, *Handbook of Medieval Exchange* (London, 1986).

Van der Wee, Herman, *The Growth of the Antwerp Market and the European Economy, Fourteenth-Sixteenth Centuries*, Vol. I: *Statistics* (The Hague, 1963).

APPENDIX 2: EUROPEAN RULERS,
1400-1650

The years given are those of the reign or regency.

POPES

Martin V (1417-1431) (Oddone Colonna)
Eugenius IV (1431-1447) (Gabriele Condulmer)
Nicholas V (1447-1455) (Tommaso Parentucelli)
Calixtus III (1455-1458) (Alonso de Borja)
Pius II (1458-1464) (Enea Silvio Piccolomini)
Paul II (1464-1471) (Pietro Barbo)
Sixtus IV (1471-1484) (Francesco della Rovere)
Innocent VIII (1484-1492) (Giovanni Battista Cibo)
Alexander VI (1492-1503) (Rodrigo de Borja)
Pius III (1503) (Francesco Todeschini-Piccolomini)
Julius II (1503-1513) (Giuliano della Rovere)
Leo X (1513-1521) (Giovanni de' Medici)
Adrian VI (1522-1523) (Adriaan Floriszn)
Clement VII (1523-1534) (Giulio de' Medici)
Paul III (1534-1549) (Alessandro Farnese)
Julius III (1550-1555) (Giovanni Maria Ciocchi del Monte)
Marcellus II (1555) (Marcello Cervini)
Paul IV (1555-1559) (Gian Pietro Caraffa)
Pius IV (1559-1565) (Giovanni Angelo de' Medici)
St. Pius V (1566-1572) (Antonio Michele Ghisleri)
Gregory XIII (1572-1585) (Ugo Buoncampagni)
Sixtus V (1585-1590) (Felice Peretti)
Urban VII (1590) (Giambattista Castagni)
Gregory XIV (1590-1591) (Niccolò Sfondrati)
Innocent IX (1591) (Gian Antonio Facchinetti)
Clement VIII (1592-1605) (Ippolito Aldobrandini)
Leo XI (1605) (Alessandro de' Medici)
Paul V (1605-1621) (Camillo Borghese)
Gregory XV (1621-1623) (Alessandro Ludovisi)
Urban VIII (1634-1644) (Maffeo Barberini)
Innocent X (1644-1655) (Giambattista Pamfili)

※ ※ ※

KINGS OF GERMANY AND HOLY ROMAN EMPERORS

House of Luxemburg
Sigmund (1410-1437)

House of Habsburg-Trastámara
Albert II (1438-1439)
Frederick III (1440-1493)
Maximilian I (1493-1519)
Charles V (1519-1556)
Ferdinand I (1556-1564)
Maximilian II (1564-1576)
Rudolph II (1576-1612)
Matthias (1612-1619)
Ferdinand II (1619-1637)
Ferdinand III (1639-1657)

※ ※ ※

DUKES OF BURGUNDY

House of Valois
Philip "the Bold" (1364-1404)
John "the Fearless" (1404-1419)
Philip "the Good" (1419-1467)
Charles "the Bold" (1467-1477)

House of Habsburg
Maximilian I (regent, 1477-1482)
Philip "the Handsome" (1482-1506)
Charles V (1506-1556)
Philip II (1556-1598)
Philip III (1598-1621)
Philip IV (1621-1655)

※ ※ ※

KINGS OF DENMARK AND NORWAY
(UNION OF KALMAR, 1397-1523)

House of Estrith
Margaret (1387-1412)
Eric VII (1412-1439)
Christopher III "of Bavaria" (1439-1448)

House of Oldenbourg
Christian I (1448-1481)
John (1481-1513)
Christian II "the Cruel" (1513-1523)
Frederick I (1523-1533)
Christian III "Father of the People" (1534-1558)
Frederick II (1558-1588)
Christian IV (1588-1648)
Christian V (1646-1699)

※ ※ ※

KINGS OF ENGLAND

House of Lancaster
Henry IV (1399-1413)
Henry V (1413-1422)
Henry VI (1422-1461)

House of York
Edward IV (1461-1483)
Edward V (1483)
Richard III (1483-1485)

House of Tudor
Henry VII (1485-1509)
Henry VIII (1509-1547)
Edward VI (1547-1553)
Mary (1553-1558)
Elizabeth I (1558-1603)

House of Stuart
James I (1603-1625)
Charles I (1625-1649)

⌗ ⌗ ⌗

KINGS OF FRANCE

House of Valois
Charles VI (1380-1422)
Charles VII (1422-1461)
Louis XI (1461-1483)
Charles VIII (1483-1498)
Louis XII (1498-1512)
Francis I (1515-1547)
Henry II (1547-1559)
Francis II (1559-1560)
Charles IX (1560-1574)
Henry III (1574-1589)

House of Bourbon
Henry IV (1589-1610)
Louis XIII (1610-1643)
Louis XIV (1643-1715)

⌗ ⌗ ⌗

KINGS OF HUNGARY AND BOHEMIA

House of Luxemburg
Sigmund (Hungary 1387-1437, Bohemia 1410-1437)

House of Habsburg
Albert (1437-1439)
Ladislaus I "Posthumus" (Hungary 1440-1444, Bohemia 1439-1457)

George Podiebrady (Bohemia 1459-1471)

House of Hunyádi
Mathias Corvinus (Hungary 1458-1490, Bohemia 1465-1490)

House of Jagiello
Ladislas II (Hungary 1490-1516, Bohemia 1471-1516)
Louis II (1516-1526)

House of Habsburg-Trastámara
Ferdinand I (1526-1564)
Maximilian (1564-1576)
Rudolph (1576-1608)
Matthias II (1608-1619)
Ferdinand II (1619-1637)
Ferdinand III (1637-1657)

❊ ❊ ❊

OTTOMAN SULTANS

House of Osman
Bayezid I "the Lightning" (1389-1403)
Mehmed I "the Restorer" (1413-1421)
Murad II (1421-1451)
Mehmed II "the Conqueror" (1451-1481)
Bayezid II (1481-1512)
Selim I "the Terrible" (1512-1520)
Suleiman I "the Magnificent" or "the Lawgiver" (1520-1566)
Selim II "the Sot" (1566-1574)
Murad III (1574-1595)
Mehmed III (1595-1603)
Ahmed I (1603-1617)
Mustapha I (1617-1618)
Osman II (1618-1622)
    Interregnum (1622-1623)
Murad IV (1623-1640)
Ibrahim I (1640-1648)
Mehmed IV (1648-1687)

※ ※ ※

KINGS OF POLAND

House of Jagiello
Wladyslaw V (1386-1434)
Wladyslaw VI (1434-1444)
Casimir IV (1447-1492)
John Albert (1492-1501)
Alexander (1501-1506)
Sigmund I (1506-1548)
Sigmund II (1548-1572)
    Interregnum (1572-1573)

House of Valois
Henry (1573-1574)
    Interregnum (1575-1576)

House of Báthory
Stephen (1575-1586)
    Interregnum (1586-1587)

House of Vasa
Sigmund III (1587-1632)
Wladislaw IV (1632-1648)
John Casimir (1648-1668)

※ ※ ※

KINGS OF PORTUGAL

House of Avis
John I "the Great" (1385-1433)
Edward (1433-1438)
Afonso V "the African" (1438-1481)
John II "the Perfect Prince" (1481-1495)
Emanuel "the Fortunate" (1495-1521)
John III (1521-1557)
Sebastian I (1557-1578)

House of Trastámara-Habsburg
Philip I (1580-1598)
Philip II (1598-1621)

House of Braganza
John IV "the Fortunate" (1640-1656)

❈ ❈ ❈

RULERS OF MUSCOVY

House of Riúrik
Basil I Dmitrievich (1389-1425)
Basil II "the Blind" (1425-1462)
Ivan III "the Great" (1462-1505)
Basil III (1505-1533)
Ivan IV "the Terrible" (1533-1584)
Theodore I (1584-1598)

House of Godunov
Boris Godunov (1598-1605)
Theodore (1605)

House of Romanov
Michael (1613-1645)
Alexis I (1645-1676)

❈ ❈ ❈

KINGS OF SCOTLAND

House of Stuart
Robert III (1390-1424)
James I (1424-1437)
James II (1437-1460)
James III (1460-1488)
James IV (1488-1513)
James V (1513-1542)
Mary of Guise (regent, 1543-1560)
Mary, "Queen of Scots" (1561-1567)

James VI (1567-1625)
Charles I (1625-1649)

※ ※ ※

KINGS OF SPAIN

House of Trastámara (Castile)
Henry III (1390-1406)
John II (1406-1454)
Henry IV (1454-1474)
Isabella "the Catholic" (1474-1504)

House of Aragon
Martin (1395-1410)
Ferdinand I "the Just" (1412-1416)
Alfonso V "the Magnanimous" (1416-1458)
John II (1458-1479)
Ferdinand II "the Catholic" (1479-1516)

House of Trastámara-Habsburg
Philip I "the Handsome" (1504-1506)
Charles I (Castile 1506-1516, Aragon 1516-1556)
Philip II (1556-1598)
Philip III (1598-1621)
Philip IV (1621-1665)

※ ※ ※

KINGS OF SWEDEN

House of Vasa
Gustavus I (1523-1560)
Eric XIV (1560-1568)
John III (1568-1592)
Charles IX (1604-1611)
Gustavus Adolphus (1611-1632)
Christina (1632-1654)
Charles X (1654-1660)

✖ ✖ ✖

SOVEREIGNS AND REGENTS OF THE HABSBURG NETHERLANDS

House of Valois
Mary of Burgundy (1477-1482)

House of Habsburg
Maximilian I (1482-1494)
Philip "the Handsome" (1494-1506)
Maximilian I (1506-1514)
Regent: Margaret of Austria (1507-1515)

House of Habsburg-Trastámara
Charles V (1514-1556)
Regents: Margaret of Austria (1517-1530)
        Mary of Hungary (1531-1555)
Philip II (1556-1598)
Regents: Emmanuel Philibert of Savoy, Gov. General (1556-1559)
        Margaret of Parma (1559-1566)
        Fernándo Alvárez de Toledo, Duke of Alba (1566-1573)

✖ ✖ ✖

SOVEREIGNS AND REGENTS OF THE SPANISH NETHERLANDS AFTER 1572

House of Habsburg-Trastámara
Philip II (1556-1598)
Regents: Luis de Requesens y Zuniga (1573-1576)
        Don Juan of Austria (1576-1578)
        Alexander of Parma (1578-1592)
        Peter Ernst von Mansfeld (1592-1594)
        Archduke Ernst of Austria (1593-1595)
        Archduke Albert of Austria (1596-1598)
Archduke Albert and Infante Isabella (1598-1621)

※ ※ ※

RULERS FOR THE UNITED PROVINCES AFTER 1572

Stadtholders of Holland and Zeeland
  House of Orange-Nassau
William I "the Silent" (1572-1584)
Maurice of Nassau (1585-1621)
Frederick Henry (1625-1647)
William II (1647-1650)

Grand Pensionaries of the States of Holland
Paulus Buys (1572-1584)
Johan van Oldenbarnevelt (1586-1618)

INDEX OF PERSONS

(b.=born; d.=died; fl.=flourished; r.=reigned)

INDEX OF PLACES

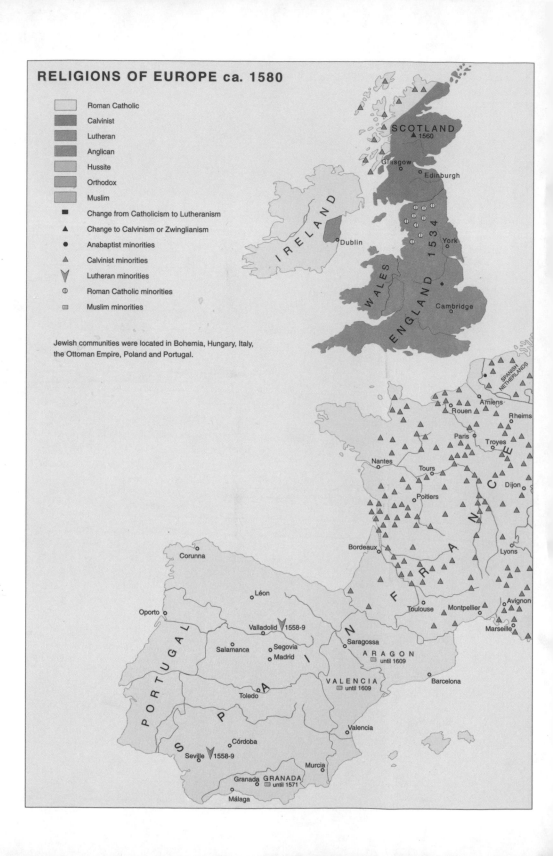

RELIGIONS OF EUROPE ca. 1580

- Roman Catholic
- Calvinist
- Lutheran
- Anglican
- Hussite
- Orthodox
- Muslim
- ■ Change from Catholicism to Lutheranism
- ▲ Change to Calvinism or Zwinglianism
- ● Anabaptist minorities
- ▲ Calvinist minorities
- ⱱ Lutheran minorities
- ⱷ Roman Catholic minorities
- ⬚ Muslim minorities

Jewish communities were located in Bohemia, Hungary, Italy, the Ottoman Empire, Poland and Portugal.

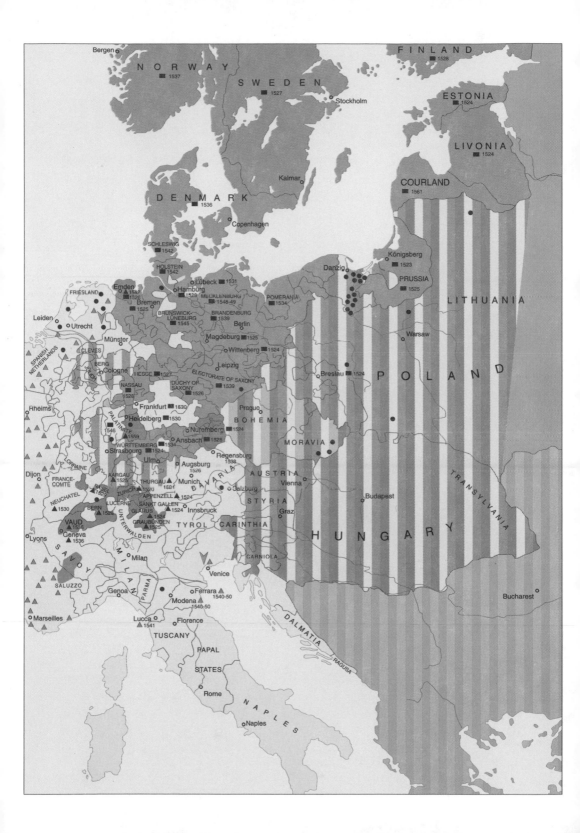

FINLAND
■ 1528

NORWAY
■ 1537

SWEDEN
■ 1527

Bergen o

Stockholm o

ESTONIA
■ 1524

LIVONIA
■ 1524

Kalmar o

DENMARK
■ 1536

COURLAND
■ 1561

Copenhagen o

Königsberg o
■ 1523

Danzig o

PRUSSIA
■ 1525

LITHUANIA

SCHLESWIG
■ 1542

HOLSTEIN
■ 1542

Lübeck o ■ 1531

Hamburg o
■ 1529

POMERANIA
■ 1534

Emden o
■ 1542
■ 1526
FRIESLAND o
Bremen o
■ 1525

MECKLENBURG
■ 1548-49

Warsaw o

Leiden o

Utrecht o

BRUNSWICK-
LUNEBURG
■ 1545

BRANDENBURG
■ 1539

Berlin o

POLAND

Münster o

Magdeburg o ■ 1525

SPANISH
NETHERLANDS

Wittenberg o ■ 1524

Breslau o ■ 1524

CLEVES

BERG

Leipzig o

Cologne o

HESSE ■ 1527

ELECTORATE OF SAXONY
■ 1539

NASSAU
■ 1528

DUCHY OF
SAXONY
■ 1526

Rheims o

Frankfurt o ■ 1630

Prague o

BOHEMIA

PALATINATE
■ 1546

Heidelberg o ■ 1530

Nuremberg o
■ 1524

MORAVIA

■ 1559

Ansbach o ■ 1528

WÜRTTEMBERG ■ 1534

Strasbourg o
■ 1524

Regensburg
1538

Ulm o

Augsburg o
1526

AUSTRIA

TRANSYLVANIA

Dijon o

FRANCE-
COMTÉ

AARGAU
■ 1525

THURGAU ▲
ZÜRICH ▲ 1520

Munich o

BAVARIA

Salzburg o

Vienna o

BASEL
■ 1529

APPENZELL ▲
■ 1524

Budapest o

NEUCHATEL
▲ 1530

LUCERNE

SANKT GALLEN ▲
■ 1524

Innsbruck o

STYRIA

BERN
■ 1528

GLARUS
▲ 1524

Graz o

VAUD
▲ 1536

GRAUBÜNDEN
▲ 1525

TYROL

CARINTHIA

HUNGARY

Geneva o ■ 1536

UNTERWALDEN

Lyons o

SAVOY

MILAN

Milan o

CARNIOLA

Venice o

Bucharest o

SALUZZO

PARMA

Genoa o

Ferrara o ▲
1540-50

DALMATIA

Marseilles o

Modena ▲
1540-50

RAGUSA

Lucca o

Florence o

▲ 1541

TUSCANY

PAPAL

STATES

Rome o

NAPLES

Naples o